C0-DAO-261

CATHERINE MCELVAIN LIBRARY SAR

2981   978.9 Hoo
The Indians of Pecos Pueblo
Hooton, Earnest.

WITHDRAWN

978.9   R.SR

PAPERS OF THE SOUTHWESTERN EXPEDITION
NUMBER FOUR

THE INDIANS OF PECOS PUEBLO

DEPARTMENT OF ARCHAEOLOGY

PHILLIPS ACADEMY · ANDOVER · MASSACHUSETTS

THE INDIANS OF PECOS PUEBLO

A STUDY OF THEIR SKELETAL REMAINS

BY

EARNEST ALBERT HOOTON

APPENDIX ON THE DENTITION BY HABIB J. RIHAN

APPENDIX ON THE PELVES BY EDWARD REYNOLDS

STATISTICAL AND LABORATORY ASSISTANTS

RUTH OTIS SAWTELL, ETHEL CLARK YATES, PEARL B. HURWITZ

NEW HAVEN

PUBLISHED FOR THE DEPARTMENT OF ARCHAEOLOGY

PHILLIPS ACADEMY · ANDOVER · MASSACHUSETTS

BY THE YALE UNIVERSITY PRESS

1930

COPYRIGHT, 1930, BY YALE UNIVERSITY PRESS

PRINTED AT THE HARVARD UNIVERSITY PRESS

CAMBRIDGE, MASS., U. S. A.

TO

ALEŠ HRDLIČKA

GREAT STUDENT OF THE
PHYSICAL ANTHROPOLOGY
OF THE AMERICAN INDIAN

PREFACE

AFTER the Andover Pecos Expedition had been in the field for several seasons an agreement was made between the Department of Archaeology of Phillips Academy and the Peabody Museum of Harvard University that the skeletal remains recovered in the excavations should be added to the collections of the latter institution. In return, on behalf of the Peabody Museum, I engaged to make a study of the skeletons, to be published as one of the *Papers of the Southwestern Expedition*. In order that I might become acquainted with the conditions under which the skeletons were exhumed, I accompanied the Pecos Expedition into the field in the summer of 1920 and spent a most profitable and enjoyable season with Dr. A. V. Kidder and his party.

I have worked intermittently upon the study of the Pecos collections for almost ten years. But with the exception of the two months actually spent at the ruined pueblo, I have never been able to devote my time and attention exclusively to the Pecos study for any protracted period. Often I have been forced to neglect it entirely for many months at a time. The work in its first phase consisted of the cleaning, mending, cataloguing, measuring, and observing of the material as it came in from the field. No statistical elaboration of the data could be begun until all skeletons to be included in the report had been measured. At the end of the 1924 season it seemed advisable to close the series, partly because of the vastness of the impending task of analysis, and partly because Dr. Kidder did not plan to continue excavations in the rubbish heaps, from which the majority of the better-preserved skeletons come. During the years of 1925, 1926, and 1927 the bulk of the statistical work was completed. I began to write the report in the summer of 1927 and the first chapters went to the printer in July, 1928. The task is now virtually completed. The report is by no means as exhaustive as I should like it to be. Large as is the collection, I have been forced to divide it into subgroups which, for statistical purposes, are in many cases too small. The considerable number of skeletons found in the nave of the church at Pecos, all of them of historical date and some of them undoubtedly the result of recent Mexican burials, have not been analyzed as a group. I have left this series open in the hope that subsequent additions to it may come from future excavations.

In this report I have not dealt with the anthropometry of the bones of the hands and the feet. I have omitted also the study of the ribs, and have been very summary in my treatment of the vertebral column and certain other skeletal parts. These omissions and abridgments have been due partially to the magnitude of the task undertaken and partially to my belief that detailed studies of such parts ought to be presented in special monographs rather than in a work designed to study the changes during a thousand years and the ethnic composition of a single village population. The tables of raw measurements of the Pecos material are to be published, in a limited edition, as a supplement to this volume.

With a single exception all of the anthropometric measurements and observations on the Pecos collection have been made by me personally, according to methods prescribed (in the case of the measurements) by the International Agreement. The cranial capacities were measured, under my direction, by two of my assistants.

During the course of this investigation I have become indebted to many for encouragement and assistance. Firstly, I wish to acknowledge my obligation to the Trustees of Phillips Academy, Andover, who have supplied all of the funds for the preparation of the skeletal material, the payment of my assistants, and the publication of this work. I am especially grateful to Professor James Hardy Ropes of the Trustees of Phillips Academy, who has been in charge of expenditures on account of the Pecos expedition. Professor Ropes has been at all times both interested in the progress of my work and ready to recommend or to authorize the expenditure for assistance of such sums as I have requested. He has made it a pleasure and a privilege to carry on research under the auspices of Phillips Academy.

Dr. Alfred V. Kidder, Director of the Andover Pecos Expedition, has been most helpful and encouraging at every stage of this work. To my frequent demands for advice and assistance he has invariably responded with characteristic cheerfulness and generosity.

I cannot adequately express my sense of obligation to the three young Radcliffe graduates who have been my principal assistants in the preparation of this report. Dr. Ruth Otis Sawtell, now of the Bureau of Educational Experiments, New York, was my sole helper from 1921 to 1925. During this period she repaired and catalogued the bulk of the Pecos collection, recorded my observations, measured the cranial capacities, and made substantial progress upon the work of statistical reduction. I am most grateful to Miss Sawtell for her skilled and efficient coöperation. Mrs. Ethel Clark Yates succeeded Miss Sawtell and devoted herself for two years to the Pecos work. During this period she completed the cataloguing of specimens, the recording of my data, and the measuring of cranial capacities. She accomplished most of the stupendous task of statistical analysis. The majority of the calculations were carried out and checked by Mrs. Yates; she compiled most of the tables. To her statistical ability and indefatigable industry must be credited much of whatever merit this work may possess. During the past year and more, I have had the assistance of Mrs. Pearl B. Hurwitz in preparing the report for the press. To her lot has fallen the arduous labor of proof-reading, checking and revising tables, ferreting out and correcting mistakes and inconsistencies, calculating additional statistical constants and compiling new tables, finding and checking bibliographical references, and all the other ungrateful tasks of an editorial and statistical assistant. Every one of these duties and others she has performed to my complete satisfaction. Each one of these three assistants has been in her turn invaluable and each has performed services far in excess of any pecuniary compensation received. All have endured with cheerfulness and apparent equanimity the vicissitudes of protracted collaboration with a none too genial personality.

I have received occasional and valuable assistance from many kindly colleagues and former students. Professor T. Wingate Todd of Western Reserve University made independent studies of the age of individual skeletons of the Pecos series, and these, together with his sex determinations, I have been privileged to use as a check upon my own work. Professor Herbert U. Williams of the University of Buffalo has devoted much time and his expert knowledge of palaeopathology to the examination of many of the Pecos pathological specimens. He has allowed me to incorporate his conclusions in my report and has offered me many helpful suggestions. He has read the proof of the chapter on pathology and has provided me with valuable illustrative material. Professor M. C. Sosman of Harvard University and the Peter Bent Brigham Hospital of Boston generously radiographed all of the more important pathological specimens of the Pecos collection and put these X-ray films, together with his diagnoses, at my disposal. Dr. A. C. Vogt, Roentgenologist of the Children's and Infants' Hospital, Boston, has been equally kind, in permitting me to publish his interesting observations on *osteoporosis symmetrica* and in providing me with illustrative material. Among the other pathologists who have examined some of the Pecos specimens and to whom I am indebted for opinions or diagnoses are: Professor F. B. Mallory of Harvard University, Professor S. B. Wolbach of Harvard University, Professor James Ewing of Cornell University, and Dr. Percy Howe, Director of the Forsyth Dental Infirmary, Boston.

Professor Habib J. Rihan, American University, Beirut, Syria, has contributed the interesting study of Pecos dentition which forms Appendix I of this volume. My colleague, Dr. Edward Reynolds, Director of the Peabody Museum, has devoted his profound knowledge of the anatomy and physiology of the human pelvis to a special monograph on the Pecos pelves, which I am privileged to include in this volume (Appendix II). Dr. Harry L. Shapiro, of the American Museum of Natural History, New York, has enabled me to enrich this investigation by utilization of his formulae for the correction of cranial deformation, worked out by him at my instigation and especially for use in the Pecos study. Dr. George D. Williams of Washington University, St. Louis, Missouri, spent an entire summer in classifying and diagnosing pathological specimens from the Pecos collection, in compiling tables, and in assisting me in the difficult task of making composite photographs of the crania.

Others who have had a part in working on the Pecos collection are: Mr. Kenneth G. Emory of the Bishop Museum of Honolulu, to whom I am indebted for most of the photographs of the Pecos crania; Dr. Arthur R. Kelly, Fellow in Anthropology, National Research Council, who assisted in the preparation of the Pecos collection; Mr. Frederick S. Hulse, Thaw Fellow, Harvard University, and Miss Dorothy Murfitt, who assisted Dr. Reynolds in his special study of Pecos pelves.

To the staff of the Harvard University Press, and especially to Mr. A. K. Wilson and Mr. Walter S. Gregson, I am indebted for splendid service and friendly coöperation in preparing this volume for the press.

Finally I wish to extend in advance to my prospective readers, if such there be, gratitude for their patience and a warning that, if they are not hardened physical anthropologists, they would best begin their perusal of this volume with, or confine it to, the last chapter.

EARNEST A. HOOTON

Peabody Museum of Harvard University
Cambridge, Massachusetts
September 11, 1929.

CONTENTS

CHAPTER I

HISTORICAL AND ARCHAEOLOGICAL SUMMARY

CHAPTER II

THE SKELETAL MATERIAL

CHAPTER III

CRANIAL MEASUREMENTS BY STRATA

CHAPTER IV

CHAPTER V

CHAPTER VI

MEASUREMENTS OF MORPHOLOGICAL CRANIAL TYPES

CHAPTER VII

OBSERVATIONS AND COMPOSITE PHOTOGRAPHS OF MORPHOLOGICAL CRANIAL TYPES

CHAPTER VIII

AFFINITIES OF THE MORPHOLOGICAL CRANIAL TYPES

CHAPTER IX

CHAPTER X

CHAPTER XI

CHAPTER XII

APPENDICES

TABLES IN THE TEXT

CHAPTER IV

CHAPTER VI

CHAPTER VII

CHAPTER VIII

CHAPTER IX

CHAPTER X

CHAPTER XI

TABLES IN THE APPENDICES

APPENDIX I

APPENDIX II

ILLUSTRATIONS

PLATES

CHAPTER VI

CHAPTER VII

CHAPTER X

FIGURES IN THE TEXT

APPENDIX II

THE INDIANS OF PECOS PUEBLO

CHAPTER I

HISTORICAL AND ARCHAEOLOGICAL SUMMARY

HISTORY [1]

THE ruins of the Indian pueblo of Pecos lie in the valley of the Pecos river in north-central New Mexico, about 7000 feet above sea level. In the distance are rugged mesas and mountains; the higher slopes are covered with pines and the river-bottom abounds in willows and cottonwoods; but the broad valley is dry, with red adobe flats and bare sandstone outcroppings. Empty arroyos cut through the cactus and pinyon covered wastes. On the flat top of a long, narrow sandstone ledge about a mile west of the river the Indians built their village, Cicuye or Pecos. The site was easily defensible and close to a never-failing spring of good water.

The village was visited by the first Spanish expedition which penetrated the Southwest in 1540 under the leadership of Francisco Vasquez de Coronado. These Spaniards were seeking for the fabulous wealth of the "Seven Cities of Cibola," reports of which had been circulated in Mexico by a certain adventurer called Cabeza de Vaca. After a long journey filled with hardships the Spanish expedition reached Hawikuh, one of the Zuñi villages in western New Mexico, and took possession of it and the surrounding country, although bitterly disappointed at the poverty of the region and its inhabitants. Here the conquerors settled down to await the submission of the peoples of the district. There soon arrived a group of Indians from Cicuye led by a tall, moustached young man whom the Spanish nicknamed Whiskers. Coronado sent one of his captains back with this party to reconnoitre the country. This captain, Alvarado, sent back the following account: [2]

Five days from here (Acoma) he came to Cicuye, a very strong village four stories high, a village of nearly five hundred warriors, who are feared throughout that country. It is square, situated on a rock, with a large court or yard in the middle, containing the estufas. The houses are all alike, four stories high. One can go over the top of the whole village without there being a street to hinder. There are corridors going all around it at the first two stories, by which one can go around the whole village. These are like outside balconies and they are able to protect themselves under these. The houses do not have doors below, but they use ladders, which can be lifted up like a drawbridge, and so go up to the corridors which are inside of the village. As the doors of the houses open on the corridor of that story, the

---

[1] This account is an abridgment and paraphrase of the fuller treatment of the subject by Dr. Kidder. Kidder, 1924, pp. 4–35.

[2] Quoted by Kidder, op. cit., from Winship's translation of Casteñada. G. P. Winship, 1896. The Coronado Expedition, 1540–1542. Fourteenth Report of the Bureau of American Ethnology, pt. 1, pp. 329–613, Washington, 1896.

corridor serves as a street. The houses that open on the plain are right back of these that open on the court, and in time of war they go through those behind them. The village is inclosed by a low wall of stone. The people of this village boast that no one has been able to conquer them and that they conquer whatever villages they wish.

The Spaniards were hospitably received by the Indians but soon got into trouble because of their greed for gold and silver, of which there was none to be had in Pecos. In order to get rid of the avaricious horde of Coronado, which in the spring of 1541 had descended upon Pecos, the Indians detailed a captive from an eastern tribe to lead the Spaniards off on a wild-goose chase after gold. This unfortunate con-

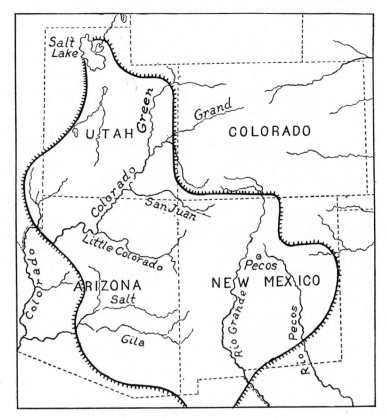

FIG. I–1.   APPROXIMATE EXTENT OF THE SOUTHWESTERN CULTURE AREA

ducted the army many weeks' march out into the buffalo plains, but they found no gold and finally, becoming exasperated, they strangled their devoted guide and wandered back to Pecos, where they were received with open hostility. However, they conquered the town without any great difficulty.

When Coronado departed from New Mexico in 1542 he left two Franciscans to convert the Indians, one of them at Cicuye. The Spaniards also left some sheep at Pecos, probably the first livestock to be introduced into the United States. The Indians killed the friars, but kept the sheep.

PLATE I–1

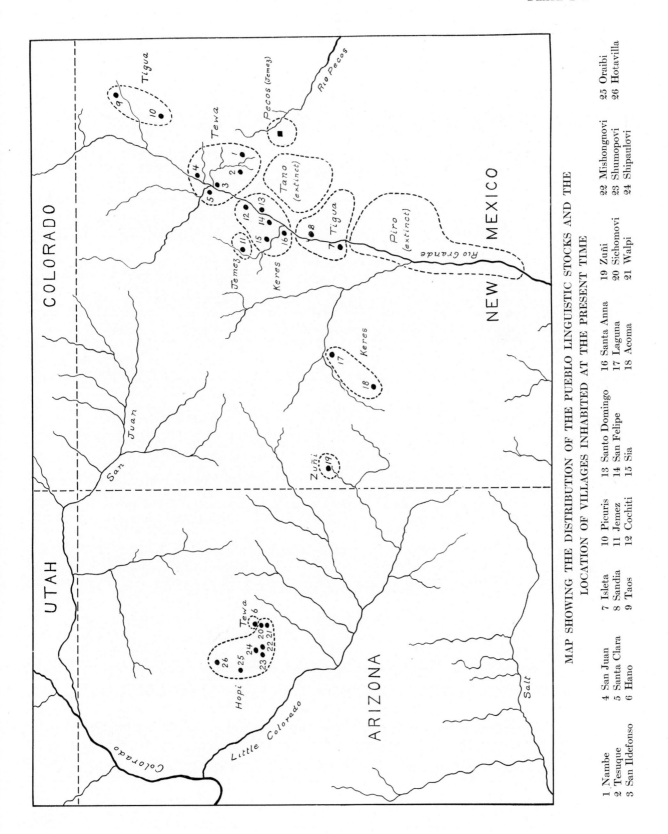

MAP SHOWING THE DISTRIBUTION OF THE PUEBLO LINGUISTIC STOCKS AND THE
LOCATION OF VILLAGES INHABITED AT THE PRESENT TIME

1 Nambe	4 San Juan	7 Isleta	10 Picuris	13 Santo Domingo	16 Santa Anna	19 Zuñi	22 Mishongnovi	25 Oraibi
2 Tesuque	5 Santa Clara	8 Sandia	11 Jemez	14 San Felipe	17 Laguna	20 Sichomovi	23 Shumopovi	26 Hotavilla
3 San Ildefonso	6 Hano	9 Taos	12 Cochiti	15 Sia	18 Acoma	21 Walpi	24 Shipaulovi	

PLATE I–2

GENERAL VIEW OF PECOS FROM THE NORTH

It was not until 1581 that the Spanish again entered New Mexico with a small armed party and three priests. After some stay the soldiers withdrew, leaving the priests to continue the work of Christianization. The next year another expedition came into the country to ascertain the fate of the three missionaries. This small party, having learned that the priests had been killed by the Indians, made a remarkable exploratory trip through the Southwest, stopping at Acoma, Zuñi, and the Hopi towns, passing through central Arizona and returning to the Rio Grande. The pueblos north of Santa Fe and Pecos were visited before this hardy group of adventurers returned to Mexico.

In 1590 Castaño de Sosa with a party of Spanish men and women entered New Mexico for the purpose of founding a colony. He sent a scouting party up to Pecos which was received with apparent friendliness and presently robbed of all its possessions. It was only by precipitate flight that the members of this advance guard managed to escape and after many vicissitudes to rejoin the main body. Whatever noble qualities the conquistadores lacked they were abundantly equipped with courage, and Sosa audaciously advanced with a party of nineteen soldiers and seventeen servants to punish the treacherous Pecos Indians. He arrived before the town on the twenty-sixth of December, 1590, and found the inhabitants on the roofs, ready to give battle. Sosa pitched his camp and planted his two brass cannon in strategic places and then advanced with flying colors to make friendly overtures. These were received with jeers by the Indians, who responded by hurling stones and shooting arrows at the Spaniards. It would seem that the Pecos Indians were quick in acquiring the elements of civilized behavior. One squaw went out on a balcony and threw ashes on the head of Sosa — an act which was greeted with great acclaim by her fellow townsmen. Sosa then tried to scare the Indians into submission by discharging firearms, but the Indians were not easily frightened. The Spaniards then got down to business. Four men carrying a cannon climbed up on a roof despite desperate resistance on the part of the defenders. With this artillery they then opened fire on the Indians while the main body of Spaniards attacked in front.

The Pecos Indians fought valiantly for a long time, but gradually became discouraged and finally gave in when the Indian followers of Sosa began to assist the Spaniards. After receiving the submission of the inhabitants, Sosa explored the pueblo.

It was found to contain five plazas and sixteen kivas, the latter being underground chambers, well plastered, which Sosa believed to have been made for protection against the cold. The houses, from four to five stories high, were built in the form of *cuarteles* (garrisons), the entrances all on the outside and the houses standing back to back. They were all connected by wooden corridors or balconies which ran from house to house throughout the village. Intersecting streets were bridged by wooden beams flung from roof to roof. Access to the houses was had by means of small ladders, which could afterward be drawn through trap-doors in the roof.

Each house was found to contain a store of grain — the village as a whole possessing an immense supply, estimated at thirty thousand *fanegas*, evidently the product of several years' harvests. The houses also contained a great deal of pottery, both gaily colored and figured, and black, some of it glazed.

As it was winter, the people were warmly clothed — the men in *mantas* of cotton and buffalo skins, while some wore also gaily figured trousers. The women wore a *manta* fastened at the shoulder, with a wide girdle round the waist, and over this another *manta*, gaily colored, and either embroidered or decorated with furs and feathers.

The pueblo had a large amount of land under cultivation, irrigated by two running streams at the side, while the pool which supplied them with water for drinking lay within a gunshot. A quarter of a league from the pubelo, the Rio Salado flowed.[1]

During the next night the Indians decamped, leaving the Spanish in possession of the village. After waiting in vain for their return for several days, Sosa and his followers departed. Soon after, the expedition was recalled to Mexico.

New Mexico was finally made the seat of a Spanish settlement in 1598 by Oñate, who was accompanied by a number of energetic Franciscans. These priests were allotted various districts for their parishes. Fray Francisco de San Miguel was in charge of the Pecos district with his headquarters in that pueblo. Oñate himself visited Pecos and received the submission of the inhabitants on the 24th of July, 1598. Nothing is known of the administration of Fray Francisco at Pecos and there is little information available concerning events in New Mexico during the first eight decades of the seventeenth century, since all records were destroyed in the revolution of 1680. About 1620 Fray Alonzo de Benavides reported that the town "contains more than two thousand souls. Here there is a monastery and a very splendid temple of distinguished workmanship and beauty, in which a Religious put very great labor and care." [2]

In 1680 the Pueblo Indians, actuated by a hatred of Spanish rule and of Christianity, revolted simultaneously, hoping to exterminate every Spaniard in the country. They almost succeeded in this endeavor although their long-laid plans were revealed to the European rulers just before the uprising. On August 10th, the appointed day, about four hundred Spanish of both sexes and all ages were killed, including twenty-one priests. The survivors fled to Santa Fe where a defense was organized by the governor. The Pecos priest, Fernando de Velasco, was informed of the impending revolt on the night of August 9th and set out to inform his superior at Galisteo, a short distance to the west. He was killed when within sight of his destination. The Spaniards in Santa Fe were besieged for five days by a band of five hundred warriors from Pecos and the other northern pueblos and then managed to retreat southward and reached the undisturbed settlements north of El Paso.

More than ten years elapsed before the Spanish again secured a foothold in New Mexico, and it was not until 1700 that all of the tribes were finally reduced to submission. During the absence of the Spanish from New Mexico the Pecos, Taos, and Keres waged war with the Tanos to the west and the Tehua to the north, but the Pecos were not active against the Spanish during the period of the reconquest. In 1692 they fled from their village at the approach of the Spanish governor, de Vargas. In 1694, the governor of Pecos, the same Indian who had warned the priest Velasco

---

[1] Kidder, 1924, pp. 11–12, quoting D. Hull, Castaño de Sosa's Expedition to New Mexico in 1590, Old Santa Fe Magazine, Vol. III, no. 12, pp. 307–322, Santa Fe, 1916.

[2] Kidder, 1924, p. 13, quoting E. A. B. Ayer. The Memorial of Fray Alonso de Benavides, 1630, Chicago, 1916.

Plate I–3

(a) THE PECOS CHURCH, SEEN FROM THE RUINS OF THE PUEBLO

(b) NORTH TERRACE EXCAVATIONS, FROM THE TOP OF THE MAIN RUIN–MOUND

THE REMAINS OF THE OLDEST SETTLEMENT LIE JUST WITHIN THE LATER DEFENSE-WALL;
FROM THE TRENCHES HERE VISIBLE THERE WERE TAKEN OVER NINETY SKELETONS.

of the impending revolt, accompanied the army of de Vargas and acted as an intermediary between the Spanish and the Indians of Taos.

The decline of Pecos, according to Kidder, set in soon after 1700, with the arrival in the southwestern plains of the warlike and predatory Comanches, who preyed incessantly upon the Pueblo Indians and especially harassed the Pecos who were on the frontier of the sedentary settlements. By 1750, it is said, the population had shrunk to one thousand. About this time, according to local legend, the Pecos organized an expedition against the Comanche and with the whole man power of the pueblo set forth into the plains and were annihilated, only one man escaping. In 1788 an epidemic of small-pox decimated the surviving population, leaving only one hundred and eighty survivors. Attacks of mountain fever further reduced the remnant until in 1805 there were only one hundred and four inhabitants.

Writing about 1840, Gregg [1] describes the dying pueblo as follows:

This village, anciently so renowned, lies twenty-five miles eastward of Santa Fe, and near the Rio Pecos, to which it gave name. Even so late as ten years ago, when it contained a population of fifty to a hundred souls, the traveler would oftentimes perceive but a solitary Indian, a woman, or a child, standing here and there like so many statues upon the roofs of their houses, with their eyes fixed on the eastern horizon, or leaning against a wall or a fence, listlessly gazing at the passing stranger; while at other times not a soul was to be seen in any direction, and the sepulchral silence was only disturbed by the occasional barking of a dog or the cackling of hens.

In 1838, the surviving inhabitants of Pecos, either seventeen or twenty in number, migrated to Jemez, eighty miles to the northwest, and cast in their lot with the people of that pueblo, who were akin to them in language. Nine of these emigrants were still living in New Mexico in 1910; the last survivor died in 1919.[2]

ARCHAEOLOGICAL SUMMARY

The Site. Dr. Kidder describes the appearance of the Pecos site before he began his excavations in the following words: [3]

The Pecos ruins occupy the more or less level top of a long, rocky ridge, which stands boldly up above the surrounding land. At the north end this *mesilla* pinches out to a narrow neck of bare sandstone (Plate I–2,); south of this there is a rise of ground and a great widening of the top, but still farther south it is again constricted and falls away in height until it merges with the uplands that stretch off toward the river.

At the extreme southern end lie the ruins of the church and monastery; the latter has crumbled to a low mound, but the massive six-foot adobe walls of the church have resisted time and vandalism, and still stand, at the transepts, to almost their original height (Plate I–3a). Directly north of the church is a pile of ruins, four hundred feet long by sixty-five or seventy feet wide (Plate I–3b). Again to the north, and occupying the highest and broadest part of the *mesilla*, is an enormous quadrangular mound five hundred and fifty feet long by two hundred and fifty wide. These two mounds are the remains of the pueblo structures

[1] Kidder, 1924, p. 15, quoting J. Gregg, Commerce of the Prairies, 2d ed., Vol. I, p. 272, N. Y., 1845.
[2] Parsons, 1925, p. 130.
[3] Kidder, 1924, p. 17.

which have fallen so completely into ruin that they appear to be nothing but vast heaps of tumbled stones. Closer examination, however, discloses the tops of walls, and here and there the protruding ends of wooden beams. The mounds are overgrown with grass and cactus. In rainy seasons the wild verbena carpets the ruins with brilliant purple.

The remains of the defense wall mentioned by Casteñada are still easily traceable (Plate I–4). It starts and ends at the church, hugging the edge of the *mesilla* and surrounding the entire settlement. Outside the wall the ground falls away more or less steeply, the slopes covered with thousands of potsherds and chips of flint.

The Rubbish Heaps. No scientific excavation of the Pecos site had been conducted when in 1915 the Department of Archaeology of Phillips Academy began work with Dr. Kidder as archaeologist in charge. He began to trench at the foot of the east slope leading up to the defense wall. The trench, which was carried down to undisturbed soil, rapidly grew deeper, until, when the defense wall had been reached, some twenty feet of rubbish were found to overlie the subsoil. It was then

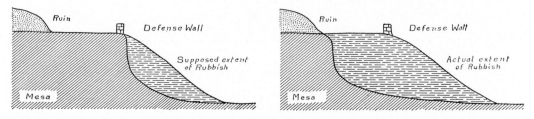

Fig. I–2. Supposed and actual extent of rubbish

ascertained that the defense wall was built not, as supposed, on the edge of the mesa, but upon accumulated rubbish, and that the actual rock mesa was entirely covered by the ruins of buildings (Fig. I–2).

This great rubbish heap on the eastern side of the site was crowded with skeletons, often lying one above another on as many as nine different levels (Plate I–5).

The "rubbish" is a dark, loamy soil, full of charcoal, streaked with ashes and containing a vast quantity of potsherds, flint chips, and animal bones. By isolating columns of earth in various parts of the diggings, marking these off in horizontal sections, and carefully excavating these sections, Dr. Kidder was able to establish an exact chronological and stratigraphic sequence of eight pottery types from the founding of the pueblo down to its abandonment in 1838. These eight types have been named as follows: Black-on-white, Glazes I, II, III, IV, V, VI, Modern [1] (Plate I–6).

Pottery Sequence. The earliest Pecos ware is the Black-on-white with which occurs black cooking ware of the corrugated type. The most strongly marked varieties of corrugated ware occur at the bottom of the stratified rubbish and gradually fade out through the upper layers. Dr. Kidder concludes that the Pecos mesa was settled toward the end of the Black-on-white period and that the Black-on-white ware preceded the use of glaze paints. For a short time glazing and Black-on-white existed side by side, but the former technique soon supplanted the latter. Kidder

[1] For a description of these wares, cf., Kidder, M. A. and A. V., 1917.

PLATE I–4

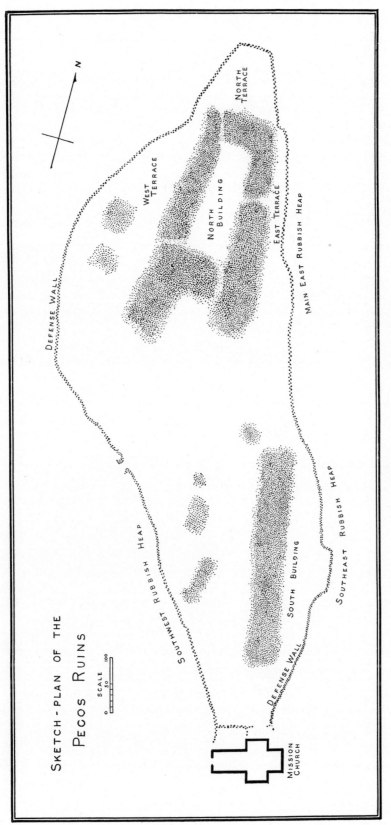

SKETCH-PLAN OF THE PECOS RUINS

PLATE I–5

A STRATIGRAPHIC SECTION IN THE DEEP RUBBISH

(a) WORKING IN CUT 3 TEST X; (b) CUT 5, TEST X PARTLY REMOVED — THE ARROWS MARK THE POSITIONS OF SKELETONS.

thinks that the sudden appearance of red ware with glazed paint may indicate influence from the west, probably from the Little Colorado.

Glaze I ware is at first a red-slipped ware over which is applied a thin black glaze paint. Later the red is replaced by yellow. Glaze II is marked by a degeneration of the glaze which becomes thicker and less adapted to the production of fine-line decoration; the clear yellow of the slip deteriorates; the rim thickens, and slashed marks and crosses and red-filled decorations appear on the exterior of bowls. It is a transitional ware, perhaps representing a shorter period of production than others of the series. Glaze III has a light-colored slip of poor and uncertain quality; the

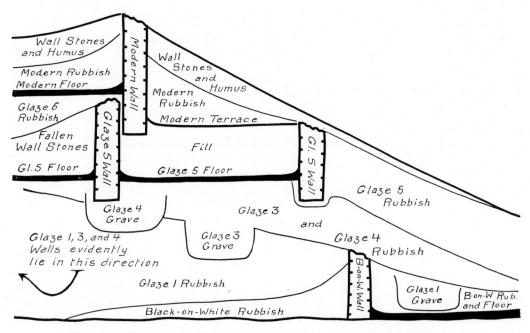

FIG. I–3. CROSS-SECTION SHOWING SUPERPOSITION OF WALLS, BURIALS, ETC.,
ON THE NORTH TERRACE AT PECOS

glaze lines are heavy and sloppy, and rusty black or greenish in color instead of the clear black of the early periods. Red-filled bird-figures or keys occur on the exterior of bowls. Glaze IV is also a three-color ware, with a slip in light red. The black glaze paint is of rather good quality and figures are filled with a much darker red than the slip; the rims are thin. This ware comes in abruptly, runs a short course and disappears. It has close resemblance to Pajaritan wares.

Glaze V is a late three-color ware with thick bowl-rims, dirty whitish slip, heavy and drippy glaze, and soft red pigment for filling of figures. The decoration is crudely and carelessly drawn. Glaze VI is of historic date and of extreme degeneration. The slip is usually light and varied in shade; it flakes badly. The glaze is thick and "runny." All attempt at precise design has been abandoned. Crude zigzags, dashes, and blobs are the only decoration. There is no red filling. Glaze V continued well into historic times as is proved by the bones of domesticated animals and objects of

European manufacture in the rubbish heaps. Glaze VI is supposed to have run its course by 1680, since it is thought that the Pueblo Indians ceased to make glazed wares after the revolt.

Lastly comes the Modern style which is a return to dull paints and is quite different in color and design from the glazed pottery. The slip is red or yellowish buff. Dull black pigment is used for decoration and red fillings are rare. This pottery closely resembles the modern wares of Santo Domingo, Cochiti, San Ildefonso, and Tesuque. Its origin is something of a mystery, but it may have been a return to the dull-painted wares of early days by way of revolt against the degenerative tendencies of the Spanish period.

Dr. Kidder bases his classification not only upon stratigraphy and upon sequence of colors and glazes, but also upon rim shapes, forms of vessels, and designs. In addition to the wares already mentioned, dull black painted ware on a white ground, of two varieties, called Biscuit A and Biscuit B, accompany the glaze paints and must be considered as successors of the prehistoric Black-on-white wares. Corrugated black cooking wares are succeeded by plain black, striated black, plain red, and polished black wares.

Thus we have for the sequence of wares on the mesa at Pecos:

1. Late archaic. Corrugated (little), strong blind corrugated, *Black-on-white*.
2. Period of the introduction of glaze. Strong and medium blind corrugated, *Glaze I*, Biscuit A.
3. Period of concentration. Faint blind corrugated, *Glazes II and III*, Biscuit B.
4. Late prehistoric ?–1600. Featureless black, Glaze IV, *Glaze V*, Biscuit B.
5. Early historic 1600–1680. Striated black, late Glaze V, *Glaze VI*, modern begins (?).
6. Late period 1680–1840. Striated black(?), plain red, polished black, *Modern*.

In general the pottery wares of Pecos are characterized by an almost consistent and steady deterioration from the earliest to the latest periods. Glaze IV, however, represents a possibly intrusive ware superior to its predecessors and approaching Glaze I in quality of finish, pigments, and design, though by no means necessarily a lineal descendant of the earliest glazes.

The Ruins on the Mesa. During the first season (1915) excavations were confined to the rubbish heap on the eastern slope, which was found to extend the full length of the mesa. The west slope was ascertained to contain little dumpage, probably because of the strong prevailing west winds which actuated the inhabitants to dump to the leeward. On the narrow neck of land where the mesa pinches away to the north beyond the main ruin mound, there was discovered unexpectedly in the season of 1916 the walls of an extensive Black-on-white pueblo, forming a three-sided structure open to the west and enclosing a large plaza. This seems to have been the first settlement built on the mesa, having succeeded earlier Black-on-white villages of considerable size which were discovered on the other side of the river Pecos. The oldest pueblo on the mesa itself, this Black-on-white village of the North Terrace, seems to have been built not long before the close of the Black-on-white period and the beginning of the next pottery phase. The bulk of the Glaze I pueblo lies to the south under the mass of the great quadrangle and covered by later structures. The

PLATE I–6

PECOS POTTERY

CHRONOLOGICAL SERIES ARRANGED TO ILLUSTRATE THE SEQUENCE OF TYPES FROM THE BLACK-ON-WHITE WARE OF EARLY PREHISTORIC TIMES (*a*), TO MODERN WARE MADE DURING THE FIRST PART OF THE NINETEENTH CENTURY (*h*).

Plate I–7

PECOS POTTERY

Chronological series of bowl designs: (a) Black-on-white; (b) Glaze I; (c) Glaze II; (d) Glaze III;
(e) Glaze IV; (f) Glaze V; (g) Glaze VI; (h) Modern.

North Terrace was apparently abandoned until the southern extension of later periods had occupied all the main portion of the mesa, when again in Glaze V a portion of it was built over. Glaze V seems to have been the period when the settlements extended over the largest part of the mesa and when the débris of occupation were deposited most abundantly. Everywhere among the buildings and outside them were encountered numerous burials, many of which are dated by the accompanying pottery.

In the third season (1920) a portion of the great quadrangular mound called the North House was uncovered. A great many rooms were excavated here in this and in succeeding seasons. Casteñada's description of the town in 1540 was verified in almost every particular. The building was, as he stated, terraced up from the plaza to a height at the rear of four stories; there were balconies at the second and third stories, and the rooms on the ground floor were without doorways. The Pecos buildings were invariably made of rough, uncoursed stones, and the later structures usually stand insecurely upon the ruins of previous habitations. Consequently the upper stories have, without exception, collapsed, leaving only the lower walls standing, and these when their fill of earth and stone is removed are so shaky that it is not possible to clear the rooms and leave the walls intact. Pecos is thus a ruin incapable of restoration. The later structures of the great North House are underlaid by remains of walls and buildings belonging to earlier periods of occupation, the whole presenting a most confusing network of buried and abandoned rooms, collapsed wooden roofs and domestic rubbish, with burials everywhere — under the floors, under the walls, in the plaza, and in the terraces. There are also in the plaza and outside of the main structure many of the subterranean circular rooms called kivas — some of them belonging to the early periods and filled with rubbish or burials of subsequent times, others which evidently had been used throughout several periods of the pueblo's habitation.

Apparently when a room became unsafe it was abandoned and filled with rubbish, or, in some instances, it was pulled down and a new structure built on the ruins. At some time subsequent to 1680 part of the outer wall of the western wing had fallen inward, crushing the rooms to the eastward. No effort had been made to rebuild this section.

The long South House which lies between the main quadrangle and the church was found to be the site of an early pueblo, upon the ruins of which another structure was erected sometime during the sixteenth or early seventeenth centuries. Here were found rooms containing bits of china, iron, copper, and other objects of European manufacture. Along the west terrace, where no surface indications of buildings were in evidence, remains of an extensive Glaze I pueblo were uncovered together with the usual profusion of burials, kivas, and so forth.

To quote Dr. Kidder:[1]

It was at first supposed that the Pecos ruins were the remains of a single structure, erected *en bloc*, occupied until 1838, and then abandoned. The excavations, however, have

[1] Kidder, 1924, p. 32.

shown that we have not only ruin piled on ruin, but that the population kept shifting about from one part of the mesa to another, building and rebuilding. We have uncovered in the course of our limited excavations portions of no less than six distinct towns. While some of these have been nearly obliterated by stone-robbing, all of them can eventually be traced out, and they can all be accurately dated relative to each other by means of the pottery and burials found in and about them.

During the first season the walls of the nave and transepts of the huge adobe church were reinforced with concrete in order to preserve them as a religious monument, and in the course of the excavations incidental to this work hundreds of skeletons were found under the floor of the nave, all of which belong to the historical period of the pueblo's occupation.

The last few seasons' work has been devoted principally to the exploration of the earlier sites across the river at Bandelier Bend and elsewhere. Not more than twelve per cent of the main mesa has been excavated, although it is probable that all of the main outlines of the pueblo's development have been traced.

Dr. Kidder is of the opinion, on the basis of intrusive potsherds from Pueblo Bonito and other prehistoric sites of which the chronological position is more or less definitely known, that the earliest settlement on the mesa dates from about A.D. 800.

Burials and Minor Objects. The present report is not intended to cover the history and archaeology of Pecos except in so far as to provide the reader with the minimum number of facts essential for a comprehension of the problems involved in the study of the skeletal remains. In future publications Dr. Kidder will treat *in extenso* the history and archaeology of Pecos and of the neighboring sites. At no time was cremation practised at Pecos. The burials show no consistent orientation and occur in all positions. Plate II–1 shows some typical examples. Extended burials are commonest in the late periods and partial or complete flexion of the body predominates in the earlier strata. The most numerous burials are those in which the legs are tightly flexed against the abdomen and the body is buried face downward. Mortuary pottery is found in about one third of the burials and occurs in a higher percentage of cases in the earlier than in the later periods of occupation. There was, apparently, little distinction as to age or sex in the matter of mortuary pottery. Such offerings range in frequency of occurrence from 92.8 per cent in middle-aged male burials of the Black-on-white period to 7.27 per cent in infant burials of Glaze V.

Objects of stone, including arrowheads, scrapers, knives, drills, and pipes, are commoner in the general diggings than in the graves. Tools of bone and antler are found in great profusion. Few wooden objects are preserved. Shells, rattles, and miscellaneous decorative or ceremonial objects are of occasional occurrence.

The Pecos seem not to have excelled either in architecture or in the arts. Their buildings were wretchedly constructed; their pottery in no period attained to the standard of excellence found among most of the Pueblo peoples in prehistoric or even in modern times; their tools, utensils, and weapons were commonplace.

Grouping of Skeletal Series according to Pottery Classifications. Owing to the multiplicity of stratigraphic periods based upon pottery classifications, and to the comparative paucity of well-preserved skeletal remains of assignable date, it has been necessary in this study to combine the skeletons of different periods into the following subgroups: (*a*) skeletons belonging to the Black-on-white and Glaze I periods, (*b*) Glazes II and III, (*c*) Glaze IV, (*d*) Glazes V and VI. Skeletons of unknown or doubtful provenience have been measured, but have not been treated as a series, nor, as yet, has any extensive study been made of the skeletal material from the nave of the church. This group includes many mixed-bloods and not a few skeletons of Mexicans buried in that consecrated ground within the last century. It is hoped to make this material the subject of a future report.

CHAPTER II

THE SKELETAL MATERIAL

STATE OF PRESERVATION

OBVIOUSLY a large number of factors contribute to the state of preservation of skeletal material. These factors may here be enumerated and discussed.

Age of the Burial. The mere length of time which has elapsed since the remains were buried is probably of little importance, except in so far as erosion, movements of the earth, and other geological changes contribute to the chances of the dispersal and destruction of bones. Human remains which have become fossilized have been known to withstand the effects of time for several hundreds of thousands of years. On the other hand the age of the burial is probably of great importance when soil conditions are unfavorable to preservation. In the present instance it is improbable that any of the bones studied are much more than one thousand years old. In the rubbish dumps the skeletons of the earlier periods are more likely to be crushed by the weight of the overlying earth and are oftener disturbed and scattered by building operations and by subsequent burials than is the case with the remains of later inhabitants. But there is little or no indication that the comparative scarcity of skeletons belonging to the Black-on-white period is due to decay caused by lapse of time.

Soil Conditions. Skeletons seem to disintegrate very rapidly when buried in damp vegetable mould. They are better preserved in wet clay soil and better still in dry sand. Skeletons buried in saturated clay or adobe are likely to be crushed or distorted by the weight of the soil and must be carefully dried before removal as they are often soft and pulpy. When exposed to the direct rays of the sun, such bones are likely to crack and split. Burials in chalk or in limestone country often last well. It seems probable that alternations of dryness and damp and changes of temperature conduce to a rapid decomposition of bone. At Pecos the pueblo was built upon a sandstone ridge and the soil is largely red clay with a good deal of sand in some places. In the summer there are heavy rains and the clay becomes saturated and then baked by the hot sun. In the winter there are severe frosts. All sorts of soil conditions, favorable and unfavorable to skeletal preservation, occur. Skeletons in the dry hard-baked clay are often well preserved, except for crushing. Skeletons in wet clay are often in fairly good condition. Skeletons resting directly upon the sandstone are invariably in a bad state of decomposition. Skeletons in the sandier soil are likely to be very friable and often suffer from erosion. On the whole the Pecos skeletal material is fairly well preserved. Its general state of preservation is inferior to that of skeletons dug up in arid sandy country such as the coast lands of

PLATE II–1

a

b

c

TYPICAL BURIALS

(*a*) EXTENDED BURIAL OF LATE PERIOD; NOTE SHALLOWNESS OF GRAVE. (*b*) PARTLY FLEXED BURIAL OF GLAZE IV PERIOD; MORTUARY BOWL BROKEN AND THE PIECES SCATTERED OVER THE BODY AT THE TIME OF INTERMENT. (*c*) CLOSELY FLEXED BURIAL ON FACE, GLAZE III PERIOD; MORTUARY BOWL UNBROKEN.

Peru and Egypt; it is better than recent Indian osteological material from New England and New York.

Age of the Individual at Death. The more organic material there is present in the bones at the time of death, the better preserved the skeleton is likely to be. In the case of infants and immature individuals, the cartilaginous state of epiphyses and the incomplete ossification of sutures, as well as the fragility of the bones themselves usually results in crushing and disarticulation. In any event the skeletons of young subjects are of comparatively little anthropological value. The bones of old persons are well known to be brittle and to have lost a certain proportion of their organic constituents. The compact layers are thinned in old age and the cancellous portions are increased. Bones of aged individuals do not resist well the wear of time and soil conditions. They are commonly fragile and friable. Persons in the prime of life have heavy bones well supplied with both organic and mineral constituents. The bones of such persons are likely to be in the best state of preservation.

Sex of the Individual. Males have heavier bones than females, with more compact tissue and less cancellous tissue relative to their size. Male bones are stronger than female bones and resist better the onslaught of time and the grave.

Cause of Death. Usually it is not possible to ascertain the cause of death in excavated skeletal material. Individuals in the prime of life whose death has demonstrably been caused by a wound or injury, usually have well preserved skeletons, all other conditions being equal. Not infrequently skeletons which exhibit inflammatory lesions of the bones are in a bad state of preservation even in the undiseased parts. Usually good teeth are associated with sound bones and *vice versa.* It seems probable that the skeletons of people who have died of wasting and chronic diseases disintegrate more rapidly than those who have succumbed to acute infections. However, I have no evidence to offer in support of this opinion.

Miscellaneous Causes. There is some evidence that the skeletons of persons buried in air-tight receptacles decay very rapidly, possibly on account of the effect of the gases formed in the decomposition of the soft parts and confined in the coffin. At Pecos, skulls or other parts of the skeleton covered by a pot or bowl are invariably in a worse state of decay than the uncovered parts of the same skeleton. Curiously enough, the hair of individuals whose skulls have been so covered is often well preserved. Skeletons under water, such as the specimens dredged up from the Sacred Cenote at Chichen Itza, Yucatan, and those recovered from the Swiss lakes, when dried, have a chocolate or slaty patina and are usually in excellent condition.

NUMBER

The number of graves excavated at Pecos and the neighboring sites during the several seasons of field work between 1915 and 1926 is as follows:

Season	Number	Season	Number
1915	200*	1924	346
1916	475	1925	264
1917 (Rowe)	17	1926	4
1920	284		
1922	233	Total	1823

* Exclusive of some 56 skeletons dug up in the nave of the church.

The material recovered during the first two seasons was sent to the Peabody Museum, regardless of its state of preservation. In the season of 1920 the author was at Pecos and had charge of the excavating and recording of skeletal material. From this time onward skeletons in a bad state of preservation were discarded after notes had been made upon their age, sex, and any features of interest which they

TABLE II–1. TOTAL PECOS SKELETAL MATERIAL RECORDED AT ANDOVER, ON FEBRUARY 1, 1924

	Old	Middle	Young	Sub-Ad. Adol.	Child	Infant	Foetus, or Stillborn	Age?	Age, sex?	Total
Males										
B.-on-W. & I	17	44	8	3	0	0	0	0	0	72
Gl. II & III	30	62	15	5	0	0	0	1	0	113
Gl. IV	12	33	5	4	0	0	0	1	0	55
Gl. V & VI	17	33	5	5	0	0	0	0	0	60
Stratum ?	22	53	12	5	0	0	0	1	0	93
Total	98	225	45	22	0	0	0	3	0	393
Females										
B.-on-W. & I	6	26	14	6	0	0	0	3	0	55
Gl. II & III	21	31	24	9	0	0	0	0	0	85
Gl. IV	12	18	8	7	0	0	0	0	0	45
Gl. V & VI	12	10	6	6	0	0	0	0	0	34
Stratum ?	16	29	13	3	0	0	0	1	0	62
Total	67	114	65	31	0	0	0	4	0	281
Sex?										
B.-on-W. & I	4	9	4	2	11	27	8	0	66	131
Gl. II & III	4	14	3	2	19	28	1	0	60	131
Gl. IV	4	1	0	6	5	11	1	0	19	47
Gl. V & VI	1	4	0	1	11	18	1	0	24	60
Stratum ?	5	27	7	12	27	59	20	0	54	211
Total	18	55	14	23	73	143	31	0	223	580
Grand total	183	394	124	76	73	143	31	7	223	1254

might present. But all skeletons exhibiting pathological features or other points of anthropological importance were shipped in as before. During the last three seasons the excavators were concerned principally with the buildings and there was little or no trenching of the rubbish heaps which yield the richest results from the standpoint of skeletal material. Most of the workable skeletal material comes from the excavations carried on during the years 1915–1924.

The material utilized in the present report is largely that gathered during the seasons up to and including 1924. It seemed advisable to close our series and to begin the work of statistical analysis in 1925 before the material of that year's excavation had been sent in. Total Series A, in which the remains are classified according to archaeological periods, includes only the skeletons of the years 1915–1924. Series B, a group of male crania classified according to morphological type, contains some few crania from the 1925 excavations.

Table II–1 records the totals of skeletons listed on the grave-cards of the Andover Pecos Expedition up to February 1, 1924. It will be noted that the grand total is 1254. The excavations of the next three seasons include some 600 additional burials. Of the 1254 on record 580 or 46.2 per cent are not identified as to sex. Of this unsexed group 270 or 46.5 per cent were adolescents, children, infants, or foetuses. Of the 1254 skeletons 223 or 17.8 per cent bear no record of identification as to sex or age. It was not possible to assign any archaeological dating to 366 skeletons, or about 29 per cent of the total number.

The recording of sex and age on the grave-cards in the field was done by a number of different observers during the several seasons of excavation. The grave-cards of skeletal material sent to the Peabody Museum, including the bulk of the material up to and including 1924, were corrected as to age and sex determination by the author's reëxamination of the bones in the laboratory. The errors of the field recorders in determining age and sex of the material were not numerous according to the check-up of the somatologist in the laboratory.

TABLE II–2. PECOS SKELETAL MATERIAL IN THE PEABODY MUSEUM

	1915–1923	1924	Total
Measured and observed wholly or in part			
Males	182	62	244
Females	142	41	183
Doubtfuls	8	6	14
Total	332	109	441
Noted, but not measured or observed			
Adults	140	171 *	311
Foetus to adolescent	221	. . .	221
Total	361	171	532
Grand total	693	280	973

* Includes all ages.

Table II–2 gives the numbers of skeletons sent to the Peabody Museum and studied as a basis for the present report. Of the total of 973 skeletons, 532 or 54.7 per cent were neither measured nor recorded according to routine of graded morphological observations on each skeletal part. This omission was due either to the incomplete and fragmentary state of the skeletons or to their immaturity.

Of the 441 skeletons actually measured and observed many were also incomplete and fragmentary so that measurements and observations were taken upon a few bones only. Skeletons of doubtful sex or of unknown archaeological provenience were measured and observed but have not been utilized in the statistical analysis of the various series.

After all necessary eliminations of fragmentary material, immature skeletons, and those of doubtful sex or of unknown archaeological date had been made, there remained no more than 250 skeletons in good condition for study. Many of the skeletons found in the nave of the church showed clear traces of European admixture and none of these have been included in the various series, with the exception of two or three crania in the "European" type group of Series B.

Of the total of 1254 burials recorded up to the end of the season of 1922 about one fifth could be fully utilized for purposes of study, being in a good state of preservation, of adult years, determinable sex, and known archaeological stratum. Only about 1.5 per cent were rejected because of the inability of the laboratory observer to determine sex.

AGE

In the laboratory the age of immature specimens was estimated from the state of eruption of the dentition and from the fusion of epiphyses. The age of adults was judged from the wear of teeth, the occlusion of cranial sutures, the growth phase of the pubic symphysis and the general texture of the bones. In the case of immature individuals it is usually possible to estimate the age within a year or two. For the older groups the following classification was used: sub-adult 18–20 years, young adult 21–34 years, middle-aged adult 35–54 years, old adult 55 years and over. Table II–1 records the number of individual skeletons in each category according to the records of 1254 grave-cards at Andover. Most of these age determinations are mine. Of 1254 grave-cards, 223 are without record as to age or sex and seven others have no designation as to age. These refer to skeletons in bad condition recorded by observers who did not feel competent to estimate age.

In 1927 Professor T. Wingate Todd of Western Reserve University visited our laboratory and with the help of Mrs. Yates and Dr. George D. Williams, my assistants, assessed the ages of 594 individuals of the Pecos series [1] (Fig. II–1). Professor Todd remarks upon the data presented in the graph: [2]

The very young children are represented by such scattered remnants that, as usual, they must be discarded. Hence our first peak falls in the second lustrum. The adolescent peak between fifteen and nineteen years is quite striking. After that there is a plateau from the later part of the fourth to the later part of the sixth decade with the median skeleton falling into age forty to forty-four years. After the sixth decade the number of deaths falls off rapidly and old age shows no peak.

Over the thousand years represented by this series there is no indication that life to old age was anything but an exception.

[1] Todd, 1927, p. 494.
[2] Loc. cit.

Table II–3 shows the association of Professor Todd's estimates of age with those previously made by me upon the same material. This table comprises only 501 individuals, since the series included in this report were closed for analysis before the arrival in the museum of some of the specimens included in Todd's survey. In general the agreement of Todd's ageing with mine, when his estimates are grouped into classes corresponding with my age groups, is fairly close. The table yields a mean square contingency coefficient of .85. A coefficient of unity would mean that every one of the determinations by the two separate observers was identical within the

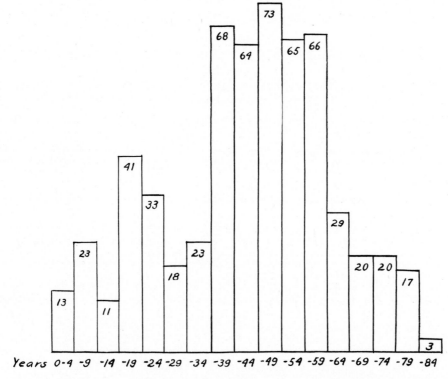

Fig. II–1. Mortality at Pecos based upon Todd's estimate of number of individuals dying at each 5-year period of age in a sample of 587 skeletons

assigned age groups. A coefficient approaching zero would mean that any agreements between the age assignments of the two observers should be taken as merely due to chance. There are two or three striking discrepancies in the table. One individual is estimated by one observer to be an "old adult" and by the other to be a sub-adult (19–20 years). This and one or two similar divergences are probably due to clerical errors. There are, however, a large number of cases in which one of us has placed skeletons in a certain age group, and the other has assigned it to the next age group above or below. Differences in judgment mostly of this sort (involving the shifting from one age group to the next) occur in 154 of 501 cases, or 30.7 per cent.

Intensity of correlation between the two sets of age assignments may again be judged by the percentages of each class falling within the correlation cell of any age group (Table II–3). These range from 92.86 in the child class down to 38.10 in the sub-adult class, 100 per cent in any class representing perfect correlation within that group. The unweighted mean of age-group agreements is 67.42 per cent. The weighted mean is 69.26 per cent.

The differences between estimates of age made by Professor Todd and by me are probably in a majority of cases due to errors in my own judgment. For it is well

TABLE II–3. AGE OF PECOS SKELETAL MATERIAL: TODD'S AGEING ASSOCIATED WITH THAT OF HOOTON

(Todd) (Hooton)	1–3 yrs.		3–10 yrs.		11–18 yrs.		19–20 yrs.		21–35 yrs.		35–55 yrs.		55 + yrs.		Total	
	No.	P. C.	No.	P. C.	No.	P. C.	No.	P. C.	No.	P. C.	No.	P. C.	No.	P. C.	No.	P. C.
Infant.......	3	75.00	1	25.00	0	0	0	0	0	0	0	0	0	0	4	100.00
Child........	0	0	13	92.86	1	7.14	0	0	0	0	0	0	0	0	14	100.00
Adolescent ...	0	0	4	23.53	11	64.71	1	5.88	1	5.88	0	0	0	0	17	100.00
Sub-adult	0	0	0	0	6	28.57	8	38.10	6	28.57	1	4.76	0	0	21	100.00
Young adult .	0	0	0	0	3	3.66	2	2.44	45	54.88	30	36.59	2	2.44	82	100.00
Middle-aged..	0	0	0	0	0	0	0	0	18	7.50	178	74.17	44	18.33	240	100.00
Old adult	0	0	0	0	0	0	1	0.81	1	0.81	32	26.02	89	72.36	123	100.00
Total......	3	0.60	18	3.59	21	4.19	12	2.40	71	14.17	241	48.10	135	26.95	501	100.00

Coefficient of contingency 0.85.

known that Professor Todd stands alone as an authority on the ageing of skeletal material and has been the first anatomist to place this problem upon a really scientific basis. Todd assigns ages to adult skeletal material within a margin of five years, while I do not feel competent to go beyond the crude groupings of young adult, middle-aged, and old adult. In the case of adult skeletons my estimates of age tend to be somewhat lower than those of the better qualified observer. Without any intention of disparaging the splendid work of Professor Todd in this field or of defending my own inaccuracies, I may point out that his correlations between age and skeletal condition in specimens of known age have been based upon Negro and white material and not upon Indian material. Hrdlička has shown that tooth eruption in Indians is slightly more precocious than in whites; Indians mature somewhat earlier and age more rapidly than do whites. It is possible that age changes identified as belonging to a certain chronological age in whites may occur earlier in Indians. In spite of this possibility, it is obviously good method to assume the applicability of Todd's correlations of age and skeletal conditions in whites and Negroes to Indian material, in the absence of any equally satisfactory data pertaining to the American Indian.

A notable contribution to the determination of chronological age in young and middle-aged adult skeletons, has been made by Professor Todd in his study of the changes which take place in the symphysial surface of the pubic bone. These changes are summarized as follows: [1]

[1] Todd, 1920, pp. 313–314.

Phase 1. Age 18–19. Typical adolescent ridge and furrow formation with no signs of margins and no ventral beveling.

Phase 2. Age 20–21. Foreshadowing of ventral beveling with slight indication of dorsal margin.

Phase 3. Age 22–24. Progressive obliteration of ridge and furrow system with increasing definition of dorsal margin and commencement of ventral rarefaction (beveling).

Phase 4. Age 25–26. Completion of definite dorsal margin, rapid increase of ventral rarefaction and commencing delimitation of lower extremity.

Phase 5. Age 27–30. Commencing formation of upper extremity with increasing definition of lower extremity and possibly sporadic attempts at formation of ventral rampart.

Phase 6. Age 30–35. Development and practical completion of ventral rampart with increasing definition of extremities.

Phase 7. Age 35–39. Changes in symphysial face and ventral aspect of pubis consequent upon diminishing activity, accompanied by bony outgrowths into pelvic attachments of tendons and ligaments.

Phase 8. Age 39–44. Smoothness and inactivity of symphysial face and ventral aspect of pubis. Oval outline and extremities clearly defined but no "rim" formation or lipping.

Phase 9. Age 45–50. Development of "rim" on symphysial face with lipping of dorsal and ventral margins.

Phase 10. Age 50 and upwards. Erosion of and erratic, possibly pathological osteophytic growth on symphysial face with breaking down of ventral margin.

Since this research of Professor Todd was published simultaneously with the beginning of my laboratory examination of the Pecos collection, I at once began to attempt to apply this method of determining age to that collection regardless of sex and of the fact that the original research applied only to male whites. Subsequently Professor Todd very kindly supplied me with an excellent set of photographs of symphyses of the several phases, thereby greatly facilitating the application of his method to the Pecos material. Table II–4 records the estimates of age on the basis of the pubic symphysis made by me on 95 male and 71 female pelves.

I confess my inability to discriminate in every instance between each of these phases, especially the earlier ones. Table II–4 shows the divisions of the various pelves into Glaze subgroups. Because of the large number of pelvic phases and small number of specimens the distribution is very irregular. It may be noted, however, that in the male series the proportion of pelves of phases 9–10 (45 years and upwards) increases throughout the archaeological periods. In the earliest subgroup the percentage of such pelves is 33.33, in the second subgroup 38.46, in the third subgroup 34.78, and in the last subgroup 54.17 per cent. In the female series this increase in the number of middle-aged and elderly persons from the early to the late periods is even more strongly marked. The proportion of pelves of phases 9–10 in the first subgroup is 41.67, in the second subgroup 67.86, in the third 76.47, and in the last 78.57. In the pelvic material there is, therefore, some evidence of an increase in the number of persons living to old age from the earlier to the later periods of the pueblo's occupation and also evidence of a larger number of females than males living to old age.

The data gathered from the grave-cards is not strictly comparable with the determinations of age on the pelves, because the former include adolescents with sub-adults and the latter include sub-adults only. Further, my classification "old" includes persons judged to be 55 years and upward, whereas Phase 10 of the pubic

TABLE II–4. Age Phase of Pubic Symphysis

	B.-on-W. and I		II and III		IV		V and VI		Total Series A	
Males	No.	P. C.	No.	P. C.	No.	P. C.	No.	P. C.	No.	P. C.
Phase 1	0	0	0	0	0	0	1	4.17	1	1.05
Phases 1–2	0	0	0	0	0	0	1	4.17	1	1.05
Phases 2–3	0	0	1	2.56	0	0	0	0	1	1.05
Phase 3	0	0	1	2.56	0	0	1	4.17	2	2.11
Phase 4	0	0	2	5.13	0	0	0	0	2	2.11
Phases 4–5	0	0	1	2.56	0	0	0	0	1	1.05
Phase 5	1	11.11	1	2.56	0	0	0	0	2	2.11
Phase 6	0	0	3	7.69	1	4.35	1	4.17	5	5.26
Phase 7	1	11.11	3	7.69	1	4.35	1	4.17	6	6.32
Phases 7–8	0	0	2	5.13	3	13.04	0	0	5	5.26
Phase 8	4	44.44	9	23.08	9	39.13	5	20.83	27	28.42
Phases 8–9	0	0	0	0	1	4.35	1	4.17	2	2.11
Phases 8–10	0	0	1	2.56	0	0	0	0	1	1.05
Phase 9	0	0	6	15.38	3	13.04	4	16.67	13	13.68
Phases 9–10	0	0	2	5.13	1	4.35	3	12.50	6	6.32
Phase 10	3	33.33	7	17.95	4	17.39	6	25.00	20	21.05
Total........	9		39		23		24		95	
Females										
Phase 1	2	16.67	0	0	0	0	1	7.14	3	4.23
Phase 2	1	8.33	3	10.71	0	0	0	0	4	5.63
Phase 3	0	0	0	0	1	5.88	1	7.14	2	2.82
Phases 3–4	0	0	1	3.57	0	0	0	0	1	1.41
Phase 4	1	8.33	1	3.57	0	0	0	0	2	2.82
Phases 5–6	0	0	0	0	1	5.88	0	0	1	1.41
Phase 6	1	8.33	1	3.57	0	0	0	0	2	2.82
Phase 7	0	0	0	0	0	0	1	7.14	1	1.41
Phases 7–8	0	0	0	0	1	5.88	0	0	1	1.41
Phase 8	2	16.67	2	7.14	1	5.88	0	0	5	7.04
Phases 8–9	0	0	1	3.57	0	0	0	0	1	1.41
Phase 9	1	8.33	5	17.86	3	17.65	1	7.14	10	14.08
Phases 9–10	2	16.67	3	10.71	2	11.76	2	14.29	9	12.68
Phase 10	2	16.67	11	39.29	8	47.06	8	57.14	29	40.85
Total........	12		28		17		14		71	

symphysis includes all specimens 50 years and over. These are, however, unimportant considerations.

From Table II–5 it may be observed that the percentages of the age groups agree fairly well in case of the males. The pelves include a slightly higher proportion of young adult and middle-aged adult males and about four per cent fewer of old males than the series recorded on the grave-cards. Since the pelvic sample includes only about one-fourth of the male series these differences may be accounted for by the possibly unrepresentative age-character of the pelvic samples as well as by the incompatibilities of classification mentioned above.

In the female series the pelvic sample includes also about one-fourth of the grave-card series. In this case there are fewer young adults and middle-aged adults in the pelvic series than in the grave-card series and many more old adults in the former. Indeed the age group including persons aged fifty-five and over comprises 24.19 per cent of the grave-card series and 40.85 per cent of the pelves. The excess of pelves adjudged to belong to old females is greater than would be expected to result from errors of the sampling process.

If age assignments of combined males, females, and doubtfuls on the grave-cards be compared with my ageing from pelves (Table II–5) it is seen that the two sets of

TABLE II–5. SEX AND AGE ACCORDING TO GRAVE–CARDS AND PELVIC
DETERMINATIONS

| | Males | | | | Females | | | | (Todd) | | | |
| | Grave-Cards | | Pelves | | Grave-Cards | | Pelves | | Males | | Females | |
Age	No.	Per cent	No.	Per cent	No.	Per cent	No.	Per cent	No.	Per cent	No.	Per cent
11–19...	22	5.64	1	1.05	31	11.19	3	4.23	4	2.70	1	1.02
20–35...	45	11.54	14	14.74	65	23.46	12	16.91	20	13.51	15	15.31
35–55...	225	57.69	60	63.16	114	41.15	27	38.03	77	52.03	61	62.24
55......	98	25.12	20	21.05	67	24.19	29	40.85	47	31.76	21	21.43
Total	390		95		277		71		148		98	

Males, Females, and Doubtfuls

| | Grave-Cards | | Pelves | | | |
| | (Kidder) | | (Hooton) | | (Todd) | |
	No.	Per cent	No.	Per cent	No.	Per cent
11–19...................	76	9.79	4	2.41	52	9.43
20–35...................	124	15.96	26	15.66	74	13.43
35–55...................	394	50.70	87	52.41	270	49.00 *
55–....................	183	23.55	49	29.51	155	29.13 *
Total...............	777		166		551	

* If the middle-aged group is taken to include 35–50, and the old group 50 and over, Todd's figures are changed so that 205 subjects or 37.20 per cent fall in the middle-aged class and 220 subjects or 39.93 per cent in the old class.

data compare very favorably. A deficiency in the youngest group of the pelvic determinations is due to the exclusion from the pelvic series of adolescents, sub-adults only being considered. There is also an excess of about 7 per cent in the oldest group as respects the determinations from the pelvis. In this table also I have calculated corresponding percentages on Todd's data for skeletons of both sexes and of the same age groups.

The percentages calculated from his age determinations agree pretty closely with my pelvic determinations. Both of these show an excess in the old-age class as compared with the grave-card data. This excess amounts to about 6 per cent. If Professor Todd's data be grouped so that the upper limit of the middle-age group is 49 instead of 54, in conformity with his gradation of pelvic phases, his groups then correspond very closely with those determined by me on female pelves, but my male pelvic series shows an excess of middle-aged individuals and a deficiency of old individuals both in comparison to my own pelvic series of both sexes and to Todd's series of both sexes in which all criteria are employed.

It is a matter of common knowledge that in most peoples the number of males born somewhat exceeds the number of females. Among the Indians of the United States, according to the Census of 1910, the total number of males exceeds the number of females in every age group up to 75 years. Thereafter in every age group the number of females exceeds the males.[1] Precisely the same condition obtains in whites. In the Negro population the females outnumber the males in every age group up to 40 years; thereafter the males outnumber the females up to 80 years, when the female sex again becomes more numerous and retains its superiority throughout the other age groups. It seems apparent, therefore, that more women than men live to an advanced age. Hence it is not strange that our age determinations on the pelvis yield a much higher proportion of females with pelves indicating the age of fifty or over than is found among the males. Neither is it remarkable that our grave-card records of age and sex show a slightly greater number of old males than females both relatively and absolutely, since male skeletons are heavier and stronger and weather better than female skeletons, and the average age of "old males" is almost certainly younger than that of "old" females. The pelvic determinations of age were made only upon well-preserved skeletons, whereas the grave-card data include all degrees of preservation.

In Table II–6 the percentages of Pecos skeletons assigned to certain age groups are compared with percentages of deaths occurring at the same periods in modern populations out of 100 born alive.[2] Here again the data are only very roughly comparable. The Pecos represent an extinct population covering a range of approximately 1000 years. The age assignments of skeletons cannot be taken to be anything more than a vague indication of the total deaths occurring during the period. Errors entering into the approximation are mistakes in the ageing of skeletons, the disappearance of skeletons through decay, lack of burial of infants or possible failure of field archaeologists to find and record all infant burials, change of the death rate within the period of the pueblo's occupation, and so forth.

For the first age group (under three years) it may be noted that the percentage of skeletons in the Pecos group (14.40) is somewhat below the lowest number of deaths of living people during the same period (14.97 per cent) noted in the comparative data. We cannot for a moment suppose that Pecos infant mortality was lower than in the Registration Area in the United States in 1910. The Pecos figures reflect two factors: loss of infant burials through decay or through failure to find and record them, and a possibility of a very great decrease in the birth rate at Pecos during the period of the Peublo's decline. The highest death rate for this period is found

---

[1] Indian Population in the United States and Alaska, 1910, p. 57. Department of Commerce, Bureau of the Census, Washington, 1915.

[2] Glover, 1921, pp. 54, 80, 86, 204.

in India (39.71). The average death rate at this age interval in Pecos was certainly less than that, but it may have been half again as high as our records show.

The periods between four and ten years and from ten to twenty years are always those in which the smallest proportion of a population dies. The percentages recorded at Pecos for these age intervals approximate to those found in India to-day and are somewhat above those of United States Negroes. The Pecos figures are perhaps elevated unduly by the disproportionate absence of the infant burials. The percentage of young adults among the Pecos corresponds fairly closely with the

TABLE II–6. Comparative Table of Percentages of Deaths Occurring at Various Age Periods

	0–3 years	4–9 years	10–19 years	20–34 years	35–54 years	55– years
Pecos skeletons..............	14.40	7.35	7.65	12.48	39.67	18.43
U. S. (Registration area, 1910)	14.97	2.57	2.38	6.95	15.57	57.56
U. S. Negroes, males, 1910....	32.15	4.59	5.06	11.26	17.89	29.05
U. S. Negroes, females, 1910 ..	28.11	4.92	6.02	10.20	17.37	33.38
India, males, 1901–1910......	39.71	10.08	6.38	12.30	16.75	14.78
Japan, males, 1898–1903	20.90	4.21	3.58	8.33	15.45	47.52
Italy, males, 1901–1910	25.01	3.66	2.75	6.62	12.12	49.84

percentage of United States Negroes and males of India dying during the same interval. Here again I think that the Pecos figures from the skeletons are probably too high.

When we come to the middle-aged group (35–54 years) we find the percentage of Pecos skeletons more than twice as large as the percentage dying during that period in any extant group. This great excess of middle-aged skeletons in the Pecos group may be referred in some measure to the better weathering and preservation of skeletons of persons dying in that age interval. There is also the possibility that I have assigned to this age group a large number of individuals who really belong in the oldest age group. But Professor Todd's age grouping shows the same lumping in this period, and that writer, on the basis of the study of ages in the Pecos and a number of other ancient and primitive peoples, concludes that the peak of old-age death is a comparatively modern achievement resulting from greater safety and improved conditions of living and that the difference between the peaks of mortality in primitive and ancient peoples on the one hand and of modern civilized humanity on the other is roughly thirty years.[1] But it would appear that more of the Pecos Indians reached old age than do modern males in India, only 14.78 per cent of whom die at the age of 55 years or older, whereas 18.43 per cent of the Pecos are assigned to that age group. If I were to hazard a guess as to significance of this high mortality in middle age among the Pecos, I should be inclined to attribute it to war and to epidemics. I suspect also the ravages of tuberculosis, evidence of which will be offered in Chapter X.

[1] Todd, 1927, pp. 495 sq.

SEX

The determination of the sex of skeletal material is not often the subject of discussion or debate among anthropologists and anatomists, for each student sexes his own material in the laboratory according to conventional criteria, and the sex determinations thus made are not likely to be questioned unless some other student has occasion to work over the same series. But every anthropologist, unless he deceives himself, must recognize that many of his decisions as to sex are questionable. The following sex differences in the skull, for example, are generally recognized. The male has larger brow-ridges and a more sloping forehead than the female; the muscular markings are more distinct in the male; the mastoids are larger, the contours and relief of the skull base are more rugged in the male; the orbital edges are more rounded; the zygomatic arches are thicker; the palate and teeth are larger, the lower jaw is more massive with a more strongly developed mental eminence. These and other differences are believed to distinguish the male from the female. But a certain number of females have well developed brow-ridges and large jaws, and among the peoples whose women carry burdens on the head the mastoid processes are likely to be well developed in females and the attachments of nuchal musculature and ligaments are frequently strongly marked. There are also some males in whom the sex characters are not well developed. It is unfortunately the case that when one skull sex criterion fails, most of the others are likely to be dubious. We expect the long bones in males to be more strongly marked and massive than in females, with larger articular heads and surfaces. But when it is really necessary to depend upon these points of distinction we usually find that specimens the sex of which is dubious show no clear differentiation in these points. Indian women from the Southwest often, even usually, show a stronger development of muscular markings of the upper extremity than the men, perhaps because of the corn-grinding activities which fall to the lot of the housewife.

Naturally the anthropologist or anatomist prefers to rely upon the pelvis for sex differentiation of skeletal material, but unfortunately in archaeological material the pelves are, of all skeletal parts, least likely to be well preserved. Moreover the orthodox pelvic criteria are not infallible. We suppose that the female pelvis should exhibit a relatively broad and circular inlet, wide ischiatic notches, ischia splayed outward, a large subpubic angle, great diameter between the ischiatic spines and a generally large development of horizontal diameters as contrasted with vertical diameters. But all of these female features do not invariably appear together in a female pelvis and some of them are found not infrequently in pelves which are certainly male.

The Pecos skeletal material offers more difficulties in the determination of sex than any other series I have studied. Of course a large number of the skeletons are clearly defined as to sex, whether male or female, but the doubtful specimens are extraordinarily puzzling and quite numerous. We expect a certain number of females to exhibit rather masculine features with respect to skull and even to pelvis, especially among primitive peoples in whom the sex differences in the pelvis are often less pronounced than among Europeans. We do not, however, expect males to have broad, low, feminine-looking pelves. Yet not infrequently in the Pecos series skeletons with exaggeratedly masculine crania and long bones have features which one expects to see only in the female pelvis.

In Tables II–7, 8, 9, 10 we may study the associations of certain recognized sex criteria in Pecos pelves adjudged to be male and female respectively. Table II–7 deals with the association of the preauricular sulcus and the ischiatic notch. The ischiatic notch is generally believed to be narrow and deep in males and broad and shallow in females. The preauricular sulcus is supposed to be absent or faintly

TABLE II–7. ASSOCIATION OF PREAURICULAR SULCUS AND ISCHIATIC NOTCH

Ischiatic Notch	Preauricular Sulcus								Total
	Slight		Medium		Pronounced		Very Pronounced		
	No.	Per cent	No.	Per cent	No.	Per cent	No.	Per cent	No.
Male									
Narrow............	98	81.67	209	16.67	2	1.67	0	00.00	120
Medium............	12	54.54	9	40.91	1	4.54	0	00.00	22
Broad.............	4	18.18	4	18.18	10	45.45	4	18.18	22
Very Broad.........	1	10.00	3	30.00	3	30.00	3	30.00	10
Total..........	115	66.09	36	20.69	16	9.20	7	4.02	174

Coefficient of mean square contingency, 0.604

Female									
Narrow............	1	25.00	1	25.00	2	50.00	0	00.00	4
Medium............	4	16.67	11	45.83	7	29.17	2	8.33	24
Broad.............	8	10.53	7	9.21	47	61.84	14	18.42	76
Very Broad.........	5	12.50	8	20.00	17	42.50	10	25.00	40
Total..........	18	12.50	27	18.75	73	50.69	26	18.06	144

Coefficient of mean square contingency 0.362

marked in males and deep and broad in females. Of the 174 cases recorded in the table, 98 exhibit the characteristically narrow notch and ill-defined sulcus of the orthodox male. But all sorts of combinations of developments of the two characters are found. No less than 20 skeletons adjudged to be male have broad notches and deep sulci. It is the privilege of the reader to suggest that these 20 pelves are incorrectly sexed. But it should be remembered that only very strong evidence of masculinity in other skeletal features of the pelvis and in other parts would lead to a decision in favor of the male sex when two pelvic criteria such as these fall into the feminine category. The coefficient of mean square contingency of these two features is .604, indicating on a scale between zero and unity the extent to which narrow notches are associated with poorly developed sulci and broad notches with deep sulci. The table shows the association of the same characters in 144 female pelves. Of this number 88 show the conventional association of deep sulci and broad notches. In this sex series 17 pelves show associations of "masculine" developments of the supposedly feminine characters. The coefficient of mean square contingency is only .362, indicating less consistency of association in the females than in the males.

Table II–8 gives the association of size of the subpubic angle with development of the preauricular sulcus. A small subpubic angle and a poorly developed sulcus are expected in males. These are realized, in combination, in 94 of 148 pelves judged to be males. Nineteen of the male pelves have either broad subpubic angles or deep sulci, or combinations of both. The coefficient of mean square contingency is .509. With respect to the association of these two features, the females again show less consistency. However, only ten of a total of 116 female pelves show male features in combinations of these two characters. A female pelvis very rarely if ever

TABLE II–8. ASSOCIATION OF SUBPUBIC ANGLE AND PREAURICULAR SULCUS

	Subpubic Angle								Total
	Small		Medium		Large		Very Large		
Preauricular Sulcus	No.	Per cent	No.	Per cent	No.	Per cent	No.	Per cent	No.
Male									
Slight.............	94	94.00	6	6.00	0	00.00	..	....	100
Medium...........	23	76.67	6	20.00	1	3.33	..	....	30
Pronounced........	4	30.77	5	38.46	4	30.77	..	....	13
Very Pronounced.....	2	40.00	2	40.00	1	20.00	..	....	5
Total..........	123	83.11	19	12.84	6	4.05	..	....	148

Coefficient of mean square contingency 0.509

	Small		Medium		Large		Very Large		Total
	No.	Per cent	No.	Per cent	No.	Per cent	No.	Per cent	No.
Female									
Slight.............	0	00.00	5	35.71	9	64.29	0	00.00	14
Medium...........	0	00.00	5	20.00	18	72.00	2	8.00	25
Pronounced........	2	3.28	6	9.84	47	77.05	6	9.84	61
Very Pronounced.....	0	00.00	5	31.25	10	62.50	1	6.25	16
Total..........	2	1.72	21	18.10	84	72.41	9	7.76	116

Coefficient of mean square contingency 0.280

has a narrow subpubic angle, but it may often have little or no development of the preauricular sulcus. The contingency coefficient is .280, showing only a feeble association.

The association of the subpubic angle with the ischiatic notch is recorded in the next table (Table II–9). Of 166 male pelves 112 have the combination of a narrow notch and a small subpubic angle. The coefficient of mean square contingency is .488. In the female series the association is less marked, 79 of 120 pelves exhibiting the orthodox feminine combination. The mean square contingency coefficient is .310

Table II–10 indicates that sacra composed of six segments are more common in males than in females but that there is no strong association between degree of curvature of the sacrum and number of segments. Strongly curved sacra are slightly more common in males than in females.

It is evident from these tables that the associations between pelvic features are more marked in males than in females, assuming the sex assignments to be approximately correct. It is also clear that the subpubic angle and the ischiatic notch are the most reliable sex indicators, the preauricular sulcus and the curvature of the sacrum being of little value for purposes of sex differentiation.

There is usually no means of checking the correctness of the laboratory sexing of skeletal material of archaeological origin. That mistakes are made, even by the most painstaking student, is certain. A great deal of care was spent by me in sexing the

Pecos collection and the doubtful cases were examined more than once. In one instance it was discovered that a skeleton to which the male sex had been assigned was reported on a grave-card as having been found with a foetal skeleton in the pelvis. Usually I have made no attempt to assign the skeletons of children and infants to a

TABLE II–9. ASSOCIATION OF SUBPUBIC ANGLE AND ISCHIATIC NOTCH

	Subpubic Angle									
	Small		Medium		Large		Very Large		Total	
Ischiatic Notch	No.	Per cent	No.	Per cent	No.	Per cent	No.	Per cent	No.	
Male										
Narrow..........	112	91.06	11	8.94	0	00.00	..	....	123	
Medium...........	14	70.00	5	25.00	1	5.00	..	....	20	
Broad.............	5	31.25	8	50.00	3	18.75	..	....	16	
Very Broad.........	3	42.86	2	28.57	2	28.57	..	....	7	
Total..........	134	80.72	26	15.66	6	3.61	..	....	166	

Coefficient of mean square contingency 0.488

	Small		Medium		Large		Very Large		Total	
Female										
Narrow..........	0	00.00	0	00.00	4	100.00	0	00.00	4	
Medium...........	0	00.00	6	30.00	13	65.00	1	5.00	20	
Broad.............	1	1.56	13	20.31	43	67.19	7	10.94	64	
Very Broad.........	1	3.13	2	6.25	26	81.25	3	9.38	32	
Total..........	2	1.67	21	17.50	86	71.67	11	9.17	120	

Coefficient of mean square contingency 0.310

TABLE II–10. ASSOCIATION OF SACRAL SEGMENTS AND SACRAL CURVATURE

	Number of Sacral Segments						Total	
	Four		Five		Six			
Sacral Curvature	No.	Per cent	No.	Per cent	No.	Per cent	No.	
Males								
Slight.................	..	.....	37	84.09	7	15.91	44	
Medium...............	..	.....	52	83.87	10	16.13	62	
Pronounced............	..	.....	21	80.77	5	19.23	26	
Very Pronounced.......	..	.....	1	100.00	0	00.00	1	
Total...............	..	.....	111	83.46	22	16.54	133	

Coefficient of mean square contingency 0.049

	Four		Five		Six		Total	
Females								
Slight.................	1	3.45	26	89.66	2	6.90	29	
Medium...............	0	00.00	40	86.96	6	13.04	46	
Pronounced............	0	00.00	12	100.00	0	00.00	12	
Very Pronounced.......	0	00.00	2	100.00	0	00.00	2	
Total...............	1	1.12	80	89.89	8	8.99	89	

Coefficient of mean square contingency 0.218

sex classification, since I am of the opinion that such sex determinations would be largely guesswork.

In Table II–11 a sample of 264 skeletons of the Pecos series sexed by me is compared with the sex assignments independently made by Todd upon the same specimens. In 207 cases or 78.41 per cent we agree as to the sex (including one case in which both observers were in doubt). In 15.15 per cent or 40 cases disagreement occurs, one observer having called a given skeleton male, and the other having pronounced it to be female. These disagreements are almost equally divided with 21 cases which I have sexed male, and which Todd has sexed as female, and 19 cases in the opposite category. There are 17 cases or 6.44 per cent in which one observer has been in doubt as to the sex of the skeleton, while the other one has assigned it either to the male or to the female sex. These again are almost equally divided both as to

TABLE II–11. COMPARISON OF SEXING OF PECOS MATERIAL BY HOOTON AND TODD

Both Male........ 129	Both Female....... 77	Both Doubtful...... 1
Hooton Male ..... ⎫ 21 Todd Female ..... ⎭	Hooton Female .... ⎫ 19 Todd Male .... ⎭	Hooton Doubtful .... ⎫ 3 Todd Male .... ⎭
Hooton Doubtful.. ⎫ 5 Todd Female ..... ⎭	Hooton Female .... ⎫ 7 Todd Doubtful..... ⎭	Hooton Male .... ⎫ 2 Todd Doubtful...... ⎭

	No.	Per cent		No.	Per cent		No.	Per cent
Agreements...	207	78.41	Differences....	40	15.15	One observer in doubt....	17	6.44

	Total Males	Total Females	Total Doubtful	Total
Todd......................	151	103	10	264
Hooton....................	152	103	9	264

TABLE II–12. COMPARISON OF SEXING OF PECOS MATERIAL BY HOOTON AND TODD BY GLAZE SUBGROUPS

		Hooton	Todd
Males:	B.-on-W. and Glaze I.............................	22	20
	Glazes II and III.................................	41	39
	Glaze IV..	24	29
	Glazes V and VI.................................	37	35
	Total.....................................	124	123
Females:	B.-on-W. and Glaze I.............................	15	20
	Glazes II and III.................................	29	34
	Glaze IV..	24	18
	Glazes V and VI.................................	19	16
	Total.....................................	87	88
Doubtful:	B.-on-W. and Glaze I.............................	4	1
	Glazes II and III.................................	5	2
	Glaze IV..	0	1
	Glazes V and VI.................................	0	5
	Total.....................................	9	9

number of cases per observer and sex assigned by the observer who committed himself upon the material of which the other was in doubt. Table II–12 shows that Todd and I arrive at almost precisely the same number of males and females in spite of having differed as to the sex of individual skeletons. These tables seem to me to indicate that where differences of opinion occur the odds are almost even as to the sex upon which each observer decides. It would seem to follow also that in debatable skeletons the criteria of sex differentiation are mixed in such a way that about half of them indicate male and the other half female.

In Table II–13 the number of males per hundred females in the Pecos series is compared with the corresponding sex ratios among the living Indians of Tanoan stock and with the Indians of Jemez who include the survivors of Pecos, nine of whom were still living at Jemez in 1910. In the age group including all under 20 years the data are not strictly comparable, owing to the exclusion from the Pecos series of children and infants of indeterminable sex. In the group including indi-

TABLE II–13. COMPARISON OF NUMBER OF MALES PER HUNDRED FEMALES IN PECOS SERIES WITH SIMILAR RATIOS OF LIVING INDIANS OF TANOAN STOCK (CENSUS OF 1910) [1]

PERCENTAGES

	Total Number	Under 20 years	20 to 50 years	51 years and over	Total
Pecos	667	70.9*	150.8	146.2	140.8
Jemez	499	104.7	152.8	142.3	128.9
All Tanoan	3137	92.4	120.6	136.2	108.7

* Includes only age 10–19 since skeletons under 10 years were not sexed.

viduals from 20 years to 50 years the ratio of males to females in the Pecos series is 150.8, in the Jemez pueblo 152.8, and in the whole Tanoan stock 120.6. Again in the old-age group the Pecos ratio is slightly higher than the Jemez ratio and both exceed the ratio in the Tanoan stock at large.

It is well known that in most countries the proportion of males born exceeds the proportion of females. Unfortunately few data as to the number of the sexes at birth among Indians are available. Hrdlička, however, found that the ratio of males to females at birth among the Apache (based upon 37 families) was 115, and among the Pima (35 families) 112.1.[2] The excess of males born at Jemez and among the Tanoan-speaking peoples in general, is probably still larger. Usually the death rate is lower among females than among males. But on the basis of Hrdlička's scanty data there is little difference between the infant mortality of the sexes among the Apache and Pima. However the figures in Table II–13 indicate among the Tanoan peoples an excess of females during childhood and adolescence. During the adult period of life deaths of women in childbirth and from exhaustion probably wipe out the excess of females.

I have been inclined to attribute the great excess of males in skeletal populations to the better weathering of male skeletons or to a possible tendency on the part of the laboratory worker to assign to the male sex skeletons of masculine appearance which were in reality female. However, the comparison of the Pecos skeletal population with the sex ratios in living peoples of the same stock indicates that the great excess of males should not be attributed to any such sources of error.

In a population which is remaining stationary or declining in numbers one expects the number of males to exceed markedly the number of females. This excess

[1] Indian Population of the United States and Alaska, 1910. Department of Commerce, Bureau of the Census, Washington, 1915.   [2] Hrdlička, 1908, p. 39.

of males is usually attributable to an actual difference of the proportions of the sexes at birth. We need not here discuss the hypothesis of the relation of nutritional factors to sex determination, but it may be remarked that if, as some think, a well nourished and increasing population produces an excess of females at birth, whereas a badly nourished and declining population produces an excess of males at birth, we may well expect the population of the extinct Pecos pueblo to manifest in a high degree the latter type of disproportion of the sexes.

We have, as a matter of fact, for the aged and sexed Pecos population, ten years of age and upwards, the following ratios of males to females during the several archaeological periods:

TABLE II–14. SEX RATIOS DURING ARCHAEOLOGICAL PERIODS

Period	Males Number	Females Number	Males per Hundred Females
B.-on-W., Glaze I	72	52	138.4
Glazes II and III	112	85	131.7
Glaze IV	54	45	120.0
Glazes V and VI	60	34	176.5
Stratum unknown	92	61	150.8
Total	390	277	140.8

This table shows that the excess of males was least during the two middle periods of the pueblo's occupation, when the population was largest and Pecos was flourishing. It also shows a notable increase in the proportion of males (176.5) during the last periods which witnessed the decline and extinction of the population.

CHAPTER III

CRANIAL MEASUREMENTS BY STRATA

CRANIAL DEFORMATION

THE total number of crania of the Pecos collection included in the present study of cranial deformation is 615. Many of these are mere fragments and quite unfit for craniometric treatment. As excavation at Pecos continued, every summer new material was shipped to the Peabody Museum, but it has been necessary to exclude the material received since 1924 from consideration in this work, since it is obviously impossible to reopen statistical series which have been subjected to analysis. Of the 615 crania included in our analysis from the point of view of deformation, only 40, or 6.50 per cent, show no deformation, artificial or pathological (Table III–2). A considerable number (149) are so little deformed that the measurements of the cranial vault are scarcely affected. This class constitutes 24.23 per cent of the series. The deformation is almost exclusively an occipital flattening, caused, presumably, by methods of cradling.

Total Series A consists of 174 male crania and 117 female crania which have been studied by archaeological strata. Table III–1 shows the degree of deformation in

TABLE III–1. DEGREE OF DEFORMATION IN TOTAL SERIES A

| | Absent | | Submedium | | Medium | | Pronounced | | Very Pronounced | | |
Males	No.	Per cent	No.	Per cent	No.	Per cent	No.	Per cent	No.	Per cent	Total
Black-on-white and Glaze I	3	10.00	9	30.00	12	40.00	5	16.67	1	3.33	30
Glazes II and III	4	6.15	16	24.62	24	36.92	20	30.77	1	1.54	65
Glaze IV	0	0	12	34.29	5	14.29	15	42.86	3	8.57	35
Glazes V and VI	3	6.82	10	22.73	14	31.82	15	34.09	2	4.55	44
Total	10	5.75	47	27.01	55	31.61	55	31.61	7	4.02	174
Females											
Black-on-white and Glaze I	1	4.35	6	26.09	11	47.83	3	13.04	2	8.70	23
Glazes II and III	0	0	12	29.27	18	43.90	11	26.83	0	0	41
Glaze IV	1	3.33	8	26.67	12	40.00	7	23.33	2	6.67	30
Glazes V and VI	1	4.35	5	21.74	14	60.87	3	13.04	0	0	23
Total	3	2.56	31	26.50	55	47.01	24	20.51	4	3.42	117

these skulls by strata and by sexes. In the male series it would appear that cranial deformation was slightly less frequent in the earliest periods of the pueblo, the Black-on-white and Glaze I periods. There are also uncertain indications that in the males cranial deformation increased in intensity throughout the succeeding archaeological periods. Thus, in the first two periods (Black-on-white and Glaze I), which are grouped together, the percentage of crania with slight or no deformation is 40; in Glazes II and III this percentage decreases to 30.77; in Glaze IV it is 34.29 and in

Glazes V and VI 29.55 per cent. Similarly, the percentages of male crania with pronounced or very pronounced deformation is as follows: Black-on-white and Glaze I, 20 per cent; Glazes II and III, 32.31 per cent; Glaze IV, 51.43 per cent; Glazes V and VI, 38.64 per cent. It would seem that cranial deformation was most pronounced and universal in Glaze IV. In the female series there seems to be little if any significant variation in the amount or intensity of cranial deformation throughout the succeeding periods. Pronounced and very pronounced deformation is less common among the females than among the males. A careful analysis of this table seems to

TABLE III–2. DEGREE OF DEFORMATION IN TOTAL PECOS COLLECTION

	Absent	Submedium	Medium	Pronounced	Very Pronounced	Total
Number	40	149	244	157	25	615
Per cent	6.50	24.23	39.67	25.53	4.07	

indicate, however, that the greatest intensity of cranial deformation in the female series also occurred during the Glaze IV period and that, as in the case of the males, there may have been a diminution in the intensity of the cranial deformation during the last two archaeological periods of the pueblo's occupation.

Apart from the foregoing differences, which may be in a large measure due to irregularities in sampling or inconsistency in judging degrees of deformation in individual crania, there is no evidence of any particular relationship between archaeological strata and cranial deformation. At all periods the majority of the population had occipitally flattened crania, and there were always a few individuals who were unaffected by this practice. There seems to have been no very marked or even certain fluctuations in extent or degree. Two interpretations of this state of affairs are possible: (1) that throughout the history of the pueblo a small and selected few, either because of considerations of race, of religion, or of social class, did not practise cranial deformation; (2) that cranial deformation was not intentionally practised and that at all times different individuals were affected in varying degrees, according to the inherited shapes of their heads, the individual plasticity of their skulls, and the hardness of their cradles. The first interpretation seems improbable. We are not aware that cranial deformation was a matter of caste or religion within Indian tribes, such that a selected few would in successive generations refrain from the practice that was almost universal for a thousand years. Nor is it probable that any racial element entering into the composition of the village population would be nonconformist in method of cradling for several centuries.

Elsewhere,[1] it has been pointed out that accidental deformation due to a hard cradle-board, is likely to affect differently shaped heads in quite diverse ways. Granting that the infant's head is not fastened to the cradle and can be moved about at will, it is obvious that a head with a protruding occiput is likely to roll over to one side or the other and come to rest upon that side, whereas a rounded head with a comparatively flat occiput naturally rests upon its back. Even if the infant were laid in every case upon its back, the long-headed child would tend to rest its head on

[1] Hooton, 1920, p. 89.

the lateral surface of the occiput rather than upon its center. It follows that artificial occipital flattening is likely to affect brachycephalic children more markedly
than dolichocephalic children, since the pressure in the case of the latter tends to be
applied to the sides of the protuberant occiput. It is difficult to stand an egg on end.
If these considerations are logical it would seem that dolichocephalic children in
Pecos pueblo should be less affected by accidental occipital deformation than brachycephalic children. In Total Series A 58.14 per cent of the male crania which are
undeformed or only very slightly deformed, are either dolichocephals or mesocephals;
24 per cent of the undeformed female crania belong in this category. Of the deformed male skulls of Total Series A, 3.30 per cent are dolichocephals or mesocephals, and of the deformed female crania 13.23 per cent. According to our interpretation, then, the excess of dolichocephals in the undeformed series is caused by a
relative immunity from occipital deformation which long-heads enjoy. Table III–3
gives the distribution by divisions of the cranial index of all crania of Series A in
which that index could be calculated. In this table all crania with very slight occipital deformation are regarded as undeformed, as it seems improbable that the
cranial index has been much altered by the slight amount of deformation suffered.
Of these "undeformed" crania 41.86 per cent of the males and 76 per cent of the
females are brachycephals. This indicates, of course, that many of the round-heads
of the Pecos series were not pronouncedly affected by occipital flattening. These
comparatively undeformed brachycephals include 18 male crania and 19 female
crania. It seems probable that in many cases the slight degree of deformation to
which these crania have been subjected has shifted them from the upper ranges of
mesocephaly to the lower ranges of brachycephaly.

In addition to variations in the hardness of the head-rest in cradles and in the
effects of the cradle-board upon differently shaped occiputs, we must consider the
variations in plasticity of the skull which individual infants manifest. Any child
that is undernourished is likely to have a skull which will be altered by occipital
pressure or any other deformative agency to a much greater degree than the skull
of the healthy child which is subjected to the same mechanical forces. Our comparatively undeformed brachycephals may represent the round-headed element of
the Pecos population, which, being most vigorous during infancy, was best able to
withstand the deformative effects of the hard cradle-board upon the occiput.

The types of cranial deformation noted include (a) an occipital flattening that
affects the whole back of the head, producing a more or less plane surface, the transverse axis of which is nearly perpendicular to the sagittal plane of the cranium;
(b) asymmetrical occipital deformations in which the right or left side of the occiput
is exaggeratedly flattened so that the transverse axis of the flattened area is not
perpendicular to the sagittal axis of the skull; (c) a flattening which affects the apex
of the occipital bone and the portions of the parietals adjacent to lambda and which
I call "lambdoid deformation."

Asymmetrical occipital flattenings are probably referable to the habits of individual children. If a baby tends to turn its head slightly to the right when it is lying
on its back in the cradle, the right side of the occiput will be flattened more than the

TABLE III–3. DIVISIONS OF LENGTH–BREADTH (CRANIAL) INDEX

		Dolichocephalic (x–74.9)	Mesocephalic (75–79.9)	Brachycephalic (80–x)	Total
Males (deformed)					
Total Series A	Number	2	1	88	91
	Per cent	2.20	1.10	96.70	
Black-on-white and Glaze I	Number	0	1	12	13
	Per cent	0	7.69	92.31	
Glazes II and III	Number	0	0	33	33
	Per cent	0	0	100.00	
Glaze IV	Number	0	0	20	20
	Per cent	0	0	100.00	
Glazes V and VI	Number	2	0	23	25
	Per cent	8.00	0	92.00	
Females (deformed)					
Total Series A	Number	2	7	59	68
	Per cent	2.94	10.29	86.76	
Black-on-white and Glaze I	Number	1	2	11	14
	Per cent	7.14	14.29	78.57	
Glazes II and III	Number	1	1	21	23
	Per cent	4.35	4.35	91.30	
Glaze IV	Number	0	2	16	18
	Per cent	0	11.11	88.89	
Glazes V and VI	Number	0	0	13	13
	Per cent	0	0	100.00	
Males (undeformed)					
Total Series A	Number	9	16	18	43
	Per cent	20.93	37.21	41.86	
Black-on-white and Glaze I	Number	1	4	5	10
	Per cent	10.00	40.00	50.00	
Glazes II and III	Number	3	7	5	15
	Per cent	20.00	46.67	33.33	
Glaze IV	Number	1	4	3	8
	Per cent	12.50	50.00	37.50	
Glazes V and VI	Number	4	1	5	10
	Per cent	40.00	10.00	50.00	
Females (undeformed)					
Total Series A	Number	0	6	19	25
	Per cent	0	24.00	76.00	
Black-on-white and Glaze I	Number	0	0	5	5
	Per cent	0	0	100.00	
Glazes II and III	Number	0	3	4	7
	Per cent	0	42.86	57.14	
Glaze IV	Number	0	2	6	8
	Per cent	0	25.00	75.00	
Glazes V and VI	Number	0	1	4	5
	Per cent	0	20.00	80.00	

left, and *vice versa*. Table III–4 gives the frequency of the various types of deformation.

A perusal of the table shows that the deformation is direct occipital in 56.15 per cent of cases. In about 22 per cent of cases the deformation is right occipital or right parieto-occipital, as contrasted with about 12.5 per cent in which the flattenings are on the left side. I suggest that the excess of right flattenings may be connected with the greater tendency of right-handed children to turn the head slightly toward the right when lying on the back if the occiput shows a moderate convexity. Occipital deformation was designated as "right" or "left" only when there was a

TABLE III–4. KINDS OF DEFORMATION — TOTAL PECOS CRANIA

	Occ.	R. Occ.	L. Occ.	Lambd.	R. Lambd.	R. Par.-Occ.	L. Par.-Occ.	Fronto-Occ.	L.-Fronto Occ.	Scaph.	L. Par.	Total
Number	315	106	65	39	2	18	5	5	2	3	1	561 *
Per cent	56.15	18.89	11.59	6.95	0.36	3.21	0.89	0.89	0.36	0.53	0.18	

* This total does not correspond to the total for *degree* of deformation (615) for the following reasons:
  1. There were 40 skulls without deformation not included in this table — leaving 575.
  2. Post mortem deformation was included in the other table, and is not included here — leaving 561.

marked asymmetry. Probably an exact measurement of the angle of plane of flattening with the sagittal plane would reveal also a tendency in those classified simply as "occipital" to show more marked flattening on the right side. But the more brachycephalic infants would perhaps be subjected to a lesser degree of asymmetrical flattening than those with rounded occiputs, because they would present naturally a large and relatively flat area perpendicular to the sagittal plane upon which the head would come to rest.

Fronto-occipital deformation was noticed in only seven cases. Three scaphoid skulls are included in the table, but this deformation is certainly pathological.

"Lambdoid" deformation occurs in about 7 per cent of all crania.

The type of deformation I have called "lambdoid" is a flattening of the "crown" of the head. The flattened area is round or oval and its transverse axis is perpendicular to the sagittal axis of the skull, but an inferior extension of the plane of flattening makes an angle of about 35° to 45° with the eye-ear plane of the skull. The flattened surface thus slopes downward and backward from the obelion region to a point somewhat below lambda. Below this flattened area the occiput may be pronouncedly or moderately protruding. If this lambdoid flattening is artificially caused it can have been effected only by pressure exerted upon the crown of the head just behind the vertex. This pressure would have to be exerted downward and forward, unless the head and the whole body were pressed up against a forward-sloping board or pad. The lambdoid deformation is a flattening of the posterior portion of the top of the cranial vault and is exactly the opposite of the flattening of the frontal bone familiar in certain Indian groups. By no conceivable contortions of the infant could this flattening be effected by lying upon the back with the head resting on the occiput. It would hardly be possible to produce such an effect even if the infant were stood upon its head or the cradle carried upon the mother's back in an inverted position.

In most instances this lambdoid flattening is certainly not caused by artificial deformation. It has been observed in the so-called "Cro-Magnon" types of the Late Palaeolithic period and it can be seen in many crania of European and non-European peoples of the present day. It is especially noticeable in the skulls of Armenoids and Finns. For some time it has been my opinion that this lambdoid flattening is a feature found in the crania of people who are the result of an intermixture of a brachycephalic and a dolichocephalic type.[1]

In such cases this lambdoid flattening may be a form of cranial disharmony brought about by mixture of contrasting cranial types. This explanation would be valid in the case of Pecos people, in whom crossings of round-heads and long-heads were very common. But a certain number of these skulls with lambdoid flattenings give one the distinct impression that artificial pressure has been exerted upon the crown of the head to produce the condition in question. A possible explanation of this apparently artificial lambdoid flattening may lie in the alternation of growth tendencies in heads of mixed types. A child which had inherited factors for head-form from strongly contrasted parents might be born with a flattened occiput which would become more flattened as a result of cradle-board deformation. Subsequently a tendency toward the development of a projecting occiput might manifest itself, with the result that the lower portion of the occipital region would be prolonged backward, leaving the earlier occipital deformation as a flattened area sloping downward and backward above the convexity of the inferior portion of the occiput. A similar explanation, but without the introduction of the cradle-board flattening, might also explain the lambdoid flattenings so common in mixed Europeans. This is, of course, a speculation. Possibly some support for it may be adduced in the well-known fact that children of mixed blond and brunet ancestry often are born with blue eyes and blond hair which subsequently darken in an irregular fashion. That seems to constitute an approximately analogous case. However, it must be confessed that I can offer at present no scientific evidence in the way of actual observations upon growing children who present lambdoid flattenings.

STATISTICAL CORRECTION FOR CRANIAL DEFORMATION

For some years it has been my impression that an approximate restoration of the vault diameters of artificially deformed crania might be attained by the use of correlation and regression formulae, if only sufficiently high correlation coefficients between diameters unaffected by deformation and those affected by it could be found. Under my direction Dr. H. L. Shapiro, now of the American Museum of Natural History, but at that time tutor in Anthropology at Harvard University, undertook the solution of the problem. He has very kindly put the results of his research at my disposal.[2] Dr. Shapiro was able to establish by comparisons of dimensions of deformed and undeformed crania belonging to the same ethnic group, that the basion-nasion diameter (length of the cranio-facial base) is apparently unaffected by occipital flattening. He was also able to show that basion-nasion

---

[1] Hooton, 1923, p. 69.   [2] Shapiro, 1928, p. 18.

length in all groups is highly correlated with glabello-occipital length (the maximum length of the cranium in the median sagittal plane). These correlations were calculated from the weighted means of a large number of series of undeformed crania. The coefficient of correlation of basion-nasion diameter with glabello-occipital length thus obtained is .71. The correction formula for head-length is as follows:

$$r\frac{\sigma x}{\sigma y} = .65\left(\frac{4.41}{1.93}\right) = 1.49.$$

That is, for every unit change in basion-nasion diameter there is a corresponding change of 1.49 units in head-length. To obtain the corrected head-length the difference between the means of basion-nasion in deformed and undeformed crania of the same group is multiplied by 1.49. This product is then subtracted from the undeformed glabello-occipital length to secure the corrected deformed length. The following example illustrates the process:

Glabello-occipital length of undeformed male crania, Series A	= 175.74
Glabello-occipital length of deformed male crania, Series A	= 164.28
Basion-nasion length of undeformed male crania, Series A	= 102.70
Basion-nasion length of deformed male crania, Series A	= 101.58

1.49(102.70 − 101.58) = − 1.67   175.74 − 1.67 = 174.07 = corrected head-length of deformed crania, Series A.

For restoring the maximum breadth of the cranium Dr. Shapiro found that an index secured by dividing the mean of the cranial module $\frac{\text{L.} + \text{B.} + \text{H.}}{3}$ by the mean glabello-occipital length gave the largest coefficient of correlation. This coefficient of correlation of cranial module-length index was ascertained to be +.71. For each change of one unit in cranial module-length index the breadth of the head is changed .99 mm.

To obtain the restored height of deformed crania the sum of the restored lengths and breadths has been subtracted from the sum of length, breadth, and height of the deformed crania. If compensation is complete the sum of the three diameters in deformed crania should be equal to the sum of the undeformed diameters. Occipital flattening should cause as much increase in height and breadth as diminution in length. It will be seen from our tables of correction that satisfactory results, or, at any rate, reasonable results, have been obtained by this method. Dr. Shapiro, however, recommends a correction based upon correlation of basion-bregma height with breadth-height index. The correlation coefficient is −.91 and the correction is −.80 mm.

In the utilization of regression formulae for the purpose of predicting values it is, of course, understood that average values only may be obtained. Such formulae are useless for the prediction of individual values. In the present instance the use of Dr. Shapiro's formulae enables us to reconstruct the approximate average values of vault diameters and vault indices of artificially deformed crania. The value of such reconstructions need not be enlarged upon.

DIAMETERS AND INDICES OF THE CRANIAL VAULT

Table III–5 gives the means, standard deviations, coefficients of variation and their probable errors for glabello-occipital length in crania of Series A. Undeformed and deformed groups are treated separately, as are also the crania of different archaeological strata. In the total male series the mean of the undeformed crania exceeds that of the deformed by 11.46 mm. In the female series the difference is only 4 mm. The differences between subgroups of the various archaeological strata are probably insignificant.

Table III–6 gives means of glabello-occipital length for deformed crania, undeformed crania, and corrected deformed crania. For the total male series the cor-

TABLE III–5. GLABELLO–OCCIPITAL LENGTH

	Number	Range	Mean	St. D.	V.
Males					
Total Series A					
deformed	95	140–187	164.28 ± 0.59	8.46 ± 0.41	5.15 ± 0.25
undeformed	46	158–198	175.74 ± 0.81	8.15 ± 0.58	4.65 ± 0.33
Black-on-white and Glaze I					
deformed	13	157–180	166.85 ± 1.37	7.34 ± 0.97	4.40 ± 0.58
undeformed	10	163–182	173.40 ± 1.38	6.45 ± 0.97	3.71 ± 0.56
Glaze II and III					
deformed	36	140–181	161.72 ± 0.90	7.99 ± 0.64	4.94 ± 0.39
undeformed	16	161–198	180.00 ± 1.41	8.39 ± 1.00	4.66 ± 0.56
Glaze IV					
deformed	21	152–176	164.29 ± 1.03	7.02 ± 0.73	4.31 ± 0.60
undeformed	9	158–182	171.33 ± 1.86	6.76 ± 1.07	3.94 ± 0.63
Glazes V and VI					
deformed	25	145–187	166.64 ± 1.30	9.60 ± 0.92	5.76 ± 0.55
undeformed	11	165–189	175.36 ± 1.47	7.24 ± 1.04	4.13 ± 0.59
Females					
Total Series A					
deformed	71	144–179	159.66 ± 0.66	8.31 ± 0.47	5.20 ± 0.29
undeformed	26	152–177	163.65 ± 0.79	5.98 ± 0.56	3.65 ± 0.34
Black-on-white and Glaze I					
deformed	15	146–178	163.20 ± 1.74	9.99 ± 1.23	6.12 ± 0.75
undeformed	5	156–171	163.40	. . . .	. . . .
Glazes II and III					
deformed	24	144–179	158.83 ± 1.10	7.96 ± 0.77	5.05 ± 0.49
undeformed	8	152–173	164.62	. . . .	. . . .
Glaze IV					
deformed	18	147–177	157.44 ± 1.17	7.34 ± 0.82	4.66 ± 0.52
undeformed	8	156–177	162.25	. . . .	. . . .
Glazes V and VI					
deformed	14	152–172	160.14 ± 1.20	6.66 ± 0.85	4.16 ± 0.53
undeformed	5	161–170	164.60	. . . .	. . . .

rected length of the deformed crania is 174.07 mm. as compared with 175.74 mm., the mean length of the undeformed. In the case of the total female series the corrected deformed length is 162.95 mm. as compared with 163.65, the mean of the undeformed. In most of the subgroups the corrected deformed lengths are slightly below those of the undeformed. This would seem to lend support to our supposition that shorter heads with more flattened occiputs are likely to be influenced more strongly by artificial deformation, unless full correction is not given by the formula.

Tables III–7, 8 deal with the maximum breadth of the skull. The restored breadths of the deformed crania consistently exceed the breadths of the undeformed

TABLE III–6. CORRECTION OF GLABELLO–OCCIPITAL LENGTH IN DEFORMED SKULLS

Males	No.	Deformed	No.	Undeformed	Corrected Deformed
Total Series A	45	164.28	46	175.74	174.07
Black-on-white and Glaze I...	13	166.85	10	173.40	175.78
Glazes II and III	36	61.721	16	180.00	174.90
Glaze IV	21	164.29	9	171.33	170.57
Glazes V and VI	25	166.64	11	175.36	174.29
Females					
Total Series A	71	159.66	26	163.65	162.95
Black-on-white and Glaze I...	15	163.20	5	163.40	162.76
Glazes II and III	24	158.83	8	164.62	163.98
Glaze IV	18	157.44	8	162.25	159.82
Glazes V and VI	14	160.14	5	164.60	167.14

TABLE III–7. MAXIMUM BREADTH

Males	Number	Range	Mean	St. D.	V.
Total Series A					
deformed	91	132–159	145.43 ± 0.43	6.13 ± 0.31	4.22 ± 0.21
undeformed	45	122–150	137.84 ± 0.62	6.14 ± 0.44	4.45 ± 0.32
Black-on-white and Glaze I					
deformed	13	139–156	147.61 ± 1.02	5.43 ± 0.72	3.68 ± 0.49
undeformed	10	125–149	137.20 ± 1.18	5.58 ± 0.83	4.02 ± 0.61
Glazes II and III					
deformed	33	133–158	144.61 ± 0.73	6.22 ± 0.52	4.30 ± 0.36
undeformed	15	122–146	139.00 ± 1.13	6.51 ± 0.80	4.68 ± 0.58
Glaze IV					
deformed	20	140–157	147.15 ± 0.79	5.22 ± 0.56	3.55 ± 0.38
undeformed	10	126–150	137.80 ± 1.55	7.29 ± 1.10	5.29 ± 0.80
Glazes V and VI					
deformed	25	132–159	144.00 ± 0.86	6.37 ± 0.61	4.42 ± 0.42
undeformed	10	132–146	136.80 ± 0.92	4.33 ± 0.65	3.16 ± 0.48
Females					
Total Series A					
deformed	68	121–154	141.35 ± 0.44	5.43 ± 0.31	3.84 ± 0.22
undeformed	25	128–150	138.04 ± 0.83	6.14 ± 0.59	4.45 ± 0.42
Black-on-white and Glaze I					
deformed	14	131–147	140.07 ± 0.91	5.05 ± 0.64	3.60 ± 0.46
undeformed	5	132–146	140.80 ...	....	....
Glazes II and III					
deformed	23	121–150	140.30 ± 0.89	6.34 ± 0.63	4.52 ± 0.45
undeformed	7	130–140	135.29	....	....
Glaze IV					
deformed	18	134–148	142.67 ± 0.62	3.88 ± 0.44	2.72 ± 0.30
undeformed	8	128–150	138.63	....	....
Glazes V and VI					
deformed	13	135–154	142.77 ± 1.03	5.52 ± 0.73	3.87 ± 0.51
undeformed	5	132–150	138.20	....	....

TABLE III–8. CORRECTION OF MAXIMUM BREADTH IN DEFORMED SKULLS

Males	No.	Deformed	No.	Undeformed	Corrected Deformed
Total Series A	91	145.43	45	137.84	137.22
Black-on-white and Glaze I	13	147.61	10	137.20	138.38
Glazes II and III	33	144.61	15	139.00	138.56
Glaze IV	20	147.15	10	137.80	140.37
Glazes V and VI	25	144.00	10	136.80	137.16
Females					
Total Series A	68	141.35	25	138.04	138.60
Black-on-white and Glaze I	14	140.07	5	140.80	141.11
Glazes II and III	23	140.30	7	135.29	136.17
Glaze IV	18	142.67	8	138.63	140.97
Glazes V and VI	13	142.77	5	138.20	139.74

crania, giving further evidence of more pronounced brachycephaly of the skulls which suffered most extreme deformation.

Tables III–9, 10, giving means of the cephalic index, show that the undeformed or relatively undeformed crania yield high mesocephalic means in case of the male series and frankly brachycephalic means in the female series. The corrected length-breadth index means of the deformed skulls indicate that their original form was more brachycephalic than in the case of the skulls which suffered little or no deformation. These corrected means are, in the case of the males, either verging upon brachycephaly or brachycephalic. In the female series they are more pronouncedly brachycephalic than the means of the undeformed skulls. Referring to Table III–3, which tabulates the divisions of the length-breadth index for deformed and undeformed crania, we note that only 20.9 per cent of undeformed male skulls are dolichocephalic, and only 4 per cent of female skulls. Almost 42 per cent of undeformed male crania are brachycephalic and 76 per cent of undeformed female crania fall into this category. This confirms the supposition made on page 35, that while brachycephalic skulls are more pronouncedly affected by occipital cradle-board flattening than dolichocephals, yet other individual constitutional factors probably affect to a considerable extent the plasticity of the skull.

Tables III–11, 12 show that the deformed crania exceed the undeformed in basion-bregma height. Corrections of the deformed heights indicate that the original heights of the skulls that suffered deformation would have been greater than those of the undeformed skulls. The height corrections are not quite as satisfactory as the length and breadth corrections, but, on the whole, give very reasonable results.

A perusal of Tables III–13, 14, and 15 shows that the length-height index in both deformed and undeformed crania is consistently hypsicephalic. Only 1.27 per cent of deformed male crania and 20.59 per cent of undeformed skulls are orthocephalic. All female crania are hypsicephalic and no skulls of either sex are chamaecephalic. If any chamaecephalic crania ever entered into the composition of this population. that element has survived only in the modified orthocephalic form. Means of the corrected length-height indices of deformed skulls are invariably hypsicephalic, although lower than means of the uncorrected deformed crania.

TABLE III–9. LENGTH–BREADTH (CRANIAL) INDEX

Males

	Number	Range	Mean	St. D.	V.
Total Series A					
deformed	91	73–102	88.93 ± 0.44	6.30 ± 0.32	7.08 ± 0.35
undeformed	43	68–88	78.30 ± 0.49	4.81 ± 0.35	6.14 ± 0.45
Black-on-white and Glaze I					
deformed	13	79–99	88.08 ± 1.00	5.34 ± 0.71	6.06 ± 0.80
undeformed	10	69–85	79.20 ± 1.00	4.64 ± 0.70	5.86 ± 0.88
Glazes II and III					
deformed	33	81–102	89.67 ± 0.68	5.78 ± 0.48	6.44 ± 0.53
undeformed	15	68–88	77.87 ± 0.89	5.13 ± 0.63	6.59 ± 0.81
Glaze IV					
deformed	20	80–97	89.85 ± 0.80	5.31 ± 0.57	5.91 ± 0.63
undeformed	8	72–88	78.88	....	....
Glazes V and VI					
deformed	25	73–102	87.40 ± 0.87	6.44 ± 0.61	7.37 ± 0.70
undeformed	10	72–84	77.60 ± 0.86	4.05 ± 0.61	5.21 ± 0.78

Females

	Number	Range	Mean	St. D.	V.
Total Series A					
deformed	68	68–104	88.90 ± 0.53	6.53 ± 0.38	7.34 ± 0.42
undeformed	25	76–96	84.32 ± 0.80	59.6 ± 0.57	7.07 ± 0.67
Black-on-white and Glaze I					
deformed	14	74–100	86.43 ± 1.39	7.70 ± 0.98	8.91 ± 1.14
undeformed	5	80–94	86.40	....	....
Glazes II and III					
deformed	23	68–104	88.96 ± 1.03	7.34 ± 0.73	8.25 ± 0.82
undeformed	7	77–90	82.43	....	....
Glaze IV					
deformed	18	79–100	90.78 ± 0.87	5.50 ± 0.62	6.06 ± 0.68
undeformed	8	76–96	84.88	....	....
Glazes V and VI					
deformed	13	85–95	88.77 ± 0.62	3.31 ± 0.44	3.72 ± 0.49
undeformed	5	78–93	84.00	....	....

TABLE III–10. CORRECTION OF LENGTH–BREADTH (CRANIAL) INDEX IN DEFORMED SKULLS

	No.	Deformed	No.	Undeformed	Corrected Deformed
Males					
Total Series A	91	88.93	43	78.30	78.83
Black-on-white and Glaze I	13	88.08	10	79.20	78.72
Glazes II and III	33	89.67	15	77.87	79.22
Glaze IV	20	89.85	8	78.88	82.29
Glazes V and VI	25	87.40	10	77.60	78.70
Females					
Total Series A	68	88.90	25	84.32	85.06
Black-on-white and Glaze I	14	86.43	5	86.40	86.70
Glazes II and III	23	88.96	7	82.43	83.04
Glaze IV	18	90.78	8	84.88	88.21
Glazes V and VI	13	88.77	5	84.00	83.76

TABLE III–11. BASION–BREGMA HEIGHT

Males

	Number	Range	Mean	St. D.	V.
Total Series A					
deferred	80	129–156	140.69 ± 0.39	5.23 ± 0.28	3.72 ± 0.20
undeformed	34	121–152	137.14 ± 0.75	6.49 ± 0.53	4.73 ± 0.39
Black-on-white and Glaze I					
deformed	10	130–150	140.10 ± 1.14	5.36 ± 0.80	3.82 ± 0.58
undeformed	8	121–139	133.25	....	....
Glazes II and III					
deformed	28	131–150	140.07 ± 0.60	4.69 ± 0.42	3.34 ± 0.30
undeformed	11	128–152	139.82 ± 1.32	6.50 ± 0.94	4.65 ± 0.67
Glaze IV					
deformed	20	129–156	142.30 ± 0.85	5.63 ± 0.60	3.96 ± 0.42
undeformed	5	130–146	136.00	....	....
Glazes V and VI					
deformed	22	129–151	140.27 ± 0.76	5.31 ± 0.54	3.78 ± 0.38
undeformed	10	132–151	138.70 ± 1.25	5.87 ± 0.88	4.23 ± 0.64

Females

	Number	Range	Mean	St. D.	V.
Total Series A					
deformed	55	127–148	135.24 ± 0.36	4.00 ± 0.26	2.96 ± 0.19
undeformed	21	127–143	133.90 ± 0.59	4.03 ± 0.42	3.01 ± 0.31
Black-on-white and Glaze I					
deformed	10	127–148	134.70 ± 1.24	5.83 ± 0.88	4.33 ± 0.65
undeformed	5	128–140	133.40	....	....
Glazes II and III					
deformed	17	131–141	135.65 ± 0.53	3.27 ± 0.37	2.41 ± 0.28
undeformed	5	130–136	133.00	....	....
Glaze IV					
deformed	14	127–143	136.07 ± 0.78	4.33 ± 0.55	3.18 ± 0.40
undeformed	6	129–137	133.17	....	....
Glazes V and VI					
deformed	14	129–137	134.29 ± 0.39	2.19 ± 0.28	1.63 ± 0.21
undeformed	5	127–143	136.00	....	....

TABLE III–12. CORRECTION OF BASION–BREGMA HEIGHT IN DEFORMED SKULLS

Males

	No.	Deformed	No.	Undeformed	Corrected Deformed
Total Series A	80	140.69	34	137.14	139.11
Black-on-white and Glaze I ...	10	140.10	8	133.25	140.40
Glazes II and III	28	140.07	11	139.82	132.94
Glaze IV	20	142.30	5	136.00	142.80
Glazes V and VI	22	140.27	10	138.70	139.46

Females

	No.	Deformed	No.	Undeformed	Corrected Deformed
Total Series A	55	135.24	21	133.90	134.70
Black-on-white and Glaze I ...	10	134.70	5	133.40	134.10
Glazes II and III	17	135.65	5	133.00	134.63
Glaze IV	14	136.07	6	133.17	135.39
Glazes V and VI	14	134.29	5	136.00	130.62

TABLE III–13. Length–Height Index

Males

	Number	Range	Mean	St. D.	V.
Total Series A					
deformed	80	72–101	85.78 ± 0.38	5.10 ± 0.27	5.94 ± 0.32
undeformed	34	70–89	78.11 ± 0.46	3.95 ± 0.32	5.06 ± 0.41
Black-on-white and Glaze I					
deformed	10	72–87	83.00 ± 0.92	4.31 ± 0.65	5.19 ± 0.78
undeformed	8	74–80	76.25 ± 0.50	2.10 ± 0.35	2.74 ± 0.46
Glazes II and III					
deformed	28	78–95	86.46 ± 0.55	4.35 ± 0.39	5.03 ± 0.45
undeformed	11	73–83	77.36 ± 0.67	3.28 ± 0.47	4.24 ± 0.61
Glaze IV					
deformed	20	76–98	87.30 ± 0.78	5.17 ± 0.55	5.92 ± 0.63
undeformed	5	76–82	78.80	....	....
Glazes V and VI					
deformed	22	77–101	84.77 ± 0.80	5.53 ± 0.56	6.52 ± 0.66
undeformed	10	70–89	79.70 ± 1.16	5.46 ± 0.82	6.85 ± 1.03
Females					
Total Series A					
deformed	55	75–95	85.14 ± 0.40	4.36 ± 0.28	5.13 ± 0.33
undeformed	21	76–88	82.00 ± 0.50	3.36 ± 0.35	4.10 ± 0.43
Black-on-white and Glaze I					
deformed	10	75–90	82.20 ± 0.99	4.64 ± 0.70	5.64 ± 0.58
undeformed	5	77–86	81.40	....	....
Glazes II and III					
deformed	17	81–95	87.00 ± 0.73	4.48 ± 0.52	5.15 ± 0.60
undeformed	5	80–86	81.80	....	....
Glaze IV					
deformed	14	79–93	86.71 ± 0.67	3.73 ± 0.48	4.30 ± 0.55
undeformed	6	78–86	83.00	....	....
Glazes V and VI					
deformed	14	79–88	83.86 ± 0.50	2.75 ± 0.35	3.28 ± 0.42
undeformed	5	76–88	82.40	....	....

TABLE III–14. Correction of Length–Height Index in Deformed Skulls

	No.	Deformed	No.	Undeformed	Corrected Deformed
Males					
Total Series A	80	85.78	34	78.11	79.92
Black-on-white and Glaze I	10	83.00	8	76.25	79.55
Glazes II and III	28	86.46	11	77.36	76.00
Glaze IV	20	87.30	5	78.80	83.72
Glazes V and VI	22	84.77	10	79.70	79.89
Females					
Total Series A	55	85.14	21	82.00	82.66
Black-on-white and Glaze I	10	82.20	5	81.40	82.21
Glazes II and III	17	87.00	5	81.80	82.10
Glaze IV	14	86.71	6	83.00	84.38
Glazes V and VI	14	83.86	5	82.40	78.44

TABLE III–15. Divisions of the Length–Height Index *

Males (deformed)		Chamaecephalic (x–69.5)	Orthocephalic (69.6–74.5)	Hypsicephalic (74.6–x)	Total
Total Series A	Number	0	1	79	80
	Per cent	0	1.25	98.75	
Black-on-white and Glaze I	Number	0	1	9	10
	Per cent	0	10.00	90.00	
Glazes II and III	Number	0	0	28	28
	Per cent	0	0	100.00	
Glaze IV	Number	0	0	20	20
	Per cent	0	0	100.00	
Glazes V and VI	Number	0	0	22	22
	Per cent	0	0	100.00	
Females (deformed)					
Total Series A	Number	0	0	55	55
	Per cent	0	0	100.00	
Black-on-white and Glaze I	Number	0	0	10	10
	Per cent	0	0	100.00	
Glazes II and III	Number	0	0	17	17
	Per cent	0	0	100.00	
Glaze IV	Number	0	0	14	14
	Per cent	0	0	100.00	
Glazes V and VI	Number	0	0	14	14
	Per cent	0	0	100.00	
Males (undeformed)					
Total Series A	Number	0	7	27	34
	Per cent	0	20.59	79.41	
Black-on-white and Glaze I	Number	0	2	6	8
	Per cent	0	25.00	75.00	
Glazes II and III	Number	0	3	8	11
	Per cent	0	27.27	72.73	
Glaze IV	Number	0	0	5	5
	Per cent	0	0	100.00	
Glazes V and VI	Number	0	2	8	10
	Per cent	0	20.00	80.00	
Females (undeformed)					
Total Series A	Number	0	0	21	21
	Per cent	0	0	100.00	
Black-on-white and Glaze I	Number	0	0	5	5
	Per cent	0	0	100.00	
Glazes II and III	Number	0	0	5	5
	Per cent	0	0	100.00	
Glaze IV	Number	0	0	6	6
	Per cent	0	0	100.00	
Glazes V and VI	Number	0	0	5	5
	Per cent	0	0	100.00	

* The series contain no chamaecephalic crania and only 8 orthocephalic crania. All of these latter are male crania and 6 of them are found in the first two subgroups — Black-on-white and Glaze I and Glazes II and III. The other 2 belong to the latest subgroup — Glazes V and VI.

TABLE III–16. Breadth–Height Index

Males

Total Series A	Number	Range	Mean	St. D.	V.
deformed	78	86–108	96.94 ± 0.36	4.74 ± 0.26	4.89 ± 0.26
undeformed	33	89–111	99.33 ± 0.57	4.90 ± 0.41	4.93 ± 0.41
Black-on-white and Glaze I .					
deformed	10	86–104	95.00 ± 1.00	4.71 ± 0.71	4.96 ± 0.75
undeformed	8	89–106	97.12 ± 1.16	4.86 ± 0.82	5.00 ± 0.84
Glazes II and III					
deformed	27	89–108	97.18 ± 0.62	4.76 ± 0.44	4.90 ± 0.45
undeformed	11	94–108	98.91 ± 0.92	4.50 ± 0.65	4.55 ± 0.65
Glaze IV					
deformed	19	90–101	96.68 ± 0.53	3.40 ± 0.37	3.52 ± 0.38
undeformed	5	98–106	100.60	....	....
Glazes V and VI					
deformed	22	86–108	98.09 ± 0.83	5.76 ± 0.58	5.87 ± 0.60
undeformed	9	94–111	101.11 ± 1.22	5.44 ± 0.86	5.36 ± 0.86

Females

Total Series A					
deformed	53	87–104	95.28 ± 0.35	4.09 ± 0.25	3.96 ± 0.26
undeformed	21	90–104	97.67 ± 0.61	4.16 ± 0.43	4.26 ± 0.44
Black-on-white and Glaze I					
deformed	10	89–103	96.00 ± 0.90	4.24 ± 0.64	4.42 ± 0.67
undeformed	5	90–101	95.00	....	....
Glazes II and III					
deformed	16	91–102	95.81 ± 0.49	2.92 ± 0.35	3.05 ± 0.36
undeformed	5	94–104	100.40	....	....
Glaze IV					
deformed	14	88–104	95.57 ± 0.74	4.08 ± 0.52	4.27 ± 0.54
undeformed	6	93–101	97.00	....	....
Glazes V and VI					
deformed	13	87–99	94.31 ± 0.70	3.73 ± 0.49	3.96 ± 0.52
undeformed	5	95–102	98.40	....	....

TABLE III–17. Correction of the Breadth–Height Index in Deformed Skulls

Males	No.	Deformed	No.	Undeformed	Corrected Deformed
Total Series A	78	96.94	33	99.33	101.38
Black-on-white and Glaze I	10	95.00	8	97.12	101.45
Glazes II and III	27	97.18	11	98.91	95.68
Glaze IV.....................	19	96.68	5	100.60	101.73
Glazes V and VI	22	98.09	9	101.11	101.46
Females					
Total Series A	53	95.28	21	97.67	97.19
Black-on-white and Glaze I	10	96.00	5	95.00	95.04
Glazes II and III	16	95.81	5	100.40	98.87
Glaze IV	14	95.57	6	97.00	95.74
Glazes V and VI	13	94.31	5	98.40	93.57

TABLE III–18. Divisions of Breadth–Height Index

		Tapeinocephalic (x–91.5)	Metriocephalic (91.6–97.5)	Acrocephalic (97.6–x)	Total
Males (deformed)					
Total Series A	Number	10	34	34	78
	Per cent	12.82	43.59	43.59	
Black-on-white and Glaze I	Number	1	6	3	10
	Per cent	10.00	60.00	30.00	
Glazes II and III	Number	3	12	12	27
	Per cent	11.11	44.44	44.44	
Glaze IV	Number	3	8	8	19
	Per cent	15.79	42.11	42.11	
Glazes V and VI	Number	3	8	11	22
	Per cent	13.64	36.36	50.00	
Females (deformed)					
Total Series A	Number	7	31	15	53
	Per cent	13.21	58.49	28.30	
Black-on-white and Glaze I	Number	2	4	4	10
	Per cent	20.00	40.00	40.00	
Glazes II and III	Number	1	12	3	16
	Per cent	6.25	75.00	18.75	
Glaze IV	Number	1	9	4	14
	Per cent	7.14	64.29	28.57	
Glazes V and VI	Number	3	6	4	13
	Per cent	23.08	46.15	30.77	
Males (undeformed)					
Total Series A	Number	1	11	21	33
	Per cent	3.03	33.33	63.64	
Black-on-white and Glaze I	Number	1	3	4	8
	Per cent	12.50	37.50	50.00	
Glazes II and III	Number	0	5	6	11
	Per cent	0	54.55	63.64	
Glaze IV	Number	0	0	5	5
	Per cent	0	0	100.00	
Glazes V and VI	Number	0	3	6	9
	Per cent	0	33.33	66.67	
Females (undeformed)					
Total Series A	Number	1	10	10	21
	Per cent	4.76	47.62	47.62	
Black-on-white and Glaze I	Number	1	3	1	5
	Per cent	20.00	60.00	20.00	
Glazes II and III	Number	0	2	3	5
	Per cent	0	40.00	60.00	
Glaze IV	Number	0	3	3	6
	Per cent	0	50.00	50.00	
Glazes V and VI	Number	0	2	3	5
	Per cent	0	40.00	60.00	

Means of the breadth-height index verge upon acrocephaly in both deformed and undeformed skulls (Tables III–16, 17, 18). They are higher in the undeformed skulls, in fact prevailingly acrocephalic. The male crania exceed the female crania in acrocephaly. Correction of the values of the breadth-height index for deformed skulls yields restored means usually exceeding those of the actual deformed values, and in case of the males, usually in excess of means of the undeformed group. It would appear that crania deformation probably increases breadth more than height.

As a result of the application of these restoration formulae it may be asserted with a fair degree of confidence that the bulk of the deformed male skulls would probably have been brachy-hypsi-acrocephals, and in the case of the females brachy-hypsi-metriocephals. Many of the male crania, however, were shifted by deformation from dolichocephaly to mesocephaly and from mesocephaly to brachycephaly. In the case of the females there were probably few original dolichocephals and about 20 per cent of mesocephals. The effect of deformation was in this sex principally to heighten or accentuate a brachycephaly already existing.

It would seem that occipital deformation tends to obscure hereditary differences in head-form rather than to obliterate them. The formulae of Dr. Shapiro for the correction of cranial deformation, in my opinion, mark a new era in the study of the craniology of the American Indian. These restorations are not, of course, absolute, but only approximate.

In the analysis of means of the minimum frontal diameter it is noted that undeformed male crania are identical with deformed crania in this respect. Males are slightly more variable than females, and in the male series there is a slight but consistent increase in this diameter from the earliest to the latest periods (Table III–19).

TABLE III–19.   MINIMUM FRONTAL DIAMETER

	Number	Range	Mean	St. D.	V.
Males					
Total Series A					
deformed	93	83–112	94.92 ± 0.34	4.83 ± 0.24	5.09 ± 0.25
undeformed	50	82–111	94.94 ± 0.60	6.27 ± 0.42	6.60 ± 0.44
Black-on-white and Glaze I	25	82–103	93.16 ± 0.65	4.79 ± 0.57	5.14 ± 0.49
Glazes II and III	51	83–112	94.43 ± 0.54	5.74 ± 0.38	6.08 ± 0.40
Glaze IV	29	85–109	95.48 ± 0.68	5.46 ± 0.48	5.72 ± 0.51
Glazes V and VI	38	89–105	95.55 ± 0.39	3.60 ± 0.28	3.77 ± 0.29
Females					
Total Series A	95	82–104	92.41 ± 0.31	4.54 ± 0.22	4.91 ± 0.24
Black-on-white and Glaze I	21	83–99	93.14 ± 0.59	4.02 ± 0.42	4.32 ± 0.45
Glazes II and III	29	83–103	91.75 ± 0.58	4.67 ± 0.41	5.09 ± 9.45
Glaze IV	26	89–104	91.96 ± 0.71	5.37 ± 0.50	5.84 ± 0.55
Glazes V and VI	19	87–98	93.26 ± 0.50	3.21 ± 0.35	3.44 ± 0.38

CRANIAL CAPACITY, CRANIAL ARCS, AND CIRCUMFERENCE

Table III–20 gives the average cranial capacities for Series A. The undeformed crania seem to be of somewhat smaller capacity than the deformed, although the differences, considered in relation to their probable errors, are not great. They are fairly consistent, however, in the subgroups. It is interesting to note, however, that the mean cranial module of undeformed skulls in the male series (Table III–21) is slightly greater than in the deformed. The difference seems to be statistically significant. Since the greater value of the cranial module in undeformed males corresponds to a smaller mean cranial capacity, it is probable that brow-ridges are larger and skulls thicker in the undeformed than in the deformed group. In horizontal circumference, as would be expected, the undeformed skulls show slightly higher means in the male series, and in the female series the difference in favor of the undeformed group is small and probably insignificant. Similar conditions obtain in the case of the nasion-opisthion arc. The transverse arcs of the undeformed crania are smaller than those of the deformed and consistently so in both sexes (Tables III–22, 23, 24).

TABLE III–20. CRANIAL CAPACITY

	Number	Range	Mean	St. D.	V.
Males					
Total Series A					
deformed	68	1110–1560	1367.94 ± 8.18	100.15 ± 5.78	7.31 ± 0.42
undeformed	31	1030–1550	1338.71 ± 14.30	118.09 ± 10.11	8.82 ± 0.76
Black-on-white and Glaze I					
deformed	11	1270–1520	1368.98 ± 17.18	84.51 ± 12.15	6.17 ± 0.89
undeformed	7	1110–1440	1312.86	....	....
Glazes II and III					
deformed	26	1110–1550	1348.46 ± 14.43	109.09 ± 10.20	8.99 ± 0.84
undeformed	11	1230–1550	1372.73 ± 19.42	95.50 ± 13.73	6.96 ± 1.00
Glaze IV					
deformed	16	1160–1560	1393.12 ± 18.95	112.40 ± 13.40	8.07 ± 0.96
undeformed	5	1030–1510	1226.00	....	....
Glazes V and VI					
deformed	15	1270–1490	1374.00 ± 11.28	64.78 ± 7.98	4.66 ± 0.57
undeformed	8	1250–1480	1376.25	....	....
Females					
Total Series A					
deformed	54	1050–1480	1254.07 ± 7.66	83.48 ± 5.42	6.66 ± 0.43
undeformed	21	1030–1380	1221.90 ± 11.94	81.16 ± 8.45	6.64 ± 0.69
Black-on-white and Glaze I					
deformed	9	1120–1370	1248.88	....	....
undeformed	5	1160–1350	1234.00	....	....
Glazes II and III					
deformed	18	1050–1340	1227.78 ± 11.72	73.70 ± 8.28	6.00 ± 0.67
undeformed	4	1130–1210	1177.50	....	....
Glaze IV					
deformed	16	1140–1480	1265.00 ± 15.33	90.90 ± 10.84	7.18 ± 0.86
undeformed	7	1030–1300	1185.71	....	....
Glaze V and VI					
deformed	11	1160–1480	1278.18 ± 17.35	85.32 ± 12.27	6.68 ± 0.96
undeformed	5	1170–1380	1274.00	....	....

TABLE III–21. CRANIAL MODULE

Males

	Number	Range	Mean	St. D.	V.
Total Series A					
deformed	80	136.67–160.67	147.96 ± 0.30	4.00 ± 0.21	2.70 ± 0.14
undeformed	33	140.00–163.33	150.48 ± 0.60	5.08 ± 0.42	3.38 ± 0.28
Black-on-white and Glaze I ..					
deformed	10	147.33–159.67	152.00	....	....	....
undeformed	8	140.00–154.33	147.88	....	....	....
Glazes II and III					
deformed	27	136.67–155.33	148.70 ± 0.50	3.82 ± 0.35	2.57 ± 0.24
undeformed	11	145.67–163.33	153.82 ± 0.81	3.97 ± 0.57	2.58 ± 0.37
Glaze IV					
deformed	20	142.33–157.00	150.95 ± 0.48	3.85 ± 0.41	2.55 ± 0.27
undeformed	5	142.00–158.00	147.20	....	....	....
Glazes V and VI					
deformed	23	142.00–160.67	149.96 ± 0.56	3.97 ± 0.39	2.65 ± 0.26
undeformed	9	144.67–154.00	150.44	....	....	....

Females

	Number	Range	Mean	St. D.	V.
Total Series A					
deformed	54	139.67–153.00	145.20 ± 0.28	3.12 ± 0.20	2.15 ± 0.14
undeformed	18	140.00–152.33	144.89 ± 0.47	2.94 ± 0.33	2.03 ± 0.23
Black-on-white and Glaze I ..					
deformed	11	141.00–153.00	146.18 ± 0.78	3.82 ± 0.55	2.61 ± 0.38
undeformed	4	142.67–152.33	146.25	....	....	....
Glazes II and III					
deformed	17	139.67–148.00	144.24 ± 0.37	2.24 ± 0.26	1.55 ± 0.18
undeformed	3	140.00–145.33	143.33	....	....	....
Glaze IV					
deformed	14	141.00–149.33	145.29 ± 0.47	2.58 ± 0.33	1.78 ± 0.23
undeformed	6	141.00–145.33	143.67	....	....	....
Glazes V and VI					
deformed	12	140.33–150.33	145.58 ± 0.66	3.38 ± 0.47	2.32 ± 0.32
undeformed	5	142.00–151.33	146.20	....	....	....

TABLE III–22. MAXIMUM CIRCUMFERENCE

(Above Brow-ridges)

Males

	Number	Range	Mean	St. D.	V.
Total Series A					
deformed	90	440–530	493.35 ± 1.06	14.90 ± 0.75	3.02 ± 0.15
undeformed	43	475–540	502.65 ± 1.52	14.80 ± 1.08	2.94 ± 0.21
Black-on-white and Glaze I					
deformed	13	477–528	499.00 ± 2.44	13.02 ± 1.72	2.61 ± 0.34
undeformed	10	475–515	495.90 ± 2.84	13.32 ± 2.01	2.69 ± 0.40
Glazes II and III					
deformed	34	440–515	488.25 ± 1.61	13.90 ± 1.14	2.85 ± 0.23
undeformed	15	485–540	509.00 ± 2.40	13.80 ± 1.70	2.71 ± 0.33
Glaze IV					
deformed	19	465–510	495.50 ± 1.88	12.15 ± 1.33	2.45 ± 0.26
undeformed	8	475–520	498.10	....	....	....
Glazes V and VI					
deformed	24	445–526	496.04 ± 2.24	16.30 ± 1.59	3.29 ± 0.32
undeformed	10	476–523	503.30 ± 3.19	14.97 ± 2.26	2.97 ± 0.45

Females

Total Series A	Number	Range	Mean	St. D.	V.
deformed	66	450–505	479.32 ± 1.04	12.52 ± 0.74	2.61 ± 0.15
undeformed	23	465–500	481.20 ± 1.96	9.80 ± 0.98	2.03 ± 0.20
Black-on-white and Glaze I					
deformed	13	459–508	484.23 ± 2.74	14.65 ± 1.94	302. ± 0.40
undeformed	5	479–496	483.60	....	....
Glazes II and III					
deformed	21	453–488	472.71 ± 1.36	9.29 ± 0.96	1.96 ± 0.20
undeformed	5	471–503	481.60	....	....
Glaze IV					
deformed	18	455–506	476.30 ± 1.86	11.70 ± 1.32	2.46 ± 0.28
undeformed	8	467–503	479.52	....	....
Glazes V and VI					
deformed	14	460–501	483.57 ± 1.99	11.05 ± 1.41	2.30 ± 0.29
undeformed	5	469–489	479.80	....	....

TABLE III–23. NASION–OPISTHION ARC

Males

Total Series A	Number	Range	Mean	St. D.	V.
deformed	85	320–380	354.62 ± 0.92	12.50 ± 0.65	3.52 ± 0.18
undeformed	36	330–410	365.97 ± 1.83	16.25 ± 1.29	4.44 ± 0.79
Black-on-white and Glaze I					
deformed	12	342–375	355.75 ± 1.91	9.82 ± 1.35	2.92 ± 0.40
undeformed	9	330–384	362.11	....	....
Glazes II and III					
deformed	32	320–376	352.03 ± 1.49	12.50 ± 1.05	3.55 ± 0.30
undeformed	10	335–410	372.00 ± 3.89	18.22 ± 2.75	4.90 ± 0.74
Glaze IV					
deformed	19	329–377	354.16 ± 1.72	11.09 ± 1.21	3.13 ± 0.34
undeformed	6	335–382	356.00	....	....
Glazes V and VI					
deformed	22	327–380	355.18 ± 1.98	13.81 ± 1.40	3.89 ± 0.39
undeformed	11	348–385	365.82 ± 2.40	11.78 ± 1.69	3.22 ± 0.46

Females

Total Series A					
deformed	62	320–370	343.71 ± 1.05	12.24 ± 0.74	3.52 ± 0.21
undeformed	25	330–360	344.20 ± 1.05	7.80 ± 0.74	2.27 ± 0.22
Black-on-White and Glaze I					
deformed	11	320–370	343.00 ± 3.19	15.71 ± 2.26	4.58 ± 0.66
undeformed	5	337–355	345.20	....	....
Glazes II and III					
deformed	20	320–365	340.50 ± 1.73	11.50 ± 1.23	3.38 ± 0.36
undeformed	8	330–360	343.75	....	....
Glaze IV					
deformed	17	325–365	343.18 ± 2.03	12.39 ± 1.43	3.61 ± 0.42
undeformed	8	333–357	343.25	....	....
Glazes V and VI					
deformed	14	325–365	346.45 ± 1.96	10.90 ± 1.39	3.15 ± 0.40
undeformed	4	345–350	347.50	....	....

TABLE III–24. TRANSVERSE ARC

Males

	Number	Range	Mean	St. D.	V.
Total Series A					
deformed	91	297–357	329.75 ± 0.90	12.80 ± 0.64	3.88 ± 0.19
undeformed	36	292–337	316.67 ± 1.37	12.22 ± 0.97	3.89 ± 0.31
Black-on-white and Glaze I					
deformed	13	308–357	333.00 ± 2.26	12.08 ± 1.60	3.63 ± 0.48
undeformed	10	290–325	308.40 ± 2.09	9.79 ± 1.48	3.17 ± 0.48
Glazes II and III					
deformed	36	297–357	327.50 ± 1.57	13.94 ± 1.11	4.26 ± 0.34
undeformed	10	312–337	324.00 ± 1.66	7.76 ± 1.17	2.40 ± 0.36
Glaze IV					
deformed	20	315–358	332.50 ± 1.77	11.75 ± 1.25	3.53 ± 0.38
undeformed	7	292–336	311.43	....	....
Glazes V and VI					
deformed	22	312–348	328.00 ± 1.37	9.53 ± 0.97	2.90 ± 0.30
undeformed	9	305–333	320.00	....	....

Females

	Number	Range	Mean	St. D.	V.
Total Series A					
deformed	68	297–340	320.59 ± 0.92	11.30 ± 0.65	3.52 ± 0.20
undeformed	21	290–345	315.12 ± 1.83	12.46 ± 1.30	3.95 ± 0.41
Black-on-white and Glaze I					
deformed	13	302–340	316.92 ± 2.16	11.53 ± 1.53	3.64 ± 0.48
undeformed	5	302–323	314.40	....	....
Glazes II and III					
deformed	23	297–338	317.74 ± 1.49	10.57 ± 1.05	3.33 ± 0.33
undeformed	3	303–307	305.00	....	....
Glaze IV					
deformed	18	300–340	323.33 ± 1.74	10.95 ± 1.23	3.39 ± 0.38
undeformed	8	293–338	313.50	....	....
Glazes V and VI					
deformed	14	307–336	322.21 ± 1.73	9.60 ± 1.22	2.98 ± 0.38
undeformed	5	290–345	319.00	....	....

MEAN DIAMETER OF FORAMEN MAGNUM AND THICKNESS
OF LEFT PARIETAL

In the tables showing mean diameter of the foramen magnum and average thickness of the left parietal 1 cm. above the squamous suture, no distinction has been made between deformed and undeformed crania. The males show slightly greater averages for the dimensions of the occipital foramen and the females seem to have slightly thicker crania, but the differences are very slight and probably insignificant (Tables III–25, 26).

TABLE III–25. Mean Diameter of Foramen Magnum

Males	Number	Range	Mean	St. D.	V.
Total Series A	102	25–35	30.93 ± 0.12	2.00 ± 0.08	5.80 ± 0.27
Black-on-white and Glaze I	17	28–35	30.71 ± 0.34	2.09 ± 0.24	6.81 ± 0.79
Glazes II and III	33	25–34	30.71 ± 0.24	2.04 ± 0.17	6.64 ± 0.55
Glaze IV	23	27–34	31.02 ± 0.23	1.66 ± 0.16	5.34 ± 0.53
Glazes V and VI	29	29–33	30.98 ± 0.17	1.40 ± 0.12	4.50 ± 0.40
Females					
Total Series A	73	26–32	29.07 ± 0.13	1.66 ± 0.13	5.73 ± 0.32
Black-on-white and Glaze I	14	26–32	29.21 ± 0.28	1.57 ± 0.20	5.37 ± 0.68
Glazes II and III	21	26–32	29.31 ± 0.28	1.93 ± 0.20	6.58 ± 0.68
Glaze IV	19	26–32	28.92 ± 0.22	1.42 ± 0.16	4.93 ± 0.54
Glazes V and VI	19	26–32	28.82 ± 0.25	1.62 ± 0.18	5.60 ± 0.61

TABLE III–26. Thickness of Left Parietal

Males	Number	Range	Mean	St. D.	V.
Total Series A	141	3–8	5.16 ± 0.05	0.96 ± 0.04	18.60 ± 0.74
Black-on-white and Glaze I	26	4–7	5.34 ± 0.10	0.79 ± 0.07	14.80 ± 1.38
Glazes II and III	51	3–7	5.22 ± 0.09	0.97 ± 0.06	18.58 ± 1.24
Glaze IV	28	3–8	5.00 ± 0.12	0.95 ± 0.08	18.92 ± 1.70
Glazes V and VI	36	3–7	5.16 ± 0.12	1.04 ± 0.08	20.15 ± 1.60
Females					
Total Series A	94	3–8	5.24 ± 0.05	0.78 ± 0.04	14.88 ± 0.73
Black-on-white and Glaze I	20	3–8	5.18 ± 0.16	1.09 ± 0.12	21.00 ± 2.24
Glazes II and III	30	3–7	5.17 ± 0.10	0.79 ± 0.07	15.28 ± 1.33
Glaze IV	26	3–7	5.42 ± 0.10	0.76 ± 0.07	13.97 ± 1.31
Glazes V and VI	18	3–8	5.11 ± 0.19	1.23 ± 0.14	23.99 ± 2.70

FACIAL DIAMETERS AND INDICES

The bizygomatic diameters in Series A show, in the case of the males, the rather high mean values one expects to find in Indians. There seems to have been an increase in this dimension during the last three archaeological periods of the pueblo. The females show much smaller values and are far less variable as may be observed from a perusal of the standard deviations and coefficients of variation of Table III–27. In the earliest periods of the Pecos population total facial heights seem to have been somewhat larger than subsequently, at any rate in the male crania (Table III–28).

It is of interest to observe that the mean value of the total facial index in females is slightly greater than in males (Table III–29). The females are also less variable. In the males the earlier archaeological periods yield higher averages of the total facial index, but this is not true in the case of the females. If the facial index be divided into its conventional subgroups (Table III–30) it is seen that leptoprosopic crania are more common in the females and that euryprosopism seems to increase among the males in succeeding periods.

No consistent changes in the nasion-prosthion height are discernible throughout the different strata. The upper facial index (Table III–32) shows again the tendency of the females to exhibit relatively longer faces than the males and it seems to show also a regular decrease in the mean value throughout successive periods in the case of the males only. The divisions of the upper facial index (Table III–33) show a higher percentage of leptene crania in the female series and a lower percentage of the euryene crania.

TABLE III–27. Maximum Bizygomatic Diameter

Males	Number	Range	Mean	St. D.	V.
Total Series A	102	122–161	138.56 ± 0.41	6.17 ± 0.29	4.45 ± 0.21
Black-on-white and Glaze I	18	128–148	136.72 ± 0.90	5.69 ± 0.64	4.16 ± 0.47
Glazes II and III	35	122–145	136.97 ± 0.61	5.37 ± 0.43	3.92 ± 0.32
Glaze IV	20	130–161	141.20 ± 1.19	7.90 ± 0.84	5.59 ± 0.60
Glazes V and VI	29	128–148	139.72 ± 0.63	5.01 ± 0.44	3.58 ± 0.32
Females					
Total Series A	68	118–138	129.87 ± 0.27	3.36 ± 0.19	2.59 ± 0.15
Black-on-white and Glaze I	13	120–134	129.38 ± 0.72	3.87 ± 0.51	2.99 ± 0.40
Glazes II and III	20	124–138	129.45 ± 0.45	2.97 ± 0.32	2.29 ± 0.24
Glaze IV	20	126–136	130.80 ± 0.40	2.68 ± 0.28	2.05 ± 0.22
Glazes V and VI	15	118–134	129.40 ± 0.53	3.07 ± 0.38	2.37 ± 0.29

TABLE III–28. Nasion–Menton Height

Males	Number	Range	Mean	St. D.	V.
Total Series A	107	107–135	119.38 ± 0.36	5.54 ± 0.26	4.64 ± 0.21
Black-on-white and Glaze I	17	113–128	121.00 ± 0.73	4.48 ± 0.52	3.71 ± 0.43
Glazes II and III	39	107–130	118.43 ± 0.50	4.62 ± 0.35	3.90 ± 0.30
Glaze IV	20	110–135	119.80 ± 1.01	6.69 ± 0.71	5.58 ± 0.60
Glazes V and VI	31	109–131	119.42 ± 0.70	5.74 ± 0.49	4.81 ± 0.41
Females					
Total Series A	71	100–125	113.31 ± 0.47	5.87 ± 0.33	5.18 ± 0.29
Black-on-white and Glaze I	16	106–123	114.56 ± 0.97	5.75 ± 0.68	5.02 ± 0.60
Glazes II and III	25	100–121	11.24 ± 0.80	5.90 ± 0.56	5.30 ± 0.50
Glaze IV	19	107–125	114.95 ± 0.66	4.25 ± 0.46	3.70 ± 0.40
Glazes V and VI	11	100–125	113.27 ± 1.37	6.73 ± 0.97	5.94 ± 0.85

TABLE III–29. Total Facial Index

Males	Number	Range	Mean	St. D.	V.
Total Series A	86	70–99	85.69 ± 0.35	4.87 ± 0.25	5.68 ± 0.29
Black-on-white and Glaze I	15	82–99	87.73 ± 0.68	3.92 ± 0.48	4.47 ± 0.55
Glazes II and III	30	80–95	87.03 ± 0.44	3.54 ± 0.31	4.07 ± 0.35
Glaze IV	16	70–95	84.38 ± 1.20	7.16 ± 0.85	8.48 ± 1.01
Glazes V and VI	25	76–97	85.36 ± 0.60	4.42 ± 0.42	5.18 ± 0.49
Females					
Total Series A	59	76–96	86.95 ± 0.38	4.29 ± 0.27	4.93 ± 0.31
Black-on-white and Glaze I	12	79–93	87.50 ± 0.80	4.11 ± 0.56	4.70 ± 0.65
Glazes II and III	19	77–93	85.32 ± 0.65	4.18 ± 0.46	4.90 ± 0.54
Glaze IV	18	82–96	87.83 ± 0.59	3.72 ± 0.42	4.24 ± 0.48
Glazes V and VI	10	76–96	87.60 ± 1.00	4.67 ± 0.70	5.33 ± 0.80

TABLE III–30. DIVISIONS OF TOTAL FACIAL INDEX

Males

	Euryprosopic (x–84.5)	Mesoprosopic (84.6–89.5)	Leptoprosopic (89.6–x)	Total
Total Series A				
Number	27	42	17	86
Per cent	31.40	48.84	19.77	
Black-on-white and Glaze I				
Number	4	8	3	15
Per cent	26.67	53.33	20.00	
Glazes II and III				
Number	6	17	7	30
Per cent	20.00	56.67	23.33	
Glaze IV				
Number	7	5	4	16
Per cent	43.75	31.25	25.00	
Glazes V and VI				
Number	10	12	3	25
Per cent	40.00	48.00	12.00	

Females

	Euryprosopic (x–84.5)	Mesoprosopic (84.6–89.5)	Leptoprosopic (89.6–x)	Total
Total Series A				
Number	18	22	19	59
Per cent	30.51	37.29	32.20	
Black-on-white and Glaze I				
Number	4	3	5	12
Per cent	33.33	25.00	41.67	
Glazes II and III				
Number	8	8	3	19
Per cent	42.11	42.11	15.79	
Glaze IV				
Number	3	8	7	18
Per cent	16.67	44.44	38.89	
Glazes V and VI				
Number	3	3	4	10
Per cent	30.00	30.00	40.00	

TABLE III–31. NASION–PROSTHION HEIGHT

	Number	Range	Mean	St. D.	V.
Males					
Total Series A	112	64–84	72.85 ± 0.25	3.95 ± 0.18	5.42 ± 0.24
Black-on-white and Glaze I	17	66–79	73.35 ± 0.63	3.83 ± 0.44	5.22 ± 0.60
Glazes II and III	41	64–81	72.41 ± 0.37	3.50 ± 0.26	4.83 ± 0.36
Glaze IV	23	65–84	74.09 ± 0.59	4.19 ± 0.42	5.66 ± 0.56
Glazes V and VI	31	66–81	72.97 ± 0.52	4.31 ± 0.37	5.91 ± 0.50
Females					
Total Series A	75	59–77	69.04 ± 0.27	3.44 ± 0.19	4.98 ± 0.27
Black-on-white and Glaze I	16	65–75	70.00 ± 0.56	3.32 ± 0.40	4.73 ± 0.56
Glazes II and III	24	63–74	68.38 ± 0.49	3.58 ± 0.35	5.24 ± 0.51
Glaze IV	22	66–77	69.64 ± 0.37	2.57 ± 0.26	3.69 ± 0.38
Glazes V and VI	13	59–76	68.08 ± 0.76	4.07 ± 0.54	5.98 ± 0.79

TABLE III-32. UPPER FACIAL INDEX

Males	Number	Range	Mean	St. D.	V.
Total Series A	90	43–59	52.09 ± 0.23	3.28 ± 0.16	6.30 ± 0.32
Black-on-white and Glaze I	15	49–57	53.27 ± 0.39	2.26 ± 0.28	4.24 ± 0.52
Glazes II and III	32	45–58	52.94 ± 0.38	3.21 ± 0.27	6.06 ± 0.51
Glaze IV	18	43–57	51.33 ± 0.66	4.18 ± 0.47	8.14 ± 0.91
Glazes V and VI	25	46–59	52.20 ± 0.38	2.80 ± 0.27	5.36 ± 0.51
Females					
Total Series A	61	46–60	53.00 ± 0.23	2.62 ± 0.16	4.95 ± 0.30
Black-on-white and Glaze I	13	49–57	53.85 ± 0.44	2.35 ± 0.31	4.36 ± 0.58
Glazes II and III	16	48–57	52.19 ± 0.44	2.58 ± 0.31	4.94 ± 0.59
Glaze IV	20	50–60	53.30 ± 0.36	2.37 ± 0.25	4.45 ± 0.47
Glazes V and VI	12	46–50	52.75 ± 0.64	3.27 ± 0.45	6.19 ± 0.85

TABLE III-33. DIVISIONS OF UPPER FACIAL INDEX

Males	Euryene (x–49.5)	Mesene (49.6–54.5)	Leptene (54.6–x)	Total
Total Series A				
Number	14	54	22	90
Per cent	15.56	60.00	24.44	
Black-on-white and Glaze I				
Number	1	11	3	15
Per cent	6.67	73.33	20.00	
Glazes II and III				
Number	4	18	10	32
Per cent	12.50	56.25	31.25	
Glaze IV				
Number	5	9	4	18
Per cent	27.68	50.00	22.22	
Glazes V and VI				
Number	4	16	5	25
Per cent	16.00	64.00	20.00	
Females				
Total Series A				
Number	6	36	19	61
Per cent	9.84	59.02	31.15	
Black-on-White and Glaze I				
Number	1	6	6	13
Per cent	7.69	46.15	46.15	
Glazes II and III				
Number	3	9	4	16
Per cent	18.75	56.25	25.00	
Glaze IV				
Number	0	15	5	20
Per cent	0	75.00	25.00	
Glazes V and VI				
Number	2	6	4	12
Per cent	16.67	50.00	33.33	

ORBITS

The orbital diameters show a slight tendency for the left orbits to be higher and narrower than the right orbits both in the males and in the females. Curiously enough in the male series the orbits both in height and breadth seem to be large in the earlier periods, then smaller in the middle period, then larger again during the Glaze V and Glaze VI periods. The females are consistent throughout (Tables III–34, 35).

The mean orbital index shows a much greater prevalency of hypsiconchy among the females (Tables III–36, 37). Here again in the intermediate archaeological periods the males tend to show a curious drop in the orbital index, but they recover from this depression in the last periods.

TABLE III–34. Orbit Height

	Number	Range	Mean	St. D.	V.
Males					
Total Series A					
right	119	31–38	34.80 ± 0.10	1.61 ± 0.07	4.62 ± 0.20
left	117	30–38	34.90 ± 0.10	1.60 ± 0.07	4.60 ± 0.20
Black-on-white and Glaze I					
right	20	32–38	35.10 ± 0.23	1.53 ± 0.16	4.36 ± 0.46
left	19	32–38	35.16 ± 0.27	1.66 ± 0.18	4.71 ± 0.52
Glazes II and III					
right	42	31–38	34.51 ± 0.15	1.44 ± 0.10	4.19 ± 0.31
left	40	32–37	34.62 ± 0.16	1.47 ± 0.11	4.25 ± 0.32
Glaze IV					
right	24	31–37	34.98 ± 0.21	1.52 ± 0.15	4.34 ± 0.42
left	24	30–36	34.62 ± 0.21	1.51 ± 0.15	4.39 ± 0.43
Glazes V and VI					
right	33	32–38	35.17 ± 0.19	1.64 ± 0.14	4.68 ± 0.39
left	34	32–38	35.28 ± 0.19	1.68 ± 0.14	4.75 ± 0.39
Females					
Total Series A					
right	80	29–37	34.22 ± 0.12	1.65 ± 0.08	4.85 ± 0.26
left	78	29–41	34.49 ± 0.14	1.85 ± 0.10	5.36 ± 0.29
Black-on-white and Glaze I					
right	15	32–36	34.07 ± 0.22	1.27 ± 0.16	3.73 ± 0.46
left	16	31–36	34.50 ± 0.26	1.53 ± 0.18	4.43 ± 0.53
Glazes II and III					
right	27	31–37	34.13 ± 0.14	1.56 ± 0.20	4.57 ± 0.42
left	25	31–38	34.42 ± 0.23	1.69 ± 0.16	4.91 ± 0.47
Glaze IV					
right	20	30–37	34.42 ± 0.24	1.56 ± 0.17	4.53 ± 0.48
left	21	29–37	34.76 ± 0.21	1.44 ± 0.15	4.17 ± 0.43
Glazes V and VI					
right	18	29–37	34.25 ± 0.33	2.07 ± 0.23	6.04 ± 0.68
left	16	30–41	34.62 ± 0.39	2.31 ± 0.28	6.67 ± 0.80

TABLE III–35. ORBIT BREADTH

Males

	Number	Range	Mean	St. D.	V.
Total Series A					
right	119	35–44	39.90 ± 0.11	1.82 ± 0.08	4.56 ± 0.20
left	117	35–49	39.47 ± 0.12	1.89 ± 0.12	4.65 ± 0.20
Black-on-white and Glaze I					
right	20	37–44	40.60 ± 0.25	1.64 ± 0.18	4.05 ± 0.43
left	19	37–42	39.79 ± 0.22	1.42 ± 0.15	3.56 ± 0.39
Glazes II and III					
right	42	35–44	39.45 ± 0.21	1.99 ± 0.15	5.04 ± 0.37
left	40	35–49	39.41 ± 0.25	2.37 ± 0.18	6.01 ± 0.45
Glaze IV					
right	24	37–43	39.80 ± 0.26	1.86 ± 0.18	4.66 ± 0.45
left	24	38–43	39.90 ± 0.20	1.48 ± 0.14	3.71 ± 0.36
Glazes V and VI					
right	33	37–43	40.11 ± 0.17	1.46 ± 0.12	3.64 ± 0.30
left	34	36–44	39.29 ± 0.19	1.66 ± 0.14	4.24 ± 0.35

Females

	Number	Range	Mean	St. D.	V.
Total Series A					
right	80	34–43	38.49 ± 0.12	1.63 ± 0.09	4.24 ± 0.22
left	77	34–42	38.14 ± 0.11	1.46 ± 0.08	3.83 ± 0.21
Black-on-white and Glaze I					
right	15	36–43	39.40 ± 0.32	1.81 ± 0.22	4.59 ± 0.56
left	16	36–42	38.66 ± 0.27	1.58 ± 0.19	4.09 ± 0.49
Glazes II and III					
right	27	36–41	38.35 ± 0.16	1.21 ± 0.11	3.16 ± 0.29
left	24	36–41	36.02 ± 0.15	1.12 ± 0.11	2.93 ± 0.28
Glaze IV					
right	20	36–42	38.35 ± 0.21	1.40 ± 0.15	3.64 ± 0.39
left	21	36–41	38.07 ± 0.16	1.10 ± 0.12	2.90 ± 0.30
Glazes V and VI					
right	18	34–43	38.53 ± 0.29	1.83 ± 0.20	4.75 ± 0.53
left	16	34–41	38.31 ± 0.31	1.85 ± 0.22	4.83 ± 0.58

TABLE III–36. MEAN ORBITAL INDEX *

Males	Number	Range	Mean	St. D.	V.
Total Series A	120	78–99	87.80 ± 0.28	4.57 ± 0.20	5.21 ± 0.23
Black-on-white and Glaze I	21	80–94	87.62 ± 0.55	3.74 ± 0.39	4.27 ± 0.44
Glazes II and III	40	78–97	87.37 ± 0.57	5.36 ± 0.40	6.13 ± 0.46
Glaze IV	25	80–93	87.12 ± 0.52	3.84 ± 0.37	4.41 ± 0.42
Glazes V and VI	34	80–99	88.82 ± 0.51	4.39 ± 0.36	4.94 ± 0.40
Females					
Total Series A	83	76–98	89.87 ± 0.36	4.81 ± 0.25	5.35 ± 0.28
Black-on-white and Glaze I	16	80–99	89.12 ± 0.96	5.67 ± 0.68	6.36 ± 0.76
Glazes II and III	27	84–97	89.22 ± 0.37	3.99 ± 0.52	4.47 ± 0.41
Glaze IV	22	86–99	91.59 ± 0.60	4.16 ± 0.42	4.54 ± 0.46
Glazes V and VI	18	77–99	89.28 ± 0.84	5.32 ± 0.60	5.96 ± 0.67

* Right or left measurements used as well as mean measurements.

TABLE III–37. Divisions of Mean Orbital Index

Males

	Chamaeconch (x–82.5)	Mesoconch (82.6–88.5)	Hypsiconch (88.6–x)	Total
Total Series A				
Number	16	54	50	120
Per cent	13.33	45.00	41.67	
Black-on-white and Glaze I				
Number	3	9	9	21
Per cent	14.29	42.86	42.86	
Glazes II and III				
Number	6	20	14	40
Per cent	15.00	50.00	35.00	
Glaze IV				
Number	4	11	10	25
Per cent	16.00	44.00	40.00	
Glazes V and VI				
Number	3	14	17	34
Per cent	8.82	41.18	50.00	

Females

	Chamaeconch	Mesoconch	Hypsiconch	Total
Total Series A				
Number	3	32	48	83
Per cent	3.61	38.55	57.83	
Black-on-white and Glaze I				
Number	1	9	6	16
Per cent	6.25	56.25	37.50	
Glazes II and III				
Number	0	11	16	27
Per cent	0	40.74	59.26	
Glaze IV				
Number	0	6	16	22
Per cent	0	27.27	72.73	
Glazes V and VI				
Number	2	6	10	18
Per cent	11.11	33.33	55.56	

NASAL DIAMETERS AND NASAL INDEX

Tables III–38, 39, 40, 41, deal with the nasal diameters and the nasal index. In nasal height the males show a slight diminution during the middle periods as compared with the first and last periods of the pueblo's occupation. In the females, nasal height seems to decrease slightly from first to last. The nasal index shows consistently higher means in the female series, which includes a much larger proportion of platyrrhine crania than the male series. No certain differences are to be observed in the period subgroups. Throughout the occupation of the pueblo platyrrhiny seems to have been predominant.

TABLE III–38. Nasal Height

Males	Number	Range	Mean	St. D.	V.
Total Series A	125	45–57	50.96 ± 0.16	2.74 ± 0.12	5.38 ± 0.23
Black-on-white and Glaze I	19	45–56	51.42 ± 0.45	2.92 ± 0.32	5.68 ± 0.62
Glazes II and III	44	46–56	50.66 ± 0.26	2.56 ± 0.18	5.05 ± 0.36
Glaze IV	26	46–55	50.71 ± 0.32	2.40 ± 0.22	4.74 ± 0.44
Glazes V and VI	36	46–57	51.28 ± 0.34	3.00 ± 0.24	5.85 ± 0.46
Females					
Total Series A	86	43–53	48.20 ± 0.16	2.24 ± 0.12	4.65 ± 0.24
Black-on-white and Glaze I	17	45–53	48.70 ± 0.31	1.92 ± 0.22	3.94 ± 0.46
Glazes II and III	27	44–52	48.54 ± 0.28	2.14 ± 0.20	4.40 ± 0.40
Glaze IV	25	46–53	48.58 ± 0.25	1.86 ± 0.18	3.82 ± 0.36
Glazes V and VI	17	43–53	47.35 ± 0.42	2.56 ± 0.30	5.41 ± 0.62

TABLE III–39. Nasal Breadth

Males	Number	Range	Mean	St. D.	V.
Total Series A	126	21–30	25.80 ± 0.09	1.57 ± 0.07	7.08 ± 0.26
Black-on-white and Glaze I	19	22–28	25.87 ± 0.24	1.52 ± 0.17	5.88 ± 0.64
Glazes II and III	45	21–29	25.82 ± 0.16	1.64 ± 0.12	6.35 ± 0.45
Glaze IV	26	22–29	25.50 ± 0.21	1.59 ± 0.15	6.23 ± 0.58
Glazes V and VI	36	23–30	26.04 ± 0.16	1.44 ± 0.11	5.55 ± 0.44
Females					
Total Series A	86	21–30	25.33 ± 0.13	1.83 ± 0.09	7.22 ± 0.37
Black-on-white and Glaze I	17	22–30	25.59 ± 0.24	1.49 ± 0.17	5.82 ± 0.67
Glazes II and III	27	21–28	25.24 ± 0.22	1.66 ± 0.15	6.58 ± 0.60
Glaze IV	25	21–29	25.34 ± 0.25	1.86 ± 0.18	7.34 ± 0.70
Glazes V and VI	17	22–28	25.50 ± 0.28	1.74 ± 0.20	6.82 ± 0.79

TABLE III–40. Nasal Index

Males	Number	Range	Mean	St. D.	V.
Total Series A	124	40–65	50.44 ± 0.26	4.27 ± 0.18	8.46 ± 0.39
Black-on-white and Glaze I	19	43–60	50.42 ± 0.63	4.05 ± 0.44	8.03 ± 0.88
Glazes II and III	43	41–60	51.07 ± 0.42	4.10 ± 0.30	8.03 ± 0.58
Glaze IV	26	44–60	50.38 ± 0.52	3.95 ± 0.37	7.84 ± 0.73
Glazes V and VI	36	40–65	50.78 ± 0.49	4.40 ± 0.35	8.66 ± 0.69
Females					
Total Series A	86	42–62	52.60 ± 0.30	4.13 ± 0.21	7.84 ± 0.40
Black-on-white and Glaze I	17	44–61	52.47 ± 0.70	4.29 ± 0.50	8.17 ± 0.94
Glazes II and III	27	45–62	52.22 ± 0.46	3.58 ± 0.33	6.86 ± 0.63
Glaze IV	25	42–60	52.12 ± 0.54	3.98 ± 0.38	7.64 ± 0.73
Glazes V and VI	17	45–62	53.94 ± 0.75	4.61 ± 0.53	8.55 ± 0.99

TABLE III–41. Divisions of Nasal Index

Males	Leptorrhine (x–46.5)	Mesorrhine (46.6–50.5)	Platyrrhine (50.6–x)	Total
Total Series A				
Number	16	43	65	124
Per cent	12.90	34.68	52.42	
Black-on-white and Glaze I				
Number	3	6	10	19
Per cent	15.79	31.58	52.63	
Glazes II and III				
Number	6	11	26	43
Per cent	13.95	25.58	60.47	
Glaze IV				
Number	3	12	11	26
Per cent	11.54	46.15	42.31	
Glazes V and VI				
Number	4	14	18	36
Per cent	11.11	38.89	50.00	
Females				
Total Series A				
Number	6	20	60	86
Per cent	6.98	23.26	69.77	
Black-on-white and Glaze I				
Number	2	2	13	17
Per cent	11.76	11.76	76.47	
Glazes II and III				
Number	2	6	19	27
Per cent	7.41	22.22	70.37	
Glaze IV				
Number	1	8	16	25
Per cent	4.00	32.00	64.00	
Glazes V and VI				
Number	1	4	12	17
Per cent	5.88	23.53	70.59	

EXTERNAL DIAMETERS AND INDEX OF THE PALATE

Throughout the various archaeological strata the male crania show larger external dimensions of the palate than the female crania. There are possible indications that the size of the palate decreased somewhat in the male crania from the earlier to the later periods. In all periods brachyurany prevailed in both sexes, but especially in the males. The females show a larger proportion of relatively long and narrow palates and a smaller proportion of broad short palates. It will be recalled that the female crania also exhibit relatively longer and narrower faces (Tables III–42, 43, 44, 45).

TABLE III–42. EXTERNAL PALATAL LENGTH

Males	Number	Range	Mean	St. D.	V.
Total Series A	100	48–63	55.04 ± 0.19	2.82 ± 0.13	5.12 ± 0.24
Black-on-white and Glaze I	14	51–61	56.00 ± 0.48	2.59 ± 0.33	4.62 ± 0.60
Glazes II and III	37	51–60	54.78 ± 0.29	2.63 ± 0.21	4.80 ± 0.38
Glaze IV	19	52–60	55.32 ± 0.34	2.23 ± 0.24	4.03 ± 0.44
Glazes V and VI	30	48–63	54.73 ± 0.40	3.29 ± 0.29	6.01 ± 0.52
Females					
Total Series A	66	48–61	53.97 ± 0.22	2.72 ± 0.16	5.04 ± 0.30
Black-on-white and Glaze I	14	49–56	53.29 ± 0.36	2.01 ± 0.26	3.77 ± 0.48
Glazes II and III	22	49–60	54.14 ± 0.37	2.56 ± 0.26	4.73 ± 0.48
Glaze IV	17	48–61	54.65 ± 0.50	3.07 ± 0.36	5.62 ± 0.65
Glazes V and VI	13	48–59	53.58 ± 0.55	2.94 ± 0.39	5.48 ± 0.72

TABLE III–43. EXTERNAL PALATAL BREADTH

Males	Number	Range	Mean	St. D.	V.
Total Series A	97	58–73	65.59 ± 0.22	3.29 ± 0.16	5.02 ± 0.24
Black-on-white and Glaze I	14	61–71	66.28 ± 0.54	3.01 ± 0.38	4.54 ± 0.58
Glazes II and III	35	59–73	65.03 ± 0.37	3.22 ± 0.26	4.95 ± 0.40
Glaze IV	19	62–72	67.47 ± 0.42	2.74 ± 0.30	4.06 ± 0.44
Glazes V and VI	29	58–70	64.69 ± 0.41	3.26 ± 0.29	5.04 ± 0.45
Females					
Total Series A	66	55–69	62.74 ± 0.22	2.69 ± 0.16	4.29 ± 0.25
Black-on-white and Glaze I	13	57–68	62.46 ± 0.56	3.00 ± 0.40	4.80 ± 0.64
Glazes II and III	23	59–69	63.26 ± 0.35	2.47 ± 0.24	3.90 ± 0.30
Glaze IV	17	55–66	62.56 ± 0.50	3.08 ± 0.36	4.98 ± 0.58
Glazes V and VI	13	59–66	62.42 ± 0.38	2.01 ± 0.27	3.23 ± 0.43

TABLE III–44. EXTERNAL PALATAL (MAXILLO–ALVEOLAR) INDEX

Males	Number	Range	Mean	St. D.	V.
Total Series A	97	103–136	119.16 ± 0.44	6.42 ± 0.31	5.42 ± 0.26
Black-on-white and Glaze I	14	108–129	118.71 ± 1.09	6.07 ± 0.77	5.11 ± 0.65
Glazes II and III	35	105–134	118.51 ± 0.83	7.25 ± 0.58	6.12 ± 0.49
Glaze IV	19	113–136	121.05 ± 0.78	5.20 ± 0.55	4.30 ± 0.46
Glazes V and VI	29	103–127	118.13 ± 0.62	4.96 ± 0.44	4.20 ± 0.37
Females					
Total Series A	65	100–132	116.32 ± 0.52	6.28 ± 0.37	5.40 ± 0.32
Black-on-white and Glaze I	13	108–132	117.15 ± 1.26	6.78 ± 0.90	5.79 ± 0.76
Glazes II and III	22	107–126	116.55 ± 0.77	5.37 ± 0.55	4.61 ± 0.49
Glaze IV	17	100–125	114.82 ± 1.05	6.43 ± 0.74	5.60 ± 0.65
Glazes V and VI	13	107–131	116.69 ± 1.27	6.81 ± 0.90	5.84 ± 0.77

TABLE III–45. Divisions of External Palatal Index

Males	Dolichuranic (x–109.5)	Mesuranic (109.6–114.5)	Brachyuranic (114.6–x)	Total
Total Series A				
Number	7	18	72	97
Per cent	7.22	18.56	74.23	
Black-on-white and Glaze I				
Number	1	4	9	14
Per cent	7.14	28.57	64.29	
Glazes II and III				
Number	4	7	24	35
Per cent	11.43	20.00	68.57	
Glaze IV				
Number	0	3	16	19
Per cent	0	15.79	84.21	
Glazes V and VI				
Number	2	4	23	29
Per cent	6.90	13.79	79.31	
Females				
Total Series A				
Number	10	18	37	65
Per cent	15.38	27.69	56.92	
Black-on-white and Glaze I				
Number	3	1	9	13
Per cent	23.08	7.69	69.23	
Glazes II and III				
Number	2	7	13	22
Per cent	9.09	31.82	59.09	
Glaze IV				
Number	3	6	8	17
Per cent	17.65	35.29	47.06	
Glazes V and VI				
Number	2	4	7	13
Per cent	15.38	30.77	53.85	

MEASUREMENTS AND INDICES RELATING TO PROGNATHISM

Tables III–46, 47, 48 give the means of the basion-nasion and basion-prosthion diameters and of the gnathic index, which expresses the relation of these two diameters. I have thought it advisable to distinguish between deformed and undeformed crania in these tables. The undeformed crania show somewhat larger means in both sexes with respect to both of these diameters. They are also slightly less prognathous. As a matter of fact, prognathism, as expressed by the alveolar or gnathic index, is very rare in the whole series. A mesognathic condition is much more frequent among the female crania than among the male crania (Table III–49) and among the females one notices a gradual increase in the gnathic index from the earliest to the latest periods. This is probably not significant, in view of the very small numbers of crania in the subgroups.

TABLE III–46. BASION–PROSTHION LENGTH

Males	Number	Range	Mean	St. D.	V.
Total Series A	90	91–106	97.80 ± 0.26	3.59 ± 0.18	3.69 ± 0.18
deformed	65	91–106	97.51 ± 0.30	3.63 ± 0.22	3.72 ± 0.22
undeformed	25	93–105	98.60 ± 0.46	3.38 ± 0.32	3.43 ± 0.33
Black-on-white and Glaze I					
deformed	8	91–101	96.62	....	....
undeformed	5	93–100	97.40	....	....
Glazes II and III					
deformed	24	91–106	97.17 ± 0.53	3.85 ± 0.38	3.96 ± 0.38
undeformed	7	94–105	98.86	....	....
Glaze IV					
deformed	18	93–104	97.89 ± 0.48	3.00 ± 0.34	3.06 ± 0.34
undeformed	4	96–105	99.00	....	....
Glazes V and VI					
deformed	15	93–104	98.07 ± 0.66	3.79 ± 0.47	3.86 ± 0.48
undeformed	9	96–105	98.88	....	....
Females					
Total Series A	61	85–107	95.05 ± 0.41	4.75 ± 0.29	5.00 ± 0.30
deformed	40	85–107	95.32 ± 0.51	4.78 ± 0.36	5.02 ± 0.38
undeformed	21	86–103	94.52 ± 0.69	4.67 ± 0.49	4.94 ± 0.51
Black-on-white and Glaze I					
deformed	6	92–103	96.67	....	....
undeformed	5	86–101	92.60	....	....
Glazes II and III					
deformed	13	85–102	95.38 ± 0.94	5.01 ± 0.66	5.25 ± 0.69
undeformed	5	90–103	94.00	....	....
Glaze IV					
deformed	10	88–102	93.40	....	....
undeformed	6	86–101	95.00	....	....
Glazes V and VI					
deformed	11	91–107	96.27 ± 0.89	4.37 ± 0.63	4.54 ± 0.65
undeformed	5	93–102	96.40	....	....

TABLE III–47. BASION–NASION LENGTH

Males	Number	Range	Mean	St. D.	V.
Total Series A	94	92–110	101.89 ± 0.26	3.67 ± 0.18	3.60 ± 0.18
deformed	67	92–109	101.58 ± 0.29	3.55 ± 0.21	3.49 ± 0.25
undeformed	27	92–110	102.70 ± 0.49	3.78 ± 0.35	3.68 ± 0.34
Black-on-white and Glaze I					
deformed	8	92–106	101.00	....	....
undeformed	5	92–103	99.40	....	....
Glazes II and III					
deformed	25	94–108	100.96 ± 0.46	3.41 ± 0.32	3.38 ± 0.32
undeformed	8	101–109	104.38 ± 0.69	2.90 ± 0.49	2.78 ± 0.47
Glaze IV					
deformed	18	95–106	101.89 ± 0.50	3.14 ± 0.35	3.08 ± 0.35
undeformed	5	97–110	102.40	....	....
Glazes V and VI					
deformed	16	97–109	102.50 ± 0.63	3.73 ± 0.44	3.64 ± 0.43
undeformed	9	99–107	103.22	....	....

Females	Number	Range	Mean	St. D.	V.
Total Series A	61	89–108	97.31 ± 0.34	4.00 ± 0.24	4.11 ± 0.25
deformed	40	89–108	97.15 ± 0.43	4.06 ± 0.31	4.18 ± 0.32
undeformed	21	91–105	97.62 ± 0.57	3.86 ± 0.40	3.95 ± 0.41
Black-on-white and Glaze I					
deformed	6	94–108	99.33	....	....
undeformed	5	93–105	98.00	....	....
Glazes II and III					
deformed	14	92–100	96.36 ± 0.50	2.77 ± 0.35	2.87 ± 0.37
undeformed	5	91–103	97.00	....	....
Glaze IV					
deformed	10	89–102	96.20	....	....
undeformed	6	94–102	97.83	....	....
Glazes V and VI					
deformed	10	93–108	97.90	....	....
undeformed	5	95–102	97.60	....	....

TABLE III–48. GNATHIC INDEX

Males	Number	Range	Mean	St. D.	V.
Total Series A	90	88–103	95.97 ± 0.24	3.37 ± 0.17	3.52 ± 0.18
deformed	65	90–103	96.00 ± 0.27	3.20 ± 0.19	3.33 ± 0.20
undeformed	25	88–102	96.00 ± 0.52	3.84 ± 0.37	4.00 ± 0.38
Black-on-white and Glaze I					
deformed	8	92–101	95.75	....	....
undeformed	5	94–101	98.00	....	....
Glazes II and III					
deformed	24	90–103	96.04 ± 0.41	2.95 ± 0.29	3.07 ± 0.30
undeformed	7	90–100	95.14	....	....
Glaze IV					
deformed	18	90–103	96.00 ± 0.60	3.80 ± 0.43	3.96 ± 0.44
undeformed	4	88–99	95.00	....	....
Glazes V and VI					
deformed	15	92–103	95.93 ± 0.51	2.93 ± 0.36	3.05 ± 0.38
undeformed	9	90–102	96.11 ± 0.90	3.98 ± 0.63	4.14 ± 0.66

Females	Number	Range	Mean	St. D.	V.
Total Series A	60	91–105	97.53 ± 0.22	2.51 ± 0.15	2.57 ± 0.16
deformed	39	91–105	97.92 ± 0.35	3.28 ± 0.25	3.35 ± 0.26
undeformed	21	91–101	96.81 ± 0.47	3.19 ± 0.33	3.30 ± 0.34
Black-on-white and Glaze I					
deformed	6	94–100	97.33	....	....
undeformed	5	92–96	94.40	....	....
Glazes II and III					
deformed	13	91–105	98.46 ± 0.67	3.59 ± 0.47	3.65 ± 0.48
undeformed	5	92–100	97.00	....	....
Glaze IV					
deformed	10	91–104	97.20	....	....
undeformed	6	93–101	97.00	....	....
Glazes V and VI					
deformed	10	93–103	98.10	....	....
undeformed	5	97–100	98.80	....	....

TABLE III–49. DIVISIONS OF GNATHIC INDEX

Males	Orthognathous (x–97.5)	Mesognathous (97.6–102.5)	Prognathous (102.5–x)	Total
Total Series A				
Number	61	26	3	90
Per cent	67.78	28.89	3.33	
Black-on-white and Glaze I				
Number	8	5	0	13
Per cent	61.54	38.46	0	
Glazes II and III				
Number	22	8	1	31
Per cent	70.97	25.81	3.23	
Glaze IV				
Number	15	6	1	22
Per cent	68.18	27.27	4.55	
Glazes V and VI				
Number	16	7	1	24
Per cent	66.67	29.17	4.17	
Females				
Total Series A				
Number	29	28	3	60
Per cent	48.33	45.90	4.92	
Black-on-white and Glaze I				
Number	8	3	0	11
Per cent	72.73	27.27	0	
Glazes II and III				
Number	7	10	1	18
Per cent	38.89	55.56	5.56	
Glaze IV				
Number	9	6	1	16
Per cent	56.25	37.50	6.25	
Glazes V and VI				
Number	5	9	1	15
Per cent	33.33	60.00	6.67	

MEASUREMENTS OF THE MANDIBLE

Tables III–50 to III–55 give means of mandibular measurements. The usual sex differences are manifest throughout. In most of the mandibular measurements the crania of the Black-on-white and Glaze I group seem to average a little smaller than those of the succeeding periods. The consistency of this difference in the subgroups seems to indicate that it may be significant, although the numbers of crania are so small that, taken in connection with the probable errors, it would be unsafe to lay any emphasis upon the apparently smaller dimensions of the mandibles of the earlier periods. The mean angle which the horizontal rami make with the ascending rami of the mandible is pronouncedly larger in the jaws of the males of the earlier periods than in subsequent strata.

TABLE III–50. Bigonial Diameter

Males	Number	Range	Mean	St. D.	V.
Total Series A	102	88–117	101.56 ± 0.47	7.11 ± 0.34	7.00 ± 0.33
Black-on-white and Glaze I	16	92–113	100.44 ± 1.01	6.00 ± 0.71	5.97 ± 0.71
Glazes II and III	32	88–116	101.25 ± 0.93	7.79 ± 0.66	7.69 ± 0.65
Glaze IV	23	90–117	102.70 ± 1.12	7.97 ± 0.79	7.76 ± 0.77
Glazes V and VI	31	90–113	101.81 ± 0.69	5.67 ± 0.48	5.57 ± 0.48
Females					
Total Series A	62	83–109	94.47 ± 0.46	5.37 ± 0.32	5.67 ± 0.34
Black-on-white and Glaze I	15	85–100	93.07 ± 0.73	4.17 ± 0.51	4.48 ± 0.55
Glazes II and III	17	87–104	96.00 ± 0.80	4.87 ± 0.56	5.07 ± 0.59
Glaze IV	16	85–98	93.44 ± 0.69	4.08 ± 0.49	4.37 ± 0.52
Glazes V and VI	14	83–109	95.28 ± 1.33	7.39 ± 0.94	7.76 ± 0.99

TABLE III–51. Bicondylar Width

Males	Number	Range	Mean	St. D.	V.
Total Series A	83	109–138	122.34 ± 0.45	6.14 ± 0.32	5.02 ± 0.26
Black-on-white and Glaze I	15	112–130	121.73 ± 0.87	4.99 ± 0.61	4.10 ± 0.50
Glazes II and III	24	111–138	122.96 ± 0.99	7.16 ± 0.70	5.82 ± 0.57
Glaze IV	18	109–131	121.83 ± 0.98	6.19 ± 0.70	5.08 ± 0.57
Glazes V and VI	26	110–137	122.46 ± 0.74	5.58 ± 0.52	4.56 ± 0.43
Females					
Total Series A	48	103–128	115.27 ± 0.60	6.12 ± 0.42	5.31 ± 0.36
Black-on-white and Glaze I	9	105–125	113.78 ± 1.36	6.07 ± 0.96	5.33 ± 0.85
Glazes II and III	12	108–121	115.92 ± 0.73	3.73 ± 0.51	3.22 ± 0.44
Glaze IV	14	106–123	115.14 ± 0.93	5.17 ± 0.66	4.49 ± 0.57
Glazes V and VI	13	103–128	115.85 ± 1.55	8.31 ± 1.10	7.17 ± 0.95

TABLE III–52. Height of Symphysis

Males	Number	Range	Mean	St. D.	V.
Total Series A	102	29–43	35.40 ± 0.17	2.50 ± 0.12	7.08 ± 0.33
Black-on-white and Glaze I	17	31–38	35.24 ± 0.34	2.10 ± 0.24	5.96 ± 0.69
Glazes II and III	38	31–43	35.50 ± 0.26	2.38 ± 0.18	6.70 ± 0.51
Glaze IV	20	29–41	35.20 ± 0.49	3.25 ± 0.35	9.23 ± 0.98
Glazes V and VI	27	31–39	35.52 ± 0.29	2.25 ± 0.21	6.33 ± 0.58
Females					
Total Series A	79	28–41	33.65 ± 0.20	2.59 ± 0.14	7.70 ± 0.41
Black-on-white and Glaze I	19	31–37	33.74 ± 0.30	1.94 ± 0.21	5.75 ± 0.63
Glazes II and III	26	28–39	33.46 ± 0.35	2.65 ± 0.25	7.92 ± 0.74
Glaze IV	19	30–39	34.47 ± 0.37	2.41 ± 0.26	6.99 ± 0.76
Glazes V and VI	15	28–41	34.73 ± 0.54	3.08 ± 0.38	8.90 ± 1.10

TABLE III–53. Mean Angle of Ascending Rami

Males	Number	Range	Mean	St. D.	V.
Total Series A	97	105–129	117.70 ± 0.35	5.12 ± 0.25	4.35 ± 0.21
Black-on-white and Glaze I	16	111–127	119.81 ± 0.86	5.07 ± 0.60	4.23 ± 0.50
Glazes II and III	32	105–127	116.86 ± 0.64	5.40 ± 0.46	4.62 ± 0.39
Glaze IV	20	111–125	117.85 ± 0.57	3.77 ± 0.40	3.20 ± 0.34
Glazes V and VI	29	107–129	117.36 ± 0.56	4.43 ± 0.39	3.78 ± 0.33
Females					
Total Series A	62	112–135	122.90 ± 0.42	4.86 ± 0.29	3.96 ± 0.24
Black-on-white and Glaze I	12	112–131	122.92 ± 1.06	5.45 ± 0.75	4.43 ± 0.61
Glazes II and III	18	115–129	122.72 ± 0.65	4.12 ± 0.46	3.36 ± 0.38
Glaze IV	18	114–135	123.06 ± 0.92	5.81 ± 0.65	4.72 ± 0.53
Glazes V and VI	14	114–130	123.14 ± 0.69	3.81 ± 0.48	3.09 ± 0.39

TABLE III–54. Minimum Breadth of Ascending Ramus

Males	Number	Range	Mean	St. D.	V.
Total Series A	125	30–44	36.92 ± 0.17	2.90 ± 0.12	7.84 ± 0.33
Black-on-white and Glaze I	20	30–39	35.25 ± 0.40	2.69 ± 0.29	7.63 ± 0.81
Glazes II and III	46	31–44	37.08 ± 0.30	3.02 ± 0.21	8.14 ± 0.57
Glaze IV	27	31–40	36.78 ± 0.31	2.39 ± 0.22	6.50 ± 0.60
Glazes V and VI	32	32–44	37.88 ± 0.33	2.74 ± 0.23	7.25 ± 0.61
Females					
Total Series A	85	29–43	35.75 ± 0.17	2.44 ± 0.13	6.82 ± 0.35
Black-on-white and Glaze I	18	29–37	34.61 ± 0.32	2.02 ± 0.23	5.84 ± 0.66
Glazes II and III	26	32–43	35.96 ± 0.33	2.46 ± 0.23	6.85 ± 0.64
Glaze IV	23	31–42	35.83 ± 0.38	2.73 ± 0.27	7.62 ± 0.76
Glazes V and VI	18	34–39	36.50 ± 0.24	1.50 ± 0.17	4.11 ± 0.46

TABLE III–55. Height of Ascending Ramus

Males	Number	Range	Mean	St. D.	V.
Total Series A	116	48–78	62.83 ± 0.38	6.01 ± 0.25	9.56 ± 0.42
Black-on-white and Glaze I	18	53–72	61.61 ± 0.84	5.28 ± 0.56	8.57 ± 0.96
Glazes II and III	43	50–78	63.07 ± 0.67	6.48 ± 0.47	10.27 ± 0.75
Glaze IV	23	54–71	63.56 ± 0.71	5.03 ± 0.50	7.91 ± 0.79
Glazes V and VI	32	48–76	62.66 ± 0.75	6.28 ± 0.53	10.02 ± 0.85
Females					
Total Series A	79	46–65	55.02 ± 0.31	4.06 ± 0.22	7.28 ± 0.40
Black-on-white and Glaze I	14	47–61	54.00 ± 0.71	3.95 ± 0.50	7.31 ± 0.93
Glazes II and III	25	48–65	55.36 ± 0.56	4.14 ± 0.39	7.48 ± 0.71
Glaze IV	22	46–64	55.18 ± 0.72	5.01 ± 0.51	9.08 ± 0.92
Glazes V and VI	18	50–61	55.39 ± 0.51	3.23 ± 0.36	5.83 ± 0.66

CRANIOMETRIC DIFFERENCES BETWEEN MALE CRANIA OF THE VARIOUS STRATA

In order to determine the significance of the craniometric variations exhibited in the several archaeological strata, the means of measurements and indices of male crania have been studied with reference to the difference of means of the subgroups from the means of the entire male series. The significance of the deviation of any subgroup with respect to a single mean from the mean of the whole series is appraised on the basis of the probable error. The deviation of a subgroup in all of its measurements and indices is considered significant or insignificant according to the number of deviating measurements and indices in excess of, or less than, expectation.

The deviations of means of the subgroups have been expressed graphically in Figures III–1, 2, 3 and are based upon Table III–56. In the figures, the mean of the total males series is represented by a heavy horizontal line. The plus and minus deviations of subgroups are plotted as dots above or below the horizontal line and in accordance with the marginal scale. The vertical hatched bands represent on either side of the mean of the whole series twice the probable error of a sample taken at random from the entire series but numerically equal to the subgroup of which the means are plotted. The horizontal broken lines represent on each side of the mean once the probable error of a random sample of the entire group numerically equal to the subgroup, and in the case of the lowest and uppermost broken lines three times the probable error of such a sample. The deviation of the mean of a subgroup from the mean of the entire group cannot be considered significant unless the dot falls outside of the hatched band, that is, unless it is in excess of twice the probable error of a random sample of the whole series of the same size as the subgroup. Expectation is that 18 per cent of means may show a deviation equal to twice the probable error on the basis of chance only. But deviations equal to three times the probable error are to be expected only four times in 100 cases. If 82 per cent of the means of the subgroups fall within the hatched bands, the deviations of the means of the subgroup from the means of the entire group are insignificant.

In this study the measurements and indices of the cranial vault that are affected by occipital deformation are divided into deformed and undeformed groups. Deformation is treated like any other cranial character on the assumption that its presence in any individual skull is an effect of both hereditary and environmental causes and that it is subject to variations in intensity which are more or less normally distributed.

BLACK-ON-WHITE AND GLAZE I

In the Black-on-white and Glaze I group of male crania deviations in excess of twice the probable error of a random sample of similar size occur in six means out of the thirty plotted, or 20 per cent of cases. One might expect 18 per cent of deviations of such magnitude in a random sample. It is then probable that the crania of this group do vary significantly, though slightly, from a random sample of the whole male

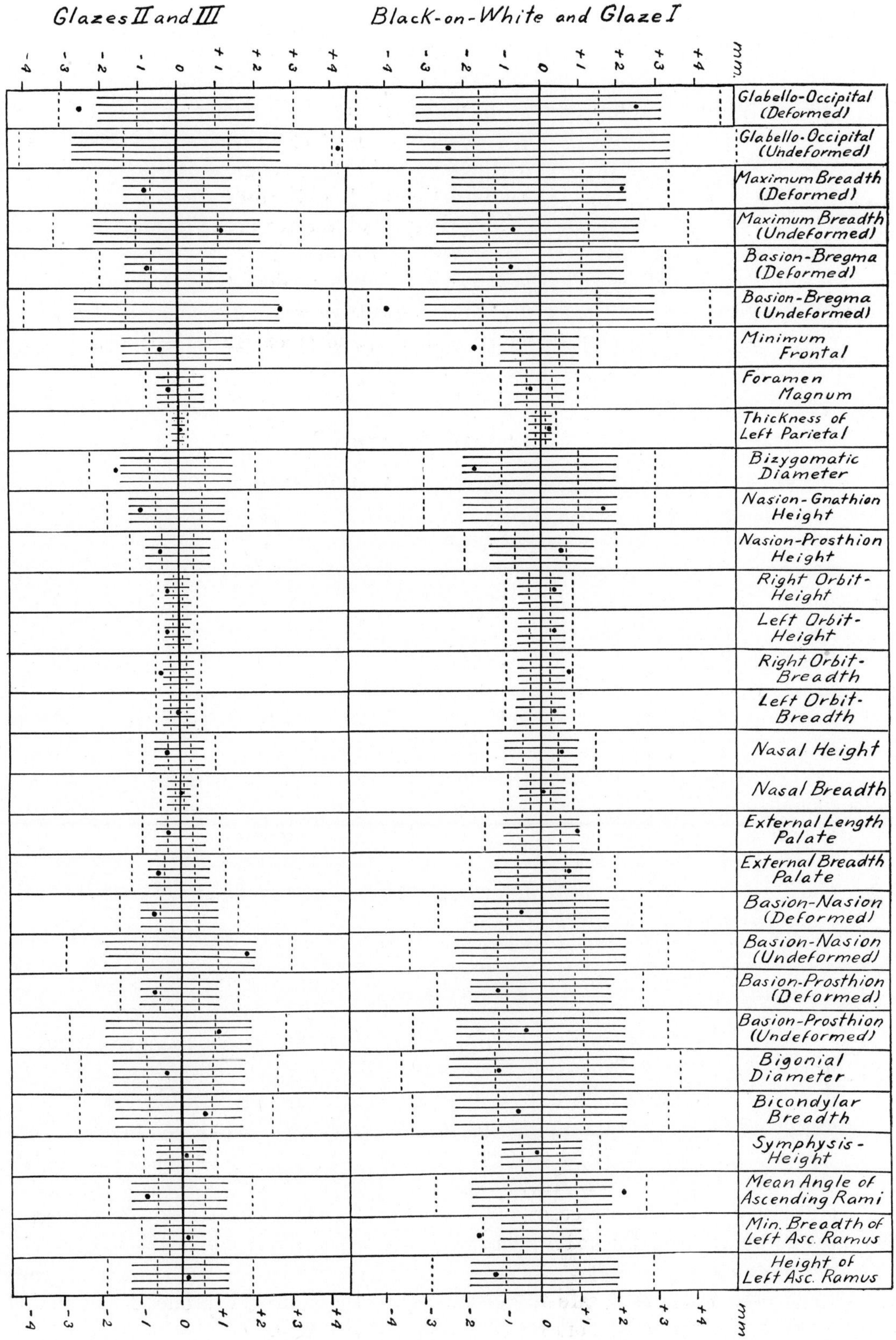

FIG. III–1. MEANS OF MEASUREMENTS OF STRATIGRAPHIC SUBGROUPS PLOTTED AGAINST MEANS OF TOTAL SERIES A. THE HEAVY HORIZONTAL LINE REPRESENTS THE MEAN OF THE ENTIRE SERIES. THE DOTS ARE THE MEANS OF THE SUBGROUPS. BLACK-ON-WHITE AND GLAZE I; GLAZES II AND III. THE HATCHED BANDS REPRESENT, BY THEIR EXTENSION ABOVE AND BELOW THE MEAN, TWICE THE PROBABLE ERRORS OF RANDOM SAMPLES OF THE ENTIRE SERIES EQUAL IN SIZE TO THE RESPECTIVE SUBGROUPS

(View from the side)

series. The significant deviations are: a deficiency in basion-bregma height in the undeformed crania; a deficiency in minimum frontal diameter in all of the crania; an excess in breadth of the right orbit in all crania; a deficiency in basion-nasion length of the undeformed skulls; an excess in the mean angle of the mandibular rami in all crania; a deficiency in the minimum breadth of the ascending rami in all crania. Deviations in excess of three times the probable error occur in minumim frontal diameter and minimum breadth of the ascending rami.

In the indices this earliest group shows significant deviations in three of thirteen indices plotted, or 23.1 per cent. These deviations are: a deficiency in the mean of the length-height index of undeformed crania, and an excess in the upper facial and total facial indices of all crania.

GLAZES II AND III

The second archaeological group of crania shows significant deviations in five of thirty measurements or 16.7 per cent. This is less than would be expected in the case of a random sample of the entire group of the same size as this subgroup. The significant deviations are: a deficiency in glabello-occipital length of deformed crania, which of course may mean only that the intensity of deformation was greater in this group; an excess in the glabello-occipital length of the undeformed; an excess in the basion-bregma height of the undeformed; a deficiency in the bizygomatic diameter of all crania; and a deficiency in the breadth of the right orbit. The only deviation in excess of three times the probable error is the great length of the undeformed group.

In the indices the Glaze II and Glaze III group of male crania show significant deviations in two cases of the thirteen recorded or 15.4 per cent. These deviations are excesses in both total facial and upper facial indices.

On the basis of probability it would not be safe to deduce that Glaze II and Glaze III crania differ more from the entire male series than any random sample of equal size would be expected to differ.

GLAZE IV

Glaze IV crania show significant deviations in five means or 16.7 per cent. These deviations are: a deficiency in glabello-occipital length of undeformed crania; an excess of basion-bregma height of deformed crania; an excess of bizygomatic diameter in all crania; an excess of nasion-prosthion height in all crania; an excess in the external palatal breadth in all crania. In no case do these deviations equal three times the probable error. In the indices the Glaze IV crania show significant excesses in two of thirteen cases, or 15.4 per cent. These deviations are an excess in the mean value of the external palatal index, and an excess in the length-height index of deformed crania.

On the whole it is safe to conclude that the Glaze IV group does not differ significantly from a random sample of the whole group.

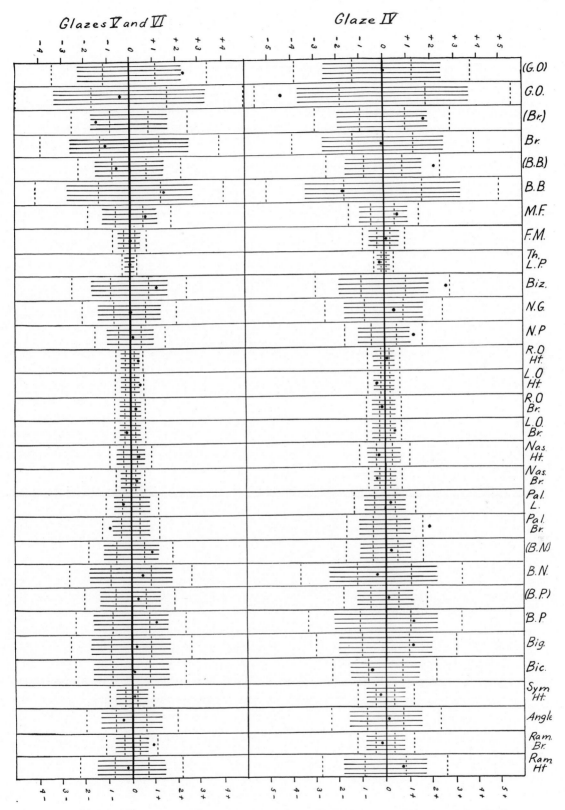

FIG. III–2. MEANS OF MEASUREMENTS OF STRATIGRAPHIC SUBGROUPS PLOTTED AGAINST MEANS OF
TOTAL SERIES A. GLAZE IV; GLAZES V AND VI

(View from the side)

Glazes V and VI

The last group of crania show in the measurements significant deviations in four means, or 13.3 per cent of those recorded. These deviations are: an excess of length in the deformed crania; an excess of height of the right orbit in all crania; a deficiency in the external breadth of the palate in all crania; an excess in the minimum breadth of the ascending rami of the mandibles.

In the indices but one possibly significant deviation is to be noted — an excess in the value of the mean orbital index equal to twice the probable error of a random sample of similar size. To all intents and purposes the crania of Glazes V and VI represent a random sample of the whole male series.

Tables III–57, 58, 59, 60 give the number of times amount of deviation in mean measure is actually observed in measurements and indices of the subgroups and of the entire groups and the number of times amount of deviation is expected if the Glaze subgroups are replaced by random samples. Table III–57 is based upon 38 measurements instead of the 30 which are plotted in Figures III–1, 2, 3.

An inspection of these tables shows that the deviations of the whole series are less than would be expected if the Glaze groups were replaced by random samples. This is true both in measurements and in indices and for every subgroup, except the earliest (Black-on-white and Glaze I). In the latter subgroup the deviations are large enough to be of possible significance both in measurements and in indices, although the deviations even in this group are not sufficiently marked so that it could be said that the crania of this group are certainly differentiated from those of the entire series.

It is clear, however, from an inspection of the graphs that the deviations from the means of the entire series are largest and most frequent in Black-on-white and Glaze I subgroup and diminish thereafter. In other words, the crania in the last periods become more and more typical of the group as a whole and more homogeneous.

The general conclusion is that the males of the Pecos population were somewhat diverse in metrical type in the early periods of the population and became more and more mixed and consequently more homogeneous as time went on. The male population in the last periods of the occupation is more representative of the entire population of the pueblo than a random sample from all periods would be. This part of our study affords no clear evidence of any radical change in the composition of the groups in different archaeological periods. It shows rather that the different types in existence in the earlier periods mixed more and more until their various metrical features were distributed among all of the individuals comprising the later population of Pecos.

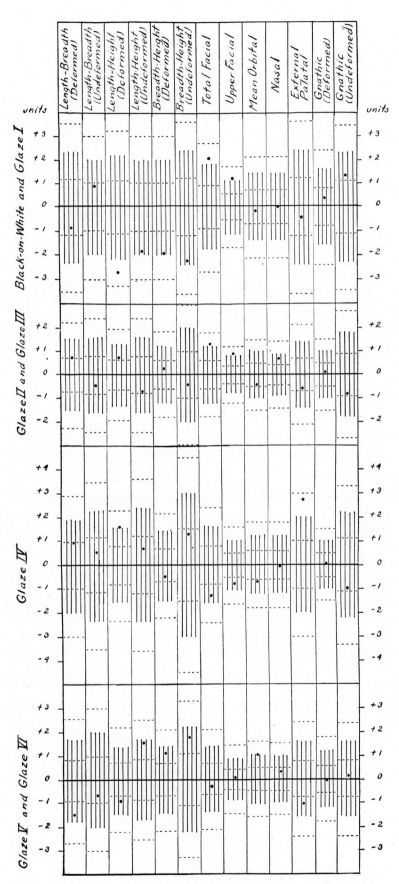

FIG. III–3. MEANS OF INDICES OF STRATIGRAPHIC SUBGROUPS PLOTTED AGAINST
MEANS OF TOTAL SERIES A

TABLE III–56. Excesses of Glaze Subgroups and Probable Errors of
Random Samples of Equal Size (Males)

Measurements	B.-on-W. and I Exc.	P. E.	II and III Exc.	P. E.	IV Exc.	P. E.	V and VI Exc.	P. E.
Glabello-occipital length (def.)	+2.57 ±	1.58	−2.56 ±	0.95	+0.01 ±	1.24	+2.36 ±	1.14
Glabello-occipital length (undef.) ..	−2.34 ±	1.74	+4.26 ±	1.37	−4.41 ±	1.83	−0.38 ±	1.66
Maximum breadth (def.)	+2.18 ±	1.15	−0.82 ±	0.72	+1.72 ±	0.92	−1.43 ±	0.83
Maximum breadth (undef.).......	−0.64 ±	1.31	+1.16 ±	1.07	−0.04 ±	1.31	−1.04 ±	1.31
Basion-bregma height (def.)	−0.74 ±	1.08	−0.77 ±	0.65	+2.16 ±	0.79	−0.57 ±	0.73
Basion-bregma height (undef.).....	−3.94 ±	1.54	+2.63 ±	1.31	−1.76 ±	1.65	+1.51 ±	1.38
Minimum frontal diameter	−1.72 ±	0.51	−0.45 ±	0.71	+0.60 ±	0.50	+0.67 ±	0.58
Cranial capacity (def.)	+1.04 ±	20.37	−19.48 ±	13.25	+25.18 ±	16.89	−6.06 ±	17.44
Cranial capacity (undef.)	−25.85 ±	30.10	+34.02 ±	24.01	−17.21 ±	35.62	+37.54 ±	28.16
Maximum circumference (def.) ...	+3.71 ±	2.94	−3.62 ±	1.76	−0.04 ±	2.37	−0.75 ±	2.16
Maximum circumference (undef.) .	−6.86 ±	2.95	+4.89 ±	2.59	−5.33 ±	3.53	+0.54 ±	2.95
Nasion-opisthion arc (def.)........	+1.13 ±	2.43	−2.59 ±	1.49	−0.46 ±	1.93	−0.56 ±	1.80
Nasion-opisthion arc (undef.)	−3.86 ±	3.65	+6.03 ±	3.46	−9.97 ±	4.47	−0.15 ±	3.30
Transverse arc (def.).............	+3.25 ±	2.40	−2.25 ±	1.44	+2.75 ±	1.93	−1.75 ±	1.84
Transverse arc (undef.)	−8.27 ±	2.61	+7.73 ±	2.61	−5.24 ±	3.12	+3.33 ±	2.75
Mean diameter of foraman magnum	−0.22 ±	0.32	−0.22 ±	0.23	+0.09 ±	0.28	+0.05 ±	0.25
Thickness of left parietal	+0.18 ±	0.13	+0.06 ±	0.09	−0.16 ±	0.12	+0 ±	0.11
Bizygomatic diameter	−1.84 ±	0.98	−1.59 ±	0.70	+2.64 ±	0.93	+1.16 ±	0.77
Nasion-menton height............	+1.62 ±	0.91	−0.95 ±	0.60	+0.42 ±	0.84	+0.04 ±	0.67
Nasion-prosthion height	+0.50 ±	0.65	−0.44 ±	0.42	+1.24 ±	0.56	+0.12 ±	0.49
Orbit height, right	+0.30 ±	0.24	−0.29 ±	0.17	+0.18 ±	0.22	+0.37 ±	0.19
Orbit height, left	+0.26 ±	0.24	−0.28 ±	0.17	−0.28 ±	0.22	+0.38 ±	0.18
Orbit breadth, right	+0.70 ±	0.27	−0.45 ±	0.19	−0.10 ±	0.25	+0.21 ±	0.21
Orbit breadth, left.............	+0.32 ±	0.29	−0.06 ±	0.20	+0.43 ±	0.26	−0.18 ±	0.22
Nasal height	+0.48 ±	0.42	−0.28 ±	0.27	−0.23 ±	0.36	+0.36 ±	0.31
Nasal breadth	+0.07 ±	0.24	+0.02 ±	0.16	−0.30 ±	0.21	+0.24 ±	0.18
External palatal length..........	+0.96 ±	0.51	−0.26 ±	0.31	+0.28 ±	0.44	−0.31 ±	0.35
External palatal breadth.........	+0.69 ±	0.59	−0.56 ±	0.38	+1.88 ±	0.51	−0.90 ±	0.41
Basion-nasion length (def.)........	−0.58 ±	0.85	−0.62 ±	0.48	+0.31 ±	0.56	+0.92 ±	0.60
Basion-nasion length (undef.)	−3.30 ±	1.14	+1.68 ±	0.90	−0.30 ±	1.14	+0.52 ±	0.85
Basion-prosthion length (def.).....	−1.18 ±	0.86	−0.63 ±	0.49	+0.09 ±	0.57	+0.27 ±	0.62
Basion-prosthion length (undef.)...	−0.40 ±	1.08	+1.06 ±	0.92	+1.20 ±	1.21	+1.08 ±	0.81
Bigonial diameter................	−1.12 ±	1.20	−0.31 ±	0.85	+1.14 ±	1.00	+0.25 ±	0.86
Bicondylar width	−0.61 ±	1.07	+0.62 ±	0.84	−0.51 ±	0.76	+0.12 ±	0.81
Height of symphysis	−0.16 ±	0.41	+0.10 ±	0.27	−0.20 ±	0.38	+0.12 ±	0.32
Mean angle of ascending rami.....	+2.11 ±	0.86	−0.84 ±	0.61	+0.15 ±	0.77	−0.34 ±	0.64
Min. breadth asc. ramus..........	−1.67 ±	0.44	+0.16 ±	0.29	−0.14 ±	0.38	+0.96 ±	0.34
Height ascending ramus	−1.22 ±	0.96	+0.24 ±	0.62	+0.73 ±	0.84	−0.17 ±	0.72
Indices								
Length-breadth (def.)	−0.85 ±	1.18	+0.74 ±	0.74	+0.92 ±	0.95	−1.53 ±	0.85
Length-breadth (undef.)	+0.90 ±	1.02	−0.43 ±	0.84	−0.58 ±	1.15	−0.70 ±	1.02
Length-height (def.).............	−2.70 ±	1.08	+0.76 ±	0.65	+1.60 ±	0.77	−0.93 ±	0.73
Length-height (undef.)	−1.86 ±	0.94	−0.75 ±	0.80	+0.69 ±	1.12	+1.59 ±	0.84
Breadth-height (def.)	−1.94 ±	1.01	+0.24 ±	0.62	−0.26 ±	0.73	+1.15 ±	0.68
Breadth-height (undef.)	−2.21 ±	1.17	−0.42 ±	1.00	+1.27 ±	1.48	+1.78 ±	1.10
Total facial	+2.04 ±	0.85	+1.34 ±	0.60	−1.31 ±	0.82	−0.33 ±	0.66
Upper facial	+1.18 ±	0.57	+0.85 ±	0.38	−0.76 ±	0.52	−0.11 ±	0.88
Mean orbital	−0.18 ±	0.67	−0.43 ±	0.49	−0.68 ±	0.61	+1.02 ±	0.53
Nasal	−0.02 ±	0.66	+0.63 ±	0.44	−0.06 ±	0.56	+0.34 ±	0.48
External palatal	−0.45 ±	1.16	−0.65 ±	0.71	+2.73 ±	1.00	−1.03 ±	0.80
Gnathic (def.)	+0.36 ±	0.76	+0.07 ±	0.46	+0.03 ±	0.54	−0.04 ±	0.59
Gnathic (undef.)	+1.28 ±	1.14	−0.83 ±	0.86	−0.97 ±	1.14	+0.14 ±	0.76

TABLE III–57. NUMBER OF TIMES AMOUNT OF DEVIATION IN MEAN MEASURE
IS OBSERVED IN GLAZE SUBGROUPS (MEASUREMENTS)

	Less than p. e.	1 x p. e. to 2 x p. e.	2 x p. e. to 3 x p. e.	3 x p. e. to 4 x p. e.	4 x p. e. to 5 x p. e.	Total
Black-on-white and Glaze I	12	18	5	3	0	38
Glazes II and III	11	20	6	1	0	38
Glaze IV	21	11	5	1	0	38
Glazes V and VI..............	22	12	4	0	0	38
Total	66	61	20	5	0	152

TABLE III–58. NUMBER OF TIMES AMOUNT MAY BE EXPECTED IF GLAZE
SUBGROUPS ARE REPLACED BY RANDOM SAMPLES (MEASUREMENTS)

	Less than p. e.	1 x p. e. to 2 x p. e.	2 x p. e. to 3 x p. e.	3 x p. e. to 4 x p. e.	4 x p. e. to 5 x p. e.	Total
Each subgroup	19	11.4	5.9	1.3	.3	37.9
Entire series	76	45.6	23.9	5.3	1.1	151.9

TABLE III–59. NUMBER OF TIMES AMOUNT OF DEVIATION IN MEAN MEASURE
IS OBSERVED IN GLAZE SUBGROUPS (INDICES)

	Less than p. e.	1 x p. e. to 2 x p. e.	2 x p. e. to 3 x p. e.	3 x p. e. to 4 x p. e.	4 x p. e. to 5 x p. e.	Total
Black-on-white and Glaze I	6	4	3	0	0	13
Glazes II and III	8	3	2	0	0	13
Glaze IV	8	3	2	0	0	13
Glazes V and VI..............	6	7	0	0	0	13
Total	28	17	7	0	0	52

TABLE III–60. NUMBER OF TIMES AMOUNT MAY BE EXPECTED IF GLAZE SUBGROUPS
ARE REPLACED BY RANDOM SAMPLES (INDICES)

	Less than p. e.	1 x p. e. to 2 x p. e.	2 x p. e. to 3 x p. e.	3 x p. e. to 4 x p. e.	4 x p. e. to 5 x p. e.	Total
Each subgroup	6.5	3.9	2	.5	.1	13
Total series	26	15.6	8.2	1.8	.4	52

SUMMARY OF CRANIOMETRIC DIFFERENCES BY ARCHAEO-
LOGICAL PERIODS

Cranial deformation. Least common in the earliest periods of the pueblo in the case of males. Seems to increase in frequency and intensity throughout later periods. In the females no certain period differences are ascertainable.

Glabello-occipital length. No certain period changes.

Maximum breadth. No apparent period changes.

Length-breadth index. Most intensive deformation effecting the highest length-breadth index seems to occur in both sexes in Glaze IV.

Basion-bregma height. No apparent differences.

Length-height index. Highest in both sexes in Glaze IV.

Breadth-height index. No certain differences.

Minimum frontal diameter. Increases in both sexes from early to late periods.

Cranial capacity. A slight and possibly insignificant increase occurs from the early to late periods in both sexes.

Circumference. No ascertainable trend.

Nasion-opisthion arc. No differences between subgroups.

Transverse arc. No differences.

Mean diameter of foramen magnum. No differences.

Thickness of left parietal. No differences.

Bizygomatic diameter. Increases in both sexes from early to late periods.

Nasion-menton height. Largest in males in the earliest period.

Nasion-prosthion height. No differences of significance.

Total facial index. Highest in males in the earliest period. Euryprosopes are commonest in the last two periods.

Upper facial index. Higher in the earlier periods in the males.

Orbits. No certain differences.

Nose. No certain differences.

Palate. Palates show a slight tendency to decrease in size from early to late periods, but this change is not certainly significant.

Prognathism. There is possibly a slight increase in prognathism in the later periods.

Mandible. The mandibles of the earliest period are perhaps slightly smaller than those of subsequent periods.

TABLE III–61. MEANS OF SKULL MEASUREMENTS: TOTAL SERIES A

Measurements	Deformed	Undeformed
Glabello-occipital length	164.28	175.74
Maximum breadth	145.43	137.84
Basion-bregma height	140.84	137.19
Minimum frontal diameter	94.88	94.92
Cranial capacity	1367.94	1338.71
Maximum circumference	495.29	502.76
Nasion-opisthion arc	355.75	365.97
Transverse arc	329.75	316.67
Mean diameter of foramen magnum	30.93	....
Thickness of left parietal	5.16	....
Maximum bizygomatic diameter	138.56	....
Nasion-menton height	119.38	....
Nasion-prosthion height	72.85	....
Orbit height, right	34.80	....
" " left	34.90	....
" breadth, right	39.90	....
" " left	39.47	....
Nasal height	50.94	....
Nasal breadth	25.80	....
External palatal length	55.04	....
External palatal breadth	65.59	....
Basion-nasion length	101.89	102.70
Basion-prosthion length	97.80	....
Bigonial diameter	101.56	....
Bicondylar width	122.34	....
Height symphysis	35.40	....
Mean angle of ascending rami	117.70	....
Minimum breadth of ascending rami	36.92	....
Height of ascending rami	62.83	....
Indices		
Length-breadth	88.93	78.30
Length-height	85.70	78.11
Breadth-height	96.94	99.33
Total facial	85.96	....
Upper facial	52.09	....
Mean orbital	87.80	....
Nasal	50.44	....
External palatal	119.16	....
Gnathic	95.97	....

PLATE III–1

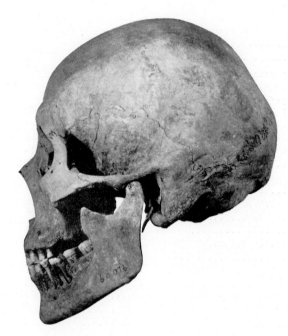

LENGTH-HEIGHT INDEX, 74.23

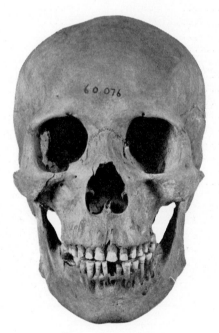

FACIAL INDEX, 91.54   CRANIAL INDEX, 83.44

No. 60,076. BLACK–ON–WHITE. BRACHYCEPHALIC MALE
VERY SLIGHT OCCIPITAL DEFORMATION

PLATE III–2

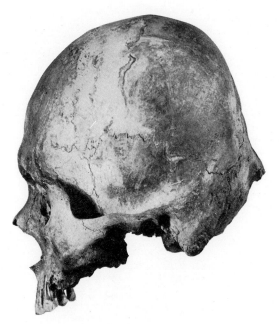

LENGTH-HEIGHT INDEX, 87.12

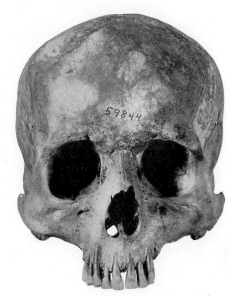

FACIAL INDEX, 88.19

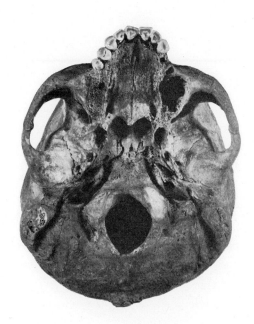

CRANIAL INDEX, 91.41

No. 59,844.   BLACK-ON-WHITE.   BRACHYCEPHALIC MALE
PRONOUNCED OCCIPITAL DEFORMATION

Plate III–3

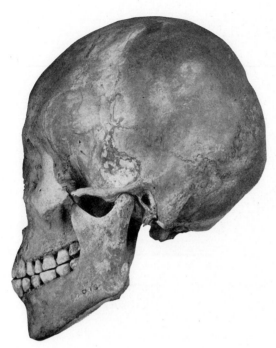

LENGTH-HEIGHT INDEX, 81.40

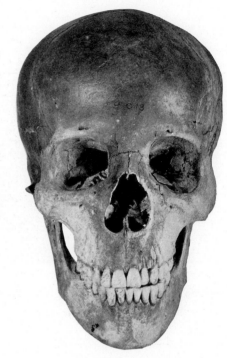

FACIAL INDEX, 93.08

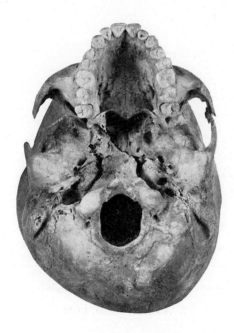

CRANIAL INDEX, 85.38

No. 60,013.   BLACK–ON–WHITE.   BRACHYCEPHALIC FEMALE
RIGHT OCCIPITAL DEFORMATION

PLATE III–4

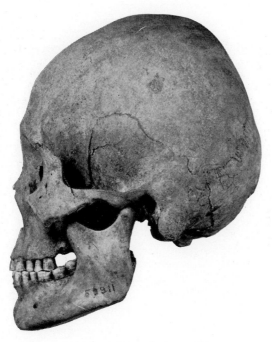

LENGTH-HEIGHT INDEX, 84.76

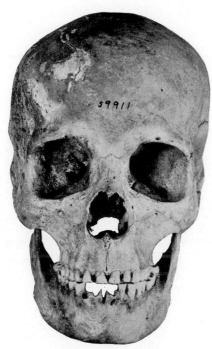

FACIAL INDEX, 90.70   CRANIAL INDEX, 85.37

No. 59,911. BLACK–ON–WHITE. BRACHYCEPHALIC FEMALE
PRONOUNCED RIGHT OCCIPITAL DEFORMATION

PLATE III-5

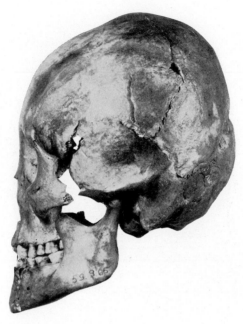

LENGTH-HEIGHT INDEX, 90.41

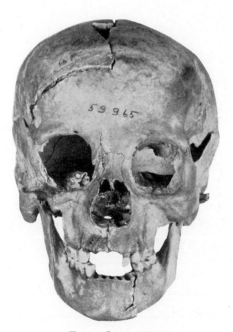

FACIAL INDEX, 79.10

CRANIAL INDEX, 99.32

No. 59,965.   BLACK–ON–WHITE.   BRACHYCEPHALIC FEMALE
FRONTO-OCCIPITAL DEFORMATION

PLATE III–6

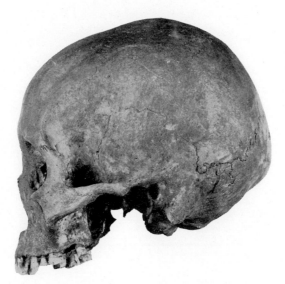

LENGTH-HEIGHT INDEX, 76.02

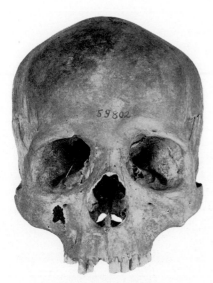

FACIAL INDEX, 88.46

CRANIAL INDEX, 79.53

No. 59,802. BLACK–ON–WHITE. MESOCEPHALIC FEMALE
RIGHT OCCIPITAL DEFORMATION

Plate III–7

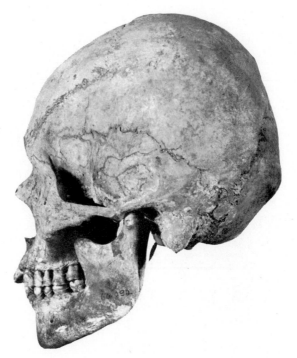

Length-Height Index, 79.43

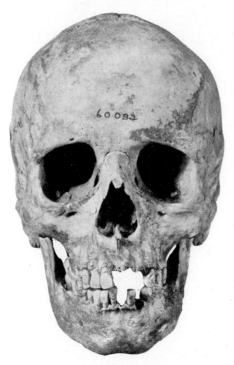

Facial Index, 88.24

Cranial Index, 85.14

No. 60,092.   GLAZE I.   BRACHYCEPHALIC MALE.   SLIGHT OCCIPITAL DEFORMATION
HEAVY, MUSCULAR TYPE

PLATE III–8

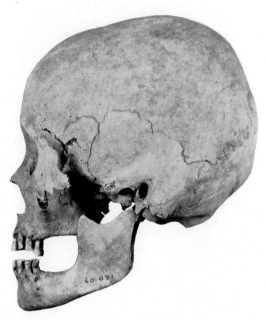

LENGTH-HEIGHT INDEX, 76.65

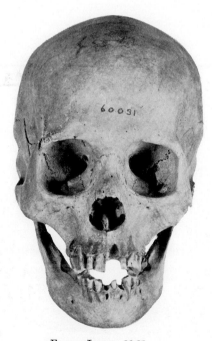

FACIAL INDEX, 82.81

CRANIAL INDEX, 80.24

No. 60,031. GLAZE I. SUB-BRACHYCEPHALIC FEMALE. NO DEFORMATION

PLATE III–9

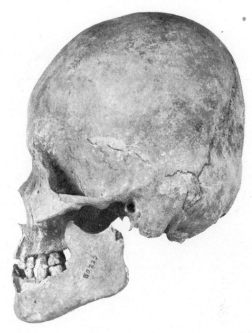

LENGTH-HEIGHT INDEX, (?)

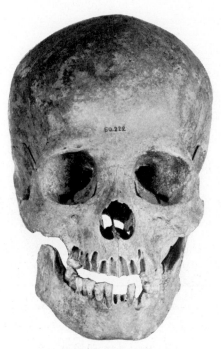

FACIAL INDEX, 83.97   CRANIAL INDEX, 100.00

No. 60,222. GLAZE I. BRACHYCEPHALIC FEMALE. PRONOUNCED
OCCIPITAL DEFORMATION

PLATE III–10

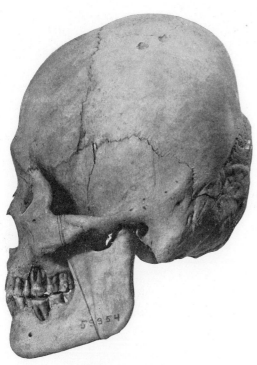

LENGTH-HEIGHT INDEX, 87.80

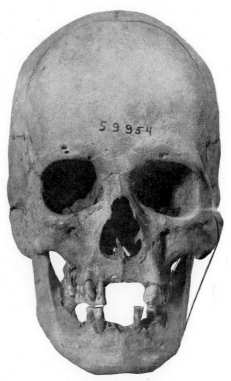

FACIAL INDEX, 82.52

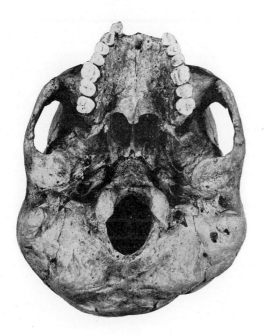

CRANIAL INDEX, 89.63

No. 59,954.   GLAZE II.   BRACHYCEPHALIC MALE.   PRONOUNCED
LEFT OCCIPITAL DEFORMATION

PLATE III–11

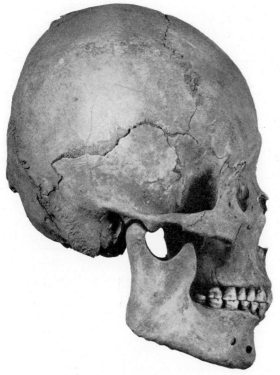

LENGTH-HEIGHT INDEX, 89.29

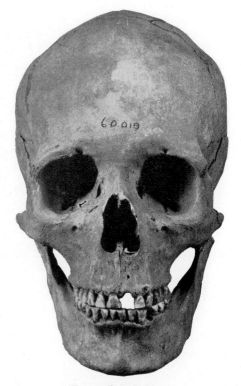

FACIAL INDEX, 91.55

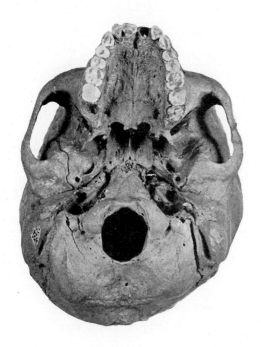

CRANIAL INDEX, 88.10

No. 60,019. GLAZE II. BRACHYCEPHALIC MALE. LEFT OCCIPITAL DEFORMATION

Plate III–12

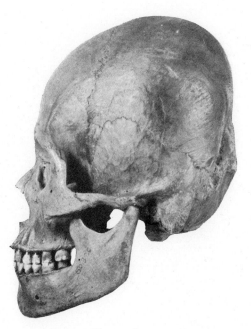

Length-Height Index, 95.00

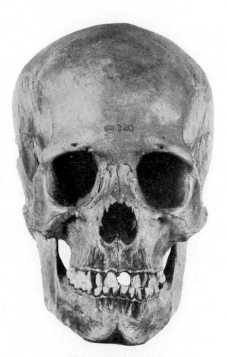

Facial Index, 87.70

Cranial Index, 97.86

No. 60,320. GLAZE II. BRACHYCEPHALIC MALE. PRONOUNCED
OCCIPITAL DEFORMATION

PLATE III–13

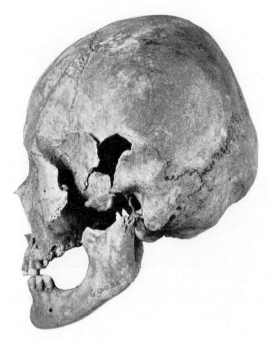

LENGTH-HEIGHT INDEX, 84.57

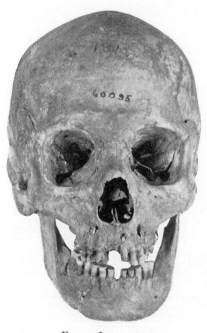

FACIAL INDEX, 90.55

CRANIAL INDEX, 85.80

No. 60,095. GLAZE II. BRACHYCEPHALIC FEMALE. OCCIPITAL DEFORMATION

PLATE III–14

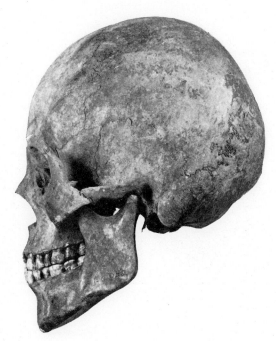

LENGTH-HEIGHT INDEX, 80.47

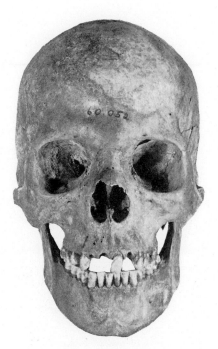

FACIAL INDEX, 89.39

CRANIAL INDEX, 77.51

No. 60,052. GLAZE II. SUB–DOLICHOCEPHALIC FEMALE. VERY SLIGHT
OCCIPITAL DEFORMATION.

PLATE III–15

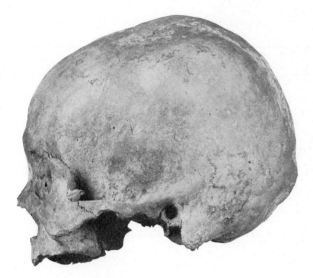

LENGTH-HEIGHT INDEX, 73.51

FACIAL INDEX, ?

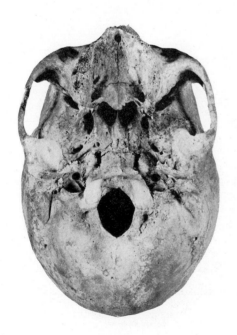

CRANIAL INDEX, 75.13

No. 59,846.   GLAZE III.   SUB–DOLICHOCEPHALIC MALE.   NO DEFORMATION

PLATE III–16

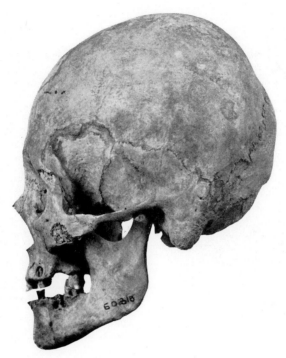

LENGTH-HEIGHT INDEX, 80.59

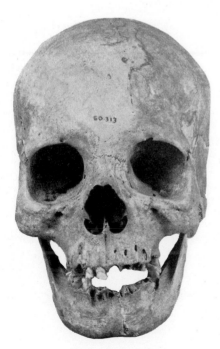

FACIAL INDEX, 85.50

CRANIAL INDEX, 81.76

No. 60,313. GLAZE III. SUB–BRACHYCEPHALIC MALE. OCCIPITAL DEFORMATION

PLATE III–17

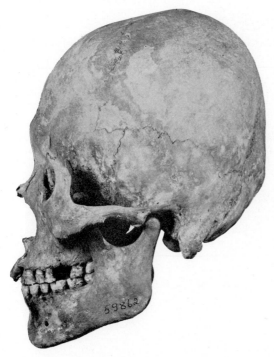

LENGTH-HEIGHT INDEX, 88.20

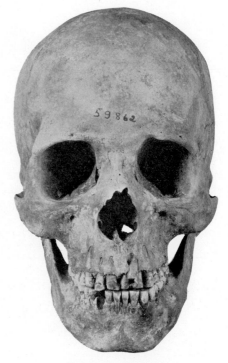

FACIAL INDEX, 87.86

CRANIAL INDEX, 86.96

No. 59,862.   GLAZE III.   BRACHYCEPHALIC MALE.   OCCIPITAL DEFORMATION

PLATE III–18

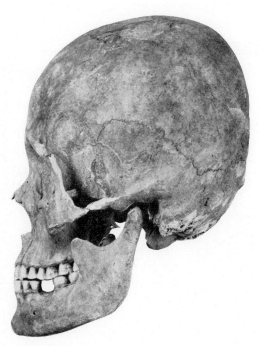

LENGTH-HEIGHT INDEX, 95.27

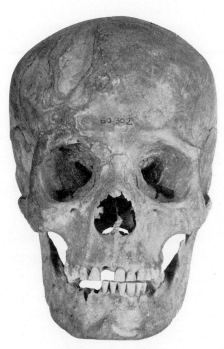

FACIAL INDEX, 85.71   CRANIAL INDEX, 98.65

No. 60,302. GLAZE III. BRACHYCEPHALIC FEMALE. OCCIPITAL DEFORMATION

PLATE III–19

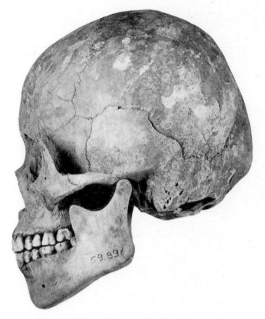

LENGTH-HEIGHT INDEX, 81.76

FACIAL INDEX, 82.95

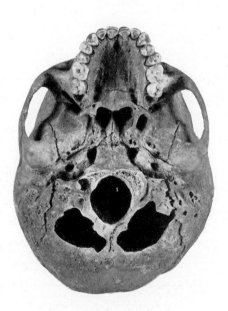

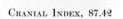

CRANIAL INDEX, 87.42

No. 59,996. GLAZE III. BRACHYCEPHALIC FEMALE. SLIGHT OCCIPITAL DEFORMATION

PLATE III–20

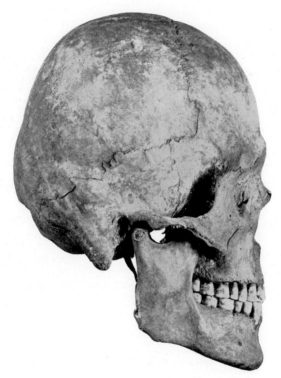

LENGTH-HEIGHT INDEX, 86.75

FACIAL INDEX, 91.91

CRANIAL INDEX, 88.62

No. 59,962. GLAZE IV. BRACHYCEPHALIC MALE
LEFT OCCIPITAL DEFORMATION

PLATE III–21

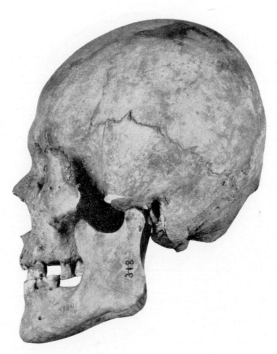

LENGTH-HEIGHT INDEX, 86.42

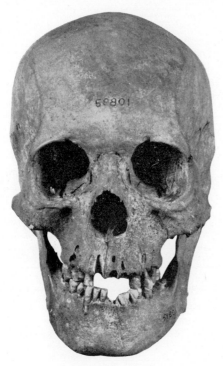

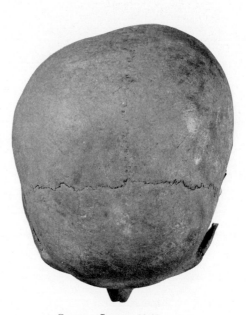

FACIAL INDEX, 91.24   CRANIAL INDEX, 88.27

No. 59,801.   GLAZE IV.   BRACHYCEPHALIC MALE.   VERY PRONOUNCED
RIGHT OCCIPITAL DEFORMATION

PLATE III–22

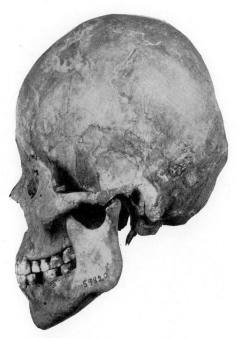

LENGTH-HEIGHT INDEX, 93.20

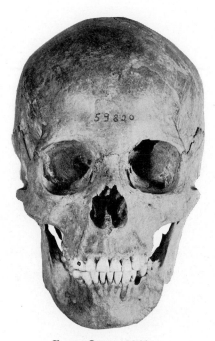

FACIAL INDEX, 86.92

CRANIAL INDEX, 94.56

No. 59,820. GLAZE IV. BRACHYCEPHALIC FEMALE. VERY PRONOUNCED
RIGHT OCCIPITAL DEFORMATION

PLATE III–23

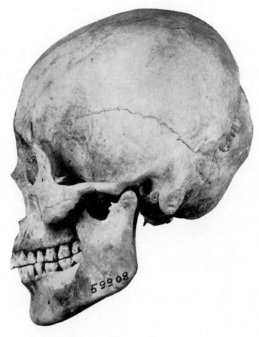

LENGTH-HEIGHT INDEX, 81.88

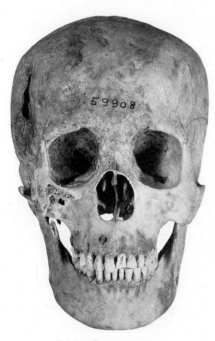

FACIAL INDEX, 92.37   CRANIAL INDEX, 89.38

No. 59,908.   GLAZE IV. BRACHYCEPHALIC FEMALE. RIGHT
OCCIPITAL DEFORMATION

PLATE III-24

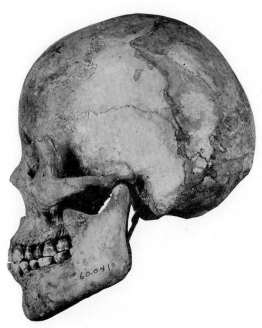

LENGTH-HEIGHT INDEX, 77.71

FACIAL INDEX, 92.91

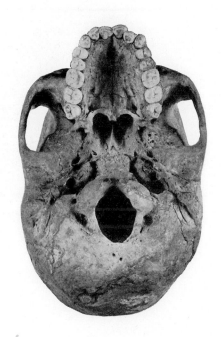

CRANIAL INDEX, 77.11

No. 60,041.   GLAZE IV.   MESOCEPHALIC FEMALE
VERY SLIGHT OCCIPITAL DEFORMATION

PLATE III–25

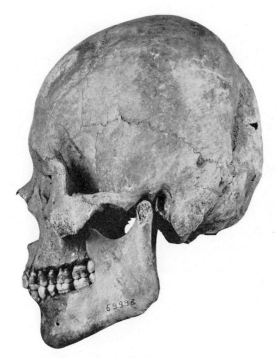

LENGTH-HEIGHT INDEX, 85.63

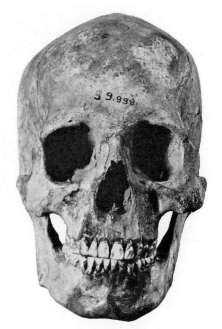

FACIAL INDEX, 84.06

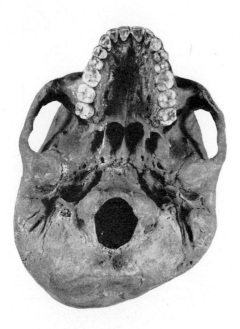

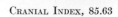

CRANIAL INDEX, 85.63

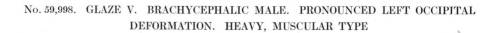

No. 59,998.   GLAZE V.   BRACHYCEPHALIC MALE.   PRONOUNCED LEFT OCCIPITAL
DEFORMATION.   HEAVY, MUSCULAR TYPE

PLATE III–26

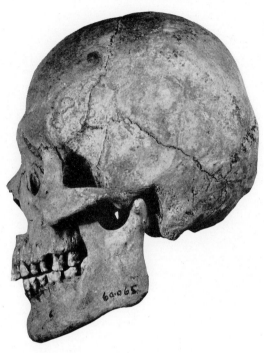

LENGTH-HEIGHT INDEX, 81.82

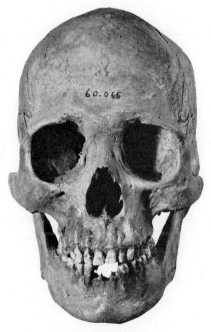

FACIAL INDEX, 85.21

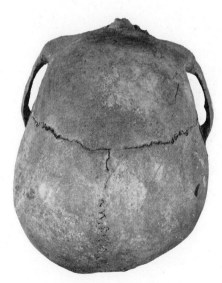

CRANIAL INDEX, 81.21

No. 60,065. GLAZE V. SUB–BRACHYCEPHALIC MALE. VERY SLIGHT
RIGHT OCCIPITAL DEFORMATION

PLATE III–27

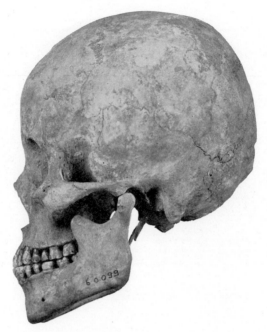

LENGTH-HEIGHT INDEX, 82.17

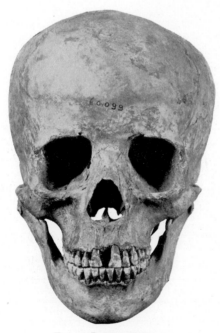

FACIAL INDEX, 83.72

CRANIAL INDEX, 94.90

No. 60,099. GLAZE V. BRACHYCEPHALIC FEMALE
RIGHT OCCIPITAL DEFORMATION

PLATE III–28

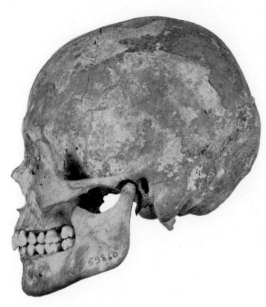

LENGTH-HEIGHT INDEX, 76.51

FACIAL INDEX, 77.52

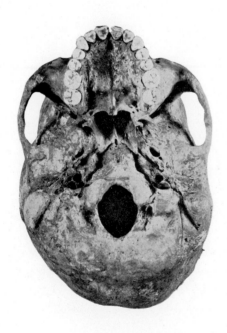

CRANIAL INDEX, 80.12

No. 59,860.   GLAZE V.   SUB–BRACHYCEPHALIC FEMALE.   SLIGHT
RIGHT OCCIPITAL DEFORMATION

PLATE III–29

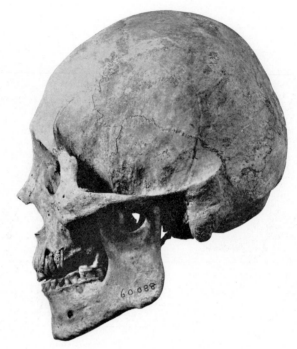

LENGTH-HEIGHT INDEX, 79.55

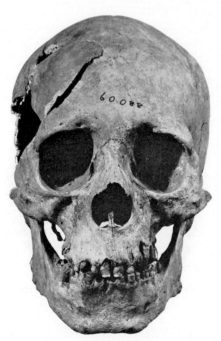

FACIAL INDEX, 86.21

CRANIAL INDEX, 85.23

No. 60,088. GLAZE VI. BRACHYCEPHALIC MALE. RIGHT
OCCIPITAL DEFORMATION

PLATE III–30

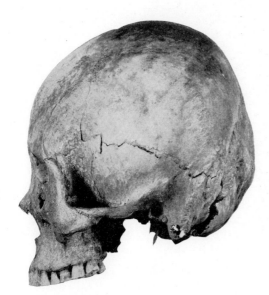

LENGTH-HEIGHT INDEX, 85.62

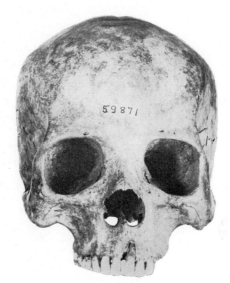

FACIAL INDEX, ?

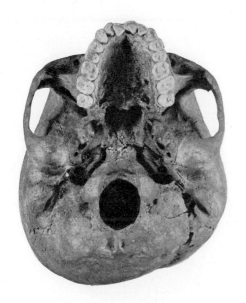

CRANIAL INDEX, 94.12

No. 59,871. GLAZE VI. BRACHYCEPHALIC FEMALE
PRONOUNCED LEFT OCCIPITAL DEFORMATION

PLATE III–31

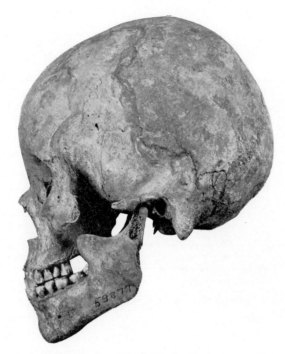

LENGTH-HEIGHT INDEX, 79.41

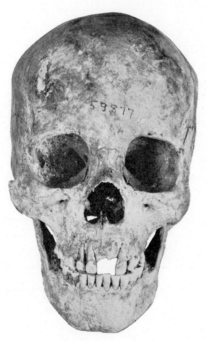

FACIAL INDEX, ?

CRANIAL INDEX, 77.65

No. 59,877.   GLAZE VI.   MESOCEPHALIC FEMALE.   NO DEFORMATION

PLATE III–32

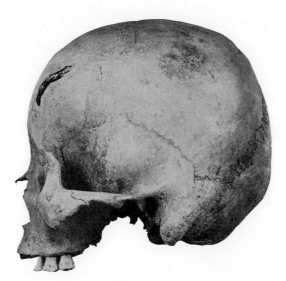

LENGTH-HEIGHT INDEX, 81.44

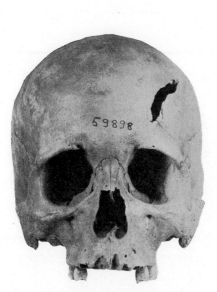

FACIAL INDEX, ?

CRANIAL INDEX, 80.84

No. 59,898. CHURCH. SUB–BRACHYCEPHALIC MALE. SLIGHT OCCIPITAL
DEFORMATION. TYPE PREDOMINATINGLY MEXICAN

PLATE III–33

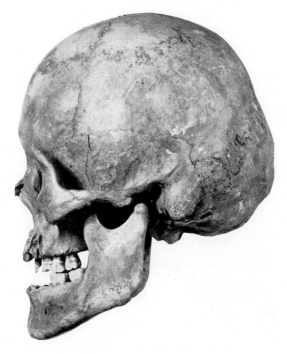

LENGTH-HEIGHT INDEX, 80.70

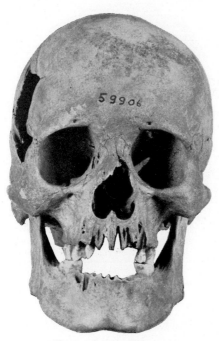

FACIAL INDEX, 84.06   CRANIAL INDEX, 81.29

No. 59,906. CHURCH. SUB–BRACHYCEPHALIC MALE. LEFT OCCIPITAL
DEFORMATION. TYPE PREDOMINATINGLY INDIAN

PLATE III–34

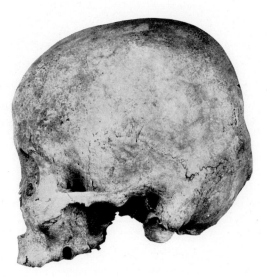

LENGTH-HEIGHT INDEX, 77.35

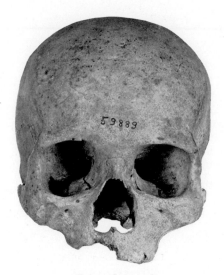

FACIAL INDEX, ?

CRANIAL INDEX, 79.56

No. 59,905. CHURCH. MESOCEPHALIC MALE. INDIAN TYPE
SLIGHT OCCIPITAL AND RIGHT PARIETO–OCCIPITAL DEFORMATION

PLATE III–35

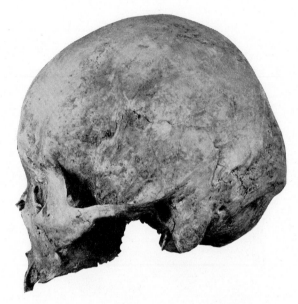

LENGTH-HEIGHT INDEX, 86.25

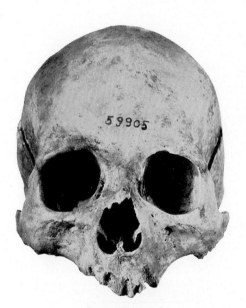

FACIAL INDEX, ?

CRANIAL INDEX, 86.25

No. 59,889. CHURCH. BRACHYCEPHALIC FEMALE. OCCIPITAL
DEFORMATION. INDIAN TYPE

CHAPTER IV

CRANIAL OBSERVATIONS BY STRATA

MORPHOLOGICAL features which can be observed and described but cannot be measured are probably of greater anthropological significance than diameters and indices. Unfortunately the personal equation of the observer inevitably enters into the gradation of such morphological observations. It has long been my custom to grade and record morphological features with respect to their development as compared with my judgment of average development in adult male Europeans. The reader may inquire, "What kind of 'adult male European' is referred to?" My conception of the adult male European is essentially that of a Northwestern European of stature 170 cm. or more, of moderate muscularity, with a cranium neither markedly dolichocephalic nor pronouncedly brachycephalic, and with a face neither short and broad nor long and narrow, but of medium proportions. Other features, such as are individually observed and graded, would conform to the mode. Brow-ridges would not be very strongly marked, for example, nor would the chin eminence be poorly developed. Taking this hypothetical average male European as a standard, I grade features on the following scale: absent, small or submedium, medium, large or pronounced, and very pronounced. I am confident that an experienced anatomical observer who has practised this method for many years, as I have done, can attain to a considerable degree of accuracy and consistency in making these morphological observations. Of course, sets of observations made by different observers are not necessarily strictly comparable. However unsatisfactory one may consider such qualitative observations, he must admit that they are better than nothing at all. They lend themselves to a measure of statistical treatment and are certainly superior to the vague and general descriptions of skull "types" which many craniologists append to their metrical studies. I therefore offer no apology for the emphasis placed upon morphological observations in this work.

CRANIAL VAULT

FRONTAL REGION

Table IV–1 gives the observations of height, breadth, and slope of the frontal region. The females show a higher percentage of crania with low frontal regions (38.38) than the males (31.66), and smaller percentages of crania with high frontal regions (females 3.03 per cent; males 14.38 per cent).

There are some peculiar features in Table IV–1 as to slope. Firstly, it is surprising that the females show more receding foreheads than the males throughout

TABLE IV–1. OBSERVATIONS ON FRONTAL REGION

	Height				Breadth				Slope			
	Submedium	Medium	Pronounced	Total	Submedium	Medium	Pronounced	Total	Steep	Medium	Receding	Total
Males												
Black-on-white and Gl. I												
Number	11	15	3	29	10	12	7	29	10	15	4	29
Per cent	37.93	51.72	10.34		34.48	41.38	24.14		34.48	51.72	13.79	
Glazes II and III												
Number	10	22	5	37	11	16	10	37	8	27	2	37
Per cent	27.03	59.46	13.51		29.73	43.24	27.03		21.62	72.97	5.41	
Glaze IV												
Number	11	14	5	30	5	13	12	30	5	20	5	30
Per cent	36.67	46.67	16.67		16.67	43.33	40.00		16.67	66.67	16.67	
Glazes V and VI												
Number	12	24	7	43	9	24	10	43	8	29	6	43
Per cent	27.91	55.81	16.28		20.93	55.81	23.26		18.60	67.44	13.95	
Total												
Number	44	75	20	139	35	65	39	139	31	91	17	139
Per cent	31.66	53.96	14.39		25.18	46.76	28.06		22.30	65.47	12.23	
Females												
Black-on-white and Gl. I												
Number	14	7	1	22	4	11	7	22	3	5	14	22
Per cent	63.64	31.82	4.55		18.18	50.00	31.82		13.64	22.73	63.64	
Glazes II and III												
Number	7	19	1	27	10	13	4	27	3	13	11	27
Per cent	25.93	70.37	3.70		37.04	48.15	14.81		11.11	48.15	40.74	
Glaze IV												
Number	12	16	1	29	11	15	3	29	4	16	9	29
Per cent	41.38	55.17	3.45		37.93	51.72	10.34		13.79	55.17	31.03	
Glazes V and VI												
Number	5	16	0	21	7	8	6	21	1	8	12	21
Per cent	23.81	76.19	0		33.33	38.10	28.57		4.76	38.10	57.14	
Total												
Number	38	58	3	99	32	47	20	99	11	42	46	99
Per cent	38.38	58.59	3.03		32.32	47.47	20.20		11.11	42.42	46.46	

the series, since one ordinarily expects the sex difference to be in the opposite direction. Secondly, there is the fact that the sex differences are at a maximum in the earliest group and diminish to a minimum in the Glaze IV period, thereafter increasing again. One may arrive at a general measure of these sex differences by adding the differences between the sexes in each category of slope for each period. By this method we arrive at the following differences: Black-on-white and Glaze I, 99.68 per cent; Glazes II and III, 70.66 per cent; Glaze IV, 28.74 per cent; Glazes V and VI, 86.37 per cent; all periods, 68.67 per cent. Of course, these differences may be nothing but an effect of the insufficiency of the samples and of possible inconsistency on the part of the observer in judging slope.

The correlation table (IV–2) shows that the commonest combination of height, breadth and slope in the male crania is a medium development of each. This combination occurs in 34 skulls or 24.5 per cent of the male series. In the females the commonest combination is height medium, breadth medium, slope receding, which occurs in 18.2 per cent of crania. The 27 different combinations of three categories of height, slope, and breadth make our classification of frontal observations too fine for the inadequate number of our cranial series.

Not much can be deduced from the relations of the glaze subgroups to combinations of observed frontal features. In the female series low foreheads are commonest in the Black-on-white and Glaze I periods, and foreheads of medium height increase from first to last. In the males high foreheads steadily increase from the earliest to latest periods. In both males and females low foreheads have two periods of maximum occurrence: the Black-on-white and Glaze I periods and the Glaze IV period. Again, both in male and female series there are two maxima for foreheads of medium height; namely, Glazes II and III, and Glazes V and VI groups, respectively.

TABLE IV–2. CORRELATION OF OBSERVATIONS ON FRONTAL REGION

Height Submedium

Males	Breadth Submedium Slope			Breadth Medium Slope			Breadth Pronounced Slope			Total
	Steep	Medium	Receding	Steep	Medium	Receding	Steep	Medium	Receding	
B.-on-W. and Gl. I										
Number	5	2	0	0	1	1	0	1	1	11
Per cent	17.24	6.90	0	0	3.45	3.45	0	3.45	3.45	37.94
Glazes II and III										
Number	1	1	0	2	2	0	2	2	0	10
Per cent	2.70	2.70	0	5.41	5.41	0	5.41	5.41	0	27.05
Glaze IV										
Number	0	2	0	1	3	1	3	1	0	11
Per cent	0	6.67	0	3.33	10.00	3.33	10.00	3.33	0	36.65
Glazes V and VI										
Number	2	2	0	1	3	1	2	1	0	12
Per cent	4.65	4.65	0	2.33	6.98	2.33	4.65	2.33	0	27.92
Total										
Number	8	7	0	4	9	3	7	5	1	44
Per cent	5.76	5.04	0	2.88	6.48	2.16	5.04	3.60	0.72	31.66

	Breadth Submedium Slope			Breadth Medium Slope			Breadth Pronounced Slope			Total
	Steep	Medium	Receding	Steep	Medium	Receding	Steep	Medium	Receding	
Females										
B.-on-W. and Gl. I										
Number	1	1	1	1	1	4	1	2	2	14
Per cent	4.55	4.55	4.55	4.55	4.55	18.18	4.55	9.09	9.09	63.54
Glazes II and III										
Number	1	2	0	1	2	1	0	0	0	7
Per cent	3.70	7.41	0	3.70	7.41	3.70	0	0	0	25.93
Glaze IV										
Number	1	2	3	2	2	2	0	0	0	12
Per cent	3.45	6.90	10.34	6.90	6.90	6.90	0	0	0	41.38
Glazes V and VI										
Number	0	1	1	0	0	0	0	0	3	5
Per cent	0	4.76	4.76	0	0	0	0	0	14.29	23.81
Total										
Number	3	6	5	4	5	7	1	2	5	38
Per cent	3.03	6.06	5.05	4.04	5.05	7.07	1.01	2.02	5.05	38.38

Height Medium

	Steep	Medium	Receding	Steep	Medium	Receding	Steep	Medium	Receding	Total
Males										
B.-on-W. and Gl. I										
Number	1	2	0	2	4	1	2	3	0	15
Per cent	3.45	6.90	0	6.90	13.79	3.45	6.90	10.34	0	51.73
Glazes II and III										
Number	1	7	0	1	9	1	1	2	0	22
Per cent	2.70	18.92	0	2.70	24.32	2.70	2.70	5.41	0	59.45
Glaze IV										
Number	1	1	1	0	8	0	0	1	2	14
Per cent	3.33	3.33	3.33	0	26.67	0	0	3.33	6.67	46.66
Glazes V and VI										
Number	1	3	0	1	13	2	1	3	0	24
Per cent	2.33	6.98	0	2.33	30.23	4.65	2.33	6.98	0	56.83
Total										
Number	4	13	1	4	34	4	4	9	2	75
Per cent	2.88	9.35	0.72	2.88	24.46	2.88	2.88	6.48	1.44	53.96
Females										
B.-on-W. and Gl. I										
Number	0	0	1	0	1	4	0	0	1	7
Per cent	0	0	4.55	0	4.55	18.18	0	0	4.55	31.83
Glazes II and III										
Number	0	4	2	0	4	5	1	1	2	19
Per cent	0	14.81	7.41	0	14.81	18.52	3.70	3.70	7.41	70.37
Glaze IV										
Number	0	5	0	1	4	3	0	2	1	16
Per cent	0	17.24	0	3.45	13.79	10.34	0	6.90	3.45	55.17
Glazes V and VI										
Number	1	3	1	0	2	6	0	2	1	16
Per cent	4.76	14.29	4.76	0	9.52	28.57	0	9.52	4.76	76.19
Total										
Number	1	12	4	1	11	18	1	5	5	58
Per cent	1.01	12.12	4.04	1.01	11.11	18.18	1.01	5.05	5.05	58.59

Height Pronounced

	Breadth Submedium Slope			Breadth Medium Slope			Breadth Pronounced Slope			Total
Males	Steep	Medium	Receding	Steep	Medium	Receding	Steep	Medium	Receding	
B.-on-W. and Gl. I										
Number	0	0	0	0	2	1	0	0	0	3
Per cent	0	0	0	0	6.90	3.45	0	0	0	10.45
Glazes II and III										
Number	0	1	0	0	1	0	0	2	1	5
Per cent	0	2.70	0	0	2.70	0	0	5.41	2.70	13.51
Glaze IV										
Number	0	0	0	0	0	0	0	4	1	5
Per cent	0	0	0	0	0	0	0	13.33	3.33	16.66
Glazes V and VI										
Number	0	1	0	0	1	2	0	2	1	7
Per cent	0	2.33	0	0	2.33	4.65	0	4.65	2.33	16.29
Total										
Number	0	2	0	0	4	3	0	8	3	20
Per cent	0	1.44	0	0	2.88	2.16	0	5.76	2.16	14.38
Females										
B.-on-W. and Gl. I										
Number	0	0	0	0	0	0	0	0	1	1
Per cent	0	0	0	0	0	0	0	0	4.55	4.55
Glazes II and III										
Number	0	0	1	0	0	0	0	0	0	1
Per cent	0	0	3.70	0	0	0	0	0	0	3.70
Glaze IV										
Number	0	0	0	0	1	0	0	0	0	1
Per cent	0	0	0	0	3.45	0	0	0	0	3.45
Glazes V and VI										
Number	0	0	0	0	0	0	0	0	0	0
Per cent	0	0	0	0	0	0	0	0	0	0
Total										
Number	0	0	1	0	1	0	0	0	1	3
Per cent	0	0	1.01	0	1.01	0	0	0	1.01	3.03

Table IV–3 gives the distribution of size of the supraorbital ridges. The usual sex difference is manifest. In the female series the size of the brow-ridges seems to diminish period by period and the number of crania in which these features are absent increases. In the males no such tendency is displayed.

The type of the supraorbital ridges is given in Table IV–4. Type I includes crania in which the brow-ridges are confined to the portion of the frontal bone above the median halves of the orbits. Type II comprises crania in which the median brow-ridges are developed and the external halves of the supraorbital margins are also thickened, but these two portions are separated from each other by a groove running up from the supraorbital notch. Type III includes all crania with brow-ridges continuous from the glabella region to the external angular process.

Type I brow-ridges are commonest among the males at all periods. Type II brow-ridges are commoner in the females of the first two periods but yield to Type I forms in the last two periods.

TABLE IV–3. SIZE OF SUPRAORBITAL RIDGES

	Black-on-white and Glaze I		Glazes II and III		Glaze IV		Glazes V and VI		Total	
Males	No.	Per cent	No.	Per cent	No.	Per cent	No.	Per cent	No.	Per cent
Absent	0	0	0	0	1	3.33	0	0	1	0.72
Submedium ..	6	21.43	8	21.05	10	33.33	12	27.91	36	25.89
Medium	18	64.29	21	55.26	10	33.33	25	58.14	74	53.23
Large	4	14.29	8	21.05	7	23.33	6	13.95	25	17.98
Very large	0	0	1	2.63	2	6.67	0	0	3	2.08
Total	28		38		30		43		139	
Females										
Absent	4	18.18	9	33.33	8	27.59	9	39.13	30	29.41
Submedium ..	14	63.64	15	53.57	17	58.62	11	47.83	57	55.88
Medium	3	13.64	4	14.29	4	13.79	2	8.70	13	12.74
Large	1	4.55	0	0	0	0	1	4.35	2	1.96
Total	22		28		29		23		102	

TABLE IV–4. TYPE OF SUPRAORBITAL RIDGES

	Black-on-white and Glaze I		Glazes II and III		Glaze IV		Glazes V and VI		Total	
Males	No.	Per cent	No.	Per cent	No.	Per cent	No.	Per cent	No.	Per cent
Absent	0	0	1	2.70	1	3.33	0	0	2	1.44
Median medium	0	0	1	2.70	1	3.33	1	2.33	3	2.16
Type I	12	41.38	18	48.65	11	36.67	17	39.53	58	41.73
Type II	8	27.59	13	35.14	10	33.33	14	32.56	45	32.37
Type III	9	31.03	4	10.81	7	23.33	11	25.58	31	22.30
Total	29		37		30		43		139	
Females										
Absent	4	21.05	8	27.59	8	29.63	9	42.86	29	31.52
Median medium	1	5.26	0	0	0	0	0	0	1	1.09
Type I	6	31.58	5	17.24	11	40.74	7	33.33	29	31.52
Type II	8	42.11	13	44.83	7	25.93	1	3.70	29	31.52
Type III	0	0	3	10.34	1	3.70	0	0	4	4.35
Total	19		29		27		17		92	

SAGITTAL REGION

Table IV–5 gives gradations of elevation of the sagittal region, breadth of the sagittal region and postcoronoid depression. Elevation of the sagittal region is much commoner in the males than in the females, probably because it is a thickening of the parietals along the sagittal margin caused by pressure of the temporal muscles, which are larger in males. This sagittal elevation raises the median longitudinal axis of the skull and may be supposed also to lessen its transverse diameter. Hence we are not surprised to find also that more of the males present submedium sagittal breadths than do females. The annular depression behind the coronal suture is usually found in a greater proportion of females than males, and the table substantiates this impression.

TABLE IV–5. OBSERVATIONS ON SAGITTAL REGION

	Elevation				Breadth				Postcoronoid Depression				
	Submedium	Medium	Pronounced	Total	Absent	Submedium	Medium	Total	Absent	Submedium	Medium	Pronounced	Total
Males													
Black-on-white and Gl. I													
Number	7	9	12	28	12	13	3	28	11	10	3	4	28
Per cent	25.00	32.14	42.86		42.86	46.43	10.71		39.29	35.71	10.71	14.29	
Glazes II and III													
Number	5	21	11	37	14	19	4	37	15	12	7	3	37
Per cent	13.51	56.76	29.73		37.84	51.35	10.81		40.54	32.43	18.92	8.11	
Glaze IV													
Number	4	15	11	30	9	16	5	30	11	14	2	3	30
Per cent	13.33	50.00	36.67		30.00	53.33	16.67		36.67	46.67	6.67	10.00	
Glazes V and VI													
Number	6	24	13	43	22	17	4	43	20	15	3	5	43
Per cent	13.95	55.81	30.23		51.16	39.53	9.30		46.51	34.88	6.98	11.63	
Total													
Number	22	69	47	138	57	65	16	138	57	51	15	15	138
Per cent	15.94	50.00	34.06		41.30	47.10	11.59		41.30	36.96	10.87	10.87	
Females													
Black-on-white and Gl. I													
Number	1	8	12	21	7	11	3	21	9	11	0	1	21
Per cent	4.76	38.10	57.14		33.33	52.38	14.29		42.86	52.38	0	4.76	
Glazes II and III													
Number	1	18	8	27	6	17	4	27	15	11	1	0	27
Per cent	3.70	66.67	29.63		22.22	62.96	14.81		55.56	40.74	3.70	0	
Glaze IV													
Number	0	13	16	29	11	15	3	29	20	7	2	0	29
Per cent	0	44.83	55.17		37.93	51.72	10.34		68.97	24.14	6.90	0	
Glazes V and VI													
Number	0	14	7	21	5	14	2	21	19	0	2	0	21
Per cent	0	66.67	33.33		23.81	66.67	9.52		90.48	0	9.52	0	
Total													
Number	2	53	43	98	29	57	12	98	63	29	5	1	98
Per cent	2.04	54.08	43.88		29.59	58.16	12.24		64.29	29.59	5.10	1.02	

Combinations of these three observations are presented in Table IV–6. The 36 possible combinations furnish too fine a grouping for our small series. The commonest combinations in males are crania of pronounced breadth with the sagittal elevation absent and the postcoronoid depression absent or submedium. In females the commonest combinations are medium or pronounced breadth with no sagittal elevation and a submedium postcoronoid depression or none at all.

With respect to period differences, it is evident that sagittal elevations tend to become less pronounced and less frequent in the males from the early to the late periods, and this is even more markedly the case in the female series.

TABLE IV–6. CORRELATION OF OBSERVATIONS ON SAGITTAL REGION

Elevation Absent

	Breadth Submedium Postcoronoid Depression			Breadth Medium Postcoronoid Depression			Breadth Pronounced Postcoronoid Depression			Total
Males	Absent	Submedium	Medium	Absent	Submedium	Medium	Absent	Submedium	Medium	
B.-on-W. and Gl. I										
Number	0	1	0	0	2	0	5	2	1	11
Per cent	0	3.57	0	0	7.14	0	17.86	7.14	3.57	39.29
Glazes II and III										
Number	2	0	0	2	3	2	1	4	1	15
Per cent	5.41	0	0	5.41	8.11	5.41	2.70	10.81	2.70	40.54
Glaze IV										
Number	0	1	0	0	2	1	3	4	0	11
Per cent	0	3.33	0	0	6.67	3.33	10.00	13.33	0	36.67
Glazes V and VI										
Number	0	1	0	4	5	1	4	3	2	20
Per cent	0	2.33	0	9.30	11.63	2.33	9.30	6.98	4.65	46.51
Total										
Number	2	3	0	6	12	4	13	13	4	57
Per cent	1.45	2.17	0	4.35	8.70	2.90	9.42	9.42	2.90	41.30
Females										
B.-on-W. and Gl. I										
Number	0	1	0	3	1	1	0	2	1	9
Per cent	0	4.76	0	14.29	4.76	4.76	0	9.52	4.76	42.86
Glazes II and III										
Number	0	0	0	2	5	2	3	3	0	15
Per cent	0	0	0	7.41	18.52	7.41	11.11	11.11	0	55.56
Glaze IV										
Number	0	0	0	3	4	0	3	8	2	20
Per cent	0	0	0	10.34	13.79	0	10.34	27.59	6.90	68.97
Glazes V and VI										
Number	0	0	0	3	9	0	1	4	2	19
Per cent	0	0	0	14.29	42.86	0	4.76	19.05	9.52	90.48
Total										
Number	0	1	0	11	19	3	7	17	5	63
Per cent	0	1.02	0	11.22	19.39	3.06	7.14	17.35	5.10	64.29

Elevation Submedium

	Breadth Submedium Postcoronoid Depression			Breadth Medium Postcoronoid Depression			Breadth Pronounced Postcoronoid Depression			Total
Males	Absent	Submedium	Medium	Absent	Submedium	Medium	Absent	Submedium	Medium	
B.-on-W. and Gl. I										
Number	0	2	0	4	1	0	1	2	0	10
Per cent	0	7.14	0	14.29	3.57	0	3.57	7.14	0	35.71
Glazes II and III										
Number	2	1	0	3	1	0	2	3	0	12
Per cent	5.41	2.70	0	8.11	2.70	0	5.41	8.11	0	32.43
Glaze IV										
Number	1	1	1	2	3	2	2	1	1	14
Per cent	3.33	3.33	3.33	6.67	10.00	6.67	6.67	3.33	3.33	46.67
Glazes V and VI										
Number	0	3	0	5	4	0	3	0	0	15
Per cent	0	6.98	0	11.63	9.30	0	6.98	0	0	34.88
Total										
Number	3	7	1	14	9	2	8	6	1	51
Per cent	2.17	5.07	0.72	10.14	6.52	1.45	5.80	4.35	0.72	36.96
Females										
B.-on-W. and Gl. I										
Number	0	0	0	1	0	1	2	7	0	11
Per cent	0	0	0	4.76	0	4.76	9.52	33.33	0	52.38
Glazes II and III										
Number	0	0	0	0	7	2	1	1	0	11
Per cent	0	0	0	0	25.93	7.41	3.70	3.70	0	40.74
Glaze IV										
Number	0	0	0	2	1	1	2	1	0	7
Per cent	0	0	0	6.90	3.45	3.45	6.90	3.45	0	24.14
Glazes V and VI										
Number	0	0	0	0	0	0	0	0	0	0
Per cent	0	0	0	0	0	0	0	0	0	0
Total										
Number	0	0	0	3	8	4	5	9	0	29
Per cent	0	0	0	3.06	8.16	4.08	5.10	9.18	0	29.59

Elevation Medium

	Breadth Submedium Postcoronoid Depression			Breadth Medium Postcoronoid Depression			Breadth Pronounced Postcoronoid Depression			Total
Males	Absent	Submedium	Medium	Absent	Submedium	Medium	Absent	Submedium	Medium	
B.-on-W. and Gl. I										
Number	0	1	0	1	0	1	0	0	0	3
Per cent	0	3.57	0	3.57	0	3.57	0	0	0	10.71
Glazes II and III										
Number	0	0	0	0	6	1	0	0	0	7
Per cent	0	0	0	0	16.22	2.70	0	0	0	18.92
Glaze IV										
Number	0	0	0	1	1	0	0	0	0	2
Per cent	0	0	0	3.33	3.33	0	0	0	0	6.67
Glazes V and VI										
Number	0	0	0	2	0	1	0	0	0	3
Per cent	0	0	0	4.65	0	2.33	0	0	0	6.98
Total										
Number	0	1	0	4	7	3	0	0	0	15
Per cent	0	0.72	0	2.90	5.07	2.17	0	0	0	10.86

	Breadth Submedium Postcoronoid Depression			Breadth Medium Postcoronoid Depression			Breadth Pronounced Postcoronoid Depression			Total
Females	Absent	Submedium	Medium	Absent	Submedium	Medium	Absent	Submedium	Medium	
B.-on-W. and Gl. I										
Number	0	0	0	0	0	0	0	0	0	0
Per cent	0	0	0	0	0	0	0	0	0	0
Glazes II and III										
Number	0	1	0	0	0	0	0	0	0	1
Per cent	0	3.70	0	0	0	0	0	0	0	3.70
Glaze IV										
Number	0	0	0	1	1	0	0	0	0	2
Per cent	0	0	0	3.45	3.45	0	0	0	0	6.90
Glazes V and VI										
Number	0	0	0	0	1	1	0	0	0	2
Per cent	0	0	0	0	4.76	4.76	0	0	0	9.52
Total										
Number	0	1	0	1	2	1	0	0	0	5
Per cent	0	1.02	0	1.02	2.04	1.02	0	0	0	5.10

Elevation High

	Absent	Submedium	Medium	Absent	Submedium	Medium	Absent	Submedium	Medium	Total
Males										
B.-on-W. and Gl. I										
Number	1	1	1	0	0	0	0	1	0	4
Per cent	3.57	3.57	3.57	0	0	0	0	3.57	0	14.29
Glazes II and III										
Number	0	0	0	2	1	0	0	0	0	3
Per cent	0	0	0	5.41	2.70	0	0	0	0	8.11
Glaze IV										
Number	0	0	0	0	3	0	0	0	0	3
Per cent	0	0	0	0	10.00	0	0	0	0	10.00
Glazes V and VI										
Number	2	0	0	2	0	0	0	1	0	5
Per cent	4.65	0	0	4.65	0	0	0	2.33	0	11.63
Total										
Number	3	1	1	4	4	0	0	2	0	15
Per cent	2.17	0.72	0.72	2.90	2.90	0	0	1.45	0	10.86
Females										
B.-on-W. and Gl. I										
Number	0	0	0	1	0	0	0	0	0	1
Per cent	0	0	0	4.76	0	0	0	0	0	4.76
Glazes II and III										
Number	0	0	0	0	0	0	0	0	0	0
Per cent	0	0	0	0	0	0	0	0	0	0
Glaze IV										
Number	0	0	0	0	0	0	0	0	0	0
Per cent	0	0	0	0	0	0	0	0	0	0
Glazes V and VI										
Number	0	0	0	0	0	0	0	0	0	0
Per cent	0	0	0	0	0	0	0	0	0	0
Total										
Number	0	0	0	1	0	0	0	0	0	1
Per cent	0	0	0	1.02	0	0	0	0	0	1.02

TEMPORAL REGION

Table IV–7 gives observations on the fullness of the temporal region. All varieties occur in both sexes and in almost the same proportions. Compressed and submedium temporal regions are more common than protuberant temporal regions. Protuberant temporals seem more common in the earliest period than subsequently. This observation is, however, dependent upon deformation.

TABLE IV–7. FULLNESS OF TEMPORAL REGION

	B.-on-W. and Gl. I		Gls. II and III		Glaze IV		Gls. V and VI		Total	
Males	No.	Per cent	No.	Per cent	No.	Per cent	No.	Per cent	No.	Per cent
Compressed	1	10.34	14	36.84	5	16.67	9	22.50	29	21.48
Submedium	6	20.69	6	15.79	7	23.33	7	17.50	26	19.26
Medium	12	41.38	10	26.32	9	30.00	14	35.00	45	33.33
Protuberant.......	8	27.59	8	21.05	8	26.67	8	20.00	32	23.70
Sphenoid Depression	0	0	0	0	1	3.33	2	5.00	3	2.22
Total	27		38		30		40		135	
Females										
Compressed	6	27.27	7	26.92	6	20.69	3	14.29	22	22.45
Submedium	3	13.64	3	11.54	9	31.03	3	14.29	18	18.37
Medium	4	18.18	14	53.85	6	20.69	11	52.38	35	35.71
Protuberant.......	7	31.82	2	7.69	7	24.14	2	9.52	18	18.37
Sphenoid Depression	2	9.09	0	0	1	3.45	2	9.52	5	5.10
Total	22		26		29		21		98	

Supramastoid crests are uncommon in both sexes and less so in the male crania. In the female series supramastoid crests seem to be more frequent in the earlier periods, but this is not true of the males. The subgroups are so small that only continuous trends in a single direction are worthy of notice (Table IV–8).

The usual sex differences are apparent in the size of the mastoid processes (Table IV–9). Again there is an indication of an increase in size of mastoids in the female series from early to late times, whereas the males vary irregularly in the several periods.

TABLE IV–8. OCCURRENCE AND SIZE OF SUPRAMASTOID CRESTS

	B.-on-W. and Gl. I		Gls. II and III		Glaze IV		Gls. V and VI		Total	
Males	No.	Per cent	No.	Per cent	No.	Per cent	No.	Per cent	No.	Per cent
Absent	26	89.66	31	79.49	26	86.67	32	76.19	115	82.14
Submedium	2	6.90	4	10.26	2	6.67	4	9.52	12	8.57
Medium	1	3.45	2	5.13	1	3.33	6	14.29	10	7.14
Pronounced	0	0	2	5.13	1	3.33	0	0	3	2.14
Total	29		39		30		42		140	

	B.-on-W. and Gl. I		Gls. II and III		Glaze IV		Gls. V and VI		Total	
Females	No.	Per cent	No.	Per cent	No.	Per cent	No.	Per cent	No.	Per cent
Absent	18	81.82	23	79.31	28	96.55	22	95.65	91	88.35
Submedium	3	13.64	4	13.79	1	3.45	1	4.35	9	8.74
Medium	1	4.55	2	6.90	0	0	0	0	3	2.91
Pronounced	0	0	0	0	0	0	0	0	0	0
Total	22		29		29		23		103	

TABLE IV–9. SIZE OF MASTOIDS

	B.-on-W. and Gl. I		Gls. II and III		Glaze IV		Gls. V and VI		Total	
Males	No.	Per cent	No.	Per cent	No.	Per cent	No.	Per cent	No.	Per cent
Small	12	41.38	12	30.77	5	17.24	17	38.64	46	32.62
Medium	12	41.38	14	35.90	15	51.72	18	40.91	59	41.84
Large	4	13.79	12	30.77	7	24.14	7	15.91	30	21.27
Very large	1	3.45	1	2.56	2	6.90	2	4.55	6	4.25
Total	29		39		29		44		141	
Females										
Small	13	76.47	24	77.42	21	75.00	12	52.17	70	70.71
Medium	3	17.65	3	9.68	5	17.86	8	34.78	19	19.19
Large	1	5.88	4	12.90	2	7.14	3	13.04	10	10.10
Total	17		31		28		23		99	

OCCIPITAL REGION

Table IV–10 shows the summary of observations of the degree of development of the occipital torus and of the curve of the occiput. A large or moderately developed occipital torus is of course commoner in males than in females. It is evident, however, that flattened and deformed occiputs are commoner among the females than among the males.

Table IV–11 gives the combinations of curve of the occiput with degree of development of the occipital torus. The occiput is flat and deformed in such an overwhelming percentage of cases that little can be deduced from the correlation, but it is fairly clear that the occipital torus is more likely to be absent when the occiput is moderately convex than when it is flattened. A flat occiput throws the skull off balance and provides less purchase for the nuchal muscles and ligaments which must find attachment on its surface. It is quite possible that the torus may develop as a secondary adaptation in flattened crania, in order to provide the necessary purchase for the muscles and ligaments which support the overbalanced head.

Table IV–11 gives also the correlation of occipital torus and slope of the occiput by archaeological periods. Small tori or lack of development of the torus seem to be associated with greater frequency of convex occiputs in the earliest periods in both sexes. It does not seem possible to go beyond this point in interpretation, in view of the small size of the subgroups.

TABLE IV–10. Observations on Occipital Region

Males	Torus					Curve				
	Absent	Small	Medium	Large	Total	Flat and Deformed	Steep	Medium Convex	Bulging	Total
Black-on-white and Gl. I										
Number..........	12	9	3	4.29	28	17	4	7	0	28
Per cent..........	42.86	32.14	10.71	14.29		60.71	14.29	25.00	0	
Glazes II and III										
Number..........	18	11	2	5	36	22	8	6	0	36
Per cent..........	50.00	30.56	5.56	13.89		61.11	22.22	16.67	0	
Glaze IV										
Number..........	9	10	6	5	30	21	8	1	0	30
Per cent..........	30.00	33.33	20.00	16.67		70.00	26.67	3.33	0	
Glazes V and VI										
Number..........	16	14	10	4	44	30	7	6	1	44
Per cent..........	36.36	31.82	22.73	9.09		68.18	15.91	13.64	2.27	
Total										
Number..........	55	44	21	18	138	90	27	20	1	138
Per cent..........	39.86	31.88	15.21	13.04		65.22	19.56	14.49	0.72	
Females										
Black-on-white and Gl. I										
Number..........	12	8	0	1	21	17	3	1	0	21
Per cent..........	57.14	38.10	0	4.76		80.95	14.29	4.76	0	
Glazes II and III										
Number..........	5	11	8	2	26	20	6	0	0	26
Per cent..........	19.23	42.31	30.77	7.69		76.92	23.08	0	0	
Glaze IV										
Number..........	11	14	1	3	29	23	5	1	0	29
Per cent..........	37.93	48.28	3.45	10.34		79.31	17.24	3.45	0	
Glazes V and VI										
Number..........	10	9	2	0	21	17	2	2	0	21
Per cent..........	47.62	42.86	9.52	0		80.95	9.52	9.52	0	
Total										
Number..........	38	42	11	6	97	77	16	4	0	97
Per cent..........	39.18	43.30	11.34	6.19		79.38	16.49	4.12	0	

TABLE IV–11. Correlation of Observations on Occipital Region

Torus Absent

Males	Curve				
	Flat and Deformed	Steep	Medium Convex	Bulging	Total
Black-on-white and Glaze I					
Number..............	6	3	3	0	12
Per cent	21.42	10.71	10.71	0	42.86
Glazes II and III					
Number..............	9	6	3	0	18
Per cent	25.00	16.67	8.33	0	50.00
Glaze IV					
Number	4	5	0	0	9
Per cent	13.33	16.67	0	0	30.00
Glazes V and VI					
Number..............	10	2	3	1	16
Per cent	22.73	4.55	6.82	2.27	36.36
Total					
Number..............	29	16	9	1	55
Per cent	21.01	11.59	6.52	0.72	39.86

	Curve				
Females	Flat and Deformed	Steep	Medium Convex	Bulging	Total
Black-on-white and Glaze I					
Number	8	3	1	0	12
Per cent	38.09	14.29	4.76	0	57.14
Glazes II and III					
Number	5	0	0	0	5
Per cent	19.23	0	0	0	19.23
Glaze IV					
Number	10	0	1	0	11
Per cent	34.49	0	3.45	0	37.94
Glazes V and VI					
Number	8	1	1	0	10
Per cent	38.09	4.76	4.76	0	47.62
Total					
Number	31	4	3	0	38
Per cent	31.96	4.12	3.09	0	39.18

Torus Small

Males	Flat and Deformed	Steep	Medium Convex	Bulging	Total
Black-on-white and Glaze I					
Number	5	0	4	0	9
Per cent	17.85	0	14.28	0	32.14
Glazes II and III					
Number	8	1	2	0	11
Per cent	22.22	2.78	5.56	0	30.56
Glaze IV					
Number	9	1	0	0	10
Per cent	30.00	3.33	0	0	33.33
Glazes V and VI					
Number	10	2	2	0	14
Per cent	22.73	4.55	4.55	0	31.83
Total					
Number	32	4	8	0	44
Per cent	23.19	2.90	5.80	0	31.88

Females	Flat and Deformed	Steep	Medium Convex	Bulging	Total
Black-on-white and Glaze I					
Number	8	0	0	0	8
Per cent	38.10	0	0	0	38.10
Glazes II and III					
Number	7	4	0	0	11
Per cent	26.92	15.38	0	0	42.30
Glaze IV					
Number	9	5	0	0	14
Per cent	31.04	17.24	0	0	48.28
Glazes V and VI					
Number	7	1	1	0	9
Per cent	33.34	4.76	4.76	0	42.86
Total					
Number	31	10	1	0	42
Per cent	31.96	10.31	1.03	0	43.30

Torus Medium

Males	Curve				
	Flat and Deformed	Steep	Medium Convex	Bulging	Total
Black-on-white and Glaze I					
Number	3	0	0	0	3
Per cent	10.71	0	0	0	10.71
Glazes II and III					
Number	2	0	0	0	2
Per cent	5.56	0	0	0	5.56
Glaze IV					
Number	4	1	1	0	6
Per cent	13.33	3.33	3.33	0	20.00
Glazes V and VI					
Number	7	3	0	0	10
Per cent	15.91	6.82	0	0	22.73
Total					
Number	16	4	1	0	21
Per cent	11.59	2.90	0.72	0	15.22
Females					
Black-on-white and Glaze I					
Number	0	0	0	0	0
Per cent	0	0	0	0	0
Glazes II and III					
Number	6	2	0	0	8
Per cent	23.08	7.69	0	0	30.77
Glaze IV					
Number	1	0	0	0	1
Per cent	3.45	0	0	0	3.45
Glazes V and VI					
Number	2	0	0	0	2
Per cent	9.52	0	0	0	9.52
Total					
Number	9	2	0	0	11
Per cent	9.28	2.06	0	0	11.34

Torus Large

Males	Flat and Deformed	Steep	Medium Convex	Bulging	Total
Black-on-white and Glaze I					
Number	3	1	0	0	4
Per cent	10.72	3.57	0	0	14.29
Glazes II and III					
Number	3	1	1	0	5
Per cent	8.34	2.78	2.78	0	13.89
Glaze IV					
Number	4	1	0	0	5
Per cent	13.33	3.33	0	0	16.67
Glazes V and VI					
Number	3	0	1	0	4
Per cent	6.82	0	2.27	0	9.09
Total					
Number	13	3	2	0	18
Per cent	9.42	2.17	1.45	0	13.04

Females	Curve				Total
	Flat and Deformed	Steep	Medium Convex	Bulging	
Black-on-white and Glaze I					
Number.................	1	0	0	0	1
Per cent	4.76	0	0	0	4.76
Glazes II and III					
Number.................	2	0	0	0	2
Per cent	7.69	0	0	0	7.69
Glaze IV					
Number.................	3	0	0	0	3
Per cent	10.35	0	0	0	10.35
Glazes V and VI					
Number.................	0	0	0	0	0
Per cent	0	0	0	0	0
Total					
Number.................	6	0	0	0	6
Per cent	6.19	0	0	0	6.19

SUTURES, WORMIAN BONES, AND FORM OF PTERION

Table IV–12 deals with the complexity of sutural serration. The usual sex difference is observable — namely, that the males show sutures of medium complexity and intricate sutures oftener than do the females. But simple sutures predominate in both series. An interesting fact is noted in the distribution by Glaze periods. In the males the sutures become more complex from the first to the last periods and in the females precisely the opposite is the case. Both of these diametrically opposite tendencies manifest themselves so consistently that it hardly seems possible that they are due to chance alone.

Table IV–13 shows the observations of external obliteration of the sutures in combinations of the sagittal, coronal, and lambdoid. "Beginning" implies that sutural obliteration is observed at a few points. "Obliterated" means that more of the suture is occluded than is open. In approximately one-third of both males and females all of the sutures are open, which implies that they were probably less than twenty-five years old. In the males the next group in order of frequency is that in which obliteration is beginning in all three sutures. This class constitutes 26.42 per cent of the whole. In 10 per cent of cases obliteration has apparently begun in the sagittal suture first; in 7 per cent of cases in the coronal, in 10 per cent of cases in the sagittal and lambdoid, and in 7.9 per cent of cases in the coronal and sagittal. In only two cases, or 1.42 per cent, is lambdoid precedence exhibited. It seems probable that obliteration began oftenest in sagittal and that the coronal tended to close next. But these orders of occlusion are not clearly marked in the males. In the females, on the other hand, occlusion begins in the coronal in 25 per cent of cases while the other two sutures are still open, whereas it begins in the sagittal in only one case. In 12 per cent of cases obliteration is manifested in coronal and sagittal before the lambdoid shows it. It seems probable then that in the Pecos males the most frequent order of sutural obliteration was sagittal, coronal, lambdoid, although there may have been no great difference in the times of obliteration of all three sutures. In the females there was certain coronal precedence. Such coronal precedence on the part of the females and sagittal precedence on the part of the males has been observed also in Canary Islands crania and in Indian crania from Madisonville, Ohio.[1]

Tables IV–14, 15 record the occurrence of Wormian bones and their location. Of the male crania 82 per cent exhibit such sutural bones, whereas only 77 per cent of female crania show this feature. In the male series fewer crania of the last Glaze subgroup show Wormian bones, whereas the highest occurrence of this feature in the female series is during Glaze II and Glaze III. These intercalated bones are found oftenest in the lambdoid suture.

The so-called Inca bone is recorded in only two cases in spite of the prevalence of occipital deformation in the series. The supposition that the transverse division of the parietal is connected with occipital flattening seems quite improbable in view of the rarity of the former and the virtual universality of the latter in the Pecos crania.

In both sexes H-forms of pterion predominate, but in the females narrow H-form and K-form are commoner than in the males. In both sexes K-formed pteria are more frequent in the last periods of the archaeological groupings (Glaze IV and Glazes V and VI). In the females there is a concurrent diminution of proportions of medium breadth H-pteria with the increase of K-forms and of narrow H-forms (Table IV–16).

TABLE IV–12. SERRATION OF SUTURES

	Simple		Medium		Complex		Total
Males	No.	Per cent	No.	Per cent	No.	Per cent	
Black-on-white and Glaze I	23	88.46	3	11.54	0	0	26
Glazes II and III	30	76.92	5	12.82	4	10.26	39
Glaze IV	22	75.86	7	24.14	0	0	29
Glazes V and VI	31	72.09	11	25.58	1	2.33	43
Total..................	106	77.37	26	18.98	5	3.65	137
Females							
Black-on-white and Glaze I	17	80.95	4	19.05	0	0	21
Glazes II and III	23	85.19	4	14.81	0	0	27
Glaze IV	25	92.59	2	7.41	0	0	27
Glazes V and VI	19	90.48	2	9.52	0	0	21
Total..................	84	87.50	12	12.50	0	0	96

[1] Hooton, 1925, p. 137; 1920, p. 101.

TABLE IV–13. OCCLUSION OF SUTURES

Males	B.-on-W. and Gl. I		Gls. II and III		Glaze IV		Gls. V and VI		Total	
	No.	Per cent	No.	Per cent	No.	Per cent	No.	Per cent	No.	Per cent
Coronal open Sagittal open Lambdoid open......	12	41.38	13	33.33	11	37.93	11	25.58	47	33.57
Coronal open Sagittal beginning Lambdoid open......	1	3.45	2	5.13	0	0	4	9.30	7	5.00
Coronal open Sagittal beginning Lambdoid beginning ..	4	13.79	2	5.13	0	0	7	16.28	13	9.29
Coronal open Sagittal obliterated Lambdoid open......	0	0	0	0	0	0	0	0	0	0
Coronal beginning Sagittal open Lambdoid open......	2	6.90	2	5.13	2	6.90	4	9.30	10	7.14
Coronal beginning Sagittal beginning Lambdoid open......	1	3.45	4	10.26	1	3.45	3	6.98	9	6.43
Coronal beginning Sagittal obliterated Lambdoid open......	0	0	0	0	0	0	1	2.33	1	0.71
Coronal beginning Sagittal obliterated Lambdoid beginning..	2	6.90	3	7.69	1	3.45	1	2.33	7	5.00
Coronal beginning Sagittal obliterated Lambdoid obliterated	0	0	0	0	0	0	1	2.33	1	0.71
Coronal obliterated Sagittal beginning Lambdoid open......	0	0	0	0	0	0	0	0	0	0
Coronal obliterated Sagittal obliterated Lambdoid beginning..	2	6.90	0	0	0	0	0	0	2	1.43
Coronal obliterated Sagittal obliterated Lambdoid obliterated	1	3.45	0	0	1	3.45	1	2.33	3	2.14
Coronal beginning Sagittal beginning Lambdoid beginning..	2	6.90	12	30.77	13	44.83	10	23.26	37	26.42
Coronal open Sagittal open Lambdoid beginning..	1	3.45	0	0	0	0	0	0	1	0.71
Coronal obliterated Sagittal beginning Lambdoid beginning..	0	0	0	0	0	0	0	0	0	0
Coronal beginning Sagittal open Lambdoid beginning..	1	3.45	0	0	0	0	0	0	1	0.71
Coronal beginning Sagittal beginning Lambdoid obliterated	0	0	1	2.56	0	0	0	0	1	0.71
Total	29		39		29		43		140	

	B.-on-W. and Gl. I		Gls. II and III		Glaze IV		Gls. V and VI		Total	
	No.	Per cent	No.	Per cent	No.	Per cent	No.	Per cent	No.	Per cent
Females										
Coronal open Sagittal open Lambdoid open......	8	36.36	10	35.71	6	21.43	9	40.91	33	33.00
Coronal open Sagittal beginning Lambdoid open......	0	0	1	3.57	0	0	0	0	1	1.00
Coronal open Sagittal beginning Lambdoid beginning..	0	0	0	0	1	3.57	0	0	1	1.00
Coronal beginning Sagittal open Lambdoid open......	6	27.27	8	28.57	8	28.57	3	13.64	25	25.00
Coronal beginning Sagittal beginning Lambdoid open......	3	13.64	4	14.29	3	10.71	2	9.09	12	12.00
Coronal beginning Sagittal obliterated Lambdoid beginning..	1	4.55	1	3.57	0	0	0	0	2	2.00
Coronal obliterated Sagittal beginning Lambdoid open......	0	0	0	0	1	3.57	0	0	1	1.00
Coronal obliterated Sagittal obliterated Lambdoid open......	0	0	1	3.57	0	0	0	0	1	1.00
Coronal obliterated Sagittal obliterated Lambdoid beginning..	0	0	0	0	1	3.57	1	4.55	2	2.00
Coronal obliterated Sagittal obliterated Lambdoid obliterated	0	0	0	0	3	10.71	1	4.55	4	4.00
Coronal beginning Sagittal beginning Lambdoid beginning..	4	18.18	2	7.14	1	3.57	4	18.18	11	11.00
Coronal open Sagittal open Lambdoid beginning..	0	0	0	0	0	0	1	4.55	1	1.00
Coronal obliterated Sagittal beginning Lambdoid beginning..	0	0	1	3.57	0	0	0	0	1	1.00
Coronal beginning Sagittal open Lambdoid beginning..	0	0	0	0	4	14.29	1	4.55	5	5.00
Total	22		28		28		22		100	

TABLE IV–14. Occurrence of Wormian Bones

	Males						Females					
	Absent		Present		Total		Absent		Present		Total	
	No.	Per cent	No.	Per cent			No.	Per cent	No.	Per cent		
Black-on-white and Glaze I..	4	16.00	21	84.00	25		5	26.32	14	73.68	19	
Glazes II and III	5	15.15	28	84.85	33		6	16.22	31	83.78	37	
Glaze IV	3	9.68	28	90.32	31		8	26.67	22	73.33	30	
Glazes V and VI	13	25.49	38	74.51	51		6	26.09	17	73.91	23	
Total.......	25	17.86	115	82.14	140		25	22.94	84	77.06	109	

TABLE IV–15. Location of Wormian Bones

	B.-on-W. and Gl. I		Gls. II and III		Glaze IV		Gls. VI and VI		Total	
	No.	Per cent	No.	Per cent	No.	Per cent	No.	Per cent	No.	Per cent
Males										
Lambdoid	11	52.38	16	57.14	17	60.71	23	60.53	67	58.26
Squamous	2	9.52	2	7.14	1	3.57	4	10.53	9	7.83
Temporo-occipital .	5	23.81	7	25.00	7	25.00	6	15.79	25	21.74
Epipteric	3	14.29	3	10.71	3	10.71	1	2.63	10	8.70
Bregmatic	0	0	0	0	0	0	3	7.89	3	2.61
Inca Bone	0	0	0	0	0	0	1	2.63	1	0.87
Total	21		28		28		38		115	
Females										
Lambdoid	10	71.43	20	64.52	13	59.09	12	70.59	55	65.48
Squamous	0	0	2	6.45	2	9.09	1	5.88	5	5.95
Temporo-occipital	2	14.29	5	16.13	3	13.64	1	5.88	11	13.10
Epipteric	2	14.29	3	9.68	1	4.55	3	17.65	9	10.71
Bregmatic	0	0	1	3.23	1	4.55	0	0	2	2.38
Inca Bone	0	0	0	0	1	4.55	0	0	1	1.19
Coronal	0	0	0	0	1	4.55	0	0	1	1.19
Total	14		31		22		17		84	

TABLE IV–16. Form of Pterion

	Large H		Medium H		Narrow H		K		Retourné		Total
	No.	Per cent	No.	Per cent	No.	Per cent	No.	Per cent	No.	Per cent	
Males											
B.-on-W. and Gl. I ...	9	36.00	8	32.00	5	20.00	2	8.00	1	4.00	25
Glazes II and III	12	35.29	16	47.06	1	2.94	5	14.71	0	0	34
Glaze IV	7	25.00	11	39.29	4	14.29	6	21.43	0	0	28
Glazes V and VI......	13	30.23	16	37.21	5	11.63	8	18.60	1	2.33	43
Total	41	31.54	51	39.23	15	11.53	21	16.15	2	1.53	130
Females											
B.-on-W. and Gl. I ...	5	31.25	6	37.50	2	12.50	3	18.75	0	0	16
Glazes II and III	9	32.14	10	35.71	6	21.43	2	7.14	1	3.57	28
Glaze IV	9	32.14	6	21.43	3	10.71	10	35.71	0	0	28
Glazes V and VI......	6	31.58	3	15.79	4	21.05	6	31.58	0	0	19
Total	29	31.87	25	27.47	15	16.48	21	23.08	1	1.10	91

PARIETAL FORAMINA

Parietal foramina are more frequently lacking in the female crania than in those of males. The combinations of number and size are so numerous as to render the subgroup distributions insignificant. But it may be deduced from the study of Table IV–17 that absence of parietal foramina and reduction in number to one only are phenomena increasingly prevalent in successive periods in both sexes.

TABLE IV–17. PARIETAL FORAMINA

	B.-on-W. and Gl. I		Gls. II and III		Glaze IV		Gls. V and VI		Total	
Males	No.	Per cent	No.	Per cent	No.	Per cent	No.	Per cent	No.	Per cent
None..................	3	10.34	3	7.69	9	30.00	6	13.64	21	14.72
One small.............	4	13.79	10	25.64	6	20.00	13	29.55	33	23.24
One medium	5	17.24	4	10.26	4	13.33	6	13.64	19	1.37
Two small	9	31.03	11	28.21	8	26.67	8	18.18	36	25.53
Two medium	4	13.79	4	10.26	0	0	3	6.82	11	7.74
Several small	0	0	3	7.69	0	0	1	2.27	4	2.81
One large	1	3.45	0	0	1	3.33	0	0	2	1.42
One small, one medium .	0	0	0	0	0	0	3	6.82	3	2.11
One small, two medium .	0	0	0	0	0	0	1	2.27	1	0.71
One small, one large	0	0	1	2.56	0	0	2	4.55	3	2.11
Two small, one medium .	0	0	1	2.56	0	0	0	0	1	0.71
Two small, one large	1	3.45	0	0	0	0	0	0	1	0.71
Doubtful	2	6.90	2	5.13	1	3.33	1	2.27	6	4.22
Total	29		39		29		44		141	
Females										
None..................	3	13.64	9	25.00	7	24.14	2	8.33	21	18.92
One small.............	2	9.09	9	25.00	9	31.03	4	17.39	24	21.62
One medium	2	9.09	1	2.78	1	3.45	3	13.04	7	6.31
Two small	6	27.27	6	16.67	7	24.14	5	21.74	24	21.62
Two medium	1	4.55	2	5.56	0	0	2	8.33	5	4.50
Several small	1	4.55	1	2.78	0	0	2	8.33	4	3.60
One large	0	0	0	0	0	0	2	8.33	2	1.80
One small, one medium .	1	4.55	1	2.78	1	3.45	0	0	3	2.70
One small, two medium .	0	0	0	0	0	0	0	0	0	0
One small, one large	0	0	0	0	1	3.45	0	0	1	0.90
Two small, one medium .	0	0	0	0	2	6.90	0	0	2	1.80
Two small, one large	0	0	1	2.78	0	0	0	0	1	0.90
Doubtful	6	27.27	6	16.67	1	3.45	4	17.39	17	15.30
Total	22		36		29		24		111	

CRANIAL BASE

SHAPE OF FORAMEN MAGNUM

Assigning shapes to the foramen magnum is a proceeding of dubious utility. Hexagonal and oval forms predominate in each sex (Table IV–18).

TABLE IV–18. SHAPE OF FORAMEN MAGNUM

	B.-on-W. and Gl. I		Gls. II and III		Glaze IV		Gls. V and VI		Total	
	No.	Per cent	No.	Per cent	No.	Per cent	No.	Per cent	No.	Per cent
Males										
Diamond shaped	4	19.05	1	4.00	2	8.70	3	10.34	10	10.20
Half diamond	3	14.29	3	8.00	1	4.35	4	13.79	11	11.22
Oval shaped	5	23.81	6	24.00	9	39.19	9	31.04	29	29.59
Half oval	0	0	1	4.00	0	0	0	0	1	1.02
Round	1	4.76	0	0	2	8.70	0	0	3	3.06
Irregular	0	0	3	12.00	2	8.70	3	10.34	8	8.16
Hexagonal	8	38.10	10	40.00	6	26.09	9	31.04	33	33.67
Pentagonal	0	0	1	4.00	1	4.35	1	3.45	3	3.06
Total	21		25		23		29		98	
Females										
Diamond shaped	0	0	2	9.09	1	5.00	2	10.53	5	6.67
Half diamond	2	14.29	3	13.64	4	20.00	1	5.26	10	13.33
Oval shaped	6	42.86	1	4.55	6	30.00	8	42.11	21	28.00
Half oval	0	0	0	0	0	0	1	5.26	1	1.33
Round	1	7.14	1	4.55	0	0	0	0	2	2.67
Irregular	1	7.14	8	36.36	1	5.00	0	0	10	13.33
Hexagonal	4	28.57	7	31.82	7	35.00	6	31.58	24	32.00
Pentagonal	0	0	0	0	1	5.00	1	5.26	2	2.67
Total	14		22		20		19		75	

GLENOID FOSSA

Tables IV–19, 20, 21, deal with the glenoid fossa. It is prevailingly of medium depth in both sexes but oftener deep in males than in females. There is a marked tendency for glenoid fossae in both sexes to become shallower in successive periods. In the first two periods in the male series glenoid fossae are as often deep as of medium depth. Shallow and medium fossae then increase at the expense of those classified as deep. A somewhat similar change takes place in the female series.

Postglenoid processes are found in about 25 per cent of males and in about 10 per cent of females. These also become much more rare in both sexes in the last two periods. Postglenoid processes usually are associated with medium or pronounced depth of the glenoid fossae, rarely with shallow fossae.

Arthritic changes in the glenoid fossae occur in 3.5 per cent of males and 9 per cent of females. These pathological conditions are distributed sporadically in the several archaeological subgroups.

TABLE IV–19. Depth of Glenoid Fossa

	Shallow		Medium		Deep		Total
Males	No.	Per cent	No.	Per cent	No.	Per cent	
Black-on-white and Glaze I ..	3	10.34	13	44.83	13	44.83	29
Glazes II and III	5	13.51	16	43.24	16	43.24	37
Glaze IV	3	10.34	18	62.07	8	27.59	29
Glazes V and VI	10	23.81	20	47.62	12	28.57	42
Total...................	21	15.32	67	48.90	49	35.77	137
Females							
Black-on-white and Glaze I ..	4	20.00	9	45.00	7	35.00	20
Glazes II and III	8	25.81	15	48.39	8	25.81	31
Glaze IV	11	39.29	12	42.86	5	17.86	28
Glazes V and VI	7	30.43	14	60.87	2	8.70	23
Total...................	30	29.41	50	49.02	22	21.57	102

TABLE IV–20. Postglenoid Process

	Absent		Submedium		Medium		Pronounced		Total
Males	No.	Per cent	No.	Per cent	No.	Per cent	No.	Per cent	
Black-on-white and Glaze I...	20	68.97	6	20.69	1	3.45	2	6.90	29
Glazes II and III	29	78.38	5	13.51	2	5.41	1	2.70	37
Glaze IV	24	82.76	4	13.79	1	3.45	0	0	29
Glazes V and VI	30	71.43	9	21.43	3	7.14	0	0	42
Total	103	75.32	24	17.53	7	5.11	3	2.19	137
Females									
Black-on-white and Glaze I...	17	85.00	3	15.00	0	0	0	0	20
Glazes II and III	26	83.87	5	16.13	0	0	0	0	31
Glaze IV	27	96.43	1	3.57	0	0	0	0	28
Glazes V and VI	22	95.65	0	0	1	4.35	0	0	23
Total	92	90.20	9	8.82	1	0.98	0	0	102

TABLE IV–21. Arthritis at Glenoid Fossa

	Males		Females		Total Crania	
	No.	Per cent	No.	Per cent	Males	Females
Black-on-white and Glaze I	0	0	3	13.64	29	22
Glazes II and III..................	3	7.69	0	0	39	36
Glaze IV	0	0	3	10.34	30	29
Glazes V and VI	2	4.45	4	16.67	44	24
Total	5	3.52	10	9.01	142	111

STYLOID PROCESSES

More male crania have large styloid processes than is the case in the female series. No period trends are observable (Table IV–22).

TABLE IV–22. SIZE OF STYLOIDS

	Absent		Small		Medium		Large		Very Large		Total
Males	No.	Per cent	No.	Per cent	No.	Per cent	No.	Per cent	No.	Per cent	
Black-on-white and Glaze I	0	0	9	33.33	8	29.63	10	37.01	0	0	27
Glazes II and III	0	0	15	41.67	13	36.11	7	19.44	1	2.78	36
Glaze IV	0	0	10	33.33	9	30.00	10	33.33	1	3.33	30
Glazes V and VI..........	1	2.44	12	29.27	13	31.71	13	31.71	2	4.88	41
Total	1	0.75	46	34.33	43	32.09	40	29.85	4	2.99	134
Females											
Black-on-white and Glaze I	0	0	13	61.90	4	19.05	2	9.52	2	9.52	21
Glazes II and III	1	3.57	15	53.57	8	28.57	4	14.29	0	0	28
Glaze IV	2	7.14	9	32.14	11	39.29	5	17.86	1	3.57	28
Glazes V and VI..........	2	8.70	11	47.83	7	30.43	2	8.70	1	4.35	23
Total	5	5.00	48	48.00	30	30.00	13	13.00	4	4.00	100

DEPRESSION OF PETROUS PARTS OF TEMPORAL BONES

When the skull is held with the base upward the amount of depression of the petrous parts of the temporal bone below the level of the basilar process of the occipital is a good measure of the development of the basal portion of the brain. Small lacerate foramina and absence of petrous depressions are inferior characters. Depression of the petrous parts is prevailingly small in both sexes of the Pecos crania. The males are somewhat superior to the females in this feature. In the later periods of the pueblo petrous depression becomes less both in males and in females (Table IV–23).

TABLE IV–23. DEPRESSION OF PETROUS PARTS OF TEMPORAL BONES

	Absent		Small		Medium		Total
Males	No.	Per cent	No.	Per cent	No.	Per cent	
Black-on-white and Glaze I ..	1	4.76	10	47.62	10	47.62	21
Glazes II and III	8	33.33	11	45.83	5	20.83	24
Glaze IV	7	26.92	13	50.00	6	23.08	26
Glazes V and VI	6	18.18	18	54.55	9	27.27	33
Total..................	22	21.15	52	50.00	30	28.85	104
Females							
Black-on-white and Glaze I ..	4	28.57	5	35.71	5	35.71	14
Glazes II and III	7	31.82	10	45.45	5	22.73	22
Glaze IV	3	14.29	13	61.90	5	23.81	21
Glazes V and VI	6	31.58	12	63.16	1	5.26	19
Total..................	20	26.32	40	52.63	16	21.05	76

MIDDLE LACERATE FORAMINA

Middle lacerate foramina are prevailingly small in both sexes. In both sexes they become smaller from period to period. In the females they are oftener of submedium size than in the males (Table IV–24).

TABLE IV–24. MIDDLE LACERATE FORAMINA

	Small		Medium		Large		Total
Males	No.	Per cent	No.	Per cent	No.	Per cent	
Black-on-white and Glaze I ..	12	54.55	10	45.45	0	0	22
Glazes II and III	16	69.57	6	26.09	1	4.35	23
Glaze IV	15	62.50	9	37.50	0	0	24
Glazes V and VI	22	68.75	10	31.25	0	0	32
Total..................	65	64.36	35	34.65	1	0.99	101
Females							
Black-on-white and Glaze I ..	9	69.23	4	30.77	0	0	13
Glazes II and III	15	71.43	6	28.57	0	0	21
Glaze IV	14	66.67	7	33.33	0	0	21
Glazes V and VI	16	88.89	2	11.11	0	0	18
Total..................	54	73.97	19	26.03	0	0	73

POSTERIOR LACERATE FORAMINA

Posterior lacerate foramina show much variability in size. In about 37.27 per cent of males and 37.33 per cent of females they are small on both sides of the skull; in 45.10 per cent of males and 49.33 per cent of females both are of medium size. In 18.62 per cent of males and in 13.33 per cent of females the paired lacerate foramina are markedly unequal in size. In males the size of the posterior lacerate foramina seems to increase somewhat from the early to the late periods. Such a tendency is absent in the female series (Table IV–25).

TABLE IV–25. POSTERIOR LACERATE FORAMINA

	B.-on-W. and Gl. I		Gls. II and III		Glaze IV		Gls. V and VI		Total	
Males	No.	Per cent	No.	Per cent	No.	Per cent	No.	Per cent	No.	Per cent
Both small	9	45.00	9	37.50	9	25.00	10	30.30	37	36.27
Both medium	8	40.00	12	50.00	10	40.00	16	48.48	46	45.10
Both large	0	0	0	0	1	4.00	3	9.09	4	3.92
One small, one medium	1	5.00	0	0	2	8.00	2	6.06	5	4.90
One small, one large	1	5.00	1	4.17	2	8.00	1	3.03	5	4.90
One medium, one large	0	0	2	8.33	0	0	1	3.03	3	2.94
One large, one very large.....	1	5.00	0	0	1	4.00	0	0	2	1.96
Total	20		24		25		33		102	
Females										
Both small	5	35.71	8	36.36	6	28.57	9	50.00	28	37.33
Both medium	7	50.00	9	40.91	15	71.43	6	33.33	37	49.33
Both large	1	7.14	2	9.09	0	0	0	0	3	4.00
One small, one medium	1	7.14	1	4.55	0	0	3	16.67	5	6.67
One small, one large	0	0	1	4.55	0	0	0	0	1	1.33
One medium, one large	0	0	1	4.55	0	0	0	0	1	1.33
One large, one very large	0	0	0	0	0	0	0	0	0	0
Total	14		22		21		18		75	

RETROMASTOID FORAMINA

Variations in number and size of retromastoid foramina are very numerous. Usually there are two or more on each side. No sex or period differences seem discernible except that in the female series retromastoid foramina are more frequently absent in the earliest period and larger and more numerous in the later periods (Tables IV–26, 27).

TABLE IV–26. RETROMASTOID FORAMINA

	B.-on-W. and Gl. I		Gls. II and III		Glaze IV		Gls. V and VI		Total	
Males	No.	Per cent	No.	Per cent	No.	Per cent	No.	Per cent	No.	Per cent
None	1	3.45	1	2.56	4	13.33	1	2.27	7	4.93
One small	1	3.45	0	0	4	13.33	0	0	5	3.52
One medium	1	3.45	0	0	5	16.67	1	2.27	7	4.93
Two or more small	5	17.24	7	17.95	5	16.67	8	18.18	25	17.61
Two or more medium	3	10.34	5	12.82	2	6.67	7	15.91	17	11.97
Two or more large	0	0	1	2.56	0	0	2	4.55	3	2.11
One small, one or more medium	1	3.45	6	15.38	1	3.33	9	20.46	17	11.97
One small, one or more large	2	6.90	0	0	1	3.33	0	0	3	2.11
One medium, one or more large	2	6.90	1	2.56	0	0	0	0	3	2.11
One medium, two or more small	5	17.24	0	0	2	6.67	4	9.09	11	7.75
Two or more small, two or more medium	1	3.45	2	5.13	1	3.33	5	11.36	9	6.34
Two or more small, one or more large	0	0	1	2.56	0	0	3	6.82	4	2.82
Two or more medium, one or more large	1	3.45	2	5.13	1	3.33	1	2.27	5	3.52
Doubtful	6	20.69	13	33.33	4	13.33	3	6.82	26	18.31
Total	29		39		30		44		142	
Females										
None	3	13.64	0	0	0	0	1	4.17	4	3.60
One small	0	0	1	2.78	2	6.90	0	0	3	2.70
One medium	0	0	1	2.78	1	3.45	2	8.33	4	3.60
Two or more small	1	4.55	6	16.67	7	24.14	7	29.17	21	18.92
Two or more medium	2	9.09	2	5.56	2	6.90	1	4.17	7	6.31
Two or more large	0	0	2	5.56	1	3.45	0	0	3	2.70
One small, one or more medium	1	4.55	4	11.11	4	13.79	4	16.67	13	11.71
One small, one or more large	0	0	0	0	3	10.34	0	0	3	2.70
One medium, one or more large	2	9.09	0	0	1	3.45	0	0	3	2.70
One medium, two or more small	1	4.55	1	2.78	1	3.45	1	4.17	4	3.60
Two or more small, two or more medium	1	4.55	3	8.33	0	0	1	4.71	5	4.50
Two or more small, one or more large	1	4.55	1	2.78	1	3.45	1	4.17	4	3.60
Two or more medium, one or more large	0	0	1	2.78	0	0	0	0	1	0.90
Doubtful	10	45.45	14	38.89	6	20.69	6	25.00	36	32.43
Total	22		36		29		24		111	

TABLE IV–27. SUMMARY OF NUMBER OF RETROMASTOID FORAMINA

	None		One		Two or more		Total
	No.	Per cent	No.	Per cent	No.	Per cent	No.
Males	7	6.03	12	10.34	97	83.62	116
Females	4	5.33	7	9.33	64	85.33	75

Postcondyloid Foramina

The variability in number and size of postcondyloid foramina is recorded in Table IV–28. Not much can be inferred from such an erratic feature.

TABLE IV–28. Postcondyloid Foramina

	B.-on-W. and Gl. I		Gls. II and III		Glaze IV		Gls. V and VI		Total	
	No.	Per cent	No.	Per cent	No.	Per cent	No.	Per cent	No.	Per cent
Males										
Two small	3	10.34	7	17.95	1	3.57	1	2.27	12	8.51
Two medium	3	10.34	12	30.77	8	28.57	14	31.11	37	26.24
Two large	4	13.79	1	2.56	4	15.38	8	17.78	17	12.06
None	0	0	0	0	0	0	1	2.22	1	0.71
One small, one medium	3	10.34	0	0	3	10.71	1	2.22	7	4.96
One small, one large	1	3.45	2	5.13	1	3.57	2	4.44	6	4.26
One medium, one large.......	5	17.24	2	5.13	1	3.57	2	4.44	10	7.09
Doubtful	8	27.59	15	38.46	7	25.00	14	31.11	44	31.21
One small, one absent	1	3.45	0	0	1	3.57	0	0	2	1.42
One medium, one absent	1	3.45	0	0	1	3.57	2	4.44	4	2.84
One medium, several small ...	0	0	0	0	1	3.57	0	0	1	0.71
Total	29		39		28		45		141	
Females										
Two small	3	13.64	5	13.89	4	13.79	2	8.33	14	12.61
Two medium	6	27.27	7	19.44	7	24.14	7	29.17	27	24.32
Two large	3	13.64	0	0	3	10.34	2	8.33	8	7.21
None	1	4.55	1	2.78	2	6.90	0	0	4	3.60
One small, one medium	0	0	3	8.33	0	0	1	4.17	4	3.60
One small, one large	2	9.09	0	0	2	6.90	1	4.17	5	4.50
One medium, one large.......	0	0	2	5.56	0	0	3	12.50	5	4.50
Doubtful	6	27.27	14	38.89	9	31.03	5	20.83	34	30.63
One small, one absent........	0	0	3	8.33	0	0	0	0	3	2.70
One medium, one absent	0	0	0	0	1	3.45	1	4.17	2	1.80
One large, one absent	1	4.55	1	2.78	1	3.45	2	8.33	5	4.50
Total	22		36		29		24		111	

Pterygo–Spinous Foramina

Pterygo-spinous foramina are fairly common in the Pecos series. They occur oftener in the males than in the females. In both sexes they are most frequent in the earliest periods and become progressively rarer throughout the succeeding periods (Table IV–29).

TABLE IV–29. Pterygo–Spinous Foramina

Males	B.-on-W. and Gl. I		Gls. II and III		Glaze IV		Gls. V and VI		Total	
	No.	Per cent	No.	Per cent	No.	Per cent	No.	Per cent	No.	Per cent
Indicated	6	26.09	2	6.90	4	13.79	3	9.09	15	13.16
Indicated on one side, absent on other	1	4.35	5	17.24	3	10.34	1	3.03	10	8.77
Complete on one side	2	8.70	1	3.45	1	3.45	1	3.03	5	4.39
Complete on both sides	0	0	0	0	0	0	1	3.03	1	0.88
Absent on both sides	14	60.87	20	68.97	21	72.41	26	78.79	81	71.05
Complete on one side, indicated on other............	0	0	1	3.45	0	0	1	3.03	2	1.75
Total	23		29		29		33		114	
Females										
Indicated	2	12.50	3	10.71	3	11.11	0	0	8	8.79
Indicated on one side, absent on other.................	4	25.00	3	10.71	0	0	2	10.00	9	9.89
Complete on one side........	1	6.25	0	0	2	7.41	0	0	3	3.30
Complete on both sides	0	0	0	0	0	0	0	0	0	0
Complete on one side, indicated on other............	0	0	0	0	0	0	1	5.00	1	1.10
Absent on both sides	9	56.25	22	78.57	22	81.48	17	85.00	70	76.92
Total	16		28		27		20		91	

Dehiscences in Floor of Auditory Meatus

Gaps in the tympanic plate which forms the hinder wall of the auditory meatus are of frequent occurrence in Indian crania. In the Pecos skulls they occur in 16 per cent of male crania and in 24 per cent of female crania. This sex difference is usual. In both sexes there are indications of a decreasing frequency of this anomaly in the last two chronological groups (Table IV–30).

TABLE IV–30. Dehiscences in Floor of Auditory Meatus

	Present		Doubtful		Absent		Total
Males	No.	Per cent	No.	Per cent	No.	Per cent	
Black-on-white and Glaze I.....	6	20.00	3	10.00	21	70.00	30
Glazes II and III	5	12.82	3	7.69	31	79.49	39
Glaze IV	5	17.24	1	3.45	23	79.31	29
Glazes V and VI	7	15.91	5	11.36	32	72.73	44
Total	23	16.20	12	8.45	107	75.35	142
Females							
Black-on-white and Glaze I.....	5	22.73	1	4.55	16	72.73	22
Glazes II and III	11	30.56	6	16.67	19	52.78	36
Glaze IV	6	20.69	1	3.45	22	75.86	29
Glazes V and VI	5	20.83	1	4.17	18	75.00	24
Total	27	24.32	9	8.11	75	67.57	111

MALARS AND ZYGOMATIC ARCHES

The malars are, of course, larger in the males than in the females. In both sexes the proportion of crania with large malars increases from the early to the late periods of the pueblo. Marginal processes on the malars are commoner in males than in females and occur more frequently in the males of the later periods (Tables IV–31, 32).

Zygomatic arches show a similar size superiority in the male series. The period distribution of zygomata according to size is extremely erratic. In both sexes an early predominance of medium development seems to give way to a more variable condition in the later periods (Table IV–33).

TABLE IV–31. SIZE OF MALARS

Males	Small No.	Small Per cent	Medium No.	Medium Per cent	Large No.	Large Per cent	Very Large No.	Very Large Per cent	Total
Black-on-white and Glaze I...	0	0	15	57.69	10	38.46	1	3.85	26
Glazes II and III	0	0	11	32.35	21	61.76	2	5.88	34
Glaze IV	0	0	7	24.14	19	65.52	3	10.34	29
Glazes V and VI	1	2.33	9	20.93	28	65.12	5	11.63	43
Total	1	0.75	42	31.82	78	59.09	11	8.33	132
Females									
Black-on-white and Glaze I....	1	5.26	15	78.95	3	15.79	0	0	19
Glazes II and III	1	3.57	21	75.00	6	21.43	0	0	28
Glaze IV	3	11.54	14	53.85	9	34.62	0	0	26
Glazes V and VI	3	14.29	11	52.38	7	33.33	0	0	21
Total	8	8.51	61	64.89	25	26.60	0	0	94

TABLE IV–32. PRESENCE OF MARGINAL PROCESS ON MALARS

	Males No.	Males Per cent	Males Total	Females No.	Females Per cent	Females Total
Black-on-white and Glaze I	1	3.45	29	2	9.09	22
Glazes II and III	5	12.82	39	1	2.78	36
Glaze IV	1	3.33	30	0	0	26
Glazes V and VI	6	13.64	44	2	8.33	24
Total	13	9.16	142	5	4.63	108

TABLE IV–33. SIZE OF ZYGOMATA

Males	Small No.	Small Per cent	Medium No.	Medium Per cent	Large No.	Large Per cent	Very Large No.	Very Large Per cent	Total
Black-on-white and Glaze I...	0	0	11	45.83	10	41.67	3	12.50	24
Glazes II and III	0	0	11	34.38	19	59.38	2	6.25	32
Glaze IV	2	7.69	7	26.92	11	42.31	6	23.08	26
Glazes V and VI	1	2.56	10	25.64	25	64.10	3	7.69	39
Total	3	2.48	39	32.23	65	53.72	14	11.57	121
Females									
Black-on-white and Glaze I...	2	11.76	10	58.82	5	29.41	0	0	17
Glazes II and III	2	7.41	21	77.78	4	14.81	0	0	27
Glaze IV	4	15.38	16	61.54	6	23.08	0	0	26
Glazes V and VI	4	19.05	10	47.62	7	33.33	0	0	21
Total	12	13.19	57	62.64	22	24.18	0	0	91

ORBITS

Orbits are oblong in the majority of cases and oftener square in females than in males. The inclination of the transverse axis of the orbit is greater in males than in females. In the females square orbits seem to increase in proportions in the last two archaeological groups. No such tendency was observed in the males (Tables IV–34, 35).

Infraorbital sutures are more common in the Pecos females than in the males. No period differences are observable. Suborbital fossae are oftener medium and deep than shallow and there are no marked sex differences. They seem to run a little deeper in the late periods in both males and females (Tables IV–36, 37).

TABLE IV–34. SHAPE AND INCLINATION OF ORBITS

	Shape						Inclination				
Males B.-on-W. and Gl. I	Square	Oblong	Rhom-boid	Oval	Round	Total	Absent	Sub-medium	Medium	Pro-nounced	Total
Number	8	17	1	0	0	26	4	4	13	5	26
Per cent	30.77	63.38	3.85	0	0		15.38	15.38	50.00	19.23	
Glazes II and III											
Number	12	20	1	1	0	34	11	12	10	1	34
Per cent	35.29	58.82	2.94	2.94	0		32.35	35.29	29.41	2.94	
Glaze IV											
Number	7	19	1	0	0	27	12	6	7	2	27
Per cent	25.93	70.37	3.70	0	0		44.44	22.22	25.93	7.41	
Glazes V and VI											
Number	14	26	1	1	1	43	8	10	14	11	43
Per cent	32.56	60.47	2.33	2.33	2.33		18.60	23.26	32.56	25.58	
Total											
Number	41	82	4	2	1	130	35	32	44	19	130
Per cent	31.54	63.08	3.08	1.54	0.77		26.92	24.62	33.85	14.62	
Females B.-on-W. and Gl. I											
Number	7	12	0	0	0	19	10	4	5	0	19
Per cent	36.84	63.16	0	0	0		52.63	21.05	26.32	0	
Glazes II and III											
Number	10	18	0	2	0	30	16	7	5	2	30
Per cent	33.33	60.00	0	6.67	0		53.33	23.33	16.67	6.67	
Glaze IV											
Number	14	12	0	2	0	28	14	8	4	2	28
Per cent	50.00	42.86	0	7.14	0		50.00	28.57	14.29	7.14	
Glazes V and VI											
Number	8	10	0	1	0	19	8	6	3	2	19
Per cent	42.11	52.63	0	5.26	0		42.11	31.58	15.79	10.53	
Total											
Number	39	52	0	5	0	96	48	25	17	6	96
Per cent	40.63	54.17	0	5.21	0		50.00	26.04	17.71	6.25	

TABLE IV–35. Correlation of Shape and Inclination of Orbits

Inclination Absent

Males		Square	Oblong	Rhomboid	Oval	Round	Total
B.-on-W. and Gl. I	Number	2	2	0	0	0	4
	Per cent	7.69	7.69	0	0	0	15.38
Glazes II and III	Number	5	6	0	0	0	11
	Per cent	14.71	17.65	0	0	0	32.35
Glaze IV	Number	3	9	0	0	0	12
	Per cent	11.11	33.33	0	0	0	44.44
Glazes V and VI	Number	3	4	0	1	0	8
	Per cent	6.98	9.30	0	2.33	0	18.60
Total	Number	13	21	0	1	0	35
	Per cent	26.92	16.15	0	0.77	0	26.92
Females							
B.-on-W. and Gl. I	Number	5	5	0	0	0	10
	Per cent	26.32	26.32	0	0	0	52.63
Glazes II and III	Number	7	8	0	1	0	16
	Per cent	23.33	26.67	0	3.33	0	53.33
Glaze IV	Number	6	7	0	1	0	14
	Per cent	21.43	25.00	0	3.57	0	50.00
Glazes V and VI	Number	4	4	0	0	0	8
	Per cent	21.05	21.05	0	0	0	42.11
Total	Number	22	24	0	2	0	48
	Per cent	22.92	25.00	0	2.08	0	50.00

Inclination Submedium

Males		Square	Oblong	Rhomboid	Oval	Round	Total
B.-on-W. and Gl. I	Number	2	2	0	0	0	4
	Per cent	7.69	7.69	0	0	0	15.38
Glazes II and III	Number	5	7	0	0	0	12
	Per cent	14.71	20.59	0	0	0	35.29
Glaze IV	Number	3	3	0	0	0	6
	Per cent	11.11	11.11	0	0	0	22.22
Glazes V and VI	Number	4	6	0	0	0	10
	Per cent	9.30	13.95	0	0	0	23.26
Total	Number	14	18	0	0	0	32
	Per cent	10.77	13.85	0	0	0	24.62
Females							
B.-on-W. and Gl. I	Number	1	3	0	0	0	4
	Per cent	5.26	15.79	0	0	0	21.05
Glazes II and III	Number	2	5	0	0	0	7
	Per cent	6.67	16.67	0	0	0	23.33
Glaze IV	Number	6	2	0	0	0	8
	Per cent	21.43	7.14	0	0	0	28.57
Glazes V and VI	Number	3	3	0	0	0	6
	Per cent	15.79	15.79	0	0	0	31.58
Total	Number	12	13	0	0	0	25
	Per cent	12.50	13.54	0	0	0	26.04

Inclination Medium

Males		Square	Oblong	Rhomboid	Oval	Round	Total
B.-on-W. and Gl. I	Number	3	10	0	0	0	13
	Per cent	11.54	38.46	0	0	0	50.00
Glazes II and III	Number	2	6	1	1	0	10
	Per cent	5.88	17.65	2.94	2.94	0	29.41
Glaze IV	Number	0	6	1	0	0	7
	Per cent	0	22.22	3.70	0	0	25.93
Glazes V and VI	Number	4	10	0	0	0	14
	Per cent	9.30	23.26	0	0	0	32.56
Total	Number	9	32	2	1	0	44
	Per cent	6.92	24.62	1.54	0.77	0	33.85

Females		Square	Oblong	Rhomboid	Oval	Round	Total
B.-on-W. and Gl. I	Number	1	4	0	0	0	5
	Per cent	5.26	21.05	0	0	0	26.32
Glazes II and III	Number	1	4	0	0	0	5
	Per cent	3.33	13.33	0	0	0	16.67
Glaze IV	Number	0	3	0	1	0	4
	Per cent	0	10.71	0	3.57	0	14.29
Glazes V and VI	Number	0	3	0	0	0	3
	Per cent	0	15.79	0	0	0	15.79
Total	Number	2	14	0	1	0	17
	Per cent	2.08	14.58	0	1.04	0	17.71

Inclination Pronounced

Males		Square	Oblong	Rhomboid	Oval	Round	Total
B.-on-W. and Gl. I	Number	1	3	1	0	0	5
	Per cent	3.85	11.54	3.85	0	0	19.23
Glazes II and III	Number	0	1	0	0	0	1
	Per cent	0	2.94	0	0	0	2.94
Glaze IV	Number	1	1	0	0	0	2
	Per cent	3.70	3.70	0	0	0	7.41
Glazes V and VI	Number	3	6	1	0	1	11
	Per cent	6.98	13.95	2.33	0	2.33	25.58
Total	Number	5	11	2	0	1	19
	Per cent	3.85	8.46	1.54	0	0.77	14.62

Females		Square	Oblong	Rhomboid	Oval	Round	Total
B.-on-W. and Gl. I	Number	0	0	0	0	0	0
	Per cent	0	0	0	0	0	0
Glazes II and III	Number	0	1	0	1	0	2
	Per cent	0	3.33	0	3.33	0	6.67
Glaze IV	Number	2	0	0	0	0	2
	Per cent	7.14	0	0	0	0	7.14
Glazes V and VI	Number	1	0	0	1	0	2
	Per cent	5.26	0	0	5.26	0	10.53
Total	Number	3	1	0	2	0	6
	Per cent	3.12	1.04	0	2.08	0	6.25

TABLE IV–36. INFRAORBITAL SUTURE

	Absent		Complete on One Side		Complete on Both Sides		Total
Males	No.	Per cent	No.	Per cent	No.	Per cent	
Black-on-white and Glaze I	15	68.18	4	18.18	3	13.64	22
Glazes II and III	19	61.29	6	19.35	6	19.35	31
Glaze IV	16	66.67	3	12.50	5	20.83	24
Glazes V and VI	27	65.85	5	12.20	9	21.95	41
Total......................	77	65.25	18	15.25	23	19.49	118
Females							
Black-on-white and Glaze I	9	52.94	3	17.65	5	29.41	17
Glazes II and III	13	40.63	7	21.88	12	37.50	32
Glaze IV	10	41.67	4	16.67	10	41.67	24
Glazes V and VI	14	66.67	1	4.76	6	28.57	21
Total......................	46	48.94	15	15.96	33	35.11	94

TABLE IV–37. SUBORBITAL FOSSAE

	Absent		Shallow		Medium		Deep		Total
Males	No.	Per cent	No.	Per cent	No.	Per cent	No.	Per cent	
Black-on-white and Glaze I ..	1	3.70	8	27.63	12	44.44	6	22.22	27
Glazes II and III	0	0	9	26.47	13	38.24	12	35.29	34
Glaze IV	1	3.57	10	35.71	9	32.14	8	28.57	28
Glazes V and VI	1	2.50	7	17.50	16	40.00	16	40.00	40
Total	3	2.30	34	26.36	50	38.76	42	32.56	129
Females									
Black-on-white and Glaze I...	0	0	4	22.22	9	50.00	5	27.78	18
Glazes II and III	1	3.33	8	26.67	11	36.67	10	33.33	30
Glaze IV	0	0	8	30.77	8	30.77	10	38.46	26
Glazes V and VI	0	0	3	14.29	8	38.10	10	47.62	21
Total	1	1.05	23	24.21	36	37.89	35	36.84	95

NOSE

In the Pecos crania as in other Indian crania nasion depressions are usually absent or slight. In female crania such depressions are usually lacking. In the male series the absence of any nasion depression becomes more frequent in the later periods. The height of the nasal bridge is prevailingly submedium in both sexes. About two thirds of the males and more than 90 per cent of the females have low noses. The breadth of the nasal bridge is medium in the majority of cases but oftener narrow than wide. The females display larger proportions of wide nasal bridges than do the males. The profile of the nasal bones is usually concavo-convex. Females show a greater proportion of concave nasal bridges than do the males (Tables IV–38, 39).

The commonest combination of height, breadth, and profile of nasal bridge is height submedium, breadth medium, slope concavo-convex, in both sexes. No period differences are discernible (Table IV–40).

The observed breadth of the nasal aperture (Table IV–41) indicates the usual sex difference in that the females show a greater prevalence of broad apertures. In the males the crania of the first period seem to show a possibly significant excess of narrow apertures, but no such fact is observable in the female series.

The lower borders of the nasal aperture are prevailingly ill-defined in both sexes and very little difference between the sexes is discernible. In both male and female crania there is a marked tendency for the proportion of ill-defined nasal apertures to increase from the early to the late periods (Table IV–42).

The nasal spine is, of course, better developed in males than in females. In the males the successive periods indicate a tendency for a medium development of the nasal spine to become more and more prevalent. In the females small spines increase in proportion from the early to the late periods (Table IV–43).

Subnasal grooves are not common in either sex, but less infrequent in females. In the males they are found oftenest in the last periods of the pueblo (Table IV–44).

TABLE IV–38. NASION DEPRESSION

	B.-on-W. and Gl. I Males	Females	Gls. II and III Males	Females	Glaze IV Males	Females	Gls. V and VI Males	Females	Total Males	Females
Absent										
Number	17	19	21	32	17	27	30	20	85	98
Per cent	62.96	95.00	60.00	100.00	56.67	93.10	71.43	90.91	63.43	95.15
Slight										
Number	9	1	13	0	11	2	11	2	44	5
Per cent	33.33	5.00	37.14	0	36.67	6.90	26.19	9.09	32.83	4.85
Medium										
Number	1	0	1	0	1	0	0	0	3	0
Per cent	3.70	0	2.86	0	3.33	0	0	0	2.24	0
Pronounced										
Number	0	0	0	0	1	0	1	0	2	0
Per cent	0	0	0	0	3.33	0	2.38	0	1.49	0
Total	27	20	35	32	30	29	42	22	134	103

TABLE IV–39. HEIGHT, BREADTH, AND PROFILE (SLOPE) OF NASAL BRIDGE

	Height				Breadth				Slope					
	Submedium	Medium	Pronounced	Total	Submedium	Medium	Pronounced	Total	Straight	Concave	Convex	Concavo-convex	?	Total
Males														
B.-on-W. and Gl. I														
Number	12	11	2	25	10	15	0	25	4	0	3	13	5	25
Per cent	48.00	44.00	8.00		40.00	60.00	0		16.00	0	12.00	52.00	20.00	
Glazes II and III														
Number	25	6	2	33	13	15	5	33	4	5	2	17	5	33
Per cent	75.76	18.18	6.06		39.39	45.45	15.15		12.12	15.15	6.06	51.52	15.15	
Glaze IV														
Number	16	9	1	26	10	13	3	26	7	3	2	12	2	26
Per cent	61.54	34.62	3.85		38.46	50.00	11.54		26.92	11.54	7.69	46.15	7.69	
Glazes V and VI														
Number	28	14	0	42	9	30	3	42	5	5	4	22	6	42
Per cent	66.67	33.33	0		21.43	71.43	7.14		11.90	11.90	9.52	52.38	14.29	
Total														
Number	81	40	5	126	42	73	11	126	20	13	11	64	18	126
Per cent	64.29	31.75	3.97		33.33	57.94	8.73		15.87	10.32	8.73	50.79	14.29	
Females														
B.-on-W. and Gl. I														
Number	18	1	1	20	3	13	4	20	4	4	2	6	4	20
Per cent	90.00	5.00	5.00		15.00	65.00	20.00		20.00	20.00	10.00	30.00	20.00	
Glazes II and III														
Number	29	1	0	30	8	19	3	30	2	7	1	12	8	30
Per cent	96.67	3.33	0		26.67	63.33	10.00		6.67	23.33	3.33	40.00	26.67	
Glaze IV														
Number	26	3	0	29	5	23	1	29	7	2	1	11	8	29
Per cent	89.66	10.34	0		17.24	79.31	3.45		24.14	6.90	3.45	37.93	27.59	
Glazes V and VI														
Number	21	1	0	22	6	9	7	22	1	3	4	12	2	22
Per cent	95.45	4.55	0		27.27	40.91	31.82		4.55	13.64	18.18	54.55	9.09	
Total														
Number	94	6	1	101	22	64	15	101	14	16	8	41	22	101
Per cent	93.07	5.94	0.99		21.78	63.37	14.85		13.86	15.84	7.92	40.59	21.78	

TABLE IV–40. CORRELATION OF HEIGHT, BREADTH, AND SLOPE OF NASAL BRIDGE

Height Submedium

	Breadth Submedium Slope					Breadth Medium Slope					Breadth Pronounced Slope					Total
Males B.-on-W. & Gl. I	St.	Conc.	Conv.	C–C.	?	St.	Conc.	Conv.	C–C.	?	St.	Conc.	Conv.	C–C.	?	
Number ...	0	0	0	5	0	0	0	0	4	3	0	0	0	0	0	12
Per cent ...	0	0	0	20.00	0	0	0	0	16.00	12.00	0	0	0	0	0	
Gls. II & III																
Number ...	2	2	0	6	0	1	1	0	4	4	0	2	0	2	1	25
Per cent ...	6.06	6.06	0	18.18	0	3.03	3.03	0	12.12	12.12	0	6.06	0	6.06	3.03	
Gl. IV																
Number ...	1	1	2	1	2	2	1	0	4	0	0	0	0	2	0	16
Per cent ...	3.85	3.85	7.69	3.85	7.69	7.69	3.85	0	15.38	0	0	0	0	7.69	0	
Gls. V & VI																
Number ...	1	0	0	2	0	1	3	2	11	5	0	2	0	1	0	28
Per cent ...	2.38	0	0	4.76	0	2.38	7.14	4.76	26.19	11.90	0	4.76	0	2.38	0	
Total																
Number ...	4	3	2	14	2	4	5	2	23	12	0	4	0	5	1	81
Per cent ...	3.18	2.38	1.59	11.11	1.59	3.18	3.97	1.59	18.25	9.52	0	3.18	0	3.97	0.79	64.29
Females B.-on-W. & Gl. I																
Number ...	0	0	1	1	0	4	1	0	4	3	0	3	0	1	0	18
Per cent ...	0	0	5.00	5.00	0	20.00	5.00	0	20.00	15.00	0	15.00	0	5.00	0	
Gls. II & III																
Number ...	0	3	0	2	3	2	3	1	8	4	0	1	0	1	1	29
Per cent ...	0	10.00	0	6.67	10.00	6.67	10.00	3.33	26.67	13.33	0	3.33	0	3.33	3.33	
Gl. IV																
Number ...	1	0	0	1	1	4	2	1	8	7	0	0	0	1	0	26
Per cent ...	3.45	0	0	3.45	3.45	13.79	6.90	3.45	27.59	24.14	0	0	0	3.45	0	
Gls. V & VI																
Number ...	0	2	1	2	0	1	1	0	6	1	0	0	2	4	1	21
Per cent ...	0	9.09	4.55	9.09	0	4.55	4.55	0	27.27	4.55	0	0	9.09	18.18	4.55	
Total																
Number ...	1	5	2	6	4	11	7	2	26	15	0	4	2	7	2	94
Per cent ...	0.99	4.95	1.98	5.94	3.96	10.89	6.93	1.98	25.74	14.85	0	3.96	1.98	6.93	1.98	93.07

Height Medium

	St.	Conc.	Conv.	C–C.	?	St.	Conc.	Conv.	C–C.	?	St.	Conc.	Conv.	C–C.	?	Total
Males B.-on-W. & Gl. I																
Number ...	0	0	0	2	1	3	0	2	2	1	0	0	0	0	0	11
Per cent ...	0	0	0	8	4	12	0	8	8	4	0	0	0	0	0	
Gls. II & III																
Number ...	0	0	0	2	0	1	0	0	3	0	0	0	0	0	0	6
Per cent ...	0	0	0	6.06	0	3.03	0	0	9.09	0	0	0	0	0	0	
Gl. IV																
Number ...	0	0	0	2	0	3	0	0	3	0	0	1	0	0	0	9
Per cent ...	0	0	0	7.69	0	11.54	0	0	11.54	0	0	3.85	0	0	0	
Gls. V & VI																
Number ...	2	0	2	2	0	1	0	0	6	1	0	0	0	0	0	14
Per cent ...	4.76	0	4.76	4.76	0	2.38	0	0	14.29	2.38	0	0	0	0	0	
Total																
Number ...	2	0	2	8	1	8	0	2	14	2	0	1	0	0	0	40
Per cent ...	1.59	0	1.59	6.35	0.79	6.35	0	1.59	11.11	1.59	0	0.79	0	0	0	31.75

Females	Breadth Submedium Slope					Breadth Medium Slope					Breadth Pronounced Slope					Total
B.-on-W. & Gl. I	St.	Conc.	Conv.	C–C.	?	St.	Conc.	Conv.	C–C.	?	St.	Conc.	Conv.	C–C.	?	
Number	0	0	0	0	0	0	0	0	1	0	0	0	0	0	0	1
Per cent	0	0	0	0	0	0	0	0	5	0	0	0	0	0	0	
Gls. II & III																
Number	0	0	0	0	0	0	0	0	1	0	0	0	0	0	0	1
Per cent	0	0	0	0	0	0	0	0	3.33	0	0	0	0	0	0	
Gl. IV																
Number	2	0	0	0	0	0	0	0	1	0	0	0	0	0	0	3
Per cent	6.90	0	0	0	0	0	0	0	3.45	0	0	0	0	0	0	
Gls. V & VI																
Number	0	0	1	0	0	0	0	0	0	0	0	0	0	0	0	1
Per cent	0	0	4.55	0	0	0	0	0	0	0	0	0	0	0	0	
Total																
Number	2	0	1	0	0	0	0	0	3	0	0	0	0	0	0	6
Per cent	1.98	0	0.99	0	0	0	0	0	2.97	0	0	0	0	0	0	5.94

Height Pronounced

Males																Total
B.-on-W. & Gl. I																
Number	1	0	1	0	0	0	0	0	0	0	0	0	0	0	0	2
Per cent	4	0	4	0	0	0	0	0	0	0	0	0	0	0	0	
Gls. II & III																
Number	0	0	1	0	0	0	0	1	0	0	0	0	0	0	0	2
Per cent	0	0	3.03	0	0	0	0	3.03	0	0	0	0	0	0	0	
Gl. IV																
Number	1	0	0	0	0	0	0	0	0	0	0	0	0	0	0	1
Per cent	3.85	0	0	0	0	0	0	0	0	0	0	0	0	0	0	
Gls. V & VI																
Number	0	0	0	0	0	0	0	0	0	0	0	0	0	0	0	0
Per cent	0	0	0	0	0	0	0	0	0	0	0	0	0	0	0	
Total																
Number	2	0	2	0	0	0	0	1	0	0	0	0	0	0	0	5
Per cent	1.59	0	1.59	0	0	0	0	0.79	0	0	0	0	0	0	0	3.97
Females																
B.-on-W. & Gl. I																
Number	0	0	1	0	0	0	0	0	0	0	0	0	0	0	0	1
Per cent	0	0	5	0	0	0	0	0	0	0	0	0	0	0	0	
Gls. II & III																
Number	0	0	0	0	0	0	0	0	0	0	0	0	0	0		0
Per cent	0	0	0	0	0	0	0	0	0	0	0	0	0	0		
Gl. IV																
Number	0	0	0	0	0	0	0	0	0	0	0	0	0	0		0
Per cent	0	0	0	0	0	0	0	0	0	0	0	0	0	0		
Gls. V & VI																
Number	0	0	0	0	0	0	0	0	0	0	0	0	0	0		0
Per cent	0	0	0	0	0	0	0	0	0	0	0	0	0	0		
Total																
Number	0	0	1	0	0	0	0	0	0	0	0	0	0	0		1
Per cent	0	0	0.99	0	0	0	0	0	0	0	0	0	0	0		0.99

TABLE IV–41. BREADTH OF NASAL APERTURE

	Narrow		Medium		Broad		Total
	No.	Per cent	No.	Per cent	No.	Per cent	
Males							
Black-on-white and Glaze I ..	5	18.52	14	51.85	8	29.63	27
Glazes II and III	3	8.82	22	64.71	9	26.47	34
Glaze IV	3	10.00	19	63.33	8	26.67	30
Glazes V and VI	1	2.44	29	70.73	11	26.83	41
Total..................	12	9.09	84	63.64	36	27.27	132
Females							
Black-on-white and Glaze I ..	1	4.76	12	57.14	8	38.10	21
Glazes II and III	3	10.00	18	60.00	9	30.00	30
Glaze IV	1	3.45	16	55.17	12	41.38	29
Glazes V and VI	1	4.55	13	59.09	8	36.36	22
Total..................	6	5.88	59	57.84	37	36.27	102

TABLE IV–42. LOWER BORDERS OF NASAL APERTURE

	Sharp		Medium		Indistinct		Absent		Total
	No.	Per cent	No.	Per cent	No.	Per cent	No.	Per cent	
Males									
Black-on-white and Glaze I...	5	17.24	13	44.83	10	34.48	1	3.45	29
Glazes II and III	1	2.94	9	26.47	24	70.59	0	0	34
Glaze IV	1	3.33	7	23.33	22	73.33	0	0	30
Glazes V and VI	7	17.07	6	14.63	27	65.85	1	2.44	41
Total	14	10.45	35	26.12	83	61.94	2	1.49	134
Females									
Black-on-white and Glaze I...	2	9.52	11	52.38	8	38.10	0	0	21
Glazes II and III	1	3.13	9	28.13	22	68.75	0	0	32
Glaze IV	5	17.86	5	17.86	16	57.14	2	7.14	28
Glazes V and VI	2	9.09	7	31.82	12	54.55	1	4.55	22
Total	10	9.71	32	31.07	58	56.31	3	2.91	103

TABLE IV–43. NASAL SPINE

	Pronounced		Medium		Submedium		Total
	No.	Per cent	No.	Per cent	No.	Per cent	
Males							
Black-on-white and Glaze I ..	5	17.86	8	28.57	15	53.57	28
Glazes II and III	3	8.82	17	50.00	14	41.18	34
Glaze IV	3	10.71	13	46.43	12	42.86	28
Glazes V and VI	3	7.32	21	51.22	17	41.46	41
Total..................	14	10.69	59	45.04	58	44.27	131
Females							
Black-on-white and Glaze I ..	1	5.56	8	44.44	9	50.00	18
Glazes II and III	3	9.68	12	38.71	16	51.61	31
Glaze IV	2	7.14	6	1.43	20	71.43	28
Glazes V and VI	2	9.09	3	13.64	17	77.27	22
Total	8	8.08	29	29.29	62	62.63	99

TABLE IV–44. Subnasal Grooves

	Absent		Doubtful		Indication		Submedium		Medium		Total
Males	No.	Per cent	No.	Per cent	No.	Per cent	No.	Per cent	No.	Per cent	
Black-on-white and Glaze I	25	86.21	2	6.90	0	0	2	6.90	0	0	29
Glazes II and III	30	76.92	5	12.82	2	5.13	1	2.56	1	2.56	39
Glaze IV	28	93.33	1	3.33	0	0	0	0	1	3.33	30
Glazes V and VI.........	31	70.45	3	6.82	2	4.55	7	15.91	1	2.27	44
Total	114	80.28	11	7.74	4	2.81	10	7.04	3	2.10	142
Females											
Black-on-white and Glaze I	20	90.91	1	4.55	0	0	1	4.55	0	0	22
Glazes II and III	33	97.06	0	0	1	2.94	0	0	0	0	34
Glaze IV	24	82.76	2	6.90	0	0	3	10.34	0	0	29
Glazes V and VI.........	21	87.50	3	12.50	0	0	0	0	0	0	24
Total	98	89.91	6	5.50	1	0.91	4	3.67	0	0	109

TEETH [1]

More of the male crania show pronounced wear of the teeth and fewer show teeth but slightly worn than is the case with the female crania (Table IV–45). This may be an effect of a high mortality among young adult females due to childbearing. In both males and females there are clear evidences of an increase in the number of crania with pronouncedly worn teeth from the early periods of the pueblo to the latest periods. Possibly one may infer that the average duration of life became somewhat longer in the course of the Pecos occupation.

Table IV–46 clearly shows that a tendency for suppression of the third molars, more strongly manifested in males than in females, became more and more marked throughout the successive archaeological periods represented in our material.

In Table IV–47 teeth are graded according to their quality. A little less than half of the crania of both sexes appear to have good teeth and of the remainder, 25 per cent are poor in the males and about 33 per cent in the females. Teeth appear to get poorer in the males throughout the successive periods, but in the females this tendency is not noticeable. The second table on the quality of dentition (Table IV–48) deals specifically with caries, alveolar abscesses, pyorrhea, and so forth. This table includes more crania than the preceding and does not substantiate the impression that the teeth of females are poorer than those of males. The females do indeed show a slightly higher percentage of caries, but fewer alveolar abscesses. Pyorrhea is clearly manifested in 5 male crania and in 3 female crania.[2] The teeth of the males become worse in the succeeding periods but no consistent tendency is observable in the female series. The teeth of Glaze IV females seem especially bad, but this may be due merely to chance.

The number of cusps on the molar teeth could be observed in a comparatively few cases only. Only 16 per cent of male and 9.5 per cent of females show the 4–4–4 formula of the upper molars. Cusp reduction seems to have been more marked in

---

[1] Much more detailed observations upon dentition will be found in Appendix I.

[2] Dr. Rihan (Appendix I) distinguishes many more cases of pyorrhea than I have found.

females than in males. In the lower molars the 5–5–5 formula appears in 21.3 per cent of males and 13.2 per cent of females (Tables IV–49, 50). One recalls, however, that a complete suppression of the third molars is commoner in males than in females.

Shovel-shaped incisors prevail in the crania where observations of this feature are possible. They are perhaps a little more frequent in females than in males. No period tendency is discernible (Table IV–51).

Crowded incisors, impacted third molars, and other irregularities of eruption are not infrequently found in both sexes (Tables IV–52, 53).

One's impression is that the Pecos people had very poor teeth for primitive people and that the quality of the teeth seemed to deteriorate slightly but steadily throughout the archaeological periods studied. Caries were common in the teeth of adults and are sometimes found in the milk dentitions. Probably the inferior quality of these Indians' teeth is to some extent referable to the diet of maize and vegetables which must have been the rule throughout the period of occupation. Some game and fish may have been added to this diet occasionally and buffalo meat may have been an exceptional luxury. It is fairly certain from a study of the teeth that the Pecos Indians were in most cases undernourished.

TABLE IV–45. WEAR OF TEETH

	Slight		Medium		Pronounced		Very Pronounced		Total
Males	No.	Per cent	No.	Per cent	No.	Per cent	No.	Per cent	
Black-on-white and Glaze I...	5	17.86	10	35.71	9	32.14	4	14.29	28
Glazes II and III	7	17.95	12	30.77	16	41.03	4	10.26	39
Glaze IV	2	5.13	15	38.46	9	30.00	4	13.33	30
Glazes V and VI	6	14.29	10	23.81	19	45.24	7	16.67	42
Total..................	20	14.39	47	33.81	53	41.01	19	13.67	139
Females									
Black-on-white and Glaze I...	4	18.18	10	45.45	6	27.27	2	9.09	22
Glazes II and III	8	23.53	16	47.06	6	17.65	4	11.76	34
Glaze IV	6	20.69	9	31.03	9	31.03	5	17.24	29
Glazes V and VI	8	38.10	2	9.52	8	38.10	3	14.29	21
Total..................	26	24.53	37	34.91	29	27.36	14	13.21	106

TABLE IV–46. CONDITION OF DENTITION

	Complete		Third Molars Imperfectly Erupted		Third Molars Absent		Total
Males	No.	Per cent	No.	Per cent	No.	Per cent	
Black-on-white and Glaze I	27	93.10	0	0	2	6.90	29
Glazes II and III	39	100.00	0	0	0	0	39
Glaze IV	27	90.00	0	0	3	10.00	30
Glazes V and VI	35	79.55	2	4.55	7	15.91	44
Total..................	128	90.14	2	1.41	12	8.45	142
Females							
Black-on-white and Glaze I	21	95.45	1	4.55	0	0	22
Glazes II and III	32	94.12	1	2.94	1	2.94	34
Glaze IV	28	96.55	0	0	1	3.45	29
Glazes V and VI	20	86.96	1	4.35	2	8.70	23
Total..................	101	93.52	3	2.78	4	3.70	108

TABLE IV–47. QUALITY OF DENTITION (1)

	Poor		Medium		Good		Total
Males	No.	Per cent	No.	Per cent	No.	Per cent	
Black-on-white and Glaze I	5	19.23	7	26.92	14	53.85	26
Glazes II and III	9	28.13	9	28.13	14	43.75	32
Glaze IV	5	20.00	7	28.00	13	52.00	25
Glazes V and VI	11	29.73	8	21.62	18	48.65	37
Total.....................	30	25.00	31	25.83	59	49.17	120
Females							
Black-on-white and Glaze I	5	26.32	4	21.05	10	52.63	19
Glazes II and III	7	22.58	10	32.26	14	45.16	31
Glaze IV	15	55.56	3	11.11	9	33.33	27
Glazes V and VI	4	22.22	3	16.67	11	61.11	18
Total.....................	31	32.63	20	21.05	44	46.32	95

TABLE IV–48. QUALITY OF DENTITION (2)

	Caries		Abscesses		Many Teeth Lost in Life		Pyorrhea		Total Crania
Males	No.	Per cent	No.	Per cent	No.	Per cent	No.	Per cent	
Black-on-white and Glaze I...	9	31.03	10	34.48	6	20.69	1	3.45	29
Glazes II and III	19	48.72	20	51.28	4	10.26	2	5.13	39
Glaze IV	16	53.33	17	56.67	7	23.33	1	3.33	30
Glazes V and VI	21	47.73	25	56.82	20	45.45	1	2.27	44
Total	65	45.77	72	50.70	37	26.77	5	3.52	142
Females									
Black-on-white and Glaze I...	13	59.09	9	40.91	3	13.64	1	4.55	22
Glazes II and III	14	38.89	13	36.11	6	16.67	0	0	36
Glaze IV	20	68.97	13	44.83	8	27.59	1	3.45	29
Glazes V and VI	8	33.33	6	25.00	9	37.50	1	4.17	24
Total	55	49.55	41	36.94	26	23.42	3	2.70	111

TABLE IV–49. NUMBER OF CUSPS OF UPPER MOLARS

	Males		Females	
	No.	Per cent	No.	Per cent
4–4–5	1	2.00	0	0
4–4–4	8	16.00	4	9.52
4–4–3	16	32.00	13	30.95
4–4–2	6	12.00	2	4.76
4–4–1	1	2.00	0	0
4–3–4	0	0	1	2.38
4–3½–3½	1	2.00	0	0
4–3–3	12	24.00	15	35.71
4–3–2	5	10.00	7	16.67
Total	50		42	

TABLE IV–50. NUMBER OF CUSPS OF LOWER MOLARS

	Males		Females	
	No.	Per cent	No.	Per cent
5–5–5	10	21.28	5	13.16
5–5–4	11	23.40	9	23.68
5–5–3	0	0	1	2.63
5–4–5	7	14.89	3	7.89
5–4–4	9	19.15	9	23.68
5–4–3	1	2.13	2	5.26
5–4–2	1	2.13	0	0
4–4–5	3	6.38	2	5.26
4–5–4	0	0	3	7.89
4–4–4	3	6.38	4	10.53
4–4–3	2	4.26	0	0
Total	47		38	

TABLE IV–51. SHOVEL INCISORS

	Absent		Doubtful		Submedium		Medium		Total
	No.	Per cent	No.	Per cent	No.	Per cent	No.	Per cent	
Males									
Black-on-white and Glaze I...	0	0	13	44.83	2	6.90	14	48.28	29
Glazes II and III	2	5.13	23	58.97	1	2.56	13	33.33	39
Glaze IV	6	20.00	15	50.00	1	3.33	8	26.67	30
Glazes V and VI	3	6.82	28	63.64	0	0	13	29.55	44
Total	11	7.75	79	55.63	4	2.82	48	33.80	142
Females									
Black-on-white and Glaze I...	4	18.18	8	36.36	0	0	10	45.45	22
Glazes II and III	1	2.78	16	44.44	2	5.56	17	47.22	36
Glaze IV	1	3.45	11	37.93	1	3.45	16	55.17	29
Glazes V and VI	0	0	15	62.50	2	8.33	7	29.17	24
Total	6	5.41	50	45.05	5	4.50	50	45.85	111

TABLE IV–52. DENTAL ABNORMALITIES NOT OBSERVED ELSEWHERE

	Impacted 3rd Molar		Reduced 3rd and 2nd Molar		Crowded Incisors		Supernumerary Tooth		Rotation of Incisors and Molars		Total Crania
	No.	Per cent	No.	Per cent	No.	Per cent	No.	Per cent	No.	Per cent	
Males											
Black-on-white and Gl. I	1	3.45	6	20.69	4	13.79	0	0	2	6.90	29
Glazes II and III	1	2.56	10	25.64	11	28.21	1	2.56	4	10.26	39
Glaze IV	1	3.33	4	13.33	3	10.00	2	6.67	0	0	30
Glazes V and VI	0	0	5	11.36	7	15.91	0	0	2	4.55	44
Total	3	2.11	25	17.61	25	17.61	3	2.11	8	5.63	142
Females											
Black-on-white and Gl. I	0	0	4	18.18	4	18.18	0	0	2	9.09	22
Glazes II and III	2	5.56	6	16.67	10	27.78	1	2.78	2	5.56	36
Glaze IV	2	6.90	5	17.24	4	13.79	0	0	1	3.45	29
Glazes V and VI	0	0	5	20.83	2	8.33	0	0	0	0	24
Total	4	3.60	20	18.02	20	18.02	1	0.90	5	4.50	111

TABLE IV–53. PRODONTISM

	Males			Females		
	No.	Per cent	Total	No.	Per cent	Total
Black-on-white and Glaze I.........	1	3.45	29	0	0	22
Glazes II and III..................	0	0	39	0	0	36
Glaze IV.........................	0	0	30	3	10.34	29
Glazes V and VI..................	1	2.27	44	0	0	24
Total.......................	2	1.41	142	3	2.70	111

PALATE

Form of the palate is classified in the following categories: parabolic, hyperbolic, U–shaped, and elliptical. The parabolic form is commonest in both sexes and the U–shape takes second rank. In the males during the first periods of the pueblo all forms of the palate are found but these gradually give way to the predominant parabolic form which increases steadily in its proportion of the population. In the females no such consistent trend is observable. Elliptical and U–shaped palates seem to be commoner in this sex than in the males.

The height of the palate is usually medium or pronounced, prevailingly the former in females and the latter in males. The height of the palate in both sexes seems to become smaller in successive periods. Height of the palate seems not to be significantly associated with palatal form (Tables IV–54, 55).

A small development of the palatine torus occurs in about 12 per cent of male crania and 13.5 per cent of female crania (Table IV–56).

TABLE IV–54. HEIGHT AND SHAPE OF PALATE

		Height				Shape				
Males		Sub-medium	Medium	Pro-nounced	Total	Parabolic	Hyper-bolic	U-shaped	Ellip-tical	Total
B.-on-W. and Gl. I	Number..	1	4	14	19	8	2	8	1	19
	Per cent..	5.26	21.05	73.68		42.11	10.53	42.11	5.26	
Glazes II and III	Number..	1	10	16	27	12	3	11	1	27
	Per cent..	3.70	37.04	59.26		44.44	11.11	40.74	3.70	
Glaze IV	Number..	0	12	11	23	18	2	2	1	23
	Per cent..	0	52.17	47.83		78.26	8.70	8.70	4.35	
Glazes V and VI	Number..	0	20	13	33	20	4	8	1	33
	Per cent..	0	60.61	39.39		60.61	12.12	24.24	3.03	
Total	Number..	2	46	54	102	58	11	29	4	102
	Per cent..	1.96	45.10	52.94		56.86	10.78	28.43	3.92	
Females										
B.-on-W. and Gl. I	Number..	0	8	8	16	12	0	4	0	16
	Per cent..	0	50.00	50.00		75.00	0	25.00	0	
Glazes II and III	Number..	0	12	12	24	11	2	9	2	24
	Per cent..	0	50.00	50.00		45.83	8.33	37.50	8.33	
Glaze IV	Number..	0	10	8	18	9	0	8	1	18
	Per cent..	0	55.56	44.44		50.00	0	44.44	5.56	
Glazes V and VI	Number..	4	7	4	15	8	0	5	2	15
	Per cent..	26.67	46.67	26.67		53.33	0	33.33	13.33	
Total	Number..	4	37	32	73	40	2	26	5	73
	Per cent..	5.48	50.68	43.84		54.79	2.74	35.62	6.85	

TABLE IV–55. CORRELATION OF HEIGHT AND SHAPE OF PALATE

Height Submedium

| | Shape | | | | | | | | | |
| | Parabolic | | Hyperbolic | | U-shaped | | Elliptical | | Total | |
Males	No.	Per cent	No.	Per cent	No.	Per cent	No.	Per cent	No.	Per cent
Black-on-white and Glaze I	0	0	0	0	1	5.26	0	0	1	5 26
Glazes II and III.........	0	0	0	0	1	3.70	0	0	1	3.70
Glaze IV.................	0	0	0	0	0	0	0	0	0	0
Glazes V and VI..........	0	0	0	0	0	0	0	0	0	0
Total	0	0	0	0	2	1.96	0	0	2	1.96
Females										
Black-on-white and Glaze I	0	0	0	0	0	0	0	0	0	0
Glazes II and III.........	0	0	0	0	0	0	0	0	0	0
Glaze IV.................	0	0	0	0	0	0	0	0	0	0
Glazes V and VI..........	1	6.67	0	0	2	13.33	1	6.67	4	26.67
Total	1	1.37	0	0	2	2.74	1	1.37	4	5.48

Height Medium

| | Parabolic | | Hyperbolic | | U-shaped | | Elliptical | | Total | |
Males	No.	Per cent	No.	Per cent	No.	Per cent	No.	Per cent	No.	Per cent
Black-on-white and Glaze I	1	5.26	0	0	3	15.79	0	0	4	21.05
Glazes II and III.........	4	14.81	1	3.70	5	18.52	0	0	10	37.04
Glaze IV.................	9	39.13	2	8.70	1	4.35	0	0	12	52.17
Glazes V and VI..........	11	33.33	0	0	8	24.24	1	3.03	20	60.61
Total	25	24.51	3	2.94	17	16.67	1	0.98	46	45.10
Females										
Black-on-white and Glaze I	8	50.00	0	0	0	0	0	0	8	50.00
Glazes II and III.........	5	20.83	1	4.17	4	16.67	2	8.33	12	50.00
Glaze IV.................	4	22.22	0	0	6	33.33	0	0	10	55.56
Glazes V and VI..........	3	20.00	0	0	3	20.00	1	6.67	7	46.67
Total	20	27.40	1	1.37	13	17.81	3	4.11	37	50.68

Height Pronounced

| | Parabolic | | Hyperbolic | | U-shaped | | Elliptical | | Total | |
Males	No.	Per cent	No.	Per cent	No.	Per cent	No.	Per cent	No.	Per cent
Black-on-white and Glaze I	7	36.84	2	10.53	4	21.05	1	5.26	14	73.68
Glazes II and III.........	8	29.63	2	7.41	5	18.52	1	3.70	16	59.26
Glaze IV.................	9	39.13	0	0	1	4.35	1	4.35	11	47.83
Glazes V and VI	9	27.27	4	12.12	0	0	0	0	13	39.39
Total	33	32.35	8	7.84	10	9.80	3	2.94	54	52.94
Females										
Black-on-white and Glaze I	4	25.00	0	0	4	25.00	0	0	8	50.00
Glazes II and III.........	6	25.00	1	4.17	5	20.83	0	0	12	50.00
Glaze IV.................	5	27.78	0	0	2	11.11	1	5.56	8	44.44
Glazes V and VI..........	4	26.67	0	0	0	0	0	0	4	26.67
Total.................	19	26.03	1	1.37	11	15.07	1	1.37	32	43.84

TABLE IV–56. PRESENCE OF PALATINE TORUS *

	Males		Females		Total	
	No.	Per cent	No.	Per cent	Males	Females
Black-on-white and Glaze I	3	10.34	3	13.64	29	22
Glazes II and III..................	7	18.92	6	16.67	39	36
Glaze IV	4	13.33	3	10.34	30	29
Glazes V and VI	3	6.82	3	12.50	44	24
Total	17	11.97	15	13.51	142	111

* One medium torus was found in a Glaze IV female. The rest were all submedium.

ALVEOLAR PROGNATHISM

A medium degree of alveolar prognathism is most characteristic of the male crania and a pronounced degree is found oftenest among the females. In the males there is a slight tendency for degree and amount of alveolar prognathism to increase in the later periods and in the case of the females this increase in prognathism is quite clear (Table IV–57).

TABLE IV–57. ALVEOLAR PROGNATHISM

	Slight		Medium		Pronounced		Very Pronounced		Total
	No.	Per cent	No.	Per cent	No.	Per cent	No.	Per cent	
Males									
Black-on-white and Glaze I...	6	25.00	15	62.50	3	12.50	0	0	24
Glazes II and III	9	27.27	15	45.45	9	27.27	0	0	33
Glaze IV	9	34.62	10	38.46	7	26.92	0	0	26
Glazes V and VI	8	22.22	19	52.78	8	22.22	1	2.78	36
Total	32	26.89	59	49.58	27	22.69	1	0.84	119
Females									
Black-on-white and Glaze I...	7	36.84	8	42.11	4	21.05	0	0	19
Glazes II and III	3	10.34	12	41.38	12	41.38	2	6.90	29
Glaze IV	1	3.57	6	21.43	18	64.29	3	10.71	28
Glazes V and VI	2	10.53	6	31.58	10	52.63	1	5.26	19
Total	13	13.68	32	33.68	44	46.32	6	6.32	95

MANDIBLE

In the male crania the size of the mandible is prevailingly medium and oftener large than small. In the female series medium-sized mandibles are also most common, but small lower jaws occur oftener than large ones. In the last two Pecos periods large jaws occur more frequently than in the earlier periods, but it is not certain that the differences are significant (Table IV–58).

The mental prominence is usually of medium development in both sexes, but frequently pronounced in males and frequently submedium in females. The distribution of this feature by periods is very irregular and probably means nothing (Table IV-59).

The sigmoid notch is shallower in females than in males. In the females the sigmoid notch seems to become shallower in succeeding periods, whereas in the males a slight tendency in the opposite direction is exhibited in the table, but is probably unimportant (Table IV–60).

The inferior dental foramen is usually about on the level of the crowns of the molars; occasionally it is lower, rarely higher. No sex difference is apparent (Table IV–61).

The mylo-hyoid ridge is usually of average development in both sexes, but is more commonly submedium in females than in males. No period differences are evident. Genial tubercles are prevailingly small in both sexes, but oftener well developed in males than in females (Tables IV–62, 63).

No consistent developmental or evolutionary trends in mandibular features are revealed by the comparison of the different subgroups.

A notable feature of the Pecos crania of both sexes and of all periods is the heaping up of irregular masses of compact bone on the lingual surfaces of the horizontal mandibular rami in the premolar region. These thickened areas assume the proportions of mandibular tori in about 14 per cent of males and 15 per cent of females, and lesser developments of the feature occur in 54 per cent of males and 43 per cent of females (Table IV–64). The mandibular torus is generally considered to be an effect of unusually strong development of the masticatory apparatus in connection with habitual chewing of very tough food. It occurs most frequently in the skulls of Eskimos and Icelanders.

In these peoples and in other flesh-eaters, it has been thought that the building up of compact tissue on the lingual face of the mandible provides a sort of buttress to reinforce the alveolar processes against the strain exerted upon the roots of the teeth in lateral movements of mastication.[1] The presence of the torus in such a large proportion of the Pecos population is puzzling. In this case it cannot be connected with a tough flesh diet, since these people probably lived to a great extent upon maize. The attachments of the masticatory muscles usually do show strong development, but not comparable with that of the Eskimo and not in excess of that usually found in North American Indians. Among the Eskimos the masticatory development is often attributed to the habit of preparing skins for clothing by chewing them, but only the women practise this habit and the masticatory development of the males exceeds that of the females. The habit of chewing grass or other material in order to prepare it for basket-making might account for the development of the masticatory muscles and especially of the mandibular torus in the Pecos Indians, were it not for the fact that baskets are usually made exclusively by the women, whereas the development under discussion is found in both sexes. Further, there is no reason for believing that the Pecos Indians were specialists in preparing material for basket-making by any such method.

On the whole, it seems doubtful that the heaping up of bone on the inner sides of the mandible can be attributed directly to function, and if it is to be attributed to such a cause we must admit ignorance of the precise nature of the latter.[2]

[1] Hooton, 1918, pp. 54–58.
[2] On this point compare the remarks of Dr. Rihan, Appendix I, p. 367.

TABLE IV–58. SIZE OF MANDIBLE

	Small		Medium		Large		Total
Males	No.	Per cent	No.	Per cent	No.	Per cent	
Black-on-white and Glaze I.....	5	18.52	17	62.96	5	18.52	27
Glazes II and III	5	13.89	21	58.33	10	27.78	36
Glaze IV	3	10.34	12	41.38	14	48.28	29
Glazes V and VI	7	16.67	20	47.62	15	35.71	42
Total....................	20	14.93	70	52.24	44	32.84	134
Females							
Black-on-white and Glaze I.....	6	30.00	11	55.00	3	15.00	20
Glazes II and III	11	36.67	15	50.00	4	13.33	30
Glaze IV	7	26.92	12	46.15	7	26.92	26
Glazes V and VI	9	42.86	8	38.10	4	19.05	21
Total....................	33	34.02	46	47.42	18	18.56	97

TABLE IV–59. MENTAL PROCESS

	Absent		Submedium		Medium		Pronounced		Total
Males	No.	Per cent	No.	Per cent	No.	Per cent	No.	Per cent	
Black-on-white and Glaze I ..	0	0	4	14.81	12	44.44	11	40.74	27
Glazes II and III	1	2.86	7	20.00	18	51.43	9	25.71	35
Glaze IV	1	3.45	4	13.79	15	51.72	9	31.03	29
Glazes V and VI............	0	0	10	23.81	22	52.38	10	23.81	42
Total	2	1.50	25	18.79	67	50.37	39	29.32	133
Females									
Black-on-white and Glaze I ..	0	0	4	20.00	15	75.00	1	5.00	20
Glazes II and III	1	3.33	12	40.00	14	46.67	3	10.00	30
Glaze IV	0	0	11	42.31	13	50.00	1	7.69	25
Glazes V and VI............	1	5.00	5	25.00	11	55.00	3	15.00	20
Total	2	2.10	32	33.68	53	55.79	8	8.42	95

TABLE IV–60. DEPTH OF SIGMOID NOTCH

	Submedium		Medium		Pronounced		Total
Males	No.	Per cent	No.	Per cent	No.	Per cent	
Black-on-white and Glaze I.....	4	16.00	13	52.00	8	32.00	25
Glazes II and III	11	31.43	12	34.29	12	34.29	35
Glaze IV	6	20.69	14	48.28	9	31.03	29
Glazes V and VI	5	12.20	24	58.54	12	29.27	41
Total	26	20.00	63	48.46	41	31.54	130
Females							
Black-on-white and Glaze I.....	4	21.05	12	63.15	3	15.79	19
Glazes II and III	7	26.92	15	57.69	4	15.38	26
Glaze IV	8	30.77	14	53.85	4	15.38	26
Glazes V and VI	8	40.00	10	50.00	2	10.00	20
Total	27	29.67	51	56.04	13	14.29	91

TABLE IV–61. LEVEL OF INFERIOR DENTAL FORAMINA WITH REFERENCE TO MOLAR CROWNS

	Low		Medium		High		Total
Males	No.	Per cent	No.	Per cent	No.	Per cent	
Black-on-white and Glaze I.....	1	3.85	23	88.46	2	7.69	26
Glazes II and III	8	22.86	26	74.29	1	2.86	35
Glazes IV	4	13.79	21	72.42	4	13.79	29
Glazes V and VI	4	9.76	36	87.80	1	2.44	41
Total	17	12.98	106	80.92	8	6.11	131
Females							
Black-on-white and Glaze I.....	4	21.05	15	78.95	0	0	19
Glazes II and III	2	7.14	24	85.71	2	7.14	28
Glaze IV	0	0	25	96.15	1	3.85	26
Glazes V and VI	1	5.00	18	90.00	1	5.00	20
Total	7	7.53	82	88.17	4	4.30	93

TABLE IV–62. DEVELOPMENT OF MYLO–HYOID RIDGE

	Absent		Submedium		Medium		Pronounced		Total
Males	No.	Per cent	No.	Per cent	No.	Per cent	No.	Per cent	
Black-on-white and Glaze I ..	0	0	8	30.77	16	61.54	2	7.69	26
Glazes II and III	0	0	12	33.33	19	52.78	5	13.89	36
Glaze IV	0	0	13	44.83	13	44.83	3	10.34	29
Glazes V and VI...........	1	2.50	17	42.50	13	32.50	9	22.50	40
Total	1	0.76	50	38.17	61	46.56	19	14.50	131
Females									
Black-on-white and Glaze I ..	0	0	5	25.00	11	55.00	4	20.00	20
Glazes II and III	1	3.33	14	46.67	13	43.33	2	6.67	30
Glaze IV	0	0	14	53.85	10	38.46	2	7.69	26
Glazes V and VI...........	0	0	8	38.10	10	47.62	3	14.29	21
Total	1	1.03	41	42.27	44	45.36	11	11.34	97

TABLE IV–63. GENIAL TUBERCLES

	Absent		Submedium		Medium		Pronounced		Total
Males	No.	Per cent	No.	Per cent	No.	Per cent	No.	Per cent	
Black-on-white and Glaze I ..	1	3.85	15	57.69	10	38.46	0	0	26
Glazes II and III	1	2.70	24	64.86	10	27.03	2	5.41	37
Glaze IV	2	6.90	23	79.31	4	13.79	0	0	29
Glazes V and VI...........	0	0	20	48.78	20	48.78	1	2.44	41
Total	4	3.01	82	61.66	44	33.08	3	2.66	133
Females									
Black-on-white and Glaze I ..	0	0	13	65.00	7	35.00	0	0	20
Glazes II and III	0	0	22	73.33	8	26.67	0	0	30
Glaze IV	0	0	20	76.92	6	23.08	0	0	26
Glazes V and VI...........	1	5.00	14	70.00	3	15.00	2	10.00	20
Total	1	1.04	69	71.88	24	25.00	2	2.08	96

TABLE IV–64. Mandibular Torus

Slight thickening of premolar region	B.-on-W. and Gl. I		Gls. II and III		Glaze IV		Gls. V and VI		Total	
	No.	Per cent	No.	Per cent	No.	Per cent	No.	Per cent	No.	Per cent
Males	10	34.48	22	56.41	20	66.67	25	56.82	77	54.22
Females	11	50.00	18	50.00	12	41.38	7	29.17	48	43.24
Mandibular torus										
Males	8	27.59	4	10.26	1	3.33	7	15.91	20	14.08
Females	0	0	3	8.33	7	24.14	7	29.17	17	15.31

MEAN SQUARE CONTINGENCY OF MORPHOLOGICAL CHARACTERS AND STRATIGRAPHIC SUBGROUPS

In order to show the extent to which the Glaze subgroups are differentiated in the development of morphological characters of the skull, mean square contingency coefficients have been calculated for some thirty characters. The coefficient of mean square contingency expresses on a scale from zero to unity the extent to which (in this case) the several archaeological subgroups differ from each other in the various morphological features beyond what may be expected under the supposition that chance alone determines the distribution of the features.[1]

This coefficient is always positive and approaches unity in value the more completely differentiated the subgroups are. Since the value of any coefficient is likely to be increased by the use of too finely subdivided categories and by the casual irregularities of no real significance that are likely to occur in very small samples, it is not advisable to attach much significance to values of the coefficient less than .30. Table IV–65 records the value of these coefficients for 31 characters. In the male series the total number of crania involved ranges from 104 to 144, and in the females from 76 to 111. The mean value of 31 coefficients for the male series is .253 and for the female series .266. It is doubtful whether the somewhat higher value of the female coefficients is really significant; it may be due to the irregularities of the smaller samples involved in that series. On the other hand, it is quite possible that here, as elsewhere, the females tend to adhere more closely to ancestral racial types, whereas the males show combinations of all ancestral characters.

Table IV–66 summarizes the values of these coefficients of mean square contingency. In the male series they exceed .3 in 8 of 31 cases or 25.81 per cent. In the female series 11 of 30 coefficients or 36.7 per cent have values equal to, or in excess of .3. We may now consider singly the characters which show apparent Glaze group differentiation, referring back to the tables from which the coefficients are calculated.

Fullness of the temporal region shows a coefficient of .313 in males and .417 in females. In the males (Table IV–65) the value seems to be an effect of the tendency of skulls with protuberant temporal regions to be disproportionately frequent in Black-on-white and Glaze I periods, and skulls with compressed temporals to be

---

[1] For the method of calculating this coefficient and for a full explanation of its significance, cf. Yule (London, 1927), pp. 64–66.

excessively abundant in Glazes II and III, together with other irregularities of distribution. Similarly in the females the irregularities are so widely distributed that no consistent trend is discernible. It would appear that the high values of coefficients in both series are probably a secondary effect of the variation in the extent and intensity of occipital deformation in the several subgroups, since bulging of the temporals is caused by extreme occipital flattening.

In the form of pterion the female series shows a coefficient of mean square contingency amounting to .354, whereas in the males it is only .207. In the females the high value of the coefficient reflects the extent to which narrow H-forms and K-forms tend to become more numerous and wide H- and medium H-forms less common from the first to the last periods. A similar tendency may be observed in the male series, but it is not so pronounced.

Type of supraorbital ridges yields a contingency of .308 in females, but only .262 in males. In the females the contingency is largely an effect of an increasing tendency of females in successive periods to show no brow-ridges at all or median brow-ridges as compared with the divided type which is more frequent in earlier groups. In the males the contingency seems to be due to chance.

In development of nasal sills (lower borders of the nasal apertures) the coefficients are .351 for males and .343 for females. In both sexes these values reflect the tendency for indistinct lower borders of the nasal aperture to become much more frequent in the last two groups and for borders of medium development to become less common.

Subnasal grooves show a contingency coefficient of .312 in males and only .201 in females. In the former case the table indicates a greater frequence of subnasal grooves in the late periods. The coefficient apparently has no significance in the female series.

The mean square contingency coefficient of size of zygomata with subgroups is, in the case of the males, .397, owing to an apparent increase of size of this portion of the skull in the later subgroups. The female coefficient, .229, is insignificant.

Alveolar prognathism increases markedly in females from the earlier to later periods. The coefficient of contingency (.507) is the largest found in either series. In the male series there is a slight increase of alveolar prognathism also, but the coefficient (.232) is of doubtful significance.

Wear on the teeth in the female series is more pronounced in the later subgroups. The coefficient of mean square contingency is .376. In the males also the later skulls appear to have teeth more deeply worn, but the coefficient is lower (.284).

Shovel incisors show a subgroup contingency of .312 in males and .344 in females. These incisors seem to be more common in the earlier periods.

Contingency coefficients for shape of palate are .385 in males and .278 in females. In the males this coefficient expresses a tendency for U-shaped palates, which are commoner in the early periods, to be replaced by parabolic forms.

A contingency of .301 of size of styloids with female subgroups is apparently an effect of casual irregularities in the distribution. The coefficient of .303 for depression of petrous parts in the male series seems to be due to a greater prevalence of medium degrees of depression in the first subgroup than in the succeeding groups. In the females a similar phenomenon is manifested to about the same degree (coefficient .293).

The coefficient of contingency of chin prominence with female subgroups is .323, but it is apparently an effect of too fine a subdivision of categories. In the females there seems to be a slight tendency for a greater development of genial tubercles in the last two periods (coefficient .347) and a similar trend is shown by the males (coefficient .316). In the females there is a lumping of mandibles with shallow sigmoid notches in the last period, causing a coefficient of .371.

TABLE IV–65. CONTINGENCIES OF STRATIGRAPHIC SUBGROUPS WITH MORPHOLOGICAL CHARACTERS

Character	Mean Square Contingency Coefficient	
	Males	Females
Size of supraorbital ridges	.299	.107
Type of supraorbital ridges	.262	.308
Fullness of temporal region	.313	.417
Development of supramastoid process	.215	.252
Size of mastoid processes	.235	.255
Serration of sutures	.273	.126
Occurrence of Wormian bones	.263	.121
Form of pterion	.207	.354
Size of styloids	.217	.302
Depression of petrous parts	.303	.293
Size of middle lacerate foramina	.080	.194
Size of malars	.243	.247
Size of zygomata	.397	.229
Presence of infraorbital suture	.106	.230
Depth of suborbital fossae	.221	.240
Depth of nasion depression	.184	.173
Breadth of nasal aperture	.203	.135
Development of nasal sills	.351	.343
Development of nasal spine	.188	.261
Subnasal grooves	.312	.201
Wear of teeth	.284	.376
Eruption of dentition	.277	.185
Presence of shovel incisors	.312	.344
Shape of palate	.385	.278
Alveolar prognathism	.232	.507
Size of mandible	.217	.181
Development of mental process	.208	.323
Depth of sigmoid notch	.214	.371
Level of inferior dental foramen	.267	.290
Development of mylo-hyoid ridge	.260	.270
Development of genial tubercles	.316	.347
Mean Value	.253	.266

TABLE IV–66. SUMMARY OF VALUE OF COEFFICIENTS OF MEAN SQUARE CONTINGENCY

	Less than .100		.100–.199		.200–.299		.300–.399		.400–.499		.500–.599		Total
	No.	Per cent	No.	Per cent	No.	Per cent	No.	Per cent	No.	Per cent	No.	Per cent	No.
Males	1	3.33	3	10.00	19	61.29	8	25.81	0	0	0	0	31
Females	0	0	7	23.33	12	40.00	9	30.00	1	3.33	1	3.33	30

SUMMARY OF DIFFERENCES IN MORPHOLOGICAL CHARACTERS

Sex Differences

While the sex differences in morphological characters in the Pecos series are ordinarily of the nature expected, it may be well to summarize them here. It should be remembered that there is a certain spurious correlation in the description of these sex differences, since in many cases they are themselves in part or entirely the criteria by which the sex of the skeletons have been determined.

Frontal Region. More receding and less steep in females. This is unusual. Brow-ridges larger in males.

Sagittal Region. Sagittal elevations more common in males. Parietal bosses more prominent in females. Postcoronoid depressions commoner in females.

Temporal Region. Supramastoid crests more common in males. Mastoids larger in males.

Occipital Region. Flat deformed occiputs commoner in females.

Sutures. Serration more complex in males. Order of occlusion in males: sagittal — coronal — lambdoid; in females: coronal — sagittal — lambdoid. Narrow H- and K-forms of pterion more common in females. Wormian bones commoner in males.

Parietal Foramina. More often lacking in females. Larger in males.

Glenoid Fossae. Deeper in males. Postglenoid processes more frequent in males.

Styloid Processes. Larger in males.

Depression of Petrous Parts. Deeper in males.

Middle Lacerate Foramina. Larger in males.

Pterygo-spinous Foramina. Commoner in males.

Dehiscences in Floor of Auditory Meatus. Commoner in females.

Malars and Zygomata. Larger in males.

Orbits. Oftener square in females than in males. Infraorbital suture commoner in females.

Nose. Bridge and root lower and narrower in females. Profile more frequently concave in females. Aperture oftener wide in females; spine less developed, and subnasal grooves commoner in females.

Teeth. Wear more pronounced in males. Third molars oftener suppressed in males. Quality better in males. Cusp reduction more marked in females. Shovel incisors commoner in females.

Palate. Parabolic form commoner in males; U-form and elliptical form commoner in females than in males.

Alveolar Prognathism. More pronounced in females.

Mandible. Larger in males. Mental prominence more pronounced in males. Sigmoid notch shallower in females. Mylo-hyoid ridge less developed in females.

PERIOD DIFFERENCES BETWEEN GLAZE SUBGROUPS

Frontal Region. High foreheads increase from first to last in both sexes. Supra-orbital ridges in the females diminish from first to last and median types become increasingly common.

Sagittal Region. Sagittal elevations diminish in frequency in both sexes from first to last.

Temporal Region. In both sexes protuberant temporals are more common in the early periods. In females supramastoid crests are more frequent in the early periods and size of mastoids increases from first to last.

Occipital Region. Occipital tori become more frequent and more marked in both sexes from the early to the late periods.

Sutures. In the males the sutures seem to be more complex in the late than in the early periods. In the females the reverse is the case. K-forms of pterion are commoner in the later periods.

Glenoid Fossae. Glenoid fossae become shallower and postglenoid processes decrease in frequency in both sexes from beginning to end.

Depression of Petrous Parts. Becomes less pronounced in the later periods.

Middle Lacerate Foramina. These decrease in size from the early to the late periods.

Posterior Lacerate Foramina. These increase in size in the males in the later periods.

Retromastoid Foramina. In females these are more frequently absent in the earlier periods and they are larger and more numerous in the later periods.

Pterygo-spinous Foramina. Fewer of these occur in the later periods.

Malars. Malars increase in size in both sexes from the early to the late periods.

Orbits. In the female series square orbits become more numerous in the later periods. Suborbital fossae grow deeper in both sexes from first to last.

Nasal Region. In both sexes dull or indistinct lower borders of the nasal aperture increase in frequency from first to last. Nasal spines diminish in size. In the males subnasal grooves become more common in the later periods and wide nasal apertures are more frequent.

Teeth. The degree of wear of the teeth increases in both sexes from early to late. Suppression of third molars is more common in the later periods. Teeth of males become poorer in the later periods. Shovel incisors diminish in frequency in both sexes.

Palate. In the males parabolic forms of the palate are more frequent in the later periods. Height of the palate decreases in both sexes.

Alveolar Prognathism. This increases in both sexes.

Mandible. The size increases in the later periods. The depth of the sigmoid notch appears to increase in males and to decrease in females. Genial tubercles appear to increase in size.

CHAPTER V

MEASUREMENTS AND OBSERVATIONS OF BONES BY STRATA

FEMUR

MEASUREMENTS AND INDICES

THE measurements of femoral lengths show extraordinarily little variation from the earliest to the latest period. In the males the maximum length of the right femur exceeds slightly that of the left, on the average, and in the females the reverse condition obtains. The femora are longest in both sexes in the Black-on-white and Glaze I group, and shortest in the Glazes V and VI group (Tables V–1, 2).

In the maximum diameter of the femoral head there is little or no difference between right and left sides. Again there is a tendency, more clearly expressed in the females, for the femora of the first period to have the largest mean head diameters and those of the last period the smallest (Table V–3).

The antero-posterior diameter in the subtrochanteric region is somewhat greater on the left side in both males and females. In both males and females the Black-on-white and Glaze I group shows larger means than the groups of the succeeding periods. In the case of the lateral subtrochanteric diameter, the contrary obtains. The smallest means occur in the earliest group (Tables V–4, 5).

The index of platymeria shows that this condition is pronounced in the series at large. It is a little lower in females than in males. In conformity with the variations of means of the diameters in the subgroups the femora of the first periods in both sexes are less platymeric than those of the succeeding periods. In both sexes the left femora are much less flattened than those of the right side (Table V–8).

The antero-posterior diameter of the shaft at the middle is somewhat larger on the left side in both males and females. In both sexes the means of the last period are smallest and in the case of the females the earliest subgroup shows markedly larger mean values. This does not obtain, however, in the male series. The mean values of the lateral shaft diameters are larger on the left side in females, but in case of the males there is little difference. These lateral shaft diameters tend to increase from the early to the late periods in both sexes (Tables V–6, 7).

The middle index is higher on the right side than on the left in males, whereas the reverse is the case in the female series. In both sexes the index rises from early to late times. The pilaster becomes more pronounced in association with a more pronounced platymeria (Table V–9).

TABLE V–1. Maximum Length of Femur

Right

Males	No.	Range	Mean	S. D.	V.
Total Series A	142	384–495	427.22 ± 1.15	20.30 ± 0.81	4.75 ± 0.19
Black-on-white and Glaze I	21	395–495	429.52 ± 3.78	25.70 ± 2.67	5.98 ± 0.62
Glazes II and III	52	393–472	425.23 ± 1.69	18.06 ± 1.69	4.25 ± 0.28
Glaze IV	31	392–470	428.77 ± 2.35	19.40 ± 1.66	4.52 ± 0.39
Glazes V and VI	38	384–463	423.16 ± 2.20	20.15 ± 1.56	4.76 ± 0.37
Females					
Total Series A	102	356–445	394.26 ± 1.14	17.00 ± 0.80	4.31 ± 0.20
Black-on-white and Glaze I	17	384–430	404.18 ± 1.88	11.50 ± 1.33	2.85 ± 0.33
Glazes II and III	35	365–445	390.14 ± 2.06	18.05 ± 1.46	4.63 ± 0.37
Glaze IV	27	356–431	387.30 ± 2.02	15.55 ± 1.43	4.02 ± 0.37
Glazes V and VI	23	358–424	393.43 ± 2.09	14.35 ± 1.43	3.65 ± 0.36

Left

Males	No.	Range	Mean	S. D.	V.
Total Series A	140	362–476	426.71 ± 1.13	19.85 ± 0.80	4.65 ± 0.19
Black-on-white and Glaze I	20	362–476	425.75 ± 4.16	27.59 ± 2.94	6.48 ± 0.69
Glazes II and III	55	394–463	425.56 ± 1.59	17.46 ± 1.12	4.10 ± 0.26
Glaze IV	29	397–463	428.38 ± 2.26	18.05 ± 1.60	4.21 ± 0.37
Glazes V and VI	36	383–463	422.78 ± 2.24	19.95 ± 1.59	4.72 ± 0.38
Females					
Total Series A	105	357–446	396.05 ± 1.15	17.50 ± 0.81	4.42 ± 0.21
Black-on-white and Glaze I	18	360–434	402.78 ± 2.55	16.02 ± 1.80	3.98 ± 0.48
Glazes II and III	38	357–446	392.53 ± 2.00	18.25 ± 1.41	4.65 ± 0.36
Glaze IV	29	358–432	390.32 ± 1.98	15.50 ± 1.40	3.97 ± 0.36
Glazes V and VI	20	358–428	396.00 ± 2.68	17.75 ± 1.89	4.48 ± 0.48

TABLE V–2. Bicondylar Length of Femur

Right

Males	No.	Range	Mean	S. D.	V.
Total Series A	145	382–492	423.90 ± 1.12	19.95 ± 0.79	4.71 ± 0.19
Black-on-white and Glaze I	21	388–492	427.19 ± 3.57	24.25 ± 2.52	5.68 ± 0.59
Glazes II and III	53	391–470	421.87 ± 1.69	18.29 ± 1.20	4.35 ± 0.28
Glaze IV	32	390–465	425.31 ± 2.25	18.85 ± 1.59	4.43 ± 0.37
Glazes V and VI	39	382–460	420.51 ± 2.17	20.10 ± 1.54	4.78 ± 0.36
Females					
Total Series A	106	352–442	391.98 ± 1.08	16.50 ± 0.76	4.21 ± 0.20
Black-on-white and Glaze I	17	377–424	400.47 ± 1.85	11.29 ± 1.31	2.82 ± 0.33
Glazes II and III	39	364–442	389.90 ± 1.86	17.20 ± 1.31	4.41 ± 0.34
Glaze IV	28	352–429	384.32 ± 1.94	15.25 ± 1.37	3.97 ± 0.36
Glazes V and VI	22	357–420	392.00 ± 2.27	15.80 ± 1.61	4.03 ± 0.41

Left

Males	No.	Range	Mean	S. D.	V.
Total Series A	142	362–473	423.24 ± 1.09	19.25 ± 0.77	4.55 ± 0.18
Black-on-white and Glaze I	21	362–473	422.81 ± 3.82	25.98 ± 2.70	6.14 ± 0.64
Glazes II and III	56	391–461	421.84 ± 1.56	17.27 ± 1.10	4.09 ± 0.26
Glaze IV	29	392–459	425.79 ± 2.21	17.65 ± 1.56	4.15 ± 0.37
Glazes V and VI	36	382–462	420.14 ± 2.24	19.90 ± 1.58	4.74 ± 0.38
Females					
Total Series A	104	354–445	393.03 ± 1.15	17.45 ± 0.82	4.44 ± 0.21
Black-on-white and Glaze I	18	357–430	399.72 ± 2.50	15.72 ± 1.77	3.93 ± 0.44
Glazes II and III	36	355–445	390.97 ± 2.16	19.20 ± 1.53	4.91 ± 0.39
Glaze IV	29	354–430	387.45 ± 1.90	15.15 ± 1.34	3.91 ± 0.35
Glazes V and VI	21	357–426	392.24 ± 2.48	16.85 ± 1.75	4.30 ± 0.45

TABLE V–3. MAXIMUM DIAMETER OF HEAD OF FEMUR

Right

Males	No.	Range	Mean	S. D.	V.
Total Series A	151	37–49	42.99 ± 0.13	2.39 ± 0.09	5.56 ± 0.22
Black-on-white and Glaze I	23	37–49	43.00 ± 0.37	2.60 ± 0.26	6.05 ± 0.60
Glazes II and III	57	37–49	42.89 ± 0.22	2.44 ± 0.15	5.69 ± 0.36
Glaze IV	34	40–47	43.19 ± 0.20	1.72 ± 0.14	3.99 ± 0.33
Glazes V and VI	37	38.5–49	42.70 ± 0.25	2.26 ± 0.18	5.28 ± 0.41
Females					
Total Series A	112	35–42	38.59 ± 0.10	1.63 ± 0.07	4.22 ± 0.19
Black-on-white and Glaze I	19	37–42	39.00 ± 0.24	1.52 ± 0.17	3.90 ± 0.43
Glazes II and III	39	35–42	38.26 ± 0.17	1.55 ± 0.12	4.05 ± 0.31
Glaze IV	28	36–42	38.52 ± 0.22	1.69 ± 0.15	4.39 ± 0.39
Glazes V and VI	26	35–42	38.85 ± 0.22	1.64 ± 0.15	4.22 ± 0.39

Left

Males	No.	Range	Mean	S. D.	V.
Total Series A	154	36–49	42.95 ± 0.14	2.64 ± 0.10	6.15 ± 0.24
Black-on-white and Glaze I	24	36–49	42.98 ± 0.30	2.15 ± 0.21	5.00 ± 0.49
Glazes II and III	60	36–49	43.05 ± 0.22	2.54 ± 0.16	5.90 ± 0.36
Glaze IV	33	40–47	43.11 ± 0.20	1.72 ± 0.14	4.00 ± 0.33
Glazes V and VI	37	39–49	43.19 ± 0.30	2.72 ± 0.21	6.29 ± 0.49
Females					
Total Series A	109	34–43	38.35 ± 0.10	1.57 ± 0.07	4.09 ± 0.19
Black-on-white and Glaze I	19	36–41	38.63 ± 0.25	1.59 ± 0.17	4.12 ± 0.45
Glazes II and III	39	36–42.5	38.37 ± 0.15	1.44 ± 0.11	3.74 ± 0.11
Glaze IV	29	36–43	38.33 ± 0.21	1.66 ± 0.15	4.33 ± 0.38
Glazes V and VI	22	34–41	38.27 ± 0.23	1.58 ± 0.16	4.14 ± 0.42

TABLE V–4. SUBTROCHANTERIC DIAMETER OF FEMUR: ANTERO–POSTERIOR

Right

Males	No.	Range	Mean	S. D.	V.
Total Series A	158	19–28	23.15 ± 0.09	1.72 ± 0.07	7.43 ± 0.28
Black-on-white and Glaze I	24	19–28	23.81 ± 0.26	1.86 ± 0.18	7.81 ± 0.76
Glazes II and III	61	19–27.5	22.78 ± 0.15	1.78 ± 0.11	7.82 ± 0.48
Glaze IV	33	20–27	23.35 ± 0.17	1.46 ± 0.12	6.23 ± 0.52
Glazes V and VI	40	20–27	23.14 ± 0.16	1.48 ± 0.11	6.42 ± 0.48
Females					
Total Series A	118	18–26	21.08 ± 0.10	1.54 ± 0.07	7.31 ± 0.32
Black-on-white and Glaze I	20	18–24	21.50 ± 0.22	1.49 ± 0.16	6.93 ± 0.74
Glazes II and III	42	18.5–26	21.15 ± 0.16	1.58 ± 0.12	7.49 ± 0.55
Glaze IV	30	19–25	20.85 ± 0.18	1.46 ± 0.13	6.98 ± 0.61
Glazes V and VI	26	18–25	20.98 ± 0.19	1.46 ± 0.14	6.96 ± 0.65

Left

Males	No.	Range	Mean	S. D.	V.
Total Series A	157	19–29	23.38 ± 0.10	1.90 ± 0.07	8.13 ± 0.31
Black-on-white and Glaze I	24	19–28	24.23 ± 0.26	1.90 ± 0.18	7.84 ± 0.76
Glazes II and III	60	19–28	23.15 ± 0.17	1.98 ± 0.12	8.55 ± 0.53
Glaze IV	34	21–29	23.66 ± 0.20	1.76 ± 0.14	7.42 ± 0.61
Glazes V and VI	39	20–27	23.08 ± 0.18	1.67 ± 0.13	7.24 ± 0.55
Females					
Total Series A	118	19–26	21.46 ± 0.10	1.57 ± 0.07	7.32 ± 0.32
Black-on-white and Glaze I	19	19–23	21.92 ± 0.19	1.20 ± 0.13	5.50 ± 0.60
Glazes II and III	43	19–26	21.66 ± 0.18	1.73 ± 0.13	7.99 ± 0.58
Glaze IV	32	19–25.5	20.97 ± 0.17	1.45 ± 0.12	6.89 ± 0.58
Glazes V and VI	24	19–24	21.38 ± 0.20	1.50 ± 0.14	6.99 ± 0.68

TABLE V–5. Subtrochanteric Diameter of Femur: Lateral

Right

Males	No.	Range	Mean	S. D.	V.
Total Series A	159	25–37	31.79 ± 0.11	2.09 ± 0.08	6.57 ± 0.25
Black-on-white and Glaze I	24	28–36	31.04 ± 0.27	1.94 ± 0.19	6.25 ± 0.61
Glazes II and III	61	28–37	31.77 ± 0.18	2.08 ± 0.13	6.55 ± 0.40
Glaze IV	34	25–36	31.91 ± 0.25	2.19 ± 0.18	6.86 ± 0.56
Glazes V and VI	40	28–37	32.16 ± 0.22	2.02 ± 0.15	6.30 ± 0.47
Females					
Total Series A	118	24–34	29.22 ± 0.11	1.74 ± 0.08	5.95 ± 0.26
Black-on-white and Glaze I	20	26–33	28.95 ± 0.26	1.70 ± 0.18	5.87 ± 0.63
Glazes II and III	42	24–34	29.19 ± 0.20	1.90 ± 0.14	6.53 ± 0.48
Glaze IV	30	27–31	29.23 ± 0.15	1.25 ± 0.11	4.28 ± 0.37
Glazes V and VI	26	25–33	29.54 ± 0.25	1.87 ± 0.17	6.33 ± 0.59

Left

Males	No.	Range	Mean	S. D.	V.
Total Series A	158	27–37.5	31.76 ± 0.12	2.15 ± 0.08	6.77 ± 0.26
Black-on-white and Glaze I	25	28–36	30.44 ± 0.24	1.74 ± 0.17	5.72 ± 0.55
Glazes II and III	60	28.5–36	31.70 ± 0.19	2.13 ± 0.13	6.72 ± 0.41
Glaze IV	34	28–36	32.24 ± 0.23	2.02 ± 0.16	6.27 ± 0.51
Glazes V and VI	39	27–37.5	32.27 ± 0.23	2.14 ± 0.16	6.63 ± 0.51
Females					
Total Series A	118	22–34	29.34 ± 0.12	1.89 ± 0.08	6.44 ± 0.28
Black-on-white and Glaze I	19	26–32	28.79 ± 0.28	1.82 ± 0.20	6.32 ± 0.69
Glazes II and III	43	26–34	29.60 ± 0.18	1.74 ± 0.13	5.88 ± 0.43
Glaze IV	32	27.5–32	29.55 ± 0.15	1.25 ± 0.11	4.23 ± 0.36
Glazes V and VI	24	22–33	29.02 ± 0.34	2.50 ± 0.24	8.61 ± 0.84

TABLE V–6. Middle Shaft Diameter of Femur: Antero-Posterior

Right

Males	No.	Range	Mean	S. D.	V.
Total Series A	159	22–35	27.89 ± 0.12	2.26 ± 0.09	8.10 ± 0.31
Black-on-white and Glaze I	24	24–35	28.42 ± 0.31	2.22 ± 0.22	7.81 ± 0.76
Glazes II and III	61	23–32	27.65 ± 0.19	2.25 ± 0.14	8.14 ± 0.50
Glaze IV	35	25–33	28.61 ± 0.23	1.98 ± 0.16	6.92 ± 0.56
Glazes V and VI	39	22–32	27.22 ± 0.24	2.26 ± 0.17	8.28 ± 0.63
Females					
Total Series A	116	21–29	24.91 ± 0.11	1.76 ± 0.08	7.07 ± 0.31
Black-on-white and Glaze I	20	23–29	25.70 ± 0.26	1.73 ± 0.18	6.73 ± 0.72
Glazes II and III	41	21–28	24.83 ± 0.17	1.64 ± 0.12	6.58 ± 0.49
Glaze IV	30	22–29	24.50 ± 0.23	1.86 ± 0.16	7.57 ± 0.66
Glazes V and VI	25	22–28	24.88 ± 0.21	1.59 ± 0.15	6.39 ± 0.61

Left

Males	No.	Range	Mean	S. D.	V.
Total Series A	156	23–34	28.13 ± 0.14	2.53 ± 0.10	8.99 ± 0.34
Black-on-white and Glaze I	25	24–34	28.02 ± 0.36	2.64 ± 0.25	9.42 ± 0.90
Glazes II and III	59	23–32.5	28.03 ± 0.20	2.27 ± 0.14	8.10 ± 0.50
Glaze IV	34	24.5–32.5	28.51 ± 0.24	2.10 ± 0.17	7.38 ± 0.60
Glazes V and VI	38	23–33	27.47 ± 0.30	2.73 ± 0.21	9.94 ± 0.77
Females					
Total Series A	119	20–29	25.00 ± 0.11	1.84 ± 0.08	7.36 ± 0.32
Black-on-white and Glaze I	19	23–29	26.53 ± 0.26	1.70 ± 0.19	6.41 ± 0.70
Glazes II and III	44	20–28	24.85 ± 0.18	1.72 ± 0.12	6.88 ± 0.49
Glaze IV	32	21–29	24.48 ± 0.21	1.78 ± 0.15	7.29 ± 0.61
Glazes V and VI	24	22–28	24.85 ± 0.22	1.58 ± 0.15	6.34 ± 0.62

TABLE V–7. MIDDLE SHAFT DIAMETER OF FEMUR: LATERAL

Right

Males	No.	Range	Mean	S. D.	V.
Total Series A	159	20–30	24.57 ± 0.10	1.91 ± 0.07	7.77 ± 0.29
Black-on-white and Glaze I	24	22–27	24.21 ± 0.18	1.28 ± 0.13	5.30 ± 0.51
Glazes II and III	61	20–29	24.18 ± 0.18	2.04 ± 0.12	8.44 ± 0.52
Glaze IV	35	22.5–30	24.80 ± 0.20	1.77 ± 0.14	7.14 ± 0.58
Glazes V and VI	39	20–29	25.18 ± 0.21	1.92 ± 0.15	7.60 ± 0.58
Females					
Total Series A	116	18–28	22.81 ± 0.10	1.59 ± 0.07	6.97 ± 0.31
Black-on-white and Glaze I	20	19–28	22.80 ± 0.33	2.18 ± 0.23	9.56 ± 1.02
Glazes II and III	41	18–25	22.63 ± 0.17	1.60 ± 0.12	7.07 ± 0.53
Glaze IV	30	21–26	22.73 ± 0.13	1.06 ± 0.09	4.66 ± 0.41
Glazes V and VI	25	21–26	23.20 ± 0.20	1.45 ± 0.14	6.25 ± 0.60

Left

Males	No.	Range	Mean	S. D.	V.
Total Series A	156	20–29	24.43 ± 0.11	2.03 ± 0.08	8.31 ± 0.32
Black-on-white and Glaze I	25	21–28	24.40 ± 0.20	1.50 ± 0.14	6.15 ± 0.59
Glazes II and III	59	20–29	24.06 ± 0.17	1.93 ± 0.12	8.02 ± 0.50
Glaze IV	34	21–28	24.59 ± 0.19	1.64 ± 0.13	6.67 ± 0.55
Glazes V and VI	38	21–29	24.90 ± 0.20	1.81 ± 0.14	7.27 ± 0.56
Females					
Total Series A	118	19–27	23.14 ± 0.09	1.46 ± 0.06	6.31 ± 0.28
Black-on-white and Glaze I	19	20–26	22.79 ± 0.24	1.54 ± 0.17	6.76 ± 0.74
Glazes II and III	43	19–27	23.35 ± 0.15	1.46 ± 0.11	6.27 ± 0.46
Glaze IV	32	19.5–26	23.16 ± 0.15	1.27 ± 0.11	5.48 ± 0.46
Glazes V and VI	24	21–27	23.08 ± 0.21	1.54 ± 0.15	6.69 ± 0.65

TABLE V–8. INDEX OF PLATYMERIA

Right

Males	No.	Range	Mean	S. D.	V.
Total Series A	158	58–96	73.24 ± 0.32	6.01 ± 0.23	8.21 ± 0.31
Black-on-white and Glaze I	24	63–87	76.79 ± 0.76	5.49 ± 0.54	7.15 ± 0.70
Glazes II and III	61	58–96	72.43 ± 0.57	6.61 ± 0.40	9.13 ± 0.56
Glaze IV	33	62–86	73.52 ± 0.69	5.85 ± 0.49	7.96 ± 0.66
Glazes V and VI	40	65–84	72.13 ± 0.48	4.48 ± 0.34	6.21 ± 0.47
Females					
Total Series A	118	58–89	72.31 ± 0.36	5.87 ± 0.26	8.12 ± 0.36
Black-on-white and Glaze I	20	67–85	74.45 ± 0.81	5.38 ± 0.57	7.23 ± 0.77
Glazes II and III	42	58–85	72.19 ± 0.61	5.88 ± 0.43	8.15 ± 0.60
Glaze IV	30	61–89	72.00 ± 0.68	5.54 ± 0.48	7.69 ± 0.67
Glazes V and VI	26	59–88	71.23 ± 0.81	6.15 ± 0.58	8.63 ± 0.81

Left

Males	No.	Range	Mean	S. D.	V.
Total Series A	157	59–93	73.85 ± 0.32	6.00 ± 0.23	8.12 ± 0.31
Black-on-white and Glaze I	24	66–93	79.29 ± 0.83	6.00 ± 0.58	7.57 ± 0.74
Glazes II and III	60	59–89	73.20 ± 0.52	5.91 ± 0.36	8.07 ± 0.50
Glaze IV	34	64–83	73.59 ± 0.52	4.49 ± 0.37	6.10 ± 0.50
Glazes V and VI	39	62–81	71.74 ± 0.53	4.91 ± 0.37	6.84 ± 0.52
Females					
Total Series A	118	62–100	73.39 ± 0.39	6.22 ± 0.27	8.48 ± 0.37
Black-on-white and Glaze I	19	68–87	76.42 ± 0.76	4.93 ± 0.54	6.45 ± 0.71
Glazes II and III	43	65–86	73.30 ± 0.55	5.32 ± 0.39	7.26 ± 0.53
Glaze IV	32	62–91	71.12 ± 0.66	5.56 ± 0.47	7.82 ± 0.66
Glazes V and VI	24	63–100	74.42 ± 1.17	8.48 ± 0.83	11.40 ± 1.11

TABLE V–9. MIDDLE INDEX OF FEMUR

Right

Males	No.	Range	Mean	S. D.	V.
Total Series A	159	69.70–111.54	88.65 ± 0.46	8.57 ± 0.32	9.67 ± 0.37
Black-on-white and Glaze I	24	71.43–100.00	85.75 ± 0.84	6.12 ± 0.60	7.14 ± 0.69
Glazes II and III	61	70.97–107.67	88.28 ± 0.77	8.91 ± 0.54	10.09 ± 0.62
Glaze IV	35	69.70–100.00	87.34 ± 0.95	8.33 ± 0.67	9.54 ± 0.77
Glazes V and VI	39	75.00–111.54	92.82 ± 0.83	7.70 ± 0.59	8.30 ± 0.63
Females					
Total Series A	116	70.37–113.64	91.60 ± 0.46	7.29 ± 0.32	7.96 ± 0.35
Black-on-white and Glaze I	20	70.37–103.70	88.30 ± 1.30	8.60 ± 0.92	9.74 ± 1.04
Glazes II and III	41	75.00–108.70	90.93 ± 0.62	5.91 ± 0.44	6.50 ± 0.48
Glaze IV	30	79.31–108.33	93.30 ± 0.88	7.15 ± 0.62	7.66 ± 0.67
Glazes V and VI	25	83.02–113.64	93.44 ± 0.98	7.30 ± 0.70	7.81 ± 0.74

Left

Males	No.	Range	Mean	S. D.	V.
Total Series A	156	68.75–116.00	86.97 ± 0.48	8.95 ± 0.34	10.29 ± 0.39
Black-on-white and Glaze I	25	72.73–100.00	84.76 ± 1.06	7.89 ± 0.75	9.31 ± 0.89
Glazes II and III	59	68.75–100.00	85.56 ± 0.65	7.44 ± 0.46	8.70 ± 0.54
Glaze IV	34	72.31–104.00	86.15 ± 0.98	8.45 ± 0.69	9.81 ± 0.80
Glazes V and VI	38	71.88–116.00	91.37 ± 1.16	10.58 ± 0.82	11.58 ± 0.90
Females					
Total Series A	118	74.14–117.39	92.24 ± 0.47	7.52 ± 0.33	8.15 ± 0.36
Black-on-white and Glaze I	19	74.14–100.00	86.11 ± 1.15	7.43 ± 0.81	8.63 ± 0.94
Glazes II and III	43	83.02–117.39	92.67 ± 0.52	5.02 ± 0.37	5.42 ± 0.39
Glaze IV	32	82.76–114.29	94.78 ± 0.93	7.77 ± 0.66	8.20 ± 0.69
Glazes V and VI	24	81.48–108.00	92.92 ± 1.00	7.26 ± 0.71	7.81 ± 0.76

OBSERVATIONS

The shape of the femoral shaft is predominatingly prismatic in both sexes and at all periods. About 65 per cent of male skeletons and 85 per cent of female skeletons show this form of femoral shaft. In the male series about 27 per cent of femora have plano-convex shafts, but only about nine per cent of females show this form. No period differences are observable. Differences in shape of shaft between right and left femora are negligible (Table V–10).

Forward curvature or bowing of the femoral shaft is more marked in male skeletons than in female skeletons. As is usually the case with Indians, this bowing of the femoral shaft is a conspicuous feature of the bone (Table V–11).

The linea aspera usually exhibits a medium development in males and a submedium development in females (Table V–12). There are no period differences.

Femoral torsion is pronounced or medium in the majority of males and is somewhat greater in right femora than in left femora. Males slightly exceed females in amount of femoral torsion. In both sexes the maximum femoral torsion seems to occur in the Glaze II and III subgroup (Table V–13).

Poiret's facet or "squatting facets" on the femoral neck are found in varying degrees of development in more than half of the male femora and in a lesser proportion of females. In the females these facets become progressively rarer from period to period but no such trend is observable in the male series (Table V–14).

Table V–15 shows the association of a *Crista hypotrochanterica* with combinations of the *Fossa hypotrochanterica*, the flange, and the third trochanter proper. The most frequent development is a moderate crest unaccompanied by any other feature. The third trochanter occurs most commonly in conjunction with an absence of a hypotrochanteric crest. Such a condition is especially common in female femora. A flange lateral to the gluteal crest does not usually occur in association with a third trochanter. The development of the *Crista hypotrochanterica* is more pronounced in males than in females.

TABLE V–10. SHAPE OF SHAFT OF FEMUR

Right

	B.-on-W. and Gl. I		Gls. II and III		Glaze IV		Gls. V and VI		Total	
Males	No.	Per cent	No.	Per cent	No.	Per cent	No.	Per cent	No.	Per cent
Prismatic	17	62.93	41	66.17	23	63.89	26	66.67	107	65.24
Plano-convex	8	29.63	14	22.58	12	33.34	11	28.21	45	27.44
Quadrilateral	1	3.70	3	4.84	1	2.78	1	2.56	6	3.66
Oval	1	3.70	4	6.45	0	0	1	2.56	6	3.66
Irregular	0	0	0	0	0	0	0	0	0	0
Total	27		62		36		39		164	

Coefficient of contingency 0.21

	B.-on-W. and Gl. I		Gls. II and III		Glaze IV		Gls. V and VI		Total	
Females										
Prismatic	17	85.00	36	85.71	27	90.00	19	79.17	99	85.34
Plano-convex	2	10.00	5	11.90	0	0	4	16.67	11	9.48
Quadrilateral	0	0	0	0	0	0	0	0	0	0
Oval	1	5.00	1	2.38	2	6.67	1	4.17	5	4.31
Irregular	0	0	0	0	1	3.33	0	0	1	0.86
Total	20		42		30		24		116	

Coefficient of contingency 0.26

Left

	B.-on-W. and Gl. I		Gls. II and III		Glaze IV		Gls. V and VI		Total	
Males										
Prismatic	17	68.00	41	66.13	20	57.14	27	69.23	105	65.22
Plano-convex	6	24.00	14	22.58	14	40.00	10	25.64	44	37.33
Quadrilateral	1	4.00	3	4.84	1	2.86	0	0	5	3.11
Oval	1	4.00	4	6.45	0	0	1	2.56	6	3.73
Irregular	0	0	0	0	0	0	1	2.56	1	0.62
Total	25		62		35		39		161	

Coefficient of contingency 0.28

	B.-on-W. and Gl. I		Gls. II and III		Glaze IV		Gls. V and VI		Total	
Females										
Prismatic	17	85.00	39	88.64	28	87.50	18	78.26	102	85.71
Plano-convex	2	10.00	4	9.09	0	0	4	17.39	10	8.40
Quadrilateral	0	0	0	0	0	0	0	0	0	0
Oval	1	5.00	1	2.27	3	9.38	1	4.35	6	5.04
Irregular	0	0	0	0	1	3.13	0	0	1	0.84
Total	20		44		32		23		119	

Coefficient of contingency 0.32

TABLE V-11. FORWARD CURVATURE OF SHAFT OF FEMUR

Right

Males	Submedium		Medium		Pronounced		Very Pronounced		Total
	No.	Per cent	No.	Per cent	No.	Per cent	No.	Per cent	No.
B.-on-W. and Glaze I	1	3.85	15	57.69	8	30.77	2	7.69	26
Glazes II and III	3	4.84	26	41.94	27	43.55	6	9.68	62
Glaze IV	1	2.94	17	50.00	16	47.06	0	0	34
Glazes V and VI	5	12.50	19	47.50	14	35.00	2	5.00	40
Total	10	6.17	77	47.53	65	40.12	10	6.17	162

Coefficient of contingency 0.22

Females	Submedium		Medium		Pronounced		Very Pronounced		Total
B.-on-W. and Glaze I	1	5.00	12	60.00	5	25.00	2	10.00	20
Glazes II and III	4	9.76	25	60.98	11	26.83	1	2.44	41
Glaze IV	2	6.67	16	53.33	11	36.67	1	3.33	30
Glazes V and VI	1	4.17	14	58.33	8	33.33	1	4.17	24
Total	8	6.96	67	58.33	35	30.43	5	4.35	115

Coefficient of contingency 0.18

Left

Males	Submedium		Medium		Pronounced		Very Pronounced		Total
B.-on-W. and Glaze I	1	4.00	14	56.00	7	28.00	3	12.00	25
Glazes II and III	3	4.84	26	41.94	27	43.55	6	9.68	62
Glaze IV	2	5.88	17	50.00	15	44.12	0	0	34
Glazes V and VI	5	12.82	20	51.28	12	30.77	2	5.13	39
Total	11	6.88	77	48.12	61	38.12	11	6.88	160

Coefficient of contingency 0.24

Females	Submedium		Medium		Pronounced		Very Pronounced		Total
B.-on-W. and Glaze I	1	5.00	12	60.00	5	25.00	2	10.00	20
Glazes II and III	4	9.09	27	61.36	12	27.27	1	2.27	44
Glaze IV	2	6.25	17	53.13	12	37.50	1	3.13	32
Glazes V and VI	1	4.17	14	58.33	8	33.33	1	4.17	24
Total	8	6.67	70	58.33	37	30.83	5	4.17	120

Coefficient of contingency 0.17

TABLE V-12. LINEA ASPERA

Right

Males	Submedium		Medium		Pronounced		Very Pronounced		Total
	No.	Per cent	No.	Per cent	No.	Per cent	No.	Per cent	No.
B.-on-W. and Glaze I	9	34.62	11	42.31	6	23.08	0	0	26
Glazes II and III	25	40.32	29	46.77	7	11.29	1	1.61	62
Glaze IV	10	28.57	17	48.57	8	22.86	0	0	35
Glazes V and VI	15	37.50	17	42.50	8	20.00	0	0	40
Total	59	36.20	74	45.40	29	17.79	1	0.61	163

Coefficient of contingency 0.18

Females	Submedium		Medium		Pronounced		Very Pronounced		Total
B.-on-W. and Glaze I	11	55.00	7	35.00	2	10.00	0	0	20
Glazes II and III	31	73.81	11	26.19	0	0	0	0	42
Glaze IV	21	70.00	9	30.00	0	0	0	0	30
Glazes V and VI	13	54.17	9	37.50	2	8.33	0	0	24
Total	76	65.52	36	31.03	4	3.44	0	0	116

Coefficient of contingency 0.25

Left

Males	Submedium		Medium		Pronounced		Very Pronounced		Total
	No.	Per cent	No.	Per cent	No.	Per cent	No.	Per cent	No.
B.-on-W. and Glaze I	10	40.00	10	40.00	5	20.00	0	0	25
Glazes II and III	24	39.34	29	47.54	7	11.48	1	1.64	61
Glaze IV	10	28.57	17	48.57	8	22.86	0	0	35
Glazes V and VI	15	38.46	16	41.03	8	20.51	0	0	39
Total	59	36.88	72	45.00	28	17.50	1	0.62	160

Coefficient of contingency 0.17

Females	Submedium		Medium		Pronounced		Very Pronounced		Total
B.-on-W. and Glaze I	10	50.00	7	35.00	3	15.00	0	0	20
Glazes II and III	31	70.45	13	29.55	0	0	0	0	44
Glaze IV	23	71.88	9	28.13	0	0	0	0	32
Glazes V and VI	13	56.52	8	34.78	2	8.70	0	0	23
Total	77	64.71	37	31.09	5	4.20	0	0	119

Coefficient of contingency 0.30

TABLE V–13. FEMORAL TORSION

Right

Males	B.-on-W. and Gl. I		Gls. II and III		Glaze IV		Gls. V and VI		Total	
	No.	Per cent	No.	Per cent	No.	Per cent	No.	Per cent	No.	Per cent
Absent	2	7.69	2	3.28	1	2.94	1	2.50	6	3.73
Submedium	3	11.54	12	19.67	8	23.53	2	5.00	25	15.53
Medium	10	38.46	14	22.95	11	32.35	20	50.00	55	34.16
Pronounced	10	38.46	27	44.26	11	32.35	16	40.00	64	39.75
Very pronounced	1	3.85	6	9.84	3	8.82	1	2.50	11	6.83
Total	26		61		34		40		161	

Coefficient of contingency 0.29

Females	B.-on-W. and Gl. I		Gls. II and III		Glaze IV		Gls. V and VI		Total	
Absent	0	0	1	2.44	0	0	2	8.70	3	2.63
Submedium	6	30.00	4	9.76	6	20.00	5	21.74	21	18.42
Medium	6	30.00	14	34.15	11	36.67	9	39.13	40	35.09
Pronounced	4	20.00	18	43.90	12	40.00	7	30.43	41	35.96
Very pronounced	4	20.00	4	9.76	1	3.33	0	0	9	7.89
Total	20		41		30		23		114	

Coefficient of contingency 0.35

Left

Males	B.-on-W. and Gl. I		Gls. II and III		Glaze IV		Gls. V and VI		Total	
Absent	2	8.00	2	3.28	2	5.71	1	2.56	7	4.38
Submedium	2	8.00	13	21.31	9	25.71	3	7.69	27	16.88
Medium	12	48.00	21	34.43	14	40.00	25	64.10	72	45.00
Pronounced	9	36.00	23	37.70	9	25.71	9	23.08	50	31.25
Very pronounced	0	0	2	3.28	1	2.86	1	2.56	4	2.50
Total	25		61		35		39		160	

Females	B.-on-W. and Gl. I		Gls. II and III		Glaze IV		Gls. V and VI		Total	
Absent	0	0	1	2.38	0	0	2	8.70	3	2.56
Submedium	6	30.00	5	11.90	9	28.13	5	21.74	25	21.37
Medium	6	30.00	19	45.24	13	40.63	12	52.17	50	42.74
Pronounced	7	35.00	15	35.71	10	31.25	4	17.39	36	30.77
Very pronounced	1	5.00	2	4.76	0	0	0	0	3	2.56
Total	20		42		32		23		117	

TABLE V–14. "Squatting Facets" on Femora

Right

Males	B.-on-W. and Gl. I		Gls. II and III		Glaze IV		Gls. V and VI		Total	
	No.	Per cent	No.	Per cent	No.	Per cent	No.	Per cent	No.	Per cent
Absent	9	34.62	26	42.62	18	51.43	14	35.00	67	44.36
Submedium	5	19.23	17	27.87	6	17.14	5	12.50	33	20.37
Medium	9	34.62	9	14.75	7	20.00	12	30.00	37	22.84
Pronounced	3	11.54	9	14.75	4	11.43	9	22.50	25	15.43
Total	26		61		35		40		162	
Females										
Absent	9	47.37	23	56.10	16	59.26	19	79.17	67	60.36
Submedium	3	15.79	11	26.83	7	25.93	3	12.50	24	21.62
Medium	6	31.58	3	7.32	4	14.81	2	8.33	15	13.51
Pronounced	1	5.26	4	9.76	0	0	0	0	5	4.50
Total	19		41		27		24		111	

Left

Males	B.-on-W. and Gl. I		Gls. II and III		Glaze IV		Gls. V and VI		Total	
Absent	8	32.00	25	40.32	18	51.43	14	35.90	65	40.37
Submedium	4	16.00	18	29.03	6	17.14	5	12.82	33	20.50
Medium	11	44.00	10	16.13	7	20.00	11	28.21	39	24.22
Pronounced	2	8.00	9	14.52	4	11.43	9	23.08	24	14.91
Total	25		62		35		39		161	
Females										
Absent	9	47.37	25	56.82	17	58.62	14	73.68	65	58.56
Submedium	3	15.79	12	27.27	8	27.59	3	15.79	26	23.42
Medium	6	31.58	3	6.82	4	13.79	2	10.53	15	13.51
Pronounced	1	5.26	4	9.09	0	0	0	0	5	4.50
Total	19		44		29		19		111	

TABLE V–15. Crista Associated with Fossa, Flange, and Third Trochanter

Right

Males	Crista Absent		Crista Submedium		Crista Medium		Crista Pronounced		Crista Very Pronounced		Total	
	No.	Per cent	No.	Per cent	No.	Per cent	No.	Per cent	No.	Per cent	No.	Per cent
Fossa	12	25.53	18	40.00	17	28.81	2	22.22	0	0	49	30.06
Fossa and third troch.	4	8.51	0	0	0	0	0	0	0	0	4	2.45
Flange	0	0	2	4.44	2	3.39	3	33.33	1	33.33	8	4.91
Flange and third troch.	3	6.38	0	0	0	0	0	0	0	0	3	1.84
Third trochanter	8	17.02	0	0	3	5.08	1	11.11	0	0	12	7.36
Crista without others.	20	42.55	25	55.56	37	62.71	3	33.33	2	66.67	87	53.37
Total	47		45		59		9		3		163	

Coefficient of contingency 0.55

Females	Crista Absent		Crista Submedium		Crista Medium		Crista Pronounced		Crista Very Pronounced		Total	
Fossa	10	31.25	22	43.14	6	19.35	0	0	0	0	38	32.76
Fossa and flange	1	3.13	0	0	1	3.23	0	0	0	0	2	1.72
Fossa and third troch.	4	12.50	1	1.96	0	0	0	0	0	0	5	4.31
Flange	1	3.13	1	1.96	2	6.45	0	0	0	0	4	3.45
Flange and third troch.	1	3.13	0	0	0	0	0	0	0	0	1	0.09
Third trochanter	8	25.00	1	1.96	0	0	0	0	0	0	9	7.76
Crista without others.	7	21.88	26	50.98	22	70.97	2	100.00	0	0	57	49.14
Total	32		51		31		2		0		116	100.00

Coefficient of contingency 0.52

Left

	Crista Absent		Crista Submedium		Crista Medium		Crista Pronounced		Crista Very Pronounced		Total	
Males	No.	Per cent	No.	Per cent	No.	Per cent	No.	Per cent	No.	Per cent	No.	Per cent
Fossa	12	29.27	16	37.21	20	31.25	0	0	0	0	48	39.19
Fossa and third troch.	2	4.88	0	0	0	0	0	0	0	0	2	1.26
Flange	0	0	2	4.65	3	4.69	2	25.00	1	33.33	8	5.03
Flange and third troch.	2	4.88	0	0	0	0	0	0	0	0	2	1.26
Third trochanter	8	19.51	0	0	1	1.56	1	12.50	0	0	10	6.29
Crista without others .	17	41.46	25	58.14	40	62.50	5	62.50	2	66.67	89	55.97
Total	41		43		64		8		3		159	
Females												
Fossa	9	29.03	26	47.27	5	15.63	0	0	0	0	40	33.33
Fossa and flange	1	3.23	0	0	1	3.13	0	0	0	0	2	1.67
Fossa and third troch.	3	9.68	1	1.82	1	3.13	0	0	0	0	5	4.17
Flange	1	3.23	0	0	4	12.50	1	50.00	0	0	6	5.00
Flange and third troch. and fossa	0	0	1	1.82	0	0	0	0	0	0	1	0.83
Third trochanter	7	22.58	0	0	0	0	0	0	0	0	7	5.83
Crista without others	10	32.26	27	49.09	21	65.63	1	50.00	0	0	59	49.17
Total	31		55		32		2		0	0	120	

TIBIA

MEASUREMENTS AND INDICES

The maximum length of the tibia seems to decline in both sexes from the earliest to the latest periods. In the female series the antero-posterior diameter at the middle of the shaft shows a similar progressive diminution, but this is not true of the males. The lateral shaft diameters in both sexes are at their maximum in the earliest period. Precisely similar conditions obtain in the case of the antero-posterior and lateral shaft diameters at the level of the nutrient foramen (Tables V–16, 17, 18, 19, 20).

The index of platycnemia and the middle index of the tibia (Tables V–21, 22) show a prevalent condition of platycnemia which becomes more pronounced in males from the early to the late periods and in the females seem to display a tendency in the opposite direction.

The tibio-femoral index (Table V–23) is somewhat lower in females than in males and lower on the left side in both sexes. This index seems to increase in the males after the first period and to decrease in the females.

TABLE V–16. MAXIMUM LENGTH OF TIBIA

Right

Males	No.	Range	Mean	S. D.	V.
Total Series A	130	312–415	357.69 ± 1.15	19.50 ± 0.80	5.45 ± 0.23
Black-on-white and Glaze I	19	320–415	359.53 ± 3.64	23.53 ± 2.58	6.54 ± 0.72
Glazes II and III	48	316–401	358.02 ± 1.91	19.64 ± 1.35	5.49 ± 0.38
Glaze IV	28	325–392	357.32 ± 1.98	15.50 ± 1.40	4.34 ± 0.39
Glazes V and VI	35	312–401	353.43 ± 2.31	20.30 ± 1.64	5.74 ± 0.46
Females					
Total Series A	90	288–369	327.22 ± 1.10	15.45 ± 0.78	4.72 ± 0.24
Black-on-white and Glaze I	14	311–363	339.14 ± 2.54	14.08 ± 1.79	4.15 ± 0.53
Glazes II and III	31	288–369	323.16 ± 2.00	16.50 ± 1.41	5.10 ± 0.44
Glaze IV	24	304–358	322.33 ± 1.74	12.65 ± 1.23	3.92 ± 0.38
Glazes V and VI	21	298–346	324.43 ± 1.88	12.80 ± 1.33	3.94 ± 0.41

Left

Males	No.	Range	Mean	S. D.	V.
Total Series A	117	311–413	357.78 ± 1.17	18.75 ± 0.83	5.24 ± 0.23
Black-on-white and Glaze I	18	338–413	360.06 ± 3.52	22.13 ± 2.49	6.15 ± 0.69
Glazes II and III	43	312–402	358.86 ± 1.90	18.52 ± 1.35	5.16 ± 0.38
Glaze IV	24	321–392	357.08 ± 2.20	16.00 ± 1.56	4.48 ± 0.44
Glazes V and VI	32	311–393	352.67 ± 2.19	18.40 ± 1.55	5.22 ± 0.44
Females					
Total Series A	81	285–362	323.83 ± 1.12	14.90 ± 0.79	4.60 ± 0.24
Black-on-white and Glaze I	14	310–359	335.21 ± 2.35	13.04 ± 1.66	3.89 ± 0.50
Glazes II and III	27	285–362	317.59 ± 1.96	15.10 ± 1.39	4.75 ± 0.44
Glaze IV	21	298–343	315.86 ± 1.95	13.25 ± 1.38	4.19 ± 0.44
Glazes V and VI	19	296–347	325.47 ± 1.91	12.35 ± 1.35	3.80 ± 0.42

TABLE V–17. MIDDLE DIAMETER OF TIBIA: ANTERO–POSTERIOR

Right

Males	No.	Range	Mean	S. D.	V.
Total Series A	146	27–40	32.69 ± 0.15	2.72 ± 0.11	8.32 ± 0.33
Black-on-white and Glaze I	21	27–37	32.24 ± 0.38	2.58 ± 0.27	8.00 ± 0.83
Glazes II and III	55	27–40	32.55 ± 0.24	2.67 ± 0.17	8.20 ± 0.53
Glaze IV	33	29–37	33.35 ± 0.29	2.44 ± 0.20	7.30 ± 0.16
Glazes V and VI	37	27–39.5	32.45 ± 0.33	2.93 ± 0.23	9.03 ± 0.71
Females					
Total Series A	105	23–34.5	27.93 ± 0.13	1.97 ± 0.09	7.05 ± 0.33
Black-on-white and Glaze I	14	27–32	28.78 ± 0.30	1.65 ± 0.21	5.73 ± 0.73
Glazes II and III	42	23–34.5	28.29 ± 0.23	2.16 ± 0.16	7.65 ± 0.56
Glaze IV	24	25–32	27.40 ± 0.24	1.76 ± 0.17	6.41 ± 0.62
Glazes V and VI	25	25–30	27.36 ± 0.19	1.42 ± 0.14	5.19 ± 0.50

Left

Males	No.	Range	Mean	S. D.	V.
Total Series A	146	27–39	32.86 ± 0.14	2.45 ± 0.10	7.46 ± 0.29
Black-on-white and Glaze I	22	29–37	33.07 ± 0.29	2.05 ± 0.21	6.20 ± 0.63
Glazes II and III	57	28–38	32.33 ± 0.21	2.34 ± 0.15	7.25 ± 0.46
Glaze IV	31	29–37	33.71 ± 0.24	1.99 ± 0.17	5.90 ± 0.50
Glazes V and VI	36	27–39	32.85 ± 0.32	2.82 ± 0.22	8.60 ± 0.68
Females					
Total Series A	107	24–33	28.06 ± 0.12	1.82 ± 0.08	6.48 ± 0.30
Black-on-white and Glaze I	15	27–31	28.87 ± 0.21	1.20 ± 0.15	4.16 ± 0.51
Glazes II and III	43	24–33	28.26 ± 0.20	1.98 ± 0.14	7.02 ± 0.51
Glaze IV	26	25–32	27.62 ± 0.23	1.74 ± 0.16	6.30 ± 0.59
Glazes V and VI	23	24–31	27.60 ± 0.23	1.62 ± 0.16	5.87 ± 0.58

TABLE V–18. MIDDLE DIAMETER OF TIBIA: LATERAL

Right

Males	No.	Range	Mean	S. D.	V.
Total Series A	146	16–26	20.51 ± 0.13	2.23 ± 0.09	10.87 ± 0.43
Black-on-white and Glaze I	21	17–26	20.95 ± 0.32	2.20 ± 0.23	10.48 ± 1.09
Glazes II and III	55	16–25	20.39 ± 0.19	2.06 ± 0.13	10.17 ± 0.65
Glaze IV	33	18–26	20.94 ± 0.26	2.24 ± 0.19	10.70 ± 0.89
Glazes V and VI	37	17–26	20.05 ± 0.23	2.09 ± 0.16	10.42 ± 0.82
Females					
Total Series A	104	16–23	18.44 ± 0.10	1.46 ± 0.07	7.92 ± 0.37
Black-on-white and Glaze I	14	17–21	18.86 ± 0.23	1.30 ± 0.17	6.89 ± 0.88
Glazes II and III	42	16–23	18.02 ± 0.17	1.59 ± 0.12	8.82 ± 0.65
Glaze IV	23	16–21	18.54 ± 0.18	1.29 ± 0.13	6.96 ± 0.69
Glazes V and VI	25	16–21	18.78 ± 0.17	1.24 ± 0.12	6.63 ± 0.63

Left

Males	No.	Range	Mean	S. D.	V.
Total Series A	146	16–29	20.06 ± 0.13	2.34 ± 0.09	11.67 ± 0.46
Black-on-white and Glaze I	22	17–25	21.00 ± 0.25	1.76 ± 0.18	8.38 ± 0.85
Glazes II and III	57	16–25	20.35 ± 0.19	2.11 ± 0.13	10.37 ± 0.66
Glaze IV	31	18–29	21.28 ± 0.32	2.60 ± 0.22	12.22 ± 1.05
Glazes V and VI	36	16–26	19.97 ± 0.26	2.30 ± 0.18	11.52 ± 0.92
Females					
Total Series A	107	16–23	18.49 ± 0.09	1.36 ± 0.06	7.36 ± 0.34
Black-on-white and Glaze I	15	18–23	19.07 ± 0.25	1.44 ± 0.18	7.55 ± 0.93
Glazes II and III	43	16–21	18.05 ± 0.14	1.38 ± 0.10	7.67 ± 0.56
Glaze IV	26	17–20.5	18.75 ± 0.15	1.12 ± 0.10	5.97 ± 0.56
Glazes V and VI	23	16.5–21	18.65 ± 0.16	1.12 ± 0.11	6.03 ± 0.60

TABLE V–19. NUTRITIVE FORAMEN DIAMETER OF TIBIA: ANTERO–POSTERIOR

Right

Males	No.	Range	Mean	S. D.	V.
Total Series A	142	28–43	35.42 ± 0.17	2.95 ± 0.12	8.33 ± 0.33
Black-on-white and Glaze I	20	29–41	35.20 ± 0.48	3.17 ± 0.34	9.01 ± 0.96
Glazes II and III	54	28–43	35.13 ± 0.30	3.22 ± 0.21	9.17 ± 0.59
Glaze IV	33	31–40	36.42 ± 0.25	2.14 ± 0.19	5.89 ± 0.49
Glazes V and VI	35	29–41	35.03 ± 0.32	2.84 ± 0.23	8.09 ± 0.65
Females					
Total Series A	100	26–35	29.96 ± 0.13	1.93 ± 0.09	6.44 ± 0.31
Black-on-white and Glaze I	14	28–34	30.86 ± 0.32	1.80 ± 0.23	5.83 ± 0.74
Glazes II and III	39	26–35	30.53 ± 0.21	1.97 ± 0.15	6.45 ± 0.49
Glaze IV	22	27–33	29.80 ± 0.23	1.60 ± 0.16	5.37 ± 0.55
Glazes V and VI	25	26.5–33	29.92 ± 0.25	1.84 ± 0.18	6.15 ± 0.59

Left

Males	No.	Range	Mean	S. D.	V.
Total Series A	144	26–45	35.53 ± 0.17	3.11 ± 0.12	8.75 ± 0.35
Black-on-white and Glaze I	22	31–43	36.09 ± 0.44	3.04 ± 0.31	8.42 ± 0.86
Glazes II and III	54	26–45	34.91 ± 0.32	3.47 ± 0.22	8.87 ± 0.58
Glaze IV	32	31–40	36.23 ± 0.25	2.13 ± 0.18	5.88 ± 0.50
Glazes V and VI	36	29–42	35.39 ± 0.36	3.21 ± 0.26	9.07 ± 0.72
Females					
Total Series A	104	26–35.5	30.45 ± 0.13	1.99 ± 0.09	6.54 ± 0.31
Black-on-white and Glaze I	15	29–35	31.40 ± 0.30	1.70 ± 0.21	5.41 ± 0.67
Glazes II and III	40	27–35.5	30.36 ± 0.21	1.98 ± 0.15	6.52 ± 0.49
Glaze IV	25	26–34	30.26 ± 0.26	1.96 ± 0.19	6.46 ± 0.62
Glazes V and VI	24	26–35	30.14 ± 0.28	2.02 ± 0.20	6.72 ± 0.65

TABLE V–20. NUTRITIVE FORAMEN DIAMETER OF TIBIA: LATERAL

Right

Males	No.	Range	Mean	S. D.	V.
Total Series A	142	17–27	21.51 ± 0.12	2.04 ± 0.08	9.48 ± 0.38
Black-on-white and Glaze I	20	19–27	21.80 ± 0.34	2.25 ± 0.24	10.32 ± 1.10
Glazes II and III	54	17–26	21.43 ± 0.19	2.08 ± 0.13	9.71 ± 0.63
Glaze IV	33	18–26	21.91 ± 0.22	1.88 ± 0.16	8.60 ± 0.71
Glazes V and VI	35	17.5–26	21.09 ± 0.23	1.98 ± 0.16	9.36 ± 0.75
Females					
Total Series A	100	16.5–24	19.51 ± 0.11	1.57 ± 0.07	8.05 ± 0.38
Black-on-white and Glaze I	14	18–24	20.07 ± 0.32	1.75 ± 0.22	8.72 ± 1.11
Glazes II and III	39	16.5–23	19.05 ± 0.16	1.50 ± 0.11	7.85 ± 0.60
Glaze IV	22	17–22	19.61 ± 0.22	1.55 ± 0.16	7.90 ± 0.80
Glazes V and VI	25	17–22	19.90 ± 0.19	1.40 ± 0.13	7.06 ± 0.67

Left

Males	No.	Range	Mean	S. D.	V.
Total Series A	143	17–28	21.59 ± 0.13	2.22 ± 0.09	10.28 ± 0.41
Black-on-white and Glaze I	21	18–26	22.00 ± 0.31	2.11 ± 0.22	9.59 ± 1.00
Glazes II and III	54	17–26	21.53 ± 0.20	2.18 ± 0.14	10.13 ± 0.66
Glaze IV	32	18–27	21.83 ± 0.26	2.14 ± 0.18	9.80 ± 0.83
Glazes V and VI	36	17–28	21.21 ± 0.26	2.27 ± 0.18	10.70 ± 0.85
Females					
Total Series A	103	17–23	19.55 ± 0.10	1.48 ± 0.07	7.57 ± 0.36
Black-on-white and Glaze I	15	19–23	20.13 ± 0.21	1.20 ± 0.15	5.96 ± 0.73
Glazes II and III	39	17–22	18.99 ± 0.16	1.49 ± 0.11	7.85 ± 0.60
Glaze IV	25	17–22	19.84 ± 0.19	1.43 ± 0.14	7.21 ± 0.69
Glazes V and VI	24	17–22	19.83 ± 0.19	1.39 ± 0.14	7.01 ± 0.68

TABLE V–21. MIDDLE INDEX OF TIBIA

Right

Males	No.	Range	Mean	S. D.	V.
Total Series A	146	49–80	63.04 ± 0.38	6.79 ± 0.27	10.77 ± 0.42
Black-on-white and Glaze I	21	52–72	64.90 ± 0.86	5.86 ± 0.61	9.03 ± 0.94
Glazes II and III	55	49–77	62.91 ± 0.53	5.87 ± 0.38	9.33 ± 0.60
Glaze IV	33	49–78	62.94 ± 0.64	7.75 ± 0.64	12.31 ± 1.02
Glazes V and VI	37	49–80	62.08 ± 0.81	7.30 ± 0.57	11.75 ± 0.92
Females					
Total Series A	104	52–83	66.30 ± 0.42	6.37 ± 0.30	9.61 ± 0.45
Black-on-white and Glaze I	14	60–75	66.07 ± 0.74	4.13 ± 0.53	6.25 ± 0.80
Glazes II and III	42	52–83	63.95 ± 0.67	6.41 ± 0.47	10.02 ± 0.74
Glaze IV	23	56–78	68.04 ± 0.96	6.85 ± 0.68	10.07 ± 1.00
Glazes V and VI	25	55–78	68.76 ± 0.73	5.38 ± 0.51	7.82 ± 0.75

Left

Males	No.	Range	Mean	S. D.	V.
Total Series A	146	49–82	62.84 ± 0.38	6.80 ± 0.27	10.82 ± 0.43
Black-on-white and Glaze I	22	52–71	63.45 ± 0.69	4.81 ± 0.49	7.58 ± 0.77
Glazes II and III	57	49–78	63.35 ± 0.54	6.07 ± 0.38	9.58 ± 0.60
Glaze IV	31	50–82	63.26 ± 0.95	7.87 ± 0.67	12.44 ± 1.06
Glazes V and VI	36	50–78	61.08 ± 0.84	7.49 ± 0.50	12.26 ± 0.97
Females					
Total Series A	107	50–80	66.08 ± 0.39	5.99 ± 0.28	9.06 ± 0.42
Black-on-white and Glaze I	15	60–74	66.00 ± 0.68	3.91 ± 0.48	5.92 ± 0.73
Glazes II and III	43	50–79	64.07 ± 0.63	6.16 ± 0.45	9.61 ± 0.70
Glaze IV	26	59–80	68.15 ± 0.80	6.04 ± 0.56	8.86 ± 0.83
Glazes V and VI	23	53–79	67.52 ± 0.77	5.45 ± 0.54	8.07 ± 0.80

TABLE V–22. INDEX OF PLATYCNEMIA

Right

Males	No.	Range	Mean	S. D.	V.
Total Series A	141	45–79	61.17 ± 0.36	6.42 ± 0.26	10.50 ± 0.42
Black-on-white and Glaze I	20	50–73	62.65 ± 1.08	7.16 ± 0.76	11.43 ± 1.22
Glazes II and III	53	45–79	61.49 ± 0.61	6.61 ± 0.43	10.75 ± 0.70
Glaze IV	33	50–72	63.73 ± 0.72	6.15 ± 0.51	9.65 ± 0.80
Glazes V and VI	35	47–76	60.40 ± 0.69	6.03 ± 0.49	9.98 ± 0.80
Females					
Total Series A	100	53–79	64.68 ± 0.41	6.03 ± 0.29	9.32 ± 0.44
Black-on-white and Glaze I	14	56–79	65.21 ± 1.11	6.15 ± –.78	9.43 ± 1.20
Glazes II and III	39	53–78	62.54 ± 0.59	5.50 ± 0.42	8.79 ± 0.67
Glaze IV	22	55–75	65.82 ± 0.83	5.78 ± 0.59	8.78 ± 0.89
Glazes V and VI	25	55–78	66.72 ± 0.80	5.93 ± 0.57	8.89 ± 0.85

Left

Males	No.	Range	Mean	S. D.	V.
Total Series A	142	45–86	61.08 ± 0.41	7.20 ± 0.29	11.79 ± 0.47
Black-on-white and Glaze I	21	49–73	61.38 ± 1.02	6.96 ± 0.72	11.34 ± 1.18
Glazes II and III	54	45–86	62.00 ± 0.70	7.63 ± 0.50	12.31 ± 0.80
Glaze IV	31	48–73	60.39 ± 0.75	6.17 ± 0.53	10.22 ± 0.88
Glazes V and VI	36	49–73	60.23 ± 0.81	7.18 ± 0.57	11.92 ± 0.95
Females					
Total Series A	103	51–85	64.59 ± 0.39	5.82 ± 0.27	9.01 ± 0.42
Black-on-white and Glaze I	15	54–70	64.20 ± 0.70	4.03 ± 0.50	6.28 ± 0.77
Glazes II and III	39	51–75	63.10 ± 0.59	5.43 ± 0.41	8.60 ± 0.66
Glaze IV	25	55–85	66.00 ± 0.94	6.97 ± 0.66	10.56 ± 1.01
Glazes V and VI	24	56–77	65.79 ± 0.75	5.42 ± 0.53	8.24 ± 0.80

TABLE V–23. TIBIO–FEMORAL INDEX

Right

Males	No.	Range	Mean	S. D.	V.
Total Series A	120	80.05–89.71	84.20 ± 0.13	2.11 ± 0.09	2.51 ± 0.11
Black-on-white and Glaze I	16	80.05–86.64	83.81 ± 0.25	1.46 ± 0.17	1.74 ± 0.21
Glazes II and III	43	80.52–89.71	84.49 ± 0.25	2.42 ± 0.18	2.86 ± 0.21
Glaze IV	27	80.59–87.38	84.00 ± 0.20	1 54 ± 0.20	1.83 ± 0.17
Glazes V and VI	34	80.81–88.61	84.21 ± 0.26	2.22 ± 0.18	2.64 ± 0.22
Females					
Total Series A	81	78.83–88.75	83.39 ± 0.14	1.89 ± 0.10	2.64 ± 0.22
Black-on-white and Glaze I	11	81.86–88.75	84.55 ± 0.41	2.02 ± 0.29	2.38 ± 0.34
Glazes II and III	28	80.46–87.47	83.36 ± 0.20	1.59 ± 0.14	1.91 ± 0.17
Glaze IV	22	80.31–85.91	83.45 ± 0.21	1.49 ± 0.15	1.78 ± 0.18
Glazes V and VI	20	78.83–86.20	82.75 ± 0.34	2.25 ± 0.24	2.72 ± 0.29

Left

Males	No.	Range	Mean	S. D.	V.
Total Series A	104	78.76–88.89	83.70 ± 0.13	2.03 ± 0.09	2.43 ± 0.11
Black-on-white and Glaze I	14	78.82–85.68	82.86 ± 0.35	1.92 ± 0.24	2.31 ± 0.30
Glazes II and III	40	79.80–88.89	84.05 ± 0.26	2.44 ± 0.18	2.90 ± 0.22
Glaze IV	21	80.54–86.22	83.67 ± 0.23	1.55 ± 0.16	1.85 ± 0.19
Glazes V and VI	29	78.76–86.95	83.66 ± 0.24	1.93 ± 0.17	2.31 ± 0.20
Females					
Total Series A	71	77.32–87.14	82.77 ± 0.16	2.02 ± 0.11	2.44 ± 0.14
Black-on-white and Glaze I	12	80.96–85.89	83.92 ± 0.28	1.44 ± 0.20	1.72 ± 0.24
Glazes II and III	23	79.23–85.52	82.87 ± 0.24	1.73 ± 0.17	2.09 ± 0.21
Glaze IV	20	77.32–87.14	82.15 ± 0.35	2.31 ± 0.25	2.81 ± 0.30
Glazes V and VI	16	79.14–85.57	82.56 ± 0.36	2.12 ± 0.25	2.57 ± 0.31

OBSERVATIONS

The shape of the tibial shaft at the center is classified according to the forms recognized by Hrdlička.[1] Type I approaches an equilateral triangle. Type II is a lateral triangle with the posterior surface of the bone oblique. In Type III the external surface of the tibia is concave. Type IV is quadrilateral, having the posterior surface of the bone divided into two parts by a vertical ridge. Type V has a convex posterior surface which is not clearly demarcated from the external and internal surfaces. The tibiae classified as "sabre-shaped" are so flattened laterally as to correspond to none of the forms mentioned above. Transitional forms between the types are very numerous.

The commonest shape of tibial shaft in both males and females is Type II, the lateral triangle. This occurs in about 26 per cent of males and 41 per cent of females of the Pecos series (Table V–24). In the males, Type III (with the external surface concave) occurs in 20 per cent of right bones and 18 per cent of left bones. This type occurs in only 5.45 per cent of female bones. The excavation of the external tibial surface which causes this concavity is probably an effect of strong development of the *Tibialis anterior* muscle and is consequently greater in males than in females and greater on the right side in right-footed persons. Type V, in which the posterior tibial surface is convex, occurs in about 18 per cent of male bones and about 21 per cent of female bones. It is a rather primitive and undifferentiated form of the bone. Type I, the equilateral triangle, is found in about 10 per cent of male bones and in about 24 per cent of female bones. It is clear that the sexes are markedly different in distribution of tibial shaft forms.

The distribution of the various types in the Glaze subgroups is extremely irregular and seems to show no definite trends.

Retroversion of the tibial head is oftenest pronounced in males and usually medium in females (Table V–25). No period differences of any intelligible character can be distinguished.

Convexity of the external tibial condyle is more marked in females than in males. This is probably a compensation for the lessened retroversion of the tibial head in females as compared with males. Both sexes squatted habitually and the tibial adaptation for this position may be effected by retroversion of the head or by a convexity of the external condyle or by a combination of both features. In both sexes the convexity of the external condyle seems to be especially marked in the earliest period of the occupation of the pueblo. This seems to be associated to some extent with a stronger retroversion of the tibial head in both sexes in the same subgroup (Table V–26).

"Squatting facets" on the anterior lip of the inferior tibial articular surface are usually present in both sexes. They are lacking in male tibiae oftener than in those of females (Table V–27). In both sexes these facets diminish in frequency in the successive periods and tend to show the maximum occurrence in the earliest subgroup.

[1] Hrdlička, 1920, pp. 120–125.

TABLE V–24. SHAPE OF SHAFT OF TIBIA

Right

	B.-on-W. and Gl. I		Gls. II and III		Glaze IV		Gls. V and VI		Total	
Males	No.	Per cent	No.	Per cent	No.	Per cent	No.	Per cent	No.	Per cent
Type I	2	9.52	8	13.33	2	5.88	2	5.41	14	9.21
" II	5	23.81	15	25.00	5	14.71	14	37.84	39	25.66
" I–III	0	0	1	1.67	0	0	0	0	1	0.66
" II–III	1	4.76	1	1.67	2	5.88	0	0	4	2.63
" III	5	23.81	10	16.67	8	23.53	7	18.92	30	19.74
" III–IV............	0	0	9	15.00	1	2.94	0	0	10	6.58
" III–V	0	0	0	0	1	2.94	0	0	1	0.66
" IV	2	9.52	3	5.00	3	8.82	4	10.81	12	7.89
" IV–V	0	0	4	6.67	4	11.76	0	0	8	5.26
" V	5	23.81	6	10.00	7	20.59	9	24.32	27	17.76
"Sabre" type	1	4.76	3	5.00	1	2.94	1	2.70	6	3.95
Total	21		60		34		37		152	

Left

	B.-on-W. and Gl. I		Gls. II and III		Glaze IV		Gls. V and VI		Total	
Males	No.	Per cent	No.	Per cent	No.	Per cent	No.	Per cent	No.	Per cent
Type I	3	14.29	8	13.79	2	6.06	2	5.71	15	10.20
" II	5	23.81	14	24.14	6	18.18	15	42.86	40	27.21
" I–III	0	0	1	1.72	0	0	0	0	1	0.68
" II–III	1	4.76	1	1.72	2	6.06	0	0	4	2.72
" III	4	19.05	10	17.24	7	21.21	5	14.29	26	17.69
" III–IV............	0	0	9	15.52	1	3.03	0	0	10	6.80
" IV	1	4.76	2	3.45	3	9.09	4	11.43	10	6.80
" IV–V	0	0	4	6.90	3	9.09	0	0	7	4.76
" V	6	28.57	6	10.34	8	24.24	8	22.86	28	19.05
"Sabre" type	1	4.76	3	5.17	1	3.03	1	2.86	6	4.08
Total	21		58		33		35		147	

Right and Left

	B.-on-W. and Gl. I		Gls. II and III		Glaze IV		Gls. V and VI		Total	
Females	No.	Per cent	No.	Per cent	No.	Per cent	No.	Per cent	No.	Per cent
Type I	4	23.53	6	14.63	7	25.93	9	36.00	26	23.64
" II	3	17.65	24	58.54	11	40.74	7	28.00	45	40.91
" III	1	5.88	3	7.32	2	7.41	0	0	6	5.45
" III–V	0	0	1	2.44	0	0	0	0	1	0.91
" IV	2	11.76	0	0	1	3.70	2	8.00	5	4.55
" IV–V	0	0	0	0	0	0	1	4.00	1	0.91
" V	6	35.29	6	14.63	5	18.52	6	24.00	23	20.91
"Sabre" type	0	0	0	0	1	3.70	0	0	1	0.91
Irregular	1	5.88	1	2.44	0	0	0	0	2	1.81
Total	17		41		27		25		110	

TABLE V–25. BACKWARD INCLINATION OF HEAD OF TIBIA

Right

	B.-on-W. and Gl. I		Gls. II and III		Glaze IV		Gls. V and VI		Total	
Males	No.	Per cent	No.	Per cent	No.	Per cent	No.	Per cent	No.	Per cent
Absent	0	0	0	0	1	3.23	0	0	1	0.08
Submedium	0	0	3	5.26	2	6.45	2	5.26	7	4.73
Medium	9	40.91	26	45.61	11	35.48	17	44.74	63	42.57
Pronounced	12	54.55	28	49.12	17	54.84	18	47.37	75	50.68
Very pronounced	1	4.55	0	0	0	0	1	2.63	2	1.35
Total	22		57		31		38		148	
Females										
Submedium	0	0	5	12.50	3	11.54	5	20.00	13	11.93
Medium	10	55.56	18	45.00	17	65.38	10	40.00	55	50.46
Pronounced	8	44.44	17	42.50	6	23.08	10	40.00	41	37.61
Total	18		40		26		25		109	

Left

	B.-on-W. and Gl. I		Gls. II and III		Glaze IV		Gls. V and VI		Total	
Males	No.	Per cent	No.	Per cent	No.	Per cent	No.	Per cent	No.	Per cent
Absent	0	0	0	0	1	3.57	0	0	1	0.71
Submedium	0	0	4	7.55	1	3.57	2	5.56	7	5.00
Medium	8	34.78	23	43.40	9	32.14	14	38.89	54	38.57
Pronounced	14	60.87	26	49.06	17	60.71	19	52.78	76	54.29
Very pronounced	1	4.35	0	0	0	0	1	2.78	2	1.43
Total	23		53		28		36		140	
Females										
Submedium	0	0	5	12.50	2	7.69	4	16.67	11	10.28
Medium	11	64.71	18	45.00	17	65.38	10	41.67	56	52.34
Pronounced	6	35.29	17	42.50	7	26.92	10	41.67	40	37.38
Total	17		40		26		24		107	

TABLE V–26. CONVEXITY OF EXTERNAL CONDYLES OF TIBIA

Right

	B.-on-W. and Gl. I		Gls. II and III		Glaze IV		Gls. V and VI		Total	
Males	No.	Per cent	No.	Per cent	No.	Per cent	No.	Per cent	No.	Per cent
Submedium convex	6	35.29	28	56.00	11	52.38	15	51.72	60	51.28
Medium convex	8	47.06	11	22.00	5	23.81	5	17.24	29	24.79
Pronouncedly convex.......	0	0	1	2.00	1	4.76	2	6.90	4	3.42
Flat	3	17.65	7	14.00	1	4.76	4	13.79	15	12.82
Concave.................	0	0	3	6.00	3	14.29	3	10.34	9	7.69
Total	17		50		21		29		117	
Females										
Submedium convex	1	7.69	17	47.22	8	38.10	7	41.18	33	37.93
Medium convex	6	46.15	13	36.11	7	33.33	8	47.06	34	39.08
Pronouncedly convex	3	23.08	2	5.56	2	9.52	0	0	7	8.05
Flat	1	7.69	3	8.33	1	4.76	2	11.76	7	8.05
Concave.................	2	15.38	1	2.78	3	14.29	0	0	6	6.90
Total	13		36		21		17		87	

Left

	B.-on-W. and Gl. I		Gls. II and III		Glaze IV		Gls. V and VI		Total	
	No.	Per cent	No.	Per cent	No.	Per cent	No.	Per cent	No.	Per cent
Males										
Submedium convex	6	33.33	27	57.45	11	50.00	14	50.00	58	50.43
Medium convex	9	50.00	10	21.28	6	27.27	5	17.86	30	26.09
Pronouncedly convex	0	0	1	2.13	1	4.55	2	7.14	4	3.48
Flat	2	11.11	6	12.77	1	4.55	4	14.29	13	11.30
Concave.................	1	5.56	3	6.38	3	13.64	3	10.71	10	8.70
Total	18		47		22		28		115	
Females										
Submedium convex	1	7.69	18	51.43	8	33.33	7	46.67	34	39.08
Medium convex	6	46.15	11	31.43	8	33.33	7	46.67	32	36.78
Pronouncedly convex	3	23.08	2	5.71	2	8.33	0	0	7	8.05
Flat	1	7.69	3	8.57	1	4.17	1	6.67	6	6.90
Concave.................	2	15.38	1	2.86	5	20.83	0	0	8	9.20
Total	13		35		24		15		87	

TABLE V–27. "SQUATTING FACETS" ON TIBIA

Right

	B.-on-W. and Gl. I		Gls. II and III		Glaze IV		Gls. V and VI		Total	
	No.	Per cent	No.	Per cent	No.	Per cent	No.	Per cent	No.	Per cent
Males										
Absent	4	20.00	8	13.56	7	21.88	10	26.32	29	19.46
Submedium	4	20.00	26	44.07	12	37.50	11	28.95	53	35.57
Medium	8	40.00	19	32.20	10	31.25	12	31.58	49	32.89
Pronounced	4	20.00	6	10.17	3	9.38	4	10.53	17	11.41
Very pronounced	0	0	0	0	0	0	1	2.63	1	0.67
Total	20		59		32		38		149	
Females										
Absent	3	17.65	6	15.00	3	14.29	5	19.23	17	16.35
Submedium	3	17.65	18	45.00	9	42.86	13	50.00	43	41.35
Medium	5	29.41	9	22.50	6	28.57	6	23.08	26	25.00
Pronounced	5	29.41	6	15.00	3	14.29	2	7.69	16	15.38
Very pronounced	1	5.88	1	2.50	0	0	0	0	2	1.92
Total	17		40		21		26		104	

Left

	B.-on-W. and Gl. I		Gls. II and III		Glaze IV		Gls. V and VI		Total	
Males										
Absent	5	21.74	8	14.29	8	25.00	10	26.32	31	20.81
Submedium	7	30.43	25	44.64	10	31.25	11	28.95	53	35.57
Medium	7	30.43	17	30.36	10	31.25	12	31.58	46	30.87
Pronounced	4	17.39	6	10.71	4	12.50	4	10.53	18	12.08
Very pronounced	0	0	0	0	0	0	1	2.63	1	0.67
Total	23		56		32		38		149	
Females										
Absent	3	16.67	7	17.50	4	17.39	5	20.00	19	17.92
Submedium	3	16.67	19	47.50	9	39.13	12	48.00	43	40.57
Medium	5	27.78	8	20.00	6	26.09	6	24.00	25	23.58
Pronounced	6	33.33	5	12.50	4	17.39	2	8.00	17	16.04
Very pronounced	1	5.56	1	2.50	0	0	0	0	2	1.89
Total	18		40		23		25		106	

FIBULA

Measurements

In the male series, left fibulae are longer than right fibulae, but the reverse obtains in case of the females. Curiously the disparity in fibular length between the two sides seems to disappear in both sexes during the last archaeological periods. Both males and females have shorter bones in the latter days of Pecos than at the beginning of its occupation (Table V–28).

TABLE V–28. Length of Fibula

Right

Males	No.	Range	Mean	S. D.	V.
Total Series A	86	306–391	350.24 ± 1.40	19.25 ± 0.99	5.50 ± 0.28
Black-on-white and Glaze I	11	317–391	347.27 ± 4.23	20.75 ± 2.99	5.98 ± 0.86
Glazes II and III	34	307–387	348.29 ± 2.23	19.29 ± 1.58	5.54 ± 0.45
Glaze IV	15	327–387	357.67 ± 2.88	16.55 ± 2.04	4.63 ± 0.57
Glazes V and VI	26	306–387	347.35 ± 2.30	17.35 ± 1.62	4.99 ± 0.47
Females					
Total Series A	44	280–360	322.39 ± 1.54	15.20 ± 1.09	4.71 ± 0.48
Black-on-white and Glaze I	11	316–357	332.91 ± 2.11	10.37 ± 1.49	3.12 ± 0.45
Glazes II and III	13	280–360	315.77 ± 3.55	19.00 ± 2.51	6.02 ± 0.80
Glaze IV	10	308–341	319.90	....	....
Glazes V and VI	10	298–334	316.80	....	....

Left

Males	No.	Range	Mean	S. D.	V.
Total Series A	72	310–391	352.36 ± 1.45	18.30 ± 1.03	5.19 ± 0.29
Black-on-white and Glaze I	10	330–389	353.70 ...	....	....
Glazes II and III	22	329–391	352.91 ± 2.80	19.49 ± 1.98	5.52 ± 0.56
Glaze IV	15	324–387	353.33 ± 3.09	17.75 ± 2.18	5.02 ± 0.62
Glazes V and VI	25	310–384	346.80 ± 2.47	18.30 ± 1.75	5.28 ± 0.50
Females					
Total Series A	39	292–342	318.41 ± 1.38	12.75 ± 0.98	4.00 ± 0.30
Black-on-white and Glaze I	8	305–335	319.00	....	....
Glazes II and III	11	300–329	313.18	....	....
Glaze IV	12	298–336	317.58 ± 2.27	11.65 ± 1.60	3.67 ± 0.50
Glazes V and VI	8	292–342	317.62	....	....

HUMERUS

Measurements and Index

In both sexes the right humerus is longer than the left, an indication of right-handedness. In both sexes the maximum length of the humerus tends to decrease from the early to the later periods, the Black-on-white and Glaze I period being distinguished by the highest mean values and the Glaze V and VI period showing the lowest averages (Table V–29).

The head of the right humerus shows larger maximum diameter than that of the left in both sexes. In the females there is a slight diminution in maximum diameter of the femoral head from period to period, but this tendency is not clear in the males.

The major diameter at the middle of the humeral shaft is also larger on the right side than on the left in both sexes. There is little sex difference in this diameter. The mean of the male diameters on the right side exceeds that of the females by .7 mm. and on the left side the female mean exceeds the male by .33 mm. No period differences are discernible (Tables V–30, 31).

TABLE V-29. MAXIMUM LENGTH OF HUMERUS

Right

	No.	Range	Mean	S. D.	V.
Males					
Total Series A	128	267–358	310.23 ± 0.92	15.40 ± 0.65	4.96 ± 0.21
Black-on-white and Glaze I	18	267–358	310.94 ± 3.41	21.46 ± 2.41	6.90 ± 0.78
Glazes II and III	48	281–337	310.27 ± 1.34	13.80 ± 0.95	4.45 ± 0.31
Glaze IV	31	288–339	309.35 ± 1.60	13.20 ± 1.13	4.27 ± 0.37
Glazes V and VI	31	271–335	306.16 ± 1.87	15.45 ± 1.32	5.05 ± 0.43
Females					
Total Series A	96	259–325	288.91 ± 0.92	13.35 ± 0.65	4.62 ± 0.22
Black-on-white and Glaze I	16	259–319	294.19 ± 2.60	15.39 ± 1.83	5.23 ± 0.62
Glazes II and III	39	266–325	288.69 ± 1.38	12.80 ± 0.98	4.43 ± 0.34
Glaze IV	24	263–316	284.04 ± 1.61	11.70 ± 1.14	4.12 ± 0.40
Glazes V and VI	17	268–304	283.88 ± 1.91	11.65 ± 1.35	4.10 ± 0.46

Left

	No.	Range	Mean	S. D.	V.
Males					
Total Series A	134	263–356	308.25 ± 0.86	14.70 ± 0.61	4.77 ± 0.20
Black-on-white and Glaze I	22	263–356	309.68 ± 2.81	19.56 ± 1.99	6.32 ± 0.64
Glazes II and III	46	276–339	308.91 ± 1.29	12.95 ± 0.92	4.19 ± 0.29
Glaze IV	29	289–331	308.28 ± 1.35	10.75 ± 0.95	3.49 ± 0.31
Glazes V and VI	37	270–334	304.05 ± 1.74	15.70 ± 1.23	5.16 ± 0.40
Females					
Total Series A	87	254–324	285.06 ± 0.89	12.30 ± 0.63	4.31 ± 0.22
Black-on-white and Glaze I	13	254–313	289.15 ± 2.97	15.90 ± 2.10	5.50 ± 0.73
Glazes II and III	33	267–324	289.73 ± 1.41	12.00 ± 1.00	4.14 ± 0.34
Glaze IV	24	260–316	280.83 ± 1.66	12.05 ± 1.17	4.29 ± 0.42
Glazes V and VI	17	267–301	281.41 ± 1.25	7.65 ± 0.88	2.72 ± 0.31

TABLE V-30. MAXIMUM DIAMETER OF SUPERIOR ARTICULAR HEAD OF HUMERUS

Right

	No.	Range	Mean	S. D.	V.
Males					
Total Series A	128	36–52	44.28 ± 0.17	2.85 ± 0.12	6.44 ± 0.27
Black-on-white and Glaze I	18	38–52	44.33 ± 0.59	3.68 ± 0.41	8.30 ± 0.93
Glazes II and III	46	36–50	44.14 ± 0.28	2.78 ± 0.19	6.30 ± 0.44
Glaze IV	31	39–48	45.53 ± 0.28	2.32 ± 0.20	5.10 ± 0.45
Glazes V and VI	33	39–51	44.21 ± 0.34	2.87 ± 0.24	6.49 ± 0.54
Females					
Total Series A	95	34.5–44	38.73 ± 0.12	1.67 ± 0.08	4.31 ± 0.21
Black-on-white and Glaze I	15	35–44	39.17 ± 0.37	2.14 ± 0.26	5.45 ± 0.55
Glazes II and III	36	36–43	39.03 ± 0.18	1.58 ± 0.13	4.05 ± 0.32
Glaze IV	25	35–41	38.52 ± 0.21	1.55 ± 0.15	4.02 ± 0.38
Glazes V and VI	19	34.5–40.5	38.05 ± 0.22	1.42 ± 0.16	3.73 ± 0.41

Left

Males	No.	Range	Mean	S. D.	V.
Total Series A	133	37–50	43.28 ± 0.14	2.46 ± 0.10	5.68 ± 0.23
Black-on-white and Glaze I	24	38–50	43.58 ± 0.42	3.04 ± 0.30	6.98 ± 0.68
Glazes II and III	47	37–48.5	43.18 ± 0.21	2.16 ± 0.15	5.01 ± 0.35
Glaze IV	25	39–46	43.20 ± 0.27	2.00 ± 0.19	4.63 ± 0.44
Glazes V and VI	37	39–49	43.26 ± 0.30	2.70 ± 0.21	6.25 ± 0.49
Females					
Total Series A	86	35–42	38.35 ± 0.11	1.58 ± 0.08	4.12 ± 0.21
Black-on-white and Glaze I	13	36–42	38.23 ± 0.33	1.76 ± 0.23	4.60 ± 0.61
Glazes II and III	33	35.5–42	38.33 ± 0.17	1.45 ± 0.12	3.78 ± 0.31
Glaze IV	22	35–41	38.50 ± 0.27	1.88 ± 0.19	4.88 ± 0.50
Glazes V and VI	18	36–41	38.11 ± 0.20	1.24 ± 0.14	3.25 ± 0.37

TABLE V–31. MIDDLE DIAMETER OF HUMERUS: MAJOR

Right

Males	No.	Range	Mean	S. D.	V.
Total Series A	146	20–30	22.53 ± 0.10	1.75 ± 0.07	7.77 ± 0.31
Black-on-white and Glaze I	21	20–30	22.81 ± 0.34	2.30 ± 0.24	10.08 ± 1.05
Glazes II and III	55	20–30	22.59 ± 0.17	1.87 ± 0.12	8.28 ± 0.53
Glaze IV	35	20–24.5	22.19 ± 0.13	1.14 ± 0.09	5.14 ± 0.41
Glazes V and VI	35	20–25.5	22.63 ± 0.16	1.44 ± 0.12	6.34 ± 0.51
Females					
Total Series A	107	18–27	21.83 ± 0.10	1.54 ± 0.07	7.05 ± 0.33
Black-on-white and Glaze I	18	19–24	21.75 ± 0.19	1.21 ± 0.14	5.56 ± 0.63
Glazes II and III	41	19–27	22.17 ± 0.18	1.72 ± 0.13	7.74 ± 0.58
Glaze IV	27	20–24	21.80 ± 0.15	1.16 ± 0.11	5.30 ± 0.49
Glazes V and VI	21	18–25	21.24 ± 0.25	1.70 ± 0.18	7.98 ± 0.83

Left

Males	No.	Range	Mean	S. D.	V.
Total Series A	148	17–27	21.10 ± 0.09	1.64 ± 0.06	7.77 ± 0.30
Black-on-white and Glaze I	24	18–27	21.67 ± 0.29	2.08 ± 0.20	9.60 ± 0.93
Glazes II and III	51	18–24	20.86 ± 0.15	1.57 ± 0.10	7.50 ± 0.50
Glaze IV	33	17–24	20.58 ± 0.17	1.45 ± 0.12	7.05 ± 0.59
Glazes V and VI	40	19–25	21.44 ± 0.14	1.34 ± 0.10	6.23 ± 0.47
Females					
Total Series A	95	18–27	21.43 ± 0.10	1.44 ± 0.07	6.72 ± 0.33
Black-on-white and Glaze I	16	19–23	21.31 ± 0.15	0.86 ± 0.10	4.06 ± 0.48
Glazes II and III	35	18–27	21.31 ± 0.19	1.62 ± 0.13	7.63 ± 0.61
Glaze IV	24	20–24	21.85 ± 0.16	1.18 ± 0.11	5.38 ± 0.52
Glazes V and VI	20	18–24	21.28 ± 0.24	1.59 ± 0.17	7.47 ± 0.80

TABLE V–32. MIDDLE DIAMETER OF HUMERUS: MINOR

Right

Males	No.	Range	Mean	S. D.	V.
Total Series A	145	13.5–21	16.37 ± 0.07	1.23 ± 0.05	7.51 ± 0.30
Black-on-white and Glaze I	20	13.5–18	16.18 ± 0.17	1.13 ± 0.12	6.99 ± 0.75
Glazes II and III	55	14–19	16.31 ± 0.10	1.12 ± 0.07	6.90 ± 0.44
Glaze IV	35	13.5–20	16.44 ± 0.15	1.31 ± 0.11	7.97 ± 0.64
Glazes V and VI	35	14.5–21	16.47 ± 0.15	1.34 ± 0.11	8.14 ± 0.66
Females					
Total Series A	107	13–19	14.77 ± 0.07	1.07 ± 0.05	7.24 ± 0.33
Black-on-white and Glaze I	18	13–17	15.14 ± 0.15	0.92 ± 0.10	6.11 ± 0.69
Glazes II and III	41	13–17	14.74 ± 0.11	1.08 ± 0.08	7.33 ± 0.55
Glaze IV	27	13–19	14.76 ± 0.15	1.19 ± 0.11	8.06 ± 0.74
Glazes V and VI	21	13–17	14.64 ± 0.12	0.80 ± 0.08	5.75 ± 0.60

Left

Males	No.	Range	Mean	S. D.	V.
Total Series A	148	12–19	15.94 ± 0.07	1.31 ± 0.05	8.22 ± 0.32
Black-on-white and Glaze I	24	14–19	16.29 ± 0.19	1.36 ± 0.13	8.29 ± 0.81
Glazes II and III	51	14–18	15.90 ± 0.12	1.24 ± 0.08	7.80 ± 0.52
Glaze IV	33	14–19	15.88 ± 0.13	1.12 ± 0.09	7.05 ± 0.59
Glazes V and VI	40	12–19	15.85 ± 0.15	1.43 ± 0.11	9.02 ± 0.68
Females					
Total Series A	95	12.5–20	14.63 ± 0.08	1.17 ± 0.06	8.00 ± 0.39
Black-on-white and Glaze I	16	12.5–16.5	14.81 ± 0.17	0.98 ± 0.12	6.62 ± 0.79
Glazes II and III	35	13–18	14.60 ± 0.13	1.14 ± 0.09	7.77 ± 0.63
Glaze IV	24	13–20	14.92 ± 0.20	1.42 ± 0.14	9.52 ± 0.93
Glazes V and VI	20	13–16	14.32 ± 0.12	0.78 ± 0.83	5.45 ± 0.58

TABLE V–33. HUMERO–FEMORAL INDEX

Right

Males	No.	Range	Mean	S. D.	V.
Total Series A	114	69.28–88.00	73.19 ± 0.15	2.38 ± 0.11	3.25 ± 0.15
Black-on-white and Glaze I	15	71.05–76.72	73.33 ± 0.24	1.35 ± 0.17	1.84 ± 0.23
Glazes II and III	41	69.28–88.00	73.76 ± 0.35	3.33 ± 0.25	4.51 ± 0.34
Glaze IV	29	69.57–76.50	72.66 ± 0.22	1.77 ± 0.16	2.44 ± 0.22
Glazes V and VI	29	69.49–76.00	72.86 ± 0.21	1.67 ± 0.15	2.29 ± 0.20
Females					
Total Series A	85	69.82–82.29	73.81 ± 0.14	1.98 ± 0.10	2.68 ± 0.14
Black-on-white and Glaze I	14	70.15–77.58	73.71 ± 0.40	2.22 ± 0.28	3.01 ± 0.38
Glazes II and III	34	71.31–76.29	73.97 ± 0.17	1.48 ± 0.12	2.01 ± 0.16
Glaze IV	22	69.82–82.29	74.27 ± 0.35	2.42 ± 0.25	3.26 ± 0.33
Glazes V and VI	15	70.32–76.19	72.87 ± 0.29	1.67 ± 0.21	2.29 ± 0.28

Left

Males	No.	Range	Mean	S. D.	V.
Total Series A	116	68.27–85.45	72.72 ± 0.15	2.37 ± 0.10	3.26 ± 0.14
Black-on-white and Glaze I	17	70.30–75.12	72.24 ± 0.21	1.26 ± 0.15	1.74 ± 0.20
Glazes II and III	42	68.68–85.45	73.38 ± 0.33	3.18 ± 0.23	4.33 ± 0.32
Glaze IV	25	68.27–75.12	72.12 ± 0.24	1.73 ± 0.17	2.40 ± 0.23
Glazes V and VI	32	68.50–76.22	72.56 ± 0.21	1.73 ± 0.15	2.38 ± 0.20
Females					
Total Series A	78	68.35–76.14	72.71 ± 0.16	2.14 ± 0.12	2.90 ± 0.16
Black-on-white and Glaze I	13	69.49–76.14	72.31 ± 0.38	2.05 ± 0.27	2.84 ± 0.38
Glazes II and III	27	70.99–75.74	73.11 ± 0.18	1.37 ± 0.13	1.87 ± 0.17
Glaze IV	23	69.05–75.85	72.91 ± 0.23	1.67 ± 0.17	2.29 ± 0.23
Glazes V and VI	15	68.35–76.12	72.00 ± 0.38	2.19 ± 0.27	3.04 ± 0.37

OBSERVATIONS

The commonest shaft shapes of the humerus are oblong, plano-convex, and prismatic, in that order. This is true of both sexes, but the females show a higher proportion of plano-convex and prismatic humeri than do the males (Table V–34). In the males the frequency of oblong forms increases and that of plano-convex forms declines from first to last. In the females oblong forms increase and plano-convex and prismatic forms diminish in frequency from the early to the late periods.

Perforation of the septum between the olecranon and coronoid fossae is commoner in the females than in the males and commoner on the left side in both sexes. It is commonest in the female series in the earliest group and least frequent among the males in that period (Table V–35).

TABLE V–34.　Shape of Shaft of Humerus

Right

Males	B.-on-W. and Gl. I		Gls. II and III		Glaze IV		Gls. V and VI		Total	
	No.	Per cent	No.	Per cent	No.	Per cent	No.	Per cent	No.	Per cent
Oblong	7	33.33	20	36.37	23	63.89	17	47.22	67	45.27
Plano-convex	10	47.62	21	38.19	6	16.67	7	19.44	44	29.73
Prismatic	2	9.52	10	18.18	4	11.11	6	16.67	22	14.86
Irregular	1	4.76	3	5.45	3	8.33	3	8.33	10	6.76
Trapezoid	0	0	1	1.82	0	0	3	8.33	4	2.70
Oval	1	4.76	0	0	0	0	0	0	1	0.68
Total	21		55		36		36		148	

Left

Males	B.-on-W. and Gl. I		Gls. II and III		Glaze IV		Gls. V and VI		Total	
Oblong	9	37.50	22	42.31	22	62.86	22	56.41	75	50.00
Plano-convex	8	33.34	16	30.77	5	64.29	3	7.69	32	21.34
Prismatic	3	12.50	10	19.23	3	8.57	7	17.94	23	15.33
Irregular	2	8.33	4	7.69	4	11.43	4	10.26	14	9.33
Trapezoid	1	4.17	0	0	1	2.86	3	7.69	5	3.33
Oval	1	4.17	0	0	0	0	0	0	1	0.67
Total	24		52		35		39		150	

Right and Left

Females	B.-on-W. and Gl. I		Gls. II and III		Glaze IV		Gls. V and VI		Total	
Oblong	3	17.65	14	40.00	9	33.33	10	62.50	36	37.89
Plano-convex	6	35.29	9	25.71	14	51.85	3	18.75	32	33.68
Prismatic	5	29.41	10	28.57	2	7.41	1	6.25	18	18.94
Irregular	2	11.76	1	2.86	2	7.41	2	12.50	7	7.37
Trapezoid	0	0	1	2.86	0	0	0	0	1	1.05
Quadrilateral	1	5.88	0	0	0	0	0	0	1	1.05
Total	17		35		27		16		95	

TABLE V–35.　Perforated Olecranon Fossae

	Males		Females	
	Right	Left	Right	Left
Black-on-white and Glaze I				
Total humerii	22	24	16	16
Perforated fossae	0	2	7	8
Per cent perforated	0	8.33	43.75	50.00
Glazes II and III				
Total humerii	56	51	42	38
Perforated fossae	7	10	8	10
Per cent perforated	12.50	19.61	19.05	26.32
Glaze IV				
Total humerii	35	35	27	28
Perforated fossae	4	11	4	5
Per cent perforated	11.43	31.43	14.81	17.86
Glazes V and VI				
Total humerii	40	40	19	18
Perforated fossae	2	1	8	7
Per cent perforated	5.00	2.50	42.11	38.89
Total				
Humerii	153	150	104	100
Perforated fossae	13	24	27	30
Per cent perforated	8.50	16.00	25.96	30.00

RADIUS, ULNA, CLAVICLE

MEASUREMENTS

The right radius is longer than the left in both sexes (Table V–36). In both sexes the highest values of radial length tend to fall in the Black-on-white and Glaze I periods. But the differences between the means of the various subgroups are quite small.

In both sexes right ulnae exceed lefts in mean length. In the females ulnar length declines from a maximum in the first period to a minimum in the last period. In the males the highest values fall in the Glaze IV group and the lowest in Glaze V and Glaze VI (Table V–37).

The left clavicles exceed the right clavicles in mean length in both sexes. The minimum length of clavicles in males and the maximum length in females occur in the earliest subgroup. In the females clavicular length apparently declines from period to period, but in males it increases and reaches its maximum in Glaze IV (Table V–38).

TABLE V–36. LENGTH OF RADIUS

Right

	No.	Range	Mean	S. D.	V.
Males					
Total Series A	91	200–270	239.56 ± 0.94	13.25 ± 0.66	5.53 ± 0.28
Black-on-white and Glaze I	14	216–268	240.21 ± 2.92	16.21 ± 2.07	6.75 ± 0.86
Glazes II and III	30	211–257	236.87 ± 1.40	11.38 ± 0.99	4.80 ± 0.42
Glaze IV	22	219–261	239.32 ± 1.67	11.60 ± 1.18	4.85 ± 0.49
Glazes V and VI	25	200–270	238.20 ± 2.03	15.05 ± 1.44	6.32 ± 0.60
Females					
Total Series A	68	193–241	219.40 ± 0.86	10.50 ± 0.61	4.79 ± 0.28
Black-on-white and Glaze I	13	200–241	225.15 ± 2.05	10.97 ± 1.45	4.87 ± 0.64
Glazes II and III	23	198–239	217.57 ± 1.37	9.75 ± 0.97	4.48 ± 0.45
Glaze IV	18	199–231	216.83 ± 1.40	8.83 ± 0.99	4.07 ± 0.46
Glazes V and VI	14	193–227	215.29 ± 1.55	8.62 ± 1.10	4.00 ± 0.51

Left

	No.	Range	Mean	S. D.	V.
Males					
Total Series A	100	214–270	238.35 ± 0.89	13.15 ± 0.63	5.52 ± 0.26
Black-on-white and Glaze I	13	214–270	239.46 ± 2.91	15.56 ± 2.06	6.50 ± 0.86
Glazes II and III	38	216–256	238.63 ± 1.21	11.08 ± 0.86	4.64 ± 0.36
Glaze IV	19	221–264	239.74 ± 1.79	11.55 ± 1.26	4.82 ± 0.53
Glazes V and VI	30	214–264	234.00 ± 1.68	13.65 ± 1.19	5.83 ± 0.51
Females					
Total Series A	57	190–240	216.59 ± 0.98	10.95 ± 0.69	5.06 ± 0.32
Black-on-white and Glaze I	8	202–240	224.62	....	....	....
Glazes II and III	20	198–237	213.00 ± 1.24	8.20 ± 0.87	3.85 ± 0.41
Glaze IV	18	196–230	213.56 ± 1.36	8.55 ± 0.96	4.00 ± 0.45
Glazes V and VI	11	190–234	217.27	....	....	....

TABLE V–37. LENGTH OF ULNA

Right

Males	No.	Range	Mean	S. D.	V.
Total Series A	79	231–284	259.10 ± 0.94	12.40 ± 0.67	4.79 ± 0.26
Black-on-white and Glaze I	14	231–283	258.57 ± 2.75	15.23 ± 1.94	5.89 ± 0.75
Glazes II and III	28	238–279	258.46 ± 1.33	10.45 ± 0.94	4.04 ± 0.36
Glaze IV	16	235–276	259.06 ± 1.87	11.10 ± 1.32	4.28 ± 0.51
Glazes V and VI	21	240–284	256.43 ± 1.85	12.55 ± 1.31	4.89 ± 0.51
Females					
Total Series A	43	212–259	237.05 ± 1.18	11.50 ± 0.84	4.85 ± 0.35
Black-on-white and Glaze I	6	244–255	249.17	....	....
Glazes II and III	13	218–259	238.00 ± 2.08	11.10 ± 1.47	4.66 ± 0.62
Glaze IV	16	214–251	232.56 ± 1.46	8.65 ± 1.03	3.72 ± 0.44
Glazes V and VI	8	212–246	227.75	....	....

Left

Males	No.	Range	Mean	S. D.	V.
Total Series A	87	223–283	254.78 ± 0.82	11.40 ± 0.58	4.47 ± 0.23
Black-on-white and Glaze I	13	232–283	254.38 ± 2.80	14.98 ± 1.98	5.89 ± 0.78
Glazes II and III	32	223–274	253.41 ± 1.33	11.15 ± 0.94	4.40 ± 0.37
Glaze IV	18	236–278	256.11 ± 1.69	10.60 ± 1.19	4.14 ± 0.47
Glazes V and VI	24	223–275	251.33 ± 1.91	13.90 ± 1.35	5.53 ± 0.54
Females					
Total Series A	51	209–264	235.18 ± 1.11	11.75 ± 0.78	5.00 ± 0.33
Black-on-white and Glaze I	8	226–263	241.50	....	....
Glazes II and III	16	219–257	231.19 ± 1.49	8.85 ± 1.06	3.83 ± 0.46
Glaze IV	17	215–264	233.53 ± 1.95	11.89 ± 1.38	5.09 ± 0.59
Glazes V and VI	10	209–254	234.20	....	....

TABLE V–38. LENGTH OF CLAVICLE

Right

Males	No.	Range	Mean	S. D.	V.
Total Series A	72	129–172	149.33 ± 0.70	8.82 ± 0.50	5.91 ± 0.33
Black-on-white and Glaze I	11	134–154	144.55 ± 1.37	6.76 ± 0.97	4.68 ± 0.67
Glazes II and III	23	137–161	149.17 ± 0.93	6.62 ± 0.66	4.44 ± 0.44
Glaze IV	18	129–172	150.11 ± 1.53	9.65 ± 1.08	6.43 ± 0.72
Glazes V and VI	20	132–163	149.25 ± 1.45	9.59 ± 1.02	6.43 ± 0.69
Females					
Total Series A	41	119–150	131.63 ± 0.80	7.57 ± 0.56	5.75 ± 0.43
Black-on-white and Glaze I	3	132–140	136.33	....	....
Glazes II and III	16	119–150	135.19 ± 1.59	9.42 ± 1.12	6.97 ± 0.83
Glaze IV	14	120–137	128.71 ± 0.83	4.61 ± 0.59	3.58 ± 0.46
Glazes V and VI	8	122–135	128.13	....	....

Left

Males	No.	Range	Mean	S. D.	V.
Total Series A	73	131–170	150.52 ± 0.67	8.49 ± 0.47	5.64 ± 0.31
Black-on-white and Glaze I	13	135–161	148.92 ± 1.62	8.64 ± 1.14	5.80 ± 0.77
Glazes II and III	23	131–159	149.26 ± 0.97	6.88 ± 0.68	4.61 ± 0.46
Glaze IV	16	132–170	153.25 ± 1.51	8.95 ± 1.07	5.84 ± 0.70
Glazes V and VI	21	132–165	149.14 ± 0.86	8.22 ± 1.21	5.51 ± 0.53
Females					
Total Series A	47	122–151	134.89 ± 0.68	6.89 ± 0.48	5.11 ± 0.36
Black-on-white and Glaze I	5	135–144	140.00	....	....
Glazes II and III	19	125–151	135.68 ± 1.26	8.17 ± 0.89	6.02 ± 0.66
Glaze IV	14	122–144	133.36 ± 0.96	5.31 ± 0.68	3.98 ± 0.51
Glazes V and VI	9	124–144	132.56	....	....

SCAPULA

MEASUREMENTS AND INDICES

Because of the fragility of scapulae only a very few are preserved in the Pecos series. The numbers in the subgroups are so small that no conclusions can be drawn from the differences in means. Left scapulae in both sexes are somewhat shorter and broader than rights (Tables V–39, 40, 41).

In the total scapular index the females exceed the males, as also in the inferior index or index of the infraspinous fossa (Tables V–42, 43).

The total scapular index yields very high means in both sexes, owing to the shortness of the Pecos scapulae and their comparatively great breadth. The Southern Utah Cliff-dwellers [1] are very close to the Pecos in measurements and indices of the scapula (Table V–44).

TABLE V-39. TOTAL HEIGHT OF SCAPULA

Right

	No.	Range	Mean	S. D.	V.
Males					
Total Series A	38	131–163	148.63 ± 0.84	7.67 ± 0.59	5.16 ± 0.40
Black-on-white and Glaze I	4	146–161	152.00	....	....
Glazes II and III	10	132–153	146.20	....	....
Glaze IV	11	143–163	151.91	....	....
Glazes V and VI	13	131–162	146.69 ± 1.65	8.83 ± 1.17	6.02 ± 0.80
Females					
Total Series A	12	127–140	133.50 ± 0.92	4.73 ± 0.65	3.54 ± 0.49
Black-on-white and Glaze I	2	134–139	136.50	....	....
Glazes II and III	3	129–140	136.33	....	....
Glaze IV	4	127–138	130.75	....	....
Glazes V and VI	3	128–135	132.33	....	....

Left

	No.	Range	Mean	S. D.	V.
Males					
Total Series A	36	130–165	147.17 ± 0.89	7.90 ± 0.63	5.37 ± 0.43
Black-on-white and Glaze I	3	136–152	145.33	....	....
Glazes II and III	12	130–154	145.00 ± 1.09	5.60 ± 0.77	3.86 ± 0.53
Glaze IV	10	144–165	153.80	....	....
Glazes V and VI	11	133–159	146.45	....	....
Females					
Total Series A	17	127–148	134.88 ± 0.92	5.62 ± 0.65	4.17 ± 0.48
Black-on-white and Glaze I	1	136–136	136.00	....	....
Glazes II and III	6	127–148	136.67	....	....
Glaze IV	8	127–142	134.00	....	....
Glazes V and VI	2	131–134	132.50	....	....

[1] Hrdlička, 1916, p. 74.

TABLE V–40. INFERIOR HEIGHT OF SCAPULA

Right

Males	No.	Range	Mean	S. D.	V.
Total Series A	42	106–133	116.57 ± 0.66	6.31 ± 0.46	5.41 ± 0.40
Black-on-white and Glaze I	4	111–129	118.50	....	....
Glazes II and III	11	106–120	113.27	....	....
Glaze IV	12	111–133	153.80 ± 1.65	7.75 ± 1.17	5.04 ± 0.76
Glazes V and VI	15	108–127	117.47 ± 0.97	5.58 ± 0.69	4.75 ± 0.58
Females					
Total Series A	18	96–123	107.72 ± 1.06	6.66 ± 0.75	6.18 ± 0.69
Black-on-white and Glaze I	3	105–110	107.00	....	....
Glazes II and III	7	96–123	109.00	....	....
Glaze IV	5	101–109	104.00	....	....
Glazes V and VI	3	105–120	111.67	....	....

Left

Males	No.	Range	Mean	S. D.	V.
Total Series A	44	100–127	116.25 ± 0.65	6.40 ± 0.46	5.50 ± 0.40
Black-on-white and Glaze I	4	106–117	113.50	....	....
Glazes II and III	13	100–121	113.69 ± 1.02	5.45 ± 0.72	4.79 ± 0.63
Glaze IV	11	111–127	119.82 ± 1.19	5.85 ± 0.84	4.88 ± 0.70
Glazes V and VI	16	103–126	117.12 ± 1.04	6.15 ± 0.73	5.25 ± 0.63
Females					
Total Series A	18	94–118	105.94 ± 0.92	5.81 ± 0.65	5.48 ± 0.62
Black-on-white and Glaze I	1	111–111	111.00	....	....
Glazes II and III	6	98–118	108.00	....	....
Glaze IV	8	94–114	104.00	....	....
Glazes V and VI	3	105–107	106.00	....	....

TABLE V–41. TOTAL BREADTH OF SCAPULA

Right

Males	No.	Range	Mean	S. D.	V.
Total Series A	41	93–110	100.49 ± 0.53	5.01 ± 0.37	4.99 ± 0.37
Black-on-white and Glaze I	4	93–100	96.50	....	....
Glazes II and III	11	94–108	101.27	....	....
Glaze IV	12	94–109	101.08 ± 0.98	5.02 ± 0.69	4.97 ± 0.68
Glazes V and VI	14	94–110	100.50 ± 1.00	5.56 ± 0.71	5.53 ± 0.71
Females					
Total Series A	18	90–104	96.17 ± 0.59	3.69 ± 0.41	3.84 ± 0.43
Black-on-white and Glaze I	3	95–102	98.33	....	....
Glazes II and III	7	90–104	96.91	....	....
Glaze IV	5	93–98	94.60	....	....
Glazes V and VI	3	92–98	95.33	....	....

Left

Males	No.	Range	Mean	S. D.	V.
Total Series A	43	90–111	101.77 ± 0.55	5.39 ± 0.39	5.30 ± 0.39
Black-on-white and Glaze I	3	94–97	95.33	....	....
Glazes II and III	13	94–111	102.38 ± 0.83	4.43 ± 0.59	4.33 ± 0.57
Glaze IV	11	95–111	103.00	....	....
Glazes V and VI	16	90–111	101.63 ± 0.95	5.56 ± 0.67	5.56 ± 0.67
Females					
Total Series A	18	92–105	97.17 ± 0.60	3.78 ± 0.42	3.89 ± 0.44
Black-on-white and Glaze I	1	99–99	99.00	....	....
Glazes II and III	6	94–102	97.67	....	....
Glaze IV	8	92–104	95.12	....	....
Glazes V and VI	3	95–105	99.00	....	....

TABLE V–42. TOTAL INDEX OF SCAPULA

Right

Males	No.	Range	Mean	S. D.	V.
Total Series A	36	62–80	67.03 ± 0.33	2.95 ± 0.23	4.40 ± 0.35
Black-on-white and Glaze I	4	63–80	68.00	....	....
Glazes II and III	10	64–77	69.20	....	....
Glaze IV	11	62–73	66.64	....	....
Glazes V and VI	11	64–73	67.09	....	....
Females					
Total Series A	12	68–79	73.50 ± 0.70	3.57 ± 0.49	4.86 ± 0.67
Black-on-white and Glaze I	2	68–76	72.00	....	....
Glazes II and III	3	68–78	72.67	....	....
Glaze IV	4	71–79	75.50	....	....
Glazes V and VI	3	71–73	72.00	....	....

Left

Males	No.	Range	Mean	S. D.	V.
Total Series A	35	64–77	68.97 ± 0.38	3.36 ± 0.27	4.87 ± 0.39
Black-on-white and Glaze I	2	64–71	67.50	....	....
Glazes II and III	12	64–77	70.58 ± 0.70	3.58 ± 0.49	5.07 ± 0.70
Glaze IV	10	65–76	67.60	....	....
Glazes V and VI	11	64–74	69.27	....	....
Females					
Total Series A	17	61–83	71.71 ± 0.46	2.78 ± 0.32	3.88 ± 0.45
Black-on-white and Glaze I	1	73–73	73.00	....	....
Glazes II and III	6	61–80	71.83	....	....
Glaze IV	8	70–83	75.00	....	....
Glazes V and VI	2	72–72	72.00	....	....

TABLE V–43. INFERIOR INDEX OF SCAPULA

Right

Males	No.	Range	Mean	S. D.	V.
Total Series A	41	72–97	85.98 ± 0.59	5.56 ± 0.41	6.47 ± 0.48
Black-on-white and Glaze I	4	78–86	81.50	....	....
Glazes II and III	11	83–97	89.46	....	....
Glaze IV	12	72–96	85.33 ± 1.21	6.21 ± 0.85	7.28 ± 1.00
Glazes V and VI	14	76–95	84.71 ± 0.83	4.62 ± 0.59	5.45 ± 0.70
Females					
Total Series A	18	74–104	89.61 ± 1.13	7.10 ± 0.80	7.92 ± 0.89
Black-on-white and Glaze I	3	89–97	92.00	....	....
Glazes II and III	7	74–104	88.29	....	....
Glaze IV	5	87–93	91.00	....	....
Glazes V and VI	3	77–91	85.67	....	....

Left

Males	No.	Range	Mean	S. D.	V.
Total Series A	43	76–101	87.72 ± 0.51	4.92 ± 0.36	5.61 ± 0.41
Black-on-white and Glaze I	3	82–92	86.33	....	....
Glazes II and III	13	84–101	90.85 ± 0.84	4.47 ± 0.59	4.92 ± 0.65
Glaze IV	11	76–96	86.09	....	....
Glazes V and VI	16	82–97	86.38 ± 0.68	4.03 ± 0.48	4.66 ± 0.56
Females					
Total Series A	18	82–105	91.83 ± 0.90	5.64 ± 0.63	6.14 ± 0.69
Black-on-white and Glaze I	1	89–89	89.00	....	....
Glazes II and III	6	82–105	92.00	....	....
Glaze IV	8	82–98	91.62 ...	....	....
Glazes V and VI	3	90–98	93.33	....	....

TABLE V–44. COMPARATIVE TABLE OF MEANS OF MEASUREMENTS AND INDICES OF
THE SCAPULA. (COMPARATIVE DATA FROM HRDLIČKA.*)

Males	No.	Total Height	Inferior Height	Breadth	Total Index	Infraspinous Index
Pecos †	74	147.4	116.4	101.1	68.34	87.13
Southern Utah	18	151	116	101.5	67.4	87.7
Pima, Pueblo	5	155	120	110.5	71	93
Mexican Indians	9	158	120	104	65.5	86.6
Peru, Indians	55	158.3	120	101.7	64.2	84.8
United States whites	70	164	122.5	107	65.3	87.3
United States Negroes	46	162.5	116	109	66.8	92.1
Females						
Pecos †	29	134.2	106.8	96.7	73.47	90.23
Southern Utah	10	137	102.5	97	70.6	94.2
Pima, Pueblo	5	138	102.5	99.5	72.00	97
Mexican Indians	12	137.5	102.5	97.5	70.7	94.9
Peru, Indians	39	137.8	104.7	91.7	66.5	87.5
United States whites	44	144	109	96	66.7	88.4
United States Negroes	18	142	102	92.5	65	90.7

* Hrdlička, 1916, p. 74.
† Means of rights and lefts.

OBSERVATIONS

Hrdlička has developed a somewhat intricate series of morphological observations on the scapula. The principal categories of these observations have been recorded in the Pecos series and are dealt with in Tables V–45, 46, 47.

The form of the superior border may be horizontal or nearly so, moderately oblique or rising, markedly so, saddle-shaped, markedly concave or semilunar, convex or concavo-convex (wavy). It is often extremely difficult to classify this feature and a certain vagueness in the categories is reflected in the ambiguities of our classifications. In the total series of males a pronounced obliquity of the upper border seems to occur in 23–25 per cent, while 39–42 per cent show slight or medium obliquity of the upper border. This border is horizontal or nearly so in 8–11 per cent. Concave or semicircular forms are present in about 13 per cent of right scapulae and a similar percentage of left scapulae. The remainder are concavo-convex or indefinite. In the females pronouncedly oblique borders are rare. Medium obliquity predominates, with a high percentage also of almost horizontal upper borders. Concave types show about the same frequency as in the males. Hrdlička notes [1] that the superior border of the left scapula is inclined to be less oblique than that of the right. This seems to be true also of the Pecos series. Similarly the superior border is less oblique in females than in males, an observation which is confirmed in the Pecos group. Clearly a submedium obliquity of this border is the prevalent condition in both males and females, but in males the pronounced obliquity is much more frequent than in the other sex. Doubt as to the coincidence of our gradations with those of Dr. Hrdlička makes it injudicious to compile a comparative table, but it is evident

[1] Hrdlička, 1916, pp. 77–78.

that the concave, saddle-shaped, and semilunar upper borders in our series approximate in proportions to the relatively small percentages found by Hrdlička in Southern Utah Cliff-dwellers, Mexican Indians, and whites, rather than to the high proportions found among Munsee, Northwest Coast Indians, and Peruvians.

The development of the scapular notch shows a clear sex difference. It is much more likely to be deep, or a complete foramen, in males than in females, as indicated by the data given in Table V–46. Only one pair of male scapulae in the Pecos series had foramina. The notch is much more frequently absent in female scapulae than in those of males.

The vertebral borders of the scapulae usually present a moderate convexity. About 53 per cent of male scapulae show some degree of convexity of the vertebral border, while about 77 per cent of female scapulae fall into this category. Straight vertebral borders occur in about 31 per cent of males and 11–15 per cent of females. Concave vertebral borders are found in 11–13 per cent of males and 19–12 per cent of females. These are the so-called "scaphoid" scapulae (Table V–47).

A well-marked process on the inferior angle of the scapula is often developed through the attachment of a strong *teres major* muscle. This is larger and better marked in males than in females (Table V–48).

In general it may be said that our lack of knowledge as to the significance of scapular variations makes any extended commentary upon them superfluous. Unfortunately we do not know what functional factors may contribute to these wide variations, nor does it seem very probable that such features as the concave vertebral border are constitutionally significant, in spite of the interesting researches of Graves and others.

TABLE V–45. Superior Border of Scapula

Right

	B.-on-W. and Gl. I		Gls. II and III		Glaze IV		Gls. V and VI		Total Series A	
	No.	Per cent	No.	Per cent	No.	Per cent	No.	Per cent	No.	Per cent
Males										
Pronounced oblique	3	37.50	1	7.69	2	15.38	6	33.33	12	23.08
Medium oblique............	2	25.00	4	30.77	3	23.08	7	38.89	16	30.77
Submedium oblique	1	12.50	2	15.38	1	7.69	1	5.56	5	9.61
Horizontal	0	00.00	2	15.38	2	15.38	2	11.11	6	11.54
Wavy	1	12.50	1	7.69	2	15.38	1	5.56	5	9.62
Concave..................	1	12.50	3	23.07	3	23.07	1	5.56	8	15.38
Total	8		13		13		18		52	
Females										
Medium oblique	2	50.00	3	50.00	1	12.50	1	20.00	7	30.43
Submedium oblique	1	25.00	2	33.33	2	25.00	0	00.00	5	21.74
Horizontal	1	25.00	0	00.00	1	12.50	1	20.00	3	13.04
Wavy	0	00.00	0	00.00	1	12.50	0	00.00	1	4.35
Concave..................	0	00.00	1	16.67	3	37.50	3	60.00	7	30.45
Total	4		6		8		5		23	

Left

Males	B.-on-W. and Gl. I		Gls. II and III		Glaze IV		Gls. V and VI		Total Series A	
	No.	Per cent	No.	Per cent	No.	Per cent	No.	Per cent	No.	Per cent
Pronounced oblique	3	42.86	1	6.67	2	16.67	7	41.18	13	25.49
Medium oblique	2	28.57	4	26.67	1	8.33	6	35.29	13	25.49
Submedium oblique	1	14.29	4	26.67	3	25.00	1	5.88	9	17.65
Horizontal	0	00.00	1	6.67	1	8.33	2	11.76	4	7.84
Wavy	0	00.00	1	6.67	3	25.00	0	00.00	4	7.84
Concave.................	1	14.29	4	26.68	2	16.67	1	5.88	8	15.68
Total	7		15		12		17		51	
Females										
Pronounced oblique	0	00.00	1	16.67	0	00.00	0	00.00	1	4.35
Medium oblique	1	33.33	3	50.00	2	22.22	0	00.00	6	26.09
Submedium oblique	1	33.33	1	16.67	3	33.33	1	20.00	6	26.09
Horizontal	1	33.33	0	00.00	1	11.11	1	20.00	3	13.04
Wavy	0	00.00	0	00.00	1	11.11	0	00.00	1	4.35
Concave.................	0		1	16.67	2	22.22	3	60.00	6	26.10
Total	3		6		9		5		23	

TABLE V–46. SCAPULAR NOTCH

Right

Males	B.-on-W. and Gl. I		Gls. II and III		Glaze IV		Gls. V and VI		Total Series A	
	No.	Per cent	No.	Per cent	No.	Per cent	No.	Per cent	No.	Per cent
Very pronounced	0	00.00	2	16.67	0	00.00	0	00.00	2	3.85
Pronounced	3	37.50	1	8.33	1	7.14	4	22.22	9	17.31
Medium	1	12.50	5	41.67	6	42.86	4	22.22	16	30.77
Submedium	3	37.50	4	33.33	5	35.71	5	27.78	17	32.69
Trace	0	00.00	0	00.00	0	00.00	1	5.56	1	1.92
Absent	1	12.50	0	00.00	1	7.14	4	22.22	6	11.54
Foramen	0	00.00	0	00.00	1	7.14	0	00.00	1	1.92
Total	8		12		14		18		52	
Females										
Very pronounced	0	00.00	0	00.00	1	12.50	0	00.00	1	4.00
Pronounced	0	00.00	1	12.50	0	00.00	1	20.00	2	8.00
Medium	1	25.00	2	25.00	4	50.00	1	20.00	8	32.00
Submedium	1	25.00	3	37.50	0	00.00	1	20.00	5	20.00
Absent	2	50.00	2	25.00	3	37.50	2	40.00	9	36.00
Total	4		8		8		5		25	

Left

Males	B.-on-W. and Gl. I		Gls. II and III		Glaze IV		Gls. V and VI		Total Series A	
Very pronounced	0	00.00	2	14.29	0	00.00	1	5.56	3	5.77
Pronounced	3	42.86	1	7.14	1	7.69	5	27.78	10	19.23
Medium	0	00.00	4	28.57	5	38.46	2	11.11	11	21.15
Submedium	3	42.86	5	35.71	5	38.46	5	27.78	18	34.62
Trace	0	00.00	1	7.14	0	00.00	1	5.56	2	3.85
Absent	1	14.29	0	00.00	2	15.38	4	22.22	7	13.46
Foramen	0	00.00	1	7.14	0	00.00	0	00.00	1	1.92
Total	7		14		13		18		52	
Females										
Very pronounced	0	00.00	1	14.29	0	00.00	0	00.00	1	4.17
Pronounced	0	00.00	0	00.00	0	00.00	2	40.00	2	8.33
Medium	1	33.33	2	28.57	4	44.44	1	20.00	8	33.33
Submedium	1	33.33	2	28.57	2	22.22	2	40.00	7	29.17
Absent	1	33.33	2	28.57	3	33.33	0	00.00	6	25.00
Total	3		7		9		5		24	

TABLE V–47. VERTEBRAL BORDER OF SCAPULA

Right

	B.-on-W. and Gl. I		Gls II and III		Glaze IV		Gls V and VI		Total Series A	
Males	No.	Per cent	No.	Per cent	No.	Per cent	No.	Per cent	No.	Per cent
Straight	3	37.50	3	18.75	5	33.33	7	36.84	18	31.03
Concavo-convex	0	0	1	6.25	0	0	0	0	1	1.72
Pronounced convex	2	25.00	1	6.25	1	6.67	1	5.26	5	8.62
Medium convex	1	12.50	7	43.75	8	53.33	5	26.32	21	36.21
Submedium convex	1	12.50	2	12.50	0	0	3	15.79	6	10.34
Pronounced concave	1	12.50	1	6.25	0	0	2	10.53	4	6.90
Medium concave	0	0	0	0	1	6.67	1	5.26	2	3.45
Submedium concave	0	0	1	6.25	0	0	0	0	1	1.72
Total	8		16		15		19		58	
Females										
Straight	0	0	2	20.00	2	25.00	0	0	4	15.38
Pronounced convex	0	0	1	10.00	0	0	1	25.00	2	7.69
Medium convex	4	100.00	6	60.00	6	75.00	2	50.00	18	69.23
Pronounced concave	0	0	0	0	0	0	1	25.00	1	3.85
Medium concave	0	0	1	10.00	0	0	0	0	1	3.85
Total	4		10		8		4		26	

Left

	B.-on-W. and Gl. I		Gls II and III		Glaze IV		Gls V and VI		Total Series A	
Males	No.	Per cent	No.	Per cent	No.	Per cent	No.	Per cent	No.	Per cent
Straight	2	28.57	4	23.53	3	25.00	8	42.11	17	30.91
Concavo-convex	0	0	1	5.88	0	0	0	0	1	1.82
Pronounced convex	2	28.57	1	5.88	1	8.33	1	5.26	5	9.09
Medium convex	1	14.29	6	35.29	7	58.33	4	21.05	18	32.73
Submedium convex	1	14.29	2	11.76	0	0	3	15.79	6	10.91
Pronounced concave	1	14.29	1	5.88	0	0	2	10.53	4	7.27
Medium concave	0	0	1	5.88	1	8.33	1	5.26	3	5.45
Submedium concave	0	0	1	5.88	0	0	0	0	1	1.82
Total	7		17		12		19		55	
Females										
Straight	0	0	2	22.22	1	11.11	0	0	3	11.54
Pronounced convex	0	0	1	11.11	1	11.11	1	20.00	3	11.54
Medium convex	2	66.67	5	55.56	7	77.78	3	60.00	17	65.38
Pronounced concave	0	0	0	0	0	0	1	20.00	1	3.85
Medium concave	1	33.33	1	11.11	0	0	0	0	2	7.69
Total	3		9		9		5		26	

TABLE V–48. TERES PROCESS OF AXILLARY BORDER OF SCAPULA

Right

	B.-on-W. and Gl. I		Gls. II and III		Glaze IV		Gls V and VI		Total Series A	
Males	No.	Per cent	No.	Per cent	No.	Per cent	No.	Per cent	No.	Per cent
Pronounced	1	12.50	5	31.25	7	50.00	6	31.58	19	33.33
Medium	4	50.00	6	37.50	4	28.57	7	36.84	21	36.84
Submedium	3	37.50	5	31.25	3	21.43	5	26.32	16	28.07
Very submedium	0	0	0	0	0	0	1	5.26	1	1.75
Total	8		16		14		19		57	
Females										
Pronounced	1	25.00	1	11.11	2	25.00	1	20.00	5	19.23
Medium	1	25.00	4	44.44	2	25.00	2	40.00	9	34.62
Submedium	2	50.00	4	44.44	3	37.50	2	40.00	11	42.31
Very submedium	0	0	0	0	1	12.50	0	0	1	3.85
Total	4		9		8		5		26	

Left

Males	B.-on-W. and Gl. I		Gls. II and III		Glaze IV		Gls. V and VI		Total Series A	
	No.	Per cent	No.	Per cent	No.	Per cent	No.	Per cent	No.	Per cent
Pronounced	1	14.29	4	23.53	5	45.45	6	31.58	16	29.63
Medium	4	57.14	8	47.06	4	36.36	8	42.11	24	44.44
Submedium	2	28.57	5	29.41	2	18.18	4	21.05	13	24.07
Very submedium	0	0	0	0	0	0	1	5.26	1	1.85
Total	7		17		11		19		54	
Females										
Pronounced	0	0	1	12.50	1	11.11	1	20.00	3	12.00
Medium	2	66.67	4	50.00	4	44.44	3	60.00	13	52.00
Submedium	1	33.33	3	37.50	3	33.33	1	20.00	8	32.00
Very submedium	0	0	0	0	1	11.11	0	0	1	4.00
Total	3		8		9		5		25	

PELVIS

Measurements and Indices

The maximum breadth of the pelvis (bi-iliac) falls in the earliest period in both sexes, and in both sexes the minimum average breadth falls in the second period. The males exceed the females in this dimension. The height of innominate bones is greatest in the Glaze IV period in males and varies irregularly throughout the periods. The greatest breadths of the innominate bones fall in the earliest subgroup in both sex series, but the specimens preserved in that group are so few as to be an unreliable basis for comparison (Tables V–49, 50, 51).

The total pelvic index (breadth-height) shows the usual sex difference in that it is higher in the male pelves. It is apparently lowest in the males of the earliest subgroup. In the female series the mean pelvic index varies only slightly in the different subgroups (Table V–52).

In the mean value of the maximum breadth of the superior strait the females exceed the males. In both series the maximum values fall in the first period subgroup and the minimum in the latest subgroup (Table V–54). In the antero-posterior diameter of the superior strait the females show lower mean values than the males. The highest values in the male series occur in the Black-on-white and Glaze I group, but in the female series in Glaze IV. The pelvic brim index is, of course, higher in males than in females, since in the latter the superior strait is relatively broader with reference to its antero-posterior diameter. The lowest values of the index fall in the earliest period in both sexes (Tables V–55, 56).

The distances between the ischiatic spines are consistently larger in the female pelves (Table V–57) and diminish in the females from the earliest to the latest period. In the males there seems to be a similar trend but the maximum average falls in the second subgroup.

The height of male sacra averages greater than that of the female bones, but the differences are insignificant in the first and last periods of our series. Male sacra are consistently wider than female sacra, except in the first period. Means of the length-breadth index of the sacrum are, of course, higher in females than in males. The variation of the index in period subgroups is very irregular (Tables V–58, 59, 60).

TABLE V–49. MAXIMUM BREADTH OF PELVIS

Males	No.	Range	Mean	S. D.	V.
Total Series A	72	242–303	270.42 ± 0.95	12.00 ± 0.67	4.44 ± 0.25
Black-on-white and Glaze I	6	259–298	276.67	....	....
Glazes II and III	26	242–291	269.77 ± 1.68	12.67 ± 1.18	4.70 ± 0.43
Glaze IV	16	254–292	275.00 ± 1.76	10.42 ± 1.24	3.79 ± 0.45
Glazes V and VI	24	251–303	272.50 ± 1.54	11.22 ± 1.09	4.12 ± 0.40
Females					
Total Series A	56	235–297	261.52 ± 1.12	12.48 ± 0.80	4.77 ± 0.30
Black-on-white and Glaze I	6	253–283	269.17	....	....
Glazes II and III	22	235–297	258.00 ± 2.09	14.50 ± 1.47	5.62 ± 0.57
Glaze IV	17	243–277	259.53 ± 1.60	9.76 ± 1.13	3.76 ± 0.43
Glazes V and VI	11	235–280	262.27	....	....

TABLE V–50. HEIGHT OF OSSA INNOMINATA

Right

Males	No.	Range	Mean	S. D.	V.
Total Series A	69	184–221	203.22 ± 0.70	8.64 ± 0.50	4.25 ± 0.24
Black-on-white and Glaze I	5	184–218	199.00	....	....
Glazes II and III	25	190–220	202.56 ± 1.07	7.92 ± 0.76	3.91 ± 0.37
Glaze IV	16	195–217	205.06 ± 1.20	7.13 ± 0.85	3.48 ± 0.41
Glazes V and VI	23	187–221	202.65 ± 1.28	9.08 ± 0.90	4.48 ± 0.45
Females					
Total Series A	54	167–205	186.07 ± 0.72	7.82 ± 0.51	4.20 ± 0.27
Black-on-white and Glaze I	6	177–200	192.33	....	....
Glazes II and III	21	167–198	184.38 ± 1.22	8.27 ± 0.86	4.49 ± 0.47
Glaze IV	16	177–205	185.00 ± 1.15	6.81 ± 0.81	3.68 ± 0.43
Glazes V and VI	11	177–201	187.45	....	....

Left

Males	No.	Range	Mean	S. D.	V.
Total Series A	71	183–230	203.54 ± 0.74	9.21 ± 0.52	4.53 ± 0.26
Black-on-white and Glaze I	6	183–230	203.33	....	....
Glazes II and III	27	192–220	203.56 ± 1.00	7.72 ± 0.71	3.79 ± 0.35
Glaze IV	15	192–219	208.60 ± 1.35	7.76 ± 0.96	3.72 ± 0.46
Glazes V and VI	23	187–219	203.65 ± 1.36	9.66 ± 0.96	4.74 ± 0.47
Females					
Total Series A	50	161–207	185.08 ± 0.73	7.70 ± 0.52	4.16 ± 0.28
Black-on-white and Glaze I	4	177–195	188.25	....	....
Glazes II and III	21	161–198	185.52 ± 1.34	9.08 ± 0.94	4.89 ± 0.51
Glaze IV	15	176–207	186.67 ± 1.46	8.42 ± 1.03	4.51 ± 0.56
Glazes V and VI	10	178–198	189.60	....	....

TABLE V–51. Breadth of Ossa Innominata

Right

Males	No.	Range	Mean	S. D.	V.
Total Series A	57	137–165	149.77 ± 0.59	6.60 ± 0.42	4.41 ± 0.28
Black-on-white and Glaze I	4	137–165	154.00	....	....
Glazes II and III	19	138–157	147.84 ± 0.79	5.09 ± 0.56	3.44 ± 0.38
Glaze IV	14	140–165	151.21 ± 1.03	5.71 ± 0.73	3.78 ± 0.48
Glazes V and VI	20	140–161	149.75 ± 0.93	6.16 ± 0.66	4.11 ± 0.44
Females					
Total Series A	44	123–156	140.50 ± 0.68	6.68 ± 0.48	4.75 ± 0.34
Black-on-white and Glaze I	5	135–156	145.60	....	....
Glazes II and III	18	123–156	140.44 ± 1.18	7.42 ± 0.83	5.28 ± 0.59
Glaze IV	12	131–145	137.92 ± 0.80	4.13 ± 0.57	2.99 ± 0.41
Glazes V and VI	9	134–150	140.78	....	....

Left

Males	No.	Range	Mean	S. D.	V.
Total Series A	60	135–164	149.02 ± 0.56	6.45 ± 0.40	4.33 ± 0.27
Black-on-white and Glaze I	5	135–164	147.40	....	....
Glazes II and III	23	135–159	148.26 ± 0.72	5.09 ± 0.51	3.43 ± 0.34
Glaze IV	12	140–163	151.92 ± 1.24	6.37 ± 0.88	4.19 ± 0.58
Glazes V and VI	20	136–161	148.55 ± 0.97	6.42 ± 0.68	4.32 ± 0.46
Females					
Total Series A	44	126–155	140.45 ± 0.60	5.91 ± 0.42	4.21 ± 0.30
Black-on-white and Glaze I	5	140–149	144.20	....	....
Glazes II and III	20	126–155	138.90 ± 0.96	6.36 ± 0.68	4.58 ± 0.49
Glaze IV	12	132–152	140.17 ± 1.08	5.55 ± 0.76	3.96 ± 0.54
Glazes V and VI	7	136–147	142.71	....	....

TABLE V–52. Total Pelvic Index

Males	No.	Range	Mean	S. D.	V.
Total Series A	69	67–83	74.91 ± 0.24	2.93 ± 0.17	3.91 ± 0.22
Black-on-white and Glaze I	6	71–77	73.67	....	....
Glazes II and III	23	69–83	75.83 ± 0.44	3.10 ± 0.31	4.09 ± 0.41
Glaze IV	16	70–78	74.50 ± 0.34	2.00 ± 0.24	2.68 ± 0.32
Glazes V and VI	24	67–82	74.63 ± 0.44	3.20 ± 0.31	4.29 ± 0.42
Females					
Total Series A	55	66–80	71.56 ± 0.29	3.15 ± 0.20	4.40 ± 0.28
Black-on-white and Glaze I	6	69–75	71.33	....	....
Glazes II and III	22	66–80	71.77 ± 0.55	3.81 ± 0.39	5.31 ± 0.54
Glaze IV	16	68–77	71.56 ± 0.47	2.78 ± 0.33	3.88 ± 0.46
Glazes V and VI	11	68–75	71.27	....	....

TABLE V–53. Innominate Index

Males	No.	Range	Mean	S. D.	V.
Total Series A	69*	69–78	73.59 ± 0.17	2.07 ± 0.12	2.81 ± 0.16
Black-on-white and Glaze I	6	72–76	74.00	....	....
Glazes II and III	25	69–78	73.24 ± 0.30	2.22 ± 0.21	3.03 ± 0.29
Glaze IV	16	72–78	74.00 ± 0.30	1.80 ± 0.21	2.43 ± 0.29
Glazes V and VI	22	69–78	73.59 ± 0.31	2.19 ± 0.22	2.98 ± 0.30
Females					
Total Series A	52	70–82	75.37 ± 0.20	2.11 ± 0.14	2.80 ± 0.19
Black-on-white and Glaze I	6	73–78	75.83	....	....
Glazes II and III	22	71–82	75.59 ± 0.34	2.35 ± 0.24	3.11 ± 0.32
Glaze IV	14	73–80	74.93 ± 0.32	1.75 ± 0.22	2.34 ± 0.30
Glazes V and VI	10	70–77	75.20	....	....

* Right or left measurements used as well as mean measurements.

TABLE V–54. Maximum Breadth of Superior Strait of Pelvis

	No.	Range	Mean	S. D.	V.
Males					
Total Series A	74	112–144	125.58 ± 0.53	6.75 ± 0.37	5.38 ± 0.30
Black-on-white and Glaze I	6	120–137	127.17	....	
Glazes II and III	26	113–144	126.46 ± 0.96	7.29 ± 0.68	5.76 ± 0.54
Glaze IV	19	118–141	125.37 ± 0.89	5.72 ± 0.63	4.56 ± 0.50
Glazes V and VI	23	112–137	124.35 ± 0.97	6.98 ± 0.69	5.54 ± 0.55
Females					
Total Series A	59	112–147	130.12 ± 0.60	6.81 ± 0.42	5.23 ± 0.32
Black-on-white and Glaze I	6	122–144	134.00	....	....
Glazes II and III	25	117–147	130.12 ± 0.87	6.42 ± 0.61	4.93 ± 0.47
Glaze IV	16	120–138	130.69 ± 0.82	4.87 ± 0.58	3.73 ± 0.44
Glazes V and VI	12	112–138	127.42 ± 1.52	8.13 ± 1.12	6.38 ± 0.88

TABLE V–55. Antero–Posterior Diameter of Superior Strait of Pelvis

	No.	Range	Mean	S. D.	V.
Males					
Total Series A	69	75–123	95.56 ± 0.78	9.62 ± 0.55	10.08 ± 0.58
Black-on-white and Glaze I	6	86–112	99.67	....	....
Glazes II and III	25	75–112	94.68 ± 1.30	9.66 ± 0.92	10.20 ± 0.97
Glaze IV	18	80–115	96.00 ± 1.53	9.63 ± 1.08	10.03 ± 1.13
Glazes V and VI	20	79–123	94.95 ± 1.38	9.14 ± 0.97	9.63 ± 1.03
Females					
Total Series A	56	77–110	93.46 ± 0.73	8.06 ± 0.51	8.62 ± 0.55
Black-on-white and Glaze I	6	83–108	94.33	....	....
Glazes II and III	23	77–108	92.30 ± 1.06	7.60 ± 0.76	8.23 ± 0.82
Glaze IV	16	83–110	94.56 ± 1.46	8.66 ± 1.03	9.16 ± 1.09
Glazes V and VI	11	77–105	93.82	....	....

TABLE V–56. Brim Index of Pelvis

	No.	Range	Mean	S. D.	V.
Males					
Total Series A	69	59–98	76.14 ± 0.66	8.08 ± 0.46	10.61 ± 0.61
Black-on-white and Glaze I	6	68–93	77.67	....	....
Glazes II and III	25	59–93	75.00 ± 1.20	8.88 ± 0.85	11.84 ± 1.13
Glaze IV	18	64–90	76.56 ± 1.08	6.79 ± 0.76	8.87 ± 1.00
Glazes V and VI	20	69–98	76.45 ± 1.11	7.38 ± 0.79	9.65 ± 1.03
Females					
Total Series A	56	58–83	71.64 ± 0.53	5.84 ± 0.37	8.15 ± 0.52
Black-on-white and Glaze I	6	64–77	70.50	....	....
Glazes II and III	23	58–80	70.61 ± 0.79	5.61 ± 0.56	7.93 ± 0.79
Glaze IV	16	65–83	72.25 ± 0.88	5.21 ± 0.62	7.21 ± 0.86
Glazes V and VI	11	58–83	73.54	....	....

TABLE V–57. Distance between Ischiatic Spines of Pelvis

	No.	Range	Mean	S. D.	V.
Males					
Total Series A	46	61–117	85.83 ± 1.09	10.95 ± 0.77	12.76 ± 0.90
Black-on-white and Glaze I	3	61–116	86.00	....	....
Glazes II and III	16	71–101	85.81 ± 1.41	8.38 ± 1.00	9.76 ± 1.16
Glaze IV	17	67–117	87.12 ± 1.95	11.90 ± 1.38	13.66 ± 1.58
Glazes V and VI	10	75–93	83.40	....	....
Females					
Total Series A	34	85–115	100.79 ± 0.87	7.66 ± 0.63	7.60 ± 0.62
Black-on-white and Glaze I	2	101–106	103.50	....	....
Glazes II and III	14	88–115	102.86 ± 1.33	7.39 ± 0.94	7.18 ± 0.92
Glaze IV	11	87–115	99.27	....	....
Glazes V and VI	7	85–109	98.29	....	....

TABLE V–58. HEIGHT OF SACRUM

Males	No.	Range	Mean	S. D.	V.
Total Series A	66	85–126	104.73 ± 0.70	8.41 ± 0.49	8.03 ± 0.47
Black-on-white and Glaze I	5	97–117	104.80	....	....
Glazes II and III	24	94–126	107.46 ± 1.03	7.48 ± 0.73	6.96 ± 0.68
Glaze IV	19	89–122	105.00 ± 1.18	7.65 ± 0.84	7.29 ± 0.80
Glazes V and VI	18	85–114	100.78 ± 1.35	8.47 ± 0.95	8.40 ± 0.94
Females					
Total Series A	46	77–118	100.78 ± 0.82	8.27 ± 0.58	8.21 ± 0.58
Black-on-white and Glaze I	5	96–114	104.20	....	....
Glazes II and III	17	82–111	99.94 ± 1.40	8.55 ± 0.99	8.56 ± 0.99
Glaze IV	14	77–118	100.57 ± 1.52	8.41 ± 1.07	8.36 ± 1.07
Glazes V and VI	10	89–111	100.80	....	....

TABLE V–59. BREADTH OF SACRUM

Males	No.	Range	Mean	S. D.	V.
Total Series A	66	98–126	115.89 ± 0.45	5.47 ± 0.32	4.72 ± 0.28
Black-on-white and Glaze I	5	112–122	114.80	....	....
Glazes II and III	24	109–126	117.08 ± 0.62	4.47 ± 0.44	3.82 ± 0.37
Glaze IV	19	98–126	115.37 ± 0.97	6.26 ± 0.68	5.43 ± 0.59
Glazes V and VI	18	104–125	115.17 ± 0.93	5.87 ± 0.66	5.10 ± 0.57
Females					
Total Series A	47	101–123	114.34 ± 0.46	4.64 ± 0.32	4.06 ± 0.28
Black-on-white and Glaze I	5	112–121	117.20	....	....
Glazes II and III	17	101–123	114.65 ± 0.94	5.73 ± 0.66	5.00 ± 0.58
Glaze IV	14	103–116	112.50 ± 0.57	3.18 ± 0.41	2.83 ± 0.36
Glazes V and VI	11	109–122	114.91	....	....

TABLE V–60. SACRAL INDEX

Males	No.	Range	Mean	S. D.	V.
Total Series A	66	88–142	111.17 ± 0.87	10.42 ± 0.61	9.37 ± 0.55
Black-on-white and Glaze I	5	96–126	110.40	....	....
Glazes II and III	24	92–126	109.00 ± 1.13	8.22 ± 0.80	7.54 ± 0.73
Glaze IV	19	88–139	110.37 ± 1.60	10.38 ± 1.14	9.40 ± 1.03
Glazes V and VI	18	98–142	115.22 ± 1.93	12.12 ± 1.36	10.52 ± 1.18
Females					
Total Series A	46	87–148	114.30 ± 1.01	10.19 ± 0.72	8.92 ± 0.63
Black-on-white and Glaze I	5	104–126	113.20	....	....
Glazes II and III	17	105–137	115.35 ± 1.38	8.42 ± 0.97	7.30 ± 0.84
Glaze IV	14	87–148	108.21 ± 0.47	2.60 ± 0.33	2.40 ± 0.31
Glazes V and VI	10	100–130	114.10	....	....

COMPARISON OF PECOS PELVES WITH THOSE OF OTHER GROUPS

Tables V–61, 62, deal with the indices and measurements of the Pecos pelves as compared with those of other Indian groups and some non-Indian groups. The Pecos innominate bones are distinguished by their small average height from most Indian and white comparative material, but the Southern Utah Cliff-dwellers, cited by Hrdlička,[1] are very close to the Pecos in innominate height, innominate breadth, and in the innominate index. The Pecos sacra are very short relative to their

[1] Hrdlička, 1916, p. 84.

breadth, but the length-breadth indices of the sacra fall within the range of other Indian groups.

Because of the extremely low innominate heights which occur both in males and in females in the Pecos series, the total pelvic index is very low in its average (Table V–62). In our comparative series only the Japanese show lower mean values for the total pelvic index. It is, however, in the dimensions of the superior strait and in the brim index that the Pecos pelves are most remarkable. The antero-posterior diameters in both sexes are absolutely and relatively so small that the brim indices fall below those of any of the groups adduced for comparison except the United States white males. Emmons,[1] however, found an average brim index of 74.01 in 57 female pelves from Arizona and this mean approximates to that of the females of our series (71.64). It is evident that the Pueblo peoples of the Southwest were marked by extraordinarily broad and shallow pelvic inlets and that their pelves in the proportions of breadth to height were remarkably low.

OBSERVATIONS

Table V–63 deals with the breadth of the ischiatic notch. A very broad notch is well-known to be a female characteristic and a narrow notch is typical of male pelves. In general the usual sex differences may be observed in this series. Some male pelves, however, show broad notches, and particularly in the Black-on-white and Glaze I subgroup. In this subgroup no less than 29 per cent of males adjudged to be male have distinctly feminine ischiatic notches. A very few females of the last two subgroups have narrow, masculine ischiatic notches. About 76 per cent of male pelves have decidedly narrow notches, whereas over 80 per cent of female pelves show the pronouncedly broad condition.

A deep preauricular sulcus with jagged edges is supposed to be a characteristically female feature by some writers, while a faintly defined sulcus, shallow and narrow, is held to be the typical condition in male pelves. Table V–64 lists the occurrences of various grades of this morphological character. Here again it may be noted that all males and all females do not conform to the anatomical convention. About ten and a half per cent of males show well marked preauricular sulci and about 15 per cent of females show little development of this feature. In the subgroups it is again notable that the preauricular sulcus frequently shows a markedly feminine development in the Black-on-white and Glaze I series of males. In the female series the last two subgroups show considerable percentages of poorly developed sulci.

Again we are taught that the subpubic angle in males is small and in females large. Table V–65 shows that this dogma is in general true, but about 16 per cent of each sex show a medium angle, which is neither characteristically male nor female, and about 3 per cent of males and 2 per cent of females show developments not in accord with the sex assigned to them. Once more the males of the first subgroup show feminine tendencies in the subpubic angles in a considerable percentage of

---

[1] Emmons, 1913, pp. 34–57.

TABLE V-61. COMPARATIVE TABLE OF PECOS INNOMINATE BONES AND SACRA
(COMPARATIVE DATA FROM HRDLIČKA *)

	Ossa Innominata — Right				Ossa Innominata — Left				Sacrum			
	No.	Height	Breadth	Index	No.	Height	Breadth	Index	No.	Height	Breadth	Index
Males												
Pecos	69	203.22	149.77	73.59†	71	203.54	149.02		66	104.73	115.89	111.17
Southern Utah Cliff-dwellers	20	205	150	73.2	20	205	150	73.3	22	108	115.5	106.9
Southwest and Mexico	12	207	152	73.7	12	207	152	73.5	15	107	113.6	106.2
Arkansas and Louisiana mounds	13	212	154	72.7	13	213	153.5	72.1	18	109.5	122	111.6
Munsee	16	213	156	73.4	16	212	145	73.2	6	107	116	108.2
United States whites	32	220.3	164.3	74.6	32	221	164.7	74.45	56	106.2	116.7	109.9
Females												
Pecos	54	186.07	140.50	75.37†	50	185.08	140.45	....	46	100.78	114.34	114.30
Southern Utah	7	190	143	75.4	7	191	142	74.6	10	101	113.3	112.2
Southwest and Mexico	12	191	146	76.6	12	192	147.5	76.8	18	104	115	110.6
Arkansas and Louisiana	8	198	150	75.7	8	199.5	151	76.1	22	102	119.6	117.2
Munsee	11	201	149.5	75.6	11	201	149	75.1	7	99	117	118.5
United States whites	20	202	157.3	77.9	20	201	157	78.1	25	101.8	117.5	115.4

* Hrdlička, 1916, p. 84.
† Mean of rights and lefts.

TABLE V–62. COMPARATIVE TABLE OF PECOS PELVES
(COMPARATIVE DATA FROM HRDLIČKA AND MARTIN [*])

	Mean Height of Ossa Innominata		Maximum Breadth		Total Pelvic Index		Superior Strait						Distance between Ischiatic Spines	
							Diam. Ant. P.		Diam. Lat.		Brim Index			
	No.	Mean	No.	Mean	No.	Mean	No.	Mean	No.	Mean	No.	Mean	No.	Mean
Males														
Pecos	70	203.35 †	72	270.42	69	74.91 †	69	95.56	74	125.58	66	76.65	46	85.83
Southern Utah	23	206	23	268.5	23	76.7	23	100	23	124	23	80.6	..	..
Southwest and Mexico	15	206	15	270	15	76.2	15	97	15	123	15	78.7	..	..
Arkansas and Louisiana	23	215.5	23	281	23	76.7	23	104	23	130	23	79.8	..	..
Munsee (Delaware)	6	212	6	267	6	78.9	6	106	6	121	6	87.8	..	..
United States whites	32	220.6	32	271	32	81.4	32	96.4	32	127	32	75.9	..	..
Europeans	..	220	..	279	..	79	..	104	..	130	..	80	..	81
Ainu	..	200	..	262	..	76.2	..	103	..	121	..	85	..	86
Japanese	..	200	..	269	..	74.3	..	103	..	120	..	86.9	..	84
Australians	..	202	..	263	..	75	..	107	..	115	..	93.4	..	..
Females														
Pecos	52	185.50 †	56	261.52	55	71.56 †	56	93.46	59	130.12	56	71.64	34	100.79
Southern Utah	7	190.5	7	254	7	74.5	7	101	7	131	7	77.4	..	..
Southwest and Mexico	12	191.5	15	257	12	74.4	12	107.5	12	129	12	83.1	..	..
Arkansas and Louisiana	12	197	12	268	12	73.5	12	107.4	12	133.3	12	81.4	..	..
Munsee (Delaware)	10	199.5	12	259	12	77.0	12	110	12	130	12	84.5	..	..
United States whites	20	201.6	12	270.5	12	74.5	12	107.3	12	133.5	12	80.4	..	..
Europeans	..	197	..	266	..	74.0	..	106	..	135	..	78.5	..	99
Ainu	..	188	..	258	..	72.8	..	111	..	129	..	85.7	..	100
Japanese	..	182	..	252	..	71.0	..	107	..	121	..	88.2	..	100
Australians	..	182	..	247	..	74.0	..	113	..	123	..	92.3	..	..

* Hrdlička, 1916, p. 86; Martin, II (1928), 1126.

† Rights or lefts used when only one bone is measurable.

cases, and the last two subgroups of females display a somewhat masculine narrowing of the subpubic angle.

If one looks from above at the pelvis held in articulation, it is usually observed that the ischia in males converge so that they may be seen through the pelvic inlet; whereas in females they diverge and may be seen jutting out below the acetabula. Table V–66 classifies the ischia, observed in this way as converging, diverging, or parallel. About 86 per cent of male pelves show converging ischia and an almost identical percentage of pelves judged to be female show the opposite condition. More than 9 per cent of males and about 8 per cent of females show a reversal of the usual sex differences. In the female series the last two subgroups show a diminished development of the female condition.

Usually the sacrum has five segments, but not infrequently six. Table 67 shows that the six-segment sacrum occurs in almost 16 per cent of male pelves but in only 5 per cent of female pelves. The sixth segment is, of course, added by the incorporation of the last lumbar. Sacra with six segments appear least common in both sexes during the earliest periods of the pueblo's occupation.

There is some difference of opinion as to whether curvature of the sacrum is more pronounced in females or in males. Table V–68 records the graded observations of this feature. About 16 per cent of females show pronounced sacral curvature and 19.5 per cent of males. Approximately 33 per cent of male and 40 per cent of female specimens show slight curvature of the sacrum or none at all. Thus it appears that the female sacrum is somewhat less curved than the male; although the differences are so slight that one may state confidently that sacral curvature, as observed here, is no reliable criterion of sex.

Table V–69 seems to show that the curve of the sacrum begins at the third segment in the majority of cases in both sexes. Female sacra occasionally show curvature beginning at the second segment whereas in males the curve begins at the fourth segment oftener than in females. But there is no marked sex difference in this character, according to our observations.

TABLE V–63.　Breadth of Ischiatic Notch

Males	B.-on-W. and Gl. I		Gls. II and III		Glaze IV		Gls. V and VI		Total Series A	
	No.	Per cent	No.	Per cent	No.	Per cent	No.	Per cent	No.	Per cent
Very pronounced	5	20.83	3	4.84	1	2.86	2	4.88	11	6.79
Pronounced	2	8.33	7	11.29	1	2.86	4	9.76	14	8.64
Medium	2	8.33	5	8.06	1	2.86	6	14.63	14	8.64
Submedium	13	54.17	44	70.97	28	80.00	26	63.41	111	68.52
Very submedium	2	8.33	3	4.84	4	11.43	3	7.32	12	7.41
Total	24		62		35		41		162	
Females										
Very pronounced	6	27.27	20	44.44	9	29.03	7	28.00	42	34.15
Pronounced	12	54.55	21	46.67	12	38.71	12	48.00	57	46.34
Medium	4	18.18	4	8.89	8	25.81	4	16.00	20	16.26
Submedium	0	0	0	0	2	6.45	2	8.00	4	3.25
Total	22		45		31		25		123	

TABLE V–64. DEVELOPMENT OF PREAURICULAR SULCUS

	B.-on-W. and Gl. I		Gls. II and III		Glaze IV		Gls. V and VI		Total Series A	
	No.	Per cent	No.	Per cent	No.	Per cent	No.	Per cent	No.	Per cent
Males										
Very pronounced	1	4.17	3	4.84	0	0	1	2.50	5	3.11
Pronounced	3	12.50	4	6.45	3	8.57	2	5.00	12	7.45
Medium	5	20.83	10	16.13	7	20.00	5	12.50	50	31.06
Submedium	6	25.00	16	25.81	11	31.43	17	42.50	9	5.59
Very submedium	2	8.33	3	4.84	0	0	4	10.00	9	5.59
Trace	3	12.50	20	32.26	8	22.86	9	22.50	40	24.84
Absent	4	16.67	6	9.68	6	17.14	2	5.00	18	11.18
Total	24		62		35		40		161	
Females										
Very pronounced	6	27.27	13	28.89	1	3.33	2	8.00	22	18.03
Pronounced	7	31.82	23	51.11	16	53.33	13	52.00	59	48.36
Medium	6	27.27	5	11.11	5	16.67	6	24.00	22	18.03
Submedium	3	13.64	1	2.22	4	13.33	3	12.00	11	9.02
Very submedium	0	0	1	2.22	0	0	0	0	1	0.82
Trace	0	0	1	2.22	3	10.00	0	0	4	3.28
Absent	0	0	1	2.22	1	3.33	1	4.00	3	2.46
Total	22		45		30		25		122	

TABLE V–65. SUBPUBIC ANGLE

	B.-on-W. and Gl. I		Gls. II and III		Glaze IV		Gls. V and VI		Total Series A	
	No.	Per cent	No.	Per cent	No.	Per cent	No.	Per cent	No.	Per cent
Males										
Pronounced	1	7.14	2	3.70	1	3.45	0	0	4	3.10
Medium	4	28.57	10	18.52	2	6.90	5	15.63	21	16.28
Submedium	9	64.29	42	77.78	25	86.21	27	84.38	103	79.84
Very submedium	0	0	0	0	1	3.45	0	0	1	.77
Total	14		54		29		32		129	
Females										
Very pronounced	1	6.67	7	19.44	1	4.17	0	0	9	9.28
Pronounced	10	66.67	24	66.67	18	75.00	18	81.82	70	72.16
Medium	3	20.00	5	13.89	5	20.83	3	13.64	16	16.49
Submedium	1	6.67	0	0	0	0	1	4.55	2	2.06
Total	15		36		24		22		97	

TABLE V–66. ISCHIA

	B.-on-W. and Gl. I		Gls. II and III		Glaze IV		Gls. V and VI		Total Series A	
	No.	Per cent	No.	Per cent	No.	Per cent	No.	Per cent	No.	Per cent
Males										
Converging	15	88.24	48	84.21	28	90.32	30	85.71	121	86.43
Diverging	2	11.76	5	8.77	2	6.45	4	11.43	13	9.29
Parallel	0	0	4	7.02	1	3.23	1	2.86	6	4.29
Total	17		57		31		35		140	
Females										
Converging	2	12.50	2	5.13	3	11.11	1	4.35	8	7.62
Diverging	14	87.50	36	92.31	23	85.19	18	78.26	91	86.67
Parallel	0	0	1	2.56	1	3.70	4	17.39	6	5.71
Total	16		39		27		23		105	

TABLE V–67. SEGMENTS OF SACRUM

	B.-on-W. and Gl. I		Gls. II and III		Glaze IV		Gls. V and VI		Total Series A	
	No.	Per cent	No.	Per cent	No.	Per cent	No.	Per cent	No.	Per cent
Males										
Six	1	9.09	6	15.00	6	24.00	4	12.50	17	15.74
Five	10	90.91	34	85.00	19	76.00	28	87.50	91	84.26
Total	11		40		25		32		108	
Females										
Six	0	0	2	6.90	1	4.76	1	5.56	4	5.00
Five	12	100.00	27	93.10	20	95.24	17	94.44	76	95.00
Total	12		29		21		18		80	

TABLE V–68. CURVATURE OF SACRUM

	B.-on-W. and Gl. I		Gls. II and III		Glaze IV		Gls. V and VI		Total Series A	
	No.	Per cent	No.	Per cent	No.	Per cent	No.	Per cent	No.	Per cent
Males										
Very pronounced	0	0	1	2.50	0	0	0	0	1	0.93
Pronounced	4	36.36	7	17.50	5	20.83	4	12.50	20	18.69
Medium	3	27.27	19	47.50	9	37.50	19	59.38	50	46.73
Submedium	4	36.36	13	32.50	9	37.50	8	25.00	34	31.78
Very submedium	0	0	0	0	1	4.17	0	0	1	0.93
Absent	0	0	0	0	0	0	1	3.12	1	0.93
Total	11		40		24		32		107	
Females										
Very pronounced	0	0	1	3.45	1	4.76	0	0	2	2.50
Pronounced	1	8.33	4	13.79	1	4.76	5	27.78	11	13.75
Medium	3	25.00	15	51.72	10	47.62	7	38.89	35	43.75
Submedium	7	58.33	7	24.14	8	38.10	5	27.78	27	33.75
Absent	1	8.33	2	6.90	1	4.76	1	5.56	5	6.25
Total	12		29		21		18		80	

TABLE V–69. BEGINNING OF SACRAL CURVATURE

	B.-on-W. and Gl. I		Gls. II and III		Glaze IV		Gls. V and VI		Total Series A	
	No.	Per cent	No.	Per cent	No.	Per cent	No.	Per cent	No.	Per cent
Males										
Four	1	9.09	7	17.50	9	37.50	9	29.03	26	24.53
Three	10	90.91	32	80.00	15	62.50	21	67.74	78	73.58
Two	0	0	1	2.50	0	0	0	0	1	0.94
One...............	0	0	0	0	0	0	1	3.23	1	0.94
Total	11		40		24		31		106	
Females										
Five	0	0	0	0	0	0	2	11.76	2	2.67
Four	3	27.27	5	18.52	5	25.00	1	5.88	14	18.67
Three	7	63.64	21	77.78	13	65.00	13	76.47	54	72.00
Two	1	9.09	1	3.70	2	10.00	1	5.88	5	6.67
Total	11		27		20		17		75	

LUMBAR COLUMN

VERTICAL INDEX

The vertical lumbar index (Table V–70) is derived by dividing the sum of the posterior heights of the lumbar centra multiplied by 100, by the sum of the anterior heights. The lower the index, the more pronounced is the anterior convexity of the lumbar curve. Indices above 100 indicate an absence of a strongly developed lumbar curve in so far as the curve is expressed by this index. It should be recalled, however, that the lumbar curve is probably brought about to a great extent by the intervertebral disks which are thicker anteriorly than posteriorly.

According to the conventional divisions of this index, below 98 is kurtorachic or anteriorly convex, from 98 to 101.9 is orthorachic or straight, and 102 and above indicates an anterior concavity (koilorachic). The Pecos lumbar columns yield kurtorachic or low orthorachic means, the females showing a lower average than the males, as is customary. In the males the index seems to increase from the early to the late periods.

Table V–71, taken from Martin,[1] indicates the position of the Pecos with reference to other groups.

TABLE V–70. LUMBAR INDEX

	No.	Range	Mean	S. D.	V.
Males					
Total Series A	67	89–112	99.18 ± 0.33	4.00 ± 0.23	4.03 ± 0.23
Black-on-white and Glaze I	6	90–103	98.17	....	....
Glazes II and III	27	89–105	98.52 ± 0.56	4.35 ± 0.40	4.42 ± 0.41
Glaze IV	14	96–104	99.00 ± 0.41	2.27 ± 0.29	2.29 ± 0.29
Glazes V and VI	20	92–112	100.50 ± 0.63	4.15 ± 0.44	4.13 ± 0.44
Females					
Total Series A	43	90–106	97.63 ± 0.34	3.31 ± 0.24	3.39 ± 0.25
Black-on-white and Glaze I	9	95–106	98.45	....	....
Glazes II and III	17	90–105	97.35 ± 0.57	3.46 ± 0.40	3.55 ± 0.41
Glaze IV	10	93–103	97.20	....	....
Glazes V and VI	7	94–104	97.86	....	....

TABLE V–71. COMPARATIVE TABLE OF VERTICAL LUMBAR INDEX
(AFTER MARTIN)

Group	Males	Females	Authority
Australians	110.1	103.1	Turner
Senoi	110	104	Martin
Andamanese	106.3	102.4	Cunningham
Veddah	103.5	99.9	Duckworth
Kwakiutl	105	98.1	Martin
Mound-builders	104	98.7	Martin
Fuegians	105	97.4	Martin
Peruvians	102.9	97.9	Martin
Masai	98.8	95.4	Martin
Pecos	*99.2*	*97.6*	*This memoir*
Europeans	96.2	93.5	Cunningham.

[1] Martin, 1928, p. 1080.

STATURE

RECONSTRUCTION OF LONG BONES

The statures of the Pecos series were calculated by the use of well-known formulae of Pearson [1] which utilize the maximum length of the femur and of the tibia.[2] The stature of each individual was calculated and the means of groups were made up from the arrays of individual statures. The applicability of these formulae to Indian groups may be questioned; but they probably are more satisfactory than those which may be substituted for them.

The mean stature of 142 males of all periods is only 161.7 cm., and the standard deviation of 4.3 cm. is exceptionally low. None of the Glaze subgroups can be said to differ significantly in stature from the mean of the series. If, however, we compare the subgroups among themselves, it is apparent that the minimum stature of males falls in the last period. But there is only 6 mm. of difference between the highest stature of subgroups and the lowest (Table V–72).

In the case of females, the stature seems to diminish somewhat in the last two periods, but probably there is no real meaning to such diminution. At any rate, the size of the series prevents any definite conclusion from the data. The females also present an exceptional constancy in stature.

TABLE V–72. STATURE

Males	No.	Range	Mean	S. D.	V.
Total Series A	142	152–176	161.74 ± 0.24	4.30 ± 0.17	2.66 ± 0.11
Black-on-white and Glaze I	22	154–176	161.86 ± 0.70	4.85 ± 0.49	3.00 ± 0.30
Glazes II and III	55	153–171	161.81 ± 0.37	4.04 ± 0.26	2.50 ± 0.16
Glaze IV	29	154–170	162.07 ± 0.47	3.79 ± 0.34	2.34 ± 0.21
Glazes V and VI	36	152–171	161.44 ± 0.49	4.39 ± 0.35	2.72 ± 0.22
Females					
Total Series A	81	143–159	150.11 ± 0.24	3.23 ± 0.19	2.15 ± 0.11
Black-on-white and Glaze I	17	147–158	152.00 ± 0.46	2.79 ± 0.32	1.84 ± 0.21
Glazes II and III	18	145–159	150.06 ± 0.52	3.29 ± 0.37	2.19 ± 0.25
Glaze IV	24	144–157	149.00 ± 0.48	3.46 ± 0.34	2.32 ± 0.23
Glazes V and VI	22	143–155	149.91 ± 0.43	3.01 ± 0.31	2.01 ± 0.20

COMPARATIVE STATURE

Tables V–73 and V–74 show the position of the Pecos population in the stature arrays of Indians of Northern Mexico and of the Southwestern United States as determined by Hrdlička.[2] From Table V–73 it may be noted that both Pecos males and females fall below all Southwestern groups in the United States but slightly exceed in stature some of the short tribes of Mexico. The Pueblo Indians of to-day exceed the mean of the Pecos males by 2.7 cm. and of the females by 2.1 cm. These differences, are, of course, small, and may conceivably be due to inapplicability of recon-

[1] Pearson, 1898, pp. 169–244.

Formula *e*.   Stature = 71.272 + 1.159 Femur + Tibia (males)
Stature = 69.154 + 1.126 Femur + Tibia (females)

[2] Hrdlička, 1908, pp. 132–137; 1909, p. 425.

struction formulae to Indian material. That this is probably not the case, is indicated, however, by Table V–74 in which the statures of different Pueblo groups are tabulated. Here again the Pecos stand at the foot of the list, but the males are only 7 mm. below the average of the Sia males, and but 1 cm. below the mean for the males of the Jemez pueblo. In 1838 the surviving remnant of the population of Pecos, seventeen in number, abandoned the ancestral home and migrated to Jemez, eighty miles to the northwest, upon the invitation of the Jemez people who were akin to them in language.

It is remarkable that the Jemez people of the present day stand nearest to the Pecos in the matter of stature (with the exception of the seven males measured by Hrdlička at the Sia pueblo). The centimeter increase in average stature manifested by the Jemez of to-day is really an insignificant difference. Stature may have increased somewhat in this area since prehistoric times, as it has increased in certain European countries. Or the Pecos may have been a little shorter than their kinsmen. Or, finally, the difference may be due to the reconstruction process. In any event, one may be confident that the means of stature obtained for the Pecos are nearly correct. Our data seem to show practically no change in the average stature of the population during the one thousand or more years of the pueblo's occupation. It seems probable that the allied Jemez, including the Pecos remnant, have changed little if any in stature during the nine decades which have elapsed since the abandonment of Pecos.

According to Hrdlička the average difference between male and female stature in Indians of the Southwest is about 12 cm. According to our figures this difference amounts to 11.6 cm. in the case of the Pecos Indians. The ratio of male to female height is about 108 for the average of Southwestern Indians according to the authority quoted above. Among the Pecos it was, by our calculations, 107. The ratio is usually lower among the shorter peoples. Among the Laguna pueblos the sex ratio is 106.4, among the Zuni and Hopi 108.7.

Dr. Hrdlička's investigations of stature among the Southwestern Indians lead him to the conclusion that hereditary rather than environmental factors are more potent in determining this bodily character. Stature in this region seems to vary independently of altitude and climate, the shortest tribes often living in juxtaposition to the tallest. With this conclusion the results of our Pecos study agree. The Pecos seem not to have varied in stature over a period of 1000 years, in spite of the fact that the last hundred years of the occupation of the village witnessed a rapid diminution and virtual extinction of the population through war, disease, and probably famine and malnutrition. Further it appears that the kindred people who received the Pecos remnant are substantially of the same stature as were the Pecos during their rise, prosperity, and decline. It is, of course, very probable that such stunted people as these Pueblos are selected for small stature and are relatively less variable in this dimension than many taller peoples. Tempting as it is to ascribe depression of stature to environmental deficiencies, it is apparent from a study of the Southwest that such an explanation cannot be invoked with any degree of success in this particular area.

TABLE V–73. Comparative Table of Average Statures of Living Indians of Northern Mexico and Southwestern United States (Hrdlička *)

	Males				Females			
	Number	Mean	Min.	Max.	Number	Mean	Min.	Max.
Otomi................	62	159.3	148.6	169.7	25	147.3	139.8	154.2
Tepecano	25	160.2	153.6	167.5	..	....	....	....
Mazahua	41	160.9	148.0	174.7	..	....	....	....
Tlahuiltec	50	161.0	153.5	172.9	30	148.9	139.5	163.3
Pecos †	*142*	*161.7*	*152*	*176*	*81*	*150.1*	*143*	*159*
Tarasco	50	163.1	155.5	175.5	30	150.8	144.7	165.2
Huichol	30	163.4	155.1	171.5	19	154.3	147.1	162.2
Cora	53	164.1	150.5	175.3	10	152.2	146.2	159.7
Tarahumare	23	164.2	153.0	174.5	10	152.7	148.6	159.6
Nahua	50	164.3	155.5	177.3	..	....	....	....
Pueblos..............	*383*	*164.5*	*148.2*	*182.3*	*59*	*152.3*	*143.5*	*168.4*
Tepehuane	40	165.3	156.6	180.8	15	151.6	145.6	157.1
Southern Ute	50	166.8	153.3	178.8	20	153.7	142.8	164.5
Opata	30	167.0	158.8	180.5	20	155.0	144.6	163.2
Mayo	53	167.3	154.7	185.1	30	155.2	147.0	166.5
Walapai, and Havasupai	47	168.4	155.1	180.2	23	157.7	134.7	172.2
Apache..............	212	169.1	151.0	182.5	70	156.8	147.2	169.3
Yaqui	50	169.6	157.0	180.4	33	154.2	146.5	161.0
Papago..............	50	170.9	155.7	180.8	30	155.9	148.8	163.3
Navaho	50	171.3	162.4	180.0	30	157.3	148.4	166.3
Mohave	45	171.6	161.8	186.2	25	158.5	147.4	169.3
Pima	53	171.8	161.7	181.4	30	157.4	146.9	164.8
Yuma	37	172.2	159.9	184.8	5	161.7	157.5	166.8
Maricopa	40	174.9	162.5	185.1	30	160.4	150.0	170.8

* Hrdlička, 1909, p. 425.
† Reconstruction from skeletons by use of Pearson's formulae.

TABLE V–74. Comparative Table of Average Statures of Living Pueblo Peoples (Hrdlička *)

	Males				Females			
	Number	Mean	Min.	Max.	Number	Mean	Min.	Max.
Pecos †	*142*	*161.7*	*152*	*176*	*81*	*150.1*	*143*	*159*
Sia	7	162.4	155	170	..	....	...	...
Jemez	40	162.7	150	175	..	....	...	...
Zuni	60	163.5	150	175	30	150.4	140	160
Laguna	65	163.7	150	175	30	153.8	145	170
Hopi	60	163.8	150	175	29	150.7	145	165
Taos	38	164.1	155	180	..	....	...	...
Acoma	14	165.0	155	170	..	....	...	...
Santo Domingo	40	165.6	155	175	..	....	...	...
San Juan	29	165.9	150	185	..	....	...	...
Isleta	30	168.3	155	180	..	....	...	...

* Hrdlička, 1908, pp. 132–137.
† Reconstruction from skeletons.

EXCESS OF GLAZE SUBGROUPS IN SKELETAL MEASUREMENTS AND INDICES

Table V–76 records the number and percentage of instances in which means of measurements and indices of Glaze subgroups exceed the means of the entire series by an amount in excess of twice the probable error of such differences. It will be recalled that less than 18 per cent of differences greater than twice the probable error are to be expected if the Glaze subgroups represent random samples of the entire series.

The first row of the table records excesses in measurements. The Black-on-white and Glaze I subgroup shows only 12.28 per cent of such excesses, and the Glaze II and III subgroup only 16.07 per cent. It, therefore, may be concluded that these subgroups are not significantly differentiated in size from the generality of the series. On the other hand Glaze IV subgroup and the Glaze V and VI subgroup show significant excesses of size in 25 per cent and 20 per cent respectively of measurements. A glance at the signs of Table V–75 shows that Glaze IV means are somewhat larger and Glaze V and VI means somewhat smaller than those of the series as a whole. It would appear that in gross dimensions the Glaze IV period marked the maximum of the pueblo population and that in the last two periods a marked or, at any rate, perceptible decline in size occurred.

The second row of the tables shows differences in indices or proportions. In this category the first subgroup shows 21 per cent of significant excesses and thus may be said to differ slightly from the entire series. The second subgroup and fourth subgroup show each 31.58 per cent of indicial differences and are thus markedly differentiated from the series at large. Glaze IV subgroup shows only 5.26 per cent of significant differences in indices.

If we consider significant differences of indices and measurements combined, (row three of the table), it is observed that the earliest subgroup shows an average of less than 15 per cent of significant differences, the second and third groups each 20 per cent, and the latest group 24 per cent. On the whole, then, the skeletal group representing the most recent members of the Pecos community differs most from the population at large. Curiously, this is exactly opposite to the results obtained in a similar survey of craniometric differences. In that case the Black-on-white and Glaze I subgroup was the most strongly, indeed the only, significantly differentiated subgroup, and the latest subgroup represented a random sample of the series. It would then appear that the Pecos people grew more and more homogeneous in craniometric features and more diversified in other skeletal measurements and proportions in the course of the pueblo's occupation. How may this fact be explained? One is tempted to infer that craniometric features are more largely controlled by genetic factors than other skeletal characters. Fluctuations in the prosperity and health of the community would, on this assumption, affect measurements and indices of other parts of the skeleton more than those of the skull. Unquestionably Glazes V and VI represent a period when the pueblo was gradually becoming depopulated through disease, attacks of enemies, and probably shortage of food. There is a slight but perceptible decrease in the gross dimensions during these periods. On the other hand, we have reason for believing that the pueblo was at once most populous and most prosperous during the Glaze IV period, skeletal remains of which are sufficiently numerous to form a single subgroup. And it is perhaps of interest to note that gross dimensions of males and stature of males reach their maximum in this period. However, one must always be on guard against attributing too much importance to slight differences of means, even when statistically significant. The maximum difference between average statures of males in different period subgroups is only .63 cm. and between female subgroups only 3 cm.

TABLE V–75. Excesses of Glaze Subgroups in Skeletal Measurements and Indices

Males	B.-on-W. and Gl. I		Gls. II and III		Glaze IV		Gls. V and VI	
	Excess	p. e.	Excess	p. e.	Excess	p. e.	Excess	p. e.
Femur								
length, max., r.	+2.30	± 2.99	−1.99	± 1.90	+1.55	± 2.46	−4.06	± 2.22
length, max., l.	−0.96	± 2.99	−1.15	± 1.80	+1.67	± 2.49	−3.93	± 2.23
length, bicond., r.	+3.29	± 2.94	−2.03	± 1.85	+1.41	± 2.38	−3.39	± 2.15
length, bicond., l.	−0.43	± 2.83	−1.40	± 1.74	+2.55	± 2.41	−3.10	± 2.16
max. diam. head, r.	+0.01	± 0.34	−0.10	± 0.21	+0.20	± 0.28	−0.29	± 0.26
max. diam. head, l.	+0.03	± 0.36	+0.10	± 0.23	+0.16	± 0.31	+0.24	± 0.29
sub. troc. diameter								
ant.-post., r.	+0.66	± 0.24	+0.37	± 0.15	+0.20	± 0.20	−0.01	± 0.18
ant. post., l.	+0.85	± 0.26	−0.23	± 0.16	+0.28	± 0.22	−0.30	± 0.20
lateral, r.	−0.75	± 0.29	−0.02	± 0.18	+0.12	± 0.24	+0.37	± 0.22
lateral, l.	−1.31	± 0.29	−0.05	± 0.19	+0.43	± 0.25	+0.52	± 0.23
middle diam. a. p., r.	+0.53	± 0.31	−0.24	± 0.19	+0.72	± 0.26	−0.67	± 0.24
middle diam. a. p., l.	−0.11	± 0.34	−0.10	± 0.22	+0.38	± 0.29	−0.66	± 0.28
middle diam. lat., r.	−0.36	± 0.26	−0.39	± 0.16	+0.23	± 0.22	+0.61	± 0.21
middle diam. lat., l.	−0.03	± 0.27	−0.37	± 0.18	+0.16	± 0.23	+0.47	± 0.22
platymeric index, r.	+3.55	± 0.83	−0.81	± 0.52	+0.28	± 0.70	−1.11	± 0.64
platymeric index, l.	+5.39	± 0.81	−0.58	± 0.52	−0.31	± 0.68	−2.16	± 0.64
middle index, r.	−1.90	± 1.18	−0.37	± 0.74	−1.31	± 0.98	+4.17	± 0.92
middle index, l.	−2.21	± 1.21	−1.41	± 0.78	−0.82	± 1.04	+4.40	± 0.98
Tibia								
length, r.	+1.84	± 3.02	+0.33	± 1.90	−0.37	± 2.48	−4.26	± 2.23
length, l.	+2.28	± 2.98	+1.08	± 1.93	−0.70	± 2.58	−5.11	± 2.23
middle diam. ant. post. r.	−0.45	± 0.40	−0.14	± 0.24	+0.66	± 0.32	−0.24	± 0.30
middle diam. ant. post. l.	+0.21	± 0.35	−0.53	± 0.22	+0.73	± 0.29	−0.01	± 0.28
middle diam., lat., r.	+0.44	± 0.32	−0.12	± 0.20	+0.43	± 0.26	−0.46	± 0.25
middle diam. lat., l.	+0.42	± 0.32	−0.23	± 0.20	+0.59	± 0.27	−0.68	± 0.25
nut. for diam.								
ant.-post., r.	−0.22	± 0.44	−0.29	± 0.27	+1.00	± 0.34	−0.39	± 0.34
ant.-post., l.	+0.56	± 0.45	−0.62	± 0.28	+0.70	± 0.37	−0.14	± 0.35
lateral, r.	+0.29	± 0.31	−0.08	± 0.19	+0.40	± 0.24	−0.42	± 0.23
lateral, l.	+0.41	± 0.33	−0.06	± 0.20	+0.24	± 0.26	−0.38	± 0.25
middle index, r.	+1.86	± 1.00	−0.11	± 0.63	−0.10	± 0.80	−0.96	± 0.76
middle index, l.	+0.71	± 0.98	+0.01	± 0.61	+0.52	± 0.82	−0.66	± 0.76
Tibio. fem. index, r.	−0.39	± 0.36	+0.29	± 0.22	−0.20	± 0.27	+0.01	± 0.24
Tibio. fem. index, l.	−0.84	± 0.36	+0.35	± 0.22	−0.03	± 0.30	−0.04	± 0.25
Fibula								
length, r.	−2.97	± 3.91	−1.95	± 2.22	+7.43	± 3.34	−2.89	± 2.55
length, l.	+1.34	± 3.90	+0.55	± 2.63	+0.97	± 3.18	−5.56	± 2.47

	B.-on-W. and Gl. I		Gls. II and III		Glaze IV		Gls. V and VI	
	Excess	p. e.	Excess	p. e.	Excess	p. e.	Excess	p. e.
Humerus								
length, r.	+0.71	± 2.45	+0.04	± 1.50	−0.88	± 1.86	−4.07	± 1.86
length, l.	+1.43	± 2.11	+0.66	± 1.46	+0.03	± 1.84	−4.20	± 1.63
max. diam. head, r.	+0.05	± 0.45	−0.14	± 0.28	+1.25	± 0.34	−0.07	± 0.33
max. diam. head, l.	+0.30	± 0.34	−0.14	± 0.28	+0.08	± 0.33	−0.02	± 0.28
middle diam. minor, r.	−0.19	± 0.18	−0.06	± 0.11	+0.07	± 0.14	+0.10	± 0.14
middle diam. minor, l.	+0.35	± 0.18	−0.04	± 0.12	−0.06	± 0.15	−0.09	± 0.14
middle diam. major, r.	+0.28	± 0.26	+0.06	± 0.16	−0.34	± 0.20	+0.10	± 0.20
middle diam. major, l.	+0.57	± 0.18	−0.24	± 0.15	−0.52	± 0.19	+0.34	± 0.17
Humero-femoral index, r.	+0.14	± 0.41	+0.57	± 0.25	−0.53	± 0.30	−0.33	± 0.30
Humero-femoral index, l.	−0.48	± 0.39	+0.66	± 0.25	−0.60	± 0.32	−0.16	± 0.28
Radius								
length, r.	+0.65	± 2.38	−2.69	± 1.63	−0.24	± 1.90	−1.36	± 1.79
length, l.	+1.11	± 2.46	+0.28	± 1.43	+1.39	± 2.03	−4.35	± 1.62
Ulna								
length, r.	−0.53	± 2.23	−0.64	± 1.57	−0.04	± 2.09	−2.67	± 1.82
length, l.	−0.40	± 2.13	−1.37	± 1.45	+1.33	± 1.92	−3.45	± 1.57
Clavicle								
length, r.	−4.78	± 1.79	−0.16	± 1.24	+0.78	± 1.40	−0.08	± 1.33
length, l.	−1.60	± 1.59	−1.26	± 1.18	+2.73	± 1.43	−1.38	± 1.25
Scapula								
total height, r.	+3.37	± 2.58	−2.43	± 1.63	+3.28	± 1.56	−1.94	± 1.43
total height, l.	−1.84	± 3.07	−2.17	± 1.54	+6.63	± 1.68	−0.72	± 1.61
inferior height, r.	+1.93	± 2.13	−3.30	± 1.28	0.00	± 1.23	+0.90	± 1.10
inferior height, l.	−2.78	± 2.09	−2.59	± 1.16	+3.54	± 1.26	+0.38	± 1.08
total breadth, r.	−3.99	± 1.69	+0.78	± 1.02	+0.59	± 0.98	+0.01	± 0.90
total breadth, l.	−6.44	± 2.10	+0.61	± 1.01	+1.23	± 1.09	−0.14	± 0.91
total index, r.	+0.28	± 1.24	+1.48	± 0.78	−1.29	± 0.94	−0.63	± 0.75
total index, l.	−1.47	± 1.60	+1.61	± 0.65	−1.37	± 0.72	+0.30	± 0.68
inferior index, r.	−4.35	± 1.86	+3.75	± 1.17	−0.52	± 1.07	−1.14	± 0.99
inferior index, l.	−2.08	± 2.07	+2.44	± 1.00	−2.32	± 1.08	−2.03	± 0.90
Pelvis								
breadth, max.	+6.25	± 3.30	−0.65	± 1.59	+4.58	± 2.02	+2.08	± 1.65
ischiatic spines	+0.17	± 4.26	+8.85	± 1.48	+1.29	± 1.79	−2.43	± 2.34
innominate bones								
breadth, r.	+4.23	± 2.22	−1.93	± 1.02	+1.44	± 1.19	−0.02	± 1.00
breadth, l.	−1.62	± 1.94	−0.76	± 0.91	+2.90	± 1.26	−0.47	± 0.97
height, r.	−4.22	± 2.60	−0.66	± 1.16	+1.84	± 1.46	−0.57	± 1.21
height, l.	−0.21	± 2.54	+0.02	± 1.19	+5.06	± 1.60	+0.11	± 1.29
superior strait								
breadth, max.	+1.59	± 1.86	+0.88	± 0.89	−0.21	± 1.04	−1.23	± 0.94
ant. post. diam.	+4.11	± 2.65	−0.88	± 1.29	+0.44	± 1.53	−0.61	± 1.45
sacrum, height	+0.07	± 2.54	+2.73	± 1.16	+0.27	± 1.30	−3.95	± 1.34
sacrum, breadth	−1.09	± 1.65	+1.19	± 0.75	−0.52	± 0.85	−0.72	± 0.87
total pelvic index	−1.24	± 0.80	+0.92	± 0.41	−0.41	± 0.49	−0.28	± 0.40
brim index	+1.02	± 2.11	−0.29	± 1.10	−0.09	± 1.22	−0.20	± 1.15
innominate index	+0.41	± 0.57	−0.35	± 0.28	+0.41	± 0.35	0.00	± 0.30
sacral index	−0.77	± 3.14	−2.17	± 1.43	−0.80	± 1.61	+4.05	± 1.66
Lumbar vertebral index	−0.01	± 1.10	−0.66	± 0.52	−0.18	± 0.72	+1.32	± 0.60

TABLE V–76. Excesses of Glaze Subgroups More Than Twice Their Probable Errors (Males)

		B.-on-W. and Gl. I		Gls. II and III		Glaze IV		Gls. V and VI	
		No.	Per cent	No.	Per cent	No.	Per cent	No.	Per cent
Measurements	(56)	7	12.28	9	16.07	14	25.00	12	21.53
Indices	(19)	4	21.05	6	31.58	1	5.26	6	31.58
Total	(75)	11	14.67	15	20.00	15	20.00	18	24.00

SUMMARY OF SIGNIFICANT EXCESSES IN MEASUREMENTS OF GLAZE SUBGROUPS. (MALES)

BLACK–ON–WHITE AND GLAZE I

The femora in this group show significantly augmented antero-posterior diameters in the sub-trochanteric region and diminished lateral diameters. In consequence the indices of platymeria on both sides are higher than in the group at large. The tibio-femoral index on the left side is markedly higher than in the entire series. The right clavicle shows a marked deficiency in length, and the left clavicle is also shorter, but not significantly so. There are some indications that the pelves of this group are lower and broader than those of the total series, but we cannot be sure that these are valid differences. The scapulae are narrower also in this earliest group and the right scapula presents a marked deficiency in the inferior index.

GLAZES II AND III

In this group the femora show on both sides deficiency in the lateral diameters and there is also an augmentation of the antero-posterior diameter of the subtrochanteric region of the right femur. The left tibiae show deficiencies of the lateral diameters. The humero-femoral index is markedly higher than the group average. In the pelvis the diameter between the ischiatic spines is excessive; the height of the sacrum is augmented, as is also the total pelvic index. Marked diminution of the inferior height of the scapula and increases in the inferior and total scapular indices are recorded.

GLAZE IV

The antero-posterior middle shaft diameter of the right femur is augmented. The tibiae show increases of the antero-posterior shaft diameters. There is an inexplicable and probably meaningless excess in length of right fibulae. The right humerus shows an enlarged head diameter. The pelves seem to be broader and to show increased diameters of the left innominate bones. The scapulae show an augmentation in height measurements and in the inferior index of the left side.

GLAZES V AND VI

The bones of the last group show, in general, diminished lengths, but many of these are statistically insignificant. The lateral subtrochanteric diameters of the femora are increased, as are those of the middle shaft; the antero-posterior diameters are diminished. The indices of platymeria are diminished and the middle index increased. Thus the femora are more platymeric and have more strongly developed pilasters than in the group at large. The tibiae and fibulae are shorter, as are also the humeri. The sacra are shorter and the sacral indices are higher. The lumbar curve is less pronounced and the scapulae are smaller and have lower inferior indices.

CHAPTER VI

MEASUREMENTS OF MORPHOLOGICAL CRANIAL TYPES

METHOD OF DIFFERENTIATING TYPES

THE study of the Pecos skeletal material by archaeological subgroups revealed certain changes which took place in the population of the pueblo during the approximate millenium of its inhabitation. But these differences in the period groups which have been set forth in detail in the foregoing chapters of the present work, are in no case sufficiently pronounced to indicate that the racial type of the population changed perceptibly from period to period. Long-heads and round-heads, deformed and undeformed crania, appear in every stratum from the earliest to the latest. There was at no time the wholesale replacement of one prevailing racial type by another, as might have been expected, if, for example, the earliest dwellers on the mesa had been people of the primitive Basket Maker type found in certain caves of Arizona and New Mexico, who were followed by brachycephalic Mongoloids, who were in turn driven out and replaced by such a physically different group as might be represented by the Comanche Indians of the plains. No marked changes of this sort seem to have coincided with our groupings of the various Glaze burials. No "New Race" appeared during the history of Pecos.

Nevertheless it is apparent to the craniologist that the skeletal population of Pecos was at no time markedly homogeneous in type. On the contrary the handling and measurement of the Glaze subgroups leaves the impression of a number of markedly diverse cranial types, found in varying proportions at all periods. Therefore upon the conclusion of the study of period groups it was decided to reanalyze the material, relying upon morphological rather than upon archaeological criteria for the differentiation of groups.

The method followed in this second analysis depended upon the sorting of all male crania into types on the basis of morphological features. All of the male crania utilized in Total Series A and a number of additional skulls which had been sent in from the excavations subsequently, were spread out in the laboratory. These were then grouped according to their mutual resemblances. The criteria of differentiation were mostly facial features, since in the majority of cases the skull-vaults had been artificially deformed. After a number of days of sorting and resorting, the series of 129 male skulls was finally divided into eight types. The first of these I called the "Basket Maker" type, because of its small face, narrow forehead, poorly developed chin and mandible, but above all because of a general resemblance, perhaps fancied, to the veritable Basket Makers of the Arizona caves. The second type was styled "Pseudo-Negroid," not because of any theory of the observer as to the presence of a Negroid strain in the American Indian, but because the skulls of this type showed flat, broad nasal bones, platyrrhiny, pronounced alveolar prognathism, and rounded frontal regions. Another type was called "Pseudo-Australoid" because it consisted of skulls with heavily marked supraorbital ridges continuous from one external angular process to the other, deeply depressed nasal roots, platyrrhiny, and facial prognathism. Still another group received the designation "Plains Indians," because of a certain robusticity of skull structure and the prevalence of long concavo-convex nasalia, prominent malars, and well developed mandibles. A further type was characterized by compressed or medium malars, very long faces and deep mandibles, straight and often high-bridged and narrow noses, high orbits, and orthognathism. I called this type "Long-faced Europeans" because it seemed to me rather un-Indian, if one may employ such an expression. Another group was christened "Pseudo-Alpine" because of its very short broad face with rounded contours, rather prominent malars, broad vertical forehead, swelling temporal regions, and broad short nose. This group also appeared to be orthognathous. A cranial type defined by massiveness, heavy projecting malars, long faces, ponderous jaws with everted gonial angles, and a number of other features not easily described but easily recognized was called the "Large Hybrid" group because of my opinion that the massive face so often seen in American Indians is due to the crossing of a long-faced type with a broad-faced type, in which the maximum diameters of both dimensions persist. Finally a number of crania with no discernible affinities with any of the groups enumerated above were "dumped" into a "Residual" class. Most of such skulls were merely nondescript specimens of a generalized Southwestern Indian appearance.

It is easy enough in racial analysis to select a few arbitrary types characterized by an alleged combination of contrasted characters and to give verisimilitude to such classifications by illustrating a few individual specimens and listing two or three means of different values. It is quite another thing to divide up a whole population into types and to prove statistically that these types actually exist and are individually homogeneous. In the present instance I have not been satisfied with setting up types for the reader to believe in or to reject according to his fancy, but have actually tested the validity of my morphological assignments by calculating means, standard deviations, and probable errors of each type and contrasting these with the same constants derived from the series as a whole. This, of course, involved a complete reworking of all of the metric data of the series. In this task only male crania were included, partly because of my opinion that racial types are usually more clearly marked in the male sex, and partly because of the tremendous labor which would have been involved in repeating the analysis of the female series also.

The following tables show the means of type subgroups, the standard deviations, coefficients of variation, and probable errors of these constants, in every case contrasted with the series as a whole. In order to demonstrate that a type is homogeneous with respect to any given mean of a measurement or index, it should be shown that the type has a smaller standard deviation and coefficient of variation than the same mean exhibits in the series as a whole. In other words the dispersion of a type should be less than that of the entire population, at any rate in those features which characterize the type.

THE SKULL VAULT

In dealing with this series of male crania, called Series B, no distinction has been made between crania with undeformed skulls and crania with deformed vaults. Cranial deformation is distributed accidentally and continuously throughout the entire Pecos population almost like any other metric or morphological character. Nevertheless Table VI–1 clearly shows that the types least affected by deformation are the "Basket Makers," "Pseudo-Negroids," "Pseudo-Australoids," and "Long-faced Europeans." The remaining types show consistent occipital flattening.

TABLE VI–1. MORPHOLOGICAL TYPES ASSOCIATED WITH DEFORMATION

	Absent		Submedium		Medium		Pronounced		Total
	No.	Per cent	No.	Per cent	No.	Per cent	No.	Per cent	
"Basket Makers"	2	25.00	4	50.00	1	12.50	1	12.50	8
"Pseudo-Negroids"	2	15.38	6	46.15	4	30.77	1	7.69	13
"Pseudo-Australoids"	3	27.27	6	54.55	1	9.09	1	9.09	11
"Plains Indians"..........	0	0	11	45.83	10	41.67	3	12.50	24
"Long-faced Europeans"...	2	11.11	5	27.78	7	38.89	4	22.22	18
"Pseudo-Alpines".........	0	0	1	1.14	4	28.57	9	64.29	14
"Large Hybrids"	0	0	3	11.11	9	33.33	15	55.56	27
"Residuals"	0	0	0	0	7	50.00	7	50.00	14
Total	9	6.98	36	27.91	43	33.33	41	31.78	129

Coefficient of contingency 0.56.

A perusal of Table VI–2, dealing with means of the glabello-occipital length in the various type groups, shows that all of these morphological groups show lower standard deviations and coefficients of variation than the series at large, with the exception of the type labelled "Pseudo-Negroid." The so-called "Basket Makers" and "Pseudo-Australoids" have much longer heads than the series at large, and a significant excess of this measurement is also displayed by the "Plains Indians" and "Long-faced Europeans"; whereas the "Pseudo-Alpines," "Large Hybrids," and "Residuals" exhibit means considerably lower than that of the entire series. This of course may be interpreted to mean that cranial deformation is more prevalent or more pronounced in the latter three groups than in the former, but, since vault formation was not a conscious criterion of type selection, it may be concluded that differences in deformation among our types are associated with facial criteria of distinction.

If we separate our type groups into deformed and undeformed (Table VI–3), we note that the same excesses appear in the head-lengths of the subgroups, whether deformed crania are taken separately or practically undeformed crania. The application of Shapiro's correction formulae to the deformed crania of the various subgroups results in a restoration of deformed crania to lengths usually somewhat less than those of the undeformed crania, but the type differences persist.

Table VI–4 shows that the standard deviations of skull breadth in the type subgroups are also significantly less than those of the series as a whole; the types which exhibit excess skull lengths show deficiencies of skull breadth, with the exception of the "Long-faced European" type. The groups which are distinguished by the shortness of their crania show excesses in breadth. When, again, the crania are divided by types into deformed and undeformed groups the type differences still persist, and the application of correction formulae to the deformed crania indicates a somewhat greater original breadth in the deformed crania of a type than in those which have not been subjected to occipital flattening.

The means of the length-breadth index of the various types are recorded in Table VI–6. The standard deviations and coefficients of variations of the types are again significantly less than those of the series as a whole, with the exception of the "Pseudo-Negroid" group. All of the type groups show means markedly different from the value of the total series. Only the "Pseudo-Australoid" and "Basket Maker" groups show approximations to dolichocephaly. When the crania of the type groups are divided into deformed and undeformed categories (Table VI–7) it may be observed that all of the subgroups of deformed skulls yield brachycephalic means, but that the undeformed means of the "Basket Makers," "Pseudo-Negroids," and "Pseudo-Australoids" are sub-dolichocephalic, and the mean of the "Plains" group is mesocephalic. Correction of the deformed crania of all groups reduces the brachycephaly — in the case of the first five types — to mesocephaly, or even to sub-dolichocephaly. Type differences are not eliminated by such correction.

Basion-bregma heights of the type subgroups (Tables VI–8, 9) usually show smaller standard deviations and significant differences from the means of the entire series. The "Basket Maker" "Pseudo-Negroid," and "Pseudo-Australoid" types have lower height values than the series at large, whereas some of the other groups show excesses. When deformed and undeformed skulls are separated the type consistency remains but the deformed groups show higher values than the undeformed. Correction of deformation does not alter the distinctiveness of the types.

The length-height index (Tables VI–10, 11) in the crude means of type groups regardless of deformation is consistently hypsicephalic, but the first three subgroups show much lower values than the remaining five. Variabilities, with one exception, are lower than in the entire series. Separation into deformed and undeformed categories and correction of values in the deformed crania gives one orthocephalic group, the so-called "Pseudo-Negroids." Type differences are maintained.

The undifferentiated means of the breadth-height index in the type subgroups (Table VI–12) shows that the "Basket Makers," "Pseudo-Australoids," "Plains," and "European" types are prevailing acrocephalic, the other groups being metriocephalic. Distinction between deformed and undeformed and correction of mean values of the former accentuate the previously existing type differences (Table VI–13), but reduce the acrocephaly of the "European" type.

Minimum frontal diameters show somewhat reduced variabilities in the type subgroups and marked excesses in the values of means in the case of "Long-faced Europeans" and "Large Hybrids." The narrowest frontals are found in the "Basket Maker" and "Plains Indian" types.

TABLE VI–2. GLABELLO–OCCIPITAL LENGTH. TOTAL SERIES B

Males	No.	Range	Mean	S.D.	V.
Total Series B	127	145–189	168.56 ± 0.55	9.16 ± 0.38	5.43 ± 0.23
"Basket Makers"	8	169–183	176.88 ± 1.30	5.46 ± 0.92	3.09 ± 0.52
"Pseudo-Negroids"	13	153–189	169.15 ± 1.89	10.04 ± 1.33	5.94 ± 0.79
"Pseudo-Australoids"	11	163–182	175.73 ± 1.12	5.51 ± 0.79	3.14 ± 0.45
"Plains Indians"	23	160–185	172.61 ± 1.07	7.63 ± 0.76	4.42 ± 0.44
"Long-faced Europeans"	17	162–187	172.71 ± 1.10	6.70 ± 0.77	3.88 ± 0.45
"Pseudo-Alpines"	14	151–173	161.21 ± 1.00	5.52 ± 0.70	3.42 ± 0.44
"Large Hybrids"	27	145–178	165.30 ± 1.02	7.87 ± 0.72	4.76 ± 0.44
"Residuals"	14	148–170	159.57 ± 1.18	6.52 ± 0.83	4.09 ± 0.52

TABLE VI–3. GLABELLO–OCCIPITAL LENGTH[1] (DEFORMED, UNDEFORMED, AND CORRECTED). TOTAL SERIES B

Males	No.	Deformed	No.	Undeformed	Corrected Deformed
Total Series B	96	165.96	31	176.61	175.88
"Basket Makers"	2	174.50	6	177.67	174.84
"Pseudo-Negroids"	10	165.60	3	177.67	175.54
"Pseudo-Australoids"	4	174.75	7	176.29	179.27
"Plains Indians"	16	170.62	7	177.14	175.49
"Long-faced Europeans"	12	171.00	5	176.80	176.43
"Pseudo-Alpines"	14	161.21	0	. . . . .	. . . . .
"Large Hybrids"	24	164.38	3	172.67	172.64
"Residuals"	14	159.57	0	. . . . .	. . . . .

[1] Cranial diameters of the "Pseudo-Alpines" and "Residual" types have not been corrected, because of the lack of a sufficient number of undeformed or slightly deformed crania in these types to furnish a basis for correction.

TABLE VI–4. MAXIMUM BREADTH. TOTAL SERIES B

Males	No.	Range	Mean	S.D.	V.
Total Series B	125	125–164	142.73 ± 0.43	7.17 ± 0.31	5.02 ± 0.21
"Basket Makers"	8	127–142	134.75 ± 1.32	5.54 ± 0.93	4.11 ± 0.69
"Pseudo-Negroids"	13	128–150	138.69 ± 0.96	5.15 ± 0.68	3.71 ± 0.49
"Pseudo-Australoids"	11	125–145	135.64 ± 1.19	5.85 ± 0.84	4.31 ± 0.62
"Plains Indians"	22	132–150	139.64 ± 0.61	4.23 ± 0.43	3.03 ± 0.31
"Long-faced Europeans"	17	132–148	141.59 ± 0.75	4.60 ± 0.53	3.25 ± 0.38
"Pseudo-Alpines"	14	139–157	148.07 ± 1.06	5.89 ± 0.75	3.98 ± 0.51
"Large Hybrids"	27	135–164	148.89 ± 0.77	5.95 ± 0.55	4.00 ± 0.37
"Residuals"	13	143–158	145.85 ± 0.76	4.05 ± 0.54	2.78 ± 0.37

TABLE VI–5. MAXIMUM BREADTH (DEFORMED, UNDEFORMED, AND CORRECTED). TOTAL SERIES B

Males	No.	Deformed	No.	Undeformed	Corrected Deformed
Total Series B	94	144.61	31	137.00	137.66
"Basket Makers"	2	140.50	6	132.83	135.24
"Pseudo-Negroids"	10	139.80	3	135.00	135.49
"Pseudo-Australoids"	4	139.50	7	133.43	133.98
"Plains Indians"	15	140.80	7	137.16	137.79
"Long-faced Europeans"	12	141.42	5	142.00	140.84
"Pseudo-Alpines"	14	148.07	0	. . . . .	. . . . .
"Large Hybrids"	24	149.08	3	147.33	147.43
"Residuals"	13	145.85	0	. . . . .	. . . . .

TABLE VI–6. Cranial Index. Total Series B

Males	No.	Range	Mean	S.D.	V.
Total Series B	124	69.44–101.94	84.71 ± 0.44	7.21 ± 0.31	8.51 ± 0.36
"Basket Makers"	8	72.57 – 82.25	76.38 ± 0.86	3.60 ± 0.61	4.71 ± 0.79
"Pseudo-Negroids" ...	13	72.02 – 96.15	82.08 ± 1.25	6.67 ± 0.88	8.13 ± 1.08
"Pseudo-Australoids"	11	69.44 – 84.67	77.27 ± 0.96	4.71 ± 0.68	6.10 ± 0.88
"Plains Indians"	22	73.33 – 88.96	81.23 ± 0.65	4.49 ± 0.46	5.53 ± 0.56
"Long-faced Europeans"	17	74.87 – 88.62	82.12 ± 0.63	3.88 ± 0.45	4.72 ± 0.55
"Alpines"	14	81.29 – 98.73	92.14 ± 0.93	5.17 ± 0.66	5.61 ± 0.72
"Large Hybrids"	26	82.22–101.92	89.31 ± 0.68	5.16 ± 0.48	5.78 ± 0.54
"Residuals"..........	13	84.12–101.94	90.92 ± 0.89	4.78 ± 0.63	5.26 ± 0.70

TABLE VI–7. Cranial Index (Deformed, Undeformed, and Corrected). Total Series B

Males	No.	Deformed	No.	Undeformed	Corrected Deformed
Total Series B	93	87.09	31	77.65	78.27
"Basket Makers"	2	80.50	6	75.00	77.35
"Pseudo-Negroids"	10	84.00	3	75.67	77.18
"Pseudo-Australoids"	4	80.00	7	75.71	74.74
"Plains Indians"	15	83.00	7	77.43	78.52
"Long-faced Europeans"	12	82.83	5	80.40	79.83
"Pseudo-Alpines"	14	92.14	0	....	....
"Large Hybrids"	23	89.83	3	85.33	85.40
"Residuals"	13	90.92	0	....	....

TABLE VI–8. Basion–Bregma Height. Total Series B

Males	No.	Range	Mean	S.D.	V.
Total Series B	106	127–156	139.63 ± 0.37	5.61 ± 0.26	4.02 ± 0.19
"Basket Makers"	7	128–144	135.57 ± 1.50	5.90 ± 1.06	4.35 ± 0.78
"Pseudo-Negroids" ...	11	127–142	133.73 ± 0.93	4.59 ± 0.66	3.43 ± 0.49
"Pseudo-Australoids"	10	133–144	137.10 ± 0.75	3.53 ± 0.53	2.57 ± 0.39
"Plains Indians"	21	131–152	138.90 ± 0.73	4.93 ± 0.51	3.55 ± 0.37
"Long-faced Europeans"	13	135–151	141.69 ± 0.84	3.99 ± 0.60	3.18 ± 0.42
"Pseudo-Alpines"	10	129–148	138.50 ± 1.03	4.84 ± 0.73	3.49 ± 0.53
"Large Hybrids"	23	136–156	144.13 ± 0.64	4.53 ± 0.45	3.14 ± 0.31
"Residuals"	11	136–148	141.00 ± 0.69	3.41 ± 0.49	2.42 ± 0.35

TABLE VI–9. Basion–Bregma Height (Deformed, Undeformed, and Corrected). Total Series B

Males	No.	Mean Deformed	No.	Mean Undeformed	Corrected Deformed
Total Series B	79	140.84	27	136.30	137.87
"Basket Makers"	2	137.00	5	135.00	141.92
"Pseudo-Negroids"	8	134.88	3	130.67	129.15
"Pseudo-Australoids"	4	140.25	6	135.00	141.25
"Plains Indians"	15	139.20	6	137.83	137.34
"Long-faced Europeans"	8	142.62	5	140.20	137.77
"Pseudo-Alpines"	10	138.50	0	.....	.....
"Large Hybrids"	21	144.57	2	137.50	137.96
"Residuals"	11	141.00	0	.....	.....

TABLE VI–10. Length–Height Index. Total Series B

Males	No.	Range	Mean	S.D.	V.
Total Series B	107	70.37–100.69	82.89 ± 0.39	5.93 ± 0.27	7.15 ± 0.33
"Basket Makers"	7	72.22 – 85.21	76.86 ± 1.10	4.32 ± 0.78	5.62 ± 1.01
"Pseudo-Negroids" ...	11	70.37 – 92.21	79.27 ± 1.35	6.66 ± 0.96	8.40 ± 1.21
"Pseudo-Australoids" .	10	73.08 – 84.66	78.20 ± 0.81	3.82 ± 0.58	4.88 ± 0.74
"Plains Indians"	21	73.74 – 89.57	80.81 ± 0.59	4.02 ± 0.42	4.97 ± 0.52
"Long-faced Europeans"	13	75.84 – 88.30	82.31 ± 0.64	3.41 ± 0.45	4.14 ± 0.55
"Pseudo-Alpines"	11	77.71 – 94.41	85.64 ± 0.93	4.56 ± 0.66	5.32 ± 0.77
"Large Hybrids"	23	78.65–100.69	87.17 ± 0.73	5.19 ± 0.52	5.95 ± 0.59
"Residuals"	11	81.18 – 92.86	87.55 ± 0.87	4.27 ± 0.61	4.88 ± 0.70

TABLE VI–11. Length–Height Index (Deformed, Undeformed, and Corrected). Total Series B

Males	No.	Deformed	No.	Undeformed	Corrected Deformed
Total Series B	80	84.71	27	77.41	78.41
"Basket Makers"	2	78.50	5	76.20	81.14
"Pseudo-Negroids"	8	81.38	3	73.67	73.30
"Pseudo-Australoids"	4	80.25	6	76.83	78.77
"Plains Indians"	15	81.60	6	78.50	78.29
"Long-faced Europeans"	8	84.25	5	79.40	78.41
"Pseudo-Alpines"	11	85.64	0	....	....
"Large Hybrids"	21	87.90	2	79.50	79.77
"Residuals"	11	87.55	0	....	....

TABLE VI–12. Breadth–Height Index. Total Series B

Males	No.	Range	Mean	S.D.	V.
Total Series B	106	86.00–111.81	98.08 ± 0.31	4.74 ± 0.22	4.83 ± 0.22
"Basket Makers"	7	91.55–111.81	100.00 ± 1.56	6.12 ± 1.10	6.12 ± 1.10
"Pseudo-Negroids" ...	11	93.53–103.73	97.36 ± 0.68	3.34 ± 0.48	3.43 ± 0.49
"Pseudo-Australoids" ..	10	95.68–106.40	100.40 ± 0.76	3.58 ± 0.54	3.57 ± 0.54
"Plains Indians"	20	93.33–111.76	99.30 ± 0.62	4.11 ± 0.44	4.14 ± 0.44
"Long-faced Europeans"	13	95.86–108.27	100.54 ± 0.61	3.25 ± 0.43	3.23 ± 0.43
"Pseudo-Alpines"	11	86.00–100.00	92.73 ± 0.92	4.53 ± 0.65	4.89 ± 0.70
"Large Hybrids"	23	89.47–107.41	97.57 ± 0.62	4.39 ± 0.44	4.50 ± 0.45
"Residuals"	11	88.61–103.50	96.64 ± 0.75	3.68 ± 0.53	3.81 ± 0.55

TABLE VI–13. Breadth–Height Index (Deformed, Undeformed, and Corrected). Total Series B

Males	No.	Deformed	No.	Undeformed	Corrected Deformed
Total Series B	79	97.43	27	99.63	100.00
"Basket Makers"	2	98.00	5	100.80	105.18
"Pseudo-Negroids"	8	97.62	3	97.00	95.56
"Pseudo-Australoids"	4	99.25	6	101.17	105.22
"Plains Indians"	14	98.64	6	100.83	99.28
"Long-faced Europeans"	8	101.88	5	98.80	97.87
"Pseudo-Alpines"	11	92.73	0	.....	.....
"Large Hybrids"	21	97.86	2	94.50	93.88
"Residuals"	11	96.64	0	.....	.....

TABLE VI–14.   Minimum Frontal Diameter.   Total Series B

Males	No.	Range	Mean	S.D.	V.
Total Series B	127	83–112	95.28 ± 0.31	5.15 ± 0.22	5.41 ± 0.23
"Basket Makers"	8	87–100	93.00 ± 1.03	4.30 ± 0.73	4.62 ± 0.78
"Pseudo-Negroids"	13	88–105	95.46 ± 0.94	5.03 ± 0.67	5.27 ± 0.70
"Pseudo-Australoids" ..	11	89–105	94.09 ± 0.93	4.56 ± 0.66	4.85 ± 0.70
"Plains Indians"	23	83–104	93.65 ± 0.63	4.45 ± 0.44	4.75 ± 0.47
"Long-faced Europeans"	18	87–105	97.00 ± 0.77	4.85 ± 0.55	5.00 ± 0.56
"Pseudo-Alpines"	14	86–103	94.50 ± 0.86	4.76 ± 0.61	5.04 ± 0.64
"Large Hybrids"	26	89–109	97.62 ± 0.65	4.95 ± 0.46	5.07 ± 0.47
"Residuals"	14	88–112	94.29 ± 1.06	5.90 ± 0.75	6.26 ± 0.80

Cranial capacities in the type subgroups show interesting deviations from the total series mean. In general the first four subdolichocephalic or mesocephalic types show lower capacities than the remaining four brachycephalic types. The extreme deviations are found in the "Pseudo-Negroid" type which shows a mean deficiency of 84 cc. and in the "Large Hybrid" type which shows an excess of 81 cc.

Tables VI–16, 17 deal with the cranial module, which is the mean of the three diameters of the brain-case. The smallest value is that of the "Pseudo-Negroid" type and the largest that of the "Large Hybrid" groups. Clear differentiation of types is observable in this table, which shows similar tendencies to those displayed in the table dealing with cranial capacity.

The means of the horizontal circumferences of type groups (Table VI–18) when compared with the mean of the whole series show, for the most part, insignificant differences and almost equal variabilities. The single exceptions occur in the "Pseudo-Australoid" and "Residual" types. On the whole it may be concluded from Table VI–18 that our types are not clearly differentiated with regard to this measurement. More clearly differentiated means and generally lessened variabilities are to be observed in the case of the nasion-opisthion or sagittal arc (Table VI–19). "Basket Makers" and "Pseudo-Australoids" show significantly larger values and "Pseudo-Alpines" and "Residuals" smaller values than those of the series in general.

Means of the transverse arc (Table VI–20) show very marked type differentiation and significantly reduced variabilities. Low values occur in the first four types, which exhibit long-headed tendencies, and significantly high means characterize the "Large Hybrids" and "Pseudo-Alpines."

TABLE VI–15.   Cranial Capacity.   Total Series B

Males	No.	Range	Mean	S.D.	V.
Total Series B	91	1120–1560	1358.79 ± 7.24	102.40 ± 5.12	7.54 ± 0.38
"Basket Makers"	6	1210–1550	1306.67 ± 31.50	114.40 ± 22.27	8.75 ± 1.70
"Pseudo-Negroids"	12	1155–1410	1274.17 ± 14.42	74.10 ± 10.20	5.82 ± 0.80
"Pseudo-Australoids" ..	8	1120–1470	1335.00 ± 24.75	103.80 ± 17.50	7.78 ± 1.31
"Plains Indians"	14	1172–1560	1332.86 ± 17.67	98.00 ± 12.49	7.35 ± 0.94
"Long-faced Europeans"	13	1240–1510	1372.31 ± 16.95	90.60 ± 11.98	6.60 ± 0.87
"Pseudo-Alpines"	10	1300–1530	1380.00 ± 15.83	74.20 ± 11.19	5.38 ± 0.81
"Large Hybrids"	22	1270–1550	1420.45 ± 11.32	78.70 ± 8.00	5.54 ± 0.56
"Residuals"	6	1239–1560	1376.67 ± 32.85	119.30 ± 23.23	8.67 ± 1.69

TABLE VI–16. Cranial Module. Total Series B

Males	No.	Range	Mean	S.D.	V.
Total Series B	105	138.67–159.67	150.27 ± 0.25	3.78 ± 0.18	2.52 ± 0.12
"Basket Makers"	7	144.00–154.67	149.40	....	....	....
"Pseudo-Negroids"	11	141.00–153.33	147.00 ± 0.65	3.27 ± 0.46	2.19 ± 0.31
"Pseudo-Australoids" ...	10	145.33–154.33	149.40	....	....	....
"Plains Indians"	20	144.33–156.67	150.15 ± 0.55	3.65 ± 0.39	2.43 ± 0.26
"Long-faced Europeans" .	13	145.00–158.00	151.38 ± 0.65	3.48 ± 0.46	2.30 ± 0.30
"Pseudo-Alpines"	10	146.67–154.33	149.80 ± 0.62	2.89 ± 0.44	1.93 ± 0.29
"Large Hybrids"	23	138.67–159.67	152.43 ± 0.57	4.02 ± 0.40	2.64 ± 0.26
"Residuals"	11	146.33–153.00	149.45 ± 0.43	2.11 ± 0.30	1.41 ± 0.20

TABLE VI–17. Cranial Module (Deformed and Undeformed). Total Series B

Males	No.	Deformed	No.	Undeformed
Total Series B	78	150.42	27	149.85
"Basket Makers"	2	150.67	5	148.80
"Pseudo-Negroids"............................	8	146.75	3	147.67
"Pseudo-Australoids"	4	151.50	6	148.00
"Plains Indians"	14	150.07	6	150.33
"Long-faced Europeans"	8	150.62	5	153.00
"Pseudo-Alpines"	10	149.80	0	.....
"Large Hybrids"	21	152.48	2	152.33
"Residuals"	11	149.45	0	.....

TABLE VI–18. Maximum Circumference. Total Series B

Males	No.	Range	Mean	S.D.	V.
Total Series B	124	445–528	495.73 ± 0.85	14.10 ± 0.60	2.84 ± 0.12
"Basket Makers"	8	485–525	500.00 ± 3.31	13.90 ± 2.34	2.78 ± 0.47
"Pseudo-Negroids"	13	469–523	492.08 ± 2.79	14.90 ± 1.97	3.03 ± 0.40
"Pseudo-Australoids" ...	11	485–517	499.09 ± 1.88	9.25 ± 1.33	1.85 ± 0.27
"Plains Indians"	22	472–520	494.27 ± 1.95	13.55 ± 1.38	2.74 ± 0.28
"Long-faced Europeans"	17	476–526	500.41 ± 2.41	14.75 ± 1.71	2.95 ± 0.34
"Pseudo-Alpines"	14	478–517	492.64 ± 1.94	10.75 ± 1.37	2.18 ± 0.28
"Large Hybrids"	25	445–528	498.60 ± 2.02	14.95 ± 2.02	3.00 ± 0.29
"Residuals"	14	470–505	487.14 ± 1.97	10.95 ± 1.40	2.25 ± 0.29

TABLE VI-19. Nasion–Opisthion Arc. Total Series B

Males	No.	Range	Mean	S.D.	V.
Total Series B	110	323–382	354.55 ± 0.84	13.00 ± 0.59	3.67 ± 0.17
"Basket Makers"	7	345–381	360.71 ± 2.77	10.85 ± 1.96	3.01 ± 0.54
"Pseudo-Negroids"	13	329–382	354.38 ± 3.10	16.55 ± 2.19	4.67 ± 0.62
"Pseudo-Australoids" ...	9	345–375	361.67 ± 2.06	9.15 ± 1.45	2.53 ± 0.40
"Plains Indians"	20	323–377	353.50 ± 2.01	13.30 ± 1.42	3.76 ± 0.40
"Long-faced Europeans" .	16	340–375	356.56 ± 1.97	11.70 ± 1.39	3.28 ± 0.39
"Pseudo-Alpines"	10	337–371	348.50 ± 2.29	10.75 ± 1.62	3.08 ± 0.46
"Large Hybrids"	24	327–382	356.38 ± 1.94	14.10 ± 1.37	3.96 ± 0.39
"Residuals"	11	334–369	349.55 ± 1.91	9.40 ± 1.35	2.69 ± 0.39

TABLE VI–20. VERTICAL TRANSVERSE ARC. TOTAL SERIES B

Males	No.	Range	Mean	S.D.	V.
Total Series B	119	293–358	322.96 ± 0.84	13.65 ± 0.60	4.23 ± 0.18
"Basket Makers"	8	296–324	308.75 ± 2.21	9.25 ± 1.56	3.00 ± 0.51
"Pseudo-Negroids"	13	293–338	316.46 ± 1.99	10.65 ± 1.41	3.37 ± 0.45
"Pseudo-Australoids"	11	300–330	315.00 ± 2.17	10.65 ± 1.53	3.38 ± 0.49
"Plains Indians"	21	298–340	315.86 ± 1.57	10.65 ± 1.11	3.37 ± 0.35
"Long-faced Europeans"	14	297–337	322.36 ± 2.34	13.00 ± 1.66	4.03 ± 0.51
"Pseudo-Alpines"	14	313–350	327.64 ± 1.85	10.25 ± 1.31	3.13 ± 0.40
"Large Hybrids"	25	317–358	336.20 ± 1.38	10.25 ± 0.98	3.05 ± 0.29
"Residuals"	13	320–340	329.23 ± 0.96	5.15 ± 0.68	1.56 ± 0.21

The means of thickness of left parietal bones (measured about 1 cm. above the squamous suture) show some significant type differentiations and decreased variabilities. "Large Hybrids" seem to have the thickest skulls; "Plains," "Alpines," and "Residuals" the thinnest (Table VI–21).

The mean diameter of the foramen magnum is much smaller in "Pseudo-Negroids" than in other groups, but in general this dimension has no value as a type character and probably not much significance from any anthropological viewpoint.

TABLE VI–21. MEAN DIAMETER OF FORAMEN MAGNUM. TOTAL SERIES B

Males	No.	Range	Mean	S.D.	V.
Total Series B	91	27.0–37.0	31.22 ± 0.13	1.90 ± 0.10	6.09 ± 0.30
"Basket Makers"	5	28.0–37.0	32.00 ± 0.83	2.76 ± 0.59	8.62 ± 1.84
"Pseudo-Negroids"	10	28.0–30.5	29.35 ± 0.19	0.87 ± 0.13	2.96 ± 0.45
"Pseudo-Australoids"	9	27.0–33.5	30.72 ± 0.47	2.10 ± 0.33	6.84 ± 1.09
"Plains Type"	17	28.0–33.5	31.65 ± 0.25	1.53 ± 0.18	4.83 ± 0.56
"Long-faced Europeans"	13	28.0–34.5	31.81 ± 0.31	1.68 ± 0.22	5.28 ± 0.70
"Pseudo-Alpines"	10	28.0–34.0	30.60 ± 0.40	1.88 ± 0.28	6.14 ± 0.93
"Large Hybrids"	20	27.5–35.0	31.65 ± 0.24	1.60 ± 0.17	5.05 ± 0.54
"Residuals"	7	27.5–34.0	31.57 ± 0.45	1.78 ± 0.32	5.64 ± 1.02

TABLE VI–22. THICKNESS OF LEFT PARIETAL. TOTAL SERIES B

Males	No.	Range	Mean	S.D.	V.
Total Series B	124	2.3–8.0	5.09 ± 0.06	0.93 ± 0.04	18.27 ± 0.78
"Basket Makers"	8	4.0–6.6	5.17 ± 0.18	0.75 ± 0.13	14.51 ± 2.45
"Pseudo-Negroids"	13	4.0–6.0	5.23 ± 0.10	0.55 ± 0.73	10.52 ± 1.39
"Pseudo-Australoids"	11	4.3–6.0	5.21 ± 0.11	0.54 ± 0.08	10.36 ± 1.49
"Plains Indians"	23	3.6–7.0	4.61 ± 0.11	0.75 ± 0.07	16.30 ± 1.00
"Long-faced Europeans"	17	2.3–6.3	5.03 ± 0.16	1.00 ± 0.12	19.88 ± 2.30
"Pseudo-Alpines"	14	3.6–6.6	4.79 ± 0.14	0.77 ± 0.10	16.18 ± 2.06
"Large Hybrids"	26	3.0–8.0	5.52 ± 0.14	1.07 ± 0.10	19.38 ± 1.81
"Residuals"	12	3.3–7.0	4.78 ± 0.18	0.92 ± 0.13	19.25 ± 2.65

THE FACE

Bizygomatic diameters in the type subgroups usually exhibit lessened variabilities as compared with the total series. This is the case in six of the eight subgroups (Table VI–23). Significant deficiency in the mean of this measurement is shown in the "Basket Maker" and "Pseudo-Negroid" subtypes, while the "Large Hybrid" group greatly exceeds the other types in the average of this dimension.

Total facial (nasion-menton) height is a distinguishing feature of most of the types. Variabilities are usually reduced in the subgroups. The most marked deviations are found in the "Pseudo-Alpine" group where total facial height is at a minimum, and in the "Long-faced European" group where it is greatest, although in this group the variability is high (Table VI–24).

The general mean of the total facial index in Series B is mesoprosopic, but two of our types are leptoprosopic: the "Basket Makers" and the "Long-faced Europeans." The "Pseudo-Alpine" type alone is frankly euryprosopic. Most of the variabilities of the types are significantly less than of the total series, and valid differences in the means of the subgroups occur in four of the subgroups (Table VI–25).

The upper facial height (nasion-prosthion) again shows reduced variabilities in all but one of the subgroups and characteristically significant deviations in means. The shortest faces are found among the "Pseudo-Australoids" and the "Pseudo-Alpines," the longest in "Europeans" and "Plains" types. The upper facial index (Table VI–27) shows type differentiations similar to those demonstrated in case of the total facial index. The type groups individually are comparatively homogeneous with the exception of the "Pseudo-Alpine" group.

TABLE VI–23.   MAXIMUM BIZYGOMATIC DIAMETER.   TOTAL SERIES B

Males	No.	Range	Mean	S.D.	V.
Total Series B	107	126–161	138.20 ± 0.41	6.24 ± 0.29	4.52 ± 0.21
"Basket Makers"	7	126–142	132.71 ± 1.22	4.77 ± 0.86	3.59 ± 0.65
"Pseudo-Negroids"	12	127–143	133.83 ± 0.92	4.74 ± 0.65	3.54 ± 0.49
"Pseudo-Australoids"	9	133–144	137.67 ± 0.83	3.68 ± 0.59	2.67 ± 0.42
"Plains Indians"	17	132–145	139.82 ± 0.58	3.52 ± 0.41	2.52 ± 0.29
"Long-faced Europeans" ..	13	130–147	137.00 ± 0.77	4.11 ± 0.54	3.00 ± 0.40
"Pseudo-Alpines"	13	130–154	138.92 ± 1.26	6.75 ± 0.89	4.86 ± 0.64
"Large Hybrids"	26	131–161	143.65 ± 0.68	5.14 ± 0.48	3.58 ± 0.33
"Residuals"	10	128–142	137.50 ± 0.87	4.10 ± 0.62	2.98 ± 0.45

TABLE VI–24.   NASION–MENTON HEIGHT.   TOTAL SERIES B

Males	No.	Range	Mean	S.D.	V.
Total Series B	107	104–145	120.01 ± 0.38	5.90 ± 0.27	4.92 ± 0.23
"Basket Makers"	6	115–128	121.17 ± 1.27	4.60 ± 0.90	3.80 ± 0.74
"Pseudo-Negroids"	13	113–125	118.31 ± 0.60	3.20 ± 0.42	2.70 ± 0.36
"Pseudo-Australoids"	10	110–121	117.70 ± 0.84	3.93 ± 0.59	3.34 ± 0.50
"Plains Indians"	17	114–131	121.35 ± 0.86	5.27 ± 0.61	4.34 ± 0.50
"Long-faced Europeans" ..	16	104–145	123.31 ± 1.51	8.97 ± 1.07	7.27 ± 0.87
"Pseudo-Alpines"	11	109–125	115.00 ± 0.96	4.70 ± 0.68	4.09 ± 0.59
"Large Hybrids"	24	112–130	121.54 ± 0.61	4.40 ± 0.43	3.62 ± 0.35
"Residuals"	10	110–127	118.30 ± 0.93	4.34 ± 0.65	3.67 ± 0.55

TABLE VI–25. TOTAL FACIAL INDEX. TOTAL SERIES B

Males	No.	Range	Mean	S.D.	V.
Total Series B	93	69.57–99.22	86.54 ± 0.35	5.04 ± 0.25	5.82 ± 0.29
"Basket Makers"	5	85.21–99.22	90.20 ± 1.45	4.82 ± 1.03	5.34 ± 1.14
"Pseudo-Negroids" ...	12	88.67–96.15	88.67 ± 0.69	3.52 ± 0.48	3.97 ± 0.55
"Pseudo-Australoids" ..	8	77.08–88.72	85.25 ± 0.86	3.60 ± 0.61	4.22 ± 0.71
"Plains Indians"	14	82.01–94.89	87.14 ± 0.61	3.36 ± 0.43	3.86 ± 0.49
"Long-faced Europeans"	12	77.61–97.93	90.00 ± 1.00	5.12 ± 0.70	5.69 ± 0.78
"Pseudo-Alpines"	10	73.38–93.85	81.90 ± 1.22	5.73 ± 0.86	7.00 ± 1.06
"Large Hybrids"	23	69.57–94.59	85.39 ± 0.69	4.88 ± 0.49	5.71 ± 0.57
"Residuals"	9	78.57–91.04	85.33 ± 0.77	3.43 ± 0.55	4.02 ± 0.64

TABLE VI–26. NASION–PROSTHION HEIGHT. TOTAL SERIES B

Males	No.	Range	Mean	S.D.	V.
Total Series B	114	64–91	73.61 ± 0.27	4.20 ± 0.19	5.71 ± 0.26
"Basket Makers"	8	68–77	73.25 ± 0.58	2.44 ± 0.41	3.33 ± 0.56
"Pseudo-Negroids"	13	67–77	72.23 ± 0.56	2.99 ± 0.40	4.14 ± 0.55
"Pseudo-Australoids" ...	9	66–75	70.67 ± 0.64	2.83 ± 0.45	4.00 ± 0.64
"Plains Indians"	19	70–81	75.74 ± 0.60	3.88 ± 0.42	5.12 ± 0.56
"Long-faced Europeans" .	15	69–91	76.67 ± 0.91	5.22 ± 0.64	6.81 ± 0.84
"Pseudo-Alpines"	12	64–78	69.75 ± 0.76	3.92 ± 0.54	5.62 ± 0.77
"Large Hybrids"	26	67–81	74.46 ± 0.46	3.46 ± 0.32	4.65 ± 0.43
"Residuals"	12	67–78	72.75 ± 0.60	3.06 ± 0.42	4.21 ± 0.58

TABLE VI–27. UPPER FACIAL INDEX. TOTAL SERIES B

Males	No.	Range	Mean	S.D.	V.
Total Series B	98	43.48–64.08	52.93 ± 0.23	3.37 ± 0.16	6.37 ± 0.31
"Basket Makers"	7	52.71–57.94	55.00 ± 0.44	1.73 ± 0.31	3.15 ± 0.57
"Pseudo-Negroids"	12	50.76–59.23	54.25 ± 0.48	2.45 ± 0.34	4.52 ± 0.62
"Pseudo-Australoids" ..	7	46.53–52.86	51.14 ± 0.52	2.03 ± 0.37	3.97 ± 0.72
"Plains Indians"	15	51.06–58.39	53.87 ± 0.34	1.93 ± 0.24	3.58 ± 0.44
"Long-faced Europeans"	12	51.49–64.08	56.17 ± 0.63	3.21 ± 0.44	5.71 ± 0.79
"Pseudo-Alpines"	11	44.80–58.46	49.45 ± 0.76	3.75 ± 0.54	7.58 ± 1.09
"Large Hybrids"	25	43.48–57.04	51.80 ± 0.41	3.01 ± 0.29	5.81 ± 0.55
"Residuals"	9	50.00–57.03	52.44 ± 0.55	2.45 ± 0.39	4.67 ± 0.74

Tables VI–28–32, record the means and other constants of the orbital dimensions and of the mean orbital index (orbital breadth measured from dacryon). The "Basket Maker" and "Long-faced European" types show relatively high indices, doubtless in correlation with their leptoprosopic faces, whereas the "Pseudo-Australoids" are very chamaeoconch. Variabilities in these measurements and in this index are in many cases as large or larger than in the total series.

TABLE VI–28. ORBIT HEIGHT (RIGHT). TOTAL SERIES B

Males	No.	Range	Mean	S.D.	V.
Total Series B	123	31.0–38.0	34.98 ± 0.10	1.64 ± 0.07	4.69 ± 0.20
"Basket Makers"	7	34.0–37.0	35.43 ± 0.28	1.08 ± 0.19	3.05 ± 0.55
"Pseudo-Negroids"	13	31.0–38.0	34.46 ± 0.39	2.07 ± 0.27	6.01 ± 0.80
"Pseudo-Australoids"	10	31.0–34.0	32.85 ± 0.19	0.87 ± 0.13	2.69 ± 0.40
"Plains Indians"	22	33.0–38.0	35.56 ± 0.21	1.47 ± 0.15	4.13 ± 0.42
"Long-faced Europeans" ..	18	31.0–38.0	35.64 ± 0.27	1.70 ± 0.19	4.77 ± 0.54
"Pseudo-Alpines"	13	32.0–38.0	35.27 ± 0.25	1.34 ± 0.18	3.80 ± 0.50
"Large Hybrids"	27	33.0–38.0	35.57 ± 0.16	1.24 ± 0.11	3.49 ± 0.32
"Residuals"	13	32.0–36.5	34.31 ± 0.23	1.22 ± 0.16	3.58 ± 0.47

TABLE VI–29. Orbit Height (Left). Total Series B

Males	No.	Range	Mean	S.D.	V.
Total Series B	122	30.5–38.0	34.44 ± 0.10	1.66 ± 0.07	4.82 ± 0.21
"Basket Makers"	8	34.0–37.0	35.25 ± 0.23	0.97 ± 0.16	2.75 ± 0.46
"Pseudo-Negroids"	13	31.0–37.0	34.58 ± 0.35	1.89 ± 0.25	5.47 ± 0.72
"Pseudo-Australoids"	11	30.5–35.0	33.14 ± 0.25	1.22 ± 0.18	3.68 ± 0.53
"Plains Indians"	23	32.0–38.0	35.20 ± 0.21	1.46 ± 0.15	4.15 ± 0.41
"Long-faced Europeans"	18	32.0–38.0	35.53 ± 0.26	1.66 ± 0.19	4.67 ± 0.52
"Pseudo-Alpines"	13	32.0–38.0	35.12 ± 0.25	1.34 ± 0.18	3.81 ± 0.50
"Large Hybrids"	26	32.0–38.0	35.19 ± 0.21	1.60 ± 0.15	4.55 ± 0.43
"Residuals"	10	31.0–37.0	34.70 ± 0.35	1.63 ± 0.25	4.70 ± 0.71

TABLE VI–30. Orbit Breadth (Right). Total Series B

Males	No.	Range	Mean	S.D.	V.
Total Series B	123	35.0–45.0	40.15 ± 0.11	1.87 ± 0.08	4.66 ± 0.20
"Basket Makers"	7	38.0–42.0	39.57 ± 0.39	1.52 ± 0.27	3.84 ± 0.69
"Pseudo-Negroids"	13	36.5–44.5	39.65 ± 0.40	2.12 ± 0.28	5.35 ± 0.71
"Pseudo-Australoids"	10	37.0–43.0	39.55 ± 0.45	2.10 ± 0.32	5.31 ± 0.80
"Plains Indians"	22	38.0–43.0	40.52 ± 0.19	1.34 ± 0.14	3.31 ± 0.34
"Long-faced Europeans"	18	37.0–45.0	40.14 ± 0.36	2.29 ± 0.26	5.71 ± 0.64
"Pseudo-Alpines"	13	37.0–44.0	40.69 ± 0.37	1.98 ± 0.26	4.87 ± 0.64
"Large Hybrids"	27	35.0–43.0	41.07 ± 0.22	1.70 ± 0.16	4.14 ± 0.38
"Residuals"	13	38.0–42.0	39.46 ± 0.25	1.34 ± 0.18	3.40 ± 0.45

TABLE VI–31. Orbit Breadth (Left). Total Series B

Male	No.	Range	Mean	S.D.	V.
Total Series B	122	35.0–44.0	39.65 ± 0.11	1.72 ± 0.07	4.34 ± 0.19
"Basket Makers"	8	35.0–40.5	38.81 ± 0.41	1.70 ± 0.29	4.38 ± 0.74
"Pseudo-Negroids"	13	37.0–42.0	39.12 ± 0.30	1.62 ± 0.21	4.14 ± 0.55
"Pseudo-Australoids"	11	37.0–42.0	39.45 ± 0.37	1.82 ± 0.26	4.61 ± 0.66
"Plains Indians"	23	37.0–42.5	39.96 ± 0.22	1.58 ± 0.16	3.95 ± 0.39
"Long-faced Europeans"	18	35.0–44.0	39.97 ± 0.38	2.40 ± 0.27	6.00 ± 0.67
"Pseudo-Alpines"	13	38.0–43.0	39.42 ± 0.25	1.36 ± 0.18	3.45 ± 0.46
"Large Hybrids"	26	37.0–42.5	40.02 ± 0.16	1.23 ± 0.12	3.07 ± 0.29
"Residuals"	10	38.0–41.0	39.25 ± 0.27	1.28 ± 0.19	3.26 ± 0.49

TABLE VI–32. Mean Orbital Index. Total Series B

Males	No.	Range	Mean	S.D.	V.
Total Series B	124	76.54–99.34	87.52 ± 0.30	4.94 ± 0.21	5.64 ± 0.24
"Basket Makers"	7	82.42–95.89	90.43 ± 1.03	4.03 ± 0.73	4.46 ± 0.80
"Pseudo-Negroids"	13	76.54–97.30	88.08 ± 1.07	5.74 ± 0.76	6.52 ± 0.86
"Pseudo-Australoids"	11	78.31–89.19	83.73 ± 0.67	3.28 ± 0.47	3.92 ± 0.56
"Plains Indians"	23	78.82–93.67	87.87 ± 0.66	4.67 ± 0.46	5.31 ± 0.53
"Long-faced Europeans"	18	76.83–99.34	89.06 ± 0.91	5.75 ± 0.65	6.46 ± 0.73
"Pseudo-Alpines"	14	78.31–96.00	87.14 ± 1.00	5.55 ± 0.71	6.37 ± 0.81
"Large Hybrids"	27	80.25–97.18	87.07 ± 0.50	3.85 ± 0.35	4.42 ± 0.41
"Residuals"	11	82.05–93.59	87.09 ± 0.78	3.82 ± 0.55	4.39 ± 0.63

The nasal diameters and nasal index (Tables VI–33, 34, 35) also show certain clear type differences. "Pseudo-Negroids," "Pseudo-Australoids," and "Pseudo-Alpines" exhibit means which are chamaerrhine, whereas the "Long-faced Europeans" are markedly leptorrhine and the "Plains" type approaches this category. Other types are prevailing mesorrhine. Variabilities are usually below that of the whole series.

TABLE VI–33. NASAL HEIGHT. TOTAL SERIES B

Males	No.	Range	Mean	S.D.	V.
Total Series B	125	44.0–62.0	51.26 ± 0.18	2.99 ± 0.13	5.83 ± 0.25
"Basket Makers"	8	49.0–54.0	51.38 ± 0.36	1.49 ± 0.25	2.90 ± 0.49
"Pseudo-Negroids"	13	44.0–53.0	48.81 ± 0.43	2.32 ± 0.31	4.75 ± 0.63
"Pseudo-Australoids"	11	46.0–54.0	49.18 ± 0.47	2.29 ± 0.33	4.66 ± 0.67
"Plains Indians"	22	49.0–57.0	53.14 ± 0.34	2.38 ± 0.24	4.48 ± 0.46
"Long-faced Europeans"	18	48.0–62.0	52.39 ± 0.50	3.14 ± 0.35	5.99 ± 0.67
"Pseudo-Alpines"	14	45.0–54.0	49.57 ± 0.48	2.69 ± 0.34	5.43 ± 0.69
"Large Hybrids"	27	45.5–57.5	51.87 ± 0.40	3.08 ± 0.28	5.94 ± 0.55
"Residuals"	12	49.0–55.0	51.04 ± 0.33	1.69 ± 0.23	3.31 ± 0.46

TABLE VI–34. NASAL BREADTH. TOTAL SERIES B

Males	No.	Range	Mean	S.D.	V.
Total Series B	126	21.0–30.0	25.81 ± 0.10	1.74 ± 0.07	6.74 ± 0.29
"Basket Makers"	8	24.0–28.0	26.12 ± 0.37	1.54 ± 0.26	5.90 ± 0.99
"Pseudo-Negroids"	13	21.5–29.0	26.38 ± 0.39	2.10 ± 0.28	7.96 ± 1.05
"Pseudo-Australoids"	11	22.0–28.0	26.18 ± 0.39	1.90 ± 0.27	7.26 ± 1.04
"Plains Indians"	22	23.0–29.0	26.07 ± 0.21	1.45 ± 0.15	5.56 ± 0.57
"Long-faced Europeans"	18	21.0–27.0	24.53 ± 0.25	1.55 ± 0.17	6.32 ± 0.71
"Pseudo-Alpines"	14	22.0–30.0	25.68 ± 0.32	1.79 ± 0.23	6.97 ± 0.89
"Large Hybrids"	27	23.0–29.5	25.94 ± 0.22	1.72 ± 0.16	6.63 ± 0.61
"Residuals"	13	24.0–28.0	26.00 ± 0.22	1.18 ± 0.16	4.54 ± 0.60

TABLE VI–35. NASAL INDEX. TOTAL SERIES B

Males	No.	Range	Mean	S.D.	V.
Total Series B	124	40.32–65.22	50.45 ± 0.27	4.45 ± 0.19	8.82 ± 0.38
"Basket Makers"	8	45.28–54.90	50.75 ± 0.72	3.02 ± 0.52	5.97 ± 1.01
"Pseudo-Negroids"	13	46.94–61.70	53.77 ± 0.81	4.32 ± 0.57	8.03 ± 1.06
"Pseudo-Australoids"	11	47.83–57.14	53.27 ± 0.65	3.19 ± 0.46	5.99 ± 0.86
"Plains Indians"	21	40.35–58.00	49.05 ± 0.60	4.07 ± 0.42	8.30 ± 0.86
"Long-faced Europeans"	18	40.32–54.17	46.78 ± 0.55	3.47 ± 0.39	7.42 ± 0.83
"Pseudo-Alpines"	14	45.28–65.22	51.93 ± 0.87	4.83 ± 0.62	9.30 ± 1.19
"Large Hybrids"	27	42.59–60.42	50.04 ± 0.55	4.23 ± 0.39	8.45 ± 0.78
"Residuals"	12	43.64–54.90	51.25 ± 0.56	2.89 ± 0.40	5.64 ± 0.78

Basion-prosthion diameters, basion-nasion diameters, and the derived gnathic index (Tables VI–36, 37, 38) indicate some type differentiation in these features. Most groups are orthognathous, but the "Pseudo-Negroids" are mesognathous and the "Basket Makers" approach this condition. The most markedly orthognathous group is that called "Long-faced European." The "Pseudo-Alpine" type also shows this feature. Variabilities are usually lower in the subgroups than in the group at large.

TABLE VI–36. BASION–PROSTHION LENGTH. TOTAL SERIES B

Males	No.	Range	Mean	S.D.	V.
Total Series B	94	90–106	97.84 ± 0.24	3.50 ± 0.17	3.58 ± 0.18
"Basket Makers"	7	91–103	98.29 ± 1.02	3.99 ± 0.72	4.06 ± 0.73
"Pseudo-Negroids"	10	96–105	100.40 ± 0.57	2.69 ± 0.41	2.68 ± 0.40
"Pseudo-Australoids" .	8	95–103	97.62 ± 0.66	2.78 ± 0.47	2.85 ± 0.48
"Plains Indians"	19	92–105	98.53 ± 0.44	2.82 ± 0.31	2.86 ± 0.31
"Long-faced Europeans"	10	90–101	95.80 ± 0.56	2.64 ± 0.40	2.76 ± 0.42
"Pseudo-Alpines"	10	91–102	95.40 ± 0.68	3.17 ± 0.48	3.32 ± 0.50
"Large Hybrids"	21	92–106	98.62 ± 0.51	3.47 ± 0.36	3.52 ± 0.37
"Residuals"	9	91–104	96.56 ± 0.85	3.80 ± 0.60	3.94 ± 0.63

TABLE VI–37. BASION–NASION LENGTH. TOTAL SERIES B

Males	No.	Range	Mean	S.D.	V.
Total Series B	96	92–110	101.90 ± 0.22	3.18 ± 0.15	3.12 ± 0.15
"Basket Makers"	7	99–103	100.86 ± 0.40	1.55 ± 0.28	1.54 ± 0.28
"Pseudo-Negroids"	10	97–105	101.10 ± 0.52	2.43 ± 0.37	2.40 ± 0.36
"Pseudo-Australoids"	8	99–105	102.00 ± 0.48	2.00 ± 0.42	7.08 ± 1.13
"Plains Indians"	19	96–109	103.58 ± 0.50	3.22 ± 0.35	3.11 ± 0.34
"Long-faced Europeans" ...	10	99–110	103.60 ± 0.67	3.14 ± 0.47	3.03 ± 0.46
"Pseudo-Alpines"	10	92–106	100.80 ± 0.78	3.68 ± 0.56	3.65 ± 0.55
"Large Hybrids"	23	97–107	102.48 ± 0.39	2.76 ± 0.27	2.69 ± 0.27
"Residuals"	9	95–103	99.67 ± 0.63	2.79 ± 0.44	2.80 ± 0.45

TABLE VI–38. GNATHIC INDEX. TOTAL SERIES B

Males	No.	Range	Mean	S.D.	V.
Total Series B	94	88.18–105.15	95.93 ± 0.24	3.51 ± 0.17	3.66 ± 0.18
"Basket Makers"	7	91.92–101.00	97.14 ± 0.88	3.44 ± 0.62	3.54 ± 0.64
"Pesudo-Negroids" ...	10	96.97–105.15	100.40 ± 0.50	2.33 ± 0.35	2.32 ± 0.35
"Pseudo-Australoids" ..	8	90.48 – 99.01	95.62 ± 0.63	2.64 ± 0.45	2.76 ± 0.47
"Plains Indians"	19	89.62–100.00	95.05 ± 0.41	2.68 ± 0.29	2.82 ± 0.31
"Long-faced Europeans"	10	88.18 – 99.34	92.50 ± 0.67	3.14 ± 0.48	3.39 ± 0.51
"Pseudo-Alpines"	10	91.18 – 98.91	94.50 ± 0.58	2.73 ± 0.41	2.89 ± 0.44
"Large Hybrids"	21	91.51–102.97	96.19 ± 0.48	3.23 ± 0.34	3.36 ± 0.35
"Residuals"	9	94.12–102.97	96.89 ± 0.58	2.60 ± 0.41	2.68 ± 0.43

The external palatal dimensions which yield the maxillo-alveolar index present some type differences of interest. "Pseudo-Negroids" have the longest palates and "Pseudo-Alpines" the shortest. "Basket Makers" have the greatest external palatal breadth and the least is found in the so-called "Pseudo-Australoids." The maxillo-alveolar index is at a minimum in the "Pseudo-Negroid" group which has the mesuranic mean of 112. All other groups are brachyuranic — the "Pseudo-Alpines" and "Basket Makers" particularly so, each of these types having means of 122.

TABLE VI–39. External Palatal Length. Total Series B

Males	No.	Range	Mean	S.D.	V.
Total Series B	96	50–63	55.62 ± 0.18	2.55 ± 0.12	4.58 ± 0.22
"Basket Makers"	6	52–58	55.17 ± 0.70	2.55 ± 0.50	4.62 ± 0.90
"Pseudo-Negroids"	11	55–61	57.68 ± 0.38	1.88 ± 0.27	3.26 ± 0.47
"Pseudo-Australoids" ...	8	52–57	54.25 ± 0.44	1.85 ± 0.31	3.41 ± 0.57
"Plains Indians"	15	51–59	55.87 ± 0.35	2.03 ± 0.25	3.63 ± 0.45
"Pseudo-Europeans"....	15	50–63	55.27 ± 0.51	2.93 ± 0.36	5.30 ± 0.65
"Pseudo-Alpines"	11	50–58	53.95 ± 0.52	2.54 ± 0.37	4.71 ± 0.68
"Large Hybrids"	22	53–60	56.41 ± 0.31	2.19 ± 0.22	3.88 ± 0.39
"Residuals"	8	53–58	55.25 ± 0.35	1.48 ± 0.25	2.68 ± 0.45

TABLE VI–40. External Palatal Breadth. Total Series B

Males	No.	Range	Mean	S.D.	V.
Total Series B	96	55–73	65.91 ± 0.22	3.17 ± 0.15	4.81 ± 0.23
"Basket Makers"	6	63–70	67.33 ± 0.69	2.49 ± 0.48	3.70 ± 0.72
"Pseudo-Negroids"	11	55–73	64.82 ± 0.96	4.71 ± 0.68	7.27 ± 1.05
"Pseudo-Australoids" ...	8	58–69	64.12 ± 0.78	3.29 ± 0.55	5.13 ± 0.87
"Plains Indians"	15	61–73	67.00 ± 0.46	2.66 ± 0.33	3.97 ± 0.49
"Long-faced Europeans" .	15	59–70	65.60 ± 0.57	3.26 ± 0.40	4.97 ± 0.61
"Pseudo-Alpines"	11	61–72	65.82 ± 0.56	2.76 ± 0.40	4.19 ± 0.60
"Large Hybrids"	21	61–71	66.81 ± 0.34	2.28 ± 0.24	3.41 ± 0.35
"Residuals"	9	61–68	64.56 ± 0.44	1.95 ± 0.31	3.02 ± 0.48

TABLE VI–41. External Palatal (Maxillo–Alveolar) Index. Total Series B

Males	No.	Range	Mean	S.D.	V.
Total Series B	96	100.00–135.85	118.61 ± 0.47	6.81 ± 0.33	5.74 ± 0.28
"Basket Makers"	6	118.87–130.19	122.00 ± 1.03	3.74 ± 0.73	3.07 ± 0.60
"Pseudo-Negroids"	11	100.00–125.86	112.45 ± 1.30	6.68 ± 0.92	5.94 ± 0.82
"Pseudo-Australoids" ...	9	108.77–126.92	118.44 ± 1.32	5.89 ± 0.94	4.97 ± 0.79
"Plains Indians"	15	112.07–132.73	120.00 ± 1.01	5.80 ± 0.71	4.83 ± 0.59
"Long-faced Europeans" .	15	103.17–132.08	119.13 ± 1.61	9.26 ± 1.14	7.77 ± 0.96
"Pseudo-Alpines"	11	113.79–135.85	122.36 ± 1.27	6.24 ± 0.90	5.10 ± 0.73
"Large Hybrids"	21	110.00–127.27	118.29 ± 0.71	4.84 ± 0.50	4.09 ± 0.43
"Residuals"	8	110.34–124.53	116.88 ± 1.03	4.34 ± 0.73	3.71 ± 0.63

Mandibular measurements show many type variations. The smallest bigonial diameters (Table VI–42) are found in the "Basket Maker" and "Pseudo-Negroid" types, the largest in "Residuals," "Large Hybrids," and "Plains" groups. Bicondylar diameters (Table VI–43) vary almost identically. Symphysial height varies only slightly, but is significantly smaller in the "Alpine" group than in any of the others (Table VI–44).

TABLE VI–42.   BIGONIAL DIAMETER.   TOTAL SERIES B

Males	No.	Range	Mean	S.D.	V.
Total Series B	86	88–117	102.36 ± 0.46	6.36 ± 0.33	6.21 ± 0.32
"Basket Makers"	5	90–103	95.40 ± 1.47	4.88 ± 1.04	5.12 ± 1.09
"Pseudo-Negroids"	10	93–103	98.60 ± 0.66	3.10 ± 0.47	3.18 ± 0.48
"Pseudo-Australoids" ..	6	94–109	100.00 ± 1.51	5.48 ± 1.07	5.48 ± 1.07
"Plains Indians"	12	98–113	104.25 ± 0.80	4.11 ± 0.57	3.94 ± 0.54
"Long-faced Europeans"	12	90–112	101.58 ± 1.37	7.03 ± 0.97	6.92 ± 0.95
"Pseudo-Alpines"	10	88–106	100.02 ± 1.20	5.62 ± 0.85	5.61 ± 0.85
"Large Hybrids"	23	96–113	105.22 ± 0.77	5.44 ± 0.54	5.17 ± 0.51
"Residuals"	8	97–117	107.25 ± 1.48	6.20 ± 1.05	5.78 ± 0.97

TABLE VI–43.   BICONDYLAR WIDTH.   TOTAL SERIES B

Males	No.	Range	Mean	S.D.	V.
Total Series B	70	106–131	121.36 ± 0.49	6.12 ± 0.35	5.04 ± 0.29
"Basket Makers"	5	109–127	116.80 ± 1.78	5.91 ± 1.26	5.06 ± 1.08
"Pseudo-Negroids" ...	9	110–125	115.78 ± 1.02	4.52 ± 0.72	3.90 ± 0.62
"Pseudo-Australoids"	6	112–131	120.17 ± 1.57	5.69 ± 1.11	4.73 ± 0.92
"Plains Indians"	10	116–130	124.60 ± 0.82	3.85 ± 0.58	3.09 ± 0.47
"Long-faced Europeans"	12	106–131	119.17 ± 1.43	7.32 ± 1.01	6.14 ± 0.85
"Pseudo-Alpines"	9	116–128	121.89 ± 1.03	4.56 ± 0.72	3.74 ± 0.59
"Large Hybrids"	13	119–131	125.85 ± 0.55	2.96 ± 0.39	2.35 ± 0.31
"Residuals"	6	117–130	123.33 ± 1.18	4.27 ± 0.83	3.46 ± 0.67

TABLE VI–44.   HEIGHT OF SYMPHYSIS.   TOTAL SERIES B

Males	No.	Range	Mean	S.D.	V.
Total Series B	92	29–42	35.87 ± 0.17	2.36 ± 0.12	6.58 ± 0.33
"Basket Makers"	6	31–38	36.00 ± 0.67	2.45 ± 0.48	6.81 ± 1.33
"Pseudo-Negroids"	12	33.5–39	36.33 ± 0.36	1.85 ± 0.25	5.09 ± 0.70
"Pseudo-Australoids" ...	6	33–37	35.68 ± 0.38	1.37 ± 0.27	3.84 ± 0.75
"Plains Indians"	13	31–40	35.15 ± 0.48	2.54 ± 0.34	7.23 ± 0.96
"Long-faced Europeans" .	15	30–42	36.07 ± 0.55	3.17 ± 0.39	8.79 ± 1.08
"Pseudo-Alpines"	10	29–36	33.65 ± 0.44	2.05 ± 0.31	6.09 ± 0.92
"Large Hybrids"	21	34–40	36.62 ± 0.21	1.43 ± 0.15	3.90 ± 0.41
"Residuals"	9	35–40	36.72 ± 0.38	1.71 ± 0.27	4.66 ± 0.74

The mean angle of the lower jaw is much higher in the "Pseudo-Negroid" type than in any other, the "Basket Makers" showing the next highest mean. The minimum value of this measurement is found in the "Pseudo-Alpines" (Table VI–45). Minimum breadth of the ascending ramus shows little variation in type groups but the highest value of the mean is found in the "Pseudo-Negroid" group (Table VI–46). The height of the ascending ramus is greatest in the "Long-faced European" type and least among the "Pseudo-Negroids." This last-named type has the largest average condylo-symphysial length; the least value of this diameter is found in the "Pseudo-Alpine" type.

TABLE VI–45. Mean Angle of Lower Jaw. Total Series B

Males	No.	Range	Mean	S.D.	V.
Total Series B	84	105–135	117.17 ± 0.34	4.66 ± 0.24	3.98 ± 0.21
"Basket Makers"	5	114–125	119.00 ± 1.36	4.52 ± 0.96	3.80 ± 0.81
"Pseudo-Negroids"	11	116–135	122.09 ± 1.04	5.09 ± 0.73	4.17 ± 0.60
"Pseudo-Australoids"	6	114–126	117.50 ± 1.14	4.15 ± 0.81	3.53 ± 0.69
"Plains Indians"	13	110–120	116.54 ± 0.56	2.98 ± 0.39	2.56 ± 0.34
"Long-faced Europeans"	14	108–130	116.21 ± 0.91	5.06 ± 0.64	4.35 ± 0.55
"Pseudo-Alpines"	10	105–128	115.90 ± 1.53	7.16 ± 1.08	6.18 ± 0.93
"Large Hybrids"	18	109–126	116.50 ± 0.70	4.40 ± 0.49	3.78 ± 0.42
"Residuals"	7	111–127	118.86 ± 1.47	5.77 ± 1.04	4.85 ± 0.87

TABLE VI–46. Minimum Breadth of Ascending Ramus. Total Series B

Males	No.	Range	Mean	S.D.	V.
Total Series B	113	30–44	37.21 ± 0.17	2.68 ± 0.12	7.20 ± 0.32
"Basket Makers"	6	31–40	36.33 ± 0.89	3.25 ± 0.63	8.95 ± 1.74
"Pseudo-Negroids"	12	34.5–42	38.21 ± 0.53	2.71 ± 0.37	7.09 ± 0.98
"Pseudo-Australoids"	9	33–41	37.00 ± 0.59	2.62 ± 0.42	7.08 ± 1.13
"Plains Indians"	20	30–42	37.05 ± 0.37	2.46 ± 0.26	6.64 ± 0.71
"Long-faced Europeans"	16	30–44	37.28 ± 0.54	3.20 ± 0.38	8.58 ± 1.02
"Pseudo-Alpines"	13	32.5–41	37.04 ± 0.42	2.24 ± 0.30	6.05 ± 0.80
"Large Hybrids"	24	32–42	37.67 ± 0.33	2.41 ± 0.23	6.40 ± 0.62
"Residuals"	13	32–40	36.31 ± 0.45	2.40 ± 0.32	6.61 ± 0.87

TABLE VI–47. Height of Ascending Ramus. Total Series B

Males	No.	Range	Mean	S.D.	V.
Total Series B	104	49–78	63.75 ± 0.36	5.37 ± 0.25	8.42 ± 0.39
"Basket Makers"	6	60–70	65.50 ± 1.02	3.69 ± 0.72	5.63 ± 1.10
"Pseudo-Negroids"	12	49–66	58.92 ± 0.88	4.54 ± 0.63	7.71 ± 1.06
"Pseudo-Australoids"	8	55–71	63.38 ± 1.26	5.27 ± 0.89	8.31 ± 1.40
"Plains Indians"	19	58–69	62.95 ± 0.46	2.98 ± 0.33	4.73 ± 0.52
"Long-faced Europeans"	16	60–77	68.12 ± 0.79	4.70 ± 0.56	6.90 ± 0.82
"Pseudo-Alpines"	11	57–74	63.45 ± 1.15	5.66 ± 0.81	8.92 ± 1.28
"Large Hybrids"	22	57–71	64.73 ± 0.56	3.87 ± 0.39	5.98 ± 0.61
"Residuals"	10	52–78	61.60 ± 1.59	7.45 ± 1.12	12.09 ± 1.82

TABLE VI–48. Condylo–Symphysial Length. Total Series B

Males	No.	Range	Mean	S.D.	V.
Total Series B	82	92–117	104.91 ± 0.31	4.22 ± 0.22	4.02 ± 0.21
"Basket Makers"	4	99–108	103.75 ...	... ...	... ...
"Pseudo-Negroids"	11	101–110	106.00 ± 0.56	2.73 ± 0.39	2.58 ± 0.37
"Pseudo-Australoids"	6	98–110	104.67 ± 1.05	3.82 ± 0.74	3.65 ± 0.71
"Plains Indians"	13	101–112	105.54 ± 0.61	3.27 ± 0.43	3.10 ± 0.41
"Long-faced Europeans"	13	92–111	104.85 ± 0.92	4.94 ± 0.65	4.71 ± 0.62
"Pseudo-Alpines"	10	95–109	102.60 ± 0.99	4.63 ± 0.70	4.51 ± 0.68
"Large Hybrids"	18	97–117	106.11 ± 0.74	4.63 ± 0.52	4.36 ± 0.49
"Residuals"	7	98–107	103.29 ± 0.68	2.66 ± 0.50	2.58 ± 0.47

STATISTICAL EVIDENCE OF THE VALIDITY OF MORPHOLOGICAL DETERMINATIONS OF TYPE

In figures VI–1 through VI–8 the means of measurements and indices of the type subgroups are plotted against the means of the entire Series B. The hatched bands represent, on either side of the mean (the horizontal line), twice the probable error of a random sample of the whole series of the same size as that of the subgroup whose deviations are being plotted. The dotted lines represent, on either side of the mean, once and three times the probable error of such a random sample. According to probability, if our type subgroups are merely random samples of the entire series, 82 per cent of their means should fall within the hatched bands, i. e., should deviate from the mean of the whole series by amounts less than twice the probable error of a random sample of the same size as that of the subgroup. This graphic method of showing deviations is the same as that employed on pages 70–75 to show deviations of the Glaze subgroups. In that series of graphs such a large percentage of subgroup means actually did fall within the limits of insignificance as to force the conclusion that, on the whole, most of the Glaze subgroups were not significantly different from what might be expected of a random sample of the same size drawn from the series at large. In the present instance, however, the reverse is the case. The reader may satisfy himself by a mere glance that the deviations of the type subgroups are too numerous and too great to be the result of chance.

Tables VI–49, 50 list the magnitude of the expected deviations and of the observed deviations in terms of the mean measure (the probable error of a random sample of size equal to that of the subgroup). In the case of the measurements every type subgroup is clearly differentiated from the series as a whole. The fewest deviations are found in the "Residual" group and the greatest number of deviations in the "Large Hybrid" group. These are, of course, deviations in gross dimensions only. Table VI–50 lists the deviations of the subgroups with respect to nine indices. Here again the deviations are numerous and great except in the "Large Hybrid" and "Residual" types. In the former case a perusal of the measurement graphs indicates that the great deviations of that group are for the most part due to excesses of size in that group. The index deviations of the "Large Hybrid" type are barely sufficient to characterize the type. In the case of "Residuals" the deviations of means of indices from those of the entire group are insufficient to demonstrate indicial individuality for the type.

Thus we may conclude that all of our type groups are clearly differentiated and valid both in gross measurements and in indices, with the exception of two. The "Large Hybrid" group is clearly differentiated from the series as a whole in size, but scarcely in proportions. The "Residual" group also shows differentiation in its measurements, but to a lesser degree than any other type subgroup; in proportions this group does not differ significantly from what might be expected of a random sample of the same size drawn from the series at large. When we consider that the

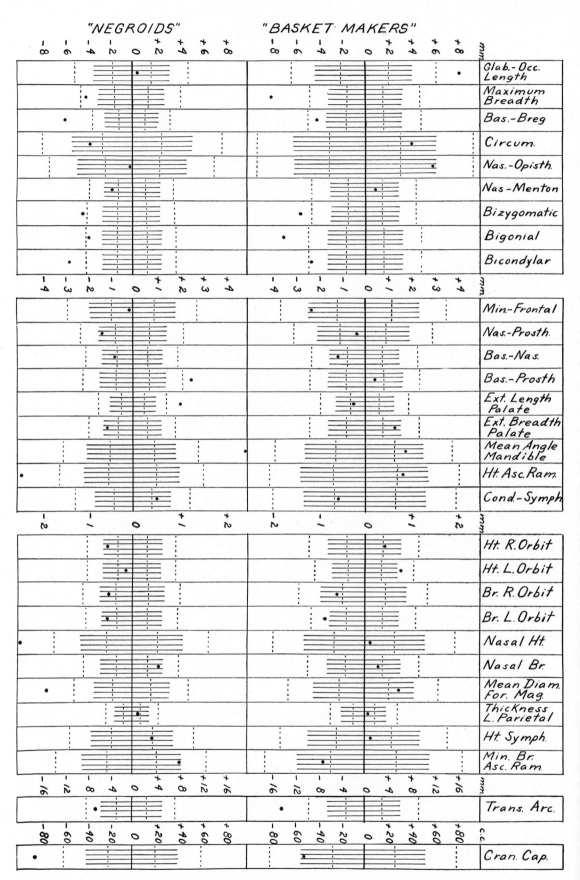

FIG. VI-1. MEANS OF MEASUREMENTS OF TYPE SUBGROUPS PLOTTED AGAINST MEANS OF TOTAL SERIES B. "BASKET MAKERS" AND "PSEUDO-NEGROIDS"

(View from the side)

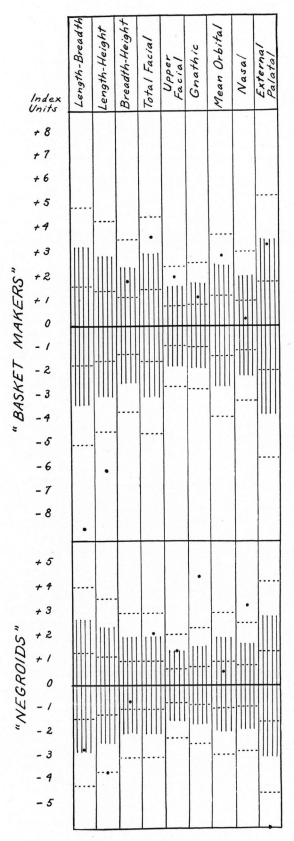

FIG. VI–2. MEANS OF INDICES OF TYPE SUBGROUPS PLOTTED AGAINST MEANS
OF TOTAL SERIES B. "BASKET MAKERS" AND "PSEUDO-NEGROIDS"

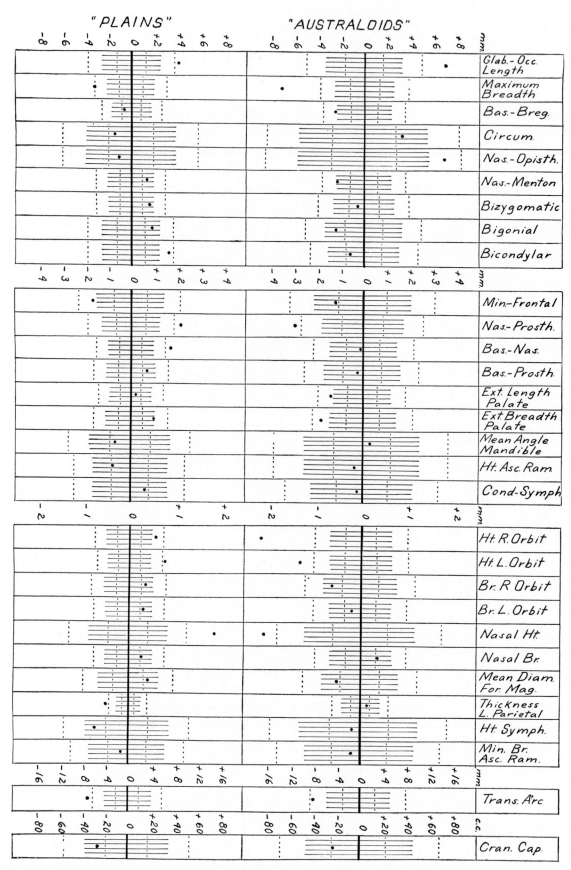

FIG. VI-3. MEANS OF MEASUREMENTS OF TYPE SUBGROUPS PLOTTED AGAINST MEANS OF TOTAL SERIES B. "PSEUDO-AUSTRALOIDS" AND "PLAINS INDIANS"

(View from the side)

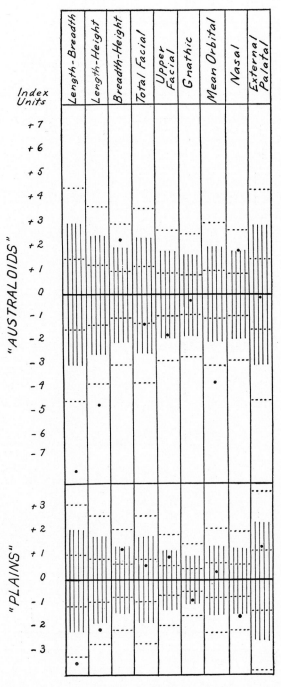

Fig. VI–4. Means of indices of type subgroups plotted against means of Total Series B. "Pseudo-Australoids" and "Plains Indians"

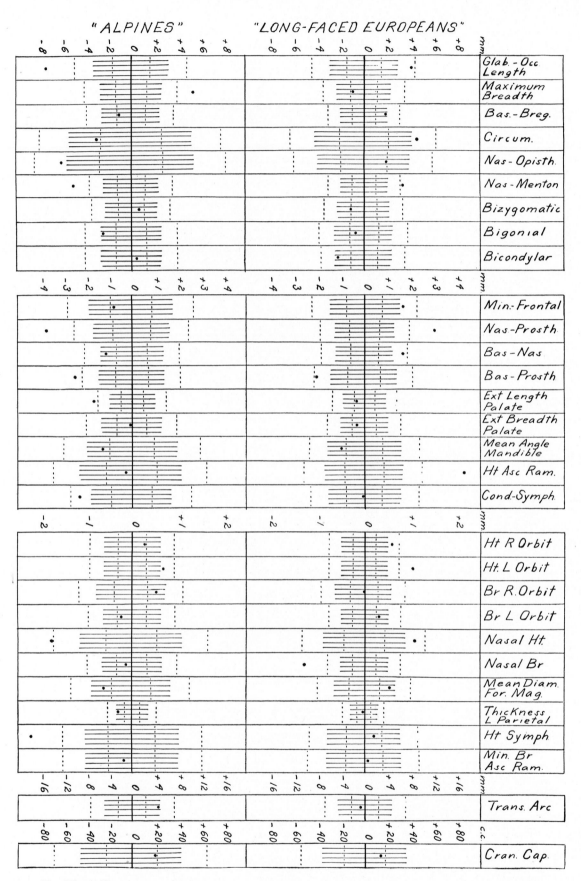

Fig. VI–5. Means of measurements of type subgroups plotted against means of Total Series B. "Long-faced Europeans" and "Pseudo-Alpines"

(View from the side)

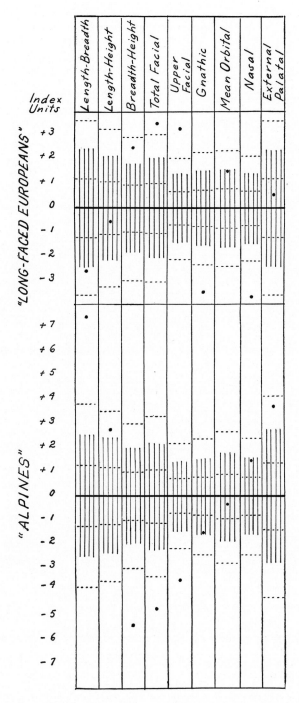

Fig. VI-6. Means of indices of type subgroups plotted against means of Total Series B. "Long-faced Europeans" and "Pseudo-Alpines"

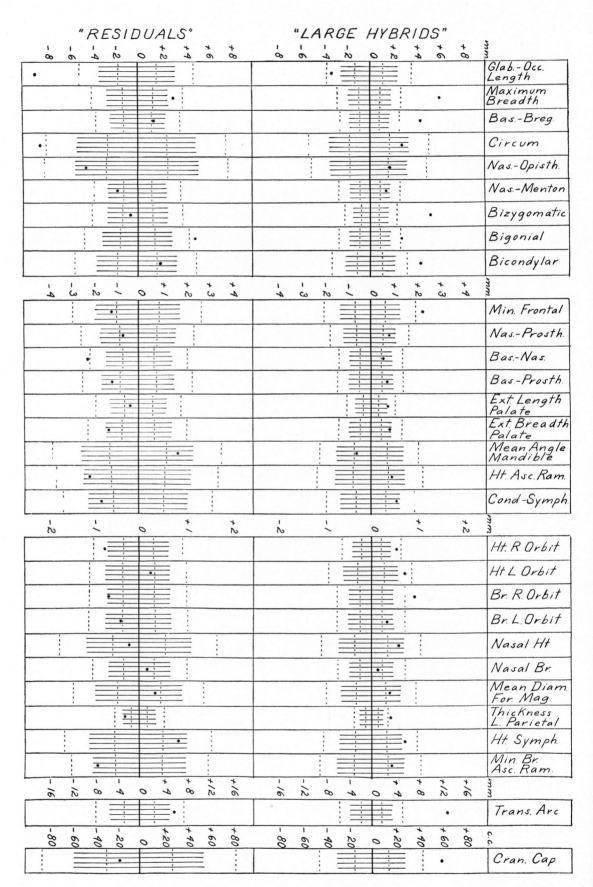

Fig. VI-7. Means of measurements of type subgroups plotted against means of Total Series B. "Large Hybrids" and "Residuals"

(View from the side)

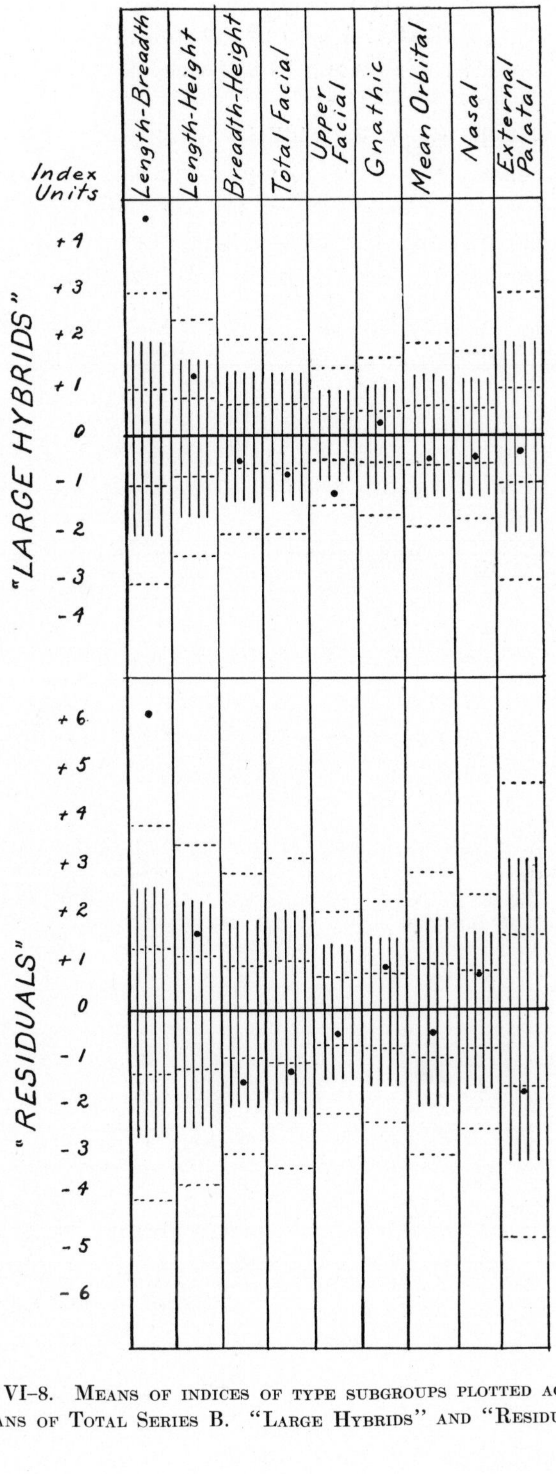

FIG. VI–8. MEANS OF INDICES OF TYPE SUBGROUPS PLOTTED AGAINST MEANS OF TOTAL SERIES B. "LARGE HYBRIDS" AND "RESIDUALS"

"Residual" type is nothing but an assortment of misfits and crania not distinguishable as to type, the result is exactly what would be expected.

It has been fully demonstrated that our morphological types are valid with respect to the deviations of their means from those of the entire series. We may now consider their average variabilities.

Table VI–51 records the mean variabilities of 28 measurements and 9 indices and the percentage of cases in which the type subgroups exceed the coefficient of variation of the entire series in the individual measurements and indices. All of the type subgroups show lower means of coefficients of variation in both measurements and indices, with the exception of the group labelled "Long-faced Europeans," which shows a higher mean variation of measurements than the series at large. The most homogeneous type groups are "Plains," "Large Hybrids" "Residuals," and "Pseudo-Australoids"; the most variable are the "Long-faced Europeans" and "Pseudo-Alpines." On the basis of variabilities we could hardly state that these last two types are distinguished from the series as a whole. Yet the deviations of their means from those of the series at large are perhaps the most numerous and striking of all the type subgroup deviations.

It may be concluded that our type sortings have resulted in subgroups significantly deviating in means of measurements and indices and in general show decreased variabilities as compared with the entire series. Two of our type groups are unsatisfactory — the "Long-faced Europeans" with respect to variability and the "Residuals" with respect to deviations of means. The variability of the former group may have been increased by the inclusion within it of two or three skulls from the church at Pecos which are almost certainly Mexican or of Mexican admixture.

TABLE VI–49. EXPECTED AND OBSERVED DEVIATIONS OF MEANS OF TYPE
SUBGROUPS (MEASUREMENTS). TOTAL SERIES B

	Less than p. e.		$1 \times$ p. e. to $2 \times$ p. e.		$2 \times$ p. e. to $3 \times$ p. e.		Greater than $3 \times$ p. e.		Total
	No.	Per cent	No.	Per cent	No.	Per cent	No.	Per cent	
Expected	15	50.00	19.50	32.00	4.20	14.00	1.20	4.00	30
Observed									
"Basket Makers"	9	30.00	12	40.00	4	13.33	5	16.67	30
"Pseudo-Negroids"	6	20.00	11	36.67	3	10.00	10	33.33	30
"Pseudo-Australoids"	12	40.00	7	23.33	5	16.67	6	20.00	30
"Plains Indians"	8	26.67	11	36.67	3	10.00	8	26.67	30
"Long-faced Europeans"	13	43.33	5	16.67	7	23.33	5	16.67	30
"Pseudo-Alpines"	11	36.67	8	26.67	3	10.00	8	26.67	30
"Large Hybrids"	2	6.67	13	43.33	5	16.67	10	33.33	30
"Residuals"	8	26.67	15	50.00	3	10.00	4	13.33	30
Total Expected	120	50.00	76.8	32.00	33.6	14.00	9.6	4.00	240
Total Observed	69	28.7	82	34.20	33	13.70	56	23.30	240

TABLE VI–50. Expected and Observed Deviations of Means of Type Subgroups (Indices). Total Series B

	Less than p. e.		1 × p. e. to 2 × p. e.		2 × p. e. to 3 × p. e.		Greater than 3 × p. e.		Total
	No.	Per cent	No.	Per cent	No.	Per cent	No.	Per cent	
Expected	4.5	50.0	2.9	32.0	1.3	14.0	0.4	4.0	9
Observed									
"Basket Makers"	1	11.1	3	33.3	3	33.3	2	22.2	9
"Pseudo-Negroids"	2	22.2	1	11.1	2	22.2	4	44.4	9
"Pseudo-Australoids" ..	2	22.2	2	22.2	2	22.2	3	33.3	9
"Plains Indians"	2	22.2	4	44.4	2	22.2	1	11.1	9
"Long-faced Europeans"	2	22.2	1	11.1	2	22.2	4	44.4	9
"Pseudo-Alpines"	1	11.1	2	22.2	2	22.2	4	44.4	9
"Large Hybrids"	5	55.5	2	22.2	1	11.1	1	11.1	9
"Residuals"	3	33.3	5	55.5	0	10.0	1	11.1	9
Total Expected	36	50.0	23	32.0	10	14.0	3	4.0	72
Total Observed	18	25.0	20	27.8	14	19.4	20	27.8	72

TABLE VI–51. Variabilities of Type Subgroups

	Mean of Coefficients of Variation		Percentage exceeding Variation of Total Series	
	Measurements	Indices	Measurements	Indices
Total Series B	5.60	6.28	....	....
"Basket Makers"	4.82	4.66	32.14	11.11
"Pseudo-Negroids"	4.80	5.70	32.14	33.33
"Pseudo-Australoids"	4.73	4.49	25.00	0
"Plains Indians"..................	4.60	4.82	7.14	0
"Long-faced Europeans"...........	5.74	5.39	50.00	22.22
"Pseudo-Alpines"	5.08	6.01	28.57	55.56
"Large Hybrids"	4.74	5.29	14.29	0
"Residuals"	4.75	4.34	17.86	0

STATURE OF TYPE SUBGROUPS

It will be recalled that our various Glaze subgroups differed not at all in stature or very slightly. Table VI–52 records the differences in means of stature between our morphological types. In a population marked by small stature the "Pseudo-Negroid" type stands out as notably dwarfish. Its calculated mean of stature is only 155.2 cm. as compared with 161.8, the mean of the entire series. Here is a difference which must be taken as significant, with due consideration of probable errors. The other short groups are the "Basket Makers" and the "Residuals," both of whom fall well below the mean of the series. "Australoids" and "Alpines" are somewhat above the series average; "Hybrids," "Plains" and "Europeans" range from 163.2 to 163.7 cm. in average stature. In a population which averages 161.8, statures of 155.2 are small and statures of 163.7 are large, but a glance at the range of stature in our various subgroups will convince the readers that in the case of "Pseudo-Negroids" only has our selection of morphological skull type isolated a relatively homogeneous stature group. The only type groups which include individuals with statures of 170 cm. or more are the "Pseudo-Australoids," "Plains," "Long-faced Europeans," and "Large Hybrid" groups.

TABLE VI–52 Stature. Total Series B

Males	No.	Range	Mean	S.D.	V.
Total Series B	101	147.82–175.23	161.83 ± 0.34	5.10 ± 0.24	3.15 ± 0.15
"Basket Makers"	6	157.45–167.79	160.50 ...	... ...	... ...
"Pseudo-Negroids"	12	147.82–159.65	155.25 ± 0.63	3.24 ± 0.45	2.09 ± 0.29
"Pseudo-Australoids" ...	10	152.81–170.95	162.50 ± 0.99	4.63 ± 0.70	2.85 ± 0.43
"Plains Indians"	18	155.01–174.32	163.72 ± 0.83	5.22 ± 0.59	3.19 ± 0.36
"Long-faced Europeans" .	10	153.45–175.23	163.20 ± 0.94	4.42 ± 0.67	2.71 ± 0.41
"Pseudo-Alpines"	11	151.59–168.98	162.00 ± 1.05	5.15 ± 0.74	3.18 ± 0.46
"Large Hybrids"	22	156.69–171.41	163.73 ± 0.51	3.57 ± 0.36	2.18 ± 0.22
"Residuals"	12	156.32–167.01	160.92 ± 0.67	3.46 ± 0.48	2.15 ± 0.30

I believe we are safe in concluding that the "Pseudo-Negroid" type actually was distinguished by low stature, even among these short Pueblo Indians, and that the "Hybrids," "Plains," and "European" groups were in reality the tallest peoples of the Pecos.

PLATE VI–1

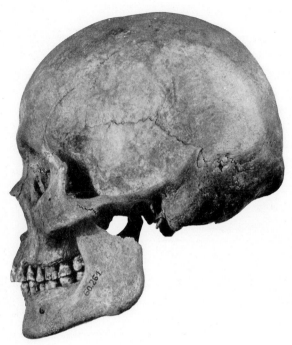

LENGTH-HEIGHT INDEX, ?

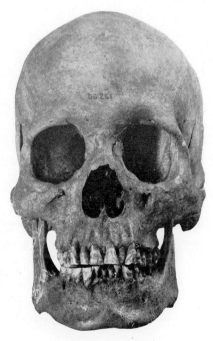

FACIAL INDEX, 91.27

CRANIAL INDEX, 69.78

No. 60,261. "BASKET MAKER" TYPE. DOLICHOCEPHALIC MALE
NO DEFORMATION. GLAZE II (?)

PLATE VI–2

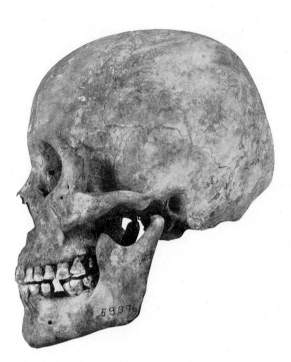

LENGTH-HEIGHT INDEX, 77.06

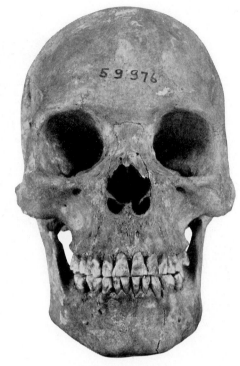

FACIAL INDEX, 86.89

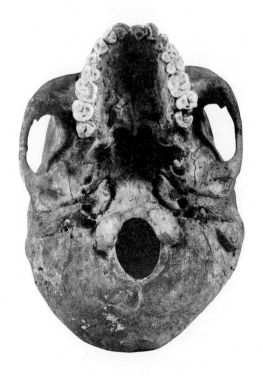

CRANIAL INDEX, 77.06

No. 59,976. "BASKET MAKER" TYPE. MESOCEPHALIC MALE
VERY SLIGHT OCCIPITAL DEFORMATION. GLAZE IV

PLATE VI–3

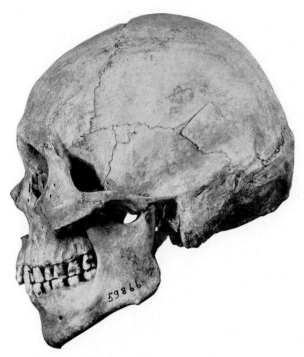

LENGTH-HEIGHT INDEX, 70.37

FACIAL INDEX, 86.01

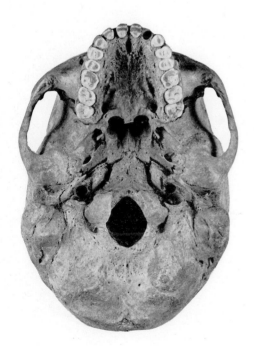

CRANIAL INDEX, 72.02

No. 59,866. "PSEUDO-NEGROID" TYPE. DOLICHOCEPHALIC MALE
NO DEFORMATION. GLAZE VI (?)

PLATE VI–4

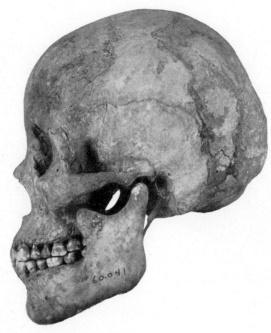

LENGTH-HEIGHT INDEX, 77.71

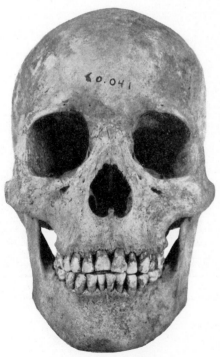

FACIAL INDEX, 92.91

CRANIAL INDEX 77.11

No. 60,041. "PSEUDO-NEGROID" TYPE. MESOCEPHALIC MALE
VERY SLIGHT OCCIPITAL DEFORMATION. GLAZE IV (?)

Plate VI–5

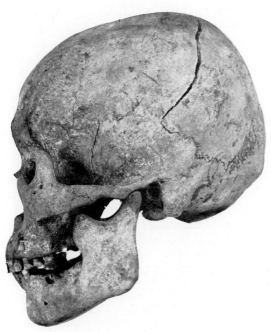

Length-Height Index, 73.03

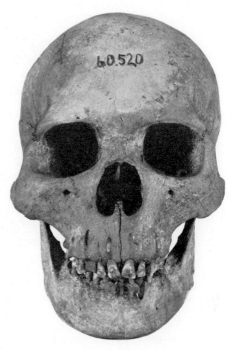

Facial Index, 84.29

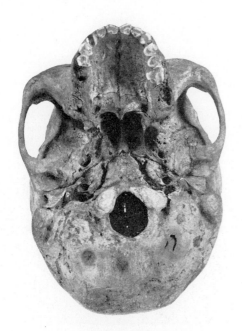

Cranial Index, 78.09

No. 60,520. "PSEUDO-NEGROID" TYPE. MESOCEPHALIC MALE
NO DEFORMATION. STRATUM DOUBTFUL

PLATE VI-6

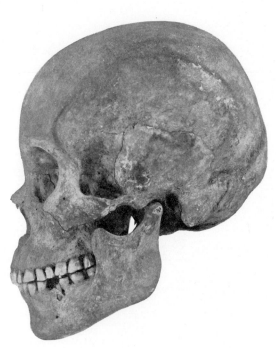

LENGTH-HEIGHT INDEX, 78.03

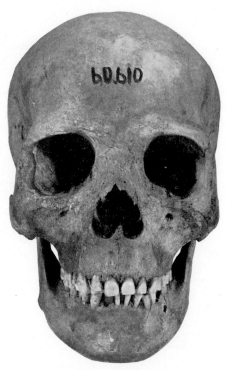

FACIAL INDEX, 91.34

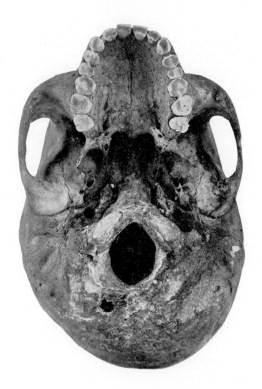

CRANIAL INDEX, 81.50

No. 60,610. "PSEUDO-NEGROID" TYPE. BRACHYCEPHALIC MALE
SLIGHT OCCIPITAL DEFORMATION. GLAZE V OR VI

PLATE VI–7

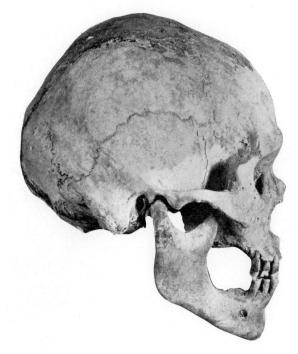

LENGTH-HEIGHT INDEX, 73.89

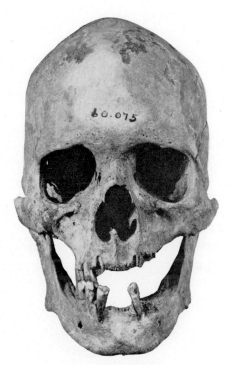

FACIAL INDEX, 88.72

CRANIAL INDEX, 69.44

No. 60,075. "PSEUDO-AUSTRALOID" TYPE. DOLICHOCEPHALIC MALE
NO DEFORMATION. GLAZE I (?)

PLATE VI–8

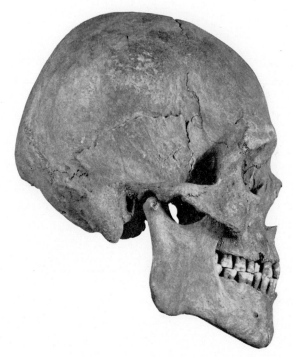

LENGTH-HEIGHT INDEX, 76.14

FACIAL INDEX, ? CRANIAL INDEX, 71.59

No. 60,283. "PSEUDO-AUSTRALOID" TYPE. DOLICHOCEPHALIC MALE
VERY SLIGHT OCCIPITAL DEFORMATION. GLAZE IV (?)

PLATE VI–9

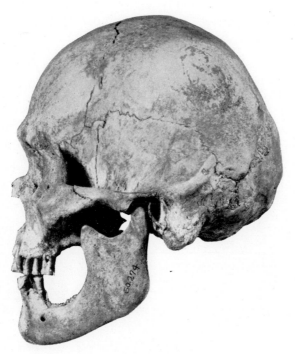

LENGTH-HEIGHT INDEX, 74.72

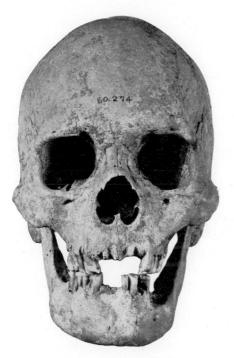

FACIAL INDEX, 87.68

CRANIAL INDEX, 76.40

No. 60,274. "PSEUDO-AUSTRALOID" TYPE. MESOCEPHALIC MALE
VERY SLIGHT OCCIPITAL DEFORMATION. GLAZE I (?)

PLATE VI–10

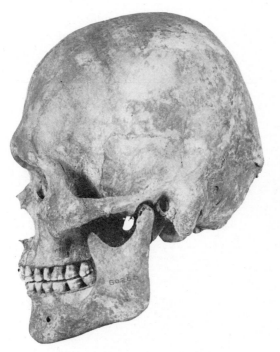

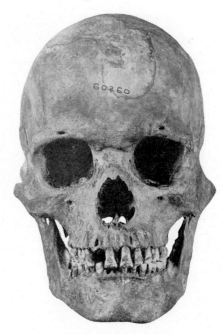

LENGTH-HEIGHT INDEX, 82.25

FACIAL INDEX, 77.08

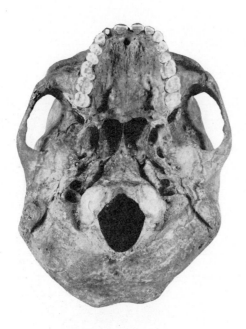

CRANIAL INDEX, 80.95

No. 60,260. "PSEUDO-AUSTRALOID" TYPE. BRACHYCEPHALIC MALE
SLIGHT LEFT OCCIPITAL DEFORMATION. GLAZE IV

PLATE VI–11

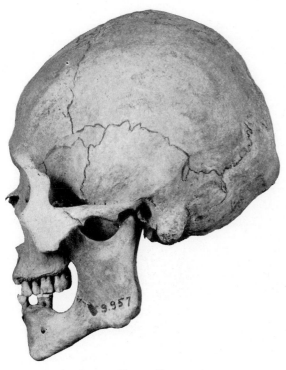

LENGTH-HEIGHT INDEX, 76.11

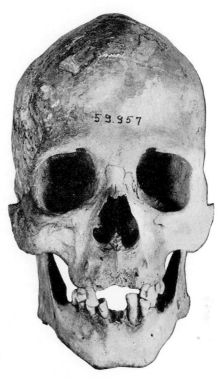

FACIAL INDEX, 88.41

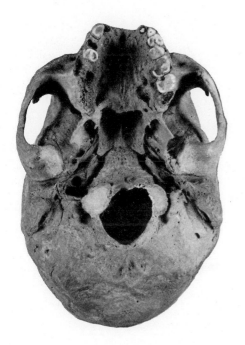

CRANIAL INDEX, 73.33

No. 59,957. "PLAINS INDIAN" TYPE. DOLICHOCEPHALIC MALE
VERY SLIGHT OCCIPITAL DEFORMATION. GLAZE V (?)

PLATE VI–12

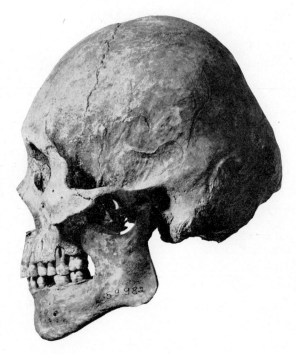

LENGTH-HEIGHT INDEX, 77.22

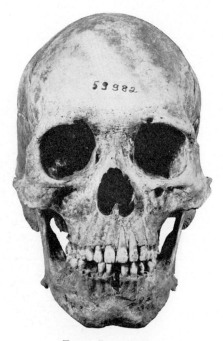

FACIAL INDEX, 84.51   CRANIAL INDEX, 73.33

No. 59,982.   "PLAINS INDIAN" TYPE.   DOLICHOCEPHALIC MALE
LAMBDOID DEFORMATION.   GLAZE VI (?)

PLATE VI–13

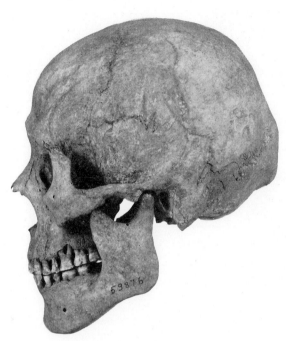

LENGTH-HEIGHT INDEX, 73.74

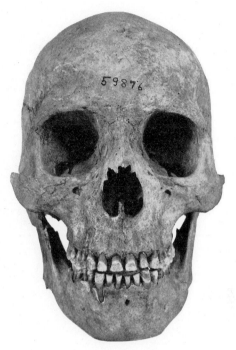

FACIAL INDEX, 89.58

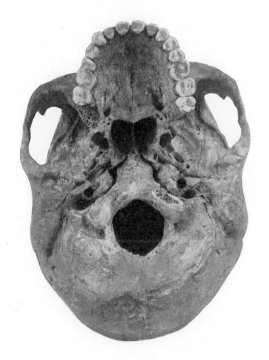

CRANIAL INDEX, 75.42

No. 59,876. "PLAINS INDIAN" TYPE. MESOCEPHALIC MALE
VERY SLIGHT DEFORMATION. GLAZE V (?)

PLATE VI–14

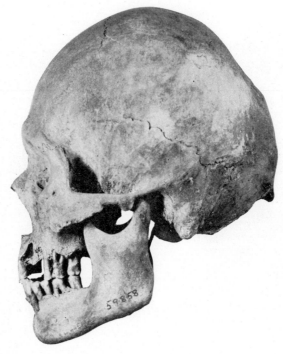

LENGTH-HEIGHT INDEX, 80.35

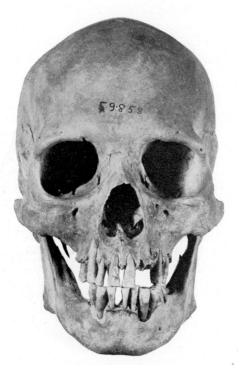

FACIAL INDEX, 84.40   CRANIAL INDEX, 80.35

No. 59,858. "PLAINS INDIAN" TYPE. BRACHYCEPHALIC MALE. PRONOUNCED
LAMBDOID DEFORMATION. BLACK-ON-WHITE

Plate VI–15

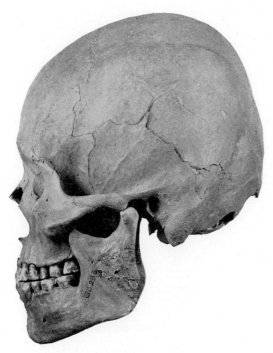

Length-Height Index, 85.12

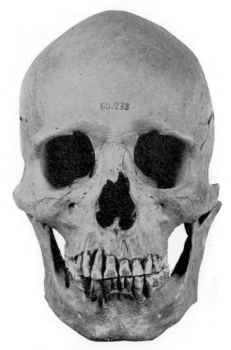

Facial Index, 85.00

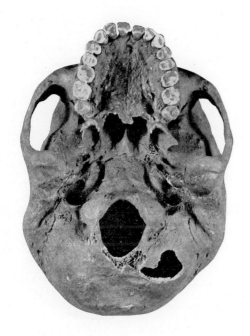

Cranial Index, 80.95

No. 60,238. "PLAINS INDIAN" TYPE. BRACHYCEPHALIC MALE
SLIGHT OCCIPITAL DEFORMATION. GLAZE III

PLATE VI–16

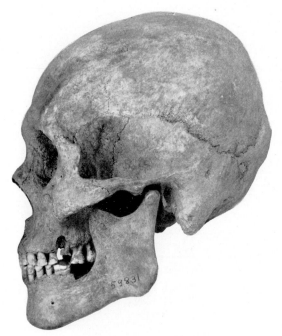

LENGTH-HEIGHT INDEX, 79.53

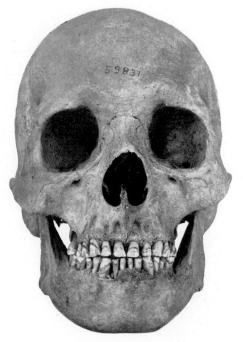

FACIAL INDEX, 85.92

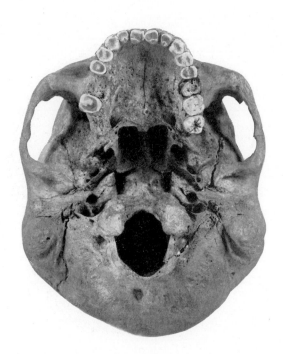

CRANIAL INDEX, 83.04

No. 59,831. "PLAINS INDIAN" TYPE. BRACHYCEPHALIC MALE
SLIGHT OCCIPITAL DEFORMATION. GLAZE VI (?)

PLATE VI–17

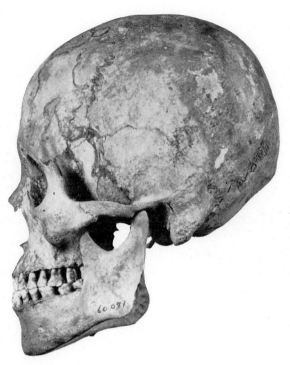

LENGTH-HEIGHT INDEX, 80.00

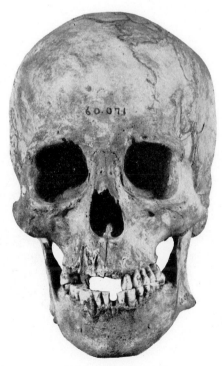

FACIAL INDEX, 93.08   CRANIAL INDEX, 81.14

No. 60,071. "LONG-FACED EUROPEAN" TYPE. BRACHYCEPHALIC MALE
VERY SLIGHT OCCIPITAL DEFORMATION. GLAZE III

PLATE VI–18

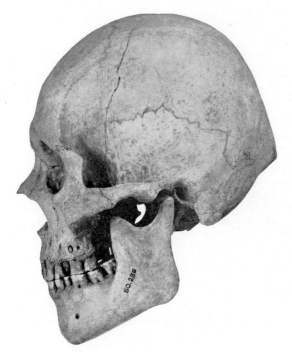

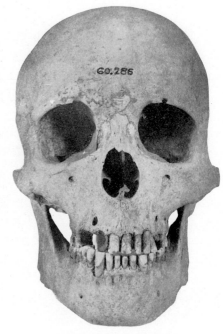

LENGTH-HEIGHT INDEX, 80.22

FACIAL INDEX, 91.84

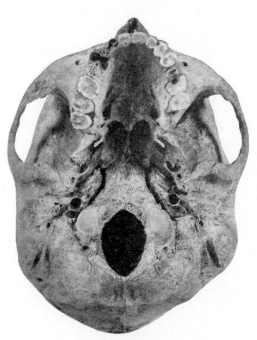

CRANIAL INDEX, 80.22

No. 60,286. "LONG-FACED EUROPEAN" TYPE. BRACHYCEPHALIC MALE
VERY SLIGHT OCCIPITAL DEFORMATION. GLAZE IV (?)

Plate VI–19

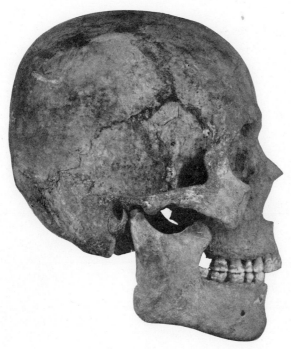

Length-Height Index, 88.30

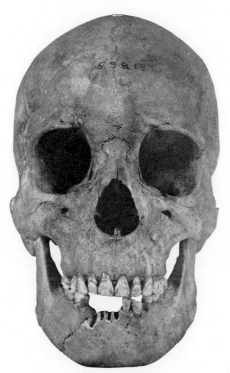

Facial Index, 97.04

Cranial Index, 81.87

No. 59,918. "LONG-FACED EUROPEAN" TYPE. BRACHYCEPHALIC MALE
SLIGHT LEFT OCCIPITAL DEFORMATION. GLAZE V (?)

PLATE VI–20

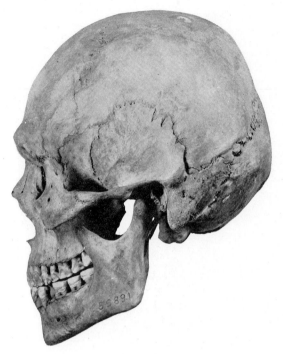

LENGTH-HEIGHT INDEX, 81.98

FACIAL INDEX, 87.59

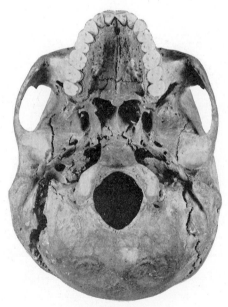

CRANIAL INDEX, 82.56

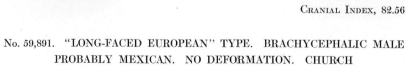

No. 59,891. "LONG-FACED EUROPEAN" TYPE. BRACHYCEPHALIC MALE
PROBABLY MEXICAN. NO DEFORMATION. CHURCH

PLATE VI–21

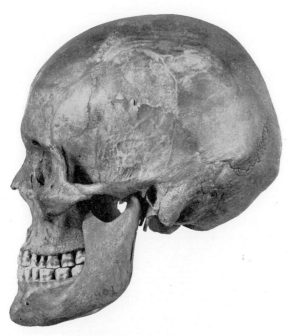

LENGTH-HEIGHT INDEX, 75.84

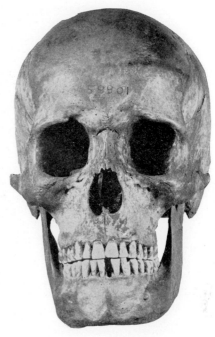

FACIAL INDEX, 77.61

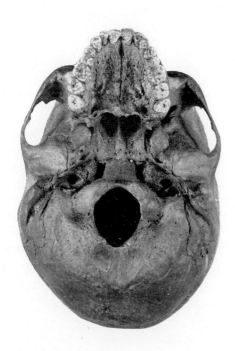

CRANIAL INDEX, 75.84

No. 59,901. "LONG-FACED EUROPEAN" TYPE. MESOCEPHALIC MALE
PROBABLY MEXICAN. NO DEFORMATION. CHURCH

PLATE VI–22

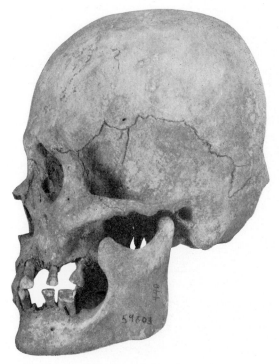

LENGTH-HEIGHT INDEX, 85.35

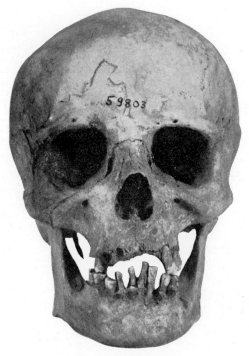

FACIAL INDEX, 86.92

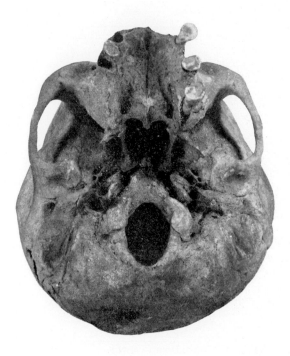

CRANIAL INDEX, 98.09

No. 59,803. "PSEUDO-ALPINE" TYPE. BRACHYCEPHALIC MALE
PRONOUNCED OCCIPITAL DEFORMATION. GLAZE I

Plate VI–23

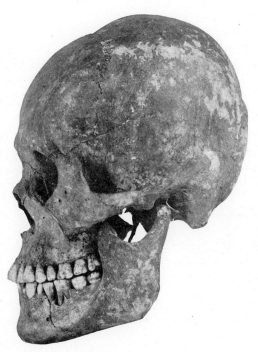

Length-Height Index, ?

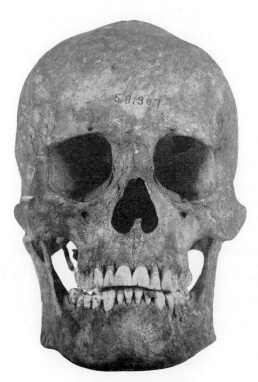

Facial Index, 82.86

Cranial Index, 88.20

No. 59,987. "PSEUDO-ALPINE" TYPE. BRACHYCEPHALIC MALE WITH
SLIGHT OCCIPITAL DEFORMATION. GLAZE II (?)

PLATE VI–24

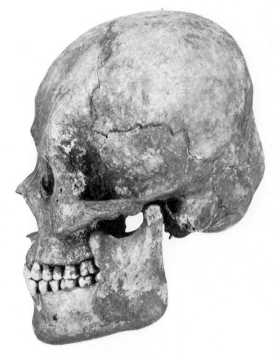

LENGTH-HEIGHT INDEX, 87.01

FACIAL INDEX, 82.39

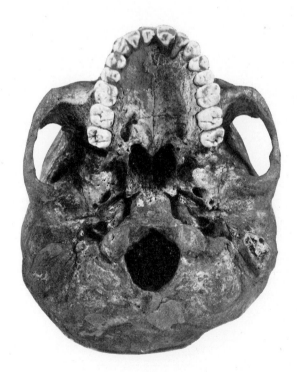
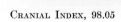

CRANIAL INDEX, 98.05

No. 60,074. "PSEUDO-ALPINE" TYPE. BRACHYCEPHALIC MALE
PRONOUNCED OCCIPITAL DEFORMATION. GLAZE III (?)

PLATE VI–25

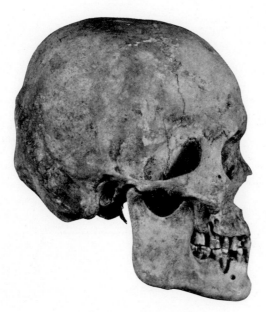

LENGTH-HEIGHT INDEX, 77.71

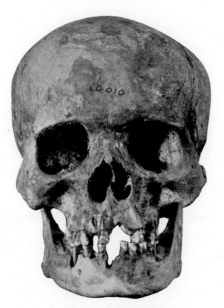

FACIAL INDEX, 79.56

CRANIAL INDEX, 90.36

No. 60,010. "PSEUDO-ALPINE" TYPE. BRACHYCEPHALIC MALE
OCCIPITAL DEFORMATION. GLAZE V

PLATE VI–26

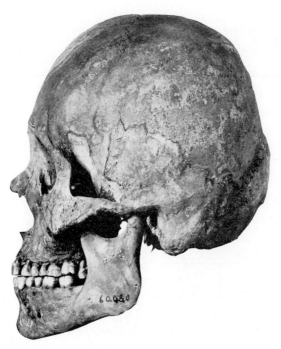

LENGTH-HEIGHT INDEX, 85.54

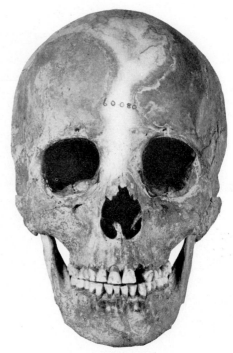

FACIAL INDEX, 84.51

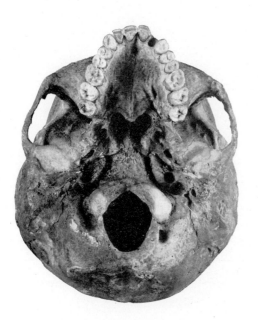

CRANIAL INDEX, 91.57

No. 60,080. "LARGE HYBRID" TYPE. BRACHYCEPHALIC MALE
OCCIPITAL DEFORMATION. GLAZE I (?)

PLATE VI–27

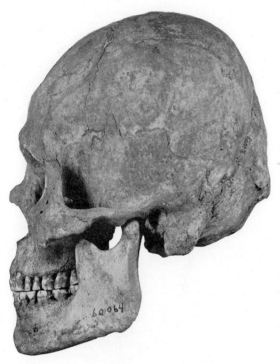

LENGTH-HEIGHT INDEX, 84.62

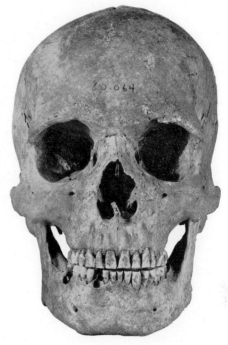

FACIAL INDEX, 83.56

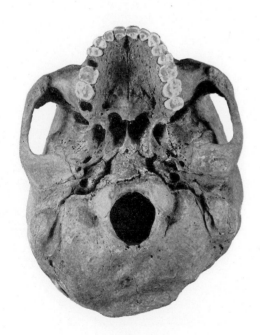

CRANIAL INDEX, 86.98

No. 60,064.   "LARGE HYBRID" TYPE.   BRACHYCEPHALIC MALE
PRONOUNCED OCCIPITAL DEFORMATION.   GLAZE IV (?)

Plate VI–28

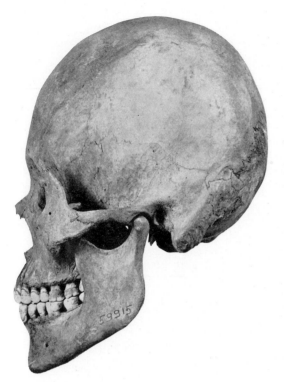

Length-Height Index, 91.41

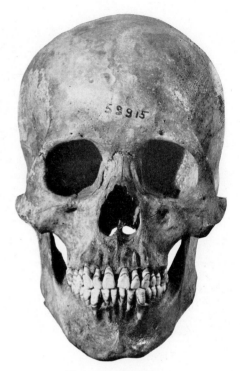

Facial Index, 88.11

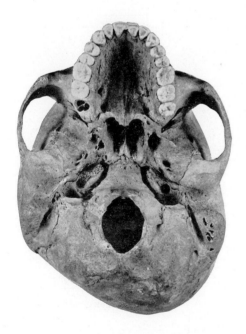

Cranial Index, 91.14

No. 59,915. "LARGE HYBRID" TYPE. BRACHYCEPHALIC MALE. PRONOUNCED
RIGHT OCCIPITAL DEFORMATION. GLAZE V

PLATE VI–29

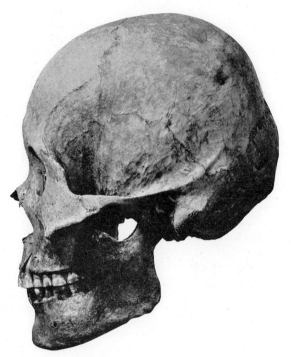

LENGTH-HEIGHT INDEX, 79.77

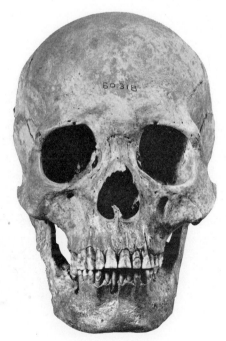

FACIAL INDEX, 88.65   CRANIAL INDEX, 84.39

No. 60,318. "LARGE HYBRID" TYPE. BRACHYCEPHALIC MALE
VERY SLIGHT OCCIPITAL DEFORMATION. GLAZE VI

PLATE VI–30

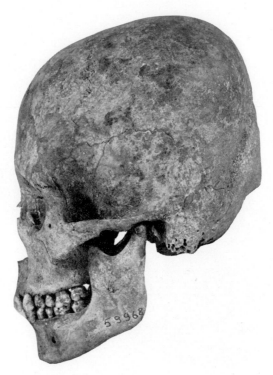

LENGTH-HEIGHT INDEX, 87.27

FACIAL INDEX, 85.40

CRANIAL INDEX, 87.27

No. 59,968. "RESIDUAL" TYPE. BRACHYCEPHALIC MALE. PRONOUNCED
LEFT OCCIPITAL DEFORMATION. STRATUM DOUBTFUL

PLATE VI-31

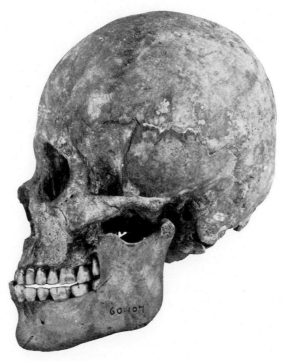

LENGTH-HEIGHT INDEX, 92.50

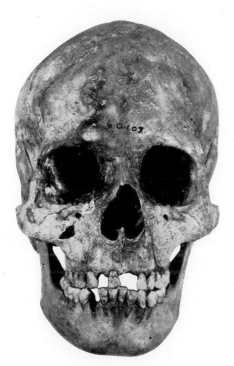

FACIAL INDEX, 85.07   CRANIAL INDEX, 89.38

No. 60,107. "RESIDUAL" TYPE. BRACHYCEPHALIC MALE. MEDIUM LEFT
OCCIPITAL DEFORMATION. GLAZE VI (?)

CHAPTER VII

OBSERVATIONS AND COMPOSITE PHOTOGRAPHS OF MORPHOLOGICAL CRANIAL TYPES

METHOD OF ANALYZING TYPE OBSERVATIONS

HAVING established the validity of our morphological types by metric criteria, we must now examine their observational features. The types should show differences in the degree of development of certain features which are observed and graded, but which cannot be measured. For purposes of this test a number of observed characters have been tabulated according to their occurrence and development in the several types. Not all morphological observations included in our routine examination of crania have been analyzed for type differences, simply because of vast labor involved in such retabulation and analysis.

The method of differentiation is based in each table upon the theory of association and the coefficient of mean square contingency. These are, or should be, familiar to all students of Physical Anthropology.[1] In the tables following, the percentages of a given grade of an observed character in any morphological type are compared with the percentage of the same grade of that character in the entire series. A significant association of a feature with a type occurs when the percentage is markedly less or greater in the type than in the entire series.

The coefficient of mean square contingency measures, on a scale from 0 to 1, the extent to which the various grades of an observational feature are distributed among the type subgroups contrary to what one might expect if chance alone operated in the assignment of grades to types. The coefficient is always positive, always more than zero, and, in the present tables, its values are somewhat enhanced by a combination of small numbers in our type subgroups and, in some instances, a rather too fine subdivision of observational categories. Hence the significance of the coefficient of mean square contingency is probably little, unless its value is at least equal to .3. In any event it merely gives a general mathematical measure of type group differentiation with regard to the character involved. A value of the coefficient less than .3 implies that altogether our morphological types are but slightly distinguished as to the character in question or not at all; a value of unity would imply an absolute distinction between all types in the development of the category in question.

[1] Yule, 1927, pp. 25–72.

THE CRANIAL VAULT

Table VII–1 deals with the observed height of the frontal region. "Medium" implies that the observer regards the cranium in question as conforming in frontal height to the average or modal skull of the adult male European of prevailingly Nordic race, but with the slight Alpine admixture which is commonly found in the crania of northwestern Europe. In the series at large 33.59 per cent of crania are classified as "submedium" in height of the forehead. But the "Hybrids" and "Residuals" show a significant deficiency of skulls belonging to this category, and conversely, the "Hybrids" show an excessive percentage of crania of "pronounced" height and the "Residuals" an excess of crania of "medium" height. We may therefore conclude that the "Hybrid" type has fewer crania with low foreheads and more with high foreheads than the series at large, and that the "Residual" type is distinguished by a prevalence of frontals of "medium" height. Similarly it is seen that the "Pseudo-Australoids" are distinguished by their very low foreheads, and that this is true to a lesser degree of the "Pseudo-Negroids" and the "Basket Makers." The coefficient of mean square contingency is .49, which indicates in general that our types are fairly well differentiated with respect to frontal height.

Table VII–2 records the observations as to the breadth of the frontal region. Here again it is to be observed that the types displaying great breadth of the forehead are the "Pseudo-Alpines," "Hybrids," and "Europeans," whereas the "Pseudo-Australoids," "Plains," "Basket Makers," and "Pseudo-Negroids" are deficient in this diameter. The table of measurements of minimum frontal diameter (Table VI–14) naturally yields similar results. The coefficient of mean square contingency of frontal breadth with morphological type (.44) shows a sharp type difference.

The slope of the frontal region (Table VII–3) is most pronounced in "Plains," "Pseudo-Australoids," and "Europeans," least so in "Pseudo-Negroids," "Large Hybrids," and "Residuals." The contingency coefficient is again high — .44.

TABLE VII–1. HEIGHT OF FRONTAL REGION. TOTAL SERIES B

Males	Very Submedium		Submedium		Medium		Pronounced		Total
	No.	Per cent	No.	Per cent	No.	Per cent	No.	Per cent	No.
"Basket Makers"	0	0	4	50.00	3	37.50	1	12.50	8
"Pseudo-Negroids"	0	0	7	53.85	5	38.46	1	7.69	13
"Pseudo-Australoids"	1	9.09	7	63.64	3	27.27	0	0	11
"Plains Indians".................	2	8.70	10	43.48	10	43.48	1	4.35	23
"Long-faced Europeans"	0	0	5	27.78	10	55.56	3	16.67	18
"Pseudo-Alpines"	0	0	6	42.86	5	35.71	3	21.43	14
"Hybrids"	0	0	3	11.11	10	37.04	14	51.85	27
"Residuals"	0	0	1	7.14	10	71.43	3	21.43	14
Total	3	2.34	43	33.59	56	43.75	26	20.31	128

Coefficient of contingency 0.49

TABLE VII–2. BREADTH OF FRONTAL REGION. TOTAL SERIES B

Males	Very Submedium		Submedium		Medium		Pronounced		Very Pronounced		Total
	No.	Per cent	No.	Per cent	No.	Per cent	No.	Per cent	No.	Per cent	No.
"Basket Makers"	1	12.50	2	25.00	4	50.00	1	12.50	0	0	8
"Pseudo-Negroids" ...	0	0	3	23.08	8	61.54	2	15.38	0	0	13
"Pseudo-Australoids" .	0	0	7	63.64	3	27.27	1	9.09	0	0	11
"Plains Indians"	2	8.70	8	34.78	8	34.78	4	17.39	1	4.35	23
"Long-faced Europeans"	0	0	3	16.67	6	33.33	8	44.44	1	5.56	18
"Pseudo-Alpines"	0	0	2	14.29	5	35.71	7	50.00	0	0	14
"Hybrids"	0	0	3	11.11	11	40.74	13	48.15	0	0	27
"Residuals"	0	0	1	7.14	10	71.43	3	21.43	0	0	14
Total	3	2.34	29	22.66	55	42.97	39	30.47	2	1.56	128

Coefficient of contingency 0.44

TABLE VII–3. SLOPE OF FRONTAL REGION. TOTAL SERIES B

Males	Protruding		Submedium		Medium		Pronounced		Total
	No.	Per cent	No.	Per cent	No.	Per cent	No.	Per cent	No.
"Basket Makers"	0	0	0	0	7	87.50	1	12.50	8
"Pseudo-Negroids"	0	0	4	30.77	7	53.85	2	15.38	13
"Pseudo-Australoids"	0	0	0	0	6	54.55	5	45.45	11
"Plains Indians".................	0	0	1	4.35	10	43.48	12	52.17	23
"Long-faced Europeans"..........	0	0	0	0	12	66.67	6	33.33	18
"Pseudo-Alpines"	0	0	3	21.43	10	71.43	1	7.14	14
"Hybrids"	1	3.70	5	18.52	16	59.26	5	18.52	27
"Residuals"	0	0	3	21.43	11	78.57	0	0	14
Total	1	0.78	16	12.50	79	61.72	32	25.00	128

Coefficient of contingency 0.44

Table VII–4 shows that a full or protuberant temporal region is especially characteristic of the "Residual," "Hybrid," and "Pseudo-Alpine" types, whereas this region is most compressed in "Pseudo-Australoids," "Basket Makers," and "Pseudo-Negroids." The coefficient of contingency is .56.

TABLE VII–4. TEMPORAL REGION. TOTAL SERIES B

Males	Compressed or very Compressed		Flat or Submedium		Medium		Pronounced or very Pronounced		Total
	No.	Per cent	No.	Per cent	No.	Per cent	No.	Per cent	No.
"Basket Makers"	4	50.00	2	25.00	2	25.00	0	0	8
"Pseudo-Negroids"	1	7.69	8	61.54	4	30.77	0	0	13
"Pseudo-Australoids"	6	54.55	4	36.36	1	9.09	0	0	11
"Plains Indians"..................	7	30.43	7	30.43	7	30.43	2	8.70	23
"Long-faced Europeans"	3	18.75	5	31.25	8	50.00	0	0	16
"Pseudo-Alpines"	1	7.14	1	7.14	6	42.86	6	42.86	14
"Hybrids"	4	15.38	4	15.38	8	30.77	10	38.46	26
"Residuals"	2	14.29	0	0	5	35.71	7	50.00	14
Total	28	22.40	31	24.80	41	32.80	25	20.00	125

Coefficient of contingency 0.56

Supraorbital ridges are largest among the "Pseudo-Australoids" and least developed in the "Pseudo-Negroids," "Pseudo-Alpines," and "Residuals" (coefficient of contingency .54) (Table VII–5). Types of supraorbital ridges may be classified as (1) median, (2) divided, (3) continuous. Table VII–6 shows a small contingency of brow-ridge types upon morphological subgroups, but clearly the continuous type is most frequent among "Pseudo-Australoids," "Pseudo-Negroids," and "Plains" types; divided brow-ridges are most frequent among the "Basket Makers"; and the "Pseudo-Alpines" and "Residuals" show largest proportions of the type of brow-ridges which are restricted to the median half of the orbits. The coefficient of contingency is only .34.

TABLE VII–5. SIZE OF SUPRAORBITAL RIDGES. TOTAL SERIES B

Males	Absent No.	Per cent	Submedium No.	Per cent	Medium No.	Per cent	Pronounced No.	Per cent	Very Pronounced No.	Per cent	Total No.
"Basket Makers"	0	0	2	25.00	6	75.00	0	0	0	0	8
"Pseudo-Negroids"	1	7.69	8	61.54	3	23.08	1	7.69	0	0	13
"Pseudo-Australoids" ..	0	0	0	0	3	27.27	6	54.55	2	18.18	11
"Plains Indians"	0	0	2	8.70	14	60.87	6	26.09	1	4.35	23
"Long-faced Europeans"	0	0	5	27.78	10	55.56	3	16.67	0	0	18
"Pseudo-Alpines"	0	0	6	42.86	7	50.00	1	7.14	0	0	14
"Hybrids"	0	0	2	7.41	20	74.07	4	14.81	1	3.70	27
"Residuals"	0	0	8	57.14	5	35.71	1	7.14	0	0	14
Total	1	0.78	33	25.78	68	53.13	22	17.19	4	3.12	128

Coefficient of contingency 0.54

TABLE VII–6. TYPE OF SUPRAORBITAL RIDGES. TOTAL SERIES B

Males	Type I No.	Per cent	Type II No.	Per cent	Type III No.	Per cent	Total No.
"Basket Makers"	2	25.00	5	62.50	1	12.50	8
"Pseudo-Negroids"	2	18.18	4	36.36	5	45.45	11
"Pseudo-Australoids"	2	18.18	3	27.27	6	54.55	11
"Plains Indians"	8	34.78	5	21.74	10	43.48	23
"Long-faced Europeans"	6	33.33	8	44.44	4	22.22	18
"Pseudo-Alpines"	7	50.00	4	28.57	3	21.43	14
"Hybrids"	10	37.04	10	37.04	7	25.93	27
"Residuals"	7	50.00	6	42.86	1	7.14	14
Total........................	44	34.92	45	35.71	37	29.37	126

Coefficient of contingency 0.34

THE FACE

Size and projection of malars is a feature of importance in studies of Indian crania. Table VII–7 records the preëminence of the "Large Hybrid" type in great malar development. The least development of malars is found in the "Basket Maker" type and in the "Long-faced Europeans." The series at large shows an excessive development of malars when compared with European race standards.

The size of zygomata is distributed quite similarly to that of malars. Again the "Hybrids" show the largest development, the "Pseudo-Australoids" ranking next. The smallest average development of zygomatic arches is found in "Basket Makers" with "Pseudo-Negroids," "Long-faced Europeans," and "Pseudo-Alpines," next in order of frequency (Table VII–8).

TABLE VII–7. MALARS. TOTAL SERIES B

Males	Submedium		Medium		Pronounced		Very Pronounced		Total
	No.	Per cent	No.	Per cent	No.	Per cent	No.	Per cent	No.
"Basket Makers"	0	0	6	75.00	2	25.00	0	0	8
"Pseudo-Negroids"	0	0	5	38.46	8	61.54	0	0	13
"Pseudo-Australoids"	0	0	4	40.00	6	60.00	0	0	10
"Plains Indians"..................	0	0	5	21.74	16	69.57	2	8.70	23
"Long-faced Europeans".........	1	5.88	7	41.18	8	47.06	1	5.88	17
"Pseudo-Alpines"	0	0	4	28.57	10	71.43	0	0	14
"Hybrids"	0	0	2	7.69	16	61.54	8	30.77	26
"Residuals"	0	0	3	23.08	10	76.92	0	0	13
Total	1	0.81	36	29.03	76	61.29	11	8.87	124

Coefficient of contingency 0.47

TABLE VII–8. ZYGOMATA. TOTAL SERIES B

Males	Submedium		Medium		Pronounced		Very Pronounced		Total
	No.	Per cent	No.	Per cent	No.	Per cent	No.	Per cent	No.
"Basket Makers"	0	0	5	62.50	3	37.50	0	0	8
"Pseudo-Negroids"	0	0	6	46.15	6	46.15	1	7.69	13
"Pseudo-Australoids"	0	0	2	22.22	6	66.67	1	11.11	9
"Plains Indians"..................	0	0	3	13.04	18	78.26	2	8.70	23
"Long-faced Europeans".........	3	17.65	5	29.41	8	47.06	1	5.88	17
"Pseudo-Alpines"	1	7.14	5	35.71	8	57.14	0	0	14
"Hybrids"....................	0	0	2	7.69	16	61.54	8	30.77	26
"Residuals"..................	0	0	3	23.08	10	76.92	0	0	13
Total	4	3.25	31	25.20	75	60.98	13	10.57	123

Coefficient of contingency 0.45

Shape and inclination of the orbits seem to be poor type criteria. Orbits are usually oblong or square. Absence of inclination of the horizontal axis is most notable in the "Pseudo-Australoids" and most pronounced in "Plains" and "Basket Maker" types, but the coefficient of contingency (.22) is scarcely significant for type differentiation in general (Tables VII–9, 10).

The absence of well-marked suborbital fossae is an anthropoidal characteristic frequently observed in Mongoloid crania. Deep fossae are commonly found in Europeans. But the development of this feature is also affected by the age of the individual, since, with the loss of teeth and the absorption of the alveolar processes, the maxillary sinus tends to be deflated, thus increasing the depth of the suborbital fossae. Table VII–11 shows the distribution of suborbital fossae according to gradations of depth. There appears to be no clear differentiation of types with respect to this feature.

TABLE VII–9. Shape of Orbits. Total Series B

Males	Oblong No.	Oblong Per cent	Square No.	Square Per cent	Rhomboid No.	Rhomboid Per cent	Oval No.	Oval Per cent	Round No.	Round Per cent	Total No.
"Basket Makers"	6	75.00	2	25.00	0	0	0	0	0	0	8
"Pseudo-Negroids"	10	76.92	3	23.08	0	0	0	0	0	0	13
"Pseudo-Australoids"	11	100.00	0	0	0	0	0	0	0	0	11
"Plains Indians"	11	47.83	9	39.13	3	13.04	0	0	0	0	23
"Long-faced Europeans"	11	61.11	7	38.89	0	0	0	0	0	0	18
"Pseudo-Alpines"	8	57.14	5	35.71	1	7.14	0	0	0	0	14
"Hybrids"	18	69.23	5	19.23	0	0	2	7.69	1	3.85	26
"Residuals"	10	71.43	3	21.43	0	0	1	7.14	0	0	14
Total	85	66.93	34	26.77	4	3.15	3	2.36	1	0.79	127

Coefficient of contingency 0.45

TABLE VII–10. Inclination of Orbits. Total Series B

Males	Absent No.	Absent Per cent	Submedium No.	Submedium Per cent	Medium No.	Medium Per cent	Pronounced No.	Pronounced Per cent	Total No.
"Basket Makers"	1	12.50	2	25.00	3	37.50	2	25.00	8
"Pseudo-Negroids"	3	23.08	7	53.85	2	15.38	1	7.69	13
"Pseudo-Australoids"	6	54.55	1	9.09	2	18.18	2	18.18	11
"Plains Indians"	4	17.39	7	30.43	6	26.09	6	26.09	23
"Long-faced Europeans"	5	27.78	6	33.33	4	22.22	3	16.67	18
"Pseudo-Alpines"	4	28.57	6	42.86	2	14.29	2	14.29	14
"Hybrids"	8	29.63	4	14.81	14	51.85	1	3.70	27
"Residuals"	7	50.00	2	14.29	4	28.57	1	7.14	14
Total	38	29.69	35	27.34	37	28.91	18	14.06	128

Coefficient of contingency 0.22

TABLE VII–11. Suborbital Fossae. Total Series B

Males	Absent No.	Absent Per cent	Submedium No.	Submedium Per cent	Medium No.	Medium Per cent	Pronounced No.	Pronounced Per cent	Very Pronounced No.	Very Pronounced Per cent	Total No.
"Basket Makers"	0	0	1	12.50	5	62.50	2	25.00	0	0	8
"Pseudo-Negroids"	0	0	3	25.00	5	41.67	4	33.33	0	0	12
"Pseudo-Australoids"	0	0	5	45.45	4	36.36	2	18.18	0	0	11
"Plains Indians"	0	0	5	21.74	9	39.13	7	30.43	2	8.70	23
"Long-faced Europeans"	0	0	8	47.06	6	35.29	3	17.65	0	0	17
"Pseudo-Alpines"	1	7.69	3	23.08	5	38.46	1	7.69	3	23.08	13
"Hybrids"	1	3.85	12	46.15	5	19.23	7	26.92	1	3.85	26
"Residuals"	0	0	4	28.57	8	57.14	2	14.29	0	0	14
Total	2	1.61	41	33.06	47	37.90	28	22.58	6	4.84	124

Coefficient of contingency 0.32

Lack of a nasion depression is a Mongoloid feature quite characteristic of American Indians. The nasion depression is absent in more than 52 per cent of our male series. It is most frequently lacking in "Residuals," "Basket Makers," "Pseudo-Alpines," and "Plains" subgroups; most frequently well developed in "Pseudo-Negroids," "Pseudo-Australoids," and "Long-faced Europeans" (Coefficient of mean square contingency .46) (Table VII–12).

Subnasal grooves, a primitive feature not commonly found in our series, seem to show little if any difference in type distribution, although the coefficient of mean square contingency is .36 (Table VII–13). The lowest nasal bridges are found in the "Pseudo-Negroids," and somewhat less frequently in the "Basket Makers." High nasal bridges are particularly characteristic of "Long-faced Europeans." The height of the nasal bridge is also well developed in "Hybrids" and in the "Plains" type. The narrowest nasal bridges are found in the "Residual" type and the broadest in the "Pseudo-Negroid" type. Concavo-convex nasal bridges are the most common form in Indians and probably in most other groups. In this series concave noses are most frequent in the "Pseudo-Negroids" and "Pseudo-Australoids"; straight noses, perhaps, among the "Basket Makers," "Hybrids," and "Europeans." But all forms other than the concavo-convex are so uncommon that to draw conclusions from their sporadic distribution would be unsafe. The breadth of the nasal aperture seems to be least in "Europeans" and greatest among "Pseudo-Australoids," "Pseudo-Negroids," and "Basket Makers" (Tables VII–14, 15, 16, 17).

As a rule Indians have rather indistinct or dull lower borders of the nasal aperture; this is true of the Pecos series (Table VII–18). "Basket Makers," "Pseudo-Alpines" and "Residuals" seem to have the sharpest lower borders, and the most primitive groups in this respect are the "Pseudo-Negroids," "Pseudo-Australoids," and "Plains" types. "Pseudo-Negroids" show the poorest development of the nasal spine, followed in this respect by "Residuals." "Hybrids," "Basket Makers," "Pseudo-Alpines" have the largest spines (Table VII–19).

TABLE VII–12. NASION DEPRESSION. TOTAL SERIES B

Males	Absent		Submedium		Medium		Pronounced		Total
	No.	Per cent	No.	Per cent	No.	Per cent	No.	Per cent	No.
"Basket Makers"	6	75.00	1	12.50	1	12.50	0	0	8
"Pseudo-Negroids"	1	7.69	8	61.54	3	23.08	1	7.69	13
"Pseudo-Australoids"	3	27.27	6	54.55	1	9.09	1	9.09	11
"Plains Indians"	14	60.87	8	34.78	1	4.35	0	0	23
"Long-faced Europeans"	8	44.44	9	50.00	0	0	1	5.56	18
"Pseudo-Alpines"	9	64.29	5	35.71	0	0	0	0	14
"Hybrids"	15	55.56	12	44.44	0	0	0	0	27
"Residuals"	11	78.57	3	21.43	0	0	0	0	14
Total	67	52.34	52	40.63	6	4.69	3	2.34	128

Coefficient of contingency 0.46

TABLE VII–13. SUBNASAL GROOVES. TOTAL SERIES B

Males	Absent		Submedium		Medium		Total
	No.	Per cent	No.	Per cent	No.	Per cent	No.
"Basket Makers"	6	75.00	0	0	2	25.00	8
"Pseudo-Negroids"	11	84.62	2	15.38	0	0	13
"Pseudo-Australoids"	10	90.91	1	9.09	0	0	11
"Plains Indians"	17	73.91	6	26.09	0	0	23
"Long-faced Europeans"	14	77.78	3	16.67	1	5.56	18
"Pseudo-Alpines"	12	85.71	0	0	2	14.29	14
"Hybrids"	22	81.48	4	14.81	1	3.70	27
"Residuals"	10	83.33	2	16.67	0	0	12
Total	102	80.33	18	14.29	6	4.76	126

Coefficient of contingency 0.36

TABLE VII–14.   HEIGHT OF NASAL BRIDGE.   TOTAL SERIES B

Males	Very Submedium		Submedium		Medium		Pronounced		Total
	No.	Per cent	No.	Per cent	No.	Per cent	No.	Per cent	No.
"Basket Makers"	2	25.00	5	62.50	1	12.50	0	0	8
"Pseudo-Negroids"	6	46.15	7	53.85	0	0	0	0	13
"Pseudo-Australoids"	1	9.09	6	54.55	4	36.36	0	0	11
"Plains Indians"................	0	0	12	52.17	11	47.83	0	0	23
"Long-faced Europeans"........	0	0	6	35.29	9	52.94	2	11.76	17
"Pseudo-Alpines"	1	7.14	9	64.29	4	28.57	0	0	14
"Hybrids"	0	0	17	62.96	8	29.63	2	7.41	27
"Residuals"	2	16.67	7	58.33	3	25.00	0	0	12
Total	12	9.60	69	55.20	40	32.00	4	3.20	125

Coefficient of contingency 0.49

TABLE VII–15.   BREADTH OF NASAL BRIDGE.   TOTAL SERIES B

Males	Submedium		Medium		Pronounced		Total
	No.	Per cent	No.	Per cent	No.	Per cent	No.
"Basket Makers"	1	12.50	6	75.00	1	12.50	8
"Pseudo-Negroids"	2	15.38	7	53.85	4	30.77	13
"Pseudo-Australoids"	3	27.27	6	54.55	2	18.18	11
"Plains Indians"	9	39.13	12	52.17	2	8.70	23
"Long-faced Europeans"	6	33.33	12	66.67	0	0	18
"Pseudo-Alpines"	5	35.71	8	57.14	1	7.14	14
"Hybrids"	12	44.44	12	44.44	3	11.11	27
"Residuals"	8	61.54	5	38.46	0	0	13
Total	46	36.22	68	53.54	13	10.24	127

Coefficient of contingency 0.35

TABLE VII–16.   PROFILE OF NASAL BRIDGE.   TOTAL SERIES B

Males	Concavo-convex		Concave		Convex		Straight		Total
	No.	Per cent	No.	Per cent	No.	Per cent	No.	Per cent	No.
"Basket Makers"	4	66.67	0	0	0	0	2	33.33	6
"Pseudo-Negroids"	7	53.85	5	38.46	1	7.69	0	0	13
"Pseudo-Australoids"	7	63.64	3	27.27	1	9.09	0	0	11
"Plains Indians"................	15	71.43	2	9.52	2	9.52	2	9.52	21
"Long-faced Europeans".........	10	71.43	1	7.14	1	7.14	2	14.29	14
"Pseudo-Alpines"	11	84.62	0	0	1	7.69	1	7.69	13
"Hybrids"	14	58.33	3	12.50	1	4.17	6	25.00	24
"Residuals"	0	0	2	50.00	0	0	2	50.00	4
Total	68	64.15	16	15.09	7	6.60	15	14.15	106

Coefficient of contingency 0.47

TABLE VII–17. BREADTH OF NASAL APERTURE. TOTAL SERIES B

Males	Submedium		Medium		Pronounced		Very Pronounced		Total
	No.	Per cent	No.	Per cent	No.	Per cent	No.	Per cent	No.
"Basket Makers"	0	0	5	62.50	3	37.50	0	0	8
"Pseudo-Negroids"	2	15.38	5	38.46	6	46.15	0	0	13
"Pseudo-Australoids"	0	0	5	45.45	6	54.55	0	0	11
"Plains Indians"	2	8.70	14	60.87	7	30.43	0	0	23
"Long-faced Europeans"	5	27.78	13	72.22	0	0	0	0	18
"Pseudo-Alpines"	1	7.14	10	71.43	3	21.43	0	0	14
"Hybrids".....................	3	11.11	17	62.96	7	25.93	0	0	27
"Residuals"	0	0	10	71.43	4	28.57	0	0	14
Total......................	13	10.16	79	61.72	36	28.13	0	0	128

Coefficient of contingency 0.38

TABLE VII–18. LOWER BORDERS OF NASAL APERTURE. TOTAL SERIES B

Males	Absent		Indistinct		Submedium		Medium		Pronounced		Total
	No.	Per cent	No.	Per cent	No.	Per cent	No.	Per cent	No.	Per cent	No.
"Basket Makers"	0	0	1	12.50	3	37.50	2	25.00	2	25.00	8
"Pseudo-Negroids" ...	1	7.69	0	0	11	84.62	0	0	1	7.69	13
"Pseudo-Australoids" .	0	0	3	27.27	7	63.64	0	0	1	9.09	11
"Plains Indians"	3	13.04	0	0	15	65.22	3	13.04	2	8.70	23
"Long-faced Europeans"	0	0	1	5.56	11	61.11	5	27.78	1	5.56	18
"Pseudo-Alpines"	1	7.14	0	0	5	35.71	6	42.86	2	14.29	14
"Hybrids"	0	0	2	7.41	16	59.26	8	29.63	1	3.70	27
"Residuals"	0	0	1	7.14	10	71.43	1	7.14	2	14.29	14
Total	5	3.91	8	6.25	78	60.94	25	19.53	12	9.38	128

Coefficient of contingency 0.40

TABLE VII–19. NASAL SPINE. TOTAL SERIES B

Males	Submedium		Medium		Pronounced		Total
	No.	Per cent	No.	Per cent	No.	Per cent	No.
"Basket Makers"	3	37.50	3	37.50	2	25.00	8
"Pseudo-Negroids"	12	92.31	0	0	1	7.69	13
"Pseudo-Australoids"	5	45.45	5	45.45	1	9.09	11
"Plains Indians"	9	39.13	12	52.17	2	8.70	23
"Long-faced Europeans"	5	27.78	10	55.56	3	16.67	18
"Pseudo-Alpines"	2	14.29	9	64.29	3	21.43	14
"Hybrids".....................	8	29.63	12	44.44	7	25.93	27
"Residuals"	8	61.54	4	30.77	1	7.69	13
Total......................	52	40.94	55	43.31	20	15.75	127

Coefficient of contingency 0.39

Alveolar prognathism, on the contrary, shows well-marked differences in the subgroups. It is by far most pronounced in the "Pseudo-Negroid" type. The "Pseudo-Australoid" type ranks next in the development of this feature. The "European" type is conspicuous for the small development of alveolar prognathism in its crania. The coefficient of mean square contingency is 0.45 (Table VII–20).

TABLE VII–20. ALVEOLAR PROGNATHISM. TOTAL SERIES B

	Submedium		Medium		Pronounced		Very Pronounced		Total
Males	No.	Per cent	No.	Per cent	No.	Per cent	No.	Per cent	No.
"Basket Makers"	2	25.00	3	37.50	3	37.50	0	0	8
"Pseudo-Negroids"	1	7.69	2	15.38	7	53.85	3	23.08	13
"Pseudo-Australoids"	1	14.29	2	28.57	4	57.14	0	0	7
"Plains Indians".................	5	25.00	11	55.00	4	20.00	0	0	20
"Long-faced Europeans".........	10	62.50	5	31.25	1	6.25	0	0	16
"Pseudo-Alpines"	7	26.92	10	38.46	8	30.77	1	3.85	26
"Hybrids"	4	30.77	6	46.15	3	23.08	0	0	13
"Residuals"....................	1	8.33	6	50.00	5	41.67	0	0	12
Total	31	26.96	45	39.13	35	30.43	4	3.48	115

Coefficient of contingency 0.45

COMPARISON OF CONTINGENCIES IN GLAZE AND TYPE SUBGROUPS

In Table VII–21 the coefficients of mean square contingency of morphological feature upon type subgroups have been compared with similar coefficients calculated for the Glaze subgroups on both male and female divisions of Series A. Included in this comparative table is also an array of coefficients of mean square contingency calculated upon groups made by combining the "Pseudo-Negroid," "Pseudo-Australoid," and "Basket Maker" types into one group, combining the "Europeans," "Large Hybrids," and "Pseudo-Alpines" into another group, and contrasting these two groups with the original "Plains" type. The "Residual" type was left out of consideration, as being a hodge-podge of remnants. The object of this regrouping was to determine the possibility of reducing the number of type subgroups without sacrificing their morphological distinctiveness. Table VII–21 shows first of all that such regrouping in every case reduces the coefficient of mean square contingency, usually to the margin of insignificance. Admitting that the large size of the coefficient when calculated upon all eight of our type subgroups is probably due, in some measure, to the small size of the groups and to too fine subdivision of morphological grades, it is nevertheless apparent that the reductions of the coefficients of contingency when calculated upon the three-group basis are probably brought about, for the most part, by the heterogeneity of the combined groups. In other words this regrouping has destroyed our type distinctions.

Again if one compares the contingency of morphological feature upon type subgroups with the contingency of the same feature upon Glaze subgroups it may be observed that in every instance except one, and in both sexes, the Glaze group contingencies are much smaller than the type contingencies. The single exception is the contingency of female Glaze subgroups upon alveolar prognathism, which yields a coefficient of 0.51, which is very high. In most cases the contingencies of morphological features upon Glaze subgroups are so small as to be of little significance. It may be concluded, therefore, that the significant associations of the morphological features here tabulated are with type subgroups rather than with archaeological or chronological subgroups.

TABLE VII–21. COEFFICIENTS OF CONTINGENCY: SERIES A COMPARED
WITH SERIES B

	Glaze Subgroups		Morphological Types (Males)	
	Series A (Males)	Series A (Females)	Series B	Series B (Three groups)
1. Height of Frontal Region	...	...	0.49	0.38
2. Breadth of Frontal Region	...	...	0.44	0.37
3. Slope of Frontal Region	...	...	0.44	0.23
4. Temporal Region	0.31	0.42	0.56	0.41
5. Size of Supraorbital Ridges	0.30	0.18	0.54	0.27
6. Type of Supraorbital Ridges	0.26	0.31	0.34	...
7. Malars	0.24	0.25	0.47	0.29
8. Zygomata	0.40	0.23	0.45	...
9. Inclination of Orbits	...	...	0.22	...
10. Suborbital Fossae	0.22	0.24	0.32	0.22
11. Nasion Depression	0.18	...	0.46	0.34
12. Subnasal Grooves	0.31	0.20	0.36	...
13. Height of Nasal Bridge	...	...	0.49	...
14. Breadth of Nasal Bridge	...	...	0.35	...
15. Slope of Nasal Bridge	...	...	0.47	...
16. Nasal Aperture	0.20	0.14	0.38	...
17. Lower Borders of Nasal Aperture	0.35	0.34	0.40	...
18. Nasal Spine	0.19	0.26	0.39	0.32
19. Alveolar Prognathism	0.23	0.51	0.45	0.31

ASSOCIATION OF MORPHOLOGICAL TYPES WITH GLAZE PERIODS

Table VII–22 records the distribution of morphological types with reference to the various archaeological periods. The "Basket Maker" type has a disproportionately large representation in Black-on-white, Glaze I, II, and III periods; it does not occur at all in the latest periods. The "Pseudo-Negroid" type is proportionately represented in the first archaeological subgroup; in Glazes II, III, and IV its representation is perhaps significantly large; in V and VI it is represented by one cranium only. The "Pseudo-Australoid" type has somewhat more than its proportionate quota in the first three groups and less in the last groups. In general it may be said that the three types just enumerated are strongly represented in the earlier periods of the pueblo's occupation and tend to disappear in the later periods. The "Plains" type shows a disproportionately small representation until Glaze V and VI, when it becomes the dominant skull type of the period. The "European" type is also represented by less than its expected quota up to the last periods, when it becomes very prominent. Of six skulls in the series belonging to the church burials, four belong to this type. One or two of these church crania are almost certainly those of Mexicans or of Indian-Mexican mixtures. The so-called "Pseudo-Alpine" type is found in every chronological group. At no time does it exceed its just representation except, possibly, in the earliest chronological group, and in the latest groups. The "Large Hybrids" are rather strongly represented in the first group and thereafter maintain their expected frequency up to the end. The "Residual" type predominates in the middle groups, Glazes II, III, and IV, and is feebly represented in the earliest and latest periods.

TABLE VII–22. MORPHOLOGICAL TYPES ASSOCIATED WITH GLAZES

	B.-on-W. and Gl. I		Glazes II and III		Glaze IV		Glazes V and VI		Church		Total	
	No.	Per cent	No.	Per cent	No.	Per cent	No.	Per cent	No.	Per cent	No.	Per cent
"Basket Makers"	2	28.57	4	57.14	1	14.29	0	0	0	0	7	6.03
"Pseudo-Negroids"	2	18.18	4	36.36	3	27.27	2	18.18	0	0	11	9.48
"Pseudo-Australoids"	2	22.22	2	22.22	4	44.44	1	11.11	0	0	9	7.76
"Plains Indians"	2	10.53	6	31.58	3	15.79	7	36.84	1	5.26	19	16.38
"Long-faced Europeans"	1	5.56	5	27.78	3	16.67	5	27.78	4	22.22	18	15.43
"Pseudo-Alpines"	3	21.43	4	28.57	2	14.29	4	28.57	1	7.14	14	12.07
"Large Hybrids"	6	24.00	8	32.00	5	20.00	6	24.00	0	0	25	21.55
"Residuals"	1	7.69	6	46.15	4	30.77	2	15.38	0	0	13	11.20
Total	19	16.38	39	33.62	25	21.55	27	23.28	6	5.17	116	

Coefficient of contingency 0.55

Summarizing this table it may be said that the types designated as "Large Hybrids" and "Pseudo-Alpines" are practically constant throughout the whole period of occupation. Together they constitute 33.6 per cent of our skeletal sample. In the first group they make up 47.4 per cent of the total; thereafter they are somewhat less prominent. The "Basket Maker" type is the first dominant type and the earliest to decline and disappear. This type, together with the "Pseudo-Negroids" and "Pseudo-Australoids," seems to form the archaic stratum of the population. The three types include 23.4 per cent of the whole skeletal population. In the earliest period they form 31.6 per cent of the population; in the second group 25.6; in the third group 32 per cent; in the fourth group only 11.1 per cent. The "European" and "Plains" types increase in importance. Together they form 31.8 per cent of the total population. In the first group they are only 15.8 per cent; in the second group 28.2; in the third group 24 per cent; in the fourth group 44.4 per cent; almost all of the post-Christian burials are skulls of these types. The "Residual" type is amorphous; its disproportionate representation in the middle periods may mean nothing; it may indicate that the periods of maximum population and of minimum selection produced the largest number of cranially undistinguished individuals.

It may well seem to the reader that I have been pushing too far differences in the distribution of very minute type groups and have been drawing from chance variations altogether unjustifiable conclusions. Let me admit at once that our small type subgroups, when subdivided according to Glaze periods, offer no adequate samples such as would warrant a fair degree of confidence that chance does not operate largely in their distribution. If each of our type subgroups were composed of as few as fifty crania, we might be sure of the significance of their distributions in the various periods. I have not been unconscious of the inadequacy of our samples in the application of this method of analysis. I have been actuated partly by the desire to demonstrate the application of the method, though upon regrettably insufficient numbers, and partly by the opinion that cumulative differences, if all in the same direction, are significant even when the magnitude of such differences is not great enough to supervene chance occurrence. Further, I believe that striking differences in small samples may often indicate equally great distinctions between adequate samples, theories of probability to the contrary notwithstanding. We have one Rhodesian skull and one calva of Pithecanthropus erectus. It is my opinion that the differences between these two early human or humanoid types would not be diminished if we possessed a dozen or twenty examples of each type.

In spite of this apologia, which will not, in all probability, commend itself to the mathematically minded, I am not desirous of putting forth as conclusive the period differences of morphological types discussed above. They may be regarded as suggestive rather than definitive, of possible but not of certain significance. The skeptic may, if he wishes, reject them entirely.

COMPOSITES OF MORPHOLOGICAL TYPES

The visual criterion of morphological type groups was likeness. Skulls which looked alike were assigned to the same type. The metrical and morphological validity of these types was established by the use of statistical methods. A final test of the reality of these type subgroups should lie in the extent to which each of them may manifest composite unity and in the differences between the composites of the several types. To this end it was determined to make composite photographs of the several types.

The method adopted was as follows. On the ground-glass focussing screen of a $6\frac{1}{2} \times 8\frac{1}{2}$ camera a vertical line was ruled dividing the field into halves. A horizontal line was ruled intersecting the vertical about two-thirds of the way from the bottom of the field. Each skull was set up in the eye-ear plane at a constant distance from the lens. The *norma frontalis* of each skull was adjusted so that the horizontal line on the ground glass coincided with the nasion point and the intersecting vertical coincided with a line drawn from nasion to gnathion (menton). Ten skulls of each type were exposed on a single plate (except in the case of the "Basket Maker" type for which only six crania were available). All of the exposures on a given plate were of equal duration. In this way composite negatives were made of seven different type groups. The "Residual" group was not included because of the fragmentary condition of most of the skulls belonging to this type. Finally a composite was made by taking at random one skull from each of the type subgroups and exposing it upon the same plate with representatives of the remaining types. After the negatives had been developed a number of experiments in composite printing were tried. A composite of composites was made by using all of the type negatives in the production of a single print. Combinations of several types were produced in the same way. In the case of the "Basket Maker," "Pseudo-Negroid," and "Pseudo-Australoid" types, composites of the *norma lateralis* were also taken, but this process was not applied to the other types because of the enormous variations in the occipital profile caused by different degrees of artificial deformation in the various crania and because of similar variations in the facial profile brought about by varying degrees of alveolar prognathism.

Photographs of the several types are juxtaposed on Plates VII–1, 2, in order that the reader may appreciate the type differences. Larger plates of the several types are to be found in the pocket at the back of the volume and should be spread out for reference. It will be seen that each type presents definite features and outlines and is not blurred and vague as are the composites of the composites (Plates VII, A–O [pocket]). Each one of the type composites is distinctly different from every other and the composite made from a skull of each type differs from all of the others.

The *norma facialis* of the "Basket Maker" type presents a frontal region of medium breadth and of rather submedium height; the orbits are high relative to their breadth and of medium inclination; the brow-ridges do not seem strongly marked; the nasal bridge seems rather low and concavo-convex; the nasal aperture is of medium breadth and distinctly piriform; the spine and lower borders are well developed. Malars are not particularly prominent; the mandible is quite shallow.

The "Pseudo-Negroid" type shows a moderately scaphoid tendency; the malars are more prominent and the mandible is deeper. The nasal bridge is very low and broad, concave in form; the nasal aperture is almost round; the lower borders poorly defined and the spine ill developed. The orbits are somewhat broader relative to their height than in the "Basket-Maker" composite.

The "Pseudo-Australoid" type at once commands attention by the extreme narrowness of its frontal region and its pronounced scaphocephaly. The glabella is very prominent and the nasion sharply depressed. The malars jut outward; the orbits are very low. The nasal bridge appears to be submedium in height and of moderate breadth; the nasal profile appears slightly concave. The nasal aperture is broad and low, but piriform rather than round. There are no clear borders of the nasal aperture and the spine is but little better developed than in the "Pseudo-Negroid" type. Suborbital fossae are strongly marked. The premaxillary region is short and the mandible shallow. The face is quite short. In the *norma lateralis* the low, sloping forehead, great brow-ridges, and concave nasal bridge may be contrasted with the rounded forehead, flat glabella, and lower nasal bridge of the "Pseudo-Negroid" type.

The "Plains" type shows higher and more strongly inclined orbits than those previously considered; the malars are more strongly protuberant. The nasal bridge is longer and higher, the aperture broad, but high; spine and lower borders are of fair development. The lower jaw is a little deeper than in any preceding type. Suborbital fossae are strongly marked.

The "Long-faced European" type is notable by reason of its elongated face, deep lower jaw, and prominent mental process. The frontal region is broad and of rather submedium height. The glabella region is strongly prominent and the nasion depression seems well marked. Orbits are broad and high and of moderate inclination. The nasal bridge is higher and longer, the aperture longer and narrower than in any preceding type. Lower borders and spine are poorly developed. Malars show a moderate projection.

The "Pseudo-Alpine" type shows a much broader and more rounded frontal region, with swelling temples. The face is very broad and short. The glabella eminence is slight and the orbits are high and very sharply inclined downward and outward. The nasal bridge seems narrow; the aperture is low, broad, and almost triangular. Lower borders and spine are poorly developed. Malars jut strongly forward and outward, and the suborbital fossae are very deep. The mandible is shallow, with a poorly developed mental eminence.

The "Large Hybrid" type has a high, broad forehead. The face seems as long as, but much broader than that of the "European type." The orbits are not as large as in the European type and are not strongly inclined. The malars are protuberant. The nasal bridge seems to be of medium height and breadth; the aperture is long, of medium breadth, and distinctly oval in shape. The spine and lower borders show a medium development. The suborbital fossae are rather shallow. The jaw is deeper than in any type but the "European." The mental prominence shows fair development.

Each one of the above types, is, as the reader may judge for himself, quite distinct and individual. By far the most primitive looking types are the "Pseudo-Negroid" and the "Pseudo-Australoid," each of which recalls strongly the racial types from which they are named. The "Basket Maker" composite resembles a somewhat negroid Mediterranean type. It is rather reminiscent of the Predynastic Egyptian. Frontal regions are comparatively narrow in all of these types. The "European," "Pseudo-Alpine," and "Large Hybrid" types have capacious frontal regions and swelling temporals, larger orbits and bigger faces. The last two give a somewhat Mongoloid impression by reason of their strongly projecting malars. The "Plains" type looks like a compromise between the three primitive types and the three advanced types.

The composite printed from the "Basket Maker," "Pseudo-Negroid," and "Pseudo-Australoid" composite negatives superimposed upon one print is strongly "Basket Maker" in appearance, with a touch, however, of the scaphocephaly of the "Pseudo-Australoid" type. The orbits, nose, and eyes are predominantly "Basket Maker," except that the nasal aperture is higher and broader at the top, and more rounded than in the veritable "Basket Maker" type. The jaws are also deeper and the orbits larger.

A composite made from the "Pseudo-Alpine," "Long-faced European," and "Large Hybrid" types shows facial characteristics strongly reminiscent of the

"Long-faced European type," but the frontal region shows several divergent outlines indicating a lack of homogeneity of these types. Similarly a composite printed from the "Plains," "Long-faced European," and "Pseudo-Alpine" types has blurred and irregular frontal and mandibular outlines.

"Basket Maker," "Pseudo-Negroid," and "Pseudo-Australoid" types superimpose more satisfactorily than do any of the more advanced types. Yet there is no doubt that the more highly evolved types have a good deal in common with each other.

We have for comparison with each other two general composite photographs, one made by taking a skull of each type, and the other by printing all of the composite negatives together. I shall call the first the single composite and the second the composite of composites. Curiously enough these two are markedly different from each other. The composite of composites is, as might be expected, very foggy, when compared with the single composite. The latter is made from ten crania, one of each type, the former from all seventy crania. The single composite looks more like our "Negroid" type than any other, but it has a narrower and higher frontal region, a much longer face, and a heavier and deeper mandible. The nasal bridge is low and broad, as in the "Negroid" type, but the aperture is higher, less rounded and has a well-developed spine and somewhat better defined lower borders. The suborbital fossae are much shallower than in any of the single types.

The composite of composites represents much more closely my general impression of the Pecos series. The forehead is of good breadth and of medium height, the orbits high and more strongly inclined, the malars more jutting, and suborbital fossae well developed. The nasal bridge is of medium breadth and height, the aperture high and broadly piriform; the spine is not in evidence and the lower borders are of submedium definition. The glabella eminence and nasion depression are more strongly marked than in the single composite and the negroid appearance is lacking. The composite of composites looks like a compromise between the "Plains," "European," "Pseudo-Alpine," and "Large Hybrid" types. The three "archaic" types do not appear to express themselves in this composite of composites. I confess myself puzzled by the difference between the single composite and the composite of composites. The former seems to bring out all the primitiveness of the "Pseudo-Negroid" and "Pseudo-Australoid" types; in the latter all of this is lost. I cannot but regard the composite of composites as more representative of the series as a whole. I am inclined to explain the negroid appearance of the single composite as a chance effect due to the choice of individual skulls from the type groups selected to make this composite. The only basis of selection was that the skulls be complete, with no parts broken away, and thoroughly characteristic of the types which they purported to represent.

On the whole I feel that the method of photographic composites offers a great deal of value in the analysis of a cranial population. It is, however, such a laborious and difficult method that it will probably never gain great favor among craniologists.

In the present instance, it has, I think, furnished the ultimate proof of the validity of our morphological types.

PLATE VII–1

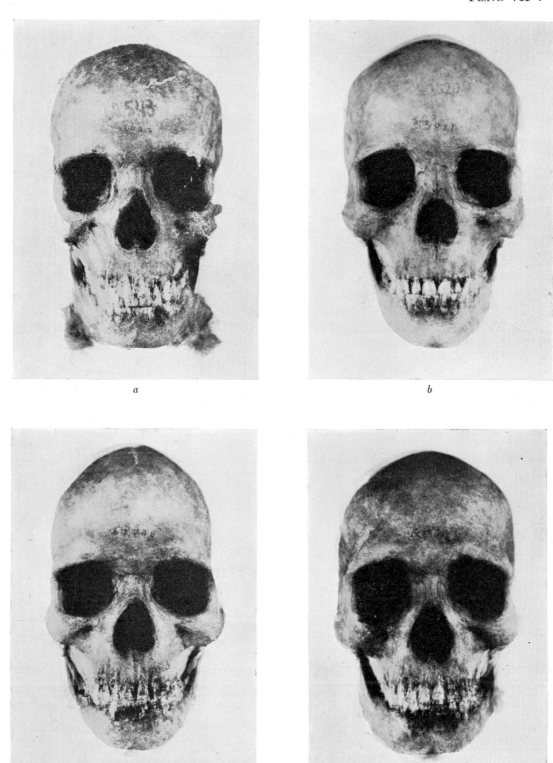

a *b*

c *d*

COMPOSITE PHOTOGRAPHS OF PECOS MORPHOLOGICAL TYPES

(*a*) "Basket Maker." (*b*) "Pseudo-Negroid." (*c*) "Pseudo-Australoid." (*d*) "Plains Indian"

PLATE VII–2

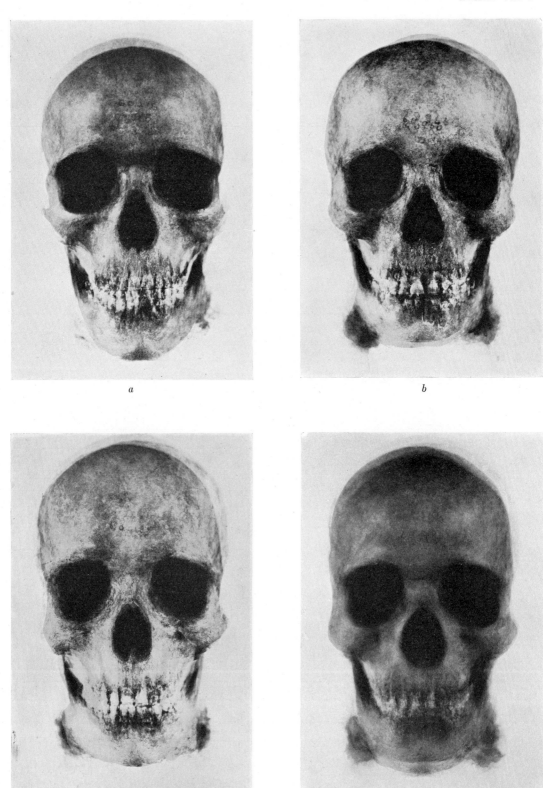

a

b

c

d

COMPOSITE PHOTOGRAPHS OF PECOS MORPHOLOGICAL TYPES

(a) "Long-faced European." (b) "Pseudo-Alpine." (c) "Large Hybrid." (d) Composite of Composites

CHAPTER VIII

AFFINITIES OF THE MORPHOLOGICAL CRANIAL TYPES

IN THE present chapter it is proposed to give a general description of each of our morphological types and to follow this description with an attempt to trace the affinities of the said types outside of the Southwestern Region and, if necessary, outside of the New World. This latter task is not only difficult but practically impossible, because craniologists have usually contented themselves with the description of entire series by means and other constants and have almost never attempted to establish and statistically to justify morphological types. All that can be done is to compare means of our morphological types with means of entire populations which have not been so distinguished.

"BASKET MAKER" TYPE

DESCRIPTION

The "Basket Maker" type consists of skulls which are rather small (length about 177 mm., breadth 135 mm., height 136 mm.). These skulls exhibit no occipital flattening or only slight flattening. The length-breadth index is very low mesocephalic, verging upon dolichocephaly, even when some slight deformation is included. Undeformed skulls are frankly dolichocephalic. The skulls are hypsicephalic and acrocephalic. The cranial capacity is usually small (mean 1306 cc.). The face is the narrowest of all the Pecos types but is fairly long; it is leptoprosopic. The orbits are rather high and narrow, and the mean orbital index is hypsiconch. The nasal index is mesorrhine. There is sufficient facial projection so that the mean gnathic index is just below the lower limit of mesognathism. The palate is of medium length and rather broad; the mean of the maxillo-alveolar index (122) is strongly brachyuranic. The bigonial diameters of the mandibles are small; the mandibles are not robust (Table VIII–1).

The "Basket Maker" type of cranium is not massive nor are the muscular markings pronounced. The height of the frontal region is prevailingly submedium; the breadth is also rather narrow and the slope usually medium, but not infrequently pronounced. The temporal regions are very flat or compressed. Occipital regions are usually convex or protuberant when not artificially flattened. Brow-ridges are of medium size or small, usually of the divided variety. Characteristically there is no nasion depression; the nasal bridge is of medium breadth and low; its profile is concavo-convex. The nasal aperture is of medium breadth and piriform in shape; the lower borders are distinct and usually without subnasal grooves. The orbits are oblong or square and varying in inclination; malars and zygomata are of medium size and projection, suborbital fossae medium or pronounced. Alveolar prognathism is medium or pronounced, less often slight. The mandible is not large and the mental eminence is rather poorly developed. Plates VII–A, B, give an accurate composite picture of the type.

This type has an average stature of 160.5 cm. and seems to have been most numerous in the earlier periods of Pecos history.

TABLE VIII–1. Means of "Basket Maker" Type

Males

Measurements				Measurements			
Glabello-occipital length *..	177.67		...	External palatal breadth ..	67.33	±	0.69
Maximum breadth *	132.83		...	Bigonial diameter	95.40	±	1.47
Basion-bregma height *....	135.00		...	Bicondylar width	116.80	±	1.78
Maximum circumference ..	500.00	±	3.31	Height of symphysis	36.00	±	0.67
Nasion-opisthion arc	360.71	±	2.77	Min. breadth of asc. ramus	36.33	±	0.89
Transverse arc	308.75	±	2.21	Height of ascending ramus	65.50	±	1.02
Thickness of left parietal ..	5.17	±	0.18	Condylo-symphysial length	103.75		...
Mean diam. of for. mag....	32.00	±	0.83	Cranial capacity	1306.67	±	31.50
Minimum frontal diameter.	93.00	±	1.03	Cranial module	149.40		...
Max. bizygomatic diam....	132.71	±	1.22				
Nasion-menton height	121.17	±	1.27	Indices			
Nasion-prosthion height ...	73.25	±	0.58	Length-breadth *	75.00		...
Orbit height, right	35.43	±	0.28	Length-height *	76.20		...
Orbit height, left	35.25	±	0.23	Breadth-height *	100.80		...
Orbit breadth, right	39.57	±	0.39	Total facial	90.20	±	1.45
Orbit breadth, left........	38.81	±	0.41	Upper facial............	55.00	±	0.44
Nasal height	51.38	±	0.36	Mean orbital	90.43	±	1.03
Nasal breadth	26.12	±	0.37	Nasal	50.75	±	0.72
Basion-nasion length	100.86	±	0.40	Gnathic	97.14	±	0.88
Basion-prosthion length ...	98.29	±	1.02	External palatal	122.00	±	1.03
External palatal length	55.17	±	0.70				

* Undeformed crania only.

COMPARISON WITH OTHER GROUPS

The Pecos "Basket Maker" type may first be compared with the authentic Basket Makers and Post-Basket Makers of Arizona.[1] In Table VIII–2 the means of the Pecos "Basket Maker" types are set against those of the Arizona crania. Inasmuch as deformation in this Pecos type is slight, deformed crania have been included, although the veritable Basket Makers of Arizona are quite undeformed. It will be observed that the mean skull length of the Arizona crania exceeds that of our Pecos type by 2.99 mm. This is, however, less than twice the probable error of the difference. Looking over the arrays of means we find that the first significant difference between the two series lies in basion-bregma height, which in our Pecos "Basket Maker" type exceeds that of the Arizona group by 5.65 mm., which is more than three times the probable error of the difference. Again the minimum frontal diameter of the Pecos group is 3.71 mm. greater than that of the Arizona Basket

[1] Series measured by the author for comparative purposes.

Makers, and the total facial height of our Pecos group exceeds that of the more primitive group by almost 5 mm. The cranio-facial base (basion-nasion length) is also greater in the Pecos group and the orbits are higher. The palate is significantly broader in our Pecos type; the mean thickness of the left parietal is greater; the transverse arc is much greater, as is also the height of the ascending ramus of the mandible. The average difference between the two series in 29 measurements is 2.28 mm.

In the indices the Pecos type shows a significant excess in the length-height index, amounting indeed to 4.24 index units. The breadth-height index is also higher in the Pecos type, but not significantly so. The total facial index and the mean orbital index are both higher in our Pecos type. Three of nine indices and nine of 29 measurements exhibit differences between the groups in excess of twice the probable errors of such differences. Since not more than 18 per cent of differences in excess of twice the probable error are to be expected when two groups are drawn at random from the same population, it must be concluded that the number and magnitude of differences between Pecos "Basket Makers" and authentic Arizona Basket Makers are sufficient to render the groups statistically distinct. The Pecos "Basket Maker" type is much more hypsicephalic, has a broader frontal region, longer and more leptoprosopic face, more hypsiconch orbits, and an absolutely broader palate. The mean difference between nine indices of the two series is 2.26 index units. While, in general, there is a marked resemblance between the two groups it cannot be said that the Pecos "Basket Makers" are true Basket Makers.

We may now compare the Pecos "Basket Maker" type with the crania from the caves of Coahuila, Mexico.[1] The culture of these Coahuila people bears marked affinities to that of the authentic Arizona Basket Makers. (Table VIII–3 records the comparative means.) In the first place it is observed that the Coahuila series exhibits a glabello-occipital length 5.65 mm. in excess of the mean of our Pecos type. The orbits in our type are narrower than in the cave series; the palatal length is greater and the transverse cranial arc is considerably larger in our pueblo type. The cranial capacity of the Coahuila group is 87 cc. larger than that of the Pecos "Basket Makers." In an array of 27 measurements the mean difference between the two groups is 1.92 mm. The Pecos group is significantly less long-headed than the Coahuila series and much more hypsicephalic and acrocephalic. The orbits of Pecos "Basket Makers" are more hypsiconch and narrower. The mean difference between the two series in nine indices is, however, only 1.96 units. It is evident that our Pecos type is significantly different also from the Coahuila group and particularly in its excessive basion-bregma height, diminished skull length, smaller capacity, and more hypsiconch orbits. Here again it appears that some factor making for diminished skull length and increased skull height operates in the Pecos group. A slight occipital deformation would tend to bring about changes in this direction, and such slight deformation does occur in several crania of our Pecos type, but it is not sufficient to account for the differences manifested.

[1] Series measured by the author for comparative purposes.

TABLE VIII–2. DIFFERENCES OF MEANS OF PECOS "BASKET MAKERS" AND ARIZONA BASKET MAKERS

Males

Measurements	Pecos	Arizona	Difference	2 p. e.
Glabello-occipital length *	176.88 ± 1.30	179.87 ± 1.00	−2.99 ± 1.64	3.28
Maximum breadth *	134.75 ± 1.32	134.53 ± 0.86	−0.22 ± 1.57	3.14
Basion-bregma height *	135.57 ± 1.50	129.92 ± 0.77	5.65 ± 1.69	3.38
Maximum circumference	500.00 ± 3.31	500.00 ± 2.02	0.00 ± 3.88	7.76
Nasion-opisthion arc	360.71 ± 2.77	361.83 ± 2.09	−1.12 ± 3.47	6.94
Transverse arc	308.75 ± 2.21	290.67 ± 1.73	18.08 ± 2.80	5.60
Thickness of left parietal	5.17 ± 0.18	4.45 ± 0.29	0.72 ± 0.34	0.68
Mean diameter of foramen magnum	32.00 ± 0.83	31.46 ± 0.25	0.54 ± 0.86	1.72
Minimum frontal diameter	93.00 ± 1.03	89.29 ± 0.72	3.71 ± 1.26	2.52
Bizygomatic diameter	132.71 ± 1.22	132.38 ± 0.80	0.33 ± 1.46	2.92
Nasion-menton height	121.17 ± 1.27	116.25 ± 1.56	4.92 ± 2.09	4.18
Nasion-prosthion height	73.25 ± 0.58	73.08 ± 0.91	0.17 ± 1.08	2.16
Orbit height, right	35.43 ± 0.28	34.23 ± 0.37	1.20 ± 0.46	0.92
Orbit height, left	35.25 ± 0.23	34.32 ± 0.41	0.93 ± 0.48	0.96
Orbit breadth, right	39.57 ± 0.39	39.00 ± 0.20	0.57 ± 0.44	0.88
Orbit breadth, left	38.81 ± 0.41	39.14 ± 0.19	−0.33 ± 0.45	0.90
Nasal height	51.38 ± 0.36	50.80 ± 0.69	0.58 ± 0.78	1.56
Nasal breadth	26.12 ± 0.37	25.40 ± 0.44	0.72 ± 0.58	1.16
Basion-nasion length	100.86 ± 0.40	99.00 ± 0.48	1.86 ± 0.62	1.24
Basion-prosthion length	98.29 ± 1.02	97.15 ± 0.92	1.14 ± 1.37	2.74
External palatal length	55.17 ± 0.70	54.69 ± 0.64	0.48 ± 0.94	1.88
External palatal breadth	67.33 ± 0.69	64.67 ± 1.01	2.66 ± 1.22	2.44
Bigonial diameter	95.40 ± 1.47	92.70 ± 0.86	2.70 ± 1.70	3.40
Bicondylar width	116.80 ± 1.78	116.45 ± 0.61	0.35 ± 1.88	3.76
Height of symphysis	36.00 ± 0.67	34.58 ± 0.50	1.42 ± 0.84	1.68
Minimum breadth of ascending ramus	36.33 ± 0.89	34.73 ± 0.38	1.60 ± 0.97	1.94
Height of ascending ramus	65.50 ± 1.02	57.42 ± 0.96	8.08 ± 1.40	2.80
Condylo-symphysial length	103.75 ...	104.44 ± 1.14	−0.69 ...	...
Mean difference			2.28	

Indices

	Pecos	Arizona	Difference	2 p. e.
Length-breadth *	76.38 ± 0.86	74.87 ± 0.64	1.51 ± 1.07	2.14
Length-height *	76.86 ± 1.10	72.62 ± 0.51	4.24 ± 1.21	2.42
Breadth-height *	100.00 ± 1.56	97.08 ± 0.49	2.92 ± 1.62	3.24
Total facial	90.20 ± 1.45	86.85 ± 0.73	3.35 ± 1.62	3.24
Upper facial	55.00 ± 0.44	54.83 ± 0.47	0.17 ± 0.64	1.28
Mean orbital	90.43 ± 1.03	87.50 ± 0.89	2.93 ± 1.36	2.72
Nasal	50.75 ± 0.72	50.13 ± 0.81	0.62 ± 1.08	2.16
Gnathic	97.14 ± 0.88	98.23 ± 1.07	−1.09 ± 1.38	2.76
External palatal	122.00 ± 1.03	118.50 ± 1.85	3.50 ± 2.11	4.22
Mean difference			2.26	

* Deformed and undeformed crania.

TABLE VIII–3. DIFFERENCES OF MEANS OF PECOS "BASKET MAKERS" AND
COAHUILA CAVE CRANIA

Males

Measurements	Pecos	Coahuila	Difference	2 p. e.
Glabello-occipital length *	176.88 ± 1.30	182.53 ± 0.62	−5.65 ± 1.44	2.88
Maximum breadth *	134.75 ± 1.32	135.12 ± 0.60	−0.37 ± 1.45	2.90
Basion-bregma height *	135.57 ± 1.50	133.82 ± 0.92	1.75 ± 1.76	3.52
Maximum circumference	500.00 ± 3.31	504.76 ± 1.73	−4.76 ± 3.73	7.46
Nasion-opisthion arc	360.71 ± 2.77	366.93 ± 1.53	−6.22 ± 3.16	6.32
Transverse arc	308.75 ± 2.21	302.94 ± 1.37	5.81 ± 2.60	5.20
Thickness of left parietal	5.17 ± 0.18	5.00 . . .	0.17 . . .	. . .
Mean diameter of foramen magnum . .	32.00 ± 0.83	33.77 ± 0.43	−1.77 ± 0.93	1.86
Minimum frontal diameter	93.00 ± 1.03	91.24 ± 0.80	1.76 ± 1.30	2.60
Bizygomatic diameter.	132.71 ± 1.22	134.23 ± 1.14	−1.52 ± 1.67	3.34
Nasion-menton height	121.17 ± 1.27	120.67 . . .	0.50 . . .	. . .
Nasion-prosthion height	73.25 ± 0.58	73.57 ± 0.65	−0.32 ± 0.87	1.74
Orbit height, right.	35.43 ± 0.28	35.36 ± 0.23	0.07 ± 0.36	0.72
Orbit height, left	35.25 ± 0.23	35.18 ± 0.27	0.07 ± 0.37	0.74
Orbit breadth, right	39.57 ± 0.39	40.86 ± 0.28	−1.29 ± 0.48	0.96
Orbit breadth, left.	38.81 ± 0.41	40.96 ± 0.35	−2.15 ± 0.54	1.08
Nasal height	51.38 ± 0.36	53.50 ± 0.57	−2.12 ± 0.67	1.34
Nasal breadth	26.12 ± 0.37	26.79 ± 0.36	−0.67 ± 0.54	1.08
Basion-nasion length.	100.86 ± 0.40	101.29 ± 0.38	−0.43 ± 0.56	1.12
Basion-prosthion length	98.29 ± 1.02	98.29 ± 0.74	0.00 ± 1.26	2.52
Palatal length	55.17 ± 0.70	54.36 ± 0.43	0.81 ± 0.82	1.64
Palatal breadth	67.33 ± 0.69	65.29 ± 0.48	2.04 ± 0.84	1.68
Bigonial diameter	95.40 ± 1.47	101.33 . . .	−5.93	. . .
Bicondylar width.	116.80 ± 1.78	116.00 . . .	0.80 . . .	. . .
Height of symphysis	36.00 ± 0.67	35.00 . . .	1.00 . . .	. . .
Minimum breadth of ascending ramus	36.33 ± 0.89	32.83 . . .	3.50 . . .	. . .
Condylo-symphysial length	103.75	104.17 . . .	−0.42 . . .	. . .
Mean difference			1.92	
Cranial capacity	1306.67 ± 31.50	1393.57 ± 21.32	−86.90 ± 38.03	76.06

Indices

	Pecos	Coahuila	Difference	2 p. e.
Length-breadth *	76.38 ± 0.86	74.35 ± 0.35	2.03 ± 0.93	1.86
Length-height *	76.86 ± 1.10	73.24 ± 0.48	3.62 ± 1.20	2.40
Breadth-height *	100.00 ± 1.56	96.94 ± 0.71	3.06 ± 1.71	3.42
Total facial	90.20 ± 1.45	91.67 ± 1.05	−1.47 ± 1.79	3.58
Upper facial	55.00 ± 0.44	55.54 ± 0.52	−0.54 ± 0.61	1.22
Mean orbital	90.43 ± 1.03	86.07 ± 0.57	4.36 ± 1.18	2.36
Nasal	50.75 ± 0.72	50.07 ± 0.77	0.68 ± 1.05	2.10
Gnathic	97.14 ± 0.88	97.00 ± 0.89	0.14 ± 1.25	2.50
External palatal.	122.00 ± 1.03	120.29 ± 1.02	1.71 ± 1.45	2.90
Mean difference			1.96	

* Deformed and undeformed crania.

For purposes of comparison with the Pecos "Basket Maker" type, I have measured a series of crania from the Santa Catalina Islands, off the coast of southern California. This series of crania may be divided into two groups; those from Santa Cruz and those from San Clemente, Santa Catalina, and the other islands of the group. The Santa Cruz crania more closely resemble the Pecos type than do the skulls from the other islands, since the Santa Cruz population seems to have been modified by the introduction of a brachycephalic element, which is not obvious in the other subseries. For our present purpose the comparison may be limited to the crania of the Santa Cruz group. The Pecos "Basket Makers" have skulls somewhat shorter (1.84 mm.) and very much narrower (3.82 mm.) than those of the Santa Cruz islanders. The basion-bregma height of the Pecos "Basket Maker" type exceeds that of the Santa Cruz group by almost 8 mm. in the mean. The faces (nasion-prosthion diameter) of the Pecos "Basket Makers" are more than 3 mm. longer than those of the Santa Cruz group, but the latter have somewhat greater bizygomatic diameters in the mean. The cranio-facial base (basion-nasion) length averages 3.7 mm. greater in the Pecos type. The transverse arc of the Pecos, in conformity with the greater vault height, largely exceeds that of the average Santa Cruz skull. In the comparison of indices eight means are available for the contrasted groups. The Pecos group is strongly divergent from the Santa Cruz group in every one of these indices. Our so-called Pecos "Basket Makers" are longer-headed relatively; they are hypsicephalic, whereas the Santa Cruz group is orthocephalic, acrocephalic as contrasted with tapeinocephalic, leptene as against mesene, orthognathous as against mesognathous, mesorrhine where the Santa Cruz crania are leptorrhine. Finally the Pecos group is much more brachyuranic than the island population. The crania of the other islands of the Santa Catalina group are even more divergent from our Pecos series than the Santa Cruz subgroup. The mean difference between the averages of fourteen measurements of the Pecos "Basket Makers" and the Santa Cruz group is 3.92 mm., and the mean difference in eight cranial indices is 3.79 index units. Thus the Pecos "Basket Makers" differ much more markedly from the Santa Cruz group than from the Coahuila cave skulls (Table VIII–4).

If we compare the indices of the authentic Arizona Basket Maker series, it may be observed that they differ from the corresponding Santa Cruz means by much less than do the means of our Pecos "Basket Maker" type (Table VIII–5). The mean difference between the Arizona series and the Santa Cruz series with respect to averages of eight cranial indices is 2.06 index units as against 3.79 units in the case of the Pecos "Basket Makers." Figure VIII–1 shows graphically the differences between these three groups with respect to the eight indices. Clearly the Pecos "Basket Maker" type is much nearer to the Arizona Basket Maker type than to the Santa Cruz series. On the whole it may be judged also that the Arizona Basket Makers and the Pecos type under discussion resemble each other a little more closely than do the former and the Santa Cruz series.

If we compare the authentic Arizona Basket Maker group with the Coahuila cave group (Table VIII–7) it is found that the former group shows cranial dimen-

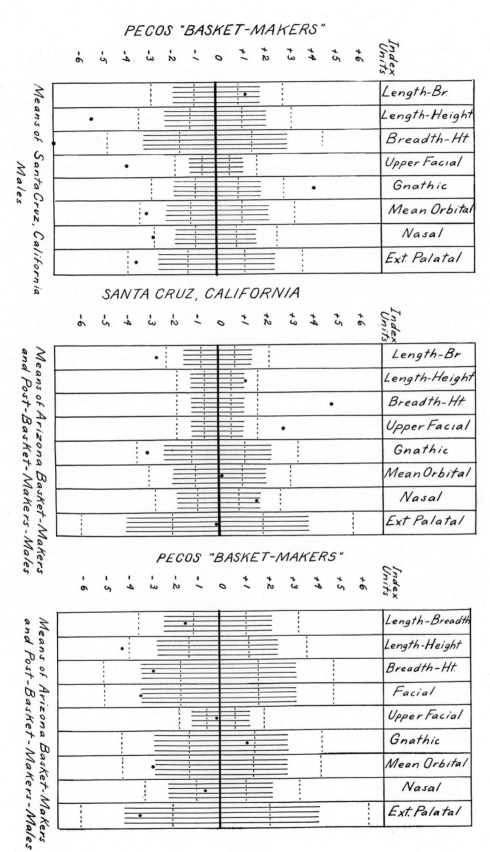

FIG. VIII–1

[237]

sions which are almost invariably smaller than the latter. The mean difference in averages of 28 measurements is 2.47 mm., whereas the similar difference between Pecos "Basket Makers" and Coahuila skulls is 1.92 mm. However, when nine cranial indices of the Arizona Basket Makers are compared with the same indices in the Coahuila group the mean difference is only 1.26 index units and but one of the indices exhibits a difference between the two groups equal to twice the probable error of such difference. In most of the cases the differences are less than their own probable errors. It is therefore reasonable to conclude that the authentic type of Arizona Basket Maker and Post-Basket Maker is substantially identical with the type found in the Coahuila caves, except that in gross size the Arizona people were smaller. The Pecos "Basket Maker" series differs in gross dimensions from the Coahuila group less than from the Arizona group; and it approaches the Coahuila type a little more closely in indicial means. Therefore it may be concluded that the Pecos "Basket Maker" type has its closest affinities with the primitive dolichocephalic group, represented perhaps best by the Coahuila cave skulls, and found in a somewhat stunted form, but otherwise almost identical, in the caves of Arizona associated with the Basket Maker and Post-Basket Maker cultures. Our Pecos "Basket Maker" type, however, seems to have been modified from the prototype to some extent by the admixture of a longer-faced and higher-headed strain which was probably brachycephalic. In our "Basket Maker" Pecos Indians the slight amount of occipital deformation which is present and not eliminated by correction probably serves to exaggerate the differences between the type and authentic Basket Makers.

The same fundamental stock, dolichocephalic and non-Mongoloid, is present in the Santa Catalina Islands, but there it has been modified locally in such a way as to make it diverge from the Coahuila "Basket Maker" type in an opposite direction, and more widely than the Pecos "Basket Makers" differ from the cave crania (Table VIII–7).

If we desire to find cranial types comparable with the Basket Maker–Coahuila group outside of the New World, it is necessary to search among dolichocephalic peoples of small stature, small cranial capacity, but with leptoprosopic faces and mesorrhine noses — peoples also who are essentially orthognathous. Such cranial characters appear among the ancient and modern Egyptians, whose crania have been subjected to a good deal of study. Dr. Cicely Fawcett's study of the crania from Naquada offers a good series for comparative purposes since the necessary statistical constants have been calculated and since that study includes the tabulation of a good deal of comparative material.[1]

[1] Fawcett and Lee, 1901, p. 426.

TABLE VIII–4. DIFFERENCES OF MEANS OF PECOS "BASKET MAKERS" AND
SANTA CRUZ

Males

Measurements	Pecos	Santa Cruz	Difference	2 p. e.
Glabello-occipital length	176.88 ± 1.30*	178.72 ± 0.45	−1.84 ± 1.37	2.74
Maximum breadth	134.75 ± 1.32*	138.57 ± 0.48	−3.82 ± 1.40	2.80
Basion-bregma height	135.57 ± 1.50*	127.69 ± 0.46	7.88 ± 1.57	3.14
Maximum circumference	500.00 ± 3.31	505.04 ± 1.08	−5.04 ± 3.48	6.96
Nasion-opisthion arc	360.71 ± 2.77	356.00 ± 0.94	4.71 ± 2.92	5.84
Transverse arc	308.75 ± 2.21	294.98 ± 0.95	13.77 ± 2.40	4.80
Thickness of left parietal	5.17 ± 0.18	5.43 ± 0.08	−0.26 ± 0.19	0.38
Minimum frontal diameter	93.00 ± 1.03	91.78 ± 0.42	1.22 ± 1.11	2.22
Bizygomatic diameter..............	132.71 ± 1.22	134.43 ± 0.56	−1.72 ± 1.34	2.68
Nasion-menton height	121.17 ± 1.27	111.33 ...	9.84 ...	...
Nasion-prosthion height...........	73.25 ± 0.58	70.22 ± 0.33	3.03 ± 0.67	1.34
Basion-nasion length	100.86 ± 0.40	97.12 ± 0.33	3.74 ± 0.52	1.04
Basion-prosthion length	98.29 ± 1.02	98.27 ± 0.41	0.02 ± 1.10	2.20
External palatal length	55.17 ± 0.70	55.75 ± 0.27	−0.58 ± 0.91	1.82
External palatal breadth	67.33 ± 0.69	65.94 ± 0.39	1.39 ± 0.77	1.54
Mean difference			3.92	

Indices

Length-breadth	76.38 ± 0.86*	77.60 ± 0.27	−1.22 ± 0.90	1.80
Length-height	76.86 ± 1.10*	71.44 ± 0.27	5.42 ± 1.13	2.26
Breadth-height	100.00 ± 1.56*	92.24 ± 0.31	7.76 ± 1.59	3.18
Upper facial	55.00 ± 0.44	52.11 ± 0.30	2.89 ± 0.53	1.06
Mean orbital	90.43 ± 1.03	87.37 ± 0.42	3.06 ± 1.11	2.22
Nasal	50.75 ± 0.72	48.37 ± 0.31	2.38 ± 0.78	1.56
Gnathic	97.14 ± 0.88	101.29 ± 0.43	−4.15 ± 0.93	1.86
External Palatal	122.00 ± 1.03	118.55 ± 0.66	3.45 ± 1.22	2.44
Mean difference			3.79	

* Deformed and undeformed crania.

TABLE VIII–5. DIFFERENCES OF MEANS OF ARIZONA BASKET MAKERS AND
SANTA CRUZ

Males

Indices	Arizona	Santa Cruz	Difference	2 p. e.
Length-breadth	74.87 ± 0.64	77.60 ± 0.27	−2.73 ± 0.69	1.38
Length-height	72.62 + 0.51	71.44 ± 0.27	1.18 ± 0.56	1.12
Breadth-height..................	97.08 ± 0.49	92.24 ± 0.31	4.84 ± 0.58	1.16
Upper facial	54.83 ± 0.47	52.11 ± 0.30	2.72 ± 0.56	1.12
Gnathic	98.23 ± 1.07	101.29 ± 0.43	−3.06 ± 1.15	2.30
Mean orbital	87.50 ± 0.89	87.37 ± 0.42	0.13 ± 0.98	1.96
Nasal	50.13 ± 0.81	48.37 ± 0.31	1.76 ± 0.86	1.72
External Palatal	118.50 ± 1.85	118.55 ± 0.66	−0.05 ± 1.96	3.92
Mean difference			2.06	

TABLE VIII–6. Differences of Means of Arizona Basket Makers and
Coahuila Cave Crania

Males

Measurements	Arizona	Coahuila	Difference	2 p. e.
Glabello-occipital length	179.87 ± 1.00	182.53 ± 0.62	−2.66 ± 1.17	2.34
Maximum breadth	134.53 ± 0.86	135.12 ± 0.60	−0.59 ± 1.05	2.10
Basion-bregma height	129.92 ± 0.77	133.82 ± 0.92	−3.90 ± 1.20	2.40
Maximum circumference	500.00 ± 2.02	504.76 ± 1.73	−4.76 ± 2.66	5.32
Nasion-opisthion arc	361.83 ± 2.09	366.93 ± 1.53	−5.10 ± 2.59	5.18
Transverse arc	290.67 ± 1.73	302.94 ± 1.37	−12.27 ± 2.21	4.42
Thickness of left parietal	4.45 ± 0.29	5.00 ...	−0.55 ...	...
Mean diameter of foramen magnum ..	31.46 ± 0.25	33.77 ± 0.43	−2.31 ± 0.49	0.98
Minimum frontal diameter	89.29 ± 0.72	91.24 ± 0.80	−1.95 ± 1.08	2.16
Bizygomatic diameter..............	132.38 ± 0.80	134.23 ± 1.14	−1.85 ± 1.39	2.78
Nasion-menton height	116.25 ± 1.56	120.67	−4.42	...
Nasion-prosthion height	73.08 ± 0.91	73.57 ± 0.65	−0.49 ± 1.12	2.24
Orbit height, right.................	34.23 ± 0.37	35.36 ± 0.23	−1.13 ± 0.43	0.86
Orbit height, left	34.32 ± 0.41	35.18 ± 0.27	−0.86 ± 0.49	0.98
Orbit breadth, right	39.00 ± 0.20	40.86 ± 0.28	−1.86 ± 0.34	0.68
Orbit breadth, left.................	39.14 ± 0.19	40.96 ± 0.35	−1.82 ± 0.40	0.80
Nasal height	50.80 ± 0.69	53.50 ± 0.57	−2.70 ± 0.89	1.78
Nasal breadth	25.40 ± 0.44	26.79 ± 0.36	−1.39 ± 0.57	1.14
Basion-nasion length	99.00 ± 0.48	101.29 ± 0.38	−2.29 ± 0.61	1.22
Basion-prosthion length	97.15 ± 0.92	98.29 ± 0.74	−1.14 ± 1.18	2.36
External palatal length	54.69 ± 0.64	54.36 ± 0.43	0.33 ± 0.72	1.44
External palatal breadth	64.67 ± 1.01	65.29 ± 0.48	−0.62 ± 1.12	2.24
Bigonial diameter	92.70 ± 0.86	101.33 ...	−8.63 ...	...
Bicondylar width	116.45 ± 0.61	116.00 ...	0.45 ...	...
Height of symphysis	34.58 ± 0.50	35.00 ...	−0.42 ...	...
Minimum breadth of ascending ramus	34.73 ± 0.38	32.83 ...	1.90 ...	...
Condylo-symphysial length	104.44 ± 1.14	104.17 ...	0.27 ...	...
Mean difference			2.47	

Indices				
Length-breadth	74.87 ± 0.64	74.35 ± 0.35	0.52 ± 0.73	1.46
Length-height	72.62 ± 0.51	73.24 ± 0.48	−0.62 ± 0.70	1.40
Breadth-height	97.08 ± 0.49	96.94 ± 0.71	0.14 ± 0.85	1.70
Total facial	86.85 ± 0.73	91.67 ± 1.05	−4.82 ± 1.28	2.56
Upper facial	54.83 ± 0.47	55.54 ± 0.52	−0.71 ± 0.70	1.40
Mean orbital	87.50 ± 0.89	86.07 ± 0.57	1.43 ± 1.68	3.36
Nasal	50.13 ± 0.81	50.07 ± 0.77	0.06 ± 1.12	2.24
Gnathic	98.23 ± 1.07	97.00 ± 0.89	1.23 ± 1.38	2.76
External Palatal	118.50 ± 1.85	120.29 ± 1.02	−1.79 ± 1.33	2.66
Mean difference			1.26	

TABLE VIII–7. Differences of Means of Coahuila Cave Crania and
Santa Catalina

Males

Indices	Coahuila	Santa Catalina	Difference	2 p. e.
Length-breadth	74.35 ± 0.35	72.27 ± 0.32	2.08 ± 0.47	0.94
Length-height	73.24 ± 0.48	67.45 ± 0.32	5.79 ± 0.57	1.14
Breadth-height...................	96.94 ± 0.71	93.14 ± 0.44	3.80 ± 0.83	1.66
Total facial	91.67 ± 1.05	87.21 ± 0.52	4.46 ± 1.17	2.34
Upper facial	55.54 ± 0.52	54.50 ± 0.38	1.04 ± 0.64	1.28
Gnathic	97.00 ± 0.89	97.63 ± 0.41	−0.63 ± 0.98	1.96
Nasal	50.07 ± 0.77	48.19 ± 0.59	1.88 ± 0.97	1.94
Mean orbital	86.07 ± 0.57	88.69 ± 0.72	−2.62 ± 0.92	1.84
External Palatal	120.29 ± 1.02	118.36 ± 0.71	1.93 ± 1.24	2.48
Mean difference			2.69	

Table VIII–8 records the differences in means of measurements and indices between the Pecos "Basket Maker" type, the Arizona Basket Makers, and the Coahuila cave skulls on one hand, and the Naquada crania, a series of "Prehistoric Egyptians" measured by MacIver, a series of Theban mummy crania, modern Egyptians, and a mixed Negro series, on the other. The table includes also a summary of mean deviations of measurements and indices. First of all it may be noted from the table that our Southwestern crania are markedly shorter than all of these comparative groups, except the modern Egyptians. In breadth the Southwestern crania differ only insignificantly from the Naquada crania; they exceed those of MacIver's "Prehistoric Egyptians" and fall below the Theban mummies and the modern Egyptians. Basion-bregma heights of our series are also generally lower than in the Egyptians. The same deficiency holds true in case of the minimum frontal diameters and the various cranial arcs. These deficiencies are generally at a maximum among the Arizona Basket Makers and at a minimum among the Coahuila crania, which are somewhat larger. The cranial capacities of the Pecos "Basket Maker" type range from 41 cc. to 81 cc. below those of the Egyptians and Negroes. The deficiencies of the Coahuila group range from 6 cc. to 46 cc., but are in general insignificant. The crania of our small series of Arizona Basket Makers were in such poor condition that the cranial capacities were not calculated.

When we consider the facial dimensions, we observe that the excesses are almost invariably in favor of our Southwestern crania. Thus the bizygomatic diameters of the American crania exceed those of the Egyptian and Negro groups by 3 to 9 mm. Total and upper facial heights are notably greater in the Southwestern crania, differences in means of the latter measurement averaging 4 to 5 mm. The basion-nasion lengths of our crania are slightly smaller than those of the Egyptians and markedly smaller than those of the Negroes. The basion-prosthion diameters of the Southwestern skulls usually exceed those of the Egyptians but fall below those of the Negroes. Both nose height and nose breadth are greater in our series than in those from Egypt, but the nasal apertures of the Negro series are markedly wider.

In summarizing the measurements it may be said that the Egyptian crania have generally longer lengths and greater heights, broader frontal regions and somewhat larger capacities. The faces of the American crania are broader and longer, and have longer and wider noses. The facial projection is somewhat greater in the American than in the Egyptian series. The mean differences range from 2.48 mm. to 4.99 mm. The minimum average difference (2.48 mm.) obtains between the Pecos "Basket Maker" type and the modern Egyptians. Generally speaking, the Coahuila crania are least divergent from the various Egyptian series and the Arizona Basket Makers most divergent. Of the three Egyptian series for which mean differences of all 14 measurements have been calculated the modern group is least divergent in measurements from the Southwestern series, the average deviation of this group from the three American groups being 3.42 mm. as against 3.93 in the Theban mummy series and 4.57 in the case of the Naquada crania. The mean difference of 10 measurements of the "Prehistoric Egyptian" series from our three Southwestern groups is only 2.61 mm., but arcs and circumferences are not included

in the comparison. The mean difference between measurements of the Negro group
and of the three American groups is 4.09 mm.

The consideration of indicial deviations yields a quite different result. The
length-breadth index is higher in the Southwestern crania than in the Naquada,
"Prehistoric Egyptian," and Negro series, generally lower than in the other Egyptian series. Except in the case of the Pecos "Basket Maker" type and in a single
Coahuila deviation the length-height indices of the American groups are less than
those of the Egyptian and Negro crania. Breadth-height indices of the American
group are generally lower. The nasal index fluctuates in the various groups. Differences between the American and Egyptian series are not consistent, but the
former fall far below the means of the Negro crania, as might be expected. Where
data for the orbital index are available it may be seen that no consistent differences
are manifested. The gnathic index is higher in the American crania than in any of
the Egyptian series except the modern group. The Negroes, of course, far exceed
both Americans and Egyptians in this index of prognathism. The upper facial
index is higher (more leptoprosopic) in the Southwestern crania than in any of the
series here adduced for comparison. The difference is least marked in the case of
the modern Egyptians. When the mean indicial deviations are considered (six to
eight indices) they are seen to be remarkably low. In no case do they exceed two
index units, with the exception of the Negro group and of the deviations of the Pecos
"Basket Maker" type from the "Prehistoric Egyptians." The minimum deviation
(1.40 index units) occurs between the Pecos "Basket Maker" skulls and the skulls
of modern Egyptians. Next is 1.45 units, the mean deviation between the Coahuila
cave skulls and the Theban mummies. The average difference between the indices
of Arizona Basket Makers and Theban mummy skulls is only 1.54 index units.
But the Negro series shows mean differences from the three Southwestern series
ranging from 2.79 to 3.09 index units.

Lest the reader fail to appreciate the significance of these very small average
indicial differences between the Southwestern Indian crania and the Egyptian
crania, it may be pointed out that the corresponding difference between Pecos and
Arizona Basket Makers (the same eight indices) is 2.10 units, between the Coahuila
and Santa Catalina crania 2.55 units, between the Pecos "Basket Makers" and the
Santa Cruz skulls 4.05 units, between Pecos "Basket Makers" and Coahuila 1.99,
and between Arizona Basket Makers and Coahuila crania 1.19 index units. With
two exceptions the differences between the means of indices of this group of American crania and of Egyptian crania are less than the inter-group differences of the
American crania.

The quite unexpected indicial similarities of the Southwestern and Egyptian
crania call for a further extension of the comparison. Thomson and MacIver have
studied more than 1500 crania from the Thebaïd, belonging to different periods.[1]
Unfortunately these authors have tabulated the means of only four indices and of
the estimated cranial capacity. In Table VIII–9 these means for indices of Egyptian
crania of the different periods are compared with the means of Southwestern doli-

---

[1] Thomson and MacIver, 1905, pp. 137–139.

TABLE VIII–8. DIFFERENCES OF MEANS OF PECOS "BASKET MAKERS," ARIZONA BASKET MAKERS, AND COAHUILA CAVE CRANIA AND EGYPTIAN AND NEGRO CRANIA (DATA OF FAWCETT)

Males

Measurements	Naquada			Prehistoric Egyptians			Theban Mummies			Modern Egyptians			Modern Negroes		
	P.	A.	C.	P.	A.	C.	P.	A.	C.	P.	A.	C.	P.	A.	C.
Glabello-occipital length	−8.25*	−5.26	−2.60	−7.62*	−4.63	−1.97	−5.06*	−2.07	0.59	−0.15*	2.84	5.50	−5.97*	−2.98	−6.32
Maximum breadth	−0.12*	−0.34	0.25	2.37*	2.15	2.74	−1.88*	−2.10	−1.51	−2.01*	−2.23	−1.64	1.60*	1.38	1.97
Basion-bregma height	0.36*	−5.29	−1.39	1.63*	−4.02	−0.12	−0.48*	−6.13	−2.23	−1.67*	−7.32	−3.42	0.26*	−5.39	−1.49
Minimum frontal diameter	1.94	−1.77	0.18	...	...	...	−0.83	−4.54	−2.59	−1.08	−4.79	−2.84	2.91	−6.62	−4.67
Maximum circumference	−11.02	−11.02	−6.26	...	...	...	−10.76	−10.76	−6.00	−1.76	−1.76	3.00	−8.47	−8.47	−3.71
Nasion-opisthion arc	−12.31	−11.19	−6.09	...	...	...	−11.73	−10.61	−5.51	−5.24	−4.12	0.98	−7.01	−5.89	−0.79
Transverse arc	−4.53	−13.55	−1.28	...	...	...	2.68	−15.40	−3.13	−3.06	−21.14	8.87	1.90	−16.18	−3.91
Bizygomatic diameter	7.08	6.75	8.60	6.26	5.93	7.78	4.38	4.05	5.90	6.89	6.56	8.41	3.24	2.91	4.76
Nasion-menton height	9.15	4.23	8.65	...	...	...	6.86	1.94	6.36	5.43	0.51	4.93	5.96	1.04	5.46
Nasion-prosthion height	5.66	5.49	5.98	2.61	2.44	2.93	4.47	4.30	4.79	4.56	4.39	4.88	5.25	5.08	5.57
Basion-nasion length	1.52	−0.34	1.95	−0.06	−1.92	0.37	0.23	−1.63	0.66	−0.09	−1.95	0.34	−2.10	−3.96	−1.67
Basion-prosthion length	3.57	2.43	3.57	2.17	1.03	2.17	2.50	1.36	2.50	0.82	−0.32	0.82	−7.04	8.18	−7.04
Nasal height	2.44	1.86	4.56	1.02	0.44	3.14	0.77	0.19	2.89	0.70	0.12	2.82	1.86	1.28	3.98
Nasal breadth	1.00	0.28	1.67	1.02	0.30	1.69	0.86	0.14	1.53	1.19	0.47	1.86	−1.17	−1.89	−0.50
Mean difference	4.92	4.99	3.79	2.75	2.54	2.55	3.82	4.66	3.30	2.48	4.18	3.59	3.91	5.09	3.27
Cranial capacity	−74.33	...	12.57	...	...	...	−80.96	...	5.94	49.43	...	37.47	−41.03	...	45.87
Indices															
Length-breadth	3.39*	1.88	1.36	4.60	3.09	2.57	1.31	−0.20	−0.72	−0.89	2.40	−2.92	3.51	2.00	1.48
Length-height	3.56*	−0.68	−0.06	4.26	−0.02	0.64	2.15	−2.09	−1.47	0.60	−4.84	−4.22	2.71	−1.53	−0.91
Breadth-height	−0.47*	−3.39	−3.53	−1.18	−4.10	−4.24	0.36	−2.56	−2.70	−0.56	−3.48	−3.62	−1.75	−4.67	−4.81
Nasal	−0.33	−0.95	−1.01	0.72	0.10	0.04	0.68	0.06	0.00	1.39	0.77	0.71	−4.68	−5.30	−5.36
Orbital	...	...	...	4.43	1.50	0.07	3.89	0.96	−0.47	5.20	2.27	0.84	3.23	0.30	−1.13
Gnathic	1.79	2.88	1.65	1.90	2.99	1.76	1.86	2.95	1.72	−0.40	0.69	−0.54	−5.16	−4.07	−5.30
Upper facial	1.20	1.03	1.74	...	...	...	1.41	1.24	1.95	0.41	0.24	0.95	2.48	2.31	3.02
Total facial	1.12	−2.23	2.59	...	...	...	1.13	2.22	2.60	−1.78	5.13	−0.31	1.22	2.13	2.69
Mean difference	1.69	1.86	1.71	2.85	1.97	1.55	1.60	1.54	1.45	1.40	2.48	1.76	3.09	2.79	3.06

* Deformed and undeformed crania.

TABLE VIII–9. DIFFERENCES OF MEANS OF INDICES OF ARCHAIC SOUTHWESTERN CRANIA AND ANCIENT EGYPTIANS (DATA OF THOMSON AND MACIVER)

	Upper Facial	Nasal	Cephalic	Cranial Capacity (Estimated)	Length-height	Mean Difference
Males						
Predynastic and Old Empire	55.61 ± 0.14	50.31 ± 0.21	72.60 ± 0.15	1406.0 ± 5.2	72.44 ± 0.13	
Middle and New Empires	56.20 ± 0.11	49.50 ± 0.19	73.64 ± 0.12	1401.6 ± 5.3	73.21 ± 0.11	
Ptolemaic and Roman Periods	55.28 ± 0.22	49.23 ± 0.24	74.39 ± 0.21	1381.8 ± 5.6	71.89 ± 0.17	
Coahuila Cave	55.54 ± 0.52	50.07 ± 0.77	74.35 ± 0.35	1393.5 ± 21.3	73.24 ± 0.48	
Arizona Basket Makers	54.83 ± 0.47	50.13 ± 0.81	74.87 ± 0.64	......	72.67 ± 0.51	
Santa Catalina	54.50 ± 0.38	48.19 ± 0.59	72.27 ± 0.32	......	67.45 ± 0.32	
Pecos "Basket Makers"	55.00 ± 0.44	50.75 ± 0.72	76.38 ± 0.86*	1306.2 ± 31.5	76.86 ± 1.10*	
Santa Cruz	52.11 ± 0.30	48.37 ± 0.31	77.60 ± 0.27	......	71.44 ± 0.27	
Coahuila Cave Crania						
Predynastic and Old Empire	-0.07 ± 0.55	-0.24 ± 0.80	1.75 ± 0.38	-12.5 ± 21.9	0.80 ± 0.50	0.72
Middle and New Empires	-0.66 ± 0.53	-0.57 ± 0.79	0.71 ± 0.37	-8.1 ± 21.9	0.03 ± 0.49	0.49
Ptolemaic and Roman Periods	0.26 ± 0.56	0.84 ± 0.81	-0.04 ± 0.41	11.7 ± 23.5	1.35 ± 0.51	0.62
Arizona Basket Makers						
Predynastic and Old Empire	-0.78 ± 0.49	-0.18 ± 0.88	2.27 ± 0.66	......	0.23 ± 0.52	0.86
Middle and New Empires	-1.37 ± 0.48	0.63 ± 0.83	1.23 ± 0.65	......	-0.54 ± 0.52	0.94
Ptolemaic and Roman Periods	-0.45 ± 0.51	0.90 ± 0.84	0.48 ± 0.67	......	0.78 ± 0.53	0.65
Santa Catalina						
Predynastic and Old Empire	-1.11 ± 0.41	-2.12 ± 0.63	-0.33 ± 0.36	......	-4.99 ± 0.34	2.14
Middle and New Empire	-1.70 ± 0.40	-1.31 ± 0.62	-1.37 ± 0.34	......	-5.76 ± 0.34	2.54
Ptolemaic and Roman Periods	-0.78 ± 0.44	-1.04 ± 0.64	-2.12 ± 0.38	......	-4.44 ± 0.36	2.10
Pecos "Basket Makers"						
Predynastic and Old Empire	-0.61 ± 0.46	0.44 ± 0.75	3.78 ± 0.87	-99.8 ± 31.9	4.42 ± 1.17	2.31
Middle and New Empires	-1.20 ± 0.46	1.25 ± 0.75	2.74 ± 0.87	-95.4 ± 31.8	3.65 ± 1.15	2.21
Ptolemaic and Roman Periods	-0.28 ± 0.49	1.52 ± 0.76	1.99 ± 0.88	-75.6 ± 31.8	4.97 ± 1.22	2.19

* Deformed and undeformed crania.

chocephals. In this group it is possible to compare differences in means with respect to the probable error of such differences. The Coahuila skulls show differences from the various chronological Egyptian subgroups in excess of twice their probable errors in two cases out of twelve indices, or 16.7 per cent. One may expect 18 per cent of such differences to occur in random samples drawn from the same population. The Arizona Basket Maker group shows the same percentage of significant indicial differences from the Egyptians (two out of twelve or 16.7 per cent). But the Pecos "Basket Makers" show 67 per cent of such differences and the Santa Catalina crania 75 per cent.

If the mean indicial differences are considered, it is seen that the Coahuila cave and Arizona Basket Maker crania differ from each of the Egyptian groups by averages of less than one index unit. The mean deviation between Coahuila crania and Egyptian crania of the Middle and New Empires is only 0.49 index units, and between Coahuila crania and crania of the Ptolemaic and Roman periods only 0.62 index units. But the Pecos "Basket Makers" and the Santa Catalina Islanders show mean differences from the Egyptian crania in excess of two index units. Taking these same four indices the mean difference between Arizona Basket Makers and Coahuila cave skulls is 0.48 units, between Pecos "Basket Makers" and Coahuila crania 1.72 units, and between Pecos "Basket Makers" and Arizona Basket Makers 1.64 index units. We are thus confronted by the fact that indicially two groups of Southwestern dolichocephals, the Arizona and Coahuila, resemble various Egyptian crania more closely than they resemble the Pecos and Santa Catalina groups. The remarkably close indicial resemblances, upon the basis of which we judged the Arizona Basket Makers and the Coahuila crania to be racially identical and to represent different groups drawn from the same population, are not perceptibly closer than resemblances between these groups and certain groups of Egyptian crania. If, however, we refer back to differences of means of measurements as demonstrated in the comparison of our crania with the series tabulated by Fawcett we find that Egyptian crania differ from the American series under consideration by larger averages than do various other American groups. Table VIII–10 presents these contrasts.

It is therefore apparent that the American groups show among themselves smaller mean differences in raw measurements than they do when compared with Egyptian groups. The single exception is the case of the Pecos "Basket Makers" and the modern Egyptians, in which the mean deviation in measurements is only 2.48 mm. and in indices only 1.40 units. If, however, we compare any of the American groups with the Negro group of Fawcett we find mean deviations of measurements ranging from 3.91 to 5.09 and of indices from 2.79 to 3.09.

TABLE VIII–10. MEAN DIFFERENCES IN MEASUREMENTS BETWEEN SOUTHWESTERN
AMERICAN AND EGYPTIAN CRANIA

Males	Pecos "B. M."	Arizona B. M.	Coahuila	Naquada	Theban Mummies	Modern Egyptians
Pecos "Basket Makers"	0	2.28	1.92	4.92	3.82	2.48
Arizona Basket Makers	2.28	0	2.47	4.99	4.66	4.18
Coahuila	1.92	2.47	0	3.79	3.30	3.59

The situation may be summarized in the statement that in indices the South-western American crania are so similar to the crania of Egyptians as to be well-nigh identical, but that in gross measurements there is a considerable divergence, in that the American group has shorter and lower brain-cases and much wider and longer faces. Are we then to conclude that these two groups so far separated geographically are related racially? If we deny any such relationship we are forced to throw into the discard once and for all the craniometric method whereby skulls are adjudged to belong to the same racial group when the differences between the means of a large number of significant indices are found to be less than would be expected were the contrasted groups random samples of the same population. But if we conclude that a racial relationship does exist we are forced to consider the strong metric divergence of the two groups in raw dimensions and the fact that the great facial lengths and breadths of the American groups, coupled with their small vault diameters, clearly demarcate them from the Old World series. Add to this the fact that we have been unable to utilize criteria of morphological observation, such as form of the nasal bridge, depth of the nasal depression and of the suborbital fossae, shape of the palate, frontal projection of the malars, and so forth, which often constitute most important means of racial differentiation.

Assuming for the moment that the similarities found are really significant, we may consider the implications of such a finding. In the first place it should be stated emphatically that these craniometric similarities cannot be interpreted as evidence that any group of American Indians were of Egyptian origin or came from Egypt, any more than it can be concluded that the Basket Makers built the pyramids of Gizeh. We cannot safely proceed beyond the supposition that the Basket Maker–Coahuila and Ancient Egyptian groups represent divergent offshoots of a common primitive race which may have sent colonies in many different directions during the neolithic period. One may suppose this primitive race to have been dolicho-cephalic, leptoprosopic, orthognathous, of short stature and possibly of brown or brunet-white pigmentation. Its migrants may have carried in solution a certain proportion of Negroid or Mongoloid blood or may have picked up such admixture either on the way or after arriving at their destination. That the predynastic Egyptians had a perceptible Negroid strain is a matter of historical record and a cranio-metric commonplace; just as it is obvious to all students that American Indians everywhere show more or less pronounced Mongoloid features. That the great facial dimensions of the Basket Maker–Coahuila group when compared with the Egyptian crania are the result of Mongoloid mixture is *a priori* probable enough. We must also consider, however, the possibilities of functional differentiation. Our Basket Makers represent a human type of which the masticatory apparatus is well developed, a type of people living in a state of nature. The Egyptians were civil-ized people — domesticated animals living on a civilized diet. Even the predynastic Egyptians were culturally far in advance of the primitive agriculturists of the Southwest and subsisted on a probably more diversified diet. Even in Europe primitive and early forms of skulls commonly show not only greater masticatory development, but particularly more prominent and projecting malars and zygomata than are found in Egyptians. It should be recalled, moreover, that the bizygomatic diameters of our Basket Maker–Coahuila type (132–134 mm.) in no way approach the great dimensions commonly found in Mongols and Mongoloid American Indians.

For the moment we may, perhaps, leave this question unsettled, except for a tentative recognition of a fundamental similarity of the two groups, due to a common origin, and of perceptible differences referable either to functional differentiation or to diverse admixtures.

TABLE VIII–11. DIFFERENCES OF MEANS OF "BASKET MAKERS" AND OTHER PECOS TYPES

Males Measurements	"Pseudo-Negroids"	"Pseudo-Australoids"	"Plains Indians"	"Long-Faced Europeans"	"Pseudo-Alpines"	"Hybrids"
Glabello-occipital length *	0.00	1.38	0.53	0.87	...	5.00
Maximum breadth *	−2.17	−0.60	−4.33	−9.17	...	−14.50
Basion-bregma height *	4.33	0.00	−2.83	−5.20	...	−2.50
Maximum circumference	7.92	0.91	5.73	−0.41	7.36	1.40
Nasion-opisthion arc	6.33	−0.96	7.21	4.15	12.21	4.33
Transverse arc	−7.71	−6.25	−7.11	−13.61	−18.89	−27.45
Thickness of left parietal	−0.06	−0.04	0.56	0.14	0.38	−0.35
Mean diam. of foramen magnum	2.65	1.28	0.35	0.19	1.40	0.35
Minimum frontal diameter	−2.46	−1.09	−0.65	−4.00	−1.50	−4.62
Maximum bizygomatic diameter	−1.12	−4.96	−7.11	−4.29	−6.21	−10.94
Menton-nasion height	2.86	3.47	−0.18	−2.14	6.17	−0.37
Nasion-prosthion height	1.02	2.58	−2.49	−3.42	3.50	−1.21
Orbit height, right	0.97	2.58	−0.13	−0.21	0.16	−0.14
Orbit height, left	0.67	2.11	0.05	−0.28	0.13	0.06
Orbit breadth, right	−0.08	0.02	−0.95	−0.57	−1.12	−1.50
Orbit breadth, left	−0.31	−0.64	−1.15	−1.16	−0.61	−1.21
Nasal height	2.57	2.20	−1.76	−1.01	1.81	−0.49
Nasal breadth	−0.26	−0.06	0.05	1.59	0.44	0.18
Basion-nasion height	−0.24	−1.14	−2.72	−2.74	0.06	−1.62
Basion-prosthion height	−2.11	0.67	−0.24	2.49	2.89	−0.33
External palatal length	−2.51	0.92	−0.70	−0.10	1.22	−1.24
External palatal breadth	−2.51	3.21	0.33	1.73	1.51	0.52
Bigonial diameter	−3.20	−4.60	−8.85	−6.18	−4.62	−9.82
Bicondylar width	1.02	−3.37	−7.80	−2.37	−5.09	−9.05
Height of symphysis	−0.33	0.32	0.85	−0.07	2.35	−0.62
Min. breadth of ascending ramus	−1.88	−0.67	−0.72	−0.95	−0.71	−1.34
Height of ascending ramus	6.58	2.12	2.55	−2.62	2.05	0.77
Condylo-symphysial length	−2.25	−0.92	−1.79	−1.10	1.15	−2.36
Mean difference	2.36	1.75	2.49	2.60	3.34	3.72
Cranial capacity	32.50	−28.33	−26.19	−65.64	−73.33	−113.78
Cranial module	2.40	0.00	−0.75	−1.98	−0.40	−3.03
Indices						
Length-breadth *	−0.67	−0.71	−2.43	−5.40	...	−10.33
Length-height *	2.53	−0.63	−2.30	−3.20	...	−3.30
Breadth-height *	3.80	−0.37	−0.03	2.00	...	6.30
Total facial	1.53	4.95	3.06	0.20	8.30	4.81
Upper facial	0.75	3.86	1.13	−1.17	5.55	3.20
Mean orbital	2.35	6.70	2.56	1.37	3.29	3.36
Nasal	−3.02	−2.52	1.70	3.97	−1.18	0.71
Gnathic	−3.26	1.52	2.09	4.64	2.64	0.95
External palatal	9.55	3.56	2.00	2.87	−0.36	3.71
Mean difference	3.05	2.76	1.92	2.76	3.55	4.07

* Undeformed crania only.

"PSEUDO–NEGROID" TYPE

DESCRIPTION

The so-called "Pseudo-Negroid" type consists of very small crania (mean uncorrected length 169 mm., breadth 138.7 mm., height 133.7 mm.). Deformation is commoner in this type than in the "Basket Maker" type, 10 of 13 skulls showing deformation. When this deformation is statistically corrected, the corrected deformed crania of the series show a mean length-breadth index of 77.35, the undeformed crania 75.67. The corrected length-height index (73 to 74) is the lowest of any of the Pecos series. Breadth-height indices are also well below the mean (undeformed 97, corrected deformed 95.6). The cranial module of this type and the cranial capacity are far below the series average and the lowest of any type (cranial capacity 1274 cc.). Bizygomatic breadth is less than that of any group except the "Basket Makers." The total facial height is small (118 mm.), but the total facial index (88.7) indicates a relatively long face. Orbits are relatively high. The nose is very short and somewhat broader than that of any other type. The mean nasal index, 53.77, is chamaerrhine. Basion-prosthion length considerably exceeds that of any other type. The mean of the gnathic index is 100.4, indicating a pronouncedly mesognathous condition. This type is the only one which includes crania that are really prognathous (gnathic indices in excess of 103). The palate of the "Pseudo-Negroid" type is significantly longer than that of any other type and the maxillo-alveolar index (mean 112.45) is by far the lowest of the series. The palate is thus more inclined to the primitive U-shape than that of any other group. In the mandible bigonial diameters are small; bicondylar width is small; the ascending rami are low and broad and the mean angles of the rami are the greatest of the series. These differences are, of course, associated with the facial projection.

Frontal regions of the "Pseudo-Negroid" type are rather low and of medium breadth; they are less sloping than those of any other type. Temporal regions are prevailingly flat or compressed. Brow-ridges are smaller than those of any other group. The nasion depression is slight; the nasal root and bridge are low and broad and usually concave or concavo-convex. The lower borders of the nasal aperture are very poorly defined and the spine is little developed. Malars and zygomata are well developed; suborbital fossae exceed medium depth and alveolar prognathism is extreme.

Composite Plates VII–C, D, show very clearly the characteristics of this type and Plates VI–3 to VI–6 give individual examples.

The mean of stature in this group is only 155.2 cm., by far the lowest of the Pecos series.

TABLE VIII–12.   MEANS OF "PSEUDO–NEGROID" TYPE

Males

Measurements

Glabello-occipital length *	177.67	...
Maximum breadth *	135.00	...
Basion-bregma height *...	130.67	...
Maximum circumference .	492.08 ±	2.79
Nasion-opisthion arc	354.38 ±	3.10
Transverse arc	316.46 ±	1.99
Thickness of left parietal .	5.23 ±	0.10
Mean diam. of for. mag. ..	29.35 ±	0.19
Minimum frontal diameter	95.46 ±	0.94
Max. bizygomatic diameter	133.83 ±	0.92
Nasion-menton height ...	118.31 ±	0.60
Nasion-prosthion height ..	72.23 ±	0.56
Orbit height, right	34.46 ±	0.39
Orbit height, left	34.58 ±	0.35
Orbit breadth, right	39.65 ±	0.40
Orbit breadth, left	39.12 ±	0.30
Nasal height	48.81 ±	0.43
Nasal breadth	26.38 ±	0.39
Basion-nasion length	101.10 ±	0.52
Basion-prosthion length ..	100.40 ±	0.57
External palatal length ..	57.68 ±	0.38

Measurements

External palatal breadth..	64.82 ±	0.96
Bigonial diameter	98.60 ±	0.66
Bicondylar width	115.78 ±	1.02
Height of symphysis	36.33 ±	0.36
Min. breadth of asc. ramus	38.21 ±	0.53
Height of ascending ramus	58.92 ±	0.88
Condylo-symphysial length	106.00 ±	0.56
Cranial capacity	1274.17 ±	14.42
Cranial module	147.00 ±	0.65

Indices

Length-breadth *	75.67	...
Length-height *	73.67	...
Breadth-height *	97.00	...
Total facial	88.67 ±	0.69
Upper facial............	54.25 ±	0.48
Mean orbital	88.08 ±	1.07
Nasal	53.77 ±	0.81
Gnathic	100.40 ±	0.50
External palatal	112.45 ±	1.30

* Undeformed crania only.

COMPARISON WITH OTHER GROUPS

Any anthropologist who selects a group of prehistoric American crania and labels it "Pseudo-Negroid" should be prepared to demonstrate the resemblance of that group to authentically Negroid crania. For we have no record of the invasion of any Negroid people into the New World during the pre-Columbian period. The crania so named were, in the present instance, given this designation in the laboratory because of their frequently swollen frontal regions, their flat, broad noses, and their alveolar prognathism. The writer is not mounted on any hobby, being committed neither to the hypothesis of the sanctity and unity of the American race nor to the heresy of its heterogeneity. Therefore if our "Pseudo-Negroid" type proves to be dissimilar to any Negroid type of known origin, we shall abandon the label without a qualm.

In Table VIII–13 the Pecos "Negroids" are compared with the Baining of New Guinea,[1] the Aetas of the Philippines,[2] the Andamanese[2] and the Fan[3] of West Africa. The Baining are Oceanic Negroes; the Aetas and Andamanese are Negritoes, and the Fan are Bantu Negroes. Let us first dispose of the Andamanese. These are pigmy brachycephals with much shorter and somewhat broader skulls than those of our Pecos type. Their measurements fall far below the corresponding dimensions in the Pecos, except in skull breadth and in skull height. The mean difference in measurements between the two groups is almost 6 mm. There is a similarly wide

[1] Bauer, 1915, pp. 145–202.   [2] Sullivan, 1921, 175–201.   [3] Poutrin, 1910, pp. 435–504.

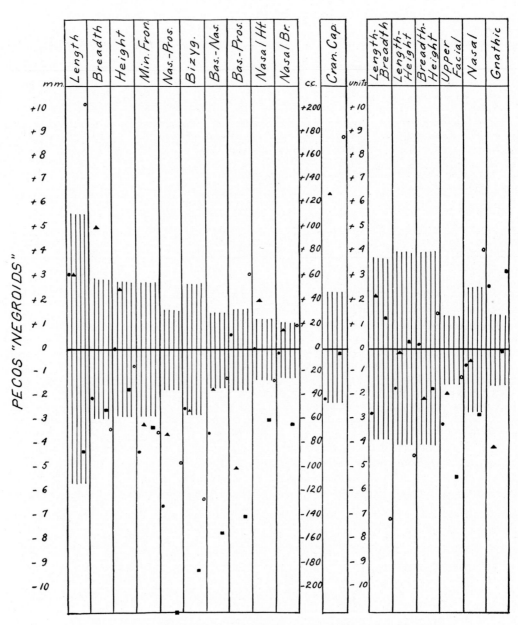

*Baining ▲ Philippine Negritoes ■ Andamanese ○ Fan

(Means plotted against Pecos "Negroids" base-line with three times the probable error of means of the latter.)

FIG. VIII–2

TABLE VIII–13. DIFFERENCES OF "PSEUDO–NEGROIDS" AND NEGROID CRANIA

Males	"Pseudo-Negroids"	New Guinea Baining (Bauer)	Philippine Aetas (Sullivan)	Andamanese (Sullivan)	Fan (Poutrin)
Measurements					
Glabello-occipital length	177.67*	172.30	172.3	164.9	180.5
Maximum breadth	135.00*	136.64	143.7	136.1	135.3
Basion-bregma height	130.67*	133.76	136.3	130.2	133.0
Minimum frontal diameter	95.46	91.12	92.3	92.2	92.0
Max. bizygomatic diameter ...	133.83	131.42	131.3	124.6	127.5
Nasion-prosthion height	72.23	65.66	68.7	61.0	67.5
Basion-nasion length	101.10	97.60	99.5	93.4	99.9
Basion-prosthion length	100.40	100.61	95.4	93.4	103.5
Nasal height	48.81	48.85	50.9	45.8	47.5
Nasal breadth	25.38	26.22	27.2	23.3	27.4
Cranial capacity	1274.17	1232.00	1409.0	1269.0	1449.0
Indices					
Length-breadth..............	75.67*	79.38	84.30	83.4	75.00
Length-height	73.67*	77.63	79.10	78.95	74.87
Breadth-height	97.00*	97.60	95.30	95.7	98.92
Upper facial	54.25	50.10	52.32	48.9	53.08
Nasal	53.77	53.10	53.30	51.0	57.89
Gnathic	100.40	103.08	96.30	100.3	103.60
Differences of Measurements					
Glabello-occipital length	...	5.37	5.37	12.77	−2.83
Maximum breadth	...	−1.64	−8.70	−1.10	−0.30
Basion-bregma height	...	−3.09	−5.63	0.47	−2.33
Minimum frontal diameter ...	...	4.34	3.16	3.26	3.46
Max. bizygomatic diameter ...	...	2.41	2.53	9.23	6.33
Nasion-prosthion height	...	6.57	3.53	11.23	4.73
Basion-nasion length	...	3.50	1.60	7.70	1.20
Basion-prosthion length	...	−0.21	5.00	7.00	−3.10
Nasal height	...	−0.04	−2.09	3.01	1.31
Nasal breadth	...	0.16	−0.82	3.08	−1.02
Mean difference	...	2.73	3.84	5.79	2.66
Cranial capacity	...	42.00	−135.00	5.00	−175.00
Differences of Indices					
Length-breadth..............	...	−3.71	−8.63	−7.73	0.67
Length-height	...	−3.96	−5.43	−5.28	−1.20
Breadth-height	...	−0.60	1.70	1.30	−1.92
Upper facial	...	4.15	1.93	5.35	1.17
Nasal	...	0.67	0.47	2.77	−4.12
Gnathic	...	−2.68	4.10	0.10	−3.20
Mean difference	...	2.63	3.71	3.76	2.05

* Undeformed crania only.

divergence in indicial means, except in the case of the gnathic index. The mean difference of six indices is almost four units. It seems to be apparent that the Andamanese in no way resemble the Pecos "Pseudo-Negroids."

The Aetas of the Philippines exhibit much shorter, broader, and higher crania than the Pecos "Pseudo-Negroids"; their facial dimensions are also consistently smaller, except, curiously enough, the nasal diameters. The mean difference in measurements between the two types is 3.84 mm. The cranial capacity of the Aetas exceeds that of the Pecos type by no less than 135 cc. A glance at the index differences shows that the two types are almost equally divergent in these ratios, the mean difference of six indices being 3.71 units. We may confidently assert that the Pecos "Pseudo-Negroids" are not in the least like the Aetas, and it may be added that our type is still further from the type of the African pigmy, although no measurements are here adduced to substantiate the statement.

The Baining of New Guinea have shorter, broader, and higher heads than the Pecos "Pseudo-Negroids." Their facial diameters are also much smaller. The mean difference in cranial measurements is, however, only 2.73 mm. In indices the Baining much exceed the Pecos group in values of the cranial and length-height means; the upper facial index is much lower in the New Guinea group and the gnathic index, indicative of prognathism, is markedly higher. The mean difference between the two groups in six indices is 2.63 index units. It may be said, therefore, that the Baining are much closer to the Pecos "Pseudo-Negroids" than either the Andamanese or the Aetas, but they are nevertheless so different that no marked resemblance can be claimed.

The Bantu Fan have longer and higher heads, narrower foreheads, shorter and narrower faces than the Pecos "Pseudo-Negroids." They have a much larger average cranial capacity. The facial projection of the African group is much greater and its nasal apertures are wider. But the mean difference in cranial measurements is only 2.66 mm. Among the indices the Negro series shows a strong divergence in its greater platyrrhiny and in its more pronounced prognathism, these, of course, being the most characteristically Negro features. The mean indicial difference is 2.05 units. On the whole, it may be concluded that the Pecos "Pseudo-Negroids" show some resemblance to the Fan but these resemblances are not sufficiently close to be very convincing.

We may next select for comparison several series of Negroes measured by Dr. Aleš Hrdlička.[1] Since our methods of measurement are identical with those of Dr. Hrdlička, the comparisons are particularly reliable and a greater array of measurements and indices can be utilized. The three Negro groups of Hrdlička (British East Africa, South Africa, and American Negro), show much larger means of head-length than our Pecos "Pseudo-Negroids." The Negro heads are also somewhat higher. The Negroes also have shorter and somewhat narrower faces than our type. The basi-nasal and basi-alveolar lengths are also larger in the Negroes. But the differences in the means of 13–15 measurements between the Negro groups and our Pecos "Negroids" are: British East Africa 1.58 mm., South Africa 2.34 mm., American Negro 2.36 mm. The cranial capacities of the Negro groups are significantly larger, owing to the greater cranial diameters.

In indices it may be noted that the Negroes are more dolichocephalic, more chamaecephalic and more acrocephalic than our type. But the differences are not great. The Negroes are more platyrrhine and more brachyuranic than our group, and the American Negroes show a higher gnathic index, indicative of greater progna-

[1] Hrdlička, 1928, p. 139.

thism. The group of Negro crania from British East Africa differs, however, from our Pecos "Pseudo-Negroids" by only 1.20 units in the average of eight indices; the South Africans show a mean indicial divergence of 2.34 index units and the American Negroes 2.17 units. Of all these Negro groups the one from British East Africa most closely approaches the Pecos "Pseudo-Negroids." The crania in the British East Africa series come from Naivasha and Kenya provinces and are likely to have some Hamitic admixture, as is usually discernible in the tribes of that region. It is probably for that reason that they are more like our Pecos series, being less platyrrhine and prognathous than the more purely Negro groups. Apparently the British East African group is Negroid rather than Negro and, if this is the case, the same must be said of our Pecos series, which closely resembles it.

TABLE VIII–14. DIFFERENCES OF MEANS OF "PSEUDO–NEGROIDS" AND NEGROID CRANIA (DATA OF HRDLIČKA)

Males	"Pseudo-Negroids" (13)	British East Africa (14)	Difference	South Africa (34)	Difference	American Negro (37)	Difference
Measurements							
Glabello-occipital length	177.67 *	183.6	−5.9	189.3	−11.6	186.1	−8.4
Maximum breadth	135.0 *	133.6	1.4	135.4	−0.4	137.2	−2.2
Basion-bregma height	130.7 *	132.1	−1.4	134.7	−4.0	133.5	−2.8
Max. bizygomatic diameter .	133.8	129.7	4.1	133.4	0.4	131.3	2.5
Nasion-menton height......	118.3	...	...	116.7	1.6	117.4	0.9
Nasion-prosthion height	72.23	70.0	2.2	69.6	2.6	69.7	2.5
Basion-nasion length	101.1	100.8	0.3	104.0	−2.9	103.0	−1.9
Basion-prosthion length	100.4	101.3	−0.9	104.4	−4.0	107.0	−6.6
Orbit height	34.5	33.0	1.5	33.2	1.3	33.4	1.1
Orbit breadth	39.4	37.9	1.5	37.9	1.5	39.0	0.4
Nasal height	48.8	49.0	−0.2	48.8	0.0	49.6	−0.8
Nasal breadth	26.48	27.0	−0.5	28.2	−1.7	26.7	−0.2
External palatal length	57.7	57.3	0.4	57.3	0.4	58.4	−0.7
External palatal breadth ...	64.8	65.1	−0.3	67.0	−2.2	68.2	−3.4
Height of symphysis	36.3	...	...	35.8	0.5	35.3	1.0
Mean difference			1.58		2.34		2.36
Indices							
Length-breadth	75.7 *	72.8	2.9	71.5	4.2	73.7	2.0
Length-height	73.7 *	72.0 †	1.7	71.2 †	2.5	71.7 †	2.0
Breadth-height	97.0 *	98.9 †	−1.9	99.5 †	−2.5	99.0 †	−2.0
Total facial	88.7	...	...	87.9	0.8	90.0	1.3
Upper facial	54.2	54.5	−0.3	52.2	2.0	53.2	1.0
Mean orbital..............	88.1	87.1	1.0	87.6	0.5	85.6	2.5
Nasal	53.8	55.1	−1.3	57.8	−4.0	54.9	−1.1
External palatal	112.4	111.9	0.5	116.9	−4.5	116.6	−4.2
Gnathic	100.4	100.4 †	0.0	100.3 †	0.1	103.8 †	−3.4
Mean difference			1.20		2.34		2.17

* Undeformed crania only.
† Calculated from the means of the measurements.

In order to press this comparison of our Pecos "Pseudo-Negroid" type still further we may bring forward a series of Negro crania of several different regions measured by Crewdson-Benington.[1] Six indices are available for comparison. The means of measurements are not republished here, but it may be said that the Negro groups have longer, narrower, and higher crania, shorter faces, broader noses, and greater facial projections.

Table VIII–15 compares the means of six indices of Pecos "Pseudo-Negroids" with Zulu, Angoni, Kaffir, and Northern Negroes. The Negro groups are a little more dolichocephalic and tend somewhat more strongly toward acrocephaly. Their orbital indices are usually somewhat lower and nasal indices decidedly higher. But the mean differences in indices are very low — in every case less than two index units and in the Angoni and Northern Negro groups only 1.56 and 1.51 index units respectively. Thus the results accord with our previous comparisons of other Negro groups.

TABLE VIII–15. Differences of Means of "Pseudo–Negroids" and Various Negro Groups (Data of Crewdson–Benington)

Males Indices	"Pseudo-Negroids" (13)	Zulu (20)	Difference	Angoni (25)	Difference	Kaffir (38)	Difference	Northern Negroes (39)	Difference
Length-breadth	75.67 *	74.27	1.40	73.05	2.62	72.13	3.54	72.87	2.80
Length-height	73.67 *	75.04	− 1.37	74.25	− 0.58	72.13	1.54	74.15	− 0.48
Breadth-height	97.00 *	98.89	− 1.89	98.21	− 1.21	99.97	− 2.97	98.28	− 1.28
Mean orbital..	88.08	85.82	2.26	88.09	− 0.01	85.81	2.27	87.20	0.88
Nasal	53.71	58.05	− 4.34	58.03	− 4.32	56.33	− 2.62	55.43	− 1.72
Gnathic	100.40	100.08	0.32	101.03	− 0.63	100.09	0.31	102.31	− 1.91
Mean difference			1.93		1.56		2.21		1.51

* Undeformed crania only.

The Pecos type which has been called "Pseudo-Negroid" is certainly not Negro in the sense that it is indistinguishable from authentically Negro crania. It is widely divergent from the Negrito crania. It shows only remote resemblances to Oceanic Negro crania as typified, for example, by the Baining. On the other hand it does exhibit close resemblances in mean measurements and in proportions to a considerable number of African Negro groups which have been brought forward for purposes of comparison. But certain differences between the Pecos "Pseudo-Negroids" and almost every African Negro group regularly obtrude themselves. The African crania are always longer, higher, relatively narrower, and of considerably larger capacities. In this connection it should be recalled that the mean stature of our Pecos "Pseudo-Negroids" is estimated at only 155 cm., which is far below the stature of most African Negro groups. As head-length is correlated with stature, the small value of that diameter in the Pecos "Pseudo-Negroids" may be, to some extent, referable to factors governing size. The Negro crania in general tend to show lower orbits, shorter faces, shorter and much broader noses, and greater prognathism than the Pecos type. Our "Pseudo-Negroids" approach most closely to those Negro groups coming from parts of Africa where the "Negroes" commonly

[1] Crewdson-Benington, 1912, pp. 293–339.

show some trace of an infusion of white blood. This usually has the effect of broadening the head a little, lengthening the face, narrowing the nose, and reducing prognathism. To several of these Negroid groups the Pecos "Pseudo-Negroid" type bears close and far-reaching resemblances.

Unless we are prepared to impugn the worth of the methods of comparison here utilized we are forced to admit that the term "Negroid" is not a misnomer. Nevertheless, it should be emphasized that prognathism and platyrrhiny may be associated in crania which need not have any Negroid admixture. If, however, it is demonstrated that our Pecos "Pseudo-Negroid" type resembles the type of the African Negro more closely than it resembles other Pecos types or any other Indian types available for comparison we are then forced to the conclusion that the "Negroid" element is real.

Table VIII–16 gives the differences between the means of 29 measurements and nine indices of the Pecos "Pseudo-Negroids" and of six other morphological types distinguished in the Pecos series. There are also recorded in this table the mean differences of measurements and indices. The mean difference between the Pecos "Pseudo-Negroids" and the other types in respect to measurements varies from 2.04 mm. to 3.92 mm. Differences between the Pecos "Pseudo-Negroids" and various groups of Negro crania vary from 1.58 mm. to 2.36 mm. There is, however, no Negro group in which a similarly large array of measurements is available for comparison. Nevertheless it may be concluded with finality that the Pecos "Pseudo-Negroids" in their raw measurements differ less from the African Negroes than they do from other morphological types in the Pecos population. Similarly in nine indices the average difference between the Pecos "Negroids" and other groups varies from 3.05 index units to 5.03 index units. The deviations of our type with respect to the same indices from three groups of Negroes measured by Hrdlička, range from 1.20 to 2.34 index units. Other indicial comparisons between the Pecos Negroids and authentic Negro groups exhibit mean differences ranging from 1.51 to 2.21 index units. It is therefore apparent that our "Pseudo-Negroid" type at Pecos is much more like the type of the African Negro than like its contemporary Pecos types. It then seems impossible to deny the legitimacy of the appellation "Negroid." Further, an inspection of Table VIII–15 reveals the fact that the Pecos "Pseudo-Negroids" diverge from other Pecos types in the same measurements and indices and in the same direction as the authentic Negroes differ from the Pecos "Pseudo-Negroids." The latter are longer-headed than other Pecos types, and their crania are generally somewhat narrower and lower. Their bizygomatic diameters are smaller, with the exception of the "Basket Maker" type; their noses are shorter and broader; their basi-alveolar diameters are much greater; their palates are longer and narrower. The Pecos "Pseudo-Negroids" are somewhat more dolichocephalic than other Pecos types, excepting the "Basket Makers," less hypsicephalic, less acrocephalic, and much more platyrrhine, prognathous, and mesuranic. Authentic Negro groups accentuate these differences from non-Negroid Pecos types which the Pecos "Pseudo-Negroids" present.

TABLE VIII–16. DIFFERENCES OF MEANS OF "PSEUDO–NEGROIDS" AND OTHER PECOS TYPES

Males Measurements	"Basket Makers"	"Pseudo-Australoids"	"Plains Indians"	"Long-faced Europeans"	"Pseudo-Alpines"	"Hybrids"
Glabello-occipital length *	0.00	1.38	0.53	0.87	...	5.00
Maximum breadth *	2.17	1.57	−2.16	−7.00	...	−12.33
Basion-bregma height *	−4.33	−4.33	−7.16	−9.53	...	−6.83
Maximum circumference	−7.92	−7.01	−2.19	−8.33	−0.56	−6.52
Nasion-opisthion arc	−6.33	−7.29	0.88	−2.18	5.88	−2.00
Transverse arc	7.71	−1.46	0.60	5.90	−11.18	−19.74
Thickness of left parietal	0.06	0.02	0.62	0.20	0.44	−0.29
Mean diam. of foramen magnum	−2.65	−1.37	−2.30	−2.46	−1.25	−2.30
Minimum frontal diameter	2.46	1.37	1.81	−1.54	0.96	−2.16
Maximum bizygomatic diameter	1.12	−3.84	−5.99	−3.17	−5.09	−9.82
Nasion-menton height	−2.86	0.61	−3.04	−5.00	3.31	−3.23
Nasion-prosthion height	−1.02	1.56	−3.51	−4.44	2.48	−2.23
Orbit height, right	−0.97	1.61	−1.10	−1.18	−0.81	−1.11
Orbit height, left	−0.67	1.44	−0.62	−0.95	−0.54	−0.61
Orbit breadth, right	0.08	0.10	−0.87	−0.49	−1.04	−1.42
Orbit breadth, left	0.31	−0.33	−0.84	−0.85	−0.30	−0.90
Nasal height	−2.57	−0.37	−4.33	−3.58	−0.76	−3.06
Nasal breadth	0.26	0.20	0.31	1.85	0.70	0.44
Basion-nasion height	0.24	−0.90	−2.48	−2.50	0.30	−1.38
Basion-prosthion height	2.11	2.78	1.87	4.60	5.00	1.78
External palatal length	2.51	3.43	1.81	2.41	3.73	1.27
External palatal breadth	−2.51	0.70	−2.18	−0.78	−1.00	−1.99
Bigonial diameter	3.20	−1.40	−5.65	−2.98	−1.42	−6.62
Bicondylar width	−1.02	−4.39	−8.82	−3.39	−6.11	−10.07
Height of symphysis	0.33	0.65	1.18	0.26	2.68	−0.29
Min. breadth of ascending ramus	1.88	1.21	1.16	0.93	1.17	0.54
Height of ascending ramus	−6.58	−4.46	−4.03	−9.20	−4.53	−5.81
Condylo-symphysial length	2.25	1.33	0.46	1.15	3.40	−0.11
Mean difference	2.36	2.04	2.45	3.13	2.59	3.92
Cranial capacity	−32.50	−60.83	−58.69	−98.14	−105.83	−146.28
Cranial module	−2.40	−2.40	−3.15	−4.38	−2.80	−5.43
Indices						
Length-breadth *	0.67	−0.04	−1.76	−4.73	...	−9.66
Length-height *	−2.53	−3.16	−4.83	−5.73	...	−5.83
Breadth-height *	−3.80	−4.17	−3.83	−1.80	...	2.50
Total facial	−1.53	3.42	1.53	−1.33	6.77	3.28
Upper facial	−0.75	3.11	0.38	−1.92	4.80	2.45
Mean orbital	−2.35	4.35	0.21	−0.98	0.94	1.01
Nasal	3.02	0.50	4.72	6.99	1.84	3.73
Gnathic	3.26	4.78	5.35	7.90	5.90	4.21
External palatal	−9.55	−5.99	−7.55	−6.68	−9.91	−5.84
Mean difference	3.05	3.28	3.35	4.23	5.03	4.28

* Undeformed crania only.

"PSEUDO–AUSTRALOID" TYPE

DESCRIPTION

The "Pseudo-Australoid" type includes some crania with occipital deformation. The uncorrected mean of the cranial index is 77.27. When correction for deformation is made, this type is dolichocephalic (index 74–75). It is also hypsicephalic and acrocephalic. The cranial capacity (1335 cc.) is somewhat below the mean of the whole series. The malars are strongly projecting and the total face height is short. The facial index is euryprosopic. Orbits are low and broad, yielding a chamaeconch (microseme) index. The nose is short, broad, and platyrrhine. There is no marked facial prognathism. The external palatal measurements are moderate, giving a brachyuranic index. The mandible is broad and rather shallow.

From the standpoint of morphological observations this type is distinguished by low, narrow, and retreating frontal region and large supraorbital ridges, usually continuous from one external angular process to the other. The nasion is depressed. The skull vault is markedly scaphoid and the temporal regions very compressed. The occiput, when not artificially flattened, is moderately projecting. The nasal root is low and of medium breadth; the bridge is usually of submedium height and of medium breadth. It is usually concavo-convex, but sometimes concave. The nasal aperture is very broad; its lower borders are poorly developed and the spine is small. Orbits are low, of oblong shape, and not inclined. Malars and zygomata are strong and projecting — much larger than in the "Pseudo-Negroid" type. Although no prognathism is indicated by the alveolar (gnathic) index, alveolar prognathism is observed to be pronounced (Plate VII-1, c).

The average stature of this type is 162.5 cm.

TABLE VIII–17. MEANS OF "PSEUDO–AUSTRALOID" TYPE

Males

Measurements

Glabello-occipital length * .	176.29		...
Maximum breadth *	133.43		...
Basion-bregma height * ...	135.00		...
Maximum circumference .	499.09	±	1.88
Nasion-opisthion arc	361.67	±	2.06
Transverse arc	315.00	±	2.17
Thickness of left parietal .	5.21	±	0.11
Mean diam. of for. magnum	30.72	±	0.47
Minimum frontal diameter	94.09	±	0.93
Max. bizygomatic diameter	137.67	±	0.83
Nasion-menton height ...	117.70	±	0.84
Nasion-prosthion height ..	70.67	±	0.64
Orbit height, right	32.85	±	0.19
Orbit height, left	33.14	±	0.25
Orbit breadth, right	39.55	±	0.45
Orbit breadth, left	39.45	±	0.37
Nasal height	49.18	±	0.47
Nasal breadth	26.18	±	0.39
Basion-nasion length	102.00	±	0.48
Basion-prosthion length ..	97.62	±	0.66
External palatal length ...	54.25	±	0.44

Measurements

External palatal breadth..	64.12	±	0.78
Bigonial diameter	100.00	±	1.51
Bicondylar width	120.17	±	1.57
Height of symphysis	35.68	±	0.38
Min. breadth of asc. ramus	37.00	±	0.59
Height of ascending ramus	63.38	±	1.26
Condylo-symphysial length	104.67	±	1.05
Cranial capacity	1335.00	±	24.75
Cranial module	149.40		...

Indices

Length-breadth *	75.71		...
Length-height *	76.83		...
Breadth-height *	101.17		...
Total facial	85.25	±	0.86
Upper facial.............	51.14	±	0.52
Mean orbital	83.73	±	0.67
Nasal	53.27	±	0.65
Gnathic	95.62	±	0.63
External palatal	118.44	±	1.32

* Undeformed crania only.

COMPARISON WITH OTHER GROUPS

The "Pseudo-Australoid" type may first be compared with real Australians. Fortunately there is available for this purpose the magnificent series of 521 crania in Australian museums recently published by Hrdlička.[1] In Table VIII–18 the means of measurements and indices of Australians, Tasmanians,[1] and New Caledonians (Sarasin's data)[2] are compared with those of our Pecos "Pseudo-Australoid"

TABLE VIII–18. DIFFERENCES OF MEANS OF "PSEUDO–AUSTRALOIDS" AND
AUSTRALIAN CRANIA (DATA OF HRDLIČKA)

Males	"Pseudo-Australoids" (11)	Australians (521)	Difference	Tasmanians (22)	Difference	New Caledonians (Sarasin)	Difference
Measurements							
Glabello-occipital length....	176.29 *	189.1	−12.8	189.3	−13.0	184.2	−7.9
Maximum breadth	133.4 *	132.2	1.2	139.4	6.0	132.2	1.2
Basion-bregma height	135.0 *	133.6	1.4	134.0	1.0	139.3	−4.3
Nasion-menton height	117.7	113.7	4.0	112.1	5.6	115.9	1.8
Nasion-prosthion height	70.7	69.6	1.1	67.7	3.0	68.6	2.1
Max. bizygomatic diameter .	137.7	135.8	1.9	136.0	1.7	136.6	1.1
Basion-nasion length	102.0	103.0	−1.0	101.6	0.4	103.5	−1.5
Basion-prosthion length	97.6	106.6	−9.0	106.6	−9.0	108.9	−11.3
Orbit height	33.0	33.4	−0.4	30.8	2.2	33.0	0.0
Orbit breadth	39.5	38.9	0.6	38.3	1.2	40.0	−0.5
Nasal height	49.2	48.8	0.4	47.9	1.3	48.4	0.8
Nasal breadth	26.2	27.3	−1.1	27.1	−0.9	26.5	−0.3
External palatal length	54.2	61.9	−7.7	62.2	−8.0	60.4	−6.2
External palatal breadth ...	64.1	68.1	−4.0	69.3	−5.2	66.3	−2.2
Height of symphysis	35.7	34.4	1.3	31.4	4.3	...	...
Mean difference			3.19		4.19		2.94
Indices							
Length-breadth	75.7 *	69.9	5.8	74.1	1.6	71.9	3.8
Length-height	76.8 *	70.6 †	6.2	70.7 †	6.1	75.8	1.0
Breadth-height	101.2 *	101.1 †	0.1	96.1 †	5.1	105.3	−4.1
Total facial	85.2	84.0	1.2	83.1	2.1	85.4	−0.2
Upper facial	51.1	51.2	−0.1	49.8	1.3	50.3	0.8
Mean orbital..............	83.7	85.9	−2.2	80.3	3.4	82.6	1.1
Nasal	53.3	56.0	−2.7	56.7	−3.4	54.8	−1.5
External palatal	118.4	110.0	8.4	111.4	7.0	110.0	8.4
Gnathic	95.6	103.5 †	−7.9	104.9 †	−9.3	105.2 †	−9.6
Mean difference			3.84		4.37		3.39

* Undeformed crania only.
† Calculated from means of measurements.

type. The crania of all of these groups are longer than those of the Pecos; the Tasmanians have wider crania and the Australians and New Caledonians show narrower breadths. The New Caledonians have greater skull heights than our type. All of the Oceanic groups have shorter and narrower faces than the Pecos "Pseudo-Australoids." They also have shorter and broader noses, palates much larger in both dimensions, and lower mandibular symphyses. In 15 measurements the Aus-

[1] Hrdlička, 1928, p. 85.   [2] Sarasin, 1916–22, pp. 524–559.

tralians show a mean difference from our series of 3.19 mm. This is not indicative of any close resemblance in gross dimensions. The Tasmanians are still farther away from the Pecos "Pseudo-Australoids" with a mean difference of 4.19 mm. The New Caledonians with an average divergence of 2.94 mm. show a somewhat closer approach to the Pecos measurements.

A consideration of the cranial indices shows that the Oceanic groups are much more dolichocephalic, and in the case of the Australian and Tasmanian skulls the length-height index is much lower. The nasal indices are more platyrrhinic in the Oceanic groups. But the greatest divergences between our Pecos type and these Australasian crania lies in the marked dolichurany and prognathism of the latter; here the indicial differences are enormous. The mean differences of seven indices range from 3.39 units in the case of the New Caledonians to 4.37 units in the Tasmanians. In consideration of these metric and indicial divergences it must be concluded that there is no real affinity between our "Pseudo-Australoids" and the authentic Australians; still less do the Pecos "Pseudo-Australoids" resemble Tasmanians. Nor can it be said that the Pecos type bears more than a very superficial resemblance to the New Caledonians.

Next a comparison may be instituted between our type and the Ainu. This people, as is well known, are a short-statured dolichocephalic group presenting some facial features reminiscent of the Australians and also some traces of Mongoloid admixture. Here are available the data of Koganei[1] (Table VIII–19).

The inspection of the means of measurements shows that the Ainu have much longer, broader, and higher crania than the Pecos "Pseudo-Australoids." The cranial capacities of the Japanese aborigines are also markedly larger. The facial dimensions of the two groups show only small and insignificant differences. The mean differences of eleven measurements is 5.79 mm. The magnitude of this difference is, however, due to the inclusion in the small array of measurements of the cranial circumference and the transverse arc, in both of which measurements the Ainu largely surpass our Pecos type.

A consideration of the seven indices shows only slight differences. The Pecos type is slightly more hypsicephalic and acrocephalic, more platyrrhine and more chamaeconch. The mean difference of seven indices is only 1.40 index units. The comparison of the two types may be summarized in the statement that the Ainu show greater dimensions of the cranial vault than the Pecos "Pseudo-Australoids," closely similar facial diameters, and only slightly divergent vault and facial indices. Were it not for the greater size of the vault dimensions we should be justified in declaring the Pecos "Pseudo-Australoids" substantially identical with the Ainu. However, these discrepancies in size must not be disregarded. They are not correlated with stature because the mean stature of male Ainu is 157.9 cm.,[2] whereas the estimated stature of the Pecos "Pseudo-Australoids" is 162.5 cm. Similar deficiency in the size of the cranial vault differentiates most of the Pecos types, not only from all foreign groups, but also from most American Indian groups. There seems to have been operative in this pueblo community some force repressing the growth of the

[1] Koganei, 1893, pp. 1–104.   [2] Montadon, 1928, p. 213.

cranial vault and bringing about a submicrocephalic condition. If a close indicial similarity is evidence of racial affiliation the Pecos "Pseudo-Australoids" stand very near to the Ainu, but if the vault size be taken into consideration and the vault and face proportions disregarded there is a very wide divergence between the two types. For the present we may say merely that of the types brought into comparison with the Pecos "Pseudo-Australoids" the Ainu alone show convincing indicial similarities.

TABLE VIII–19. DIFFERENCES OF MEANS OF "PSEUDO–AUSTRALOIDS" AND AINU
(DATA OF KOGANEI)

Males

Measurements	"Pseudo-Australoids"		Ainu	Difference
Glabello-occipital length	176.29 *	...	185.0	−8.71
Maximum breadth	133.43 *	...	141.2	−7.77
Basion-bregma height	135.00 *	...	139.5	−4.50
Minimum frontal diameter	94.09 ± 0.93		96.2	−2.11
Max. bizygomatic diameter	137.67 ± 0.75		137.3	0.37
Maximum circumference	499.09 ± 1.88		522.5	−23.41
Transverse arc	315.00 ± 2.17		328.5	−13.50
Nasion-menton height	117.70 ± 0.84		118.3	−0.60
Nasion-prosthion height	70.67 ± 0.64		69.8	0.87
Nasal height	49.18 ± 0.47		50.5	−1.32
Nasal breadth	26.18 ± 0.39		25.6	0.58
Mean difference				5.79
Cranial capacity	1335.00 ± 24.75		1462.0	−127

Indices

Length-breadth	75.71 *	...	76.5	−0.79
Length-height	76.83 *	...	75.6	1.23
Breadth-height	101.17 *	...	98.8	2.37
Total facial	85.25 ± 0.86		86.2	−0.95
Upper facial	51.14 ± 0.52		50.8	0.34
Nasal	53.27 ± 0.65		50.7	2.57
Mean orbital	83.73 ± 0.67		85.3	−1.57
Mean difference				1.40

* Undeformed crania only.

For comparison with the Pecos "Pseudo-Australoids" within the American area, I have selected a group of small dolichocephalic crania from the highlands of Peru, the raw measurements of which have been published by MacCurdy.[1] Table VIII–20 records the means, differences, and probable errors. An inspection of the array of means of measurements shows that the Paucarcancha crania have notably smaller facial diameters than the Pecos type, but that the differences in vault dimensions are slight. Particularly noticeable, however, is the difference in orbits, those of the Peruvians being narrow and high, whereas our Pecos "Pseudo-Australoids" have low, broad orbits. The mean difference in seventeen measurements is 2.70 mm., a figure which is rather low. The indices show a more marked acrocephalic condition in the Peruvians, relatively shorter and broader faces, less platyrrhiny, more prognathism, and an extraordinary difference of 12.3 mm. in the orbital

[1] MacCurdy, 1923, pp. 218–329.

index. The mean difference in seven indices is 3.52 units, the most of which is due to the great divergence in the orbital index. If the differences in means of indices and measurements are considered with respect to the probable errors of such differences, it is seen that twelve of seventeen measurements show differences in excess of twice the probable error. The indices also show significant deviations. The "Pseudo-Australoid" series includes a few crania with slight occipital flattenings. If the vault measurements of the undeformed crania of the series are substituted for those of the series as a whole, the differences in vault diameters and indices are reduced to insignificance, and the mean indicial differences are reduced from 3.52 units to 3.08 units. In a general way this Peruvian series resembles the Pecos "Pseudo-Australoid" type, but not more closely than does the series of New Caledonians studied by Sarasin, the metric deviations of which from our Pecos type average 2.94 mm. and the indicial deviations 3.39 mm. Actually the Oceania group is a little more like our type than the South American group. The small faces of the Paucarcancha group and the high, narrow orbits differentiate them markedly from our Southwestern type.

TABLE VIII–20.   DIFFERENCES OF MEANS OF "PSEUDO–AUSTRALOIDS" AND PAUCARCANCHA (PERU) (DATA OF MACCURDY)

Males

Measurements	"Pseudo-Australoids"	Paucarcancha	Difference	2 p. e.
Glabello-occipital length	175.73 ± 1.12 *	177.08 ± 0.52	−1.35 ± 1.23	2.46
Maximum breadth	135.64 ± 1.19 *	133.66 ± 0.38	1.98 ± 1.25	2.50
Basion-bregma height	137.10 ± 0.75 *	136.82 ± 0.46	0.28 ± 0.88	1.76
Minimum frontal diameter	94.09 ± 0.93	91.09 ± 0.37	3.00 ± 1.00	2.00
Nasion-prosthion height	70.67 ± 0.64	67.05 ± 0.39	3.62 ± 0.76	1.52
Max. bizygomatic diameter	137.67 ± 0.83	132.63 ± 0.54	5.04 ± 0.98	1.96
Basion-nasion length................	102.00 ± 0.48	97.88 ± 0.34	4.12 ± 0.59	1.18
Basion-prosthion length	97.62 ± 0.66	95.56 ± 0.38	2.06 ± 0.76	1.52
Orbit height, right..................	32.85 ± 0.19	34.98 ± 0.16	−2.13 ± 0.25	0.50
Orbit height, left..................	33.14 ± 0.20	34.97 ± 0.17	−1.83 ± 0.26	0.52
Orbit breadth, right	39.55 ± 0.45	36.62 ± 0.14	2.93 ± 0.47	0.94
Orbit breadth, left.................	39.45 ± 0.37	36.32 ± 0.15	3.13 ± 0.41	0.82
Nasal height	49.18 ± 0.47	48.66 ± 0.24	0.52 ± 0.52	1.04
Nasal breadth	26.18 ± 0.39	24.33 ± 0.12	1.85 ± 0.41	0.82
Mean diameter of foramen magnum ..	30.72 ± 0.47	32.37 ± 0.18	−1.65 ± 0.50	1.00
Maximum circumference	499.09 ± 1.88	490.51 ± 1.29	8.58 ± 2.27	4.54
Nasion-opisthion arc	361.67 ± 2.06	363.41 ± 0.75	−1.74 ± 2.18	4.36
Mean difference			2.70	
Indices				
Length-breadth	77.27 ± 0.96 *	75.40 ± 0.25	1.87 ± 0.99	1.98
Length-height	78.20 ± 0.81 *	77.16 ± 0.28	1.04 ± 0.85	1.70
Breadth-height....................	100.40 ± 0.76 *	102.48 ± 0.32	−2.08 ± 0.80	1.60
Upper facial	51.14 ± 0.52	49.00 ...	2.14 ...	...
Mean orbital	83.73 ± 0.67	96.05 ± 0.43	−12.32 ± 0.79	1.58
Nasal	53.27 ± 0.65	50.20 ± 0.31	3.07 ± 0.72	1.44
Gnathic	95.62 ...	97.71 ...	2.09 ...	...
Mean difference...................			3.52	
Cranial capacity	1335.00 ± 24.75	1352.83 ± 8.69	−17.83 ± 11.68	23.36

* Deformed and undeformed crania to compare with deformation in some of Peruvian crania.

Any resemblances which our "Pseudo-Australoid" type bears to real Australians or Tasmanians become rather faint in the light of the foregoing analysis of the metrical and indicial differences which distinguish this pueblo group from the aborigines of Oceania. Actually I have never seen an American Indian skull which I should mistake for that of an Australian. While it would be a romantic and striking discovery to identify an American skull type with the low human forms found in the Antipodes, the results of the present investigation do not support any such identification. Of course, if one wishes, he may argue with considerable plausibility that the earlier strata of American Indians may have carried among other strains some of the Australoid blood and that these Pecos "Pseudo-Australoids" represent a segregation of such strains. Candidly, however, I do not think that our Pecos Australoids sufficiently resemble real Australians to justify even this moderate opinion. Large brow-ridges and platyrrhine noses together with short, broad faces may not always mean Australians, although they suggest such a type. The total absence of prognathism in our "Pseudo-Australoids" is a strong argument against the identification.

I am much more impressed with the resemblance of our "Pseudo-Australoids" to the Ainu, since here the indicial similarities are very marked. But if we were disposed to lay stress upon the resemblances in cranial and facial dimensions and indices which exist between the two groups, we should have to suppose that some frightful brain shrinkage had taken place among the descendants of the Ainu migrants to America. Yet, as a matter of fact, we encounter this same difficulty when we compare any of the Pecos crania with skulls of American Indians from other areas. The Pecos brain-cases are simply too small for their faces! For this reason it is very difficult to identify the Pecos with any other group whatsoever. I entertain a suspicion that some of the strains which are common to the Ainu and the Australians and which create a certain general resemblance between the two races may indeed crop out in the primitive long-headed American Indians, but in our present state of knowledge I do not see how this suspicion can be substantiated.

If we turn to the comparison of the Pecos "Pseudo-Australoids" with the other Pecos types (Table VIII–21) we note that metrically the "Pseudo-Australoids" diverge from no one of the Pecos morphological types (with the sole exception of the "Large Hybrid" type) in any such marked degree as they diverge from any of the foreign types brought forward for comparison. In measurements the "Pseudo-Australoid" type differs in the mean from the "Basket Maker" type by 1.75 mm. only, from the "Pseudo-Negroid" type by 2.04 mm., from the "Plains" type by 2.21 mm. In indices, however, it most closely resembles the "Plains" type and diverges widely from the "Pseudo-Negroid" group. It somewhat resembles the "Pseudo-Alpine" group in the shortness and breadth of its face.

TABLE VIII–21.   DIFFERENCES OF MEANS OF "PSEUDO–AUSTRALOIDS" AND
OTHER PECOS TYPES

Males

Measurements	"Basket-Makers"	"Pseudo-Negroids"	"Plains Indians"	"Long-faced Europeans"	"Pseudo-Alpines"	"Hybrids"
Glabello-occipital length *	−1.38	−1.38	−0.85	−0.51	...	3.62
Maximum breadth *	0.60	−1.57	−3.73	−8.57	...	−13.90
Basion-bregma height *	0.00	4.33	−2.83	−5.20	...	−2.50
Maximum circumference	−0.91	7.01	4.82	−1.32	6.45	0.49
Nasion-opisthion arc	0.96	7.29	8.17	5.11	13.17	5.29
Transverse arc	6.25	−1.46	−0.86	−7.36	−12.64	−21.20
Thickness of left parietal	0.04	−0.02	0.60	0.18	0.42	−0.31
Mean diam. of foramen magnum	−1.28	1.37	−0.93	−1.09	0.12	−0.93
Minimum frontal diameter	1.09	−1.37	0.44	−2.91	−0.41	−3.53
Maximum bizygomatic diameter	4.96	3.84	−2.15	0.67	−1.25	−5.98
Nasion-menton height	−3.47	−0.61	−3.65	−5.61	2.70	−3.84
Nasion-prosthion height	−2.58	−1.56	−5.07	−6.00	0.92	−3.79
Orbit height, right	−2.58	−1.61	−2.71	−2.79	−2.42	−2.72
Orbit height, left	2.11	−1.44	−2.06	−2.39	−1.98	−2.05
Orbit breadth, right	−0.02	−0.10	−0.97	−0.59	−1.14	−1.52
Orbit breadth, left	0.64	0.33	−0.51	−0.52	0.03	−0.57
Nasal height	−2.20	0.37	−3.96	−3.21	−0.39	−2.69
Nasal breadth	0.06	−0.20	0.11	1.65	0.50	0.24
Basion-nasion length	1.14	0.90	−1.58	−1.60	1.20	−0.48
Basion-prosthion length	−0.67	−2.78	−0.91	1.82	2.22	−1.00
External palatal length	−0.92	−3.43	−1.62	−1.02	0.30	−2.16
External palatal breadth	−3.21	−0.70	−2.88	−1.48	−1.70	−2.69
Bigonial diameter	4.60	1.40	−4.25	−1.58	−0.02	−5.22
Bicondylar width	3.37	4.39	−4.43	1.00	−1.72	−5.68
Height of symphysis	−0.32	−0.65	0.53	−0.39	2.03	−0.94
Min. breadth of ascending ramus	0.67	−1.21	−0.05	−0.28	−0.04	−0.67
Height of ascending ramus	−2.12	4.46	0.43	−4.74	0.07	−1.35
Condylo-symphysial length	0.92	−1.33	−0.87	−0.18	2.07	−1.44
Mean difference	1.75	2.04	2.21	2.49	2.24	3.46
Cranial capacity	28.33	60.83	2.14	−37.31	−45.00	−85.45
Cranial module	0.00	2.40	−0.75	1.98	−0.40	−3.03

Indices

	"Basket-Makers"	"Pseudo-Negroids"	"Plains Indians"	"Long-faced Europeans"	"Pseudo-Alpines"	"Hybrids"
Length-breadth *	0.71	0.04	−1.72	−4.69	...	−9.62
Height-length *	0.63	3.16	−1.67	−2.57	...	−2.67
Height-breadth *	0.37	4.17	0.34	2.37	...	6.67
Total facial	−4.95	−3.42	−1.89	−4.75	3.35	−0.14
Upper facial	−3.86	−3.11	−2.73	−5.03	1.69	−0.66
Mean orbital	−6.70	−4.35	−4.14	−5.33	−3.41	−3.34
Nasal	2.52	−0.50	4.22	6.49	1.34	3.23
Gnathic	−1.52	−4.78	0.57	3.12	1.12	−0.57
External palatal	−3.56	5.99	−1.56	−0.69	−3.92	0.15
Mean difference	2.76	3.28	2.09	3.89	2.47	3.00

* Undeformed crania only.

"PLAINS INDIAN" TYPE

DESCRIPTION

The group of skulls assigned to the "Plains" type is one of the most numerous in our series. Its undeformed members are mesocephalic (77.4) and its artificially deformed crania, which are in the majority, yield also a mesocephalic mean when correction formulae are applied. Breadth is moderate, as is also length, and the basion-bregma height is above the mean of the series. These crania are strongly hypsicephalic and also tend toward acrocephaly. The mean of cranial capacity is about 1333 cc. and the cranial module is just at the mean of the entire series (150).

TABLE VIII–22.　MEANS OF "PLAINS INDIAN" TYPE

Males

Measurements

Glabello-occipital length *	177.14	...	
Maximum breadth *	137.16	...	
Basion-bregma height *	137.83	...	
Maximum circumference	494.27	±	1.95
Nasion-opisthion arc	353.50	±	2.01
Transverse arc	315.86	±	1.57
Thickness of left parietal	4.61	±	0.11
Mean diam. of for. mag.	31.65	±	0.25
Minimum frontal diameter	93.65	±	0.63
Max. bizygomatic diameter	139.82	±	0.58
Nasion-menton height	121.35	±	0.86
Nasion-prosthion height	75.74	±	0.60
Orbit height, right	35.56	±	0.21
Orbit height, left	35.20	±	0.21
Orbit breadth, right	40.52	±	0.19
Orbit breadth, left	39.96	±	0.22
Nasal height	53.14	±	0.34
Nasal breadth	26.07	±	0.21
Basion-nasion length	103.58	±	0.50
Basion-prosthion length	98.53	±	0.44
External palatal length	55.87	±	0.35

Measurements

External palatal breadth	67.00	±	0.46
Bigonial diameter	104.25	±	0.80
Bicondylar width	124.60	±	0.82
Height of symphysis	35.15	±	0.48
Min. breadth of asc. ramus	37.05	±	0.37
Height of ascending ramus	62.95	±	0.46
Condylo-symphysial length	105.54	±	0.61
Cranial capacity	1332.86	±	17.67
Cranial module	150.15	±	0.55

Indices

Length-breadth *	77.43	...	
Length-height *	78.50	...	
Breadth-height *	100.83	...	
Total facial	87.14	±	0.61
Upper facial	53.87	±	0.34
Mean orbital	87.87	±	0.66
Nasal	49.05	±	0.60
Gnathic	95.05	±	0.41
External palatal	120.00	±	1.01

* Undeformed crania only.

Malars are very prominent and the face is of somewhat more than average length (121 mm.). The total facial index is mesoprosopic (87.1). The upper facial height is relatively great (75.7 mm.) and the index is in the upper ranges of the mesene category (53.87). Orbits are rather large, inclining toward hypsiconchy (mean orbital index 87.87). The nasal skeleton is of more than average length and of moderate breadth. The nasal index is mesorrhine (49.05). The cranio-facial base is long, but there is little facial protrusion. The palate is of moderate length, but somewhat broad, yielding a brachyuranic index (120). The gonial angles are flaring and the bicondylar width is large.

The frontal region in the "Plains" type is usually rather low and of medium breadth, but oftener narrow than wide. It is generally receding. The temporal regions tend to be flat or compressed. Brow-ridges are of medium size or larger, and of all types. The continuous type (Type 3) occurs most frequently. Usually the nasion depression is absent or slight. The nasal bridge is of medium breadth or narrow; its height is submedium or medium. The profile of the nasal bones is generally concavo-convex. The nasal aperture is usually of medium breadth, but sometimes wide. Lower borders of the nasal aperture and the nasal spine show poor development. Orbits are somewhat large and often strongly inclined. Malars are as a rule very projecting and zygomata robust. Suborbital fossae in this type are prevalently deep and alveolar prognathism is moderate.

The "Plains" type is not as primitive as any of the three long-headed types and shows characteristics intermediate between them and the brachycephals. The stature (163.7) is higher than that of any other type except the "Large Hybrids."

COMPARISON WITH OTHER GROUPS

It seems unnecessary to look outside of the American area for crania with which to compare our "Plains" type. These skulls are typically and unmistakably Indian, with jutting malars and powerful jaws. The large number of cranial measurements published by Hrdlička in the Catalogue of Human Crania in the United States National Museum Collection, [1] provides ample comparative material.

Table VIII–23 gives the means and differences of those series which most closely resemble our type. As usual the vault dimensions of the Pecos group are inferior. Closest to our type is the series of miscellaneous Algonkin crania from Illinois. The difference in ten measurements is only 1.7 mm. and the average indicial difference (seven indices) is only 1.03 units. The Illinois crania have larger vaults and a superior average capacity, but otherwise present only slight and insignificant differences. A group from Kentucky deviates more strongly from the Pecos "Plains" type, particularly because of its smaller facial dimensions and relatively shorter and broader face. From this group the mean differences of the "Plains" type are in the case of measurements 2.74 mm. and in indices 1.81 units.

None of the Siouan groups closely resembles our "Plains" type. The Arikara, who are allied to the Sioux, have been selected as the most similar group. The Arikara have longer, broader, and much lower crania than the Pecos "Plains" group. In general the Siouan crania are differentiated from our type by much lower vault heights, as well as by larger capacities. None of the Sioux are acrocephalic. The mean differences between Arikara and our type are in measurements 2.08 mm. and in indices 2.53 units. The Alaskan Eskimo are rather nearer to the Pecos "Plains" than are the Sioux. The term "Plains" is a poor selection for the type as far as the Sioux are concerned, and there are unfortunately no Blackfoot crania available. But the Piegan, who are Algonkin, are more like the Sioux than like our "Plains" types. No adequate series of Caddoan crania can be adduced for comparative purposes.

This Pecos type is unmistakably allied with the Eastern dolicho-hypsicephals

---

[1] Hrdlička, 1924, p. 26; 1927, pp. 46, 77.

and especially those which have been modified in the direction of a diminished head-length by brachycephalic admixture.

I regard our "Plains" type, which is mesocephalic, as a group derived by admixture of the fundamental Southwestern dolichocephals — the "Basket Maker," "Pseudo-Negroid," and "Pseudo-Australoid" groups — with some of the Mongoloid brachycephals. From this admixture resulted, in this type, mesocephaly and a pronounced broadening of the face. The "Plains" type is thus transitional between our archaic dolichocephals and the brachycephalic Mongoloid types.

In Table VIII–24 the means of the "Plains" type (with undeformed cranial diameters) are set against a number of small groups of Indian crania measured by Hrdlička.[1] The facial dimensions of the Pecos type accord well with those of most of the other Indian groups, but as in our other types, the diameters of the cranial vault are so much smaller in the Pecos as to differentiate them strongly from otherwise similar Indian groups. But taking the dimensions and proportions of the face alone, the "Plains" type may be duplicated in almost any of the eastern Indian groups.

Table VIII–25 gives the differences in means and the mean differences of the "Plains" type from other Pecos types. Evidently this type resembles most closely the "Long-faced European" and "Basket Maker" types, although from the last named it diverges most markedly in gross dimensions.

TABLE VIII–23. DIFFERENCES OF MEANS OF "PLAINS INDIANS" AND OTHER INDIAN GROUPS (DATA OF HRDLIČKA)

Males Measurements	"Plains Indians"	Illinois (30)	Difference	Kentucky (34)	Difference	Arikara (53)	Difference	Alaskan Eskimo (27)	Difference
Glabello-occipital lgth.	177.1*	183.0	−5.9	177.0	0.1	182.8	−5.7	182.9	−5.8
Maximum breadth	137.2*	139.1	−1.9	135.8	1.4	142.5	−5.3	139.0	−1.8
Basion-bregma height .	137.8*	142.1	−4.3	139.5	−1.7	134.6	3.2	137.6	0.2
Max. bizygomatic diam.	139.8	140.5	−0.7	136.0	3.8	141.5	−1.7	141.0	−1.2
Nasion-menton height .	121.4	123.4	−2.0	115.7	5.7	122.1	−0.7	128.0	−6.6
Nasion-prosthion height	75.7	74.9	0.8	70.4	5.3	76.0	−0.3	75.3	0.4
Mean orbit height.....	35.4	35.2	0.2	32.6	2.8	36.4	−1.0	36.5	−1.1
Mean orbit breadth ...	40.2	39.8	0.4	38.1	2.1	39.9	0.3	40.2	0.0
Nasal height	53.1	53.3	−0.2	50.9	2.2	55.6	−2.5	54.2	−1.1
Nasal breadth	26.1	25.5	0.6	23.8	2.3	26.2	−0.1	24.7	1.4
Mean difference.......			1.70		2.74		2.08		1.96
Cranial capacity	1333.0	1499.0	−166.0	1432.0	−99.0	1485.0	−152.0	1466.0	−133.0
Cranial module	150.2	154.8	−4.6	151.0	−0.8	153.3	−3.1	153.2	−3.0
Indices									
Length-breadth	77.4*	76.0	1.4	76.7	0.7	77.9	−0.5	76.0	1.4
Length-height	78.5*	77.6†	0.9	78.8†	−0.3	73.8†	4.7	75.2†	3.3
Breadth-height	100.8*	102.2†	−1.4	102.7†	−1.9	94.4†	6.4	99.0†	1.8
Total facial	87.1	88.7	−1.6	84.7	2.4	86.1	1.0	91.9	−4.8
Upper facial	53.9	53.5	0.4	51.7	2.2	53.7	0.2	53.7	0.2
Mean orbital	87.9	88.5	−0.6	84.9	3.0	90.9	−3.0	92.9	−5.0
Nasal................	49.0	48.1	0.9	46.8	2.2	47.1	1.9	45.8	3.2
Mean difference.......			1.03		1.81		2.53		2.81

* Undeformed crania only.   † Calculated from means of measurements.

[1] Hrdlička, 1916, pp. 22–31, 110–126; 1922, p. 95.

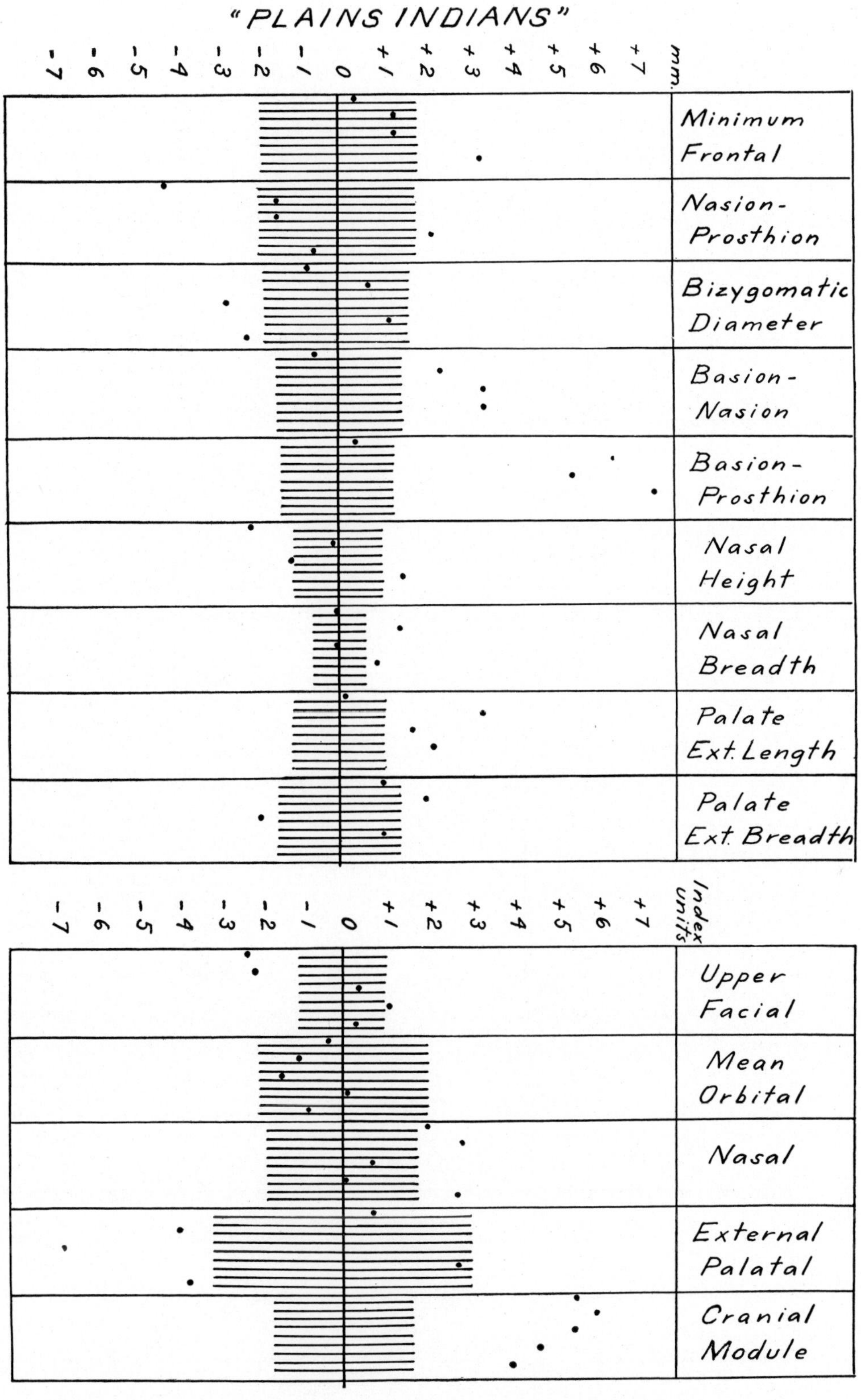

FIG. VIII–3. MEANS OF MEASUREMENTS AND INDICES OF VARIOUS EASTERN INDIAN GROUPS PLOTTED AGAINST MEANS OF PECOS 'PLAINS INDIAN' TYPE.

In each compartment from left to right: (1) Munsee; (2) New York; (3) Massachusetts; (4) Southeastern Canada; (5) Iroquois

TABLE VIII–24. DIFFERENCES OF MEANS OF "PLAINS INDIANS" AND EASTERN INDIAN GROUPS (DATA OF HRDLIČKA)

Males

Measurements	"Plains Indians"	Delaware Munsee (7-8)	Diff.	New York (2-17)	Diff.	Mass. (7-12)	Diff.	S.E. Canada (4-14)	Diff.	Iroquois (14-32)	Diff.	Florida Brachys (69)	Diff.	Florida Dolichos (40)	Diff.	Seminoles (11)	Diff.
Glabello-occipital length	177.14*	190.5	-13.36	...	...	...	...	...	...	...	...	178.7	-1.56	182.4	-5.26	179.1	-1.96
Maximum breadth	137.16*	141.0	-3.84	...	...	...	...	...	...	...	...	147.1	-9.94	142.0	-4.84	138.0	-0.84
Basion-bregma height	137.83*	139.0	-1.17	...	...	...	...	...	...	...	...	141.3	-3.47	142.3	-4.47	138.9	-1.07
Minimum frontal diameter	93.65	94.0	-0.35	95.0	-1.35	95.0	-1.35	97.0	-3.35	...	...	...	...	...	...	...	...
Nasion-menton height	121.35	121.5	-0.15	...	...	...	...	...	...	...	...	126.4	-5.05	123.0	-1.65	...	...
Nasion-prosthion height	75.74	71.5	4.24	74.0	1.74	74.0	1.74	78.0	-2.26	74.5	1.24	74.9	0.84	74.0	1.74	71.0	4.74
Max. bizygomatic diameter	139.82	139.0	0.82	140.5	-0.68	137.0	2.82	141.0	-1.18	137.5	2.32	142.8	-2.98	139.6	0.22	135.0	4.82
Basion-nasion length	103.58	103.0	0.58	106.0	-2.42	107.0	-3.42	107.0	-3.42	...	...	...	...	...	...	...	...
Basion-prosthion length	98.53	99.0	-0.47	105.0	-6.47	104.0	-5.47	106.0	-7.47	...	...	...	...	...	...	...	...
Nasal height	53.14	51.0	2.14	53.0	0.14	52.0	1.14	54.6	-1.46	...	...	52.9	0.24	52.2	0.94	51.8	1.34
Nasal breadth	26.07	26.0	0.07	27.5	-1.43	26.0	0.07	27.0	-0.93	...	...	24.8	1.27	24.8	1.27	26.2	-0.13
External palatal length	55.87	56.0	-0.13	59.2	-3.33	57.5	-1.63	58.0	-2.13	...	...	...	...	...	...	...	...
External palatal breadth	67.00	68.0	-1.00	69.0	-2.00	65.0	2.00	68.0	-1.00	...	...	...	...	...	...	...	...
Mean difference			2.18		2.17		2.18		2.58		1.78		3.17		2.55		2.13
Indices																	
Length-breadth	77.43*	73.9	3.53	...	...	...	...	...	...	...	...	82.4	-4.97	77.9	-0.47	77.0	0.43
Length-height	78.50*	73.1	5.40	...	...	...	...	...	...	...	...	79.3	-0.80	78.5	0.00	77.6	0.90
Breadth-height	100.83*	98.9	1.93	...	...	...	...	...	...	...	...	96.6	4.23	100.8	-0.03	100.7	-0.13
Total facial	87.14	87.6	-0.46	...	...	...	...	...	...	...	...	88.0	-0.86	87.9	-0.76	...	...
Upper facial	53.87	51.5	2.37	51.7	2.17	54.3	-0.43	55.2	-1.33	54.2†	-0.33	52.5	1.37	52.0	1.87	52.5	1.37
Mean orbital	87.87	87.5	0.37	86.8	1.07	86.3	1.57	87.8	0.07	87.0	0.87	...	...	...	...	...	...
Nasal	49.05	51.1	-2.05	51.8	-2.75	49.7	-0.65	49.1	0.05	51.7	-2.65	47.0	2.05	47.6	1.45	50.6	-7.55
External palatal	120.00	120.7	-0.70	116.0	4.00	113.2	6.80	117.3	2.70	116.2	3.80	...	...	...	...	...	...
Mean difference			2.10		2.50		2.36		1.04		1.91		2.38		0.76		0.88
Cranial module	150.15	155.6	5.50	156.2	6.00	155.6	5.45	154.8	4.65								

* Undeformed crania only.   † Index calculated from means of measurements.

TABLE VIII–25. DIFFERENCES OF MEANS OF "PLAINS INDIANS" AND OTHER
PECOS TYPES

Males

Measurements	"Basket Makers"	"Pseudo-Negroids"	"Pseudo-Australoids"	"Long-faced Europeans"	"Pseudo-Alpines"	"Large Hybrids"
Glabello-occipital length *	−0.53	−0.53	0.85	0.34	...	4.47
Maximum breadth *	4.33	2.16	3.73	−4.84	...	−10.17
Basion-bregma height *	2.83	7.16	2.83	−2.37	...	0.33
Maximum circumference	−5.73	2.19	−4.82	−6.14	1.63	−4.33
Nasion-opisthion arc	−7.21	−0.88	−8.17	−3.06	5.00	−2.88
Transverse arc	7.11	−0.60	0.86	−6.50	−11.78	−20.34
Thickness of left parietal	−0.56	−0.62	−0.60	−0.42	−0.18	−0.91
Mean diam. of foramen magnum	−0.35	2.30	0.93	−0.16	1.05	0.00
Minimum frontal diameter	0.65	−1.81	−0.44	−3.35	−0.85	−3.97
Maximum bizygomatic diameter	7.11	5.99	2.15	2.82	0.90	−3.83
Nasion-menton height	0.18	3.04	3.65	−1.96	6.35	−0.19
Nasion-prosthion height	2.49	3.51	5.07	−0.93	5.99	1.28
Orbit height, right	0.13	1.10	2.71	−0.08	0.29	−0.01
Orbit height, left	−0.05	0.62	2.06	−0.33	0.08	0.01
Orbit breadth, right	0.95	0.87	0.97	0.38	−0.17	−0.55
Orbit breadth, left	1.15	0.84	0.51	−0.01	0.54	−0.06
Nasal height	1.76	4.33	3.96	0.75	3.57	1.27
Nasal breadth	−0.05	−0.31	−0.11	1.54	0.39	0.13
Basion-nasion length	2.72	2.48	1.58	−0.02	2.78	1.10
Basion-prosthion length	0.24	−1.87	0.91	2.73	3.13	−0.09
External palatal length	0.70	−1.81	1.62	0.60	1.92	−0.54
External palatal breadth	−0.33	2.18	2.88	1.40	1.18	0.19
Bigonial diameter	8.85	5.65	4.25	2.67	4.23	−0.97
Bicondylar width	7.80	8.82	4.43	5.43	2.71	−1.25
Height of symphysis	−0.85	−1.18	−0.53	0.92	1.50	−1.47
Min. breadth of ascending ramus	0.72	−1.16	0.05	−0.23	0.01	−0.62
Height of ascending ramus	−2.55	4.03	−0.43	−5.17	−0.50	−1.78
Condylo-symphysial length	1.79	−0.46	0.87	0.69	2.94	−0.57
Mean difference	2.49	2.45	2.21	1.99	2.39	2.26
Cranial capacity	26.19	58.69	−2.14	−39.45	−47.14	−87.59
Cranial module	0.75	3.15	0.75	−1.23	0.35	−2.28

Indices

	"Basket Makers"	"Pseudo-Negroids"	"Pseudo-Australoids"	"Long-faced Europeans"	"Pseudo-Alpines"	"Large Hybrids"
Length-breadth *	2.43	1.76	1.72	−2.97	...	−7.90
Length-height *	2.30	4.83	1.67	−0.90	...	−1.00
Breadth-height *	0.03	3.83	−0.34	2.03	...	6.33
Total facial	−3.06	−1.53	1.89	−2.86	5.24	1.75
Upper facial	−1.13	−0.38	2.73	−2.30	4.42	2.07
Mean orbital	−2.56	−0.21	4.14	−1.19	0.73	0.80
Nasal	−1.70	−4.72	−4.22	2.27	−2.88	−0.99
Gnathic	−2.09	−5.35	−0.57	2.55	0.55	−1.14
External palatal	−2.00	7.55	1.56	0.87	−2.36	1.71
Mean difference	1.92	3.35	2.09	1.99	2.70	2.63

* Undeformed crania only.

"LONG–FACED EUROPEAN" TYPE

DESCRIPTION

The "Long-faced European" type consists of crania which, when undeformed, have a mean length-breadth index of 80.4. Deformed crania of this group yield a mean of 82.8 and, when correction is made, of 79.8. It is evident therefore that the group is on the lower border of brachycephaly. The corrected length-height index

TABLE VIII–26.　MEANS OF "LONG–FACED EUROPEAN" TYPE

Males

Measurements				Measurements		
Glabello-occipital length * .	176.80	...		External palatal breadth ..	65.60 ±	0.57
Maximum breadth *	142.00	...		Bigonial diameter	101.58 ±	1.37
Basion-bregma height * ...	140.20	...		Bicondylar width	119.17 ±	1.43
Maximum circumference ..	500.41 ±	2.41		Height of symphysis	36.07 ±	0.55
Nasion-opisthion arc	356.56 ±	1.97		Min. breadth of asc. ramus	37.28 ±	0.54
Transverse arc	322.36 ±	2.34		Height of ascending ramus	68.12 ±	0.79
Thickness of left parietal..	5.03 ±	0.16		Condylo-symphysial length	104.85 ±	0.92
Mean diam. of for. mag. ..	31.81 ±	0.31		Cranial capacity	1372.31 ±	16.95
Minimum frontal diameter	97.00 ±	0.77		Cranial module	151.38 ±	0.65
Max. bizygomatic diameter	137.00 ±	0.77				
Nasion-menton height	123.31 ±	1.51		Indices		
Nasion-prosthion height ..	76.67 ±	0.91		Length-breadth *	80.40	...
Orbit height, right	35.64 ±	0.27		Length-height *	79.40	...
Orbit height, left	35.53 ±	0.26		Breadth-height *	98.80	...
Orbit breadth, right	40.14 ±	0.36		Total facial	90.00 ±	1.00
Orbit breadth, left	39.97 ±	0.38		Upper facial.............	56.17 ±	0.63
Nasal height	52.39 ±	0.50		Mean orbital	89.06 ±	0.91
Nasal breadth	24.53 ±	0.25		Nasal	46.78 ±	0.55
Basion-nasion length	103.60 ±	0.67		Gnathic	92.50 ±	0.67
Basion-prosthion length ..	95.80 ±	0.56		External palatal	119.13 ±	1.61
External palatal length ...	55.27 ±	0.51				

* Undeformed crania only.

averages between 78.4 and 79.4, and the breadth-height index means for undeformed and corrected deformed crania are 98.8 and 97.9 respectively. The group is therefore hypsicephalic and verging upon acrocephaly. The average cranial capacity (1372 cc.) is considerably above the mean of the series. The minimum frontal diameter is large. The face is somewhat below the group average in breadth, being considerably narrower than that which prevails in the "Pseudo-Alpine," "Plains," and "Large Hybrid" types. The total height of the face (123.3) is the greatest in the Pecos series, as is also the upper facial height (76.7 mm.). The facial index is both leptoprosopic and leptene. The term "long-faced" is amply justified. Orbits are high, yielding a hypsiconch or megaseme index. The nose is not as long as in the "Plains" type but is much narrower. The mean nasal index (46.8) is leptorrhine. The cranio-facial base is the longest of the group (basion-nasion 103.6 mm.) but the gnathic index yields the lowest value of the Pecos series (92.5), so that the type may be said to be hyperorthognathous. The external palatal dimensions are those of the series at large, giving a brachyuranic index (119.1). The mandible is of moderate breadth and is otherwise not remarkable except for its long ascending ramus, which surpasses that of any other group.

The "Long-faced European" type usually has a forehead of medium height and of pronounced breadth. The slope of the frontal region is prevailingly moderate but sometimes marked. The temporal region is of medium fullness in about half of the group and flat or compressed in the rest. Supraorbital ridges are prevalently of medium size and of the divided type. The nasion depression is submedium or absent. The nasal bridge is usually of medium height and breadth, but high nasal bridges occur more frequently in this type than in any other. Concavo-convex noses are the mode, but all other types are found. The breadth of the nasal aperture is medium or, not infrequently, small. Lower borders, as in most other types at Pecos, are somewhat dull in most of the cases, and the nasal spines show only moderate development. Orbits are not especially characteristic in size or shape or inclination. Malars are usually medium but more often small than in other types. Zygomata are less robust than in other Pecos Indians. Suborbital fossae are commonly shallow, but of medium depth and deep in some cases. Alveolar prognathism is generally slight.

This type was called "European" because of its long "horse face," lack of malar prominence, and because of a more leptorrhine and higher bridged nose than is usually associated with Mongoloid types. The mental eminence of the chin region is often well developed in this group.

COMPARISON WITH OTHER GROUPS

The type called "Long-faced European" is disharmonic. To a small brachycephalic and hypsicephalic brain-case is attached a moderately broad and extremely long face with a leptorrhine nasal aperture and with no prognathism. While the face in this type strongly suggests the Northern European, there is of course no such combination with a small brachycephalic brain-case in that area with the possible exception of the so-called Frisian type of skull. But the Frisian type is markedly chamaecephalic and our Pecos type is strongly hypsicephalic. I am now convinced that the "European" type at Pecos really is quite non-European. At any rate I am unable to find any group of European crania which presents any detailed resemblances to it.

One thinks of the combination of a small brachycephalic, hypsicephalic brain-case and a long, narrow face as being particularly characteristic of the Armenoid or Near Eastern type of skull. For this reason I have brought forward such Armenian series as I have been able to secure for comparative purposes — a number of very small groups studied by Chantre.[1] Table VIII-27 gives these comparisons in detail. In this table I have disregarded the occipital deformation found in the Pecos type since it is probable that similar deformations occur in the Armenian and Kurdish groups. All of the Near Eastern groups have much smaller skull heights

[1] Chantre, 1895, pp. 72–73.

TABLE VIII–27. DIFFERENCES OF MEANS OF "LONG–FACED EUROPEANS" AND CRANIA OF ARMENOID TYPE (DATA OF CHANTRE)

Males	"Long-faced Europeans"	Armenians (5)	Diff.	Armenians (5)	Diff.	Armenians (6)	Diff.	Armenians (6)	Diff.	Kurds (6)	Diff.
Measurements											
Glabello-occipital length, ...	172.7*	173	-0.3	170	2.7	165	7.7	164	8.7	175	-2.3
Maximum breadth	141.6*	144	-2.4	146	-4.4	138	3.6	142	-0.4	143	-1.4
Basion-bregma height	141.7*	136	5.7	133	8.7	130	11.7	133	8.7	132	9.7
Minimum frontal diameter .	97.0	98	-1.0	102	-5.0	96	1.0	93	4.0	94	3.0
Maximum circumference	500.4	509	-8.6	520	-19.6	488	12.4	483	17.4	500	0.4
Transverse arc	322.4	322	0.4	332	-9.6	320	2.4	332	-9.6	322	0.4
Max. bizygomatic diameter .	137.0	132	5.0	130	7.0	128	9.0	128	9.0	131	6.0
Nasion-prosthion height	76.7	78	-1.3	72	4.7	68	8.7	73	3.7	75	1.7
Nasal height	52.4	59	-6.6	52	0.4	48	4.4	52	0.4	55	-2.6
Nasal breadth	24.5	24	0.5	22	2.5	24	0.5	24	0.5	26	-1.5
Orbital height	35.6	37	-1.4	40	-4.4	32	3.6	35	0.6	34	1.6
Orbital breadth	40.0	40	0.0	42	-2.0	36	4.0	38	2.0	39	1.0
Mean difference			2.77		5.92		5.75		5.42		2.63
Cranial capacity	1372.0	...	...	...	...	1344.0	28.0	1411.0	-39.0	1455	-83.0
Cranial module	151.4	151	0.40	149.6	1.80	144.3	7.1	146.3	5.1	150	1.4
Indices											
Length-breadth............	82.12*	83.23	-1.11	85.88	-3.76	83.63	-1.51	86.68	-4.56	81.71	0.41
Length-height.............	82.31*	78.61	3.70	80.59	1.72	78.78	3.53	81.09	1.22	75.42	6.89
Breadth-height............	100.54*	94.44	6.10	93.93	6.61	94.20	6.34	93.65	6.89	92.30	8.24
Upper facial	56.17	59.54†	-3.37	55.38†	-0.79	53.13†	3.04	57.03†	-0.86	57.25†	-1.08
Nasal	46.78	40.68	6.10	46.15	0.63	50.00	-3.22	46.15	0.63	47.27	-0.49
Nasal orbital	89.06	92.50	-3.44	95.24	-6.18	88.89	0.17	92.10	-3.04	87.17	1.89
Mean difference			3.97		3.28		2.97		2.87		3.17

* Deformed and undeformed crania used to compare with deformation in Armenoid crania.
† Calculated from means of measurements.

than the Pecos type and much smaller bizygomatic diameters. The least mean difference is 2.63 mm. This obtains between the half-dozen Kurdish skulls and the Pecos group. The Armenian groups differ more strongly from our Southwestern type. Indices show a marked divergence in the breadth-height means, the Near Eastern skulls falling six to eight index units below our type. The mean indicial divergences range from 2.87 to 3.97 units. We may therefore conclude that, in spite of the fact that both groups are brachycephalic, hypsicephalic, leptoprosopic and

TABLE VIII–28. DIFFERENCES OF MEANS OF "LONG–FACED EUROPEANS" AND DZUNGARIANS OF KULJA, EASTERN TURKESTAN (DATA OF QUATREFAGES AND HAMY)

Males

Measurements	"Long-faced Europeans"	"Dzungarians" (23)	Difference
Glabello-occipital length	176.8 *	179	−2.2
Maximum breadth	142.0 *	140	2.0
Basion-bregma height	140.2 *	143	−2.8
Maximum circumference	500.4	513	−12.6
Transverse arc	322.4	305	17.4
Mean diameter foramen magnum	31.8	31.5	.3
Minimum frontal diameter	97.0	92	5.0
Maximum bizygomatic daimeter	137.0	131	6.0
Nasion-prosthion height	76.7	76	0.7
Orbit, height	35.5	36	−0.5
Orbit, breadth	40.0	38	2.0
Nasal height	52.4	55	−2.6
Nasal breadth	24.5	26	−1.5
Basion-nasion length	103.6	102	1.6
External palatal length	55.3	54	1.3
Mean difference			3.9

Indices

Length-breadth	80.4 *	78.2	2.2
Length-height	79.4 *	79.9	−0.5
Breadth-height	98.8 *	97.7	1.1
Upper facial	56.2	58.0 †	−1.8
Mean orbital	89.1	94.7	−5.6
Nasal	46.8	47.3	−0.5
Cranial module	151.4	154.0 †	−2.6
Mean difference			2.0

* Undeformed crania only.   † Calculated from means of measurements.

leptorrhine, resemblances are not sufficiently close to warrant any inference of relationship. It is notable, however, that among these Armenians and Kurds we have at last found a cranial type, which, like the Pecos types, has a small brain-case associated with a large face.

Table VIII–28 compares the means of the "Long-faced European" type with those of a series of 23 Dzungarian crania from Kulja in Eastern Turkestan.[1] The latter are probably of mixed Mongoloid origin. They have longer, narrower, and higher crania than our Pecos type, with somewhat greater vault diameters except the minimum frontal, which is far below that of the "Long-faced Europeans."

[1] Quatrefages and Hamy, 1882, p. 434.

Their faces are considerably narrower than those of our type and the orbits are relatively higher and narrower. The mean difference of 16 measurements of the two groups is 3.9 mm., which is rather large. But the mean difference of seven indices is only 2.00 units. This indicates a close similarity in proportions. At any rate this Turkestan people resembles the Pecos type much more closely than do Kurds or Armenians.

Table VIII–29 brings forward for comparison the large series of St. Lawrence Island Eskimo and the large Mongol series measured by Hrdlička.[1] Both of these

TABLE VIII–29. DIFFERENCES OF MEANS OF "LONG–FACED EUROPEANS" AND CRANIA OF OTHER GROUPS (DATA OF HRDLIČKA)

Males	"Long-faced Europeans" (17)	St. Lawrence Island Eskimo (158)	Difference	Mongols (114)	Difference
Measurements					
Glabello-occipital length	176.8 *	184.0	−7.2	184.0	−7.2
Maximum breadth	142.0 *	141.4	0.6	150.1	−8.1
Basion-bregma height	140.2 *	137.0	3.2	131.0	9.2
Nasion-menton height	123.3	127.0	−3.7	125.8	−2.5
Nasion-prosthion height	76.7	76.6	0.1	77.6	−0.9
Max. bizygomatic diameter	137.0	140.8	−3.8	142.0	−5.0
Orbit height	35.6	36.9	−1.3	35.9	−0.3
Orbit breadth	40.0	40.4	−0.4	39.3	0.7
Nasal height	52.4	55.4	−3.0	56.6	−4.2
Nasal breadth	24.5	24.7	−0.2	27.5	−3.0
Mean difference	...	...	2.35	...	4.11
Cranial capacity	1372.0	1506.0	−134	1573.0	−201.0
Cranial module	151.4	154.2	−2.8	155.1	−3.7
Indices					
Length-breadth	80.4 *	76.9	3.5	81.4	−1.0
Length-height	79.4 *	74.5 †	4.9	71.2 †	8.2
Breadth-height	98.8 *	96.5 †	2.3	87.3 †	−11.5
Total facial	90.0	90.2	−0.2	88.8	1.2
Upper facial	56.2	54.5	1.7	54.5	1.7
Mean orbital	89.1	91.3	−2.2	91.5	−2.4
Nasal	46.8	44.6	2.2	48.6	−1.8
Mean difference			2.43		3.97

* Undeformed crania only. † Calculated from means of measurements.

groups have much larger brain-cases than the Pecos "Europeans." They also have broader and longer faces and are more markedly Mongoloid. The mean differences in measurements are not as large as they would be if arcs and circumferences were included in the comparison. The Eskimo are much more like the Pecos type than are the Mongols, since the former have high heads. Indicial differences between the Pecos "Europeans" and the Eskimo amount to 2.43 index units in the means, whereas the Mongols differ in indices from the Pecos type by an average of 3.97 index units. While it cannot be said that the Pecos "Long-faced Europeans" closely resemble either Eskimo or Mongols, there is certainly affinity to the Eskimo type in general proportions.

[1] Hrdlička, 1924, pp. 26, 50.

In Table VIII–30 the Pecos "Long-faced Europeans" are compared with Tibetans, Chinese, and Northern Chinese.[1] The table shows that the Pecos are not at all like the Tibetans, but resemble the Chinese rather closely and the Northern Chinese in particular. The mean difference between the Pecos and Northern Chinese in eight indices is only 1.99 units. The difference in measurements is 3.72 mm., largely owing to the longer, narrower, and lower crania of the Northern Chinese. On the whole the "Long-faced" Pecos type is more like Northern Chinese than like any of the contemporary types at Pecos, with the exception of the "Plains" type.

TABLE VIII–30. Differences of Means of "Long–Faced Europeans" and Tibetan and Chinese Crania (Data of Morant)

Males Measurements	"Long-faced Europeans"	Tibetan B	Difference	Chinese	Difference	Northern Chinese	Difference
Glabello-occipital length	176.8 *	185.5	−8.7	177.1	−0.3	177.9	−1.1
Maximum breadth	142.0 *	139.4	2.6	139.5	2.5	38.8	3.2
Basion-bregma height	140.2 *	134.1	6.1	136.9	3.3	136.7	3.5
Maximum circumference	500.4	525.6	−25.2	508.5	−8.1	504.6	−4.2
Nasion-opisthion arc	356.6	378.6	−22.0	370.3	−13.7	370.3	−13.7
Transverse arc	322.4	312.9	9.5	321.2	1.2	317.6	4.8
Minimum frontal diameter ...	97.0	94.3	2.7	93.9	3.1	92.6	4.4
Nasion-prosthion height	76.7	76.5	0.2	71.2	5.5	72.5	4.2
Orbit height, right	35.6	36.5	−0.9	33.8	1.8	35.8	−0.2
Orbit breadth, right.........	40.1	41.2	−1.1	38.3	1.8	38.3	1.8
Nasal height	52.4	54.9	−2.5	53.1	−0.7	54.5	−2.1
Nasal breadth	24.5	27.1	−2.6	25.5	−1.0	25.2	−0.7
Basion-nasion length	103.6	99.2	4.4	99.1	4.5	99.7	3.9
Basion-prosthion length	95.8	97.2	−1.4	97.7	−1.9	91.8	4.0
Max. bizygomatic diameter ..	137.0	137.5	−0.5	131.8	5.2	133.0	4.0
Mean difference			6.03		3.64		3.72
Cranial module	151.4	153.0	−1.6	151.0	0.4	152.1	−0.7
Indices							
Length-breadth	80.4 *	75.3	5.1	78.9	1.5	78.1	2.3
Length-height	79.4 *	72.1	7.3	77.4	2.0	76.8	2.6
Breadth-height	98.8 *	104.5	−5.7	102.4	−3.6	101.5	−2.3
Nasal	46.8	49.5	−2.7	48.9	−2.1	46.6	0.2
Orbital, right	89.1	88.6	0.5	88.4	0.7	93.5	4.4
Upper facial	56.2	55.6	0.6	54.0	2.2	54.5	1.7
Gnathic	92.5	98.0	−5.5	98.6	−6.1	92.1	0.4
Mean difference			3.91		2.60		1.99

* Undeformed crania only.

Table VIII–31 shows the mean differences of the Pecos "Long-faced European" type from other contemporary types in the pueblo. This type is strongly divergent from the "Pseudo-Negroids," "Pseudo-Australoids," "Pseudo-Alpines," and "Large Hybrids." It closely resembles the "Plains" type and does not diverge very markedly from the "Basket-Maker" type.

[1] Morant, 1924, pp. 28–29.

My conclusion as to the affinities of this type is that they are not in any sense "European." It is not a pure Mongolian type but resembles such mixed Mongoloid peoples as the Dzungarians and Northern Chinese in whom Mongoloid elements have been blended with some non-Mongoloid long-headed, leptorrhine stock.

TABLE VIII–31. DIFFERENCES OF MEANS OF "LONG–FACED EUROPEANS" AND OTHER PECOS TYPES

Males	"Basket Makers"	"Pseudo-Negroids"	"Pseudo-Australoids"	"Plains Indians"	"Pseudo-Alpines"	"Large Hybrids"
Measurements						
Glabello-occipital length *	−0.87	−0.87	0.51	−0.34	...	4.13
Maximum breadth *	9.17	7.00	8.57	4.84	...	−5.33
Basion-bregma height *	5.20	9.53	5.20	2.37	...	2.70
Maximum circumference	0.41	8.33	1.32	6.14	7.77	1.81
Nasion-opisthion arc	−4.15	2.18	−5.11	3.06	8.06	0.18
Transverse arc	13.61	5.90	7.36	6.50	−5.28	−13.84
Thickness of left parietal	−0.14	−0.20	−0.18	0.42	0.24	−0.49
Mean diam. of foramen magnum	−0.19	2.46	1.09	0.16	1.21	0.16
Minimum frontal diameter	4.00	1.54	2.91	3.35	2.50	−0.62
Maximum bizygomatic diameter	4.29	3.17	−0.67	−2.82	−1.92	−6.65
Nasion-menton height	2.14	5.00	5.61	1.96	8.31	1.77
Nasion-prosthion height	3.42	4.44	6.00	0.93	6.92	2.21
Orbit height, right	0.21	1.18	2.79	0.08	0.37	0.07
Orbit height, left	0.28	0.95	2.39	0.33	0.41	0.34
Orbit breadth, right	0.57	0.49	0.59	−0.38	−0.55	−0.93
Orbit breadth, left	1.16	0.85	0.52	0.01	0.55	−0.05
Nasal height	1.01	3.58	3.21	−0.75	2.82	0.52
Nasal breadth	−1.59	−1.85	−1.65	−1.54	−1.15	−1.41
Basion-nasion height	2.74	2.50	1.60	0.02	2.80	1.12
Basion-prosthion height	−2.49	−4.60	−1.82	−2.73	0.40	−2.82
External palatal length	0.10	−2.41	1.02	−0.60	1.32	−1.14
External palatal breadth	−1.73	0.78	1.48	−1.40	−0.22	−1.21
Bigonial diameter	6.18	2.98	1.58	−2.67	1.56	−3.64
Bicondylar width	2.37	3.39	−1.00	−5.43	−2.72	−6.68
Height of symphysis	0.07	−0.26	0.39	0.92	2.42	−0.55
Min. breadth of ascending ramus	0.95	−0.93	0.28	0.23	0.24	−0.39
Height of ascending ramus	2.62	9.20	4.74	5.17	4.67	3.39
Condylo-symphysial length	1.10	−1.15	0.18	−0.69	2.25	−1.26
Mean difference	2.60	3.13	2.49	1.99	2.67	2.34
Cranial capacity	65.64	98.14	37.31	39.45	−7.69	−48.14
Cranial module	1.98	4.38	1.98	1.23	1.58	−1.05
Indices						
Length-breadth *	5.40	4.73	4.69	2.97	...	−4.93
Length-height *	3.20	5.73	2.57	0.90	...	−0.10
Breadth-height *	−2.00	1.80	−2.37	−2.03	...	4.30
Total facial	−0.20	1.33	4.75	2.86	8.10	4.61
Upper facial	1.17	1.92	5.03	2.30	6.72	4.37
Mean orbital	−1.37	0.98	5.33	1.19	1.92	1.99
Nasal	−3.97	−6.99	−6.49	−2.27	−5.15	−3.26
Gnathic	−4.64	−7.90	−3.12	−2.55	−2.00	−3.69
External palatal	−2.87	6.68	0.69	−0.87	−3.23	0.84
Mean difference	2.76	4.23	3.89	1.99	4.52	3.12

* Undeformed crania only.

"PSEUDO–ALPINE" TYPE

DESCRIPTION

In the "Pseudo-Alpine" type heads are very short and broad and deformation is at its maximum. Not one undeformed skull offers a basis for comparison of vault diameters. This type is undoubtedly hyperbrachycephalic and probably hypsicephalic. Judging from the uncorrected mean of the breadth-height index (92.7) this type is originally tapeinocephalic or nearly so. The cranial capacity (1380 cc.) is the second largest of any type group. Bizygomatic diameters are great (138.9 mm. on the average). The upper and total facial lengths are by far the smallest of the Pecos series. The facial index (81.9) is markedly euryprosopic. Orbits are,

TABLE VIII–32.   MEANS OF "PSEUDO–ALPINE" TYPE

Males

Measurements

Maximum circumference .	492.64	±	1.94
Nasion-opisthion arc	348.50	±	2.29
Transverse arc	327.64	±	1.85
Thickness of left parietal .	4.79	±	0.14
Mean diam. of for. mag. ..	30.60	±	0.40
Minimum frontal diameter	94.50	±	0.86
Max. bizygomatic diameter	138.92	±	1.26
Nasion-menton height	115.00	±	0.96
Nasion-prosthion	69.75	±	0.76
Orbit height, right	35.27	±	0.25
Orbit height, left	35.12	±	0.25
Orbit breadth, right	40.69	±	0.37
Orbit breadth, left	39.42	±	0.25
Nasal height	49.57	±	0.48
Nasal breadth	25.68	±	0.32
Basion-nasion length	100.80	±	0.78
Basion-prosthion length ..	95.40	±	0.68
External palatal length ..	53.95	±	0.52

Measurements

External palatal breadth..	65.82	±	0.56
Bigonial diameter	100.02	±	1.20
Bicondylar width	121.89	±	1.03
Height of symphysis	33.65	±	0.44
Min. breadth of asc. ramus	37.04	±	0.42
Height of ascending ramus	63.45	±	1.15
Condylo-symphysial length	102.60	±	0.99
Cranial capacity	1380.00	±	15.83
Cranial module	149.80	±	0.62

Indices

Total facial	81.90	±	1.22
Upper facial.............	49.45	±	0.76
Mean orbital	87.14	±	1.00
Nasal	51.93	±	0.87
Gnathic	94.50	±	0.58
External palatal	122.36	±	1.27

however, mesoconch (mean index 87.1). The nose is short and of moderate breadth so that the nasal index is chamaerrhine (51.9). The gnathic index indicates no prognathism. The palate is very short and relatively the broadest of any of our types. The maxillo-alveolar index averages 122.4. Noteworthy features of the mandible are its low symphysial height and small angle of the ascending ramus with the mandibular body. In both of these measurements the "Pseudo-Alpine" type is at the extreme of the Pecos series. The condylo-symphysial length is also the least of the series.

The frontal region of the "Pseudo-Alpine" type is oftener of submedium height than medium or high, but it is usually broad or of medium breadth. It is rarely receding, usually of medium slope, and not infrequently steep. The temporal region, when not of medium fullness, is usually very protuberant. Supraorbital ridges are small or medium and generally of the median type. The nasion depression is generally absent; when present it is slight. The nasal bridge is usually low, of medium breadth and concavo-convex. The nasal aperture is of medium breadth, or less often broad; lower borders are variable in development and the nasal spine is prevailingly of medium size, and oftener large than small. Malars are usually very projecting and zygomata well developed. Suborbital fossae average deeper than in any other type. Alveolar prognathism is extremely variable.

The stature of this type averages 162 cm., which is a trifle above the series mean.

COMPARISON WITH OTHER GROUPS

It is not possible to compare the means of cranial vault diameters of the "Pseudo-Alpine" type with those of other types, since the skulls of this group are all deformed and offer no basis for comparison with undeformed types. In Table VIII–33 means of the facial dimensions, indices, cranial capacity, and cranial module have been compared with those of other groups, including Canary Island brachycephals,[1] Swiss Disentis type,[2] Bavarians,[3] Telengets, and Kalmucks[2] and Apaches.[4] The few means of facial dimensions available for comparison indicate that our Pecos type is radically different from the European and Canary types but shows very marked similarities to the Mongoloid types represented by the Apaches, Telengets, and Kalmucks. The differences in indices tell the same story. The affinities of the Pecos "Pseudo-Alpine" type are not with "Alpine" crania, but with crania of Mongoloid origin.

Table VIII–34 compares the means of the Pecos "Pseudo-Alpines" with those of various Oriental series measured by Morant,[5] including Tibetans, Chinese, Malays, and three small groups of Burmese crania. The cranial capacity of the Pecos series is smaller than that of any Oriental group and the vault dimensions of the Pecos type are undoubtedly inferior, although, because of deformation, no direct comparison can be made. All of the Oriental series have longer and narrower faces than the Pecos type. The mean differences of 10 or 11 facial measurements range from 2.73 mm. in the Burmese B series to 3.67 mm. in the Burmese C series. The differences in means of four facial indices range from 1.02 units in the Burmese B series to 4.95 units in the Burmese C series. Both the Burmese A and the Tibetan B groups are very close to the Pecos "Pseudo-Alpines" in the indices considered and in the measurements of the face differ markedly from the Southwestern type only in their diminished bizygomatic diameters.

Table VIII–35 compares the means of the "Pseudo-Alpine" type with those of other Pecos types. Evidently this type is least divergent in means of measurements from the "Pseudo-Australoid" type and in means of indices from the "Large Hybrid" type. The close approach to the "Pseudo-Australoid" type is due to the fact that both of these types have low, broad faces and broad noses. If the diameters and indices of the cranial vault were brought into the comparison marked differences would be apparent.

[1] Hooton, 1925, pp. 88–128.　　　　[2] Reicher, 1913, pp. 421–562.
[3] Reid, 1911, pp. 1–113.　　　　[4] Hrdlička, 1924, p. 38.
[5] Morant, 1924, pp. 48–49.

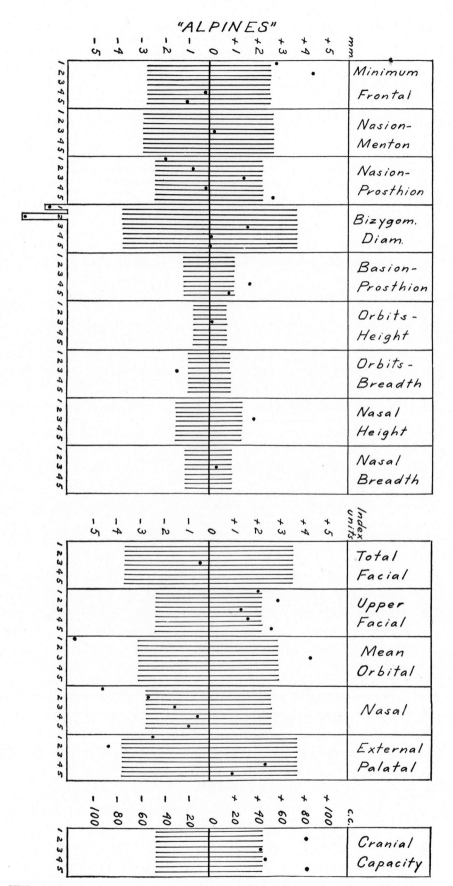

Fig. VIII–4. Means of various brachycephals plotted against means of Pecos "Pseudo-Alpine" type.

In each compartment from left to right: (1) Canary brachycephals (Hooton); (2) Bavarians (Reid); (3) Apaches (Hrdlička); (4) Telengets (Reicher); (5) Kalmucks (Reicher)

TABLE VIII-33. DIFFERENCES OF MEANS OF "PSEUDO-ALPINES" AND ALPINE AND MONGOLOID CRANIA

Males Measurements	"Pseudo-Alpines"	Canary Brachys (Hooton)	Diff.	Swiss Disentis (Reicher)	Diff.	Bavarians (Reid)	Diff.	Apaches (Hrdlička)	Diff.	Telengets (Reicher)	Diff.	Kalmucks (Reicher)	Diff.
Minimum frontal diameter	94.50	97.44	−2.94	99.0	−4.50	99.00	−4.50	...	...	94.3	0.20	93.5	1.00
Max. bizygomatic diameter	138.92	132.04	6.88	...	...	131.0	7.92	140.6	−1.68	140.0	−1.08	138.9	0.02
Nasion-menton height	115.00	...	...	...	...	...	...	115.2	−0.20	...	...	...	...
Nasion-prosthion height	69.75	67.84	1.91	66.9	2.85	69.0	0.75	71.3	−1.55	69.6	0.15	72.5	−2.75
Basion-prosthion length	95.40	...	...	...	...	...	...	...	...	97.2	−1.80	96.3	−0.90
Orbit height	35.19	...	...	...	...	...	...	35.08	0.11	...	...	...	...
Orbit breadth	40.06	...	...	...	...	...	...	38.66	1.40	...	...	...	...
Nasal height	49.57	...	...	...	...	...	...	51.6	−2.03	...	...	...	...
Nasal breadth	25.68	...	...	...	...	...	...	26.0	−0.32	...	...	...	...
Mean difference			3.91		3.68		4.39		1.34		0.56		1.17
Cranial capacity	1380.00	...	...	...	...	1464.0	−84.00	1425.0	−45.00	1429.0	−49.00	1466.0	−86.00
Cranial module	149.80	152.29	−2.49	...	...	151.0	−1.20	150.3	−0.50	151.0	−1.20	150.33	−0.53
Indices													
Total facial	81.90	...	...	...	...	...	...	81.5	0.40	...	...	...	...
Upper facial	49.45	51.58	−2.13	50.0	−0.55	52.4	−2.95	50.9	−1.45	51.0	−1.55	52.2	−2.75
Mean orbital	87.14	81.42	5.72	...	...	...	...	91.5	−4.36	...	...	...	...
Nasal	51.93	47.46	4.47	47.1	4.83	49.3	−2.63	50.4	1.53	51.4	0.53	51.0	0.93
External palatal	122.36	119.96	2.40	117.7	4.66	118.1	4.26	...	...	124.8	−2.44	123.4	−1.04
Mean difference			3.68		3.35		3.28		1.94		1.51		1.57

TABLE VIII-34. DIFFERENCES OF MEANS OF "PSEUDO-ALPINES" AND MONGOLOID CRANIA (DATA OF MORANT)

Males

Measurements	"Pseudo-Alpine"	Tibetan A	Diff.	Chinese	Diff.	Malayan	Diff.	Burmese C	Diff.	Burmese B	Diff.	Burmese A	Diff.
Maximum circumference	492.6	502.2	−9.6	508.5	−15.9	505.7	−13.1	503.1	−10.5	497.7	−5.1	505.7	13.1
Minimum frontal diam.	94.5	92.2	2.3	93.9	0.6	93.4	1.1	90.4	4.1	89.7	4.8	94.3	0.2
Max. bizygomatic diam.	138.9	131.0	7.9	131.8	7.1	133.2	5.7	126.7	12.2	131.7	7.2	134.0	4.9
Nasion-prosthion height	69.8	68.7	1.1	71.2	−1.4	70.1	−0.3	74.5	−4.7	68.2	1.6	71.4	−1.6
Nasal height	49.6	51.3	−1.5	53.1	−3.5	51.9	−2.3	55.1	−5.5	52.3	−2.7	53.4	−3.8
Nasal breadth	25.7	25.7	0.0	25.5	0.2	26.1	−0.4	25.5	0.2	26.6	−0.9	28.1	−2.4
Orbit height, right	35.3	34.0	1.3	33.8	1.5	33.5	1.8	35.6	−0.3	33.6	1.7	35.0	0.3
Orbit height, left	35.1	34.3	0.8	33.8	1.5	33.5	1.8	35.9	−0.8	34.3	0.8	35.0	0.1
Orbit breadth, right	40.7	39.6	1.1	38.3	2.4	39.1	1.6	39.4	1.3	39.1	1.6	39.6	1.1
Basion-nasion length	100.8	96.9	3.9	99.1	1.7	99.5	1.3	100.5	0.3	98.8	2.0	98.5	2.3
Basion-prosthion length	95.4	92.9	2.5	97.7	−2.3	98.2	−2.8	95.9	−0.5	93.8	1.6	96.6	−1.2
Mean difference			2.91		3.66		3.04		3.67		2.73		2.82
Cranial capacity	1380.0	1452.0	−72.0	1468.0	−88.0	1424.0	−44.0	1442.0	−62.0	1415.0	−35.0	1407.0	−27.0

Indices

Measurements	"Pseudo-Alpine"	Tibetan A	Diff.	Chinese	Diff.	Malayan	Diff.	Burmese C	Diff.	Burmese B	Diff.	Burmese A	Diff.
Nasal	51.9	50.2	1.7	48.9	3.0	50.4	1.5	46.4	5.5	51.2	0.7	52.8	−0.9
Orbital, right	87.1	86.2	0.9	88.4	−1.3	86.0	1.1	91.1	−4.0	87.7	−0.6	88.4	−1.3
Upper facial	49.4	52.4	−3.0	54.0	−4.6	52.6	−3.2	58.8	−9.4	51.8	−2.4	53.3	−3.9
Gnathic	94.5	95.9	−1.4	98.6	−4.1	98.7	−4.2	95.4	−0.9	94.9	−0.4	98.1	−3.6
Mean difference			1.75		3.25		2.5		4.95		1.02		2.42

TABLE VIII–35. DIFFERENCES OF MEANS OF "PSEUDO–ALPINES" AND OTHER PECOS TYPES

Males Measurements	"Basket Makers"	"Pseudo-Negroids"	"Pseudo-Australoids"	"Plains Indians"	"Long-faced Europeans"	"Large Hybrids"
Maximum circumference	−7.36	0.56	−6.45	−1.63	−7.77	−5.96
Nasion-opisthion arc	−12.21	−5.88	−13.17	−5.00	−8.06	−7.88
Transverse arc	18.89	11.18	12.64	11.78	5.28	−8.56
Thickness of left parietal	−0.38	−0.44	−0.42	0.18	−0.24	−0.73
Mean diam. of foramen magnum	−1.40	1.25	−0.12	−1.05	−1.21	−1.05
Minimum frontal diameter	1.50	−0.96	0.41	0.85	−2.50	−3.12
Maximum bizygomatic diameter	6.21	5.09	1.25	−0.90	1.92	−4.73
Nasion-menton height	−6.17	−3.31	−2.70	−6.35	−8.31	−6.54
Nasion- prosthion height	−3.50	−2.48	−0.92	−5.99	−6.92	−4.71
Orbit height, right	−0.16	0.81	2.42	−0.29	−0.37	−0.30
Orbit height, left	−0.13	0.54	1.98	−0.08	−0.41	−0.07
Orbit breadth, right	1.12	1.04	1.14	0.17	0.55	−0.38
Orbit breadth, left	0.61	0.30	−0.03	−0.54	−0.55	−0.60
Nasal height	−1.81	0.76	0.39	−3.57	−2.82	−2.30
Nasal breadth	−0.44	−0.70	−0.50	−0.39	1.15	−0.26
Basion-nasion height	−0.06	−0.30	−1.20	−2.78	−2.80	−1.68
Basion-prosthion height	−2.89	−5.00	−2.22	−3.13	−0.40	−3.22
External palatal length	−1.22	−3.73	−0.30	−1.92	−1.32	−2.46
External palatal breadth	−1.51	1.00	1.70	−1.18	0.22	−0.99
Bigonial diameter	4.62	1.42	0.02	−4.23	−1.56	−5.20
Bicondylar width	5.09	6.11	1.72	−2.71	2.72	−3.96
Height of symphysis	−2.35	−2.68	−2.03	−1.50	−2.42	−2.97
Min. breadth of ascending ramus	0.71	−1.17	0.04	−0.01	−0.24	−0.63
Height of ascending ramus	−2.05	4.53	0.07	0.50	−4.67	−1.28
Condylo-symphysial length	−1.15	−3.40	−2.07	−2.94	−2.25	−3.51
Mean difference	3.34	2.59	2.24	2.39	2.67	2.92
Cranial capacity	73.33	105.83	45.00	47.14	7.69	−40.45
Cranial module	0.40	2.80	0.40	−0.35	−1.58	−2.63
Indices						
Total facial	−8.30	−6.77	−3.35	−5.24	−8.10	−3.49
Upper facial	−5.55	−4.80	−1.69	−4.42	−6.72	−2.35
Mean orbital	−3.29	−0.94	3.41	−0.73	−1.92	0.07
Nasal	1.18	−1.84	−1.34	2.88	5.15	1.89
Gnathic	−2.64	−5.90	−1.12	−0.55	2.00	−1.69
External palatal	0.36	9.91	3.92	2.36	3.23	4.07
Mean difference	3.55	5.03	2.47	2.70	4.52	2.26

There seems to be no reason for doubting that the type called "Pseudo-Alpine" is a small brachycephalic, euryprosopic, and platyrrhine Mongoloid type. It resembles such crania as the Tibetan, Burmese, Telenget, and Kalmuck series rather more closely than it resembles any contemporary Pecos type. But it seems to show also very close affinity to the existing Apache tribe of the Southwest. Like all of our Pecos types, the brain-case of the "Pseudo-Alpine" type is small when compared with that of any other similar type outside of the Southwestern area.

"LARGE HYBRID" TYPE

DESCRIPTION

The "Large Hybrid" type is the most numerous in the Pecos series. Usually the crania of this type are strongly deformed. The skull length is short (172.7 undeformed and corrected deformed), its breadth large (147 undeformed and corrected deformed). The undeformed height is about 137.5. Cranial capacities are the maximum of the series (mean 1420 cc.). The undeformed crania of the series have a length-breadth index of 85 in the mean, and the correction brings the mean index of the deformed crania to the same figure. In their undeformed state these crania

TABLE VIII–36. MEANS OF "LARGE HYBRID" TYPE

Males

Measurements			
Glabello-occipital length *	172.67		...
Maximum breadth *	147.33		...
Basion-bregma height *	137.50		...
Maximum circumference	498.60	±	2.02
Nasion-opisthion arc	356.38	±	1.94
Transverse arc	336.20	±	1.38
Thickness of left parietal	5.52	±	0.14
Mean diam. of for. mag.	31.65	±	0.24
Minimum frontal	97.62	±	0.65
Max. bizygomatic diameter	143.65	±	0.68
Nasion-menton height	121.54	±	0.61
Nasion-prosthion height	74.46	±	0.46
Orbit height, right	35.57	±	0.16
Orbit height, left	35.19	±	0.21
Orbit breadth, right	41.07	±	0.22
Orbit breadth, left	40.02	±	0.16
Nasal height	51.87	±	0.40
Nasal breadth	25.94	±	0.22
Basion-nasion length	102.48	±	0.39
Basion-prosthion length	98.62	±	0.51
External palatal length	56.41	±	0.31

Measurements			
External palatal breadth	66.81	±	0.34
Bigonial diameter	105.22	±	0.77
Bicondylar width	125.85	±	0.55
Height of symphysis	36.62	±	0.21
Min. breadth of asc. ramus	37.67	±	0.33
Height of ascending ramus	64.73	±	0.56
Condylo-symphysial length	106.11	±	0.74
Cranial capacity	1420.45	±	11.32
Cranial module	152.43	±	0.57

Indices			
Length-breadth *	85.33		...
Length-height *	79.50		...
Breadth-height *	94.50		...
Total facial	85.39	±	0.69
Upper facial	51.80	±	0.41
Mean orbital	87.07	±	0.50
Nasal	50.04	±	0.55
Gnathic	96.19	±	0.48
External palatal	118.29	±	0.71

* Undeformed crania only.

are hypsicephalic (79.5) and on the lower borders of acrocephaly (94.5). Deformation accentuates both of these conditions. The frontal region is broad. The faces are exaggeratedly broad because of their very large malars. The mean bizygomatic diameter is 143.6 mm., the maximum of the Pecos series. The total and upper facial lengths are large, but do not reach the means found in the "Long-faced European" group. The facial index is, on the average, mesoprosopic and the upper facial index mesene. The orbits are broader than those of any other group and yield a high mesoconch mean orbital index (87). The dimensions of the nose are moderate; the average nasal index is mesorrhine (50.0). There is no facial prognathism. Palatal dimensions are ordinary; yielding, as usual, a brachyuranic index (118.3). The mandibles are the broadest of our series and the longest.

The frontal region is higher than in any other type, broad and usually of medium slope. The temporal regions are of medium fullness or swelling. Brow-ridges are usually of medium size but of all types. The nasion depression is absent or slight. The nasal bridge is of submedium or medium height and variable in breadth. The commonest nasal profile is concavo-convex. The nasal aperture is variable, but usually of medium breadth. Lower borders are poorly developed, but the nasal spine is large oftener than in any other group, though even in this type usually of medium size. Malars are most projecting and zygomata the most massive of any of the groups. Suborbital fossae are shallow. Alveolar prognathism is usually of medium grade, but oftener slight than pronounced. The crania of this type are the largest of the Pecos series and the most brutal in appearance. The "Large Hybrid" type shares with the "Plains" type the honor of the tallest stature average in the Pecos population (163.7 cm.).

Comparison with Other Groups

Anyone who is familiar with North American Indian crania will immediately recognize the Pecos "Large Hybrid" type as similar to one which is found throughout the Mississippi Valley and the Gulf States in the burials of the Mound Culture, the Tennessee Stone Graves, and other prehistoric and protohistoric Indian sites. It is a hyperbrachycephalic type, usually much deformed and with a face both long and broad. I am inclined to regard it as the result of an intermixture of an eastern dolichocephalic long-faced type with a western brachycephalic broad and short-faced type. It is almost certainly hypsicephalic although the scarcity of undeformed crania of the type make it difficult to adduce evidence of this condition. The dolichocephalic type which contributes to the admixture is hypsicephalic, and I am inclined to regard the brachycephalic type as high-headed also.

Table VIII–37 compares the means of various groups of crania east of the Mississippi with those of the Pecos "Large Hybrid" type. These series come from the prehistoric burials of Arkansas, Louisiana, Tennessee, and Ohio [1] and are brachycephals of the type mentioned, with the exception of the Madisonville series, which is mixed and of somewhat later date than the other groups. A perusal of the means of indices and measurements and of the mean differences of the same, will convince the reader of the essential identity of our Pecos types with these very similar groups of eastern Indian crania.

Our "Large Hybrid" type resembles all of these Eastern groups more closely than it resembles any one of its contemporary Pecos types. Of the latter it is closest to the "Pseudo-Alpine" type, as may be observed from Table VIII–38.

I have not attempted to trace the affinities of this type outside of the American area, but there is no doubt that it bears general resemblances to the crania of Asiatic Mongoloids.

[1] Hooton, 1920, pp. 83–137.

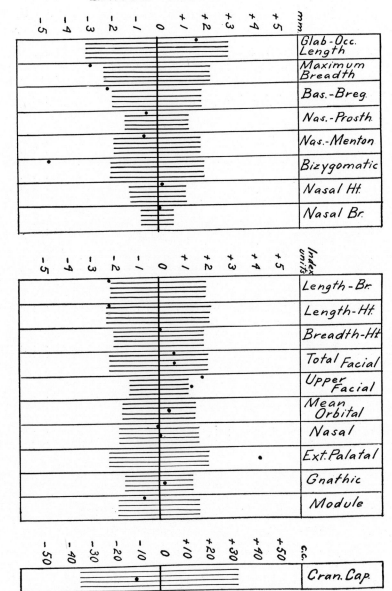

Fig. VIII–5. Means of measurements and indices of Tennessee Stone Grave groups plotted against means of Pecos "Large Hybrid" type.

(1) in the first space of each compartment, Tennessee Stone Grave brachycephals (Hrdlička)
(3) in the third space of each index compartment, Tennessee Stone Graves mixed types (Fuller).

TABLE VIII–37. DIFFERENCES OF "LARGE HYBRIDS" AND OTHER INDIAN GROUPS

Measurements	"Large Hybrids"	Madisonville Ohio (Hooton)	Diff.	Arkansas Boyott's Field (Hrdlička)	Diff.	Arkansas Nat. Mus. (Hrdlička)	Diff.	Louisana (Hrdlička)	Diff.	Tennessee Stone Graves (Fuller)	Diff.	Tennessee Stone Graves (Hrdlička)	Diff.
Glabello-occipital length	172.7	177.4	−4.7	…	…	…	…	…	…	…	…	167.0	5.7
Maximum breadth	147.3	146.1	1.2	…	…	…	…	…	…	…	…	146.0	1.3
Basion-bregma height	137.5	136.9	0.6	…	…	…	…	…	…	…	…	142.0	−4.5
Minimum frontal diameter	97.6	94.8	2.8	96.0	1.6	94.5	3.1	96.0	1.6	93.0	4.6	…	…
Maximum circumference	498.6	513.0	−14.4	500.0	−1.4	502.0	−3.4	504.0	−5.4	512.0	−13.4	…	…
Nasion-opisthion arc	356.4	361.0	−4.6	352.0	4.4	356.0	0.4	355.0	1.4	359.0	−2.6	…	…
Transverse arc	336.2	316.0	20.2	…	…	…	…	…	…	310.0	26.2	…	…
Mean diam. of foramen magnum	31.6	32.8	−1.2	33.0	−1.4	33.3	−1.7	34.5	−2.9	…	…	…	…
Nasion-prosthion height	74.5	72.0	2.5	70.5	4.0	70.6	3.9	75.5	−1.0	…	…	74.0	0.5
Nasion-menton height	121.5	117.9	3.6	117.5	4.0	125.0	−3.5	123.5	−2.0	…	…	121.0	0.5
Max. bizygomatic diameter	143.6	141.0	2.6	139.5	5.1	138.5	4.1	142.0	1.6	…	…	139.0	4.6
Basion-nasion length	102.5	…	…	104.0	−1.5	103.5	−1.0	106.0	−3.5	…	…	…	…
Basion-prosthion length	98.6	…	…	102.0	−3.4	99.5	−0.9	105.0	−6.4	…	…	…	…
Nasal height	51.9	…	…	49.8	2.1	54.9	−3.0	51.6	0.3	…	…	52.0	−0.1
Nasal breadth	25.9	…	…	25.4	0.5	26.9	−1.0	26.2	−0.3	…	…	26.0	−0.1
External palatal length	56.4	…	…	55.7	0.7	57.5	−1.1	57.5	−1.1	…	…	…	…
External palatal breadth	66.8	…	…	65.6	1.2	70.2	−3.4	66.5	0.3	…	…	…	…
Bigonial diameter	105.2	103.4	1.8	105.0	0.2	107.0	−1.8	107.0	−1.8	…	…	…	…
Bicondylar width	125.8	129.0	−3.2	…	…	…	…	…	…	…	…	…	…
Height of symphysis	36.6	36.5	0.1	36.5	0.1	37.5	−0.9	37.5	−0.9	…	…	…	…
Minimum breadth of asc. ramus	37.7	35.5	2.2	…	…	…	…	…	…	…	…	…	…
Mean difference			4.38		2.11		2.16		1.95		11.70		2.16
Cranial capacity	1420.0	1435.0	−15.0	1455.0	−35.0	…	…	…	…	…	…	…	…
Indices													
Length-breadth	85.3	…	…	…	…	…	…	…	…	…	…	87.2	−1.9
Length-height	79.5	…	…	…	…	…	…	…	…	…	…	85.0	−5.5
Breadth-height	94.5	…	…	…	…	…	…	…	…	…	…	97.6	−3.1
Total facial	85.4	83.0	2.4	85.0	0.4	86.0	−0.6	86.0	−0.6	86.0	−0.6	86.0	−0.6
Upper facial	51.8	51.1	0.7	51.0	0.8	54.5	−2.7	53.0	−1.2	53.2	−1.4	53.7	−1.9
Mean orbital	87.1	…	…	…	…	…	…	…	…	87.5	−0.4	…	…
Nasal	50.0	51.6	−1.6	51.0	−1.0	49.4	0.6	51.0	−1.0	50.1	−0.1	50.0	0.00
External palatal	118.3	117.6	0.7	118.0	0.3	122.0	−3.7	116.0	2.3	122.6	−4.3	…	…
Cranial module	152.4	153.5	−1.1	153.6	−1.2	155.4	−3.0	155.5	−3.1	…	…	151.7	0.7
Mean difference			1.3		0.94		2.12		1.62		1.36		1.96

TABLE VIII–38. DIFFERENCES OF MEANS OF "LARGE HYBRIDS" AND OTHER PECOS TYPES

Measurements	"Basket Makers"	"Pseudo-Negroids"	"Pseudo-Australoids"	"Plains Indians"	"Long-faced Europeans"	"Pseudo-Alpines"
Glabello-occipital length *	−5.00	−5.00	−3.62	−4.47	−4.13	. . .
Maximum breadth *	14.50	12.33	13.90	10.17	5.33	. . .
Basion-bregma height *	2.50	6.83	2.50	−0.33	−2.70	. . .
Maximum circumference	−1.40	6.52	−0.49	4.33	−1.81	5.96
Nasion-opisthion arc	−4.33	2.00	−5.29	2.88	−0.18	7.88
Transverse arc	27.45	19.74	21.20	20.34	13.84	8.56
Thickness of left parietal	0.35	0.29	0.31	0.91	0.49	0.73
Mean diam. of foramen magnum	−0.35	2.30	0.93	0.00	−0.16	1.05
Minimum frontal	4.62	2.16	3.53	3.97	0.62	3.12
Maximum bizygomatic diameter	10.94	9.82	5.98	3.83	6.65	4.73
Nasion-menton height	0.37	3.23	3.84	0.19	−1.77	6.54
Nasion-alveon height	1.21	2.23	3.79	−1.28	−2.21	4.71
Orbit height, right	0.14	1.11	2.72	−0.01	−0.07	0.30
Orbit height, left	−0.06	0.61	2.05	−0.01	−0.34	0.07
Orbit breadth, right	1.50	1.42	1.52	0.55	0.93	0.38
Orbit breadth, left	1.21	0.90	0.57	0.06	0.05	0.60
Nasal height	0.49	3.06	2.69	−1.27	−0.52	2.30
Nasal breadth	−0.18	−0.44	−0.24	−0.13	1.41	0.26
Basion-nasion length	1.62	1.38	0.48	−1.10	−1.12	1.68
Basion-prosthion height	0.33	−1.78	1.00	0.09	2.82	3.22
External palatal length	1.24	−1.27	2.16	0.54	1.14	2.46
External palatal breadth	−0.52	1.99	2.69	−0.19	1.21	0.99
Bigonial diameter	9.82	6.62	5.22	0.97	3.64	5.20
Bicondylar width	9.05	10.07	5.68	1.25	6.68	3.96
Height of symphysis	0.62	0.29	0.94	1.47	0.55	2.97
Min. breadth of ascending ramus	1.34	−0.54	0.67	0.62	0.39	0.63
Height of ascending ramus	−0.77	5.81	1.35	1.78	−3.39	1.28
Condylo-symphysial length	2.36	0.11	1.44	0.57	1.26	3.51
Mean difference	3.72	3.92	3.46	2.26	2.34	2.92
Cranial capacity	113.78	146.28	85.45	87.59	48.14	40.45
Cranial module	3.03	5.43	3.03	2.28	1.05	2.63
Indices						
Length-breadth *	10.33	9.66	9.62	7.90	4.93	. . .
Height-length*	3.30	5.83	2.67	1.00	0.10	. . .
Height-breadth *	−6.30	−2.50	−6.67	−6.33	−4.30	. . .
Total facial	−4.81	−3.28	0.14	−1.75	−4.61	3.49
Upper facial	−3.20	−2.45	0.66	−2.07	−4.37	2.35
Mean orbital	−3.36	−1.01	3.34	−0.80	−1.99	−0.07
Nasal	−0.71	−3.73	−3.23	0.99	3.26	−1.89
Gnathic	−0.95	−4.21	0.57	1.14	3.69	1.69
External palatal	−3.71	5.84	−0.15	−1.71	−0.84	−4.07
Mean difference	4.07	4.28	3.00	2.63	3.12	2.26

* Undeformed crania only.

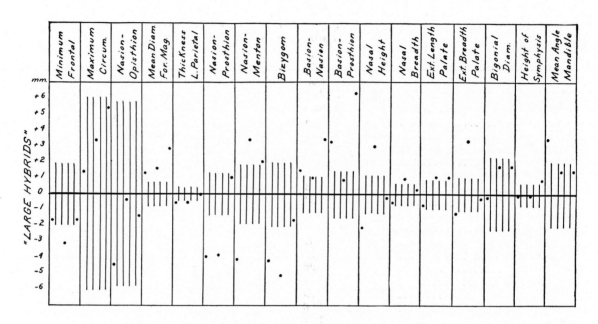

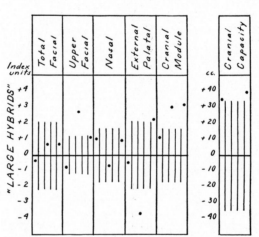

Figs. VIII–6, 7. Means of measurements and indices of Arkansas and Louisiana Male Crania
plotted against means of Pecos "Large Hybrid" type.

Left to right in each compartment: (1) first space — Boyott's Field, Arkansas.
(2) third space — National Museum Arkansas.
(3) fifth space — Louisiana crania.

Skip[288]

CHAPTER IX

CORRELATIONS, ASSOCIATIONS, AND CONTINGENCIES

CORRELATIONS

High correlations presumably imply an interdependence of variables, whereas low correlations indicate, on the contrary, an independence of variables. Neither high nor low correlations necessarily connote heterogeneity on the one hand or homogeneity on the other. High correlations of measurements do not mean that the group manifesting them is racially pure.

In the case of the cranial measurements of the male series most of the coefficients of correlation have been calculated by the ordinary product-moment method. In the correlations of long bones and of female cranial measurements, with a few exceptions, I have used the coefficient of variation method, which can be employed when coefficients of variation of two measurements and of an index derived from these two measurements are available.[1]

The numbers of measurements utilized for correlations in the Pecos series are necessarily small, but the coefficients are, in general, rather high.

Correlations of Cranial Measurements

The first group of correlations (Table IX–1) pertains to the diameters and capacity of the cranial vault. I have had the temerity to have calculations of coefficients of correlation worked out on the deformed skulls as well as on the undeformed skulls. The result shows that cranial deformation reduces correlation markedly but does not destroy it. The highest correlations between diameters found in this group are .693 ± .06 (in the case of the males) between basion-bregma height and minimum frontal diameter in the undeformed group, and .576 ± .09 between glabello-occipital length and basion-nasion diameters (Table IX–5), also in the undeformed group. In the female series (Table IX–1) the coefficients of correlation, calculated by the coefficient of variation method, yield two or three values worthy of remark. In the deformed group the correlation between glabello-occipital length and maximum breadth is negative (−.303 ± .07). In the undeformed group the coefficient (−.519 ± .10) is high. In the male series, on the contrary, the coefficient of correlation of undeformed lengths and breadths is positive but insignificant (.090 ± .10), and in the deformed group it is, as in the female series, negative (−.134 ± .07).

---

[1] If V_a and V_b are the coefficients of variation of two variables, a and b, and if V_{Iab} is the coefficient of variation of an index derived from a and b, then $r = \dfrac{(V^2_a + V^2_b) - V^2_{Iab}}{2V_aV_b}$. Karl Pearson and Julia Bell, 1919, p. 192.

In the male series cranial capacity is highly correlated with breadth and with basion-bregma height. The values of the coefficients are higher in the undeformed than in the deformed group.

In the male series correlations of bizygomatic diameter with various other facial dimensions yield, as a rule, high values (Tables IX–3, 5). A notable exception is nasal breadth, the correlation coefficient of which with bizygomatic diameter is insignificant (.101 ± .07). The extremely high correlation of bizygomatic diameter with breadth of orbits (.598 ± .04) is notable, as is also its negative correlation

TABLE IX–1. CORRELATION OF CRANIAL VAULT AND CAPACITY MEASUREMENTS

Males: Total Series A	Glabello-occipital	Maximum breadth	Basion-bregma height	Minimum frontal	Cranial capacity
Glabello-occipital					
deformed	....	−.134 ± .07 (91)	.133 ± .07 (80)	.231 ± .07 (85)	....
undeformed	....	.090 ± .10 (43)	.418 ± .10 (34)	.363 ± .09 (44)	....
Maximum breadth					
deformed	−.134 ± .07 (91)	....	.246 ± .07 (78)	.375 ± .06 (82)	.421 ± .07 (60)
undeformed	.090 ± .10 (43)	....	.425 ± .10 (33)	.481 ± .08 (39)	.631 ± .08 (29)
Basion-bregma height					
deformed	.133 ± .07 (80)	.246 ± .07 (78)	....	.345 ± .07 (75)	.480 ± .07 (62)
undeformed	.418 ± .10 (34)	.425 ± .10 (33)	....	.693 ± .06 (34)	.646 ± .04 (28)
Minimum frontal					
deformed	.231 ± .07 (85)	.375 ± .06 (82)	.345 ± .07 (75)	....	....
undeformed	.363 ± .09 (44)	.481 ± .08 (39)	.693 ± .06 (34)	....	....
Cranial capacity					
deformed	....	.421 ± .07 (60)	.480 ± .07 (62)	....	....
undeformed	....	.631 ± .08 (29)	.646 ± .04 (28)	....	....
Females: Total Series A					
Glabello-occipital					
deformed	....	−.303 ± .07 (68)	.308 ± .08 (55)	....	....
undeformed	....	−.519 ± .10 (25)	.253 ± .14 (21)	....	....
Maximum breadth					
deformed	−.303 ± .07 (68)	....	.344 ± .08 (53)	....	....
undeformed	−.519 ± .10 (25)	....	.409 ± .12 (21)	....	....
Basion-bregma height					
deformed	.308 ± .08 (55)	.344 ± .08 (53)	....	....	....
underformed	.253 ± .14 (21)	.409 ± .12 (21)	....	....	....

TABLE IX–2. CORRELATION OF CRANIAL ARC MEASUREMENTS

Males: Total Series A	Maximum circumference	Nasion-opisthion	Transverse arc
Maximum circumference			
deformed	.....	.808 ± .03 (81)	.252 ± .07 (89)
undeformed	.....	.703 ± .06 (32)	.497 ± .09 (35)
Nasion-opisthion			
deformed	.808 ± .03 (81)	.....	.301 ± .07 (82)
undeformed	.703 ± .06 (32)	.....	.277 ± .11 (32)
Transverse arc			
deformed	.252 ± .07 (89)	.301 ± .07 (82)	.....
undeformed	.497 ± .09 (35)	.277 ± .11 (32)	.....
Females: Total Series A			
Maximum circumference	.....	.789 ± .03 (84)	.440 ± .06 (86)
Nasion-opisthion	.789 ± .03 (84)	.....	.....
Transverse arc	.440 ± .06	.....	.....

with mean angle of mandible (−.300 ± .07). Bizygomatic diameter is much more closely correlated with basion-nasion length (.464 ± .06) than with basion-prosthion length (.268 ± .07).

The total height of the face (nasion-menton) in the male series is most closely correlated with other height dimensions of the facial skeleton such as nasal height, symphysial height, and height of orbits. The correlation with condylo-symphysial length (.401 ± .06) is naturally high also. Upper facial height (nasion-prosthion) behaves similarly in its correlations (Tables IX–3, 5).

Basion-nasion and basion-prosthion lengths are very highly correlated in the female series (.859 ± .02) (Tables IX–3, 5), but the coefficient in the male series is much lower (.534 ± .05). Both external dimensions of the palate are significantly correlated in the male series with basion-prosthion length. On the other hand, the total facial height shows a low correlation with basion-prosthion length (.157 ± .07). Basion-nasion length is less closely correlated with palatal dimensions than is basion-prosthion length.

Nasal breadth shows no significant correlation with other dimensions in either male or female series. But nasal height in the males is related to orbital height and to orbital breadth (Table IX–3).

The group of correlations in the male series involving mandibular measurements (Tables IX–4, 5) presents several interesting features. Bigonial diameter, for example, is markedly correlated with nasion-prosthion height (.402 ± .06). But it is not significantly correlated either with minimum breadth of the ascending ramus or with mean angle of the mandible. Bicondylar width is not highly correlated with

TABLE IX-3. CORRELATION OF MEASUREMENTS OF FACE AND CRANIO-FACIAL BASE

	Bizygomatic	Nasion-menton	Nasion-prosthion	Nasal height	Nasal breadth	Orbital height	Orbital breadth	Basion-nasion	Basion-prosthion
Males: Total Series A									
Bizygomatic	....	.220±.07 (86)	.197±.07 (90)	....	.101±.07 (101)	....	.598±.04 (98)	.464±.06 (83)	.268±.07 (79)
Nasion-menton	.220±.07 (86)	....	....	.672±.04 (105)	....	.427±.06 (99)	....	.238±.07 (81)	.157±.07 (82)
Nasion-prosthion	.197±.07 (90)	....	....	.869±.02 (110)	....	.486±.05 (103)	....	.412±.06 (89)	.302±.06 (89)
Nasal height	....	.672±.04 (105)	.869±.02 (110)	....	−.086±.06 (124)	.439±.05 (111)	.246±.02 (112)	....	....
Nasal breadth	.101±.07 (101)	....	....	−.086±.06 (124)	....	.165±.06 (115)	.023±.06 (114)	....	....
Orbital height	....	.427±.06 (99)	.486±.05 (103)	.439±.05 (111)	.165±.06 (115)	....	.360±.05 (120)	....	....
Orbital breadth	.598±.04 (98)	....	....	.246±.02 (112)	.023±.06 (114)	.360±.05 (120)	....	....	....
Basion-nasion	.464±.06 (83)	.238±.07 (81)	.412±.06 (89)	....	....	....	....	....	.534±.05 (90)
Basion-prosthion	.268±.07 (79)	.157±.07 (82)	.302±.06 (89)	....	....	....	....	.534±.05 (90)	....
Females: Total Series A									
Bizygomatic	....	.344±.08 (59)	.272±.08 (61)	....	....	....	....	....	....
Nasion-menton	.344±.08 (59)	....	....	....	....	....	....	....	....
Nasion-prosthion	.272±.08 (61)	....	....	....	....	....	....	....	....
Nasal height	....	....	....	....	.183±.05 (86)	....	....	....	....
Nasal breadth	....	....	....	.183±.05 (86)	....	....	....	....	....
Orbital height	....	....	....	....	....	....	.332±.07 (83)	....	....
Orbital breadth	....	....	....	....	....	.332±.07 (83)	....	....	....
Basion-nasion	....	....	....	....	....	....	....	....	.859±.02 (60)
Basion-prosthion	....	....	....	....	....	....	....	.859±.02 (60)	....

TABLE IX–4. CORRELATION OF PALATAL AND MANDIBULAR MEASUREMENTS

Males: Total Series A

	External palatal length	External palatal breadth	Bicondylar	Bigonial	Height of ascending ramus	Minimum breadth of ascending ramus	Height of symphysis	Condylo-symphysial	Mean angle of lower jaw
External palatal length	....	.429 ±.06 (97)	....	....	....	....	....	....	....
External palatal breadth	.429 ±.06 (97)	....	....	....	....	....	....	....	....
Bicondylar	....	....	....	.542 ±.05 (79)	.107 ±.07 (83)	.149 ±.07 (83)	.199 ±.08 (66)	.120 ±.07 (81)	−.135 ±.07 (83)
Bigonial	....	....	.542 ±.05 (79)	....	.142 ±.07 (97)	.028 ±.07 (102)	.375 ±.06 (84)	.056 ±.08 (88)	−.010 ±.07 (91)
Height of ascending ramus	....	....	.107 ±.07 (83)	.142 ±.07 (97)	....	.393 ±.05 (116)	.117 ±.07 (95)	−.115 ±.07 (94)	−.580 ±.04 (97)
Minimum breadth of ascending ramus	....	....	.149 ±.07 (83)	.028 ±.07 (102)	.393 ±.05 (116)	....	.252 ±.06 (101)	.145 ±.07 (93)	−.290 ±.06 (96)
Height of symphysis	....	....	.199 ±.08 (66)	.375 ±.06 (84)	.117 ±.07 (95)	.252 ±.06 (101)	....	.184 ±.07 (79)	.039 ±.08 (79)
Condylo-symphysial	.342 ±.07 (72)	....	.120 ±.07 (81)	.056 ±.08 (88)	−.115 ±.07 (94)	.145 ±.07 (93)	.184 ±.07 (79)	....	.411 ±.06 (79)
Mean angle of lower jaw	....	....	−.135 ±.07 (83)	−.010 ±.07 (91)	−.580 ±.04 (97)	−.290 ±.06 (96)	.039 ±.08 (79)	.411 ±.06 (93)	....

Females: Total Series A

	External palatal length	External palatal breadth	Bicondylar	Bigonial	Height of ascending ramus	Minimum breadth of ascending ramus	Height of symphysis	Condylo-symphysial	Mean angle of lower jaw
External palatal length	....	.339 ±.07 (65)	....	....	....	....	....	....	....
External palatal breadth	.339 ±.07 (65)	....	....	....	....	....	....	....	....
Bicondylar	....	....	....	....	....	.114 ±.10 (47)	.141 ±.10 (42)	....	....
Bigonial	....	....	....	....	....	....	....	....	.279 ±.09 (50)
Minimum breadth of ascending ramus	....	....	.114 ±.10 (47)	....	....	....	....	....	....
Height of symphysis	....	....	.141 ±.10 (42)	....	....	....	....	....	....
Mean angle of lower jaw	....	....	....	.279 ±.09 (50)	....	....	....	....	....

TABLE IX–5. CORRELATION OF FACIAL AND CRANIO-FACIAL WITH MANDIBULAR
MEASUREMENTS

Males: Total Series A	Bizygo-matic	Nasion-menton	Nasion-prosthion	Basion-nasion	Basion-prosthion
Glabello-occipital length .... (undeformed)	....	....	....	.576 ± .09 (27)	....
External palatal length	....	....	....	.215 ± .07 (77)	.453 ± .06 (78)
External palatal breadth	....	....	....	.200 ± .07 (76)	.233 ± .07 (74)
Bicondylar	.658 ± .05 (71)	.142 ± .08 (70)	....	....	....
Bigonial	.554 ± .05 (79)	.298 ± .07 (87)	.402 ± .06 (85)	....	....
Height of ascending ramus...	.319 ± .06 (87)	.163 ± .07 (99)	.215 ± .06 (97)	....	....
Minimum breadth of ascend-ing ramus	.222 ± .07 (92)	.114 ± .07 (103)	....	....	....
Height of symphysis	.343 ± .07 (75)	.609 ± .04 (89)	....	....	....
Condylo-symphysial	.224 ± .07 (79)	.401 ± .06 (81)	.250 ± .07 (79)	....	....
Mean angle of lower jaw ....−.300 ± .07 (79)		.064 ± .07 (83)	....	....	....
Cranial capacity............ (undeformed)	....	....	....	.797 ± .05 (23)	....
Cranial capacity .... (deformed)	....	....	....	.308 ± .08 (55)	....

other mandibular dimensions, except bigonial diameter (.542 ± .05). Height of
ascending ramus is strongly correlated with minimum breadth, with bizygomatic
diameter, and negatively with the mean angle of the lower jaw (−.580 ± .04).
Condylo-symphysial length [1] is more closely related to bizygomatic diameter and to
total facial (nasion-menton) height than to any mandibular diameter except the
mean angle. It shows a moderately close relationship to external palatal length
(.342 ± .07).

The mean angle of the lower jaw naturally is correlated with condylo-symphysial
length because the greater the mandibular angle the greater the distance between
the tangents to the condyles and the mental prominence. A negative correlation
between mean angle and minimum breadth of the ascending ramus (−.290 ± .06)
perhaps reflects the extent to which, in aging individuals, the mandibular angle
opens out and the ramus is diminished in strength.

[1] Means, standard deviations, coefficients of variation, and their probable errors for condylo–symphysial length,
which was not included in Chapter III are:

Total Series A	No.	Range	Mean	S. D.	V.
Males	94	92–117	104.62 ± 0.32	4.53 ± 0.22	4.33 ± 0.21
Females	61	90–114	101.48 ± 0.44	5.10 ± 0.31	5.03 ± 0.31

CORRELATIONS OF LONG-BONE, PELVIC, AND SCAPULAR MEASUREMENTS

These correlations have all been calculated by the coefficient of variation method. In both sexes the correlations of shaft diameters of the femur at the subtrochanteric level and in the middle are positive and significant. Curiously enough, in the male series these correlations are higher on the left side than on the right, whereas the opposite is the case in the female group. Again in the males the subtrochanteric correlations are higher than the mid-shaft correlations, while the opposite is true in the females. Males show much higher correlations in shaft diameters of the tibiae than do the females.

Tibio-femoral and humero-femoral correlations are high in both sexes (Table IX–7). Pelvic measurements exhibit high correlations of breadth and height of the innominate bones. Innominate heights are also closely correlated with total pelvic breadth. The two diameters of the pelvic brim show a low coefficient of correlation in the male series (.166 ± .08), which is considerably higher in the female series (.391 ± .08) (Table IX–8). This suggests that the proportions of the female inlet are less varied than those of the male and perhaps more stabilized by function. Sacral length and sacral breadth show no correlation in either sex. This is probably due in part to the fact that the conventional length measurement of the sacrum does not take into account the degree of its curvature, but is in fact merely the distance from the middle of the superior edge of the promontory to the middle of the inferior edge of the last sacral vertebra. Since this dimension represents merely the length of the chord of the arc represented by the sacral concavity, it cannot be expected to bear any constant relationship to the morphological breadth of the sacrum.

The scapula is such a fragile bone that the number of specimens preserved is too small for effective correlation. So far as our scanty data go, it appears that scapular diameters are more closely correlated in males than in females and that the total height (or length) of the scapula in males is more closely correlated with the breadth (true morphological length) on the right side than on the left, whereas the reverse is the case with the correlation of inferior height and breadth. What this means, if it means anything at all, I do not know (Table IX–9).

It would be possible of course to adduce a good deal of comparative data for the correlations which have been tabulated and discussed above. Frankly, I do not think this worth while in a general monograph upon the skeletal characteristics of a population, interesting as it may be in a detailed and special study. Important as the method of correlation undoubtedly is in studying the relationships of parts and proportions in individuals and groups, it seems to me that it is, at the present state of our knowledge, quite useless for purposes of racial analysis.

TABLE IX–6. Correlation of Long-Bone Measurements — Femur

	Subtrochanteric diameter of femur	Subtrochanteric diameter of femur	Middle shaft diameter of femur	Middle shaft diameter of femur
Males: Total Series A	Antero-posterior	Lateral	Antero-posterior	Lateral
Subtrochanteric diameter of femur				
Antero-posterior, right	....	.317 ± .05 (158)	....	....
Antero-posterior, left	....	.418 ± .04 (157)	....	....
Lateral, right..............	.317 ± .05 (158)	....	....	....
Lateral, left	.418 ± .04 (157)	....	....	....
Middle shaft diameter of femur				
Antero-posterior, right......	....	....	....	.258 ± .05 (159)
Antero-posterior, left	....	....	....	.296 ± .05 (156)
Lateral, right..............	....	....	.258 ± .05 (159)	....
Lateral, left	....	....	.296 ± .05 (156)	....
Females: Total Series A				
Subtrochanteric diameter of femur				
Antero-posterior, right	....	.263 ± .06 (118)	....	....
Antero-posterior, left	....	.245 ± .06 (118)	....	....
Lateral, right	.263 ± .06 (118)	....	....	....
Lateral, left..............	.245 ± .06 (118)	....	....	....
Middle shaft diameter of femur				
Antero-posterior, right	....	....	....	.357 ± .05 (116)
Antero-posterior, left	....	....	....	.297 ± .06 (118)
Lateral, right..............	....	....	.357 ± .05 (116)	....
Lateral, left	....	....	.297 ± .06 (118)	....

TABLE IX-7. CORRELATION OF LONG-BONE MEASUREMENTS — TIBIA HUMERUS, FEMUR

	Middle diameter of tibia Antero-posterior	Middle diameter of tibia Lateral	Max. length of humerus	Max. length of femur	Max. length of tibia
Males: Total Series A					
Middle diameter of tibia					
Antero-posterior, right	....	.395 ± .05 (146)	....	....	....
Antero-posterior, left	....	.429 ± .05 (146)	....	....	....
Lateral, right	.395 ± .05 (146)	....	....	....	....
Lateral, left	.429 ± .05 (146)	....	....	....	....
Maximum length of humerus					
Right..............	....	....	....	.777 ± .02 (114)	....
Left	....	....	....	.761 ± .03 (116)	....
Maximum length of femur					
Right..............	....	....	.777 ± .02 (114)		.888 ± .01 (120)
Left	....	....	.761 ± .03 (116)		.886 ± .01 (104)
Maximum length of tibia					
Right	....	....	....	.888 ± .01 (120)	....
Left	....	....	....	.886 ± .01 (104)	....
Females: Total Series A					
Middle diameter of tibia					
Antero-posterior, right	....	.180 ± .06 (104)	....	....	....
Antero-posterior, left	....	.148 ± .06 (107)	....	....	....
Lateral, right........	.180 ± .06 (104)	....	....	....	....
Lateral, left	.148 ± .06 (107)	....	....	....	....
Maximum length of humerus					
Right..............	....	....	....	.822 ± .02 (85)	....
Left	....	....	....	.780 ± .03 (78)	....
Maximum length of femur					
Right	....	....	.822 ± .02 (85)		.833 ± .02 (81)
Left	....	....	.780 ± .03 (78)		.855 ± .02 (71)
Maximum length of tibia					
Right..............	....	....	....	.833 ± .02 (81)	....
Left	....	....	....	.855 ± .02 (71)	....

TABLE IX–8. CORRELATION OF PELVIC MEASUREMENTS

	Maximum breadth of pelvis	Height of ossa innominata	Breadth of ossa innominata	Maximum breadth of superior strait of pelvis	Anterior-posterior diameter of superior strait of pelvis	Height of sacrum	Breadth of sacrum
Males: Total Series A							
Maximum breadth of pelvis	……	.608 ±.05 (69)	……	……	……	……	……
Height of ossa innominata	.608 ±.05 (69)	……	.794 ±.03 (69)	……	……	……	……
Breadth of ossa innominata	……	.794 ±.03 (69)	……	……	……	……	……
Max. breadth of sup. strait of pelvis	……	……	……	……	.166 ±.08 (69)	……	……
Ant.-post. diam. of sup. strait of pelvis	……	……	……	.166 ±.08 (69)	……	……	……
Height of sacrum	……	……	……	……	……	……	−.014 ±.08 (66)
Breadth of sacrum	……	……	……	……	……	−.014 ±.08 (66)	……
Females: Total Series A							
Maximum breadth of pelvis	……	.523 ±.07 (55)	……	……	……	……	……
Height of ossa innominata	.523 ±.07 (55)	……	.793 ±.04 (52)	……	……	……	……
Breadth of ossa innominata	……	.793 ±.04 (52)	……	……	……	……	……
Max. breadth of sup. strait of pelvis	……	……	……	……	.391 ±.08 (56)	……	……
Ant.-post. diam. of sup. strait of pelvis	……	……	……	.391 ±.08 (56)	……	……	……
Height of sacrum	……	……	……	……	……	……	.065 ±.08 (46)
Breadth of sacrum	……	……	……	……	……	.065 ±.08 (46)	……

TABLE IX–9. CORRELATION OF SCAPULAR MEASUREMENTS

Males: Total Series A	Total height of scapula	Total breadth of scapula	Inferior height of scapula	Inferior breadth of scapula
Total height of scapula				
Right	....	.625 ± .07 (36)	....	....
Left	....	.583 ± .08 (35)	....	....
Total breadth of scapula				
Right	.625 ± .07 (36)	....	....	....
Left	.583 ± .08 (35)	....	....	....
Inferior height of scapula				
Right	....	....	....	.228 ± .10 (41)
Left	....	....	....	.461 ± .08 (43)
Inferior breadth of scapula				
Right	....	....	.228 ± .10 (41)	....
Left	....	....	.461 ± .08 (43)	....
Females: Total Series A				
Total height of scapula				
Right	....	.135 ± .19 (12)	....	....
Left	....	.538 ± .12 (17)	....	....
Total breadth of scapula				
Right	.135 ± .19 (12)	....	....	....
Left	.538 ± .12 (17)	....	....	....
Inferior height of scapula				
Right	....	....	....	− .204 ± .15 (18)
Left	....	....	....	.175 ± .15 (18)
Inferior breadth of scapula				
Right	....	....	− .204 ± .15 (18)	....
Left	....	....	.175 ± .15 (18)	....

ASSOCIATIONS AND CONTINGENCIES OF OBSERVED MORPHOLOGICAL CHARACTERS

METHOD AND EXAMPLES

In the following pages are presented some examples of the method used to ascertain the interrelationship between pairs of observed morphological features, each classified according to several gradations or categories. In each cell of the association table the frequency in the male series of a certain grade of the two associated characters is recorded. Set against this observed frequency is the independence frequency. The independence frequency is obtained for each cell by multiplying the total number of the observed frequencies of a single category of one of the two associated characters by the total number of observed frequencies in the corresponding gradation of a single category of the other associated character, and dividing this product by the total number of observations of all categories of both characters, or the total number of observations in the series. Thus if the two associated characters be designated as A and B, and A_m and B_n be the frequencies of any two categories or gradations of these associated characters $(A_m B_n)$ will be the observed frequency of individuals or things possessing both characters. Then if A's and B's are totally independent in the universe of things at large, $(A_m B_n) = \dfrac{(A_m)(B_n)}{N} = (A_m B_n)_0$ where N = the total observations in the entire series. The expression $\dfrac{(A_m)(B_n)}{N}$ or $(A_m B_n)_0$ is the independence frequency. But if A and B are not completely independent $(A_m B_n)$ and $(A_m B_n)_0$ will not be identical for all values of m and n.[1]

The contingency or association table must be interpreted according to the deviations of the observed frequencies in any one cell from the independence frequency or expected frequency calculated for that cell. If the difference between the observed frequency and the expected frequency is great there is an implication of some association between the two characters apart from that due merely to chance. The coefficient of mean square contingency measures on a scale from zero to unity the extent to which two characters or the various subcategories of two characters are associated over and beyond what might be expected through the operation of mere chance. It does not specify the nature of such association. Since the coefficient of mean square contingency is always positive and its value is enhanced by the chance irregularities of distribution found in small samples, it must be interpreted conservatively.

The number of graded observational characters recorded for the series of Pecos crania is so large that the labor of calculating coefficients of mean square contingency for all possible combinations of pairs of characters is too great to be undertaken. In the present case only a few of the more promising characters have been investigated.

---

[1] Yule, 1927, p. 64.

In the total male series there is a perceptible relationship between the size of the nasal spine and the observed breadth of the nasal aperture. Large spines are positively associated with narrow apertures and small spines with broad nasal apertures. The size of the coefficients when calculated on the small subgroups is somewhat increased because of insufficiency of numbers. Small spines and broad apertures are primitive features; large spines and small apertures are more highly evolved characters.

TABLE IX–10. DEVELOPMENT OF NASAL SPINE AND OBSERVED BREADTH OF NASAL APERTURE

Males: Total Series A	Nasal Spine						
	Small		Medium		Large		
Nasal aperture	No.	I. F.	No.	I. F.	No.	I. F.	Total
Narrow....................	3	6.32	7	7.11	5	1.58	15
Medium	36	34.95	39	39.32	8	8.74	83
Broad	17	14.74	17	16.58	1	3.68	35
Total	56		63		14		133

Coefficient of mean square contingency 0.28

Black-on-white and Gl. I	Glazes II and III	Glaze IV	Glazes V and VI
0.41	0.54	0.42	0.29

The primitive feature of an ill-defined or dull nasal sill is likely to occur in association with a broad nasal aperture. The contingency of these features is shown in Table IX–11. The coefficient 0.33 for the total male series is largely the expression of the tendency for the narrower forms of noses to have sharper lower borders and for broad nasal apertures to have indistinct or absent lower borders. The higher coefficients in the subgroups are due to the very small size of the samples and are not significant.

TABLE IX–11. DEVELOPMENT OF LOWER BORDERS OF NASAL APERTURE AND OBSERVED BREADTH OF NASAL APERTURE

Males: Total Series A	Lower Borders								
	Absent or Indictinct		Dull		Medium		Sharp		
Breadth of nasal aperture	No.	I. F.	No.	I. F.	No.	I. F.	No.	I. F.	Total
Narrow	0	1.17	5	6.59	7	3.16	0	1.08	12
Medium	5	8.31	51	46.65	21	22.37	8	7.67	85
Broad	8	3.52	17	19.76	7	9.47	4	3.25	36
Total	13		73		35		12		133

Coefficient of mean square contingency 0.33

Black-on-white and Gl. I	Glazes II and III	Glaze IV	Glazes V and VI
0.45	0.51	0.39	0.42

Table IX–12 shows the tendency for orbits of square shape to have their long axes horizontal or but slightly inclined downward and outward, of oblong orbits to show a medium inclination, and of the less common rhomboidal shape to be strongly inclined.

TABLE IX–12. Shape of Orbits and Inclination of Orbits

Males: Total Series A	Inclination								
	None		Slight		Medium		Pronounced		
Shape	No.	I.F.	No.	I.F.	No.	I.F.	No.	I.F.	Total
Square	13	11.12	13	9.85	10	13.98	5	6.04	41
Oblong...............	21	21.98	18	19.47	31	27.63	11	11.93	81
Rhomboidal	1	1.90	0	1.69	3	2.39	3	1.03	7
Total	35		31		44		19		129

Coefficient of mean square contingency   0.26

Black-on-white and Gl. I	Glazes II and III	Glaze IV	Glazes V and VI
0.44	0.37	0.46	0.48

A perusal of Table IX–13 shows that there is little consistent relationship between the inclination of the orbits and the size of the malars. One expects to find little or no inclination of the long axes of the orbits when the malars are large or very large, but this expectation is not fulfilled. The size of the coefficient (0.24) is due to irregularity of association rather than definite trend of correlation.

TABLE IX–13. Size of Malars and Inclination of Orbits

Males: Total Series A	Inclination of Orbits								
	None		Slight		Medium		Pronounced		
Size of malars	No.	I.F.	No.	I.F.	No.	I.F.	No.	I.F.	Total
Small to medium	12	12.43	9	10.08	17	14.78	4	5.71	43
Large	18	21.39	20	17.34	23	25.44	13	9.83	74
Very large	6	3.18	1	2.58	4	3.78	0	1.46	11
Total	37		30		44		17		128

Coefficient of mean square contingency   0.24

Black-on-white and Gl. I	Glazes II and III	Glaze IV	Glazes V and VI
0.28	0.30	0.33	0.52

Table IX–14 shows that there is no perceptible relationship between observed shape of orbits and observed size of malars.

It is to be expected that small brow-ridges go with small malars and large brow-ridges with larger malars. Table IX–15 shows that the association between size of brow-ridges and size of malars is marked.

TABLE IX–14. SIZE OF MALARS AND SHAPE OF ORBITS

Males: Total Series A	Shape of Orbits						
	Square		Oblong		Rhomboidal		Total
Size of malars	No.	I. F.	No.	I. F.	No.	I. F.	
Small to medium	14	13.56	28	26.46	0	1.98	42
Large	23	23.57	45	45.98	5	3.45	73
Very large	4	3.87	7	7.56	1	0.57	12
Total....................	41		80		6		127

Coefficient of mean square contingency 0.16

Black-on-white and Gl. I	Glazes II and III	Glaze IV	Glazes V and VI
0.33	0.34	0.16	0.44

TABLE IX–15. SIZE OF MALARS AND SIZE OF SUPRAORBITAL RIDGES

Males: Total Series A	Size of Supraorbital Ridges						
	Absent to small		Medium		Large or very large		Total
Size of malars	No.	I. F.	No.	I. F.	No.	I. F.	
Small to medium	22	11.91	17	22.49	4	8.60	43
Large	14	21.05	43	39.75	19	15.20	76
Very large	0	3.04	8	5.75	3	2.20	11
Total....................	36		68		26		130

Coefficient of mean square contingency 0.37

Black-on-white and Gl. I	Glazes II and III	Glaze IV	Glazes V and VI
0.36	0.63	0.64	0.44

Table IX–16 shows that size of malars is independent of depth of suborbital fossae.

TABLE IX–16. SIZE OF MALARS AND DEPTH OF SUBORBITAL FOSSAE

Males: Total Series A	Size of Malars						
	Small to medium		Large		Very large		Total
Depth of suborbital fossae	No.	I. F.	No.	I. F.	No.	I. F.	
Absent or submedium	13	12.97	19	21.11	6	3.92	38
Medium	17	15.70	28	25.56	1	4.75	46
Deep	13	14.33	23	23.33	6	4.33	42
Total....................	43		70		13		126

Coefficient of mean square contingency 0.20

Black-on-white and Gl. I	Glazes II and III	Glaze IV	Glazes V and VI
0.33	0.65	0.31	0.49

In the total male series there is no significant relationship between size of brow-ridges and amount of alveolar prognathism. A similar lack of association between type of brow-ridge and degree of alveolar prognathism is indicated by a coefficient of mean square contingency of 0.20. The contingency table from which this coefficient is calculated may be omitted (Table IX–17).

TABLE IX–17. SIZE OF SUPRAORBITAL RIDGES AND DEVELOPMENT OF ALVEOLAR PROGNATHISM

Males: Total Series A	Size of Supraorbital Ridges						
	Absent to small		Medium		Large or very large		Total
Alveolar prognathism	No.	I. F.	No.	I. F.	No.	I. F.	
Submedium	7	8.02	16	16.84	8	6.15	31
Medium	13	14.74	34	30.96	10	11.30	57
Large	10	7.24	13	15.21	5	5.55	28
Total..................	30		63		23		116

Coefficient of mean square contingency 0.15

Black-on-white and Gl. I	Glazes II and III	Glaze IV	Glazes V and VI
0.46	0.35	0.47	0.26

Table IX–18 shows a marked association between wear of the teeth and estimated quality of the teeth. Teeth that are much worn are likely to be classified as "poor" and teeth little worn as "good." These associations are doubtless influenced by the fact that with advancing age and increased dental erosion, caries arising from wear and alveolar abscesses resulting from exposure of the pulp cavities bring about deterioration and loss of teeth. The young person who has teeth of medium quality is likely to have poor teeth in old age.

TABLE IX–18. WEAR OF TEETH AND QUALITY OF TEETH

Males: Total Series A	Wear of Teeth						
	Slight		Medium		Pronounced		Total
Quality	No.	I. F.	No.	I. F.	No.	I. F.	
Poor	1	4.87	8	12.04	22	14.09	31
Medium	4	5.02	12	12.43	16	14.55	32
Good	14	9.11	27	22.25	17	26.36	58
Total..................	19		47		55		121

Coefficient of mean square contingency 0.34

Black-on-white and Gl. I	Glazes II and III	Glaze IV	Glazes V and VI
0.49	0.32	0.27	0.49

Table IX–19 shows the marked extent to which worn teeth are associated with multiple alveolar abscess and conversely the negative association of slightly worn teeth with such abscesses. This is the highest contingency of observed features found in the associations examined.

TABLE IX–19. WEAR OF TEETH AND NUMBER OF ALVEOLAR ABSCESSES

Males: Total Series A	Wear of Teeth						Total
	Submedium		Medium		Pronounced		
Abscesses	No.	I. F.	No.	I. F.	No.	I. F.	
None	12	6.88	27	17.40	12	26.71	51
Few	5	5.94	14	15.02	25	23.05	44
Many	0	4.18	2	10.58	29	16.24	31
Total..................	17		43		66		126

Coefficient of mean square contingency 0.48

Black-on-white and Gl. I	Glazes II and III	Glaze IV	Glazes V and VI
0.63	0.49	0.59	0.55

OTHER CONTINGENCIES

A number of other associations were tabulated and coefficients of mean square contingency were calculated. Most of these latter were insignificant and the tables from which they were derived need not be printed. Shape of the palate (parabolic, hyperbolic, U-shaped, or elliptical) shows a low contingency upon alveolar prognathism (0.25). This value of the coefficient indicates principally the extent to which in this series parabolic palates are positively associated with pronounced alveolar prognathism and U-shaped palates with a medium degree of alveolar prognathism. The contingency coefficient of 0.16 between shape of palate and height of palatal roof shows the virtual independence of these features. Similarly, size of styloid processes shows no significant association with depression of petrous parts of the temporal bones (coefficient of mean square contingency 0.13), and the depth of the glenoid fossa is independent of the development of the postglenoid tubercle (coefficient 0.16).

The foregoing associations and contingencies are of such small value as to warrant the conclusion that apart from some crude size relations most of the morphological cranial features observed are inherited independently in individuals of this series. The higher value of the coefficients in the small subgroups seems to mean nothing, since a perusal of the tables upon which they are based shows that the values of the coefficients have been enhanced by the random irregularities of the very inadequate samples.

CHAPTER X

PATHOLOGY

INTRODUCTION

The pathology of dry bones is a sadly neglected field of investigation. The clinicians of to-day manifest but slight interest in the subject. A few of the commoner diseases which affect the bones are easily diagnosed even by an anthropologist with no claim to any special knowledge of pathology. Confronted with the more interesting bone lesions the most expert pathologist is usually at a loss and invariably non-committal. During the routine of measurement and observation of the skeletons I made brief notes upon the pathology of each specimen. These notes are recorded in the raw tables of Appendix III. All of the puzzling and interesting specimens were laid aside for examination by experts. During the summer of 1926, George D. Williams, M.D., reëxamined the bulk of the Pecos material and made independent notes upon the pathology which are listed at the end of the present chapter. The tables included in the chapter were made up from Dr. Williams' observations. At various times most of the skeletons exhibiting pathological features of interest were submitted to the expert examination of various pathologists — among them Professor Frank B. Mallory and Professor Simeon B. Wolbach of Harvard University, and Professor Herbert U. Williams of the University of Buffalo. Dr. M. C. Sosman of the Peter Bent Brigham Hospital and of the Harvard Medical School, and Dr. E. C. Vogt of the Children's Hospital, Boston, took X-ray photographs of all of the important specimens and pronounced upon them from the point of view of the roentgenologist.

We shall never be able to acquire any satisfactory basis for the study of palaeopathology until clinical pathologists and anatomists coöperate in the preservation of skeletal material of known clinical history. At the present time pathologists cannot distinguish in dry bones the lesions left by diseases which they easily and correctly diagnose in the living. The few exceptions to this generalization include only arthritis, osteomyelitis, Pott's disease, osteomalacia, and a few other ailments.

ARTHRITIS

Serious arthritic affection of the vertebrae is known as *spondylitis deformans* or "poker back." The condition varies from moderate marginal exostoses on the lumbar vertebrae to extensive bony growths involving the larger part of the spine and causing a complete rigidity. This disease is common among primitive people and occurs sporadically in most series of Indian skeletons. Table X–1 records its incidence in a group of 503 adult or sub-adult Pecos skeletons. It actually occurs in 13.12 per cent of this sample of the population. It seems to have been least prevalent in the earliest periods (Black-on-white and Glaze I), in which groups only 9 per cent

PLATE X–1

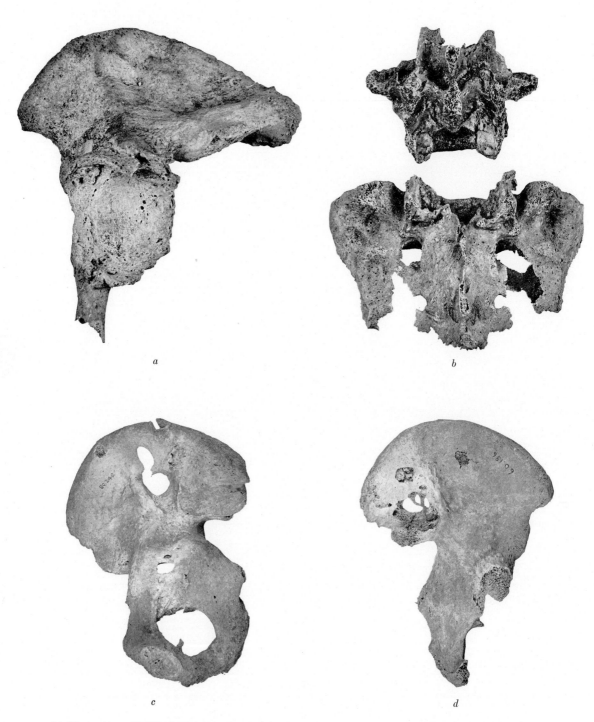

a

b

c

d

(*a*) No. 59,967. UNHEALED ARTHRITIC FRACTURE OF ACETABULUM. MALE. GLAZE III
(*b*) No. 60,196. POTT'S DISEASE. MALE. GLAZE VI.   (*c*) No. 60,242. HEALED FRACTURE
OF ILIUM AND ACETABULUM. MALE. GLAZE IV.   (*d*) No. 60,136. OSTEOMYELITIS OF
LEFT SACRO-ILIAC JOINT

of the sample are affected. The differences between the other period groups in respect to the per cent affected by this disease are probably not significant. No sub-adults (18–21 years) manifested this disease and only two young adults (21–35 years). Of the males affected, 60.42 per cent were classified as "old" (more than 50 years of age). In the female group, 66.67 per cent of those who suffered from this disease were judged to be old.

Arthritic affection of long bones, short bones, and joints is recorded in Table X–2. Of 503 sub-adult and adult skeletons 20, or 3.98 per cent, show some manifestation of the disease. Here again the earliest periods seem to show the least prevalence of the disorder. Of the 20 cases only two are recorded in the skeletons of "young adults," both of these being females. In the male cases 15.38 per cent occur in skeletons judged to be "middle-aged" and 84.62 per cent in "old" individuals. Among the female cases, on the other hand, 57.14 per cent were estimated to be "middle-aged" and only one case (14.29 per cent) was found in the skeletons aged 50 years or over. The apparently greater incidence of this disease in the younger females as compared with the males may be merely the chance result of the small size of our sample. It seems worth while, however, to call attention to its possible significance.

Usually the cases of degenerative arthritis affecting joints and long bones manifest also spondylitis deformans and, in a number of cases, osteomyelitis is an associated condition. Fractures accompanied by arthritic changes are also relatively common. Skeleton No. 59967, a middle-aged male belonging to the Glaze III period, shows, in addition to spondylitis deformans, a fracture of the left acetabulum which is unhealed with the formation of a new acetabular surface at the juncture of the ilium and pubis and above the ununited ischial portion of the original acetabulum. The left femur in this specimen also shows a vertical fracture of the head and arthritic changes have taken place in all of the bones (Plate X–1 a).

Table X–3 records the cases in which arthritic changes appear only on the occipital condyles. There are only five such cases.

TABLE X–1. SPONDYLITIS DEFORMANS

Male and Female	Young Adult No.	Per cent Affected	Per cent Glaze	Middle-Aged No.	Per cent Affected	Per cent Glaze	Old No.	Per cent Affected	Per cent Glaze	Total Affected No.	Per cent Glaze
B.-on-W. and Glaze I (total 122)	0	0	0	4	36.36	3.28	7	63.63	5.74	11	9.02
Glazes II and III .... (total 173)	1	3.57	0.58	9	32.14	5.20	18	64.28	10.40	28	16.18
Glaze IV .... (total 115)	1	7.69	0.87	1	7.69	0.87	11	84.62	9.56	13	11.30
Glazes V and VI .... (total 93) ...	0	0	0	9	64.29	9.68	5	35.71	5.38	14	15.05
Total .... (total 503)	2	3.03	0.40	23	34.85	4.57	41	62.12	8.15	66	13.12

Total (by sexes)											Per cent of Total Affected
Male	1	2.08		18	37.50		29	60.42		48	72.73
Female	1	5.56		5	27.78		12	66.67		18	27.27

TABLE X–2. DEGENERATIVE ARTHRITIS DEFORMANS

Male and Female	Young Adult			Middle-Aged			Old			Total Affected	
	No.	Per cent Affected	Per cent Glaze	No.	Per cent Affected	Per cent Glaze	No.	Per cent Affected	Per cent Glaze	No.	Per cent Glaze
B.-on-W. and Glaze I (total 122)	0	0	0	1	50.00	0.82	1	50.00	0.82	2	1.64
Glazes II and III ... (total 173)	1	14.29	0.58	1	14.29	0.58	5	71.43	2.89	7	4.05
Glaze IV .... (total 115)	1	14.29	0.87	2	28.57	1.74	4	57.14	3.48	7	6.09
Glazes V and VI .... (total 93)	0	0	0	2	50.00	2.15	2	50.00	2.15	4	4.30
Total .... (total 503)	2	10.00	0.40	6	30.00	1.19	12	60.00	2.39	20	3.98

Total (by sexes)						Per cent of Total Affected
Male	0	0	2	15.38	11	84.62	13	65.00
Female	2	28.57	4	57.14	1	14.29	7	35.00

TABLE X–3. DEGENERATIVE ARTHRITIS DEFORMANS (ARTHRITIC CONDYLES OF OCCIPITAL BONE ONLY)

Male and Female	Young Adult			Middle-Aged			Old			Total Affected	
	No.	Per cent Affected	Per cent Glaze	No.	Per cent Affected	Per cent Glaze	No.	Per cent Affected	Per cent Glaze	No.	Per cent Glaze
B.-on-W. and Glaze I (total 122)	1	50.00	0.82	0	0	0	1	50.00	0.82	2	1.64
Glazes II and III .... (total 173)	0	0	0	0	0	0	0	0	0	0	0
Glaze IV .... (total 115)	0	0	0	1	50.00	0.87	1	50.00	0.87	2	1.74
Glazes V and VI ..... (total 93)	0	0	0	0	0	0	1	100.00	1.08	1	1.08
Total .... (total 503)	1	20.00	0.20	1	20.00	0.20	3	60.00	0.60	5	0.99

Total (by sexes)						Per cent of Total Affected
Male	1	33.33	0	0	2	66.67	3	60.00
Female	0	0	1	50.00	1	50.00	2	40.00

INFLAMMATORY LESIONS

LONG BONES

Periostitis, usually affecting both tibiae, and not infrequently the femora or other long bones, was found in 13 of 503 skeletons, especially examined for pathology. Table X–4 records the distribution of this disease by age groups, periods, and sexes. It occurs at all ages. The total number of cases recorded is too small to be significant from the point of view of stratum. Of the sample series, 2.58 per cent showed evidence of this disease. It seems to have been most common in the latest period of the pueblo. This condition may have been due to some non-specific infection such as streptococcus or staphylococcus, or possibly syphilis. Indians living bare-legged on a rocky mesa would of course be liable to injuries of shins which in some cases would develop into acute or chronic inflammations. Four cases of osteomyelitis occurred in the 503 skeletons especially examined (Table X–5).

Professor Herbert U. Williams has examined minutely a number of the more interesting pathological long bones. Three of these seemed to him to indicate probable syphilis. These were a left femur and left tibia of No. 60318, a middle-aged male of Glaze VI ("historical" stratum); the right femur of No. 60455, a middle-aged female of Glaze I or Black-on-white period; and No. 60268, a left tibia of a middle-aged male of Glaze III.

TABLE X–4. PERIOSTITIS (LONG BONES)

Male and Female	Sub-adult No.	Per cent Affected	Per cent Glaze	Young Adult No.	Per cent Affected	Per cent Glaze	Middle-Aged No.	Per cent Affected	Per cent Glaze	Old No.	Per cent Affected	Per cent Glaze	Total Affected No.	Per cent Glaze
B.-on-W. and Gl. I (total 122)	1	20.00	0.82	1	20.00	0.82	2	40.00	1.64	1	20.00	0.82	5	4.10
Glazes II and III (total 173)	0	0	0	0	0	0	0	0	0	1	100.00	0.58	1	0.58
Glaze IV (total 115)	1	100.00	0.87	0	0	0	0	0	0	0	0	0	1	0.87
Glazes V and VI (total 93)	0	0	0	1	16.67	1.08	4	66.67	4.30	1	16.67	1.08	6	6.45
Total (total 503)	2	15.38	0.40	2	15.38	0.40	6	46.15	1.19	3	23.08	0.60	13	2.58

Total (by sexes)	No.	Per cent		No.	Per cent		No.	Per cent		No.	Per cent		No.	Per cent of Total Affected
Male	0	0		1	12.50		5	62.50		2	25.00		8	61.54
Female	2	40.00		1	20.00		1	20.00		1	20.00		5	38.46

TABLE X–5. OSTEOMYELITIS (LONG BONES)

Male and Female	Sub-adult No.	Per cent Affected	Per cent Glaze	Young Adult No.	Per cent Affected	Per cent Glaze	Middle-Aged No.	Per cent Affected	Per cent Glaze	Old No.	Per cent Affected	Per cent Glaze	Total Affected No.	Per cent Glaze
B.-on-W. and Gl. I (total 122)	0	0	0	0	0	0	2	100.00	1.64	0	0	0	2	1.64
Glazes II and III (total 173)	1	100.00	0.58	0	0	0	0	0	0	0	0	0	1	0.58
Glaze IV (total 115)	0	0	0	0	0	0	0	0	0	1	100.00	0.87	1	0.87
Glazes V and VI (total 93)	0	0	0	0	0	0	0	0	0	0	0	0	0	0
Total (total 503)	1	25.00	0.20	0	0	0	2	50.00	0.40	1	25.00	0.20	4	0.80

Total (by sexes)	No.	Per cent		No.	Per cent		No.	Per cent		No.	Per cent		No.	Per cent of Total Affected
Male	1	33.33		0	0		1	33.33		1	33.33		3	75.00
Female	0	0		0	0		1	100.00		0	0		1	25.00

CRANIA

The most interesting cranial lesions of an inflammatory character are found in crania Nos. 59814, 59864, and 60455.

No. 59814 is a fragment of the skull of a young adult female of the Glaze III stratum. This fragment includes the palate, most of the face, and the larger portion of the frontal bone. The roof of the palate shows evidence of inflammation and a pathological deposition of bone. The posterior third of the palate is perforated by a hole almost square in shape, but with the corners rounded and with the edges beveled and cicatrized. This hole is about 2 cm. square. The nasal orifice is a round, cicatrized hole of about the same size as the perforation through the hard palate, with which it is continuous. The borders of the nasal aperture have been covered with a thick, bony deposit which is beveled inward, and the lower halves of the nasal bones are involved in this cicatrix. It is hard to escape the conclusion that the soft parts of the nose must have been almost completely eaten away by some sort of ulcer. Plate X–2a, 2b show the nature and extent of these lesions. Plate X–3 reproduces the X-ray film of this specimen.

Professor James Ewing of Cornell Medical College, upon examination of this specimen, stated his inability to give a valid opinion as to the nature of the lesion. He was not certain that ulceration had taken place and suspected it to be a congenital deformity. He did not consider it of syphilitic origin.

No. 59864 is the cranium of a middle-aged female originating from the Glaze II stratum. In this specimen again the nasal cavity has been the seat of an extensive inflammation which has destroyed the lower portions of the nasalia and the borders of the aperture. This abscess has perforated the alveolar borders through the alveoli of the right canine and the lateral incisors. The roof of the palate is cicatrized. There are a number of erosions on the left half of the frontal bone and the left supra-orbital ridge. There are also thickened areas on the frontal bone, the malars, and the orbital walls. Professor Ewing was unable to satisfy himself as to the nature of this affection, but did not think it syphilitic (Plate X–4a).

No. 60455 is the skull of a middle-aged female of the Glaze I or Black-on-white period. In this specimen the nasal bones are only slightly involved, but the frontal bone is extensively scarred and pitted and covered with cicatrizations. On the left half of the frontal bone the *tabula externa* and the diploë have been eaten away over a large irregular area, the borders of which are cicatrized. Plates X–2c, X–4b, X–7, 8 illustrate this specimen. In this case again Professor Ewing is of the opinion that the lesion is not syphilitic.

Professor Herbert U. Williams of the University of Buffalo, who for a number of years has been engaged in a study of the osteological evidence relating to the origin of syphilis, has examined several times the three cranial specimens under discussion. Professor Williams has very kindly prepared for this publication a statement of his opinion as to the nature of the lesions which they present.

Your three bone specimens from Pecos: 59814, 59864, and 60455 were examined by me carefully. In my opinion the pathological changes in the last two were probably produced

PLATE X–2

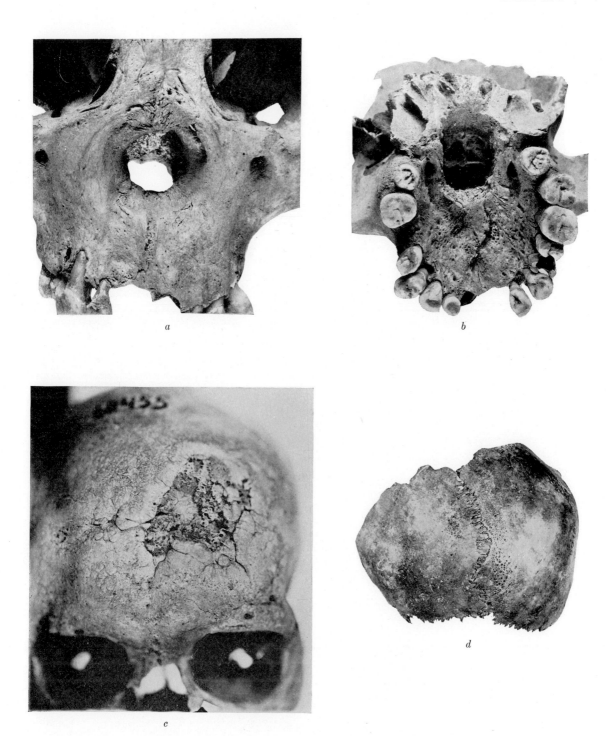

(a) No. 59,814. CICATRIZED NASAL APERTURE. FEMALE. GLAZE III.   (b) No. 59,814. PER-
FORATION AND INFLAMMATORY CHANGES OF PALATE. FEMALE. GLAZE III. (c) No. 60,455.
INFLAMMATORY LESION. FEMALE. BLACK-ON-WHITE OR GLAZE I.   (d) No. 60,184. OSTEO–
POROTIC PITTING OF PARIETALS. DOUBTFUL SEX. GLAZE V

PLATE X–3

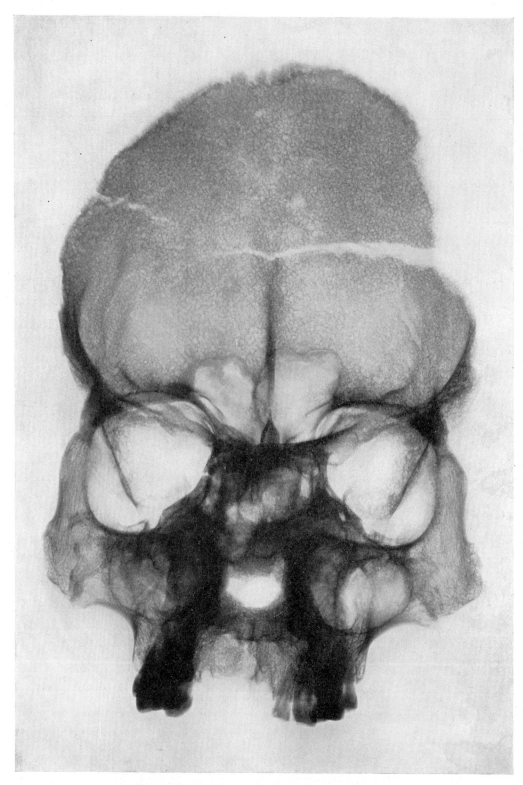

No. 59,814. ROENTGENOGRAM OF FACE AND FRONTAL FRAGMENT OF CRANIUM
WITH CICATRIZED NASAL APERTURE AND PERFORATED PALATE
FEMALE. GLAZE III

Photograph by Dr. M. C. Sosman, Peter Bent Brigham Hospital, Boston

Plate X–4

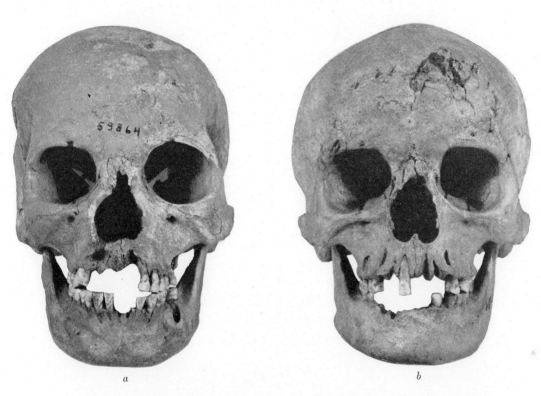

a   *b*

(*a*) No. 59,864. INFLAMMATION OF NASAL CAVITY AND FRONTAL BONE.
FEMALE. GLAZE II. (*b*) No. 60,455. INFLAMMATORY LESION OF FRONTAL
BONE. FEMALE. BLACK-ON-WHITE OR GLAZE I

PLATE X–5

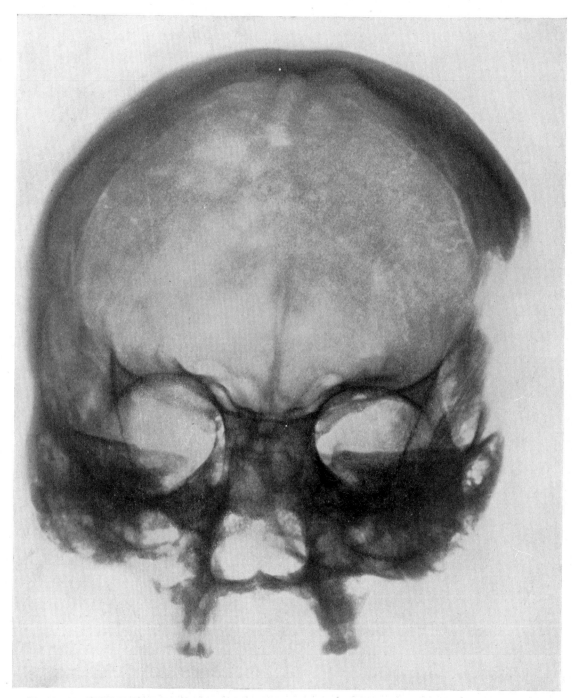

No. 59,864. ROENTGENOGRAM OF CRANIUM WITH INFLAMMATION OF NASAL CAVITY AND
FRONTAL BONE. FEMALE. GLAZE II. FRONTAL VIEW

Photograph by Dr. M. C. Sosman, Peter Bent Brigham Hospital, Boston

PLATE X–6

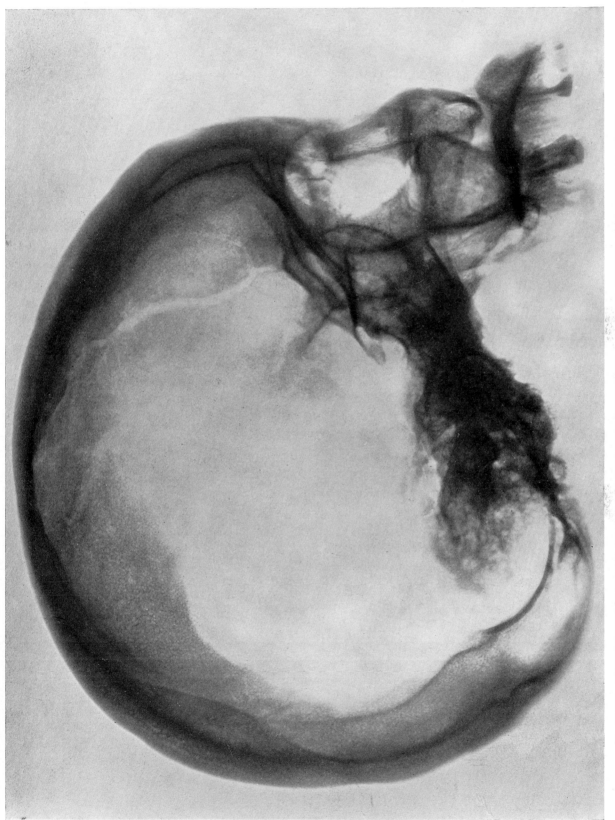

No. 59,864. ROENTGENOGRAM OF CRANIUM WITH INFLAMMATION OF NASAL CAVITY AND FRONTAL BONE
FEMALE. GLAZE II. LATERAL VIEW

Photograph by Dr. M. C. Sosman, Peter Bent Brigham Hospital, Boston

PLATE X–7

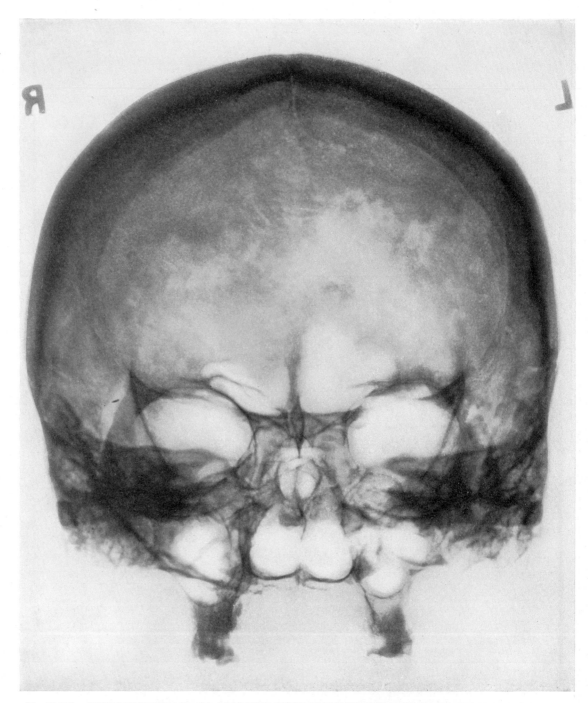

No. 60,455. ROENTGENOGRAM OF CRANIUM WITH INFLAMMATORY LESION ON FRONTAL BONE
FEMALE. BLACK-ON-WHITE OR GLAZE I. FRONTAL VIEW

Photograph by Dr. M. C. Sosman, Peter Bent Brigham Hospital, Boston

PLATE X–8

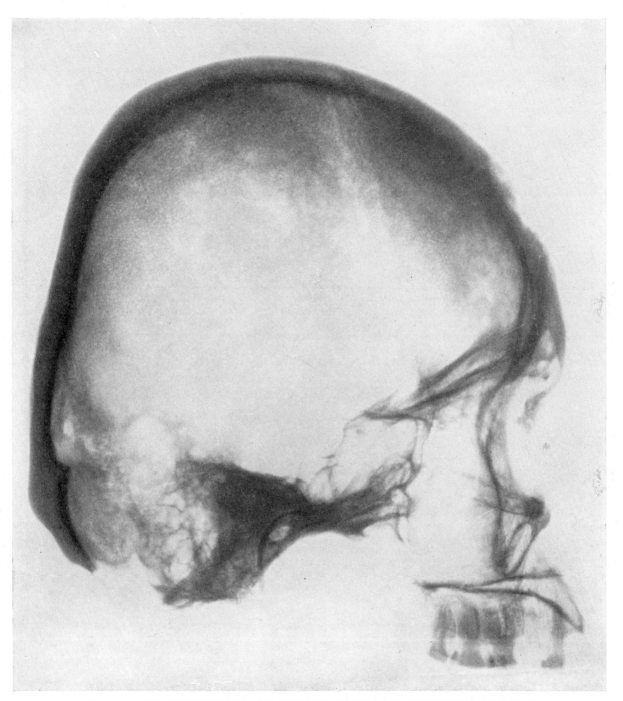

No. 60,455. ROENTGENOGRAM OF CRANIUM WITH INFLAMMATORY LESION ON
FRONTAL BONE. FEMALE. BLACK-ON-WHITE OR GLAZE I. LATERAL VIEW

Photograph by Dr. M. C. Sosman, Peter Bent Brigham Hospital, Boston.

by syphilis. The condition of the nasal region in 59814 might have been the result of injury, but the perforation of the palate is more consistent with syphilis. Case 60455 is the most characteristic of the three.[1] I remember also that you had various long bones with irregular thickenings or hyperostoses.

Tertiary syphilis when very severe or not treated often produces erosion of bone accompanied or followed by new formation of bone. On the outer surface of the vault of the cranium the result is very striking, and is almost distinctive of syphilis; this has long been considered the classical example of syphilitic bone disease in adults. Changes in the long bones are frequent, but similar changes may be brought about by so many diseases that the long bones are much less valuable for diagnostic purposes than the cranium; however, irregular thickening of the tibia is important. Involvement of the nasal region is not so common but it is by no means rare.

It is possible, though not probable, that the lesions in your cases were due to injury followed by suppurative infection, with subsequent healing. Such infections as tuberculosis, leprosy and actinomycosis should be kept in mind, though it is most unlikely that any of them was concerned in your cases.

The tropical disease, yaws or framboesia (including the allied or identical conditions, gangosa and rhinopharyngitis mutilans), may, it is said, cause extensive erosion of and about the nose, with involvement of the bones (Bittner, "Tertiary Lesions of Yaws," *Am. Journ. Tropical Med.*, Vol. VI, p. 123, March, 1926.) Castellani and Chalmers state that gangosa may cause a chronic ostitis like that seen in syphilis (*Handbook of Tropical Medicine*, 3rd. ed. 1919, p. 1879. See also Maul in *Philippine Journ. Sci.*, Section B, Vol. XII, p. 258, Sept. 1917, on "Bone Lesions in Yaws"; also Howard in *Journ. Tropical Med. and Hyg.*, Vol. XVIII, p. 25, Feb. 1915.) I have had no experience with yaws and have made only a cursory examination of the literature. It seems that bone lesions in this disease have not yet been studied so extensively as those of syphilis. Some have regarded yaws as a form of syphilis.

The disease known in Peru as Uta, which sometimes causes destruction in the nasal region, should also be considered. Strong and his colleagues regard it as a form of leishmaniasis. (Harvard Expedition to Peru, 1913.)

I do not believe that we are warranted in saying of any single dried bone specimen that it is certainly syphilitic. However, your three cases having marked erosion and bony thickening of the nasal region, and especially case 60455 showing quite typical involvement of the frontal bone, together with the various thickenings of long bones from other cases, make powerful evidence for the existence of syphilis among the people from whom the bones were derived.

HERBERT U. WILLIAMS.
Laboratory of Pathology, School of Medicine,
University of Buffalo.

June 16, 1926.

From the foregoing statement and discussion it is evident that the existence of syphilis among the American Indians in pre-Columbian times cannot be proved until pathologists become more certain of their diagnoses from dry bones of the lesions caused by this disease. It is unfortunate that qualified experts should have disagreed in the three cases under discussion, since all of them are definitely and indisputably prehistoric — a statement which cannot be made concerning most

[1] Professor Williams has recently examined the right femur of this same specimen (No. 60455) and in a communication to me, dated March 15, 1929, states that it is "probably syphilitic. Dr. E. C. König of the University of Buffalo X-rayed this femur for me and we agree that the bony thickening came from a chronic periostitis, very likely syphilitic. The association of lesions in the skull and the femur is important and is in favor of syphilis."

remains of American Indians thought to be syphilitic. Pecos is the largest and most clearly stratified site in the New World containing human burials. The three crania in question all belong to the prehistoric periods of the pueblo, Black-on-white, Glazes I, II, and III. Europeans came into the Southwest in 1540, which is the Pecos Glaze V period. In the absence of any certain diagnosis, it is obviously futile to discuss here the historical evidence of an American origin of the disease, which, to my mind, is quite impressive. Indirect evidence of a historical nature will never settle the question.

TRAUMATIC LESIONS

FRACTURES

Fractures other than those of the skull were noted in 19 skeletons of the 503 specially examined for pathological features and definitely assigned to certain Glaze periods. Two other cases occurred in skeletons of doubtful provenience. Table X–6 records the main facts relative to these fractures. The commonest fractures are those of the humerus and femur. Fractures seem to be much more common on the right side than on the left, but this is probably due to chance. The largest number of limb bone and pelvic bone fractures occur in the oldest age group, where naturally bones are most brittle and rheumatic conditions may have contributed to the liability to traumatisms of this kind. Altogether 3.78 per cent of the 503 dated skeletons examined showed evidence of having suffered fractures of the long bones or pelvis. All sorts of conditions are met with as respects the healing of the fractured bones. Some cases show a complete lack of union, others show excellent union practically without displacement; some show very marked displacement; often the the wound seems to have suppurated, and there is much pathological formation of bone.

Skull fractures, usually linear or marked by depressed and healed lesions, are even more common than fractures of the limb bones (Table X–7). No less than 23 of 581 skeletons, or 3.96 per cent, exhibit such fractures. Most of the skull fractures occur in middle-aged or elderly males and may be presumed to have been suffered in warfare or other physical conflict. However, five female crania show fractures, three of them belonging to sub-adult or young individuals. Whether these were accidental, due perhaps to falls from the mesa or from the housetops, or to the collapse of dwellings (which apparently occurred very frequently), or whether they were the result of marital disagreements, the anthropologist is unable to determine.

Table X–8 lists all fractures observed by Dr. G. D. Williams in 581 skeletons, including 78 of doubtful date. Altogether 42 fractures were recorded by him, affecting 7.23 per cent of the population. In a few instances, however, one skeleton showed more than one fracture, so the percentage of persons affected would not be quite so large as indicated in the table. The ratio of fractures to the total population seems to have been highest in the last group (Glazes V and VI), but almost as high in the first two periods (Black-on-white and Glaze I). Skull fractures are commonest in these two groups. One wonders whether or not this indicates more warfare during these periods of the peublo's occupation.

TABLE X–6. FRACTURES (NOT SKULL)

Male and Female	Young Adult			Middle-Aged			Old			Total Affected	
	No.	Per cent Affected	Per cent Glaze	No.	Per cent Affected	Per cent Glaze	No.	Per cent Affected	Per cent Glaze	No.	Per cent Glaze
B.-on-W. and Glaze I (total 122)	0	0	0	2	50.00	1.64	2	50.00	1.64	4	3.28
Glazes II and III ... (total 173)	1	10.00	0.58	4	40.00	2.31	5	50.00	4.10	10	5.78
Glaze IV .... (total 115)	0	0	0	0	0	0	1	100.00	0.87	1	0.87
Glazes V and VI .... (total 93)	2	50.00	2.15	1	25.00	1.08	1	25.00	1.08	4	4.30
Total .... (total 503)	3	15.79	0.60	7	36.84	1.39	9	47.37	1.79	19	3.78

Total (by sexes)										Per cent of Total Affected	
Male	0	0		5	41.67		7	58.33		12	63.16
Female	3	42.86		2	28.57		2	28.57		7	36.84

POSITION OF FRACTURE	Right		Left	
	No.	Per cent	No.	Per cent
Femur	5	38.46	1	12.50
Humerus	4	30.77	4	50.00
Innominate bone	1	7.69	1	12.50
Radius	1	7.69	1	12.50
Tibia	2	15.38	0	0
Ulna	0	0	1	12.50
Total	13		8	

TABLE X–7. SKULL FRACTURES

Male and Female and Doubtful	Sub-adult			Young Adult			Middle-Aged			Old			Total Affected	
	No.	Per cent Affected	Per cent Glaze	No.	Per cent Affected	Per cent Glaze	No.	Per cent Affected	Per cent Glaze	No.	Per cent Affected	Per cent Glaze	No.	Per cent Glaze
B.-and-W. and Gl. I (total 122)	1	14.29	0.82	0	0	0	5	71.43	4.10	1	14.29	0.82	7	5.74
Glazes II and III . (total 173)	0	0	0	1	50.00	0.58	0	0	0	1	50.00	0.58	2	1.16
Glaze IV .... (total 115)	1	25.00	0.87	0	0	0	1	25.00	0.87	2	50.00	1.74	4	3.48
Glazes V and VI . (total 93)	1	14.29	1.08	0	0	0	4	57.14	4.30	2	28.57	2.15	7	7.53
Doubtful .... (total 78)	0	0	0	1	33.33	1.28	2	66.67	2.56	0	0	0	3	3.85
Total.............. (total 581)	3	13.04	0.52	2	8.70	0.34	12	52.17	2.06	6	26.09	1.03	23	3.96

Total (by sexes)											Per cent of Total Affected	
Male	1	5.88		0	0		11	64.71		5	29.41	17	73.91
Female	1	20.00		2	40.00		1	20.00		1	20.00	5	21.74
Doubtful	1	100.00		0	0		0	0		0	0	1	4.35

TABLE X–8. ALL FRACTURES

Male and Female and Doubtful	Sub-adult			Young Adult			Middle Aged			Old			Total Affected	
	No.	Per cent Affected	Per cent Glaze	No.	Per cent Affected	Per cent Glaze	No.	Per cent Affected	Per cent Glaze	No.	Per cent Affected	Per cent Glaze	No.	Per cent Glaze
B.-and-W. and Gl.I (total 122)	1	9.09	0.82	0	0	0	7	63.64	5.74	3	27.27	2.46	11	9.02
Glazes II and III (total 173)	0	0	0	2	16.67	1.16	4	33.33	2.31	6	50.00	3.47	12	6.94
Glaze IV (total 115)	1	20.00	0.87	0	0	0	1	20.00	0.87	3	60.00	2.61	5	4.35
Glazes V and VI (total 93)	1	9.09	1.08	2	18.18	2.15	5	45.45	5.38	3	27.27	3.23	11	11.83
Doubtful (total 78)	0	0	0	1	33.33	1.28	2	66.67	2.56	0	0	0	3	3.85
Total (total 581)	3	7.14	0.52	5	11.90	0.86	19	45.24	3.27	15	35.71	2.58	42	7.23

Total (by sexes)	No.	Per cent Affected		No.	Per cent Affected		No.	Per cent Affected		No.	Per cent Affected		No.	Per cent of Total Affected
Male	1	3.45		0	0		16	55.17		12	41.38		29	69.05
Female	1	8.33		5	41.67		3	25.00		3	25.00		12	28.57
Doubtful	1	100.00		0	0		0	0		0	0		1	2.38

OTHER TRAUMATIC LESIONS

Depressed cranial lesions, or less frequently elevated cranial lesions, of probably traumatic origin are also very common. These occur 28 times in 581 skeletons or

TABLE X–9. SKULL LESIONS (TRAUMATIC?)

Male and Female and Doubtful	Sub-adult			Young Adult			Middle-Aged			Old			Total Affected	
	No.	Per cent Affected	Per cent Glaze	No.	Per cent Affected	Per cent Glaze	No.	Per cent Affected	Per cent Glaze	No.	Per cent Affected	Per cent Glaze	No.	Per cent Glaze
B.-on-W. and Gl. I (total 122)	1	12.50	0.82	0	0	0	6	75.00	4.92	1	12.50	0.82	8	6.56
Glazes II and III (total 173)	0	0	0	2	50.00	1.16	0	0	0	2	50.00	1.16	4	2.31
Glaze IV (total 115)	1	20.00	0.87	0	0	0	2	40.00	1.74	2	40.00	1.74	5	4.35
Glazes V and VI (total 93)	1	12.50	1.08	0	0	0	5	62.50	5.38	2	25.00	2.15	8	8.60
Doubtful (total 78)	0	0	0	1	33.33	1.28	2	66.67	2.56	0	0	0	3	3.85
Total (total 581)	3	10.71	0.52	3	10.71	0.52	15	53.57	2.58	7	25.00	1.20	28	4.82

Total (by sexes)	No.	Per cent Affected		No.	Per cent Affected		No.	Per cent Affected		No.	Per cent Affected		No.	Per cent of Total Affected
Male	1	4.76		0	0		14	66.67		6	28.57		21	75.00
Female	1	16.67		3	50.00		1	16.67		1	16.67		6	21.43
Doubtful	1	100.00		0	0		0	0		0	0		1	3.57

POSITION OF LESION	No.	Per cent
Right side	11	39.29
Left side	11	39.29
Mid-line	6	21.43
Total	28	

in 4.62 per cent of the series. They are much more common in the crania of males than in those of females; 21 of 28 cases observed are found in male skulls. Again most of the lesions of male skulls are found in the middle-aged or elderly group, while three of six females suffering from such injuries were young adults (Table X–9). The majority of these lesions show clear evidence of healing and probably did not cause death. They occur with equal frequency on both sides of the cranial vault. As in the case of fractures, cranial lesions are most frequent in the first and last groups dated by pottery deposits, indicating, perhaps, more warlike activity during these periods.

One of the most interesting lesions of probably traumatic origin is that observed in the innominate bone of the skeleton of an old male (No. 60226) belonging to the Glaze VI or post-Christian epoch. It consists of a hole just above the acetabulum and inside the inferior anterior tuberosity of the ilium, probably a bullet-hole. There is evidence of some infection, involving the sacrum.

MISCELLANEOUS

BUTTON OSTEOMATA

Small bony tumors ("button osteomata") were observed in the skulls of 13 individuals, or 2.24 per cent of the series. Table X–10 records the incidence of this type of lesion. These osteomata seem to increase in frequency from the early to the late periods of the Pecos history and are found as often in the crania of females as of males. They are probably due in some cases to disease rather than to traumatism.

TABLE X–10. BUTTON OSTEOMATA

Male and Female	Young Adult			Middle-Aged			Old			Total Affected	
	No.	Per cent Affected	Per cent Glaze	No.	Per cent Affected	Per cent Glaze	No.	Per cent Affected	Per cent Glaze	No.	Per cent Glaze
B.-on-W. and Glaze I (total 122)	0	0	0	1	50.00	0.82	1	50.00	0.82	2	1.64
Glazes II and III ... (total 173)	1	50.00	0.58	0	0	0	1	50.00	0.58	2	1.16
Glaze IV .... (total 115)	0	0	0	3	75.00	2.61	1	25.00	0.87	4	3.48
Glazes V and VI .... (total 93)	1	25.00	1.08	2	50.00	2.15	1	25.00	1.08	4	4.30
Doubtful .... (total 78)	0	0	0	1	100.00	1.28	0	0	0	1	1.28
Total .... (total 581)	2	15.38	0.34	7	53.85	1.20	4	30.77	0.69	13	2.24

Total (by sexes)											Per cent of Total Affected
Male	1	16.67		2	33.33		3	50.00		6	46.15
Female	1	14.29		5	71.43		1	14.29		7	53.85

OSTEOPOROSIS SYMMETRICA

The mysterious disease known as *osteoporosis symmetrica* occurs in several Pecos skeletons. The etiology of the disease is uncertain. Its osseous symptoms in their minimum manifestation include honeycomb-like patches on the roofs of the orbits called *cribra orbitalia*. These occur with varying frequency in the crania of most racial groups and are always more common in the crania of immature subjects than in adults. Martin[1] gives the following frequencies for various groups: Socotranese, 47.6 per cent; Negroes of the East Sudan, 35 per cent; Malays 22.5 per cent, Ainu 16.8 per cent, Chinese 13.4 per cent, Mongols 8 per cent; Japanese 11 per cent (children 27 per cent), ancient Peruvians 8.9 per cent, ancient Egyptians 7.1 per cent, Europeans 3.1–4.7 per cent. He seems, however, to have been unaware of the essentially pathological nature of this condition and of its further extensions familiar to all students of the craniology of American Indians.

The typically honeycombed condition which involves a hyperostosis of the diploë and a destruction of the external table of compact bone, frequently extends to the parietals, where it may be seen in symmetrical patches sometimes extending over the greater portion of both bones and causing a thickening of ten to fifteen millimeters in the middle portions of the areas affected. On the base of the skull it may be observed in the form of numerous small pits on the palatine roof and on the wings of the sphenoid. Traces of the condition may also be observed in some crania on the temporal bones just above the auditory meatus. The most pronounced osteoporotic conditions, in my experience, are found in the crania of immature subjects from ancient Peru and from the Sacred Cenote of Chichen Itza in Yucatan. In 21 well-preserved crania of children between the ages of about 6 years and 12 years from the latter site, marked osteoporosis was noted in no less than 14 cases, or 66.67 per cent. From the crania of older individuals recovered from this same sacred well it was possible to distinguish various less active phases of the disease terminating in the complete healing of the lesions. Healed osteoporotic patches on the parietals are characterized by a transformation of the outer portion of the spongy bone into a very thick layer of compact tissue, or by a proliferation of the *tabula externa* over the diseased portion. The healed patches are pitted and cicatrized to some extent, and the thickness of the bones is very great, often 15 mm. or more. Typically, these healed symmetrical osteoporotic patches are found on the parietals and on the superior part of the occipital. Often the parietals are so thickened in the center as to leave the sagittal suture depressed in a deep furrow. The elevations of the central portions of the thickened parietals give the skull a bilobed appearance as one regards it in the *norma verticalis*. Whenever osteoporosis is observed in adult crania it manifests itself either in almost obliterated *cribra orbitalia* and thickened and scarified parietal and occipital patches or both. Evidently the disease is one of childhood and adolescence. I have never been able to satisfy myself that the bones other than those of the skull are affected, although some of the children's long bones display multiple small pits at the extremities of the diaphyses

---

[1] Martin, 1928, p. 970.

PLATE X–9

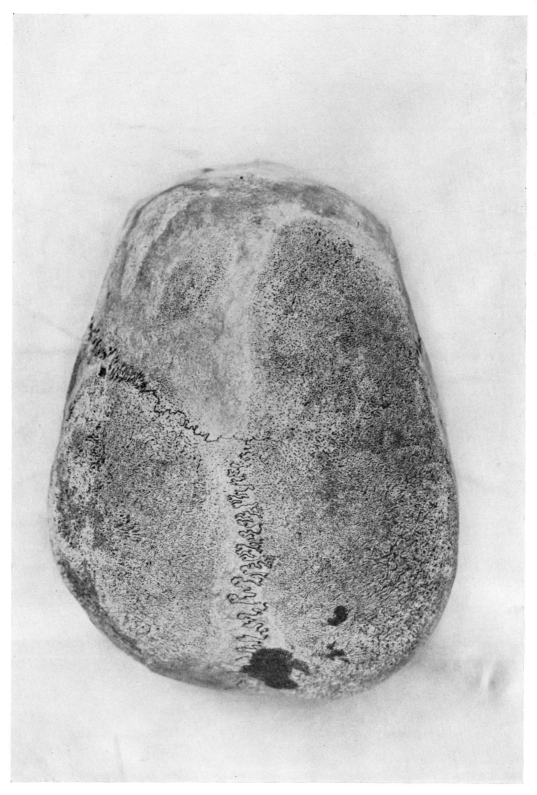

UNIVERSITY OF BUFFALO, No. 4367. SKULL OF UNKNOWN ORIGIN, PROBABLY
INDIAN, SHOWING EXTENSIVE OSTEOPOROSIS

Courtesy of Professor Herbert U. Williams

PLATE X–10

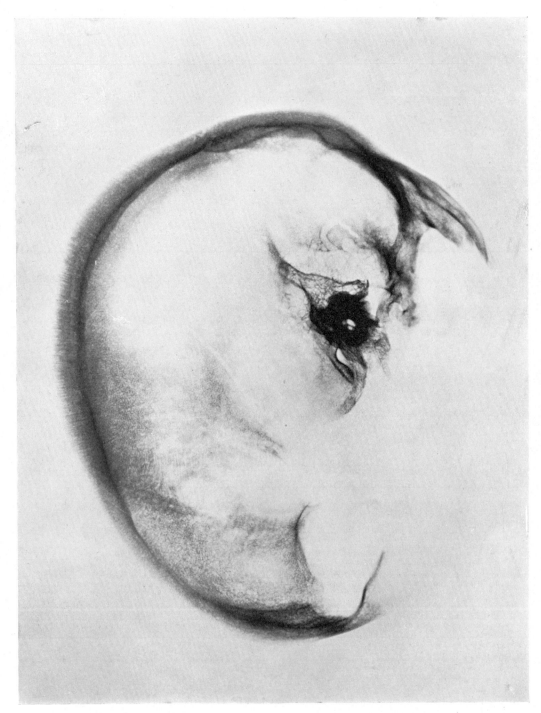

UNIVERSITY OF BUFFALO, No. 4367. ROENTGENOGRAM OF OSTEOPOROTIC SKULL, SHOWING DESTRUCTION OF THE OUTER TABLE AND CHARACTERISTIC COLUMNAR APPEARANCE OF THE DIPLOË

Courtesy of Professor Herbert U. Williams

PLATE X–11

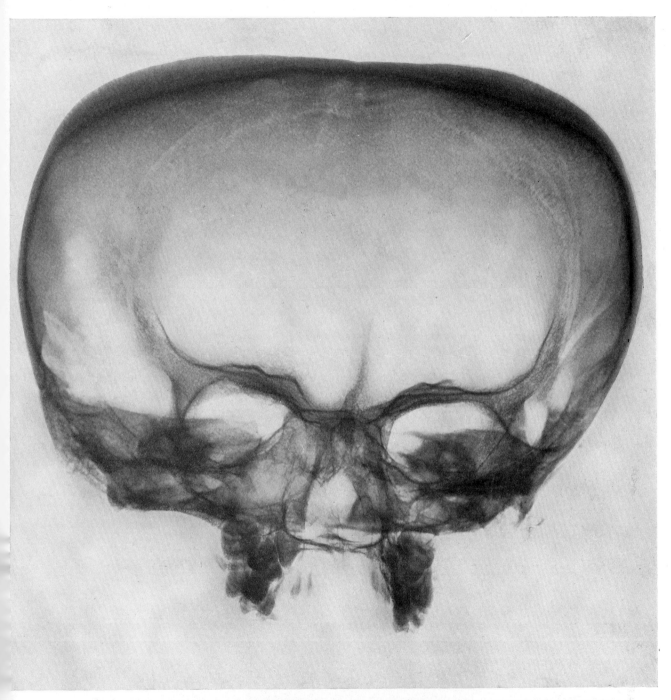

No. 58,203. ROENTGENOGRAM OF CALVARIUM OF CHILD FROM THE SACRED CENOTE, CHICHEN ITZA, YUCATAN, SHOWING OSTEOPOROTIC THICKENING OF PARIETALS WITH COLUMNAR APPEARANCE OF THE DIPLOË. FRONTAL VIEW

Photograph by Dr. M. C. Sosman, Peter Bent Brigham Hospital, Boston

PLATE X–12

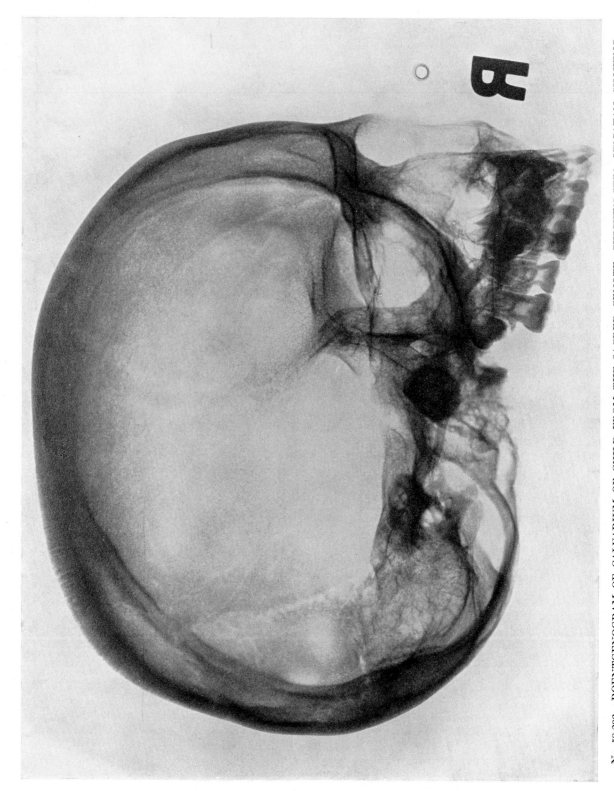

No. 58,203.   ROENTGENOGRAM OF CALVARIUM OF CHILD FROM THE SACRED CENOTE, CHICHEN ITZA, YUCATAN, SHOWING OSTEOPOROTIC THICKENING OF PARIETALS WITH COLUMNAR APPEARANCE OF THE DIPLOË.   LATERAL VIEW

PLATE X-13

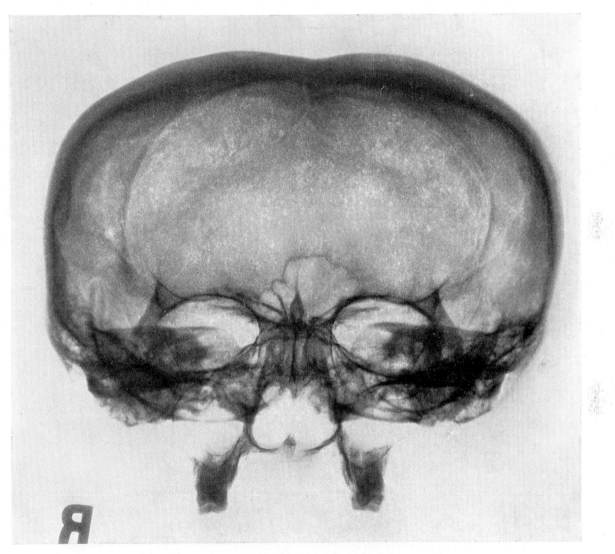

No. 58,217. ROENTGENOGRAM OF CALVARIUM OF ADOLESCENT FROM THE SACRED CENOTE,
CHICHEN ITZA, YUCATAN, SHOWING HEALED OSTEOPOROTIC THICKENING OF
THE PARIETALS. FRONTAL VIEW

Photograph by Dr. M. C. Sosman, Peter Bent Brigham Hospital, Boston

PLATE X–14

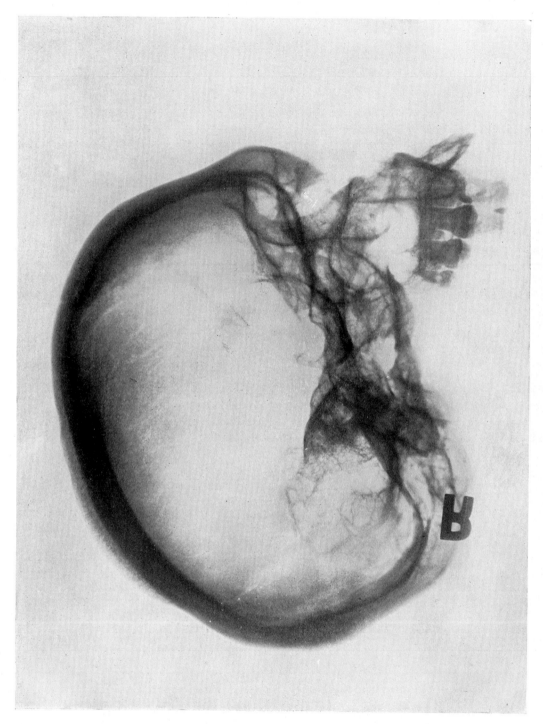

No. 58,217. ROENTGENOGRAM OF CALVARIUM OF ADOLESCENT FROM THE SACRED CENOTE, CHICHEN ITZA, YUCATAN, SHOWING HEALED OSTEOPOROTIC THICKENING OF THE PARIETALS. LATERAL VIEW

Photograph by Dr. M. C. Sosman, Peter Bent Brigham Hospital, Boston

adjacent to the epiphysial caps. These pits resemble those sometimes found on the crania in the alisphenoidal, temporal, and palatal regions, but there is no real osteoporosis.

Dr. H. U. Williams has recently summarized existing knowledge as to the distribution and nature of this disease so admirably that I am content merely to add the interesting opinions of other authorities to whom I have submitted specimens.[1] With characteristic generosity Dr. Williams has permitted me to reproduce two photographs from that work, one the view of the upper surface of a cranium, probably of a New York Indian, which is the most extensive example of osteoporosis I have seen (Plate X–9), and the other a roentgenogram of the same skull showing a distinctive appearance of the diploë (Plate X–10).

Dr. Sosman of the Peter Bent Brigham Hospital of Boston very kindly took X-ray photographs of several of the most characteristic specimens of the disease in the Cenote crania. Plates X–11, 12 clearly show the condition. In the roentgenograms the osteoporotic patches are plainly marked by the peculiarly columnar appearance of the diploë. Evidently the outer compact table is entirely destroyed but the inner table is intact. This disease seemingly is restricted to those bones which are of membranous origin. Dr. Sosman has observed a similar columnar appearance of the parietal region in skiagraphs of recent patients in the Peter Bent Brigham Hospital, whom he suspects to have suffered from deficiency diseases, possibly scurvy.

Plates X–13, 14 show the appearance in the X-ray film of what I take to be a healed osteoporosis. The surface of the bone is cicatrized.

Considerable light is thrown upon the osteoporosis problem by the experiments conducted upon the diet of various animals by Dr. Percy Howe of the Forsyth Dental Infirmary of Boston. Dr. Howe has shown me skulls of monkeys which have been kept upon a scorbutic diet. These skulls show characteristic osteoporotic changes, especially in the roofs of the orbits, which are almost entirely eaten away, and in the squamae of the temporal bones. The osteoporotic condition does not, howiever, manifest itself to the same extent in the parietals. Dr. Howe is of the opinon that osteoporosis is due to scurvy or to rickets, but probably it is more scorbutic than rachitic. The condition is certainly bound up with an unsatisfactory relationship between calcium and phosphorus components in the diet and, probably, vitamins C and D. Dr. Howe thinks that a diet restricted chiefly to maize may have caused this disease in the children of such agricultural populations as the Pueblo Indians, the Mayas, and the ancient Peruvians. Such a deficiency disease would, of course, manifest itself particularly in the period of growth between weaning and late adolescence. Typical active osteoporosis is not observable in the crania of adults.

The characteristic manifestation of osteoporosis in the bones of the cranial vault may be connected with the fact that these portions of the skull are ossified from membrane rather than from cartilage. The fact that the lesions usually appear on the orbital plates of the frontal and upon the summits of the frontal and the parietals

---

[1] Williams, 1929, pp. 839–902.

may possibly be connected with the absence of important muscular attachments in those areas. Under conditions of deficient calcification it is reasonable to suppose that the osseous parts lacking important muscular attachments will be decalcified first. The parts of the parietals covered by the temporal muscles do not usually exhibit the osteoporotic condition.

Osteoporosis does not usually affect the internal table of the skull bones, but the diploë is characteristically thickened and honeycombed and the external table is resorbed. Recovery from the condition is marked by a deposition of a very thick compact layer of bone over the extended diploë and the latter becomes to a considerable depth compact. The healed surface of the bones is rough, to some extent pitted, and has the appearance of scarification.

I am indebted to Dr. E. C. Vogt, Roentgenologist of the Children's Hospital, Boston, for the X-ray pictures (Plates X-15, 16) of skulls of children showing bone changes which seem to be identical with those in osteoporosis. In a personal communication, dated July 11, 1929, Dr. Vogt writes:

These films represent changes due to erythroblastic anemia, described by Cooley (Thomas B. Cooley, *Am. Journ. Dis. Child*, Vol. XXXVI, pp. 1257–1262), 1928. We have also seen these changes in one case of congenital hemolytic icterus. The clinical picture of this disease is well described by Dr. Wilder Tilston (*Medicine*, 1922, Vol. I, tb 355–386). It has been observed in some cases of sickle-cell anemia.

All three of these diseases mentioned above are classified as hemolytic anemias. That is, there is evidently something in the blood or spleen which causes an increased hemolysis of the red blood cells. They are all congenital and familial. Two are racial. The sickle anemia is seen only in the colored race. Erythroblastic anemia, as far as we have been able to find out, occurs only in children of Mediterranean race descent. Twelve cases of this disease have been studied in the Infants' and Children's Hospital within the last three years. Seven of these cases are of Greek parentage. Five are of Italian parentage, but it is interesting to note that even these five have at least one grandparent who is Greek.

According to Dr. Tilston there is no racial tendency in congenital hemolytic icterus. Two of our cases of erythroblastic anemia were in brothers aged seven and nine years. Two were twin sisters six months of age. Two were cousins. Two died in the hospital from thrombosis of the portal vein following splenectomy. The essential pathology — aside from the thrombosis of the portal vein — was marked hyperplasia of the bone marrow and blood-forming elements, and evidence of increased hemolysis of the red cells. We believe with Dr. Cooley that the X-ray changes are due only to hyperplasia of the red bone marrow. It seems to be far in excess of that seen in any other disease.

These changes are evidently constant in erythroblastic anemia but only occasional in sickle-cell anemia and congenital hemolytic icterus. The hyperplastic bone marrow causes a thinning of the cortex of the long bones and of the outer table of the cranial vault. In some cases this is so marked that the outer table seems to be completely eroded. I have been unable to find any evidence or reports of similar roentgenographic changes in any other disease except these hemolytic anemias. I think therefore that they have a special significance.

Dr. Louis Diamond has been studying these cases very thoroughly from a clinical and hematological standpoint and he is of the opinion that erythroblastic anemia is a disease similar to leukemia, except that it affects the red cells instead of the white.

Typical active manifestation of osteoporosis were observed in a considerable number of the crania of infants and children from the Pecos collection (Plate X–2).

PLATE X–15

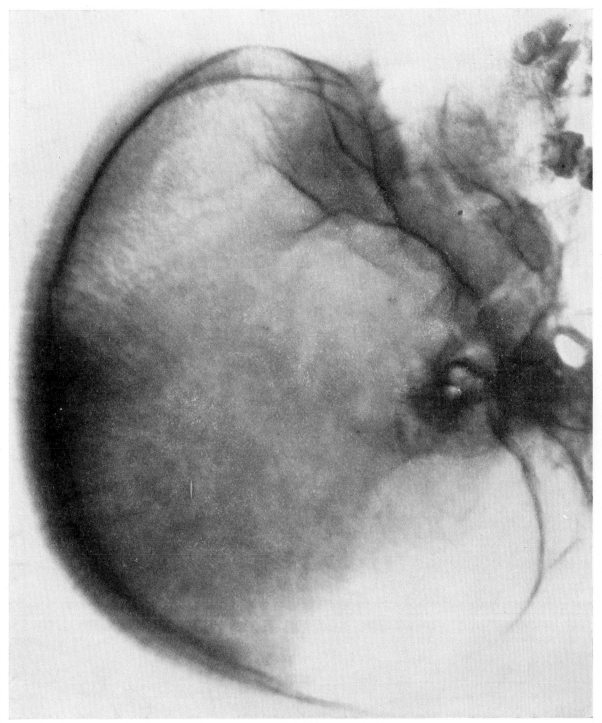

ROENTGENOGRAM OF HEAD OF GREEK CHILD SUFFERING FROM ERYTHROBLASTIC ANEMIA,
SHOWING COLUMNAR APPEARANCE OF THE DIPLOË

Courtesy of Dr. E. C. Vogt, Children's Hospital, Boston

PLATE X–16

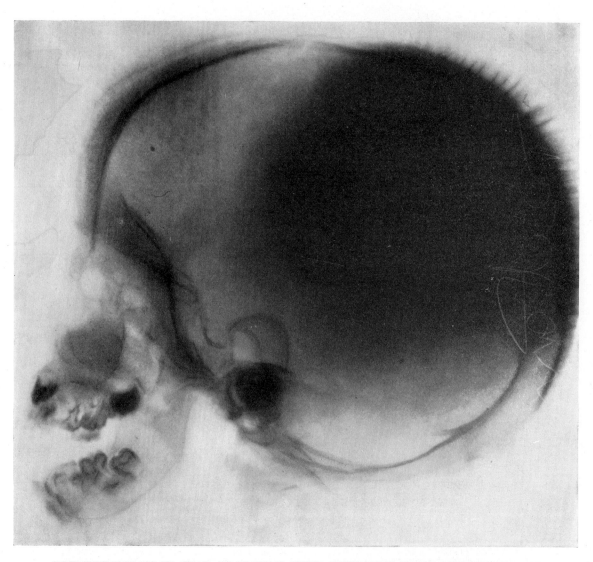

ROENTGENOGRAM OF HEAD OF ITALIAN CHILD SUFFERING FROM ERYTHROBLASTIC
ANEMIA, SHOWING COLUMNAR APPEARANCE OF THE DIPLOË

Courtesy of Dr. E. C. Vogt, Children's Hospital, Boston

PLATE X–17

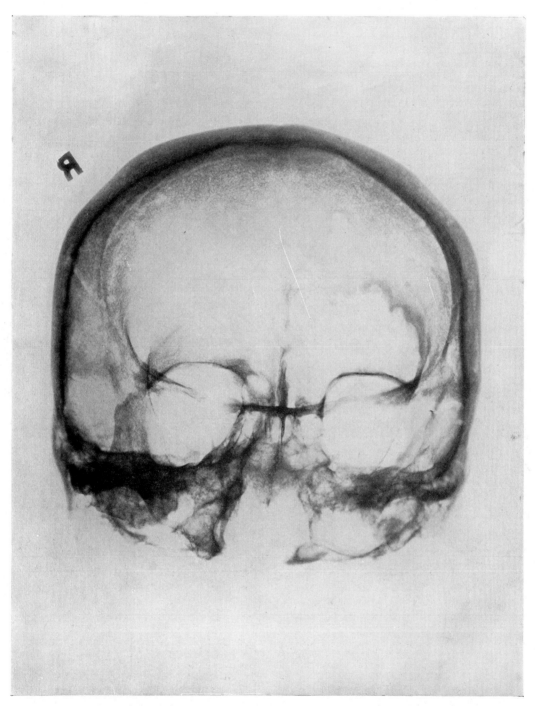

No. 60,196. ROENTGENOGRAM OF CALVARIUM WITH ENLARGED LEFT FRONTAL SINUS
WITH THICKENED EDGES. CHRONIC SINUSITIS. MALE. GLAZE VI. FRONTAL VIEW

Photograph by Dr. M. C. Sosman, Peter Bent Brigham Hospital, Boston

PLATE X–18

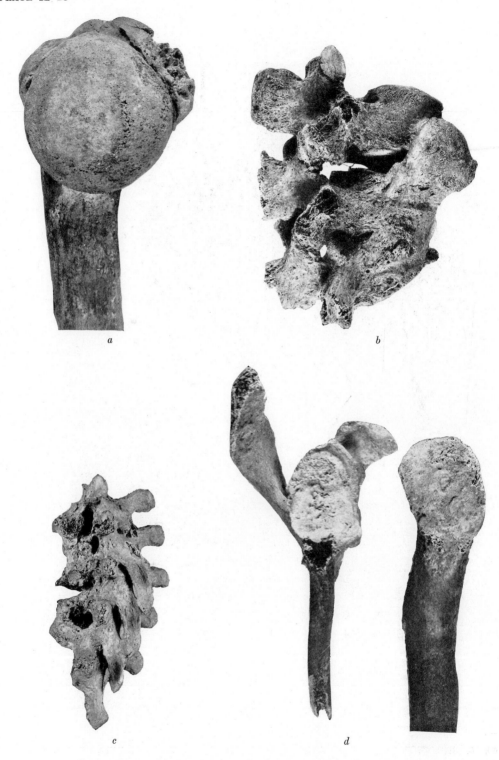

(a) No. 60,241.   FRACTURE OF HEAD OF HUMERUS.   GLAZE III (?)
(b) No. 60,189.   SPONDYLITIS DEFORMANS.   MALE.   GLAZE II (?)
(c) No. 60,280.   POTT'S DISEASE (?) OR SPONDYLITIS DEFORMANS.
FEMALE.   GLAZE IV (?).   (d) No. 60,280.   DEGENERATIVE ARTHRITIS.
FEMALE.   GLAZE IV (?)

PLATE X–19

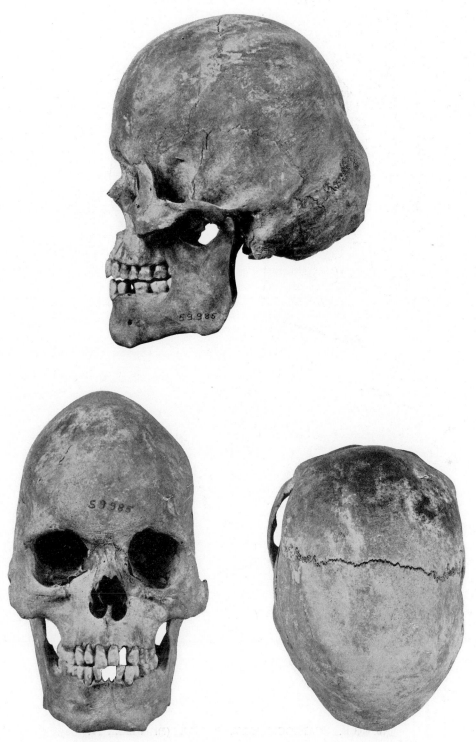

No. 59,985.   SCAPHOCEPHALY.   MALE.   DOUBTFUL STRATUM

PLATE X–20

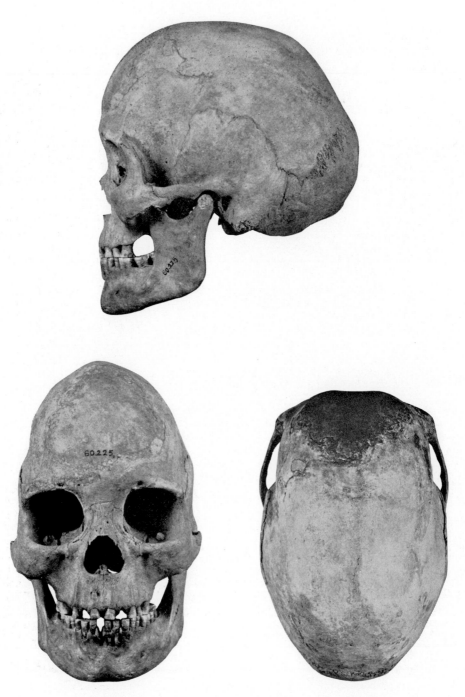

No. 60,255. SCAPHOCEPHALY. FEMALE (?). GLAZE IV.

PLATE X–21

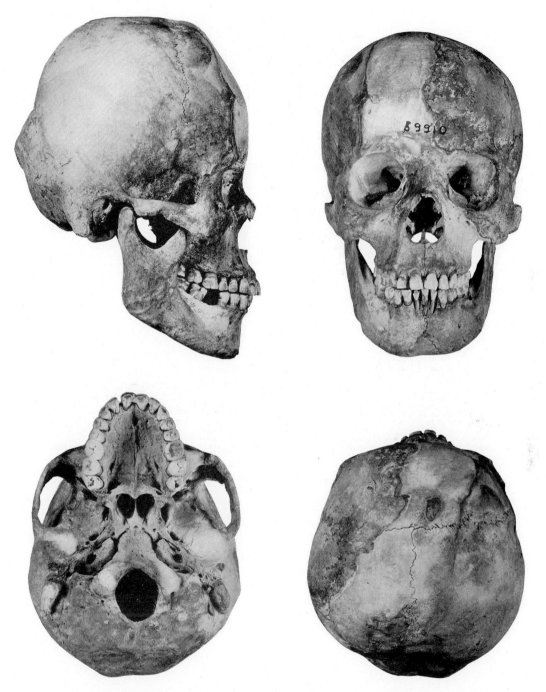

No. 59,910. PATHOLOGICAL THICKENING OF SKULL VAULT. FEMALE. GLAZE III

Traces in the orbits and porotic thickenings of the skull vault are common among the adult specimens. In the series of 581 skeletons examined by Dr. G. D. Williams, porotic thickenings or other definite traces of the disease were observed in 19 individuals, or 3.17 per cent, and 9 skeletons of immature or young adult subjects (1.54 per cent) showed active manifestations of the disorder.

OTHER LESIONS

No. 60196, the skeleton of a middle-aged male of the Glaze VI or post-Spanish period, shows a swelling of the left supraorbital region. The left half of the frontal sinus has been greatly expanded and has evidently been the seat of an inflammation. This cavity opens into the nose through a large aperture (Plate X–17). The same skeleton shows possible evidence of Pott's disease (tuberculosis of the spine). The late date of this skeleton makes the specimen inconclusive with respect to the origin of tuberculosis.

No. 60280, the skeleton of a middle-aged female of Glaze IV period, possibly shows Pott's disease and an arthritic condition of the right shoulder joint (Plate X–18c, 18d.

No. 59834, a young adult female of Glaze III, exhibits not only a fracture of the right femur with marked displacement, but also frontal and parietal lesions, metastatic tumor of the vertebrae, and a carious condition of the distal end of the right humerus. It seems almost certain that this individual was the victim of cancer.

SUMMARY

The most common disease affecting the bones of the Pecos population was arthritis. Spondylitis deformans was noted in 13.12 per cent of a sample of 503 adult or sub-adult skeletons. It was least common in the earlier periods of the pueblo and was almost confined to middle-aged and elderly persons. Arthritic affections of long bones, short bones, and joints occur in 3.98 per cent of the sample.

Inflammatory lesions of the long bones such as periostitis and osteomyelitis occur in 2.58 per cent of the sample and seem also to have been commoner in the later periods of the pueblo's occupation.

Skull lesions of an inflammatory character occur in a few instances. At least three of the crania affected, all belonging to the pre-Spanish period, show inflammatory changes suggestive of syphilis. But none of these cases can be diagnosed with certainty.

Fractures of the long bones or pelvis occur in 3.78 per cent of the 503 skeletons. Skull fractures were found in 3.96 per cent of the sample. Altogether 581 skeletons, including 78 of doubtful date, show 7.23 per cent of fractures. Fractures are commonest in the skeletons of elderly persons and more persons seem to have suffered these injuries in the last two periods of the pueblo than in the middle periods.

Depressed cranial lesions, probably due to blows, occur in 4.82 per cent of 581 skeletons examined. They are much commoner in male skulls than in female skulls, and commoner in the late and early periods than in the middle periods.

Small bony tumors on the skull occur in 2.24 per cent of the series. These are most frequent in the later periods.

Traces or marked manifestations of the disease known as *osteoporosis symmetrica* were found in 3.27 per cent of cases. According to present knowledge, conditions closely resembling symmetrical osteoporosis, as shown in Indian crania, may be caused by such deficiency diseases as rickets or scurvy, or by hemolytic anemias.

Possible indications of Pott's disease, and cancer, and clear evidence of sinusitis, and mastoiditis were found in a few cases.

Pathological deformation of the skull was rare, but three adult crania, No. 59985 (Plate X–19), No. 60225 (Plate X–20), and No. 60311, show marked scaphocephaly. The skull of one child (No. 60155) also manifests this disorder. No. 60186, the skull of a newborn infant or foetus buried in a pot, is hydrocephalous.

The pathology of the teeth is treated elsewhere (Chap. IV, pp. 118–122), and also forms the subject of an appended paper by Dr. Habib Rihan (Appendix I). Caries and alveolar abscess were common and increased in prevalence from the earlier to the later periods of the pueblo. Dr. Rihan found 47.9 per cent of adult crania with one or more carious teeth and 59 per cent with pyorrhea.

In general, the study of the Pecos pathology indicates that the health of the inhabitants declined during the closing periods of the settlement. Almost all diseases which can be diagnosed from the skeletal remains occur in a higher percentage of the late inhabitants than of the earlier dwellers. One suspects that continual undernourishment may have had the effect of lowering the resistance of the people and allowing them to fall prey to the epidemics which are recorded to have been one of the principal causes of the virtual extinction of the population.

TABLE X–11. GENERAL PATHOLOGY

Catalogue No.	Glaze	Age (Hooton)	Age (Todd)	Sex (Hooton)	Sex (Todd)	Diagnoses
59802	B.-on-W.	middle-aged	...	female	...	1. Metastatic tumor involving right lower dorsal vertebrae, right and left radius, right ulna. H. U. Williams: "osteomyelitis"
59803	I	old	45–49	male	female	1. Spondylitis deformans 2. Degenerative arthritis deformans 3. Depressed lesion 1 cm. diameter at left stephanion
59805	V	middle-aged	40–44	male	male	1. Spondylitis deformans 2. Porotic thickening at bregma
59807	III	adolescent	16	male	male	1. Osteomyelitis of left tibia affecting entire shaft. Has sequestrum. Left fibula seems affected. H. U. Williams: "osteomyelitis"
59810	VI?	middle-aged	50–54	male	male	1. Button osteoma at lambda
59811	IV?	middle-aged	35–39	female	female	1. Left sacro-iliac articulation — osteomyelitis. Absorption and perforation

Catalogue No.	Glaze	Age (Hooton)	Age (Todd)	Sex (Hooton)	Sex (Todd)	Diagnoses
59814	III	young	...	female	...	1. Extensive inflammatory changes of palate and perforation of roof, 2 cm. in diameter 2. Nasalia flattened so that bridge is eliminated; edges beveled; great deposit of bone above nose; lower borders of aperture and nasal spine (whole circumference) incorporated in cicatrix
59816	V	middle-aged	40–44	male	male	1. Healed fracture 7 mm. below trochanters on right femur 2. Depressed lesion of left frontal 2 cm. in diameter (probably traumatic)
59817	III	young adult	40–44	doubtful	female	1. Spondylitis deformans 2. Degenerative arthritis of lumbars and sacrum 3. Button osteoma of 2 mm. 4. Depressed lesion on left frontal
59823	IV	young adult	25–29	male	male	1. Spondylitis deformans
59825	IV	old	50–54	male	male	1. Spondylitis deformans
59834	III	young adult	30–34	female	doubtful	1. Fracture of right femur, $\frac{3}{4}$ inch displacement and shortening 2. Metastatic tumor of vertebrae, head of left ulna, above right orbit 3. Frontal lesions over orbit and on left parietal 4. Carious condition at distal end of right humerus
59836	IV	...	65–69	male	male	1. Degenerative arthritis deformans of both sacro-iliac joints; humero-ulna articulation 2. Spondylitis deformans
59838	II	old	55–59	male	male	1. Spondylitis deformans
59839	IV?	old	70–74	doubtful	male	1. Thickening of sagittal suture
59840	V?	...	50–54	...	male	1. Smooth holes through left humerus and right radius
59842	I	middle-aged	70–74	male	male	1. Right horizontal ramus of mandible shows on its buccal face an excavation 14 mm. long and 11 mm. wide, oval in shape, 16 mm. below level of alveolar border directly at base of coronoid process. Sides of excavation beveled and smooth; no apparent inflammation
59844	B.-on-W. or I	middle-aged	30–34	male	male	1. Septic fracture of right humerus 2. Healed fracture of right tibia 3. Abscess involving all upper left molars with extensive perforation of left antrum 4. Traumatic depressed lesion of left brow-ridge

Catalogue No.	Glaze	Age (Hooton)	Age (Todd)	Sex (Hooton)	Sex (Todd)	Diagnoses
59851	I	old	65–69	male	male	1. Spondylitis deformans
59853	IV	old	70–74	male	male	1. Spondylitis deformans
59854	II?	old	70–74	female	female	1. Spondylitis deformans 2. Degenerative arthritis deformans of femora
59855	VI?	old	75–79	female	male	1. Spondylitis deformans 2. Compression fracture of dorsal vertebrae
59857	V?	old	50–54	female	female	1. Fracture of right humerus with backward displacement of entire trochlear surface 2. Spondylitis deformans 3. Thickening of sagittal suture. Porosis around bregma and lambda
59863	III	middle-aged	...	male	...	1. Spondylitis deformans
59864	II	middle-aged	35–39	female	female	1. Nasal cavity seat of extensive inflammatory process — abscess, perforating alveolar borders through right canines and lateral incisors. Nasal bones destroyed. Maxilla has large alveolar abscesses, as has mandible at level of first premolar. Roof of hard palate cicatrized. Supraorbital area, malars, and orbit walls affected. Center of affection nose rather than teeth 2. Thickening of sagittal margins
59866	VI	middle-aged	35–39	male	male	1. Periostitis of upper half of both tibiae
59868	III	old	74–79	male	male	1. Spondylitis deformans
59870	IV	middle-aged	44–49	male	male	1. Non-porotic thickening near bregma on right parietal
59874	IV	old	74–79	male	male	1. Spondylitis deformans
59876	V?	middle-aged	45–49	male	male	1. Spondylitis deformans 2. Old healed lesion in front of bregma, probably traumatic
59877	VI?	middle-aged	35–39	female	female	1. Degenerative arthritis deformans
59908	IV	middle-aged	30–34	female	female	1. Button osteoma of right parietal 2. Arthritic facet between condyles on site of third condyle
59910	III	young adult	35–39	female	female	1. Porotic thickening 1 cm. high along coronal suture from pterion a little past bregma. Right pterion has 2 cm. depression (traumatic)
59915	V?	young adult	20–24	male	doubtful	1. Button osteoma (frontal) 2. Osteoporosis symmetrica on orbits, around bregma, and inside the parietal bosses; also on petrous parts of temporal bone

Catalogue No.	Glaze	Age (Hooton)	Age (Todd)	Sex (Hooton)	Sex (Todd)	Diagnoses
59919	early?	middle-aged	70–74	male	female	1. Healed depressed lesion (traumatic) of right frontal bone 2. Thickening of sagittal suture. Porosis around bregma
59920	III	old	55–59	male	female	1. Spondylitis deformans
59922	IV?	old	35–39	female	female	1. Small multiple button osteomata 2. Porotic thickening of sagittal suture 3. Healed lesion at distal extremities of nasals
59952	B.-on-W.	old	70–74	female	male	1. Thickening of sagittal suture 2. Multiple small exostoses (frontal) like button osteomata
59953	IV?	. . .	25–29	. . .	male	1. Humeri, radii, fibulae bent
59957	V?	middle-aged	55–59	male	male	1. Spondylitis deformans 2. Degenerative arthritis deformans 3. Arthritic changes in right glenoid fossa
59967	III	middle-aged	40–44	male	male	1. Spondylitis deformans 2. Fracture of left acetabulum unhealed with formation of new acetabulum for head of femur. Accompanied by arthritic changes. Vertical fracture of left femoral head with arthritic changes
59975	III	middle-aged	55–59	male	male	1. Spondylitis deformans
59977	V?	old	55–59	female	female	1. Spondylitis deformans
59985	?	young adult	35–39	male	male	1. Scaphoid skull; complete premature ossification of sagittal suture involving bending downwards of posterior half of parietals; annular constriction above lambdoid suture
59991	III?	middle-aged	74–79	female	male	1. Degenerative arthritis deformans of humerus, ulna, left femur 2. Spondylitis deformans
59995	IV?	middle-aged	55–59	female	female	1. Button osteoma (frontal) of 15 mm. diameter 2. Porotic thickening at bregma
60004	I	young adult	40–44	male	male	1. Arthritis of right glenoid fossa of skull
60006	IV?	old	65–69	female	female	1. Spondylitis deformans
60008	IV?	middle-aged	40–44	female	female	1. Thickening of right side of palate with marked deviation to left of nasal septum and elevation of right nasal floor
60009	VI	old	70	female	female	1. Spondylitis deformans 2. Arthritis of right glenoid fossa and occipital condyles
60018	II?	. . .	45–49	. . .	male	1. Healed fracture of right femur, middle shaft
60023	V?	sub-adult	. . .	male	. . .	1. Depressed lesion of 15 mm. diameter on right frontal (traumatic)
60024	B.-on-W.	old	55–59	male	male	1. Spondylitis deformans

Catalogue No.	Glaze	Age (Hooton)	Age (Todd)	Sex (Hooton)	Sex (Todd)	Diagnoses
60028	VI	old	74–79	male	female	1. Degenerative arthritis deformans 2. Spondylitis deformans 3. Periosititis of lower thirds of tibiae; of lower halves of femora with marked 2 cm. depression on anterior surface above condyles; of median ends of clavicles. Depressed lesion of left parietal near bregma
60039	IV	old	...	male	...	1. Button osteoma 2. Spondylitis deformans
60040	V?	old	55–59	doubtful	male	1. Degenerative arthritis deformans; sacro-iliac articulation 2. Healed lesion (probably traumatic) on right temporal crest, of 2 cm. diameter
60041	IV?	young adult	...	female	...	1. Degenerative arthritis deformans of left sacro-iliac joint
60050	B.-on-W. or I	old	70–74	female	female	1. Periostitis of lower ends of both radii and left ulna, and of lower ends of tibiae and fibulae
60051	II	middle-aged	50–54	male	male	1. Spondylitis deformans 2. Jagged L-shaped depressed lesion of middle frontal; area 2 sq. cm. 3. Healed thickening of sagittal suture
60057	?	middle-aged	...	female	...	1. Button osteoma (frontal) of 16 mm.
60058	II	old	70–74	male	male	1. Spondylitis deformans 2. Degenerative arthritis deformans of right sacro-iliac joint and right calcaneo-scaphoid joint
60061	VI?	middle-aged	35–39	male	female	1. Spondylitis deformans 2. Periostitis of mid-shaft of left tibia. H. U. Williams: "probably ostitis fibrosa"
60066	IV?	old	60–64	female	female	1. Spondylitis deformans
60075	I	old	50–55	male	male	1. Spondylitis deformans
60077	B.-on-W.	...	15–19	female	...	1. Periostitis with heavy deposition of bone (symmetrical) of femora and tibiae
60097	IV	sub-adult	20–21	female	doubtful	1. Periostitis of upper half of left tibia 2. Two depressed lesions on right parietal near bregma, of 1 and 2 cm. diameter respectively
60101	V?	middle-aged	55–59	male	male	1. Spondylitis deformans
60103	II	...	45–49	...	male	1. Distal extremity of humerus curved forward
60136	B.-on-W.	middle-aged	50–54	male	male	1. Left sacro-iliac articulation — osteomyelitis with sequestra 2. Right acromion perforated

Catalogue No.	Glaze	Age (Hooton)	Age (Todd)	Sex (Hooton)	Sex (Todd)	Diagnoses
60144	V	young adult	35–39	female	female	1. Fracture of distal extremity of left humerus and of superior extremity of left ulna at joint
60155	III	. . .	8	doubtful	. . .	1. Scaphoid skull; complete synostosis of sagittal suture
60156	III	old	55–59	male	male	1. Spondylitis deformans 2. Periostitis of mid-shaft, medial and lateral surfaces of both tibiae
60159	B.-on-W.	old	70–74	female	female	1. Spondylitis deformans
60163	III	old	80–84	male	male	1. Degenerative arthritis deformans of femoral heads 2. Spondylitis deformans
60167	III or IV	old	. . .	female	. . .	1. Spondylitis deformans
60173	?	middle-aged	. . .	doubtful	. . .	1. Spondylitis deformans
60184	V	2–3	2	doubtful	doubtful	1. Osteoporosis symmetrica of orbits, parietals, base of skull
60185	?	2–3mos.	. . .	doubtful	. . .	1. Osteoporosis symmetrica of orbits, parietals, base of skull
60186	IV	foetus	doubtful	. . .	. . .	1. Hydrocephaly. (N.B. Buried in a pot)
60189	II?	old	70–74	male	male	1. Healed fracture of head of right humerus 2. Arthritis deformans; marked arthritic changes of long bones 3. Spondylitis deformans
60190	I?	. . .	11–12	doubtful	doubtful	1. Osteoporosis symmetrica (almost obliterated) on left orbit (right broken away)
60192	I	middle-aged	55–59	female	female	1. Periostitis of right femur (mushroomed), also of tibiae and left humerus
60194	V	old	40–44	male	male	1. Button osteoma (frontal) with several similar ones near bregma
60196	VI(P. C.)	middle-aged	50–54	male	female	1. Large swelling in left supraorbital region with extension of left half of sinus. Opens by large hole into nasal cavity 2. Pott's disease
60198	IV	middle-aged	60–64	male	male	1. Healed depressed lesion of external side of left mastoid 2. Thickening of sagittal suture. Porosis of middle of sagittal suture
60199	B.-on-W.	middle-aged	30–34	female	female	1. Very marked osteomyelitis of right tibia, submedium on left tibia
60201	III	middle-aged	30–34	male	male	1. Thickening of coronal and sagittal sutures. Porosis around bregma
60202	II	. . .	45–49	male	female	1. Degenerative arthritis deformans of left ulna
60211	III	old	55–59	female	doubtful	1. Spondylitis deformans
60212	IV	old	60–64	male	male	1. Spondylitis deformans 2. Osteomyelitis of left ulna. H. U. Williams: "osteomyelitis" 3. Degenerative arthritis deformans

Catalogue No.	Glaze	Age (Hooton)	Age (Todd)	Sex (Hooton)	Sex (Todd)	Diagnoses
60216	IV?	old	75–79	doubtful	female	1. Spondylitis deformans
60219	III	old	55–59	male	male	1. Spondylitis deformans
60223	III	middle-aged	...	male	...	1. Spondylitis deformans
60225	IV	middle-aged	45–49	doubtful	female	1. Scaphoid skull
60226	VI (P. C.)	old	65–69	male	male	1. Scar just above acetabulum inside inferior anterior tuberosity. Bullet hole? Probably infected, involving sacrum
60227	I	middle-aged	35–39	female	female	1. Healed lesion at distal extremities of nasals; some deformity 2. Depressed lesion (traumatic) on right frontal near temporal crest
60228	IV	old	45–49	female	female	1. Circular depressed lesion of 8 mm. diameter on right parietal boss (traumatic)
60229	V?	old	60–64	female	female	1. Porotic thickening of sagittal suture
60230	IV	old	50–54	male	male	1. Spondylitis deformans
60231	III	old	...	male	...	1. Spondylitis deformans
60235	I	middle-aged	35–39	male	male	1. Periostitis of medial and lateral surfaces of middle of shaft of tibiae 2. Porotic condition around bregma (mild) 3. Small healed lesion, probably traumatic, on right parietal bone
60236	II	middle-aged	50–54	male	male	1. Spondylitis deformans
60241	III?	...	50–54	...	male	1. Healed fracture of head of right humerus
60242	IV	old	80–84	male	male	1. Degenerative arthritis deformans of left femur, right humeral head (mushroomed) 2. Healed fracture of acetabulum and ilium (right); arthritic changes
60248	II	middle-aged	50–54	female	female	1. Porotic thickening of middle of sagittal suture
60249	I?	...	35–39	...	female	1. Healed fracture of left femur below trochanter
60254	I	...	75–79	...	male	1. Healed fracture of right femur about mid-shaft; distal extremity bent laterally
60255	III	old	75–79	female	male	1. Spondylitis deformans 2. Healed fracture with very marked displacement and bowing of right femur. H. U. Williams: "probably osteomalacia; other alternatives ostitis deformans, rickets"
60268	III	middle-aged	55–59	male	male	1. H. U. Williams: "probably syphilis"

Catalogue No.	Glaze	Age (Hooton)	Age (Todd)	Sex (Hooton)	Sex (Todd)	Diagnoses
60274	I	middle-aged	55–59	male	male	1. Spondylitis deformans 2. Porotic thickening of sagittal suture 3. Healed depressed lesion of left frontal, 5 mm. in diameter
60276	II	old	...	male	...	1. Healed depressed lesion of 13 mm. diameter on base of skull, right of obelion
60277	III	...	30–34	...	male	1. Degenerative arthritis deformans
60278	III	old	55–59	male	male	1. Spondylitis deformans 2. Healed fracture with medial displacement and 1 mm. shortening at distal third of right tibia
60279	III	old	65–69	male	male	1. Spondylitis deformans
60280	IV?	middle-aged	45–49	female	female	1. Degenerative arthritis deformans of right humerus, glenoid fossa 2. Pott's disease (?) or spondylitis deformans
60282	V?	middle-aged	55–59	female	female	1. Spondylitis deformans
60286	IV?	old	55–59	male	male	1. Depressed lesion (traumatic) over 1 cm. in diameter just back of left coronal, 25 mm. from sagittal suture 2. Healed linear fracture from above lesion to lower part of temporosphenoidal suture 3. Arthritic exostoses of condyles 4. Raised lesion in middle of frontal
60292	VI	young adult	21–22	female	doubtful	1. Colles fracture of right radius 2. Periostitis of right tibia — middle third of shaft 3. Marked porotic thickening of both parietals
60294	III	old	45–49	male	male	1. Degenerative arthritis deformans of left ulna 2. Spondylitis deformans 3. Trochanter of left humerus bent anteriorly
60301	V?	middle-aged	60–64	male	male	1. Inflammatory area over entire left temporal region, irregular thickening and much scarification. Parietal absorption of left mastoid. Right temporal region and margins of right orbit thickened; same for hard palate 2. Periostitis of right femur, distal half of shaft and supracondylar region; of left femur with very marked thickening of whole shaft; of right humerus with very marked thickening of whole shaft; of left humerus with localized thickening just above inferior condyle

Catalogue No.	Glaze	Age (Hooton)	Age (Todd)	Sex (Hooton)	Sex (Todd)	Diagnoses
60311	III	middle-aged	45–49	female	male	1. Scaphoid skull 2. Fracture with marked medial displacement of lower extremity of left humerus 3. Left tibia bent convexly outward
60318	VI (P. C.)	middle-aged	45–49	male	male	1. Periostitis of all surfaces of lower half of right femur, lower ends of fibulae, both tibiae. H. U. Williams: "syphilis?" 2. Depressed lesion on left frontal of 2 cm. diameter. Depressed lesion of left parietal boss 1½ cm. in diameter, and punch hole 3 cm. inferior to it 3. Thickening of parietals
(401)	I	old	. . .	male	. . .	1. Mastoiditis? of right temporal
60426	IV or early V	young adult	30–34	male	male	1. Porotic thickening of sagittal suture
60431	IV or V	12–14	14	male?	doubtful	1. Osteoporosis symmetrica of orbits; suggested at long bone epiphyses
60436	III, IV or V	old	75–79	male	female	1. Fracture with callus; very marked displacement — left radius
60437	IV?	old	60–64	male	male	1. Degenerative arthritis deformans of ulna and humerus
60441	B.-on-W.	middle-aged	65–69	male	male	1. Extensive necrosis of mandible
60451	I	middle-aged	50–54	doubtful	female	1. Spondylitis deformans 2. Degenerative arthritis deformans of radius and ulna 3. Button osteoma 4. Arthritis of right glenoid fossa (skull)
60453	II	old	55–59	male	male	1. Spondylitis deformans 2. Button osteoma of 6 mm. diameter (frontal) 3. Porotic thickening of sagittal suture and bregma
60454	II?	middle-aged	70–74	male	male	1. Spondylitis deformans
60455	B.-on-W. or I	middle-aged	ca. 33	female	female	1. Extensive inflammatory process of frontal bone; left half eaten away over large area; nasal bones only slightly involved; extensive cicatrization. H. U. Williams: "syphilis" 2. Lesion of right femur. H. U. Williams: probably "syphilitic"
60456	I	young adult	45–49	. . .	male	1. Very marked osteomyelitis of left femur, left tibia, left fibula, right ulna, distal end of right humerus

Catalogue No.	Glaze	Age (Hooton)	Age (Todd)	Sex (Hooton)	Sex (Todd)	Diagnoses
60463	I	young adult	30–34	male	female	1. Porotic thickening of sagittal suture. Porosis (?) around bregma and on brow-ridges
60478	doubtful	young adult	19	female	male	1. Healed depressed lesion of left frontal bone 3 cm. in diameter
60479	B.-on-W.?	. . .	20–24	. . .	female	1. Osteoporosis symmetrica (almost obliterated) on orbits only
60482	IV?	old	50–54	male	male	1. Spondylitis deformans
60485	III?	old	50–54	. . .	male	1. Healed fracture of mid-shaft of left humerus; twisted spirally
60486	I	. . .	13–14	. . .	doubtful	1. Depressed lesion (traumatic) of 1 cm. diameter of middle of frontal bone
60488	doubtful	. . .	60–64	. . .	male	1. Depressed lesion 2 cm. long, 1 cm. wide of right frontal (traumatic)
60490	B.-on-W.?	old	65–69	male	male	1. Spondylitis deformans 2. Healed fracture of head and surgical neck of humerus
60502	V	middle-aged	45–50	male	male	1. Thickening of sagittal and coronal sutures with extensive porosis over upper frontal and upper parietals
60513	III	old	45–49	male	male	1. Depressed healed lesion 3 cm. in diameter of right frontal; over-proliferation at rim of lesion
60518	III	old	70–74	male	male	1. Spondylitis deformans
60523	?	. . .	13	doubtful	doubtful	1. Osteoporosis symmetrica on orbits only
60541	V	middle-aged	40–44	male	male	1. Button osteoma (frontal) 2. Depressed lesion of right parietal boss
60542	I	middle-aged	45–49	female	male	1. Spondylitis deformans
60548	III	old	65–69	male	male	1. Spondylitis deformans
60556	V or VI	middle-aged	45–49	male	male	1. Depressed lesion of 1 cm. diameter of right parietal boss
60561	I	. . .	25–29	. . .	female	1. Osteoporosis symmetrica (almost obliterated) on orbits only
60562	doubtful	middle-aged	55–59	male	male	1. Depressed lesion of 1 cm. diameter of left stephanion
60566	V?	. . .	15–19	. . .	female	1. Osteoporosis symmetrica on orbits only
60569	VI	middle-aged	40–44	male	male	1. Spondylitis deformans 2. Porotic thickening around bregma
60582	B.-on-W. or I	young adult	20–24	female	female	1. Osteoporosis symmetrica on orbits only 2. Thickening of sagittal suture
60583	B.-on-W.	old	55–59	male	male	1. Arthritic occipital condyle
60585	I	1½	. . .	doubtful	. . .	1. Osteoporosis symmetrica on orbits only
60593	I	middle-aged	55–59	male	doubtful	1. Broken cyst-like cavity projecting from right frontal sinus into right orbit; covering bone has porosity

Catalogue No.	Glaze	Age (Hooton)	Age (Todd)	Sex (Hooton)	Sex (Todd)	Diagnoses
60602	I	middle-aged	60–64	male	male	1. Spondylitis deformans
60608	doubtful	middle-aged	55–59	doubtful	male	1. Spondylitis deformans 2. Arthritis of left glenoid fossa (skull) 3. Depressed lesion of frontal 1 cm. in diameter (probably traumatic)
60615	VI?	middle-aged	70–74	male	male	1. Spondylitis deformans
60621	II	6?	8	doubtful	doubtful	1. Osteoporosis symmetrica on orbits only
60783	floater	. . .	. . .	. . .	. . .	1. Healed fracture of left humerus at distal extremity; backward displacement

CHAPTER XI

RECONSTRUCTION OF THE GROWTH AND DECLINE OF THE PECOS POPULATION

THE PROBLEM

IT IS incumbent upon the anthropologist who has been privileged to study the archaeologically dated skeletal remains of a site from its founding to its abandonment to attempt some reconstruction of the growth and decline of the population. It is important to form an estimate of the total number of persons who inhabited the pueblo from its beginning to the time of its desertion and of the approximate size of the population during each of the several archaeological periods. If the chronological dates of each archaeological period were known and if the remains of every person who lived and died in Pecos had been recovered, such a task would be simple. Unfortunately these conditions are not fulfilled, since the archaeological dating of the burials is principally a sequence dating and the site has been excavated only partially.

As a preliminary to the attack upon the problem the data utilized in reconstruction may be classified and enumerated. These may be grouped into three categories: (*a*) known factors, (*b*) deduced factors, (*c*) unknown factors.

KNOWN FACTORS IN THE POPULATION PROBLEM

Date of Abandonment. Pecos pueblo was abandoned in 1838.

Date of Discovery by Europeans. Pecos was discovered by Alvarado, an officer of the Coronado expedition, in 1540.

Intermediate Dates in the Historical Period.
    1542. Friar Luis, a lay Franciscan brother, martyred at Pecos.
    1581–1582. Pecos visited by priests.
    1590. De Sosa conquers Pecos, but immediately withdraws.
    1598. Oñate receives the submission of Pecos; a friar is assigned to the parish.
    1620. De Benavides refers to the church and monastery at Pecos.
    1680. The Pueblo revolt. Spanish priest of Pecos slain.
    1694. Pecos evidently again under Spanish rule. The governor of Pecos allied with de Vargas.
    1750. Population reduced to one thousand by Comanche raids.
    1788. Epidemic of smallpox in Pecos.
    1805. Population estimate.
    1830. Population estimate.

Estimates of Population during the Historical Period.

1540. Alvarado: "a village of five hundred warriors." (Total population 2500?)
1620. De Benavides: "more than two thousand souls."
1750. Population estimate one thousand.
1788. Population 180.
1805. Population 104.
1830. Population 50–100.
1838. Population 17.

From the foregoing it is evident that the historical period of Pecos lasted 298 years, from 1540 to 1838.

Number of Burials Excavated Belonging to Each Archaeological Period (End of 1925 season).

	Number	Per cent
Black-on-white	98	7.55
Glaze I	224	17.25
Glaze II	220	16.95
Glaze III	287	22.11
Glaze IV	243	18.72
Glaze V	177	13.64
Glaze VI	49	3.78
Total	1298	

The numbers of burials given above are those excavated by the Andover Pecos Expedition and definitely assigned to Glaze periods. They do not include "floaters" or undated burials. If, as we have every reason for believing, the burials excavated constitute a random but representative sample of the population during the several periods, we may then accept the percentages as approximately indicating the proportions of the total Pecos population living during the successive periods.

DEDUCED FACTORS

Date of the Founding of Pecos. Dr. A. V. Kidder postulates the founding of Pecos at about A.D. 800 to 850. In a personal communication to the writer he says:

The 1000 year estimate (c. A.D. 800–A.D. 1830) is based on the finding at the immediately pre-Pecos ruin at Bandelier Bend ("Forked Lightning" ruin) of trade pieces from the Mesa Verde. The Mesa Verde culture is known to be roughly contemporaneous with that of Chaco Canyon, and it is assumed, from the finding of materials thought to show Toltec influence, that Pueblo Bonito, a Chaco ruin, was inhabited around A.D. 900–1000. The above is pretty vague, but the exact age of many of the early phases may be expected to be determined from tree-ring materials, now in the hands of Douglass, in the near future. I am beginning to think that 800 years might be a better guess than 1000 years.

Synchronization of Sequence Dating with Chronological Date. Dr. Kidder has definitely determined that the historical period, evidenced by the appearance in the rubbish of objects of Spanish manufacture, begins in the earlier part of the Glaze V period. Since Pecos was discovered in A.D. 1540, Glaze V period may be considered to have begun about A.D. 1500. Further, the last period of glaze-decorated pottery,

Glaze VI, begins shortly before the Pueblo revolt of 1680 and ends soon after the revolt. Glaze VI may therefore be said to extend from about A.D. 1650 to about 1700. Thereafter, until the abandonment of the pueblo, "modern" ware, ornamented with dull red and black paints, was made. .

UNKNOWN FACTORS

Mean Annual Death Rate. In attempting to estimate the mean annual death rate of the inhabitants of the Madisonville, Ohio, Indian village as revealed by the burials, I utilized the known distributions of deaths per thousand in various age groups and the average annual death rate as determined in several European countries, arguing that a close correlation exists between the average annual death rate and the distribution of ages at death, especially in the age group from 0 to 10 years.[1]

TABLE XI–1. AGE AT DEATH AND AVERAGE ANNUAL DEATH RATE

	Years	Age 0–10 Per cent	Age 10–20 Per cent	Age 20– Per cent	Average annual death rate Years	Per cent
Russia	1870–74	62.33	4.13	33.54	1865–75	3.67
Austria	1865–77	52.38	4.05	43.57	1865–78	3.18
Spain	1865–70	51.86	4.37	43.77	1865–70	3.12
Bavaria	1871–77	52.61	2.22	45.17	1865–78	3.09
Italy	1872–77	52.37	4.22	43.41	1865–78	2.99
Prussia	1875–77	52.43	3.51	44.06	1865–78	2.72
France	1866–77	32.28	4.25	63.47	1865–77	2.46
Pecos	(800–1700)?	31.99	6.93	61.98	. . . . .	. . .
Madisonville, Ohio	(1570–1670)?	35.20	3.70	61.10	. . . . .	. . .
Switzerland	1873–77	36.94	3.72	59.33	1870–78	2.38

The distribution of ages at death during the Glaze periods at Pecos corresponds closely with that in France during the years 1866–77, when the death rate was 2.46 per hundred. If we allow for a number of infant burials which have disappeared and the addition of which would augment the proportion in the group 0–10 years, it is nevertheless probable that the average annual death rate per hundred for the period of the Pecos pueblo from its founding to 1700 would be something under three.

If then we assume the Black-on-white and Glaze periods to have extended from A.D. 800 to 1700 and the mean annual death rate to have been 2.5 to 3 per annum per hundred, an average population of 1000 souls during those nine centuries would have produced 22,500 or 27,000 burials, and an average population of 1500, 37,500 to 45,000 burials.

Proportion of Total Burial Area Excavated. Dr. Kidder estimates, on the basis of progress maps, that from 15 to 20 per cent of the burial area on the Pecos mesa has been excavated. The total number of burials found was approximately 1800. Upon this basis there would have been only 9000 to 12,000 burials on the mesa to represent the population from A.D. 800 to 1700. An average population of four hun-

---

[1] Hooton, 1920, pp. 20–23.

dred with a mean annual death rate of three would fill a cemetery containing the larger number in 1000 years, and an average population of 450 would fill such a cemetery in a little more than 900 years. After 1700 and perhaps for some time before, burials of Pecos Indians were made in the nave of the church and, as this has not been excavated in such a way as to record separate burials, the Christian burials cannot be used in our estimates. It will be shown that estimates of total population, based upon percentage of burials excavated, are far too low.

Estimates of Late Glaze and Post-Christian Population. For the period from 1540, almost the beginning of Glaze V, up to the time of the abandonment of Pecos we

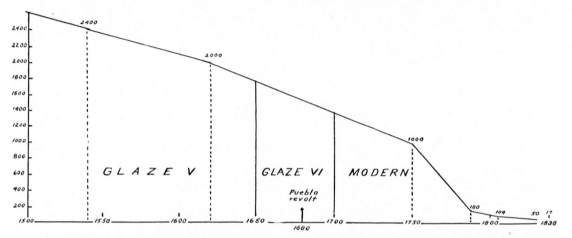

FIG. XI–1. TAIL OF PECOS POPULATION CURVE. (DOTTED LINES ARE CONTEMPORARY ESTIMATES)

have both dates and estimates of population by contemporary observers. These enable us to construct Fig. XI–1, a graph showing the size and decline of the population during this terminal period. From this graph we may arrive at a rough estimate of the number of persons who died at Pecos during the historical period by the following process. From our skeletal material the individuals represented may be placed in the following age groups: 0–34 years, 41.88 per cent; 34–55 years, 39.67 per cent; 55– years, 18.43 per cent.[1] It is obvious, however, that the percentage in the first group is much too low and that in the last group too high, for many infant burials have undoubtedly disappeared entirely and are not represented on the grave cards or in our skeletal collections. In India between the years 1901–1910 about 67 per cent of the population died between the ages 0–34 years.[2] Probably the mean death rate was not so high during the entire period of the Pecos pueblo, but it may be assumed that 50 per cent of the population died during the first 33 years of life. In India, during the period 1901–1910, about 6.8 per cent of the population lived to the age of 67 years or more.[2] Our skeletal figures give 18.43 per cent of the Pecos population as 55 years and more in age. We may then guess that in reality about 10 per cent of the population may have lived to the age of 66 or more, allowing the other 8 per cent to be added to the lowest mortality group. Therefore

[1] Cf. Chapter II, Table II–6.   [2] Glover, 1921, pp. 204–215.

if we suppose that 50 per cent of the Pecos people died in the first third of any century, 40 per cent in the second third of a century, and 10 per cent in the last third of the century, we may not be greatly in error. At any rate let us work upon this assumption. We may now consider Fig. XI–2. In this figure let the line OM equal any century, the line AO representing the population at the beginning of the century, and the line Bx the population at the beginning of the second third of the century, the line Cy the population at the beginning of the last third of the century, and the line DM the population at the end of the same century or the beginning of

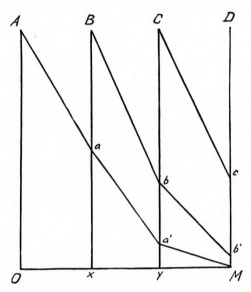

Fig. XI–2. Stationary population during any century

the next. Then if 50 per cent of the initial population AO dies in the first 33 years, let the line Aa cut off from the lower portion of line Bx an amount equal to the number of the AO population surviving into the second third of the century. That is, line ax = .5 line AO. Then line Ba equals the population born since the beginning of the century and alive at x, the beginning of the second third of the century. Then let line aa′ cut off from Cy (the population at the beginning of the third 33 years of the century) a′y, an amount equal to 10 per cent of AO, the proportion of the initial population surviving into the last third of the century. Similarly let line Bb cut off from Cy, line ba′, an amount equal to 50 per cent of Ba, the population born after the beginning of the century and surviving into the last third of the century. Then the population born after the beginning of the second third of the century and surviving into the last third equals line Cb, or Cb = Cy − ba′ − a′y. Then if X represents the total number of deaths occurring during the century:

$$X = AO + .9\,Cb \quad \text{or} \tag{1}$$

$$X = AO + .9\,(Bx − .5\,AO) + .5\,[Cy − .5\,(Bx − .5\,AO) − .1\,AO] \tag{2}$$

Then if AO, Bx, Cy, and DM each equal 1000, or, in other words, if the population remains stationary throughout the century, substituting in the above formula, we have for the number of deaths occurring in the course of the century:

$$X = 1000 + .9\,(1000 - 500) + .5[1000 - .5\,(1000 - 500) - .1\,(1000)]$$
$$= 1000 + 450 + 325$$
$$= 1775$$

But this formula assumes that all of the population at the beginning of the century are young, whereas at least 10 per cent are very old persons left over from the preceding century. Therefore in order to correct for this error we must add to the number of deaths about 10 per cent of the initial population. Thus the formula becomes:

$$X = AO + .9\,(Bx - .5AO) + .5\,[Cy - .5\,(Bx - .5\,AO) - .1\,AO] + .1\,AO \qquad (3)$$

This is the approximate number of deaths occurring in the course of the century if 50 per cent of the initial population dies in the first 33 years, 40 per cent in the second 33 years, and 10 per cent in the last 33 years. We may now proceed to the application of the formula to our Pecos problem.

For Glazes V and VI we have contemporary population estimates at various periods, from which Fig. XI–1, a graph representing the decline of the Pecos population, has been constructed. Interpolating from this graph we have the following approximate numbers of the Pecos population at the various 33-year intervals from A.D. 1500 to 1700:

Date	Population	Date	Population
1500	2600	1633	1920
1533	2440	1666	1640
1566	2280	1700	1400
1600	2120		

Applying Formula (3) for each century, we obtain for the period A.D. 1500–1600 a total number of deaths of 4611 persons and for the next century a total of 3605 deaths, or a total for two centuries of 8216 deaths.

Another method of obtaining the total number of deaths is by following the number of survivors classified according to age group through the two centuries, as follows in Table XI–2.

In this method the deaths are collected by adding the 10 per cent of old individuals who have survived from the preceding period, 50 per cent of the young survivors of the preceding period, and the difference between the middle-aged survivors of the preceding period and the number of old survivors in the next period. This method carries the population straight through the two centuries and avoids the error of assuming a completely young population at the beginning of the second century. It does not, however, avoid the error of assuming that all of the population at the beginning of the initial period are young. It necessitates the addition of about 10 per cent of deaths to compensate for the erroneous assumption of

TABLE XI–2. DECLINE OF THE PECOS POPULATION, A.D. 1500–1700

Date	Population (total)	Old Deaths	Old Survivors	Middle-aged Deaths	Middle-aged Survivors	Young Deaths	Young Survivors	Deaths (total)
1500	2600	...	...	...	...	...	2600	...
		...	...	...	...	1300	...	1300
1533	2440	...	...	...	1300	...	1140	...
		...	...	1040	...	570	...	1610
1566	2280	...	260	...	570	...	1450	...
		260	...	456	...	725	...	1441
1600	2120	...	114	...	725	...	1281	...
		114	...	580	...	641	...	1335
1633	1920	...	145	...	640	...	1135	...
		145	...	512	...	568	...	1225
1666	1640	...	128	...	567	...	945	...
		128	...	454	...	473	...	1055
1700	1400	...	113	...	472	...	815	...

Plus 10 per cent initial population

	7966
Plus 10 per cent initial population	260
	8226

the age of the population at the beginning of the first century. The 10 per cent correction is secured by comparing the results of applying Formula (3) twice — once for each century — and the present method of carrying the population straight through the two centuries. This gives:

Formula (3) A.D. 1500–1600 total deaths uncorrected 4351
Age-group method " " " " 4351
Formula (3) A.D. 1600–1700 " " " 3393
Age-group method " " " carried through 3615
Difference 222

This difference is approximately 10 per cent of 2120, the population at the beginning of 1600. Therefore about 10 per cent of the initial population at the beginning of the century must be added to each application of Formula (3) and 10 per cent of the initial population of the first century must be added when the age-group method is carried through the two centuries. If the two methods are compared we find that the age-group method with correction yields a total population of 8226 for the two centuries, and the formula twice applied with the corrections a total of 8216 deaths.

In order to obtain the number of deaths between 1700 and the abandonment of the pueblo in 1838 we reapply Formula (3) to the population estimates derived from the graph based upon the recorded estimates. These are:

Date	Population	Date	Population
1700	1400	1800....................	120
1733	1140	1838....................	17
1766	620		

For the years 1700–1800 Formula (3) with correction yields a total of 2216 deaths, to which must be added 103 deaths between 1800 and 1838, making a total of 2319 deaths with 17 survivors left in 1838 at the time of abandonment.

Estimate of Total Deaths at Pecos.   The only archaeological periods for which we have both contemporary population estimates and random samples of excavated skeletal material are Glazes V and VI. During the Modern period (1700–1838) most burials were probably made in the church and these have not been excavated, except the few which came to light in the process of restoring the walls of the nave. We must therefore depend upon the skeletal sample of Glazes V and VI if we are to attempt to find the ratio between skeletons excavated and persons dying at Pecos.

For Glazes V and VI together, we have (at the end of the 1926 season) a total of 226 dated burials. But we have found from our population estimates that a total of approximately 8226 deaths probably took place during this period. We therefore have only 2.75 per cent of the population of the two periods represented by dated burials. Figure XI–3 shows the percentages of the dated burials assigned to each Glaze period. Those of the combined Glaze V and Glaze VI burials constitute 17.4 per cent of the entire skeletal sample. But we have actually arrived at 8226 as the approximate number of deaths which took place at this period. If then 8226 deaths equals 17.4 per cent of the total number of deaths during the occupancy of the pueblo, that total would be 47,276. Then if the deaths of the Modern period (2319) are added, a grand total of 49,595 deaths is obtained.

This estimate of nearly 50,000 deaths does not accord well with Dr. Kidder's guess that he has excavated from 15 to 20 per cent of the burial area. For upon this basis only 8000 to 12,000 burials would have been made on the mesa during the entire habitation period. But the percentage of infant burials (0–3 years) included in the grave-card sample is only 14.40, which is actually less than the infant mortality for the same ages in the registration area of the United States in 1910[1] and less than half of the Negro infant mortality for the same period.[2] The probabilities are that at least half of the infant burials in the area excavated by

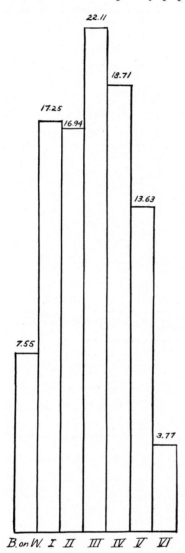

Fig. XI–3.   Histogram showing the percentage distribution of burials of known stratigraphic period

[1] Glover, 1921, p. 54.   [2] Glover, 1921, p. 80.

Dr. Kidder have disappeared entirely and consequently were not recorded. Infant bones disintegrate very rapidly. Aside from the infants a very considerable proportion of other burials must have been disturbed and destroyed during subsequent burial periods and many may have rotted away without leaving any trace whatsoever. Also many of the individuals born at Pecos must have died away from home. We know, for example, that about 1750, when the population of the pueblo still numbered 1000, the Pecos organized an expedition against the Comanche, consisting of the entire man-power of the village. This expedition was entirely cut to pieces, only one man escaping. It seems probable that during the entire period of the pueblo some thousands must have died away from home.

The contemporary estimates of the size of Pecos during the historical period are utterly inconsistent with the supposition that any such insignificant number as 12,000 could account for the deaths occurring during the ten centuries of the pueblo's occupation. An average population of 1500 souls during ten centuries with an average death rate of 30 per annum per thousand would produce 45,000 deaths in the stated period. And the average population of Pecos during the decline, from 1500 when it is estimated at 2600 souls to 1800 when it had shrunk to about 120, was about 1680, calculated at 33-year intervals. I am therefore of the opinion that the estimate of approximately 50,000 deaths through the entire period of the pueblo is altogether reasonable.

Now if we accept the estimate given above, we may calculate the approximate number of deaths to be assigned to each archaeological period, if it is admitted that the percentages of burials actually excavated and assigned to each period represent, in each case, the nearly correct proportions of the population dying in the respective periods. We might expect, perhaps, that the ratio of graves found to the number of persons who actually were buried would be smaller in the earlier periods than in the later periods, but I do not think that this is the case, because such an assumption would necessitate the supposition that the Pecos population was largest in Black-on-white and Glaze I periods and declined steadily thereafter, whereas the archaeological evidence indicates that population did not reach its maximum until Glaze II times, at any rate.

Using the recorded percentage of dated graves for the various periods we obtain the following estimates:

TABLE XI–3. DATED BURIALS AND ESTIMATED DEATHS BY PERIODS

	Approximate dates	Dated burials		Estimated deaths
		No.	Per cent	
Black-on-white	800–950	98	7.55	3569
Glaze I	950–1100	224	17.26	8159
Glaze II	1100–1200	220	16.95	8013
Glaze III	1200–1350	287	22.11	10452
Glaze IV	1350–1500	243	18.72	8849
Glaze V	1500–1650	177	13.64	6448
Glaze VI	1650–1700	49	3.78	1786
Modern	1700–1838	...	...	2319

In order to obtain the average population during any period we must find the ratio of total deaths per century to the average population for the century. The estimated total of deaths during the century 1500–1600 was 4611. The average population (2360) is about 51 per cent of this figure. For the next century the average population was 1770 and the total estimate of deaths 3615. The population is about 49 per cent of the deaths. If the population is stationary at 1000 persons for a century, according to our Formula (3) the deaths equal 1875 and the average population is 53.3 per cent of the total deaths. We may then assume roughly that the average population is about 50 per cent of the deaths occurring in any century. This enables

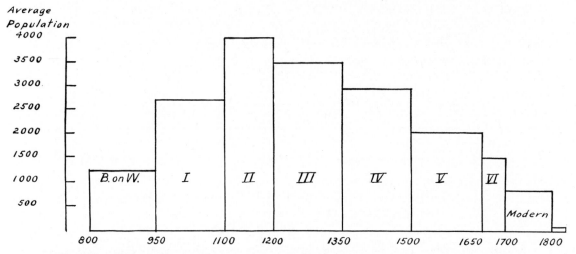

Fig. XI–4. Histogram of estimated average population at Pecos during the successive
Stratigraphic Periods

us to reconstruct Fig. XI–4, a histogram showing our guess at the average population during the several periods.

The limiting dates of the last three periods are known approximately from historical and archaeological data. Black-on-white, Glaze I, Glaze III, Glaze IV, and Glaze V are assigned periods of 150 years each. Glaze II, a shorter period according to the rubbish heaps, is assigned a length of 100 years, and Glaze VI, on the same basis, only 50 years. Then upon this basis the average populations were as follows: Black-on-white, 1189; Glaze I, 2720; Glaze II, 4006; Glaze III, 3484; Glaze IV, 2950; Glaze V, 2149; Glaze VI, 1520; Modern (A.D. 1700–1800) 829.

In this chapter I have built up a house of cards. The assumptions made and the methods employed are all questionable, perhaps erroneous. The reader need not attach much importance to this effort, nor rely at all upon its conclusions. I have merely attempted to reach a plausible solution of an impossible problem.

Taking the mean, weighted by centuries, of the average period populations obtained above, we find for the entire period of Pecos (880–1838) an average population of 2388. But I am inclined to think that this figure is too high. For the minimum mean annual death rate 2.5 per hundred would yield in 1000 years with an average population of 2388, a total of 59,700 deaths. And our estimate is only 50,000 deaths.

According to our calculation of deaths during the period 1500–1700 when the Pecos population was declining, the annual death rate was 4 per hundred. In order to make the number of deaths conform to the calculated mean population of Pecos throughout its habitation period the average death rate would have to be about 2 per hundred.

The death rate for the two centuries 1500–1700, based upon the assumption of 50 per cent dying during the first third of the century, 40 per cent in the second third, and 10 per cent in the last third, works out according to the contemporaneous population estimates at 4 per hundred per year, and this of course is for a period during which the population declined from 2600 at the beginning to 1400 at the end. A death rate of 2 per hundred is not uncommon among modern civilized people, but seems too low for the average rate of a millenium in a primitive population.

But if we raise the death rate we must also raise the total number of persons necessary to keep up the known average of the population during the historical period and consequently the total population of the pueblo. Unless the contemporaneous estimates are far too high or the period of 1000 years assigned by Dr. Kidder as the maximum period of occupancy is too short, it is difficult to avoid the conclusion that our total estimate of 50,000 deaths is nearly correct. We can of course speculate as to the unrepresentative character of the numbers of burials excavated during the several periods. The Glaze V and VI burials excavated represent, according to our calculations, only 2.75 per cent of the deaths which actually took place in that period. Perhaps the graves from the earlier periods represent a higher percentage of the population which died during those periods.

If we think that the percentage of the total population represented, for example, in our Glaze II sample is too high, we are merely forced to transfer a larger number of deaths to some other period. Our estimate must stand, therefore, unless more centuries can be added to the period of the pueblo's occupancy, or unless it can be shown that the pueblo was much smaller in all of the periods prior to Glaze V than our burial samples indicate. If for some reason the burial samples of Glazes V and VI are disproportionately small, so that instead of representing only 17.4 per cent of the total population the full count of deaths of those periods should represent, let us say, 33 per cent of the total deaths, our population estimate would be reduced to about 25,000 for the entire period of occupancy, but such a supposition would carry with it the assumption that in all periods prior to Glaze V Pecos was a very small community. If enough Glaze V and VI burials were made in the church seriously to disturb the validity of the excavated burial sample of those periods, the population count might be reduced by some thousands. But if we assume that Glaze V ended about 1600 instead of 1650, or if we assume that few Glaze V burials were made in the church, which was not built until 1610 or thereabouts, we can refigure the total population on the basis of the ratio of burial sample to calculated deaths for that century. We find that the Glaze V (sixteenth-century) excavated burials constitute 3.83 per cent of the calculated deaths during that period. Then if the 1800 excavated burials equal 3.63 per cent of the total burials, the total burials for the whole period are approximately 47,000, which is not far short of our previous estimate.

ADDENDA

By E. A. Hooton

As this volume is about to go to press, there come to hand the long-awaited data of Dr. Andrew E. Douglass, whereby absolute dates for prehistoric ruins in the Southwest are obtained from the study of tree-ring growth based upon logs taken from the ruins.[1] The article in question does not include dates for Pecos or other Rio Grande pueblos. However, it places the various Mesa Verde ruins between A.D. 1073 and A.D. 1272. On page 332 of this chapter, Dr. Kidder was quoted to the effect that his estimate of A.D. 800 for the beginning of the pueblo on Pecos mesa was based on the finding of trade pottery from Mesa Verde in the immediately pre-Pecos ruin across the river from Pecos at Bandelier Bend. The Mesa Verde culture was thought to be roughly contemporaneous with that of Pueblo Bonito, assumed from alleged Toltec material found there to have been inhabited around A.D. 900–1000. Dr. Douglass now dates Pueblo Bonito A.D. 919–1127. But if his dates for the Mesa Verde culture (A.D. 1073–1272) are correct, and if the pueblo on the mesa at Pecos was built after the abandonment of the Bandelier Bend settlement, then the founding of Pecos would have to be set at some time subsequent to A.D. 1073 — say A.D. 1100 at earliest. This would mean a reduction of 300 years in the period of occupation of the pueblo.

Now we know that Pecos was discovered in A.D. 1540, in the earlier part of the Glaze V period, which must then have begun about A.D. 1500. Glazes V and VI lasted from approximately A.D. 1500 to 1700. But the burials of these two periods together constitute only 17.4 per cent of all dated burials of the pre-Modern occupation period. Then approximately 82.6 per cent of the population up to A.D. 1700 would have died in Black-on-white, Glazes I, II, III, and IV periods. Taking the date A.D. 1100 as the founding of the pueblo, we have but four centuries, or twice the length of Glaze V and Glaze VI periods, into which to crowd all of the lives and nearly all of the deaths of the five earlier stratigraphic periods. The deaths for these first five periods were, according to my estimate, 39,042. This would give an average number of deaths for the first four centuries of 9,760 deaths per century and would require an average population of nearly half of that number or 4,880 for each century. This, to my mind, is an impossibly high figure. Further, since the Black-on-white pueblo was certainly smaller than the settlements of the subsequent periods, it would be necessary to adjust these figures in such a way as to raise the average population in some of the later pre-Spanish periods to a figure in excess of 6,000. I do not believe that Pecos was ever so large. In short, it seems impossible to collapse our estimated population for the first five periods into a space of four centuries without raising the size of the town to an incredible figure.

Again, while it is outside of my province to pass judgment upon the relative length of the various Pecos periods on the basis of the rubbish heaps and of the house ruins, it is my privilege to remark that in view of the known lapse of time during the Glaze V, Glaze VI, and Modern periods, it is hardly possible that four-fifths of the people should have lived and died and that five-eighths of the pottery development should have been completed in a little more than one-half of the period of the pueblo's occupation.

---

[1] Douglass, 1929, pp. 736–770.

By Dr. A. V. Kidder

after 1100

Dr. Douglass's findings have thrown a bombshell not only into Dr. Hooton's calculations as to population, but into all my previous estimates as to the rapidity of the cultural changes which took place at Pecos. It is very difficult to conceive how, in a period of four hundred and fifty years (which is about the earliest date for the founding of Pecos consistent with Dr. Douglass's figures) there could have been crowded the later phases of Black-on-white, the development of Glaze I and its archaeologically demonstrable very slow transition into Glaze II. And to these must be added Glaze II itself, Glaze III, and Glaze IV (the latter, according to finds made on the Pajarito and elsewhere, having evidently been an important and apparently a fairly long period). But I have nevertheless so firm a confidence in the soundness of Dr. Douglass's method, and I trust so implicitly the accuracy of his results, that I am forced to believe that Pueblo culture was capable of changing much more rapidly than I had ever thought possible. Many ideas must be rearranged and much evidence must necessarily be reinterpreted, not only in the Pecos country, but in other parts of the Southwest.

CHAPTER XII

RESULTS OF THE STUDY OF THE PECOS
SKELETAL MATERIAL

SUMMARY OF PREVIOUS CHAPTERS

NUMBER, AGE, AND SEX

MORE than 1800 graves have been excavated at Pecos by Dr. Kidder and his assistants. In the present report the skeletal material sent to the Peabody Museum prior to 1925 has been utilized. This includes remains of almost 1000 individuals, about 44 per cent of which are adult skeletons sufficiently well preserved to be studied metrically and morphologically. Skeletons of infants, children, and adolescents were observed but not measured.

Studies of the ages of individual skeletons were based upon the records made upon grave-cards in the field by a number of observers and upon examination of the skeletal material sent to the Peabody Museum. Independent estimates of the age of skeletons in the latter collection were made by Professor T. Wingate Todd and by me. These estimates agree fairly well, on the whole, but exhibit a considerable number of differences in individual judgments. The outstanding facts which emerged from the age studies are that the Pecos population shows a comparatively small proportion of individuals who survived to the age of 55 years or over; that the death rate in middle life (between the ages of 35 and 54 years) was very high — more than twice as great as in modern populations whose death rates are recorded; that the number of infant burials found and recorded at Pecos is so small that it cannot give any adequate idea of the actual infant mortality. The deficiency in infant remains may be due in part to their complete decay and disappearance and in part to a possible failure to give infants proper burials. The excess of middle-aged skeletons may be attributed partially to the better weathering of skeletons of individuals in middle life. But it is clear that comparatively few of the Pecos Indians lived to old age. Here as elsewhere, apparently, females enjoyed a greater longevity than males.

The problem of assigning sex to the Pecos skeletons presented the usual difficulties. None of the conventional anatomical criteria of sex in the skeleton are infallible. The same subject not infrequently presents contradictory sexual features, even in the pelvis. The subpubic angle and the ischiatic notches seem to afford the most reliable indications of sex. In the Pecos material male skeletons with somewhat feminine pelvic features are not very uncommon. In a sample of 264 skeletons independently sexed by Todd and by me, 15 per cent of disagreements in judgment were recorded. Yet the total numbers of males and females distinguished by the two observers differ only by one.

The number of males per hundred females in the Pecos skeletal material is 140.8 and this does not include skeletons of children under 10 years of age. That this great excess of males is not attributable to mistakes in sexing or better weathering of male skeletons is demonstrated by the fact that the allied Jemez tribe in 1910 showed almost as great a numerical superiority of males. Inability to determine sex in skeletons of infants and children by no means accounts for the overbalanced sex ratio in the Pecos skeletons, since in all populations more males than females are born and the ratio of males to females declines through successive age periods. Taking the Pecos skeletons by stratigraphic periods it was found that the number of males per hundred females increased tremendously during the period of the pueblo's decline.

The Study of the Skeletons by Archaeological Strata

The skeletal material was first studied by stratigraphic subgroups with the object of discovering what changes in the population may have taken place during the ten centuries of the pueblo's occupation. A great majority of the crania of both sexes show some degree of accidental occipital deformation. This condition was least common in the earliest stratigraphic group and more pronounced in males than in females. Evidence has been presented indicating that occipital deformation affected original brachycephals more markedly than long-heads, and that this flattening has commonly changed mesocephals to brachycephals and dolichocephals to mesocephals, rather than effected a complete transformation from long-headedness to round-headedness. This conclusion has been confirmed by the application of Shapiro's correction formulae to various subgroups in the series, whereby it has been possible to restore approximate means of the original head dimensions.

The four stratigraphic subgroups into which the skeletal material was divided are: Black-on-White and Glaze I, Glazes II and III, Glaze IV, Glazes V and VI. This grouping of the stratigraphic material was necessitated by the comparatively small number of dated and measurable adult skeletons. The metric data were discussed from the point of view of their variations in the several chronological subgroups and according to sex.

Rigorous statistical methods were applied in order to ascertain whether or not the stratigraphic subgroups as units could be shown to possess craniometric individuality. Of the different subgroups it was found that the earliest, Black-on-white and Glaze I, alone showed a sufficient number of significant differences from the series at large to justify the conclusion that such differences were not due to the sampling process. It was demonstrated that the successive subgroups became more and more homogeneous until the last in almost every respect conformed to what would be expected of a random sample of the whole series. It therefore was apparent that the thousand years of Pecos history involved a continuous process of amalgamation through inbreeding of the somewhat heterogeneous types of the earliest population.

Some individual measurements showed definite trends throughout the successive periods. Minimum frontal diameter and bizygomatic diameter increased. Facial indices were lowered so that the faces were proportionately broader and shorter; mandibles and palates probably decreased in size and prognathism seemed to show a slight increase.

The graded morphological observations of each skull were similarly subjected to statistical analysis from the point of view of stratigraphic differences and sex differences. A few rather unusual sex differences were established. For example, foreheads are more receding in the females than in the males: U-shaped and elliptical palates are commoner in the females. Males have better teeth, but show a greater frequency of suppression of the third molars. Females show more frequent cusp reduction and more numerous shovel incisors. Most of the other sex differences were of the expected nature.

Morphological features taken from period to period clearly show a deterioration of the Pecos population toward a brutal but rather degenerate type. It is true that foreheads increase in height, that sagittal elevations become less common, and that mastoids increase in size. But occipital tori also increase in frequency and the form of the nasal bridge and nasal aperture becomes more primitive. Malars become larger and alveolar prognathism more frequent and more pronounced. Teeth seem to deteriorate and third molars are oftener suppressed. The foramina of the skull base grow smaller from the early to the late periods.

Measurements, indices, and morphological observations of the bones other than cranial were also studied by stratigraphic subgroups. The results were diametrically opposed to those of the cranial investigation in that the last two subgroups were found to be most clearly differentiated from the series at large with respect to size and proportion of bones, whereas the first subgroup alone was significantly differentiated in cranial features. It thus appears that in the course of Pecos history the population became more and more homogeneous in cranial characters and more and more diversified in other skeletal features. It was suggested as an explanation of these phenomena that cranial features may be controlled more by hereditary than by environmental factors, whereas the reverse may obtain in respect to many features of the other bones, especially size and proportions. The fact that the male population seems to have been tallest during Glaze IV times, presumably the optimum period of the pueblo, and shortest during the final period of decline may lend plausibility to such a suggestion. A waning population, fighting a losing battle against disease, shortage of food, and enemies, and a population which is just at the peak of its material and physical prosperity, might be expected to vary more from the series average than their ancestors who were developing normally under more or less stable environmental restrictions. This of course is a suggestion and nothing more.

As a matter of fact differences in stature and in gross size of parts from earliest Pecos times to the final abandonment are so slight as to be statistically insignificant. Yet the diminution in maximum lengths of long bones during the period represented by the last Glaze subgroups is so consistent in the different bones as to impress the student with its validity in spite of probable errors. The Pecos Indians were at all times short in stature and inferior to the averages of all living Pueblo tribes. The kindred Jemez Indians seem to be, of all living Pueblo tribes, the closest in average stature to the extinct Pecos.[1]

Almost no consistent metric and morphological trends through successive stratigraphic periods could be discerned from the study of the bones. Apparently long bones became shorter; pelves flatter and relatively broader, and certain morphological features, such as platymeria and femoral pilaster, were more and more accentuated. But every conclusion on period trends is necessarily tentative, since our series, when divided into sex groups and stratigraphic subgroups, does not afford sufficiently large subgroups to yield wholly reliable means.

DETERMINATION OF MORPHOLOGICAL TYPES

The study of the Pecos population by periods revealed no coincidence of cultural change with alteration of physical type, such as might be expected to mark the infusion of a new racial element into the population. It became clear that the investigation of the skeletal remains by stratigraphic subgroups would yield little or nothing in the way of information as to the different physical types of which the population was composed. At the termination of the period study, I therefore began another investigation on different lines. I selected all of the fairly well-preserved male crania and divided them into groups according to their mutual resemblances as judged by visual observation. After some days of sorting there emerged eight subgroups of crania. One of these I called the "Residual" group because into it were put all crania otherwise unclassified. The other groups I called by names selected because of a real or fancied resemblance to some type of Indian skull or to crania of other races. The next step was to test the metric validity of these morphological subgroups. This was done by calculating the means and other constants of the cranial measurements and indices of each subgroup and comparing the percentage of significant divergences of these means from means of a random sample of the total series identical in size with each subgroup. Contrary to the experience in the case of the Glaze subgroups, these morphological subgroups, with two exceptions, yielded overwhelming statistical evidence of being metrically and indicially individual. One of these exceptions was the "Residual" group, which was, of course, merely a collection of irreconcilables and misfits and featureless crania. This quite properly proved to be amorphous except for a moderate size differentiation. The other was a group called "Large Hybrids" which was strongly differentiated by its great size, but in indices or proportions was scarcely distinguishable from a random sample of the series at large. A study of the morphological features of these type subgroups showed that they also possessed individuality with respect to observed characters, as might be expected from the nature of the sorting upon which the subgroups were based. In order to convince myself and my readers of the actual validity and integrity of these morphological types, I made composite photographs of ten crania of each type. These composite photographs (cf. plates in pocket at back of volume) seem conclusively to justify the type selections.

[1] With the exception of the males from Sia pueblo, whose mean of stature, according to Hrdlička, is based upon measurements of 7 individuals only.

Finally I undertook to trace the affinities of these seven morphological types (omitting the "Residual" type) with other Indian groups, and if necessary outside of the American area. A type which I had called "Basket Maker" proved to be very similar to the authentic Basket Maker crania of Arizona but resembled somewhat more closely the crania from the caves of Coahuila, Mexico. This type also bore a strong general resemblance to crania of the so-called "Mediterranean" race, especially various Egyptian groups.

A subgroup named the "Pseudo-Negroid" group was clearly distinct from any authentic Negro or Negrito type but nevertheless manifested, generally, such metrical and indicial likeness to all Negro groups brought into comparison as to justify the conjecture that some of the early American long-heads may have brought with them from the Old World a Negroid strain in solution. A group dubbed "Pseudo-Australoid" proved to have been misnamed. It resembled the Ainu type much more closely than the Australian type, but it was by no means identical with that type and I was unable to satisfy myself as to its affinities outside of the New World. Another morphological group called the "Plains Indian," turned out to bear a close relationship to various of the eastern dolichocephals and mesocephals of the United States, but it was not very similar to any group of Plains Indians.

A long, narrow-faced, un-Indian looking type of brachycephal, I somewhat rashly nicknamed "Long-faced European." But it did not prove to be metrically or indicially similar to any European group which I could find. Nor did it seem to bear any relationship to the Armenoid type of skull. I found it most similar to the crania of Northern Chinese and of mixed Mongoloids from East Turkestan. Again, another of my types, named "Pseudo-Alpine" because of its globular head, short, broad face and other features, was found to be distinctly unlike the European Alpine type, when judged by metrical and indicial criteria. Its affinities were unmistakably with the Mongoloids. Finally, my "Large Hybrid" group, which seemed to me to typify the conventional North American Indian, proved to be virtually identical with the massive brachycephals of the Mound Area. I shall return to these morphological types in my concluding discussion.

PATHOLOGY

Arthritis was the commonest disease among the Pecos in so far as diagnoses could be made from the skeletal material. It was least common in the earliest period. Inflammatory bone lesions seem to have affected the inhabitants of the latest periods to a greater degree than in early times. This is also true of long bone and pelvic fractures and small bony tumors of the skull. Dental pathology notably increased in the later periods of the pueblo's life. Several stratigraphically pre-Spanish crania strongly suggest syphilis, but apparently, in the present state of knowledge, a definite diagnosis cannot be made. Pott's disease seems to have been present in a few cases, but even here reservations as to the correctness of the diagnoses are necessary. *Osteoporosis symmetrica*, probably a deficiency disease, occurred in a number of immature specimens, but it seems to have been much less common than among the early Mayas and Peruvians.

In general the picture of Pecos pathology from period to period is one of a struggling population, apparently afflicted by the ordinary ailments of life which were neither ameliorated by a well-balanced and adequate diet nor by any effective knowledge of medicine or surgery. While the end of the pueblo's life was probably caused by epidemics and warfare, it is yet possible to trace from the skeletal remains an increased prevalence of certain diseases and a general deterioration in physique during the period of decline.

Growth and Decline of the Pecos Population

In Chapter XI, I have attempted to arrive at estimates of the total number of persons who lived at Pecos during the approximate millennium of its occupancy, and the total and average population of each stratigraphic period. The tail end of the population curve was obtained from contemporaneous population estimates during the historical period. The total of individuals required to support the population during its decline was deduced from an assumption with regard to death rates based upon modern life tables. A further assumption that the number of skeletons recovered from each archaeological period represents a constant proportion of the number of persons who actually died during that period and that the total of burials found for each period represents the true proportion of the entire Pecos population which died during the period, enabled me to reach estimates of the number of deaths occurring in each stratigraphic period and the average population during each period. The duration of each period on the basis of historical or archaeological data was estimated by me and then checked by Dr. Kidder's estimates, which were found to be identical with mine. Of this chapter it may be said that reasonable results have been obtained by methods which are at best dubious, based upon assumptions which are, to say the least, questionable.

I arrived at the conclusion that nearly 50,000 individuals must have lived at Pecos between about A.D. 800, the approximate time of its founding, and A.D. 1838, the date of its abandonment. The average populations were estimated as follows: Black-on-white, 1189; Glaze I, 2720; Glaze II, 4006; Glaze III, 3484; Glaze IV, 2,950; Glaze V, 2,149; Glaze VI, 1,520; Modern (A.D. 1700–1800), 829. On this basis, the average population for the entire life of the Pueblo was 2,388, a figure which is probably a little too high. The mean annual death rate throughout the entire period was probably between 20 per thousand and 25 per thousand. I need hardly say that I should be loath to present my methods and these results to a congress of vital statisticians. I have no doubt that I have rushed in where they would fear to tread. I trust that this rash foray into a hostile and unknown field will pass unobserved by its professional occupants and will be smiled upon indulgently by my anthropological readers. If anyone wishes to pounce upon my tethered and defenseless victim, let him pounce. I am as indifferent to its fate as I am to my present sin of metaphorical mixture.

After traversing all of this weary waste of tables and statistical comparisons of measurements, indices, and anatomical details, I feel justified in permitting myself the luxury of expounding my present views on the anthropology and prehistory of the American Indian, based upon sixteen years of intermittent study of American cranial material, and especially upon the analysis of the Pecos series which has occupied no little of my research leisure for the past ten years. I think it highly probable that another decade of study will modify and perhaps radically alter many of these opinions. The study of the physical anthropology of the American Indian is still in its infancy.

CONCLUSIONS ON THE AMERICAN RACE PROBLEM

The Peopling of the New World

The antiquity of man in the New World will doubtless continue to be a subject of acrimonious discussion among anthropologists and geologists until human skeletal remains are found undisturbed and *in situ* in a geological stratum universally admitted to be of Pleistocene date and in which also occur bones of unquestionably Pleistocene animals. No such irrefutable evidence of the presence in the American continents of geologically ancient man has yet been adduced. Even the most ardent believer in the antiquity of man in America can scarcely argue that any of the alleged finds of "ancient man" hitherto reported establish a valid case. On the other hand it has always seemed to me that there is no inherent improbability in the supposition that man may have reached the New World in late Pleistocene times. Certainly it scarcely can be denied that during the last interglacial period human types existed in the Old World which were perfectly capable of migrating from one area to another, supposing that such migrations did not involve long sea voyages. But it is perfectly evident that if man reached the New World before the present climatic epoch, he must have come in the last interglacial period or in some preceding interglacial period, since the barriers against migration imposed by the ice sheet in the northern part of Asia and of America would have been unsurmountable.

The question then arises as to the type of man which might have entered the New World in one of the later interglacial periods, if indeed such a migration took place. Few anthropologists today believe that modern forms of man have evolved from the Neanderthal type. The principal remaining adherent to this theory of descent is, perhaps, my distinguished colleague, Dr. Aleš Hrdlička. Presumably Dr. Hrdlička would expect an interglacial human migrant into America to be of a Neanderthaloid type. But Dr. Hrdlička is convinced that the New World was not peopled until post-glacial times. In the opinion of perhaps most students of ancient man, the modern types of man evolved from a non-Neanderthaloid stock sometime before the end of the Pleistocene, and, during the last glacial retreat, entered Europe and definitely supplanted the Mousterian Neanderthal race. Since several essentially modern types of man are found in Europe during the Aurignacian, Solutrian, and Magdalenian archaeological periods of the final glacial retreat, we are almost forced to assume the development of such modern types outside of the European area at least as early as the last interglacial period. And a number of authorities, chief among whom is Sir Arthur Keith, have argued convincingly in favor of a much earlier origin of the modern forms of man, both from theoretical considerations and on the evidence of the alleged high antiquity of such fossil finds as that of the Galley Hill man and others. I myself am strongly inclined to this view of an early emergence of essentially modern human forms. However, even if we adhere to the more conservative viewpoint, it is not unreasonable, but on the contrary most probable, that migrants into the New World during the third interglacial period would be comparable in evolutionary development to the Galley Hill type, the Cro-Magnon type, the Grimaldi type, or other late fossil types of essentially modern anatomical conformation. For this reason I cannot admit that a requisite of the geological antiquity of human remains found in the Americas would be an inferior morphological status, comparable to that exhibited by Neanderthal man. The fact that human skeletons, supposedly of Pleistocene date, have been invariably those of Indians differing in no significant respect from recent Indian skeletons does not refute the claim of their antiquity. I should expect a late glacial or third interglacial type of man in America to display "Indian" characteristics. Nevertheless there is no case yet on record which, on the basis of geological and palaeontological evidence, can be admitted as proof of the glacial antiquity of man in the New World.

Another argument seems to weigh negatively against the possibility of a high antiquity of man in the American area. That is the absence, hitherto, of convincing evidence of the geological antiquity of man in the Central Asiatic area and in Northeastern Asia. In spite of the claims of the proponents of the Asiatic theory of the origin of man, with one or two possible exceptions, no geologically ancient human remains have yet been found in Central or Northeastern Asia. Furthermore, no palaeolithic cultures have been found in that region, unless the claim of a Mousterian culture discovered by Teilhard de Chardin in the loess formation of Shensi can be substantiated.

It should be noted however that Fathers Licent and Teilhard de Chardin have also announced the discovery of human remains at a depth of 60 meters in a river deposit in northern Kansu, China, through which the river Osso Goh has cut a deep gorge. These include parts of six skeletons, including one well-fossilized skull of inferior morphological status, associated with small and rude implements of quartzite, and with bones of the elephant, rhinoceros, bison, camel, deer, horse and other mammals. These again are attributed to the Mousterian age.

In October, 1927, a slightly worn left lower permanent molar tooth was discovered during the investigation of a supposed Early Pleistocene deposit in a cave at Chou Kou Tien near Peking, China. Professor Davidson Black concluded that this tooth is morphologically distinct from any known human or anthropoid molar and proposes a new genus — "Sinanthropus Pekinensis." [1] The scientific world has been a little skeptical of new anthropoid genera based on finds of single teeth since the fiasco of "Hesperopithecus Harold Cookii." But a few days ago newspaper accounts announced that this same cave in the neighborhood of Peking, China, has

[1] Black, 1927, pp. 2–28.

yielded abundant skeletal remains of a new type of pre-human or protohuman primate, including a mandible with teeth *in situ*. While we must await more definite information as to this find, it should be admitted that, if it is of the nature reported in the press, there can be no longer any doubt of the geological antiquity of man in Northeastern Asia, and, consequently, the argument for a late peopling of the American continents, so far as it is based upon the absence of ancient man in Northeastern Asia, breaks down utterly.[1]

That America, when it was peopled, derived its inhabitants from Northeastern Asia by way of the present Bering Straits, is admitted by every careful student of the subject. The affinities of the modern American Indians are most obviously with the Asiatic Mongoloids. If we abandon as unprofitable the discussion as to the presence of man in the New World during geologically ancient times, we must nevertheless grapple with the question of the age of human culture in the Americas during the recent period. At least ten or twelve thousand years have elapsed since the final recession of the ice sheet. Less than half a millennium has passed since the discovery of America by Columbus. When the Europeans first came into contact with aboriginal American cultures the most notable civilizations of the New World were already dead or decadent. In South America the megalithic ruins of Tiahuanaco had been abandoned and desolate for many centuries; the coastal and highland cities of Peru had already passed through a long course of political, economic, and general cultural development; and the empire of the Incas was probably ripe for dissolution. Most of the great cities of the Mayas were already overgrown by the jungles; the civilization of the Toltecs had become legendary, and the Aztecs had passed the heyday of their power and vigor. In the Southwest the admirably built pueblos of Chaco canyon had been abandoned and desolate for about as long a time as has elapsed between the landing of Columbus and the present; Pecos had been declining in population for three centuries and had already lived three score and ten of its allotted span of a hundred decades.[2] The Southwest retained only a remnant of the population which had inhabited it in 1000 A.D. The Hopewell culture in Ohio had probably been extinct for some centuries when the Pilgrims landed at Plymouth. We may then admit that in 1500 A.D. the apogee of native American culture had been passed by at least three centuries.

Probably not more than two thousand years should be allowed for the development from a primitive agricultural status of the highest American civilizations — the Mayan, the Andean, the Toltecan, the Aztecan, and the Chaco canyon civilization of the Southwest. The Sumerian civilization rose and declined between 5000 B.C. and 2000 B.C. Egypt developed from a primitive level to a great height and sunk into decline between 3500 B.C. and 663 B.C. Crete rose from a neolithic stage and fell into utter collapse between 3800 B.C. and 1200 B.C. If we allow three thousand years for the cycle of American civilization, from a primitive agricultural level up to

---

[1] As this book goes to press, the antiquity of man in Eastern Asia seems definitely established by a new find (December 2, 1929) of the greater part of an uncrushed skull of *Sinanthropus pekinensis* at Chow Kow Tien. The stratum is said to be Lower Quaternary.

[2] But cf. Addenda, p. 342.

the time of its decline, varying between 1000 and 1500 A.D., we arrive at the approximate date 1500 B.C. or 2000 B.C. This leaves 8000 to 10,000 years in the recent period for the peopling of the New World and the development of agriculture.

There is nothing in the present archaeological and cultural record of the New World inconsistent with the supposition that these continents have been inhabited only within the recent geological period. In the Old World twelve thousand years ago man had not, so far as we know, passed the hunting and fishing stage. The kitchen-middens of Denmark are widely paralleled in the New World and it is quite possible that American kitchen-middens are as old as those of Europe. But thus far no widespread cultures which seem to precede the kitchen-middens have been found in the New World. With the possible exception of the Lagoa Santa caves, no traces of human occupation in the caverns of the New World seem to be of any great antiquity. Nor have the river gravels yielded any indisputable evidence of the presence of early man either in the form of skeletal remains or of artifacts. When we consider the thick deposits in the European caves showing many superimposed layers exhibiting the débris of human culture, and the numerous gravel pits which turn out year after year in great quantities the easily recognizable flint implements chipped in the Pleistocene period by early man, it is difficult to avoid the conclusion that palaeolithic implements would have been found in American gravels if palaeolithic man had been here to make the implements.

There is still hope that some fortunate find may establish conclusively once and for all the presence of geologically ancient man in America. But I am afraid that we must reconcile ourselves to the idea that if man did reach the New World in palaeolithic times, he must have come in such small numbers as to leave almost no trace of his culture, and that the ancestors of the present day Indians, for the most part, must have migrated from Asia within the past ten or twelve thousand years.

RELATION OF BLOOD-GROUPING TO THE AMERICAN PROBLEM

One of the most interesting developments in physical anthropology is the geographical and ethnic distribution of the blood-groups. Serologists divide mankind into four groups: I (Jansky), the blood cells of which contain no agglutinogen and which is designated R or O; II, which contains the agglutinogen A; III, which contains the agglutinogen B; and IV, which contains both A and B. The scheme of inheritance most favored is that of triple allelomorphs, although this subject is still under discussion.[1]

It is generally admitted that Group I, which lacks both agglutinogens, is recessive for that reason to all other groups, and that A and B, the two agglutinogens, represent mutations of later occurrence, the former probably originating in Europe, the latter in Asia. Evidence clearly indicates that Group I (R or O) is the primitive human blood grouping, since it occurs in fifty per cent or more of almost all races and peoples heretofore investigated. The agglutinogen A is most strongly represented in Western European peoples, B in Mongoloids and natives of India; AB is

---

[1] Furuhata, 1929, pp. 109–130. In this discussion I have utilized the Jansky blood-group classification rather than that of Moss for the reason that the authors referred to have adopted the former system.

a combination proportionately insignificant, but seems to be strongest among certain Near-eastern peoples. Negroes are not distinctive in their blood groupings, since they show a high percentage of R, and moderately large and approximately equal percentages of both A and B.

Our present interest in the blood groups lies in the fact that Snyder [1] has discovered that American Indians, when selected pure bloods are examined, belong almost exclusively in Group I and show percentages of R rising to 95.5. It seems possible and even probable that all pure-blood Indians belong in Group I, which shows neither the A nor the B agglutinogen. But the B agglutinogen is most strongly represented in the East Asiatic Mongoloids to whom the American Indians are obviously akin in anatomical characters. If there is one physical fact about the American Indian of which we are certain it is that he is at least partially Mongoloid. Therefore we are forced to the conclusion that America was peopled by the Indians before the B agglutinogen originated in Eastern Asia. Only the Western Eskimo, who are perhaps to be regarded as the most recent of the Asiatic immigrants to the New World, show a large proportion of the agglutinogen B. [2]

Are we then to regard the American Indians as a race of high antiquity in their present habitat? I do not think so. There is reason for believing that both A and B agglutinogens are of comparatively recent origin. The Icelanders of today show a very high percentage of R, a percentage of A which is small considering their Northwestern European origin, and little of B, the Asiatic agglutinogen. Iceland could not have been colonized long before the fifth century A.D. and it seems probable that at that time the A agglutinogen had not been widely diffused even in its area of characterization. It is quite possible that agglutinogen A did not originate much before the Christian era. It seems almost certain that the peopling of the New World was largely accomplished before the year 1 A.D., and that immigrants of any period prior to that would naturally lack the A agglutinogen which had not as yet originated. The B agglutinogen seems to have arisen in Eastern Asia somewhat later than A in Europe. Certain outlying peoples, such as the native Australians, show in addition to a high percentage of R, a considerable proportion of A and very little B, although they are contiguous to the B area and far from the A area. Agglutinogen B is then probably of very recent origin. If we allow the American Indians as little as eight or ten thousand years of occupation of the New World, most of the Asiatic immigrants must have arrived, and native American cultures must have been largely evolved, before either of these blood group mutations took place in the Old World.

I do not think that the fact that full-blood Indians all seem to belong to the same serological group indicates that the Indians are a pure race in the sense that they are a primary race and unmixed with other strains. For if the agglutinogens are of recent origin, the crossing of racial strains are none the less very ancient, and the diversity of physical type which is manifested by the present American Indians could scarcely have been developed within the few thousands of years during which they have inhabited the New World.

[1] Snyder, 1926, pp. 233–263.   [2] Gates, 1929, pp. 475–485.

Among the so-called "Basket Makers" it ordinarily appears in association with the types I have called Pseudo-Australoid and Pseudo-Negroid. Actually I do not think that I have ever seen the skull of a "Basket Maker" which I could mistake for that of a Predynastic Egyptian: the faces of the American crania are always too large and the brain-cases are too small. But I cannot doubt that that same fundamental stock of mankind which is predominant in North Africa and in Southern Europe, contributed in some considerable degree to the more ancient peoples of the New World. And I am confident that this "Basket Maker" type, whatever its affinities may be, was the most numerous single type among the early Americans.

These three early dolichocephaic types, then, the Pseudo-Australoid, the Pseudo-Negroid and the Basket Maker, probably together constituted the earliest American population. I cannot over-emphasize my conviction that they do not represent separate migrations of different races but rather a general mélange of strains fused together in the early invaders before their departure from the Asiatic continent. Their identification in the New World as separate and distinct craniometric and morphological types is due to the segregation of features in occasional individuals. The bulk of this Palae-American population must have consisted of people in whom the features of these three types were combined in various ways. If I were to hazard a guess as to their appearance it would be that they were not unlike some of the Dravidian inhabitants of Southern India — short statured, slender in build, dolichocephalic, mesorrhine or platyrrhine, mesognathous, and with faces lacking the massive size and jutting malars characteristic of the later Indians. The skin color was probably brown and the hair form more inclined to wave or to curl than in existing American Indian types.

The next element added to the early American mixtures was probably a Mongoloid strain. The origin of the Mongoloid type of man is by no means clear, but its diffusion seems certainly later than that of primitive Negroid and primitive long-headed white types. It is possible that the long-headed Palae-American population may have been partially Mongolized before arriving in the New World and it is hard to see how it could have escaped infusions of this strain unless we suppose the Mongoloid type to have been evolved at a very late period indeed — less than ten thousand years ago. I am by no means convinced of the correctness of the view which identifies as Mongoloid the Magdalenian man of Chancelade, and other skeletons found in France during the Upper Palaeolithic period and within the last glacial retreat. If this view is correct, it would mean that Mongoloid types spread into Europe twenty thousand years ago. I am prepared however to recognize certain Mongoloid affinities in the Azilian skeletons of Ofnet and it is not impossible that this type may have evolved west of the Central Asiatic Plateau and may not yet have extended to the eastern part of the continent at the time the first invaders passed northward to cross into America.

Of course the evidence that the earliest inhabitants of America were non-Mongoloid lies in the stratigraphic priority of dolichocephalic forms of types such as I have described at Pecos. But there are Mongoloids who are long-headed — some of the Southern Chinese, for example, and the Eskimo. I am nevertheless of the opinion that the Mongoloid type *par excellence* is essentially brachycephalic and that long-headed Mongoloids owe their dolichocephaly to admixture with non-Mongoloid stocks. The early dolichocephalic types in America which I have described do show often a robusticity of the malars and a lack of nasion depression which is reminiscent of the Mongoloid. Many of the dolichocephalic Indians are, indeed, plainly Mongoloid. But in the forms which seem earliest and purest in type, the great size of the Mongoloid face, the jutting of the malars, and the broad flat palatal form of the Mongoloid are absent, as are also the smooth frontal region and the flat suborbital area.

So it seems to me that the hypothesis which best accords with anthropological and archaeological data is that a second wave of migrants to the New World brought with them brachycephaly and the familiar Mongoloid complex of physical features. Support for this view is offered by the marginal distribution of dolichocephals which Dixon has worked out. This Mongoloid type must have pushed southward along the Cordillera and extended eastward across the plains of North America. I should think that its spread was in the nature of a gradual and peaceful penetration rather than a rapid military invasion.

The Mongoloid type seems to have had a greater capacity for civilization and cultural development than the preceding American inhabitants. To this type is to be assigned the credit for the development of all the high material cultures found in the New World. I think it probable that the introduction and development of agriculture was due to the Mongoloid element. It seems quite probable that these later comers brought with them from the Old World certain knowledge of higher material culture than heretofore existed in the Americas, but this is a subject which I am not competent to discuss.

Of the eight morphological skull types distinguished by me in the Pecos population, all except the long-headed "Basket Makers," Pseudo-Australoids, and Pseudo-Negroids show clear evidence of Mongoloid admixture, and most of them are in fact predominatingly Mongoloid in features. The type which I have called "Residual" is Mongoloid in every respect save one:—in its brachycephaly, smooth forehead lacking strong development of brow-ridges, lack of nasal depression, jutting malars, low nasal bridge and mesorrhine nasal form, brachyuranic palate, flat suborbital region, and so forth. It is a somewhat gracile Mongoloid type of skull. The face, as in most Mongoloids, is rather long, as well as broad. The skull is sphenoid, rather than spheroid. The temporal planes diverge posteriorly but are not protuberant or even full. The head length is very short, and, at Pecos, almost invariably artificially deformed. But, contrary to the prevalent form in Asiatic Mongoloids, the head height is great and the length-height index is frankly hypsicephalic. We have so few undeformed crania that it is difficult to draw conclusions concerning original head height, especially since this dimension, as well as breadth, is increased by deformation. In the Pecos series chamaecephals (skulls with low length-height index) do not occur; virtually all crania, whether dolichocephalic or brachycephalic, are hypsicephals. Nor do I believe that this is due to cranial deformation in most cases, since the undeformed crania available for examination are also, almost without exception, hypsicephalic. Chamaecephalic crania are, however, common among the Plains Indians (the real Plains Indians, not my "Plains" type). Chamaecephaly is very characteristic of the crania of true Mongols, although it does not prevail among all Mongoloid peoples. I am of the opinion that neither the length-height nor the breadth-height indices have the value as racial criteria that the length-breadth index of the skull and head seems to possess.[1] Cranial height is individually most variable and seems to be affected in a compensatory way by the hereditarily more significant variations of cranial length and cranial breadth. I am therefore not inclined to lay great emphasis upon either of the height indices which are likely to vary over all of the three subcategories into which they are divided, even in a pure type.

The brachycephalic Mongoloid types which mixed with the earlier American dolichocephals were probably several in number. At Pecos I have distinguished four such types according to morphological metrical criteria, but, as I have stated, none of them are chamaecephalic. The two which approach most closely to my conception of a fully Mongoloid type are the "Residual" type, referred to above, and the "Pseudo-Alpine" type. The latter I named from a fancied resemblance to the brachycephalic "Alpine" race of Europe. The cranial vault is higher and more globular than one expects to find in Mongoloids; the face is much shorter, and the nasal skeleton is higher and more inclined to leptorrhiny. Comparisons with Alpine types from Europe on the basis of metric features did not, however, justify the type appellation, and I am satisfied that, on the whole, the closest affinities of this type are, indeed, with Mongoloids. Cranial deformation in this type is universal and in most cases very pronounced. Hence I have been unable to utilize Shapiro's formulae for reconstructing original average vault dimensions.

One of the most outstanding Mongoloid features is a very low nasal root and bridge — often accompanied by an epicanthic fold obscuring the inner corner of the eye. These are features notable by their absence in the majority of American Indians. Both features do indeed occur, especially in women and children, but the nasal skeleton of the North American Indian is characteristically high-bridged and concavo-convex. The nose is broad at the aperture and narrow at the root. The tip is generally long and depressed rather than elevated as in the somewhat infantile Mongoloid nose. It is not as a rule as thick as that of the Armenoid nose, nor is the septum convex. I do not think that the prominent nose of the North American Indian can be identified with the Armenoid nose, but it is in many respects at the furthest remove from the typical Mongoloid nose. Whence did the American Indian acquire this noble aquilinity of nose? It certainly cannot be derived from any of the three early dolichocephalic types which I have recognized.

Among the Pecos I distinguished a cranial type which I unhappily called "Long-faced European." In this type the cranial vault is brachycephalic, as a rule; the face is prodigiously long and not very broad; the chin is strongly developed and the nose is elongated and leptorrhine, with a high bridge. This cranial type impressed me as non-Indian in appearance. The facial skeleton looked Armenoid or Nordic in its

[1] Cf. Cameron, 1929, pp. 139–153, 154–170.

elongation and in its nasal conformation. But I have been unable to find any Nordic cranial material or any other European cranial material which is metrically allied to this type. Such Armenian crania as I have been able to bring forward for comparison are quite far removed from this type. Crania of the so-called Dinaric race would be desirable for comparison, but I have been unable to find any published series which could be used. However this "Long-faced European" type at Pecos does show clear affinities with certain series of Northern Chinese skulls and even more marked affinities with a series of skulls of Zungarians from Kulja in Chinese Turkestan. There is certainly something non-Mongoloid in this Pecos type, although it is mixed with Mongoloid strains. I am inclined to think that it may be either Proto-Nordic or Armenoid, and more probably the former. I base this opinion upon the dimensions and proportions of the face and upon the nasal characters and chin prominence. Whatever this high nosed leptorrhine element may have been, its Mongoloid admixture must have been added before it arrived in the New World.

The type at Pecos which I have called the "Plains" type is again unfortunately named; it resembles more closely some of the Algonquian mesocephals further to the east — notably a series from Illinois. It is clearly a type resulting from the intermixture of the earlier dolichocephalic strains with the later-coming brachycephals. It is much more like the long-heads than like the round-heads and probably represents a larger proportion of the long-headed strains. It shows affinities to "Basket Makers," Pseudo-Negroids and Pseudo-Australoids alike, but is much more Mongoloid than any of these types. When undeformed, or when deformation is corrected, this type is, on the average, mesocephalic.

Finally the type I have called "Large Hybrid" is the North American Indian skull type *par excellence* and is especially to be identified with the massive round-heads of the Mound Area. It is a heavy and muscular type with huge jutting malars, very long and enormously broad face, robust jaws and a great beak-like nose, high, broad and long, and usually strongly concavo-convex. It is, of course, largely Mongoloid, but shows, to my mind, the influence of the admixture of the heavy-browed long-heads of the earlier American stratum, as well as the horse-face and high nose inherited from that problematical type which I have miscalled "Long-faced European." It is the end result of the blending of all Pecos types, with Mongoloid features generally dominant, but with a non-Mongoloid nose. I have no doubt that this type is to be found in Asia also, but it does not show the flatness of visage usually so characteristic of Mongoloids. It may be called a combination of all dominant characters in the various physical types which peopled the New World.

The Eskimo present a peculiar problem in American anthropology. In many respects Eskimo are the most Mongoloid of all Americans. In spite of the exaggerated narrowness of the nasal aperture they have extremely Mongoloid faces in flatness, in forward and lateral malar projection, and in palatal and mandibular form. The nose is very low and narrow at the root, and, I believe, the epicanthus is commoner among the Eskimo than in any other American group. The brow region shows the smoothness and lack of supraorbital ridges which is essentially Mongoloid. The extreme dolichocephaly and scaphoid form of the skull vault is most puzzling.

I have little confidence in the theory which attributes the dolichocephaly of the Eskimo to hypertrophy of the temporal muscles. In fact recent investigations of this and other problems pertaining to the relation of diet and masticatory functioning to skull form in the Eskimo, lead me to discard entirely the hypothesis of an elongation and lateral compression of the Eskimo skull through these agencies. The results of this study will be published elsewhere. Here it may be stated only that there is no mathematical correlation between the length-breadth index of the Eskimo skull and the area of the skull vault covered by the temporal muscles, and that the breadth of the skull is positively and highly correlated with temporal muscle area; not negatively correlated, as would be expected, if increased size and hyperfunctioning of the temporal muscles had the effect of restricting the lateral expansion of the skull.

I suspect that the dolichocephaly and leptorrhiny of the Eskimo are the result of some ancient admixture with a long-headed narrow-nosed type resembling the Nordic or Mediterranean races. In crosses of round-heads and long-heads, brachycephaly seems usually to survive at the expense of dolichocephaly, although there is certainly no simple Mendelian inheritance of the length-breadth index as such. If the Mongoloid strains in the Eskimo came from a typical Mongoloid brachycephalic type, as seems probable, the preservation and accentuation of the long-headedness of the non-Mongoloid strain must be accounted for. The Mongoloid features in the Eskimo are so strong that we cannot invoke a supposed preponderance in numerical proportions of the non-Mongoloid strain to explain the survival of dolichocephaly and leptorrhiny. We may have to concede to the northern environment and to the hypertrophy of the masticatory apparatus the rôle of preserving and fostering dolichocephaly and leptorrhiny, where the former would ordinarily tend to be recessive. Of course extreme dolichocephaly is characteristic of the Eastern Eskimo only and these Eskimo may have mixed to some extent not only with the long-headed Eastern Indians, but also with the Nordic dolichocephals who colonized Greenland.

I adhere to the consensus of American anthropological opinion that the Eskimo represent the last wave of Asiatic immigration to the New World and are not to be considered as racially diverse from the other American peoples, although presenting certain combinations of accentuated features that are peculiar to the type.

Briefly, then, my present opinion as to the peopling of the American continent is as follows: At a rather remote period, probably soon after the last glacial retreat, there straggled into the New World from Asia by way of the Bering Straits groups of dolichocephals in which were blended at least three strains: one very closely allied to the fundamental brunet European and African long-headed stock called "Mediterranean"; another a more primitive form with heavy brow-ridges, low broad face and wide nose, which is probably to be identified with an archaic type represented today very strongly (although mixed with other elements) in the native Australians, and less strongly in the so-called "Pre-Dravidians" such as the Veddahs, and also in the Ainu; thirdly an element almost certainly Negroid (not Negro). These people, already racially mixed, spread over the New World carrying with them a primitive fishing and hunting culture. Their coming must have preceded the occupation of eastern Asia by the present predominantly Mongoloid peoples, since the purer types of these dolichocephals do not show the characteristic Mongoloid features.

At a somewhat later period there began to arrive in the New World groups of Mongoloids coming by the same route as their predecessors. Many of these were probably purely Mongoloid in race, but others were mixed with some other racial element notable because of its high-bridged and often convex nose. This may have been either Armenoid or Proto-Nordic (or neither one). These later invaders were capable of higher cultural development than the early pioneers and were responsible for the development of agriculture and for the notable achievements of the New World civilization. In some places they may have driven out and supplanted the early long-heads, but often they seem to have interbred with them, producing the multiple and varied types of the present American Indians — types which are Mongoloid to a varying extent, but never purely Mongoloid. Last of all came the Eskimo, a culturally primitive Mongoloid group, already mixed with some non-Mongoloid strain before their arrival in North America.

Of course if the reader prefers he may accept one of the following alternative theories:

(1) that man originated in America and there differentiated into the various types which American Indians present;

(2) that a generalized type of primitive man came to the New World and there differentiated into the present varieties of the American race;

(3) that every existing physical type of man reached America before its discovery by Europeans, and that the Indians represent the end result of a process of panmixia and selection;

(4) that all of the aboriginal inhabitants of America were from first to last Mongoloids or mixed Mongoloids.

As to man originating in America, the only primate evidences in favor of such a hypothesis are the discovery of the ill-fated "Hesperopithecus" which turned out to be a peccary, and the recent alleged find of an anthropoid ape in South America, which does not even enjoy the status of the Hesperopithecus find — that of an honest blunder — but seems to be a palpable fraud.

That early man came to America and here evolved into a number of diverse types is more probable, but lacks the support of any convincing evidence of geologically ancient human occupation of the New World. It would seem that a much longer time than has elapsed since the last glacial retreat would be necessary to bring about such a physical diversification through natural evolutionary processes.

The theory calling for successive migrations of Negroids, Australoids, Mediterraneans, Nordics, Mongols, and so forth, through all the gamut of human races, involves, in my opinion, a disregard of the geographical difficulties involved in getting from the Eastern to the Western Hemisphere and in making this trip without undergoing en route considerable contamination through intermixture with intervening races.

The theory of the originally and perpetually Mongoloid character of the American population is difficult to accept in view of the decidedly non-Mongoloid character of the stratigraphically early types. Further the Mongoloid type seems to be dominant in so many of its features that if it were here from the beginning, we should expect a greater homogeneity of the American race than is exhibited. At Pecos Mongolization seems to have been a cumulative process not yet completed at the end of the pueblo's life.

APPENDICES

APPENDIX I

DENTAL AND ORTHODONTIC OBSERVATIONS ON 289 ADULT AND 53 IMMATURE SKULLS FROM PECOS, NEW MEXICO [1]

By Habib Y. Rihan, B.A., D.M.D.

Professor of Prosthetic Dentistry and Orthodontia, American University of Beirut, Syria

Adult Skulls

The general bony development of the Pecos adult skulls is good. No cases of receding or underdeveloped chins were observed. The goniomandibular angle, about 115°, does not show much variation. Examples of an enlarged angle are skulls 59,855, 59,890, 60,007, 60,163. The enlargement in the case of 59,855 is due to the loss of teeth and their occlusal support, the muscular pull being exerted on the angle region. The eminentia and the glenoid fossae of this skull are transformed in shape as a result of the same abnormal conditions and will be discussed later. The other skulls show a mesial or anterior relation of the mandibular arch and a consequently enlarged angle.

Lingual surface protrusions (mandibular torus) are found in 47.4% of mandibles and are absent in 38.7%. In the remaining 13.9% the lingual process is evenly thickened. The median point of the palatal processes of the maxilla presents a slight ridge (palatine torus) in 20% of the cases and no ridge in the remaining 80%. It has been explained by many that such protrusions and ridges are the natural response to masticatory stimulation, in an effort to reënforce the bony structure in those parts which are sustaining the strain transmitted by the teeth. My observations have led me to believe that this is probably incorrect. For the mandibular protrusions are found mostly lingual to the premolars, which have a limited occlusal surface and consequently bear less strain than the molars, and which therefore need no special bony reënforcement. The explanation has been offered by some that the lower jaw is a lever of the third class and that the weight is anterior to the power and that consequently the strain is carried forward toward the symphysis. But it has been shown lately that the lower jaw is a suspended millstone and that the resultant masticatory forces are perpendicular to the occlusal plane and along the bony axes of the teeth; that the fulcrum of the mandible is not at the condyles, but that the condyles slide along the glenoid articular surface as a guide plane.

Similarly, the palatine ridge is found usually near the anterior palatine foramen, or it is most prominent there. This fact would indicate that it is not a reënforcement, since it is anterior to the area where reënforcement is needed.

Then again these mandibular and palatine growths or ridges are absent in a great many cases that show marked attrition, a condition which would mean necessarily excessive strain and which would call for bony reënforcement. By reference to the table below, one will find marked attrition present in 97% of the cases.

In attempting to explain the etiology of these cases, I would say that the median palatal ridge may be considered as a benign growth, the result of continued activity on the part of embryonic osteoblasts that brought about the union of the bony plates of the palatal processes and the vomer bone.

---

[1] This work was carried on under the auspices of the Orthodontic Department of Harvard University Dental School and with the courtesy and advice of Professor Hooton of the Peabody Museum of Harvard University.

The mandibular protrusions also may be considered benign growths due to traumatic masticatory or periodontal irritations. Their unevenness is a further proof of their non-physiological nature.

However, the evenly thickened lingual process in 13.9% of cases could be considered a structural response to functional stimulation.

Nasal development was observed to be in harmony with the general development of the face except that 43.5% of the cases showed deviation of the septum. But in no case were there bony obstructions sufficient to lead to mouth-breathing and no indications of such a condition are to be found.

The relation of the dental arches is quite interesting. The table shows that, of the 207 skulls where definite observations could be made, 140 or 61.7% are normal and 29% are cases of neutro-occlusion. No. 59,908 presents unilateral disto-occlusion. The left side, which is distal, shows more attrition than the right and the left condyle path has a smaller angle, with a certain amount of bone deposited on the glenoid fossa. No. 60,007 is a distinct case of mesio-occlusion with an enlarged goniomandibular angle, an underdeveloped maxilla, a reduced condyle path angle, and condyles that are flattened externo-internally. No. 59,813 shows unilateral mesio-occlusion of the right side. The right goniomandibular angle is greater than the left and the right condyle path angle is smaller than the left. In this case also deposition of bone to raise the floor of the glenoid fossa is noticeable. The remaining cases of slight mesial relation of the lower arch to the upper are probably due to mutilation and malpositions of teeth.

The form of the arch is a wide parabola in 66.5%, a hyperbola in 30.7%, and elliptical in 2.8%. The average width of the arch is:

Canine to canine	26 mm.
First molar to first molar	36 mm.
Second molar to second molar	40 mm.

The range of variation in width is considerable even though the alignment is normal. The minimum width is 23–33–37 and the maximum is around 29–39–41. It was observed that a great many have the ratio of a 10 mm. difference between canine and first molar widths and a 4 mm. difference between the first and second molar widths. But variations ranging from 7 mm. to 13 mm. and from 3 mm. to 5 mm. respectively were observed. I have also found that the arc of the anterior teeth, in the case of most of the square and ovoid large teeth, is usually an arc with one radius (the sum width of the three anterior teeth on one side) whereas in the case of tapering and comparatively small teeth it is made up of two overlapping arcs having the same radius but different centers. These variations, present in all human mouths, demonstrate the inexactness of the definite predetermination of the dental arch in orthodontic operations. But at the same time such close ratios of arch widths and similar measurements help in bringing about approximate results.

The teeth are mostly of the shovel type but in their forms they vary between the square (63.6%), ovoid (14.4%), and tapering (22%).

The vault form does not show much variation. Normal development of the palate is easily noticeable. The edentulous cases, however, are quite flat, due to the almost total resorption of the alveolar processes. This is due to the fact that pyorrhea must have been the usual cause of the loss of teeth.

In about 33% the articular eminence is reduced in size by resorption. Simultaneously the angle of the condyle path is reduced. This is due to the lack of molar support as a result of attrition or loss of teeth. Ordinarily the tooth occlusal surfaces receive all the work-force exerted by the muscles; but when the molar occlusal plane is reduced appreciably by attrition, or by loss of the molar teeth altogether, a certain amount of the force is transmitted through the condyle to the cartilages and the glenoid articular surface, especially during lateral mastication. This causes resorption of the eminence and a harmonious resorption of the condyloid head of the mandible and a reduction of the articular angle. In some instances the character of the bony tissue shows that arthritic conditions must have existed as a result of frictional pressure from the condyle. But in some cases resorption did not take place, probably because of long overbite, muscular habits, flattening of the manibular angle, or exceptionally thick articular cartilages. The thickness of these cartilages was estimated on these skulls by the distance between the articular surfaces of the condyle and the glenoid fossa when the teeth were placed in occlusion. It varies from 2 to 4 mm. The angle of the condyle path was observed to have undergone other alterations by the building up of the deep surface of the glenoid fossa articular surface. This and the above show the liability to alteration and mutilation of the parts of this joint.

Deformed skulls having one side of the back pressed forward showed a forward position of the glenoid fossa on that side in advance of the other glenoid fossa by about half the difference between the antero-posterior lengths of the two sides of the skull.

The tympanic plate was observed at the suggestion of some orthodontist friends who were under the impression that disto-occlusion, attrition, or a general infra-occlusion may cause enough friction by the condyle on the tympanic plate to cause perforation of the latter. My observations showed me that the perforations were rudimentary openings, the result of the failure of the tympanic plate to complete its ossification. The immature skulls helped me to estimate that ossification is usually completed between the ages of 8 and 10. However, I am unable to say what sort of conditions existed in cases of extreme disto-occlusion as none were found among these skulls. Fully 20% have one or both tympanic plates still open. It is easy to see how in these cases inflammation of the temporo-mandibular joint might extend to the ear.

As the condyloid heads are mostly mutilated I have taken measurements between the centres of the glenoid fossae to take the place of the intercondylar distance. The interglenoidal breadth or distance averaged 94 mm. in 162 cases, varying from 84 to 106 mm.

Marked attrition of the occlusal surfaces of the teeth is found in 97.2%. This general condition indicates the character of the food used by these peoples as well as their powerful muscular development. Although part of the wear may be due to the fine stony grit that came off their corn grinders, the greater part is the result of the rough and raw vegetable and fruit foods they used. A certain amount of it may be due also to interdental friction, especially after wear had started. Corn was one of their main food materials and there is no question as to its wearing effect.

The limited variety of the food of this people may be given as the reason for the comparative prevalence of caries, the large loss of teeth, and the frequent occurrence of pyorrhea. Malnutrition, rapid senility, and lack of mouth hygiene are quite evident. The Pecos Indians must have owed their good development to heredity, exercise, the open air, and simple living. But work, exertion, food insufficiency, and lack of hygiene must usually have brought on the decline.

Caries is present in 47.9% and loss of teeth (one or more) is found in 47.6%. Periodontal disease is present in 72%. Marked pyorrhea is present in only 13.3% and is shown by the resorption of the gingival process horizontally and in pockets, but mostly by the former. The alveolar abscesses are largely due to attrition, and consequent exposure and infection of the pulp, or death of the pulp without exposure. Caries is mostly occlusal and is the result of wear cups or, in some cases, the imperfection of enamel formation. Proximal caries is also present and may be estimated at 30% of the teeth infected with this disease.

IMMATURE SKULLS

The skulls of the Pueblo children and adolescents represent ages from 7 months to 16 years. Development is generally good. Two cases 60,726 and 60,509, both about 7 years old, showed a slight palatine ridge or "torus." This furnishes another argument against the belief mentioned above that this ridge is a structural reënforcement to meet functional demands and at the same time supports the view that it is the result of continued activity on the part of the embryonic osteoblasts. No. 60,726 shows marked development of this feature, and one may even see beginnings of lingual mandibular protrusions on the left side. This case has a supernumerary tooth, mesio-lingual to the superior left central incisor.

One case, No. 60,187–7, however, is rachitic. The malalignment of the teeth and the lack of development of the alveolar processes are clear symptoms of the condition.

The goniomandibular angle seems to be small until the deciduous teeth erupt and then it is even greater than later, when the permanent set is fully erupted. The adult angle was estimated to be about 115°.

The nasal development is good and only one case, No. 60,621, was found with deviation of the septum.

As to the relation of the arches, 25 cases, 75.8%, are normal and 8 cases, 24.2%, present neutro-occlusion. No cases of disto-occlusion or mesio-occlusion were found.

The angle of the condyle path increased with age and was observed to be a few degrees at the age of 2 years.

The tympanic plate in No. 60,184 is quite open and incomplete. The estimated age of this case is 3 years. No. 60,712, 7 to 8 years, No. 60,621, 8 to 9 years, No. 60,217, 9 to 10 years, have completely ossified plates. These and other cases would set the complete ossification at about 8 years of age.

Attrition of the temporary teeth in cases above the age of five is the rule. Caries in deciduous teeth are found in about 12%. No premature loss of deciduous teeth was observed. No symptoms of disease of the alveolar process are present.

The crypts of the permanent anterior teeth, lingual to the deciduous teeth, begin to have bony septa separating them from each other and from the deciduous teeth at the age of about 10 months. The gubernacular foramina are widely open at birth and narrow down to small foramina about the age of 2 years and then get larger as the time of eruption of these permanent teeth comes. I have been unable to find in literature any definite statement as to the location of the foramina of the bicuspids. These cases helped me to locate them. The foramina of the superior bicuspids are usually near the mesio-palatal angle of the palatal root. Their crypts are mesial to the palatal roots of the temporary molars. The inferior bicuspids have their foramina lingual to the lingual median depression that leads to the bifurcation of the roots of the temporary molars. The crypts are slightly lingual and median. Occasionally in the case of bicuspids the foramina are on the alveolar socket surface but very near the gingival edge.

The dental bands connecting the gubernacula of the deciduous and those of the permanent teeth lie alongside each other up to the first months after birth. With the eruption of the deciduous set their band is resorbed or transformed in character and in function. The band of the permanent set connects the gubernacular necks that emerge from the foramina lingual to the deciduous teeth and dips down into the crypts of the permanent molars. This conclusion was made after observing that grooves existed between the permanent molar crypts, which suggested the presence of a band connecting the bud-sacs.

Separation or spacing of the deciduous anterior teeth is not present in every case at the proper age. In some cases, instead, the process shows labial bulging at the position of the crowns of the erupting permanent teeth, partly due to the enlargement of the process around the crowns and partly to the bending labially of the deciduous roots.

Observations as to the positions of unerupted calcified caps of permanent anterior teeth were made. It was seen that, as the buds in their crypts assumed positions in which the lateral incisors were lingual to the central incisors and canines, and the canines labial and tipped labially to them, the law of inertia governed their final eruption in that arrangement unless the inherent directing power, stimulated by exercise and good circulation, and endowed with hereditary physical well-being, helped them to arrange themselves as intended by nature. Again many cases showed the calcified caps in rotated and impacted positions in their crypts. These caps could rarely if ever correct their own positions but would naturally erupt irregularly. These two causes of malocclusion might fall under cell metabolism, but the separation and definition of such important conditions is quite necessary and to my knowledge has not been made before.

Notes of the observation of the stage of development at different ages are as follows:

TABLE 1. NOTES ON DENTAL DEVELOPMENT IN IMMATURE CRANIA

Age 7 to 8 months.

> The permanent central and lateral incisor caps are partly formed and calcified.
> Cusps of the first permanent molar are calcified.

Age 17 months.

> The second deciduous molars have not erupted yet.
> The alignment of the deciduous teeth is abnormal.
> The development of the alveolar process is abnormal.
> This is the case (60,187–7) of rachitis.

Age 2 years.

> The permanent first molar crowns are calcified.
> The second molar crypts are well defined.
> Arch width is intercanine 25 mm. and inter-second-molar 30 mm.
> The angle of the condyle path is about 5°.
> The tympanic plate is open.
> Anomaly: (60,204) inferior right central and lateral incisors are fused together.

Age 4–5 years.

> Cusps of the permanent second molars are calcified.
> The angle of the condyle path is about 10°.
> The tympanic plate is open.

Age 6–7 years.

> The deciduous anterior teeth do not show much spacing.
> The roots are bent labially.
> The unerupted permanent anteriors have the lateral in a lingual position.
> The interglenoidal distance is nearly 8.5 cm.
> The angle of the condyle path is a little over 10°.
> Attrition of the temporary molar cusps is apparent.
> Temporary canine and second molar widths are 24–30 mm.
> The tympanic plate is still open.

Age 7–8 years.

> The third molar crypts are present and vary from 2 to 5 mm. in diameter.
> Arch widths vary from 22–29–31 (intercanine, inter-temporary second molar, inter-permanent first molar) to 29–35–37.
> The temporary lateral incisors, canines, and molars are still present.
> The interglenoidal distance is quite variable but it approximates 9 cm.
> The angle of the condyle path is about 15°.
> The tympanic plate is closed in some cases.
> Anomalies: (60,726, 60,263) temporary centrals having two root canal branches and canines having three canal branches for about the length of the apical third of the root.

Age 9 years.

> The superior third molar crypts are larger than those in the mandible.
> The temporary canines and molars are still present.
> The arch widths average 25–30–32.
> The angle of the condyle path is about 20°.
> The interglenoidal distance is about 8.7 cm.

Age 9–10 years.

The temporary canines and molars are not yet shed.

The arch widths are 27–34–36.

The maxillary third molar crypts are 6–8 mm., and the mandibular are 4 to 5 mm.

The tympanic plate has completed its ossification.

Age 11–12 years.

Third molar crowns started calcification.

Permanent canines and second molars are erupting (bone resorbed over surface).

The temporary molars are present.

The arch widths are 28–32–35.

The angle of the condyle path is about 22°.

Age 12–13 years.

The temporary second molars are still present.

Age 15 years.

Third molars are half calcified.

Age 16 years.

The third molars have not erupted.

The arch widths are 26–37–40 (canine, first molar, second molar).

The angle of the condyle path is near 28°.

The interglenoidal distance is above 9 cm.

TABLE 2. TABLE OF STATISTICS

ADULTS (289)

Bony development

	Number	Per cent
Maxilla		
Overdeveloped	17	6.7
Underdeveloped	5	2.0
Edentulous	18	7.0
Normal	215	84.3
Median Raphé (Palatine torus)		
Present	53	20.0
Absent	211	80.0
Mandible		
Overdeveloped	22	9.4
Underdeveloped	2	.8
Deformed	1	.4
Normal	209	89.4
Goniomandibular angle		
Normal	200	92.7
Greater than normal	13	6.0
Asymmetrical	3	1.3
Chin		
Normal (no receding chins)	216	100.0
Lingual surface protrusions (Mandibular torus)		
Present	119	47.4
Absent	97	38.7
Evenly thickened lingual process	35	13.9
Nasal bridge		
Narrow	78	31.8
Medium	128	52.2
Broad	39	16.0
Nasal septum		
Deviated	80	43.5
Normal	104	56.5

	Number	Per cent
Relation of arches		
Normal	140	67.6
Neutro-occlusion	60	29.0
Unilateral disto-occlusion	1	.5
Mesio-occlusion	1	.5
Mesio-occlusion (slight)	4	1.9
Unilateral mesio-occlusion	1	.5
Tooth positions		
Normal	140	61.7
Abnormal	52	22.9
Abnormal posteriors	23	10.2
Disturbed by loss of teeth	12	5.2
Relation of jaws		
Normal	232	99.2
Mesial	2	.8
Arch form		
Parabolic	187	66.5
Hyperbolic	87	30.7
Elliptical	8	2.8
Arch average widths		
Intercanine		26 mm.
Inter-first molar		36 mm.
Inter-second molar		40 mm.
Vault		
Normal	..	100.0
Tooth form		
Square	75	63.6
Ovoid	17	14.4
Tapering	26	22.0
Articular eminence		
Normal	162	66.7
Prominent	3	1.2
Reduced	47	19.3
Asymmetrical	31	12.8
Angle of condyle path		
Above 30°	163	67.0
Below 30°	49	20.0
Asymmetrical	31	13.0
Tympanic plate		
Normal	210	80.0
Perforated (incomplete)	54	20.0
Interglenoidal breadth		
Aveolar of 162		94 mm.
Attrition		
Marked attrition	248	97.2
Unilateral attrition	2	.8
No attrition	5	2.0
Caries		
Absent	137	52.1
Present	126	47.9
Loss of teeth		
No loss	149	52.5
With loss	135	47.5
Periodontal diseases		
Present	200	72.0
Pyorrhea	165	59.0
Alveolar abscess	73	26.0
Absent	78	28.0

APPENDIX II

A STUDY OF THE PECOS PELVES WITH SPECIAL REFERENCE TO THE BRIM

By Edward Reynolds

THE pelvic girdle, like the hand and foot, is a structure of functional importance composed of a number of distinct and individual bones, which are in life attached to each other by non-osseous connective tissues of one sort and another.

In the human race the girdle as a whole furnishes the base and origin for each and every impulse in terrestrial locomotion. It gives origin to all the most important muscles which maintain the erect posture, and to all those which constitute the pelvic floor of the abdomen. The efficiency of each of these muscles is mechanically dependent upon the degree of leverage afforded to it by its pelvic attachment. The action of some one or other of these muscles must then be increased or decreased by each variation in the shape of the pelvic bones.

The functions of the pelvic girdle just enumerated are best studied in combination with the characteristics of the hind limb and spine and by comparison with the pelves and posterior limbs of the quadrupeds. Such a study forms the subject of another paper now in preparation. Nothing then will be said here of the Pecos pelves from this point of view, other than that they do not appear to differ radically from those of the other races on which information is at hand.

The shape of the pelvic girdle is, however, important in its relation to another all-important matter. In the female, the canal, or true pelvis, must be fitted for the transmission of the foetus or the species perishes.

Human labor differs from the parturition of any other animal in that in all other cases[1] the soft and compressible body is so much larger than the head that the pelvis need only be adapted to the body of the foetus, since the small cranium offers no obstacle of importance. In the human foetus the case is reversed, the diameters of the relatively incompressible head are always much larger than those of the compressible body, and the head therefore offers the only obstacle which normally needs be considered.

The shape of the foetal head in its relation to normal labor may be comprehended by the use of two cross-sections. When it is fully flexed with the chin upon the chest it presents a nearly circular outline with the suboccipito-bregmatic (9.50 cm.)[2] and biparietal (9.25 cm.) diameters at right angles to each other and of nearly equal length. When the head is extended, i. e., with the occipito-frontal approximately at right angles to the axis of the body, the contour is approximately ovate (Fig. 1), and the diameters which present are the occipito-frontal (12 cm.), the biparietal (9.25), and the bitemporal (8 cm.).[3] This somewhat extended position is that in which the head usually presents at the brim. Since the condyles, through which a great part of the pressure of the uterus is transmitted to the head, are nearer to the occipital than to the frontal end, the head tends to become flexed during its progress through the pelvis.

---

[1] Certain highly specialized bulldogs are said to be an exception.

[2] The diameter is drawn from the great fontanelle to the junction of the head and neck below the occipital protuberance.

[3] These are the accepted statements of the obstetrical textbooks.

That the adaptation of the human pelvis to these exclusively human conditions of labor is less complete than it might be is evident from the fact that the human female is exposed to more danger, and also probably suffers more in labor, than any other mother. This somewhat incomplete sexual adaptation is evident'y due to the existence of a certain amount of antagonism between the modifications of the pelvis which are favorable to stability and activity in erect bipedal progression and those which ease and expedite labor.

The special survey of the pelvis which has been made upon the Pecos series has involved the use of twenty-four measurements upon each of 118 pelves,[1] the greater part of which were measured by Mr. F. S. Hulse. It will be seen that but a small part of these measurements have been utilized in this present report.

All study of the dimensions and shape of the pelvis as a whole is complicated in the case of dried specimens by the absence of the cartilages of the synchondroses and symphysis, which of course increase all the transverse and oblique diameters considerably. In some such studies the observer has filled in these spaces with an estimated amount of packing before measuring each pelvis. In others all the pelves have been fitted together without packing. The latter method has been used here and the technique used will now be described.

After assembling the pelvis, a piece of elastic tape was passed around it several times at considerable tension. It passes just above the posterior superior spines of the ilia, across the acetabula and the descending rami of the pubes, and the end is tucked under at any convenient point. The height at which it should lie anteriorly and posteriorly varies somewhat in the several pelves. The knack of applying this tape quickly and effectively comes with practice, and we have found that in the great majority of cases pelves so fixed can be handled freely and conveniently.

A cross was then placed at each of the following points:

> The laterally most prominent point of the iliac tuberosity (bi-iliac).
> The laterally most prominent point of the posterior superior spine of the ilium (bi-spinal).
> The middle point of the line which separates the attachments of the hamstring muscles on the tuberosities of the ischia (bi-ischiatic).
> The subpubic angle, internal surface.
> The ends of the greatest transverse diameter of the brim. (This was ascertained by the use of a pair of internal calipers and the level selected was at the point where this diameter is least, usually a little below the ilio-pectineal line, the obstetrical, or practically useful, transverse.)
> The point on the inner surface of the pubes nearest to the centre of the upper edge of the promontory (i. e., the anterior end of the obstetrical conjugate or antero-posterior diameter of the brim).
> The centre of the upper edge of the promontory.
> The so-named halfway point, ascertained and marked by placing a straight-edge between the two last-named points and marking the brim at the obstetrical level at a point rectangularly opposite the halfway distance as shown on the straight-edge.
> The point at which the ilio-pectineal line meets the synchondrosis, or, if the line divides, a point midway between its two parts (ilio-pectineo-sacral point).
> The point at which the sacral wing at the brim is farthest posterior to the promontory (mid-sacral wing).

The following measurements were then taken with the pelvis in hand:

> Bi-iliac
> Bispinal
> Anterior superior spine to iliac tuberosity

---

[1] Our Pecos collection contains skeletal remains of 943 individuals, but only 118 pelves which are reasonably complete and unbroken. The whole collection of innominates and sacra have been examined as separate bones by Dr. Hooton and reported upon in Chapter V.

> Bi-ischiatic
> Perpendicular to posterior superior spine [1]
> Bi-ischial spinal
> Transverse
> Conjugate
> Halfway transverse
> Synchondrosis to halfway diagonal [2]
> Ilio-pectineal line to ischial spine (of same side)
> Ilio-pectineal line to tuberosity of ischium inside.

The pelvis was then placed on a measuring board,[3] resting on the ischial tuberosities with the halfway point and ilio-pectineo-sacral point at the same vertical height, for the following measurements:

> Bi-ischial spinal perpendicular to sacral tip (distance from its central point to sacral tip)
> Bi-ischiatic inside [4]
> Bi-ischiatic (inside) perpendicular to sacral tip
> Height of brim
> Angle between axes [5]
> Angle between spines and brims [6]
> Height of subpubic angle
> Symphysis to centre of transverse
> Symphysis to centre of halfway transverse
> Height of iliac blade above brim anterior to projection of promontory (beyond posterior point of sacral wing).

It seems probable that as the study progresses all these measurements will be found useful in the study of the two functions of the pelvis, but, to date, the pressure of other work has prevented the completion of any study other than that of the form of the brim.

This has been taken up by comparison of the Pecos brims, male and female, with those of a series of Whites and one of Negroes [7] on which the same measurements have been made. Both of these latter series are too small to warrant final conclusions, but since many of the characters shown vary with much regularity, they are suggestive and are presented for what they are worth. It is hoped that in the near future it may be possible to examine a larger series of Whites, and if possible of Negroes.

In studying and reporting these observations two methods have been employed, and these to some extent check each other. The statistical investigation by comparison of indices and a graphic representation of the relation of the marked points of the brim by use of the means have both been made for the whole series of White, Negro, and Pecos pelves for the separated sexes (Tables I–8; Figs. 2–3).

[1] Lay ruler from top of sacro-sciatic notch to posterior superior spine, measure greatest perpendicular distance from this to posterior superior spine. (Experimentally adopted for study of the sacro-sciatic notch.)

[2] From one ilio-pectineo-sacral point to the halfway point of the opposite side.

[3] It is convenient to use a measuring board on which millimeter paper has been fastened to both the vertical and horizontal plates. With a millimeter measure attached vertically to a stand, it is then easy to take all these measurements with rapidity.

[4] Bi-ischiatic inside is the transverse distance between the inner edges of the ischial tuberosities, taken from the point at which these edges begin to turn outwards at their dorsal ends, i. e., the bi-ischial (inside) diameter from an obstetrical point of view.

[5] The axes here referred to may be defined as (a) the line of intersection of the median plane and of that which passes through the points taken for the bi-iliac and bi-ischiatic measurements, and (b) that of the intersection of the median plane and that which passes through the posterior superior spines of the ilia and the pubes. With the position of all the points known on the measuring board these angles can be obtained by a clinometer.

[6] This is the angle made by the plane which passes through the anterior superior and the anterior inferior spines of the ilia, with that of the brim.

[7] Considered by Dr. Hrdlička as probably of unmixed descent.

In the White and Negro series the numbers in the separated sexes are entirely too small to warrant deductions from any but extremely evident factors and can be at most only suggestive there. Sexual variations are, however, of such great importance in the pelvis that it seemed desirable to observe and report them even upon this basis.

It will be observed that even in the means the sexual variations exceed the racial but that on most points the races vary from each other in the same way in both sexes. This is especially true as between the Whites and Pecos.

When individual variations are added, the particular points to be described here are not sufficient for a definite determination of the race to which an individual pelvis belongs. There seems reason to hope, however, that when this study of the pelvis embraces a larger number of characters a satisfactory racial complex may perhaps be made out.

The following indices have seemed to be of value:

$$\text{I} \quad \frac{\text{Symphysis to centre of transverse}}{\text{Conjugate}}$$

II   Projection of promontory [1]

$$\text{III} \quad \frac{\text{Symphysis to centre of halfway transverse}}{\text{Conjugate}}$$

$$\text{IV} \quad \frac{\text{Halfway transverse}}{\text{Transverse}}$$

$$\text{V} \quad \frac{\text{Ilio-pectineal line to ischial spine}}{\text{Transverse}}$$

The importance of these indices (Tables 8–12) can hardly be made apparent without some reference to the mechanism of labor in its relation to the brim, which will, therefore, be briefly recapitulated here. The writer has, however, found no reference to any definite study of the mechanism of labor in other than Whites. All that follows must then be understood as referring to Whites unless otherwise stated.

When the foetal head is fully flexed, with the chin upon the breast, its transverse section is approximately circular. It is not, however, normally presented to the brim in this position. It habitually enters the brim in a partially extended position, in which the cross-section of the head made by the plane of the brim is ovate (Fig. 1).

The transverse is normally the greatest diameter of the brim, but owing to the projection of the promontory into the available space, the long diameter of the oval which the foetal head presents to the brim cannot occupy the transverse. It is therefore forced to enter with its long diameter in the diagonal diameter of the brim, which is approximately the synchondrosis to halfway point of these measurements. It will be seen that there are four positions in which the head may enter diagonally.[2] The most favorable of these positions are, however, the occipito-anteriors, in which the relatively narrow bifrontal region passes between the promontory and the region of the pectineal eminence, while the broader biparietal occupies approximately the opposite diagonal diameter of the brim. A glance at Figures 1 and 3 will make this clear.

The anterior positions are fortunately the most frequent. In a not small minority of labors, however, the head enters in one of the occipito-posterior positions. The large biparietal diameter is thus in apposition to the comparatively narrow pectineo-promontorial

---

[1] A mean inserted with the indices for convenience.

[2] I. e., with the larger end of the head either anterior or posterior and this in either of the diagonal diameters. (OLA, ORA, ORP, OLP), cf. page 374 ff.

diameter. If of normal size, the head can then pass only by extreme moulding under pressure, which is preceded usually by its slipping forward along the diagonal diameter in which it lies until this motion is arrested by impact of the frontal region against the region of the half-way point. The frontal region then becomes arrested and advance ceases until flexion and moulding together reach a point at which the biparietal can pass.

In short, and in other words: in these posterior positions the occipital end of the head is usually unable to utilize the space about the posterior end of the diagonal diameter since it is held away from it by the inability of the biparietal diameter to pass the brim unless the bosses are somewhat anterior to the pectineo-promontorial diameter, and then usually only after undergoing extreme moulding. It is easy to see why occipito-posterior positions usually involve a slow and difficult entrance to the brim.

I $\dfrac{\text{Symphysis to centre of transverse}}{\text{Conjugate}}$

II   Projection of promontory.

The importance of these two means is then that the usefulness of the greatest diameter of the brim, the transverse, decreases with the degree of its proximity to the promonitory, and that that is determined both by the position of the transverse itself in the brim as a whole and by the degree to which the promontory projects into the brim.

It will perhaps be conducive to clearness if the sexual modifications of the Pecos and Negro pelves are discussed separately and as variants from the White.

Reference either to the statistical tables or to the graphic representation of the means of Whites and Pecos will show that the racial variation in these points is chiefly limited, as would perhaps be expected, to the female pelves. In the male the differences between the Whites and Pecos are very slight; in point of fact, so very small as to be negligible when derived from so small a series (Figure 2).

The sexual modifications of the female pelves in these two races are in general similar, but one definite difference is readily observed. Its meaning is perhaps most easily under-stood in the graphic representation of the means (Figure 3), but it will be seen that the sta-tistical studies give similar and confirmatory results (Tables 1–12).

In the graph it will be readily perceived that if the superposition of the outlines had been made with the pubes as a centre, the shapes would have been similar within the limits to be expected from the short White series, except in the great projection of the promontory in the Pecos, and since position of the transverse in the pelvis as a whole is essentially the same in both races, it will be evident that the promontory approaches much more nearly to the transverse in the Pecos than in White.[1] This is functionally a very important change, since relationship of the promontory to the transverse plays so dominant a part in governing the entrance of the head. As a result of this difference, entrance of the extended head with its long diameter (the occipito-frontal) in the transverse is even less possible in the Pecos female than in the White. If the outline of the extended head were superimposed upon the outline of the pelvis with the occipito-frontal diameter in the transverse, it would be seen at once that in both races the posterior end of the biparietal would overlap or be in too close contact with the sacro-iliac curves, while its anterior end would have abundant space; also that the anterior end of the bifrontal would be in contact with the pectineal portion of the brim while its posterior end would have comparatively ample room afforded by the sacrum. This is in

---

[1] This would not be so evident in an index because the shortened conjugate and the increased projection of the promontory in fact diminish the divisor and dividend of the equation in such similar proportions that the quotient remains essentially the same.

addition to the fact already referred to that the whole posterior side of the head would in this position be arrested by the promontory. It is at once evident that in the Pecos pelvis, entrance of the extended head with its long diameter in the oblique is even more essential than in the White, and will occur with equal certainty and probably with more readiness in the Pecos under the influence of the intrapelvic pressure as the head is urged down upon the brim by uterine contraction. Further, since the greater projection of the promontory in the Pecos prolongs and somewhat narrows the already scanty space at the posterior end of the oblique, the entrance of the head in a posterior position, i. e., with the longer biparietal diameter opposite this narrow space instead of the shorter bitemporal, is even more unfavorable to Pecos labor than to White. It will be remembered, too, from what was said in the summary of labor, that in the posterior positions the inability of the biparietal to pass without excessive moulding commonly forces the head towards the centre of the oblique diameter and consequently shortens that as a whole. The actual lengths of the obliques are alike in the two races, but for the reason just given, the effective length of the oblique in posterior positions of the head will be less in the Pecos than in the White.

In the Negro series a different and very curious sexual variation obtains in the fact that in the Negress the necessary adaptation of the female pelvis to labor not only shows a curiously greater transformation of the shape of the inlet from that of the male than is the case in the other two races, but that this variation also results in a shape which is radically different from that of the other two races in the opportunity which it offers to the entrance of the head.

In the Negro male the pelvis is smaller, and in addition proportionately much narrower, than in the White or Pecos, and also differs from them in that the situation of the transverse is much more posterior in the pelvis as a whole. In the Negress, on the other hand, the transverse is much further forward than in any of the other pelves. The brim as a whole is still somewhat smaller than in the White, but in spite of that, this very important change of shape makes it capable of affording, in all probability, an easier entrance to the head.

It will be remembered that in all pelves the transverse is longer than the oblique. This is true of the Negress as of the other races, but it will be seen in the graph that although the transverse of the Negress is shorter than that of the other races, it is almost precisely the length of their obliques. Now in the Negress, as in the Negro, the oblique remains both relatively and actually shorter than in the other races, but if the outline of the head is superimposed upon that of the Negro pelvis, it will be seen that it is quite easily adaptable to the inlet when its longer diameter is coincident with the transverse diameter. This is in great contrast with the conditions in the other two races. It will be seen too that both the biparietal and the bitemporal have fairly ample space through which to enter; and this is the more especially true since the sweeping curves of the ileo-pectineal line of either side of the situation of the transverse makes the whole length of that diameter mechanically useful to the head.

The actual result of the change of shape is then that since the forward position of the transverse of the Negress makes this a useful diameter, the head should be able to pass the brim of her pelvis in a transverse position as easily or more easily than it can pass the White brim in the oblique, which is there the only available diameter.

Since the variation in the antero-posterior position of the transverse in the Negro series is rather great, it is, however, probable that in some Negresses the entrance of the head would be in a position between the transverse and the oblique, i. e., that the degree of obliquity will show considerable individual variation.

Throughout the consideration of this whole matter, it must of course be remembered that all the lines which bound the brim are in fact curves and not straight lines and angles, as represented in the graphs. For readers who are not obstetricians it may be well to add that all these diameters are modified by the presence of the encroaching soft parts and that the average head can pass the average pelvis either at the brim or in the subsequent passage of the canal only after undergoing a not inconsiderable degree of moulding. Further, since the actual differences in measurement of the various diameters are not large, it may be proper to observe that the adaptation between the head and pelvis is always so snug that the smallest of full-term heads probably never passes through the largest of normal pelves without performing all the complicated movements which are grouped together under the title of "mechanism of labor." Very slight variations in the lengths of diameters are, then, of great importance.

The passage of the brim is the first step in this mechanism. It is succeeded by an extreme flexion of the head which brings the chin closely against the chest and presents to the canal the nearly circular outline of the section through the suboccipito-bregmatic and biparietal diameters. By the process of flexion this cross-section is brought to a lower level in the canal than that which follows it, which is a cervico-frontal and bitemporal cross-section.

The head can then make no further advance until impact of these two cross-sections at different levels against the opposite sides of the pelvic canal causes a rotation of the head which brings it to the so-called plane of the outlet, with the occipital protuberance in the median line and in immediate relation to the subpubic arch.

These movements of flexion and rotation of the head are necessary preliminaries to its expulsion in both the anterior and posterior positions of normal labor. Their occurrence is determined by the existence of the inclined planes anterior to the spines of the ischium, the elasticity of the soft parts which close in the sacro-sciatic notches, the anterior curve of the sacrum, and the position of the inner surface of the ischial tuberosities.

Consideration here of these complicated relations and of their variation in the three races from which these several series of observations have been drawn has been prevented, first, by the pressure of other unexpected work; second, because the number of female pelves in the White and Negro series is unduly small; and third, because a change of method, adopted as preferable in the Pecos series, has unexpectedly made the comparison of the positions of the ischial tuberosities difficult as between the Pecos and the other two races in this series of observations.

It has therefore been postponed to a later paper for which it is hoped that measurements of a larger series of White female pelves and perhaps of those of Negresses can be obtained.

TABLE 1. Conjugate

Males	No.	Range	Mean	S. D.	V.
Pecos	53	77–112	95.00 ± 0.75	8.07 ± 0.53	8.50 ± 0.56
White	20	79–119	97.55 ± 1.53	10.13 ± 1.08	10.38 ± 1.11
Negro	17	80–100	90.18 ± 0.91	5.57 ± 0.64	6.18 ± 0.72
Females					
Pecos	62	75–120	96.73 ± 0.71	8.31 ± 0.50	8.59 ± 0.52
White	13	85–122	105.69 ± 1.62	8.68 ± 1.15	8.21 ± 1.09
Negro	7	85–112	99.43 ± 2.74	10.77 ± 1.94	10.83 ± 1.95

TABLE 2. Symphysis to Transverse

Males	No.	Range	Mean	S. D.	V.
Pecos	55	55–80	65.44 ± 0.56	6.13 ± 0.39	9.37 ± 0.60
White	21	55–84	69.48 ± 1.24	8.39 ± 0.87	12.08 ± 1.26
Negro	17	49–83	68.94 ± 1.18	7.23 ± 0.84	10.49 ± 1.21
Females					
Pecos	63	50–82	65.68 ± 0.52	6.16 ± 0.37	9.38 ± 0.56
White	13	56–93	71.15 ± 2.11	11.29 ± 1.49	15.87 ± 2.10
Negro	7	53–74	62.29 ± 1.89	7.40 ± 1.33	11.88 ± 2.14

TABLE 3. Transverse

Males	No.	Range	Mean	S. D.	V.
Pecos	55	105–138	120.49 ± 0.68	7.48 ± 0.48	6.21 ± 0.40
White	21	100–140	123.33 ± 1.68	11.38 ± 1.18	9.23 ± 0.96
Negro	16	86–124	108.00 ± 1.76	10.44 ± 1.24	9.67 ± 1.15
Females					
Pecos	63	118–144	129.64 ± 0.50	5.91 ± 0.36	4.56 ± 0.27
White	14	106–150	124.57 ± 2.06	11.40 ± 1.45	9.15 ± 1.17
Negro	7	100–128	115.71 ± 2.03	7.96 ± 1.43	6.88 ± 1.24

TABLE 4. Symphysis to Halfway Transverse

Males	No.	Range	Mean	S. D.	V.
Pecos	55	16–35	23.80 ± 0.34	3.79 ± 0.24	15.92 ± 1.02
White	21	20–39	26.86 ± 0.88	6.00 ± 0.62	22.33 ± 2.32
Negro	17	18–37	25.71 ± 0.73	4.46 ± 0.52	17.35 ± 2.01
Females					
Pecos	62	15–34	23.21 ± 0.28	3.27 ± 0.20	14.09 ± 0.85
White	13	17–39	27.92 ± 1.12	5.97 ± 0.79	21.38 ± 2.83
Negro	7	17–35	25.00 ± 1.62	6.35 ± 1.14	25.40 ± 4.58

TABLE 5. Halfway Transverse

Males	No.	Range	Mean	S. D.	V.
Pecos	55	70–94	81.47 ± 0.40	4.42 ± 0.28	5.42 ± 0.35
White	21	56–100	85.24 ± 1.50	10.22 ± 1.06	11.99 ± 1.25
Negro	17	74–106	81.06 ± 1.30	7.97 ± 0.92	9.83 ± 1.14
Females					
Pecos	62	74–98	84.48 ± 0.41	4.74 ± 0.29	5.61 ± 0.34
White	14	72–104	86.86 ± 1.69	9.37 ± 1.19	10.79 ± 1.38
Negro	7	64–92	81.14 ± 2.29	8.99 ± 1.62	11.08 ± 1.99

TABLE 6. Half Width of Sacrum

Males	No.	Range	Mean	S. D.	V.
Pecos	32	52–63	57.38 ± 0.31	2.63 ± 0.22	4.58 ± 0.39
White	21	40–62	52.24 ± 0.90	6.09 ± 0.63	11.66 ± 1.21
Negro	17	32–55	45.59 ± 0.98	6.01 ± 0.70	13.18 ± 1.52
Females					
Pecos	33	50–63	57.15 ± 0.35	2.98 ± 0.25	5.21 ± 0.43
White	13	45–63	51.46 ± 0.88	4.68 ± 0.62	9.09 ± 1.20
Negro	7	40–54	46.14 ± 1.19	4.67 ± 0.84	10.12 ± 1.82

TABLE 7. Diagonal of Synchondrosis to Halfway Transverse

Males	No.	Range	Mean	S. D.	V.
Pecos	55	97–131	114.16 ± 0.57	6.30 ± 0.40	5.52 ± 0.36
White	20	…	114.43 …	… …	… …
Negro	17	…	106.19 …	… …	… …
Females					
Pecos	62	104–129	118.00 ± 0.45	5.22 ± 0.32	4.42 ± 0.27
White	13	…	120.76 …	… …	… …
Negro	7	…	110.18 …	… …	… …

TABLE 8. Projection of Promontory

Males	No.	Range	Mean	S. D.	V.
Pecos	53	4–20	10.98 ± 0.33	3.57 ± 0.23	32.51 ± 2.13
White	18	5–20	10.33 ± 0.75	4.72 ± 0.53	45.69 ± 5.14
Negro	17	7–20	11.24 ± 0.68	4.15 ± 0.48	36.92 ± 4.27
Females					
Pecos	62	6–21	13.45 ± 0.26	3.07 ± 0.19	22.82 ± 0.19
White	11	3–18	8.64 ± 0.90	4.42 ± 0.64	51.16 ± 7.36
Negro	7	4–15	7.86 ± 1.05	4.12 ± 0.74	52.42 ± 9.45

TABLE 9. Symphysis to Centre of Transverse / Conjugate

Males	No.	Range	Mean	S. D.	V.
Pecos	53	57–78	69.04 ± 0.49	5.31 ± 0.35	7.69 ± 0.50
White	20	59–90	72.10 ± 1.35	8.96 ± 0.96	12.43 ± 1.33
Negro	17	56–85	76.35 ± 1.15	7.05 ± 0.82	9.23 ± 1.07
Females					
Pecos	62	54–84	68.11 ± 0.47	5.44 ± 0.33	7.99 ± 0.48
White	13	57–88	68.38 ± 1.81	9.68 ± 1.28	14.16 ± 1.87
Negro	7	58–68	62.71 ± 0.99	3.92 ± 0.71	6.25 ± 1.13

TABLE 10. Symphysis to Centre of Halfway Transverse / Conjugate

Males	No.	Range	Mean	S.D.	V.
Pecos	53	16–39	25.17 ± 0.34	3.72 ± 0.24	14.74 ± 0.97
White	20	19–38	27.75 ± 0.79	5.24 ± 0.56	18.88 ± 2.01
Negro	17	20–38	28.94 ± 0.64	3.90 ± 0.45	13.48 ± 1.56
Females					
Pecos	61	15–31	24.00 ± 0.26	2.96 ± 0.18	12.33 ± 0.75
White	12	17–37	25.83 ± 1.16	5.93 ± 0.82	22.96 ± 3.16
Negro	7	20–33	24.86 ± 1.09	4.26 ± 0.77	17.14 ± 3.09

TABLE 11. **HALFWAY TRANSVERSE**
TRANSVERSE

Males	No.	Range	Mean	S. D.	V.
Pecos	55	62–72	67.64 ± 0.21	2.28 ± 0.15	3.37 ± 0.22
White	21	52–82	69.24 ± 1.02	6.94 ± 0.72	10.02 ± 1.04
Negro	16	66–91	75.88 ± 1.24	7.37 ± 0.88	9.71 ± 1.16
Females					
Pecos	62	58–74	65.21 ± 0.26	3.02 ± 0.19	4.63 ± 0.28
White	14	60–81	70.07 ± 1.40	7.75 ± 0.99	11.06 ± 1.41
Negro	7	63–77	70.14 ± 1.39	5.46 ± 0.98	7.78 ± 1.40

TABLE 12. **ILIO-PECTINEAL LINE TO ISCHIAL SPINE**
TRANSVERSE

Males	No.	Range	Mean	S. D.	V.
Pecos	47	45–65	57.19 ± 0.44	4.45 ± 0.31	7.78 ± 0.54
White	10	46–60	52.70 ± 0.92	4.34 ± 0.66	8.24 ± 1.24
Negro	15	52–72	58.80 ± 0.80	4.62 ± 0.57	7.86 ± 0.97
Females					
Pecos	58	41–59	48.31 ± 0.28	3.21 ± 0.20	6.64 ± 0.42
White	10	37–54	44.90 ± 1.09	5.13 ± 0.77	11.42 ± 1.72
Negro	6	44–62	51.33 ± 1.70	6.18 ± 1.20	12.04 ± 2.34

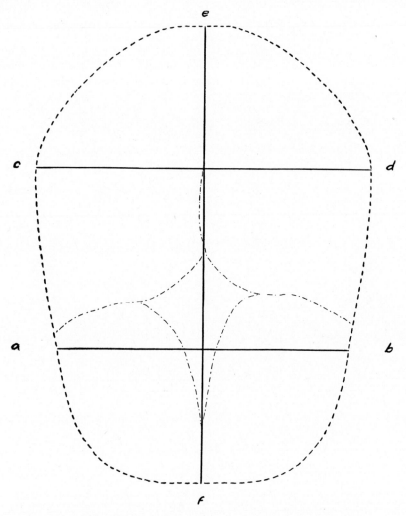

Fig. 1. Graph of white foetal head, nine months. Norma Verticalis

a b. bitemporal   *c d*. biparietal   *e f*. occipito-frontal

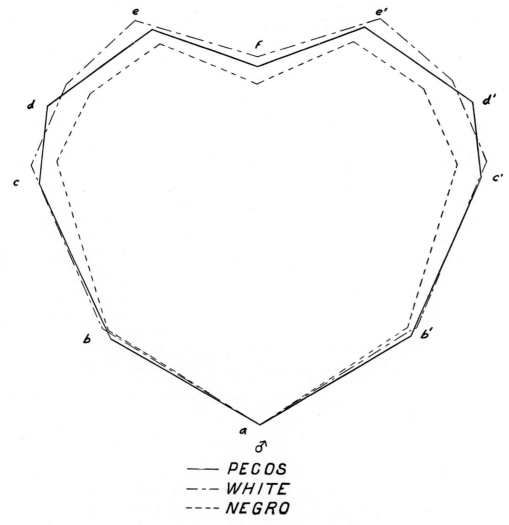

FIG. 2. GRAPH OF MALE PELVIC BRIM MEASUREMENTS

a. Symphysis   *b b'*. Half way transverse   *c c'*. Transverse
d and *d'*. Ilio-pectineo-sacral points (points at which ilio-pectineal line meets synchondrosis)
e and *e'*. Mid-sacral wing points (points at which sacral wing at brim is farthest posterior to promontory)
f. Promontory

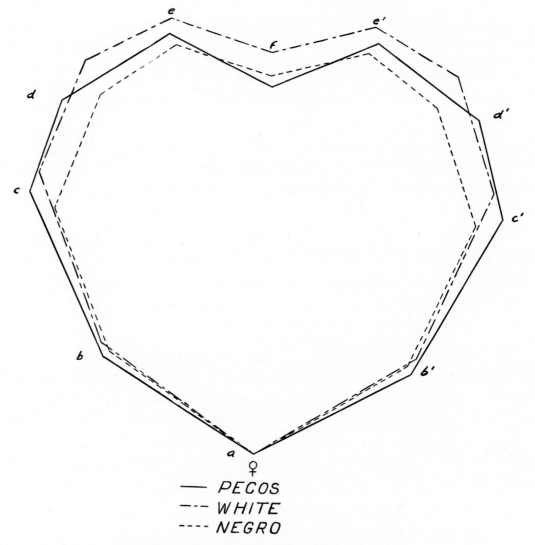

Fig. 3. Graph of female pelvic brim measurements

a. Symphysis   *b b'.* Half way transverse   *c c'.* Transverse
d and *d'.* Ilio-pectineo-sacral points (points at which ilio-pectineal line meets synchondrosis)
e and *e'.* Mid-sacral wing points (points at which sacral wing at brim is farthest posterior to promontory)
f. Promontory

BIBLIOGRAPHY

BIBLIOGRAPHY

BAUER, L.
  1915. Beitrage zur Kraniologie der Baining (Neu-Pommern). Archiv. für Anthropologie, XLII, 145–202. Braunschweig, 1915.

BLACK, D.
  1927. On a lower molar hominid tooth from the Chou Kou Tien Deposit. Palaeontologica Sinica, series D, fasc. I, pp. 2–28. Peking, 1927.

CAMERON, J.
  1929. A survey of the length-height cranial index in diverse racial types of the Hominidae. American Journal of Physical Anthropology, vol. XIII, no. 1, pp. 139–153. Philadelphia, 1929.
  1929. A survey of the breadth-height cranial index in diverse racial types of the Hominidae. American Journal of Physical Anthropology, vol. XIII, no. 1, pp. 154–170. Philadelphia, 1929.

CHANTRE, E.
  1895. Recherches anthropologiques dans l'Asie occidentale. Missions scientifiques en Transcaucasie, Asie Mineure, et Syrie. Archives du Museum d'Histoire Naturelle, vol. VI. Lyon, 1895.

CREWDSON-BENINGTON, R.
  1912. A study of the Negro skull with special reference to the Congo and Gaboon crania. Biometrika, VIII, 293–339. London, 1912.

DOUGLASS, A. E.
  1929. The secret of the Southwest solved by talkative tree rings. National Geographic Magazine (December, 1929), pp. 736–770. Washington, 1929.

FAWCETT, C. and LEE, A.
  1901. A second study of the variation and correlation of the human skull with special reference to the Naqada crania. Biometrika, I, 408–468. London, 1901.

FURUHATA, T.
  1929. A summarized review of the gen-hypothesis of the blood-groups. American Journal of Physical Anthropology, vol. XIII, no. 1, pp. 109–130. Philadelphia, 1929.

GATES, R.
  1929. Blood groups of Canadian Indians and Eskimos. American Journal of Physical Anthropology, vol. XII, no. 3, pp. 475–485. Philadelphia, 1929.

GLOVER, J. W.
  1921. United States Life Tables, 1890, 1901, 1910, and 1901–1910. Department of Commerce, Bureau of the Census. Washington, 1921.

HRDLIČKA, A.
  1908. Physiological and medical observations among the Indians of southwestern United States and northern Mexico. Bureau of American Ethnology, Bull. 34. Washington, 1908.
  1909. The stature of the Indians of the Southwest and northern Mexico. Putnam Anniversary Volume, pp. 405–426. New York, 1909.
  1916. Physical anthropology of the Lenape or Delawares and of the eastern Indians in general. Bureau of American Ethnology, Bull. 62. Washington, 1916.
  1920. Anthropometry. Philadelphia, 1920.

1922. The anthropology of Florida. Publications of the Florida State Historical Society, No. 1. Deland, 1922.

1924. Catalogue of human crania in the United States National Museum Collections. The Eskimo, Alaskan and related Indians, northeastern Asiatics. Proceedings of the United States National Museum, vol. LXIII, art. 12, pp. 1–51. Washington, 1924.

1927. Catalogue of human crania in the United States National Museum Collections. The Algonkin and related Iroquois; Siouan, Caddoan, Salish and Sahaptin, Shoshonean, and Californian Indians. Proceedings of the United States National Museum, vol. LXIX, art. 5, pp. 1–127. Washington, 1927.

1928. Catalogue of human crania in the United States National Museum Collections. Australians, Tasmanians, South African Bushmen, Hottentots, and Negro. Proceedings of the United States National Museum, vol. LXXI, art. 24, pp. 1–140. Washington, 1928.

HOOTON, E. A.

1918. On certain Eskimoid characters in Icelandic skulls. American Journal of Physical Anthropology, vol. I, no. 1, pp. 53–76. Philadelphia, 1918.

1920. Indian village site and cemetery near Madisonville, Ohio. With notes on the artifacts by C. C. Willoughby. Papers of the Peabody Museum of American Archaeology and Ethnology, vol. VIII, no. 1, pp. 1–137. Cambridge, 1920.

1923. Observations and queries as to the effect of race mixture on certain physical characteristics. Eugenics in Race and State. Scientific Papers of the Second International Congress of Eugenics, pp. 64–74. Baltimore, 1923.

1925. The ancient inhabitants of the Canary Islands. Harvard African Studies, vol. VII. Cambridge, 1925.

KIDDER, A. V.

1924. An introduction to the study of Southwestern archaeology, with a preliminary account of the excavations at Pecos. New Haven, 1924.

KIDDER, M. A. and KIDDER, A. V.

1917. Notes on the pottery of Pecos. American Anthropologist, n. s., XIX, 325–360. Lancaster, 1917.

KOGANEI, Y.

1893. Beitrage zur physischen Anthropologie der Aino. Mitteilungen aus der medicinischen Facultät der Kaiserlich-Japänischen Universität, II, 1–404. Tokio, 1893.

MARTIN, R.

1928. Lehrbuch der Anthropologie. Second edition. Jena, 1928.

MORANT, G. M.

1924. A study of certain Oriental series of crania including the Nepalese and Tibetan series in the British Museum. Biometrika, XVI, 28–29. London, 1924.

MacCURDY, G. G.

1923. Human skeletal remains from the highlands of Peru. American Journal of Physical Anthropology, VI, no. 3, 218–329. Philadelphia, 1923.

MONTADON, G.

1928. Au pays des Ainou. Paris, 1928.

PARSONS, E. C.

1925. The pueblo of Jemez. New Haven, 1925.

PEARSON, K.

1898. On the reconstruction of the stature of prehistoric races. Philosophical Transactions of the Royal Society, series A, CXCII, 169–244. London, 1898.

PEARSON, K. and BELL, J.
1919. A study of the long bones of the English skeleton. Part I, The femur. London, 1919.

POUTRIN.
1910. Les Negrilles du Centre africain. L'Anthropologie, XXI, 435–504. Paris, 1910.

QUATREFAGES DE A. and HAMY, E. T.
1882. Crania ethnica. Paris, 1882.

REICHER, M.
1913– Untersuchung uber die Schädelform der alpenlandischen und mongolischen. Stuttgart, 1914.
1914. Brachycephalen. Zeitschrift für Morphologie und Anthropologie, XV, 421–562; XVI, 1–64. Stuttgart, 1914.

RIED, A.
1911. Beitrage zür Kraniologie der Bewohner der Vorberge der bayrischen Alpen. Beitrage zür Anthropologie und Urgeschichte Bayerns, XVIII, 1–113. München, 1911.

SARASIN, F.
1916– Anthropologie der Neu-Caledonier und Loyalty-Insulaner. Berlin, 1916–1922.

SHAPIRO, H. L.
1928. A correction for artificial deformation of skulls. Anthropological Papers of the American Museum of Natural History, vol. XXX, part I, pp. 1–38. New York, 1928.

SULLIVAN, L. R.
1921. A few Andamanese skulls with comparative notes on Negrito craniometry. Anthropological Papers of the American Museum of Natural History, XXIII, 175–201. New York, 1921.

SNYDER, L. H.
1926. Human blood groups: their inheritance and racial significance. American Journal of Physical Anthropology, vol. IX, no. 2, pp. 233–263. Philadelphia, 1926.

TODD, T. W.
1920. Age changes in the pubic bone. Part I, The white male pubis. American Journal of Physical Anthropology, vol. III, no. 3, pp. 285–334. Philadelphia, 1920.
1927. Skeletal records of mortality. Scientific Monthly, XXIV, 481–496. Lancaster, 1927.

THOMSON, A. and RANDALL-MacIVER, D.
1905. The ancient races of the Thebaid. Oxford, 1905.

WILLIAMS, H. U.
1929. Human paleopathology. Archives of Pathology, VII, 839–902. Buffalo, 1929.

YULE, G. U.
1927. An introduction to the theory of statistics (eighth ed.) London, 1927.